Communications in Computer and Information Science 1903

Rationale

The CCIS series is devoted to the publication of proceedings of computer science conferences. Its aim is to efficiently disseminate original research results in informatics in printed and electronic form. While the focus is on publication of peer-reviewed full papers presenting mature work, inclusion of reviewed short papers reporting on work in progress is welcome, too. Besides globally relevant meetings with internationally representative program committees guaranteeing a strict peer-reviewing and paper selection process, conferences run by societies or of high regional or national relevance are also considered for publication.

Topics

The topical scope of CCIS spans the entire spectrum of informatics ranging from foundational topics in the theory of computing to information and communications science and technology and a broad variety of interdisciplinary application fields.

Information for Volume Editors and Authors

Publication in CCIS is free of charge. No royalties are paid, however, we offer registered conference participants temporary free access to the online version of the conference proceedings on SpringerLink (http://link.springer.com) by means of an http referrer from the conference website and/or a number of complimentary printed copies, as specified in the official acceptance email of the event.

CCIS proceedings can be published in time for distribution at conferences or as postproceedings, and delivered in the form of printed books and/or electronically as USBs and/or e-content licenses for accessing proceedings at SpringerLink. Furthermore, CCIS proceedings are included in the CCIS electronic book series hosted in the SpringerLink digital library at http://link.springer.com/bookseries/7899. Conferences publishing in CCIS are allowed to use Online Conference Service (OCS) for managing the whole proceedings lifecycle (from submission and reviewing to preparing for publication) free of charge.

Publication process

The language of publication is exclusively English. Authors publishing in CCIS have to sign the Springer CCIS copyright transfer form, however, they are free to use their material published in CCIS for substantially changed, more elaborate subsequent publications elsewhere. For the preparation of the camera-ready papers/files, authors have to strictly adhere to the Springer CCIS Authors' Instructions and are strongly encouraged to use the CCIS LaTeX style files or templates.

Abstracting/Indexing

CCIS is abstracted/indexed in DBLP, Google Scholar, EI-Compendex, Mathematical Reviews, SCImago, Scopus. CCIS volumes are also submitted for the inclusion in ISI Proceedings.

How to start

To start the evaluation of your proposal for inclusion in the CCIS series, please send an e-mail to ccis@springer.com.

Luca Longo

Editor

Explainable Artificial Intelligence

First World Conference, xAI 2023
Lisbon, Portugal, July 26–28, 2023
Proceedings, Part III

 Springer

Editor
Luca Longo 🆔
Technological University Dublin
Dublin, Ireland

ISSN 1865-0929   ISSN 1865-0937 (electronic)
Communications in Computer and Information Science
ISBN 978-3-031-44069-4   ISBN 978-3-031-44070-0 (eBook)
https://doi.org/10.1007/978-3-031-44070-0

This Springer imprint is published by the registered company Springer Nature Switzerland AG
The registered company address is: Gewerbestrasse 11, 6330 Cham, Switzerland

Paper in this product is recyclable.

Preface

This is an exciting time to be a researcher in eXplainable Artificial Intelligence (xAI), a scholar's discipline that has undergone significant growth and development over the past few years. xAI has evolved from a mere topic within Artificial Intelligence (AI) to a multidisciplinary, interdisciplinary and transdisciplinary fermenting field of research. AI-driven technologies, Machine Learning (ML) and specifically Deep Learning (DL) applications have entered our everyday lives and society, with exponential, incessant growth. These have been successfully applied in various real-world contexts such as finance, education and healthcare, just to mention a few. The reasons are the great capability of these technologies to learn patterns from complex, non-linear multi-dimensional data, thus enabling the design of solutions for real-world problems such as forecasting, recommendation, classification, prediction and data generation. However, these solutions are often too opaque, non-transparent and non-interpretable, with a negative impact on the explainability of their inferences and outputs. As a consequence, this has led regulators and policymakers to increase pressure for the design of AI-based technologies that are better aligned with humans and our rights and that do not have a negative effect on society. This call for transparency, interpretability and ethics has made xAI an active and necessary research area. As a consequence, many reviews are published every year, and an abundance of theoretical and practical contributions are appearing every month, some application-dependent, some method or discipline-specific, and some context-agnostic. Similarly, various workshops around the world are organised by independent scholars at larger events, each focused on certain aspects of the explainability of AI-based systems. Unfortunately, these are scattered, often organised at a national level, thus attracting only local scholars. This motivated the creation of a larger event, the first World Conference on eXplainable Artificial Intelligence (xAI 2023). The aim was and is to bring together researchers, academics and professionals from different disciplines, and to promote the sharing and discussion of knowledge, new perspectives, experiences and innovations in xAI.

Against the initial expectations whereby a few dozen authors and attendees were forecasted, xAI 2023 broke several records. Firstly, more than 220 articles were submitted to the different tracks. Secondly, authors and attendees were from more than 35 countries, making this conference a truly world event. Thirdly, the acceptance rate of submitted articles was already relatively low (~40%), despite this being only the first edition of, hopefully, a long series of conferences, with 94 manuscripts being accepted. It is thus a great privilege to present the proceedings of the first World Conference on eXplainable Artificial Intelligence, held in Belem, Lisbon, Portugal, from the 26th to the 28th of July at the beautiful Cultural Congress Center of Belem. Split over three volumes, this book aggregates a collection of the best contributions received and presented at xAI 2023, describing recent developments in the context of theoretical and practical models, methods and techniques in eXplainable Artificial Intelligence. The accepted articles were selected through a strict, single-blind peer-review process. Each article received at least three reviews from scholars in academia and industry, with 99% of them holding a PhD in an area relevant to the topics of the conference. The general chair of the conference, along with the programme committee chairs, carefully selected the top contributions by ranking articles across several objective criteria and evaluating and triangulating the qualitative feedback left by the 188 international reviewers. The reviewing process was intensive, and it ensured that xAI 2023 adhered to the highest standards of quality. All accepted contributions are included in these proceedings and were invited to give oral presentations. Besides the main technical track, several special tracks were introduced, each proposed and chaired by one or more scholars, to allow the identification of highly innovative areas within the larger field of eXplainable Artificial Intelligence. Special track chairs were encouraged to be innovative in designing their topics to attract relevant scholars worldwide. Similarly, a parallel track was designed to give a chance to scholars to submit novel late-breaking pieces of work that are specific in-progress research studies relevant to xAI, and present them as posters during the main event. A demo track was also organised, providing a mechanism for scholars to demo software prototypes on explainability or real-world applications of explainable AI-based systems. A doctoral consortium was organised, with lectures delivered by renowned scientists to PhD scholars who submitted their doctoral proposals on future research related to eXplainable Artificial Intelligence. A separate programme committee was set up for the late-breaking work, demo and doctoral consortium tracks.

Finally, a panel discussion was held with renowned scholars in xAI and all in all, the 1st World Conference on eXplainable Artificial Intelligence offered a truly multi-disciplinary view while inspiring the attendees to come up with solid recommendations to tackle hot-topic challenges of current technologies built with Artificial Intelligence. As the Monument of the Discoveries, right outside the conference centre, celebrates the Portuguese Age of Discovery during the 15th and 16th centuries, xAI 2023 symbolises a new mechanism for exploring and presenting novel directions for the design of the explainable intelligent systems of the future that are transparent, sustainable and ethical and have a positive impact on humans.

Luca Longo

Organizing Committee

General Chair

Luca Longo   Technological University Dublin, Ireland

Programme Committee Chairs

Francisco Herrera	Granada University, Spain
Javier Del Ser	Tecnalia & University of the Basque Country, Spain
Luca Longo	Technological University Dublin, Ireland

Doctoral Consortium Chairs

Luis Paulo Reis	University of Porto, Portugal
Sarah Jane Delany	Technological University Dublin, Ireland

Inclusion and Accessibility Chair

Alessandra Sala   Shutterstock, Ireland

Student Support Chair

Federico Cabitza   University of Milano-Bicocca, Italy

Programme Committee

Arianna Agosto	University of Pavia, Italy
Jaumin Ajdari	South East European University, Rep. of Macedonia
Jose M. Alonso	University of Santiago de Compostela, Spain
Andrea Apicella	Federico II University, Italy
Annalisa Appice	University Aldo Moro of Bari, Italy

Hamed Ayoobi	University of Groningen, The Netherlands
Omran Ayoub	Scuola Universitaria Professionale della Svizzera Italiana, Switzerland
Mohammad Reza Bahrami	Innopolis University, Russia
Javier Bajo	Universidad Politécnica de Madrid, Spain
Marília Barandas	Fraunhofer Portugal AICOS, Portugal
Sylvio Barbon Junior	University of Trieste, Italy
Francesco Barile	Maastricht University, The Netherlands
Nick Bassiliades	Aristotle University of Thessaloniki, Greece
Shahina Begum	Mälardalen University, Sweden
Juri Belikov	Tallinn University of Technology, Estonia
Antonio Berlanga	Universidad Carlos III de Madrid, Spain
Floris Bex	Utrecht University, The Netherlands
Przemek Biecek	Polish Academy of Science, University of Wroclaw, Poland
Stefano Bistarelli	Università di Perugia, Italy
Alessandro Bitetto	University of Pavia, Italy
Szymon Bobek	AGH University of Science and Technology, Poland
Romain Bourqui	Université Bordeaux 1, INRIA Bordeaux-Sud Ouest, France
Nicolas Boutry	EPITA Research Laboratory (LRE), France
Bojan Božić	Technological University Dublin, Ireland
Mario Brcic	University Of Zagreb, Croatia
Rob Brennan	University College Dublin, Ireland
Adrian Byrne	CeADAR UCD/Idiro Analytics, Ireland
Federico Cabitza	Università degli Studi di Milano-Bicocca, Italy
Roberta Calegari	Alma Mater Studiorum–Università di Bologna, Italy
Andrea Campagner	Università degli Studi di Milano-Bicocca, Italy
Andrea Capotorti	University of Perugia, Italy
F. Amílcar Cardoso	University of Coimbra, Portugal
Ramon Alberto Carrasco	Universidad Complutense de Madrid, Spain
Giuseppe Casalicchio	Ludwig Maximilian University of Munich, Germany
Aniello Castiglione	University of Salerno, Italy
Danilo Cavaliere	Università degli Studi di Salerno, Italy
Paola Cerchiello	University of Pavia, Italy
Debaditya Chakraborty	University of Texas at San Antonio, USA
Angelos Chatzimparmpas	Northwestern University, USA
Sharma Chetan	University of Texas at San Antonio, USA
Jaesik Choi	Korea Advanced Institute of Science and Technology, South Korea

Ikram Chraibi Kaadoud	IMT Atlantique, Lab-STICC, France
Giovanni Ciatto	University of Bologna, Italy
Philipp Cimiano	Bielefeld University, Germany
Mario Giovanni C.A. Cimino	University of Pisa, Italy
Oana Cocarascu	King's College London, UK
Paulo Cortez	University of Minho, Portugal
Jane Courtney	Technological University Dublin, Ireland
Sabatina Criscuolo	University of Naples Federico II, Italy
Fisnik Dalipi	Linnaeus University, Sweden
Elizabeth M. Daly	IBM, Ireland
Javier Del Ser	Tecnalia Research & Innovation, Spain
Sarah Jane Delany	Technological University Dublin, Ireland
Alexandros Doumanoglou	Information Technologies Institute, Greece
Pietro Ducange	University of Pisa, Italy
Ivana Dusparic	Trinity College Dublin, Ireland
Telmo-M. Silva Filho	University of Bristol, UK
Oliver Eberle	Technische Universität Berlin, Germany
Cristofer Englund	Halmstad University, Sweden
Lina Fahed	IMT Atlantique - Lab-STICC, France
Brígida Mónica Faria	Higher School of Health/Polytechnic of Porto, Portugal
Ad Feelders	Utrecht University, The Netherlands
Mexhid Ferati	Linnaeus University, Sweden
Gianna Figà-Talamanca	University of Perugia, Italy
Duarte Folgado	Fraunhofer, Portugal
Kary Främling	Umeå university, Sweden
Timo Freiesleben	Ludwig-Maximilians-Universität München, Germany
Alberto Freitas	University of Porto, Portugal
Pascal Friederich	Karlsruhe Institute of Technology, Germany
Angelo Gaeta	Università di Salerno, Italy
Mariacristina Gallo	University of Salerno, Italy
Hugo Gamboa	PLUX Biosignals, Portugal
Esteban García-Cuesta	Universidad Politécnica de Madrid, Spain
Gizem Gezici	Scuola Normale Superiore, Italy
Massimiliano Giacomin	University of Brescia, Italy
Giles Hooker	Cornell University, USA
Romain Giot	LaBRI Université de Bordeaux, CNRS, France
Paolo Giudici	University of Pavia, Italy
Rocio Gonzalez-Diaz	University of Seville, Spain
Mara Graziani	HES-SO Valais-Wallis, Switzerland
Grégoire Montavon	Freie Universität Berlin, Germany

Adrian Groza	Technical University of Cluj-Napoca, Romania
Riccardo Guidotti	University of Pisa, Italy
Miguel A. Gutiérrez-Naranjo	University of Seville, Spain
Mark Hall	Airbus, UK
Barbara Hammer	Bielefeld University, Germany
Yoichi Hayashi	Meiji University, Japan
Fredrik Heintz	Linköping University, Sweden
Jorge Henriques	University of Coimbra, Portugal
Jose Antonio Iglesias	Carlos III University of Madrid, Spain
Francesco Isgro	Università degli Studi di Napoli Federico II, Italy
Florije Ismaili	SEEU, Republic of Macedonia
Lundström Jens	Halmstad University, Sweden
Richard Jiang	Lancaster University, UK
Jose M. Juarez	Universidad de Murcia, Spain
Martin Jullum	Norwegian Computing Center, Norway
Zenun Kastrati	Linnaeus University, Sweden
Abhishek Kaushik	Dublin City University, Ireland
Hassan Khosravi	University of Queensland, Australia
Christophe Labreuche	Thales R&T, France
Markus Langer	Philipps-Universität Marburg, Germany
Thi Thu Huong Le	Pusan National University, South Korea
Philippe Lenca	IMT Atlantique, France
Andrew Lensen	Victoria University of Wellington, New Zealand
Francesco Leofante	Imperial College London, UK
David Lewis	Trinity College Dublin, Ireland
Paulo Lisboa	Liverpool John Moores University, UK
Weiru Liu	University of Bristol, UK
Henrique Lopes Cardoso	University of Porto, Portugal
Ana Carolina Lorena	Instituto Tecnológico de Aeronáutica, Brazil
Brian Mac Namee	University College Dublin, Ireland
Luis Macedo	University of Coimbra, Portugal
Lucie Charlotte Magister	University of Cambridge, UK
Giancladio Malgieri	Consiglio Nazionale delle Ricerche, Italy
Avleen Malhi	Bournemouth University, UK
Eleni Mangina	University College Dublin, Ireland
Francesco Marcelloni	University of Pisa, Italy
Stefano Mariani	Università di Modena e Reggio Emilia, Italy
Goreti Marreiros	ISEP/IPP-GECAD, Portugal
Manuel Mazzara	Innopolis University, Russia
Kevin McAreavey	University of Bristol, UK
Susan McKeever	Technological University Dublin, Ireland
Yi Mei	Victoria University of Wellington, New Zealand

Lucas Rizzo	Technological University Dublin, Ireland
Marcel Robeer	Utrecht University, The Netherlands
Mohammad Rostami	University of Southern California, USA
Araceli Sanchis	Universidad Carlos III de Madrid, Spain
Carsten Schulte	University of Paderborn, Germany
Christin Seifert	University of Marburg, Germany
Pedro Sequeira	SRI International, USA
Edwin Simpson	University of Bristol, UK
Carlos Soares	University of Porto, Portugal
Timo Speith	Universität Bayreuth, Germany
Gregor Stiglic	University of Maribor, Slovenia
Gian Antonio Susto	Università degli Studi di Padova, Italy
Jacek Tabor	Jagiellonian University, Poland
Nava Tintarev	University of Maastricht, The Netherlands
Alberto Tonda	Université Paris-Saclay, France
Alicia Troncoso	Universidad Pablo de Olavide, Spain
Matias Valdenegro-Toro	University of Groningen, The Netherlands
Zita Vale	GECAD - ISEP/IPP, Portugal
Jan Vanthienen	Katholieke Universiteit Leuven, Belgium
Katrien Verbert	Katholieke Universiteit Leuven, Belgium
Gianni Vercelli	University of Genoa, Italy
Giulia Vilone	Technological University Dublin, Ireland
Fabio Vitali	University of Bologna, Italy
Marvin Wright	Leibniz Institute for Prevention Research and Epidemiology - BIPS & University of Bremen, Germany
Arjumand Younus	University of Galway, Ireland
Carlos Zednik	Eindhoven University of Technology, The Netherlands
Bartosz Zieliński	Jagiellonian University, Poland

Acknowledgements

A thank you goes to everyone who helped in the organising committee for the 1st World Conference on eXplainable Artificial Intelligence (xAI 2023). A special thank you goes to the PC chairs, the doctoral committee chairs, the inclusion & accessibility chair and the student support chair. Also special thanks to the keynote speaker, Peter Flach, who, with Paolo Giudici and Grégoire Montavon took part in the conference's interesting panel discussion and provided their lectures during the doctoral consortium. A word of appreciation goes to the organisers of the special tracks, and those who chaired them during the conference. We are grateful to the members of the organisation and the volunteers who helped sort out the logistics and last-minute challenges behind organising such a large conference with great enthusiasm, effort and professionalism. A special thank you goes to the researchers and practitioners who submitted their work and committed to attending the event and turning it into an opportunity to meet and share findings and new avenues of research.

Contents – Part III

Human-Centered Explanations and xAI for Trustworthy and Responsible AI

Explainable and Interpretable AI with Argumentation, Representational Learning and Concept Extraction for xAI

xAI for Time Series and Natural Language Processing

Opening the Black Box: Analyzing Attention Weights and Hidden States in Pre-trained Language Models for Non-language Tasks

Mohamad Ballout[✉], Ulf Krumnack, Gunther Heidemann,
and Kai-Uwe Kühnberger

Institute of Cognitive Science, University of Osnabrück, Osnabrück, Germany
mohamad.ballout@uni-osnabrueck.de

Abstract. Investigating deep learning language models has always been a significant research area due to the "black box" nature of most advanced models. With the recent advancements in pre-trained language models based on transformers and their increasing integration into daily life, addressing this issue has become more pressing. In order to achieve an explainable AI model, it is essential to comprehend the procedural steps involved and compare them with human thought processes. Thus, in this paper, we use simple, well-understood non-language tasks to explore these models' inner workings. Specifically, we apply a pre-trained language model to constraithmetic problems with hierarchical structure, to analyze their attention weight scores and hidden states. The investigation reveals promising results, with the model addressing hierarchical problems in a moderately structured manner, similar to human problem-solving strategies. Additionally, by inspecting the attention weights layer by layer, we uncover an unconventional finding that layer 10, rather than the model's final layer, is the optimal layer to unfreeze for the least parameter-intensive approach to fine-tune the model. We support these findings with entropy analysis and token embeddings similarity analysis. The attention analysis allows us to hypothesize that the model can generalize to longer sequences in ListOps dataset, a conclusion later confirmed through testing on sequences longer than those in the training set. Lastly, by utilizing a straightforward task in which the model predicts the winner of a Tic Tac Toe game, we identify limitations in attention analysis, particularly its inability to capture 2D patterns.

Keywords: Pre-trained language model · Transformers · XAI · Attention analysis · BERT

1 Introduction

Pre-trained Language models, based on transformer architecture [1], have surpassed previous benchmarks in the majority of language-related tasks, demonstrating their superiority over earlier sequence networks like RNNs. Models such

L. Longo (Ed.): xAI 2023, CCIS 1903, pp. 3–25, 2023.
https://doi.org/10.1007/978-3-031-44070-0_1

as BERT [2], T5 [3], BART [4], and GPTs [5] are now extensively employed in various language tasks and have expanded into other domains, including vision [6] and audio processing [7]. One contributing factor to the success of transformers is their attention mechanism, a feature that essentially allows the model to focus on and assign different degrees of importance to various parts of an input sequence when generating the output. This mechanism not only brings inherent interpretability but also allows researchers to visualize and comprehend the relationships between different components of the transformers, providing insights into how the model processes and weighs various features during its decision-making process. However, as these models continue to grow in scale, featuring billions of parameters, the longstanding challenge of deep learning's explainability resurfaces. Can we truly comprehend the reasoning behind a model's predictions?

Numerous studies have been conducted to reveal and interpret the network output on language tasks. Earlier research focused on attention analysis within the linguistic context [8–10]. However, with the advancements in these models, such as GPT-4's [11] demonstrated ability to tackle various problem types including arithmetic and logical reasoning, we explore the interpretability of pre-trained language models in non-language tasks. Many prior studies have encountered challenges when attempting to examine explainability in language data due to its inherent complexity, often yielding inconclusive results. Some previous work went further, stating that attention analysis could not be perceived as an explanation for the model's decisions [12]. To our knowledge, there is a lack of literature exploring the analysis of pre-trained language models in non-linguistic tasks. Therefore, in this study, we fine-tune BERT on non-linguistic tasks, such as arithmetic datasets like ListOps [13], and to predict the winner of a basic Tic Tac Toe game, and examine the outcomes of attention heads and token representations. Our findings reveal interesting results that were not apparent when examining attention in language contexts. For example, in numerous instances, it was possible to deduce the model's predicted response solely by examining the attention heat maps. Furthermore, by analyzing the attention mechanism, we hypothesize that BERT's approach to solving an hierarchical arithmetic tasks closely resembles the process a human would follow.

Our examination centered on BERT, a pre-trained language model that is extensively employed in the literature. BERT uses a bidirectional context encoder for learning textual representations. We aim to investigate BERT's attention and representation in tasks unrelated to language to better understand the workings of pre-trained language models. Our objective is to enhance the models' interpretability, applicability, and reliability across various domains. This analysis as, shown later in the paper, lead to more efficient fine-tuning, better understanding of the model's decision making and its limitations. Upon publication, the code, model, and datasets used in our experiments will be made available as open source resources.[1]

---

[1] https://github.com/BalloutAI/Attention-Analysis.git.

The main contributions of this paper are:

- Conducting a comprehensive interpretability assessment of the BERT model fine-tuned on three non-linguistic tasks, employing four visualization methods: token-to-token analysis, attention heatmap analysis, token embeddings similarity analysis, and entropy analysis. In addition, by performing a layer-by-layer examination using these methods, we are able to make inferences about decision-making processes in pre-trained language models.
- In contrast to attention analysis on language data, where drawing conclusions from visual representations can be challenging, we find that the various techniques used in this study provided clear evidence of the attention models' effectiveness. We observe clear examples demonstrating the effectiveness of attention models, as we could discern the model's predictions from the heatmaps or token embeddings.
- The explainability analysis enabled us to formulate hypotheses about the model's generalization capabilities and fine-tuning techniques, which were later confirmed through testing.

2   Related Work

There is extensive research in the literature focused on analyzing the attention mechanisms within transformer models, with many researchers attempting to explain and examine the output of these models. For example, [14] introduced a visualization tool designed to investigate the attention weights and contextual representations of transformer-based models. This tool represents the attention weights of each token relative to other tokens using curved lines, allowing users to explore attention within input sequences. A similar tool was also developed by [15] for visualizing self-attention. In this work, we refer to this type of analysis as token-to-token analysis to differentiate it from heat map analysis.

Many previous studies have concentrated on identifying the linguistic skills acquired by pre-trained language models. These studies typically analyze attention weights to interpret such linguistic abilities by carefully selecting specific inputs and examining the corresponding outputs. For instance, [16] found that BERT consistently assigned higher scores to correct verb forms when fed both correct and incorrect subject-verb compositions, suggesting that BERT possesses syntactic capabilities. Similarly, the study in [8] proposed using probing tasks, which are diagnostic tasks specifically designed to examine the representation of particular types of linguistic information within a model. These tasks are employed to explore the unique properties and characteristics of linguistic details, including phrase-level information, syntactic structures, and semantic relationships, as encoded by different layers within the BERT model.

[17] conducted a more in-depth investigation into understanding what aspects BERT focuses on, discovering common behaviors across attention heads. While no attention head excelled at multiple syntactic relations, specific heads were found to correspond well with particular semantic and syntactic relations like finding direct objects of verbs, determiners of nouns, etc. In [9], the authors

demonstrated BERT's capacity to capture various types of linguistic information. Furthermore, they utilized their analysis to improve BERT's performance on language tasks, demonstrating absolute performance increases of up to 3.2% on specific tasks, such as Recognizing Textual Entailment (RTE).

Conversely, some studies in the literature express skepticism about the impact of attention weights on the system's output, as seen in [10,12]. Both studies observed that higher attention weights do not significantly influence model predictions. In fact, [12] concluded that attention modules do not offer meaningful explanations for the model's output. However, [18] challenged the tests conducted in [12] and proposed alternative tests to determine if attention can be used for explanation. The authors claim that their proposed tests disprove the assertions made in [12].

Another area of research closely related to this work involves utilizing pre-trained language models for non-linguistic tasks [19–21]. For instance, [20] proposed a novel pre-trained model called MathBERT, trained with both mathematical formulas and their contexts. The empirical findings show that MathBERT substantially surpasses the performance of current techniques on all evaluated math-related tasks. In addition, [21] demonstrated that pre-trained language models can serve as universal computational engines to solve tasks across various domains, requiring only 0.1% of GPT-2's parameters. This work aims to explain the remarkable success of pre-trained language models in these non-language tasks.

In light of this discussion and considering that linguistic probing tasks have been thoroughly explored in the literature, we build upon previous work conducted in the language context, analyzing pre-trained language transformers on arithmetic tasks. Our analysis includes both local and global attention weight analysis, which means we examine individual tokens and their target attention, as well as the attention heatmap for the entire sequence.

We demonstrate that this type of task clearly highlights the importance of attention and, in many instances, reveal decision-making processes in a pre-trained language model like BERT. We observed that the model often does not attend to tokens that do not influence the results, whereas attention is focused on tokens that are crucial for the output. Additionally, we investigated token embeddings and their similarity to each other across layers. We found that embedding similarities align with attention analysis, as the decisive tokens-those that determine the model's output-exhibit higher similarities than tokens deemed less important.

We also discovered that the last layers, especially and surprisingly the 10th layer rather than the last one, in the encoder transformer encodes the most apparent attention weights, allowing us to determine the answer by simply examining the attention maps. Based on these findings, we compared fine-tuning of BERT in two settings: by freezing all parameters except those in layers 10 and 12. We discovered that unfreezing the parameters in layer 10 outperforms unfreezing them in layer 12. Overall, this method reduced the number of parameters in the base version of BERT, which originally had approximately 109 million parameters, to just 7 million. Despite this reduction, we achieved competitive results with only a minor decrease in accuracy on non-linguistic tasks in both of the mentioned fine-tuning settings.

3 Model and Datasets

In this section, we briefly discuss the model used which is BERT, the datasets used to test the model, and the fine-tuning process.

3.1 Model-BERT

We chose to analyze BERT, or Bidirectional Encoder Representations from Transformers, on non-language tasks because it is one of the most renowned and early pre-trained language models introduced by [2]. It is based on the transformer architecture by [1], utilizing the encoder component exclusively. BERT's bidirectional design facilitates the simultaneous consideration of both, the preceding and following context in a given text, resulting in a more nuanced and comprehensive representation of linguistic information. This model is extensively employed for fine-tuning a wide range of NLP tasks, including but not limited to question answering [22], sentiment analysis [23], and named entity recognition [2].

3.2 Datasets

We choose to evaluate BERT on three non language datasets including two versions of the ListOps and a Tic Tac Toe game winner prediction. The reasoning behind selecting these tasks is that we require challenges for which we possess a clear understanding of the solution process, as opposed to language and vision tasks, where the human brain's processing mechanisms remain less comprehensible. The three non-language datasets are:

– **ListOps** The Long ListOps dataset is a classification task initially developed by [25] and later extended by [13] to create longer sequences in order to test transformers in long-range scenarios. Designed to test a model's capability to handle hierarchical data in a longer setup, the dataset comprises mathematical operations on natural numbers such as Modular Addition, Minimum, Maximum, and Median. A short example of a sequence is:

[SUM [MIN 0 1 [MED 5 2 1] 4] 1 2 [MAX 1 5 4]]

To solve this sequence, the model must process it hierarchically, as some subsequences within the longer sequence need to be resolved first, as illustrated in Fig. 1. Additionally, in order to obtain the correct answer, the model must attend to every token in long scenarios. Previous studies have shown that transformers have difficulties in processing this type of data, as the model must remember the order of every token to accurately predict the answer.

Input: [SUM [MIN 0 1 [MED 5 2 1] 4] 1 2 [MAX 1 5 4]]

Step 1:   [SUM [MIN 0 1 2 4] 1 2 [MAX 1 5 4]

Step 2:   [SUM 0 1 2 5]

Answer: 8

Fig. 1. Figure illustrates the standard process of solving a sequence in ListOps.

The dataset features a 10-class classification, where the classes are the integers from 0 to 9. For simplicity, we limit the range of the number of tokens per sequence to 200–400. The model is trained on 98k sequences and tested on 2k samples adopting this approach from the original work by [13]. BERT scores an accuracy of 61.6% on this dataset.

– **Modified ListOps**
This task is similar to the original ListOps [13], but we modified it to create an easier task. The primary reason for this modification is that we observed the model's inability to solve the modular addition, an intriguing problem worth investigating in the future. To enable a clearer attention analysis, where the model can solve all operators, we replaced the SUM and MED operators with simpler ones, including FIRST and LAST. The First and Last operators require the model to simply choose the first and last elements in the sequence or sub-sequence, respectively. A short example of a sequence would be:

[LAST 2 [MIN 0 5 4] 3 [FIRST 5 1] 4 9 [MAX 1 5]]

In this example, the answer is the last element in the sequence, which is 5. It is important to note that the actual training and testing samples have lengths ranging from 200 to 400, making the problem more complex. The model scores an accuracy of 95.1% on this dataset.

– **Tic Tac Toe**
Finally, the model is fine-tuned to determine the winner of a Tic Tac Toe game. This is a binary classification problem, and the sequence input consists of a flattened 1D representation of the game. An example input is as follows:

-	x	x
x	x	o
o	o	o

$\rightarrow$ $- x x \mid x x o \mid o o o \mid$

The symbol " - " to an unfilled space whereas the vertical bar is the delimiter of each dimension. In the example shown above the correct output is o, since the player filled the third row completly. This is an easy task where the model scores 100%.

3.3   Fine-Tuning BERT

In our experiments, we fine-tuned the BERT model on all of the tasks above using the Hugging Face [24] implementation of the BERT-base model. The model consists of 12 layers (i.e., 12 transformer blocks) and uses 12 attention heads in each of those layers. We fine-tuned BERT with learning rate of 2e-5 and the remaining hyper-parameters were adopted from [26]. We fine-tune all of the model's parameters, totaling approximately 109 million, except in certain cases where we specify that we freeze all parameters except for a particular layer. In such cases, we freeze all parameters with the exception of the specified layer and the norm layer in all layers. This training strategy was adopted from [21]. We follow the data splitting approach for training and validation from [13], which trains on 98% of the data and validates on the remaining 2%. The various analyses we have performed are summarized in Fig. 2.

Fig. 2. Figure shows the type of analysis done on non-language tasks.

4   Analysis and Results

We visualize the attention mechanisms in BERT using two methods: first, by employing the ExBert tool provided by [14], and second, by generating heatmaps of the attention score matrix. Both approaches offer valuable insights into the relationships and dependencies among input tokens. ExBERT provides an attention view option that enables us to examine each token's attention and its targets, while the attention heatmaps offer a comprehensive snapshot of the attention patterns in a single image. Both methods utilize attention weights, denoted by the matrix α, which are computed using the scaled dot-product attention formula:

$$\alpha_{ij} = \frac{\exp(\mathbf{q}_i^T \mathbf{k}j)}{\sum_{l=1}^{n} \exp(\mathbf{q}_i^T \mathbf{k}_l)} \qquad (1)$$

Here, α_{ij} denotes the attention weight between the i-th query and the j-th key, signifying the importance assigned by the model to each input token when generating the output token. By visualizing the attention weights matrix α, we can visually interpret the model's focus and the underlying structure of the token relationships. Each element in the matrix corresponds to the attention weight between the i-th and j-th tokens, effectively capturing the dependencies among them.

Another important aspect to consider is that BERT models introduce special tokens (e.g.,"[CLS]", "[SEP]") for downstream classification or generation tasks. The "[CLS]" token (short for "classification") is added at the beginning of the input sequence and is used to aggregate information from the entire input sequence for tasks that require a single output, such as classification or sentiment analysis. The "[SEP]" token (short for "separator") is used to separate different parts of the input sequence, such as individual sentences in a sentence-pair classification task or the context and the question in a question-answering task. These tokens often receive substantial attention and function as a null operation, as explained by [17]. We followed the suggestion by [14] to hide these special tokens of the model and re-normalize based on the other attentions to provide easier visualization of subtle attention patterns.

4.1   Token-to-Token Analysis

We start our analysis by exploring the token-to-token mappings in a fine-tuned BERT model on ListOps, utilizing the ExBERT tool. The visualizations reveal interesting findings. In the network's initial layers, each operator (e.g. "MAX", "MIN", etc.) attends to its corresponding numbers, neighbors, and brackets, while in the last layers, all tokens focus on the first operator and/or the answer. It is crucial to recognize that, in the ListOps dataset, the sequence's initial operator is responsible for predicting the answer and should be resolved last. We propose that this observation indicates BERT's ability to comprehend the problem's hierarchical nature and resolve it in a manner similar to the one depicted earlier in Fig. 1.

Given the short sequence for the sake of the visualization:

$$[MAX \ \ 2 \ 3 \ [MIN \ 1 \ 5 \ 6 \ 1 \ 2] \ 1 \ [FIRST \ 1 \ 4 \ 2 \ ] \ 8 \ ]$$

In the initial layers, ranging from 1 to 4, it is apparent that the tokens attend to their neighbors without recognizing the boundaries established by brackets and sub-sequences. This suggests that the tokens lack a well-defined objective. We hypothesize that, in these early layers, the tokens attempt to discern their positions within the sequences.

In layers 5 and 6, it becomes evident that the model has identified the boundaries of each sub-sequence. Consequently, in these layers, for the provided example, we observe that tokens attend to their respective operators. For instance, the "MAX" operator is attended by token 2, while the "MIN" operator is attended by tokens 1, 5, 6, 1, and 2, and the "FIRST" operator is attended by tokens 1, 4, and 2. It is important to note that this is not always flawless, as evidenced by the maximum operator not attending to token "3" in this case. Furthermore, in some instances, the opening and closing brackets also attend to their corresponding operators. Figure 3 illustrates the distribution of attention weights in layer 6, given the same input sequence as above. The green rectangles surrounding the tokens signify that we are exclusively displaying the attentions correlated with these specific tokens.

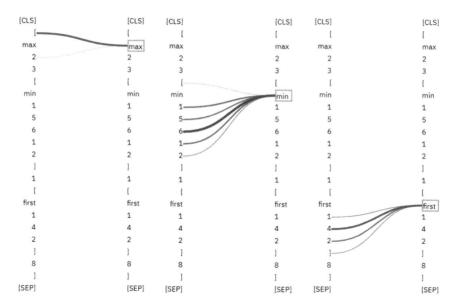

Fig. 3. Figure shows that operators inside each sub-sequence are attended by their tokens in layer 6.

From layers 7 to 12, it is strikingly apparent that the system's focus shifts towards determining the correct answer. As a result, we observe that the majority of attention is directed to the correct answer in most of these layers. The most attended token is the correct answer, and it is therefore obvious that one could predict the system's output simply by examining these attention patterns. The attention of tokens towards the correct answer, which is 8 in the given example, is illustrated in layers 10, 11, and 12 in Fig. 4.

In Fig. 4, we only illustrate the attention given to the actual answer tokens, but other tokens also receive attention. Upon closer inspection of layers 10, 11, and 12 within the model, using various examples, we uncover some interesting features. It appears that the tokens receiving the most attention tend to be the answers for each sub-sequence. This simplification step bears resemblance to step 2 in the process shown in Fig. 1 of how a person might approach solving the problem. This particular behavior is prominently observed in layer 10. For example, consider the following sequence:

[FIRST 2 3 [Max 1 5 6 1 2] 0 [MIN 1 0 2]]

The simplified problem after solving the sub-sequences would become:

[FIRST 2 3 6 0 0]

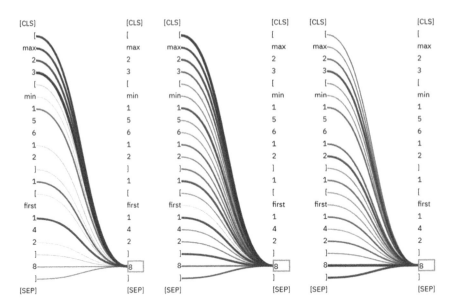

Fig. 4. Figure shows that most of the tokens attend to the correct answer in layers 10, 11, and 12 from left to right

The tokens of the simplified version match the most attended tokens in layer 10, with the token "2" receiving the highest attention. This token is the correct answer, as demonstrated in Fig. 5.

A more challenging instance occurs when the answer is not as apparent as in the previous example, as it is embedded within a sub-sequence. Nevertheless, we observe a similar pattern in which the model nearly attends to the simplified sequence version, with one token missing only. The example is presented as follows:

$$[\text{LAST } 2\ 3\ [\text{MIN } 1\ 5\ 6\ 1\ 2]\ 0\ [\text{MAX } 1\ 8\ 2\ ]\ ]$$

The simplified problem after solving the sub-sequences would become

$$[\text{LAST } 2\ 3\ 1\ 0\ 8\ ]$$

As depicted in Fig. 4, the most attended tokens are nearly identical to the simplified version, with the exception of 0. Once again, we observe that the predominantly attended token is "8" which represents the correct answer. It is crucial to acknowledge that this is not always the case, but we have noticed that it is a common pattern in layer 10. Interestingly, we discovered that this distinct pattern is not evident in layer 12, where we initially anticipated clearer observations. Although the tokens in layer 12 still attend to the correct answer, we detect more noise in the attention given to tokens that are not crucial for determining the answer.

In light of this unanticipated finding, we experimented with a novel fine-tuning technique as an alternative to the traditional method. Conventionally, the least parameter-intensive approach to fine-tuning a model involves freezing all model parameters except for the last layer. However, given our observation that the attention in layer 10 is clearer and more easily explained than in layer 12, we compared the model performance under two conditions: freezing all parameters except layer 10 and freezing all parameters except layer 12. The results presented in table 1 are both surprising and unconventional. Although both options yield lower scores than the fully fine-tuned model, the version fine-tuned with layer 10 outperforms the one with layer 12 by 5.3% on the modified ListOps dataset, with respective scores of 86.1% and 80.8%. It also outscores on the original ListOps dataset with respective scores of 54.5% and 52.8%.

Table 1. Table shows the accuracy of fine-tuned BERT

Fine-tune Settings	Modified ListOps	ListOps
Fine-tuned-layer-12	80.8%	52.8%
Fine-tuned-layer-10	86.1%	54.5%
Fully-fine-tuned	95.1%	61.6%

4.2 Heatmap Analysis

To obtain a thorough understanding of the tokens on which the model focuses and pinpoint the most attended tokens in a specific layer, we create heatmaps of the attention scores. These heatmaps offer a visual representation of the model's attention patterns, facilitating the identification of areas with high or low focus.

We employed the same formula for computing the attention map as used in the token-to-token analysis discussed earlier. As a result, we expect similar findings but with a distinct visualization method. The heatmaps display the attention of all tokens concurrently in a single image, enhancing the transparency and interpretability of the analysis. This comprehensive perspective enables us to better comprehend the model's attention patterns throughout the entire input sequence. Moreover, the heatmap allows for a clearer visualization of longer sequences, ensuring that the conclusions drawn from previous sections remain valid for extended sequences. The example shown in Fig. 6, 7, and 8 is:

[LAST 2 3 4 5 [MAX 3 9 1 1 7] [MIN 9 5 0 8 2] [MAX 1 5 8 3 5][MIN 1 0 2 3 5]]

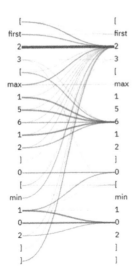
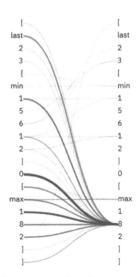

(a) Most attended tokens are the answers of sub-sequences and the answer of the whole sequence "2"

(b) Most attended tokens are the answers of sub-sequences and the answer of the whole sequence "8"

Fig. 5. Most attended tokens are the answers of sub-sequences and the answer of the whole sequence "2"

We will concentrate on layers 6, 10, and 12, where we drew significant conclusions in the previous section. In the generated heatmaps, lighter colors indicate higher attention scores. It is essential to note that the y-axis represents queries, while the x-axis represents keys. Attention heatmaps are not asymmetric: the horizontal axis of a token illustrates what it is attending to, while the vertical axis reveals which tokens it is attended by. For example, if the horizontal axis of the token "MAX" is entirely yellow, this indicates that it is attending to all tokens. Conversely, if the vertical axis of the same token "MAX" is yellow, it means that it is being attended to by all tokens.

In layer 6, as we anticipate each token to attend to its respective operator of each sub-sequence, we generate an attention heatmap for a longer sequence containing five operators. Indeed, as expected, Fig. 6 displays five blocks, corresponding to the number of operators, where each block refers to a sub-sequence signifying that the model is dividing the sequences into sub-sequences. A vertical green line is also visible at the beginning of each block, demonstrating that the most attended token is the operator for each sub-sequence.

For layer 10, the results once again align with our previous conclusions, as evidenced by the heatmap in Fig. 7. In most blocks (sub-sequences), the most attended token is the correct token for the sub-sequence. For example, token 9 of the first "MAX" operator in the sequence is primarily attended to within its sub-sequence, similar to zero in the first "MIN" sub-sequence and 8 in the second "MAX" sub-sequence. Ultimately, the overall most attended token is the correct answer for the entire sequence, which is zero.

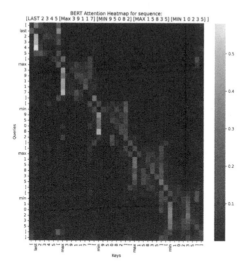

Fig. 6. The attention heat map in the 6th layer: the tokens inside each sub-sequence are attending to each other and to their operators, forming attention blocks.

Lastly, for the final layer depicted in Fig. 8, we observe that although the correct token 0 is attended to by most tokens, there are additional tokens that receive attention even though they are not crucial for the answer, such as tokens 2 and 3 in the last sub-sequence. These findings support our earlier conclusion from the token-to-token analysis, where we proposed that some noise exists in the last layer, making fine-tuning with the 10th layer achieving higher results.

4.3 Entropy Analysis

To solidify our attention analysis, we cross validate it with entropy analysis. By measuring the entropy of attention heads, we can determine whether the attention heads in each layer exhibit focused or broad attention. Theoretically, high entropy means that the attention is spread more evenly across the input elements, implying that the model is uncertain about which element is more important in the given context. This can also mean that the attention head is not specialized, as it does not focus on specific parts of the input. Low entropy, on the other hand, means that the attention is more focused or peaked on certain input elements, indicating that the model is more certain about which elements are important. This can signify that the attention head is specialized, as it concentrates on specific aspects of the input. Entropy in attention is calculated as

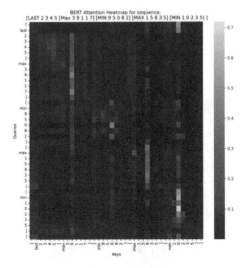

Fig. 7. The attention heat map in the 10th layer: the tokens that represent the correct answer in each sub-sequence are the most attended to.

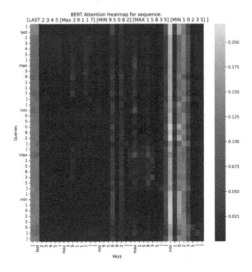

Fig. 8. The attention heat map in layer 12 (last layer): token "0", which is the correct answer among other noises are the most attended to tokens.

the sum of attention weights multiplied by their logarithms, reflecting the uncertainty or dispersion of the attention distribution across input elements. Figure 9 and 10 show the entropy average across 12 layers for the two analyzed sequences in the attention analysis.

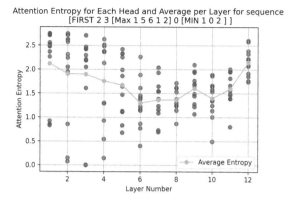

Fig. 9. Figure shows the entropy scores of each attention head in blue, as well as their layer-wise average in orange Notably, the lowest entropy values are predominantly found in layers 6 to 11. (Color figure online)

The findings align with what we observed during the attention analysis: layer 6 is evidently specialized in identifying the sub-sequences where all tokens attend to their respective operators. The entropy plot reveals that layer 6 has the lowest entropy for both analyzed sequences. Additionally, layer 10 also exhibits a low entropy score, which can be attributed to its role in selecting the correct answer for each sub-sequence, as indicated in the attention analysis. Lastly, the broad attention in the final layer could be attributed to the model's attempt to attend to all tokens and piece them together in order to predict the correct answer.

Moreover, Fig. 11 confirms that our entropy analysis remains consistent not only for the analyzed short sequence but also for a longer sequence from the validation dataset. The same characteristics discussed earlier persist, with layers 6 and 10 displaying some of the lowest entropy scores.

4.4   Representation Analysis

Finally, in this section we analyze the similarity between the embeddings of the tokens to gain more insight about the decision making in BERT for non-language tasks. In a language model, when tokens have similar representations, it means that their corresponding embedding vectors in the model's vector space are close to each other. These similar representations generally indicate that the language model has learned to associate the tokens with similar semantic or syntactic properties, and they may have comparable roles or meanings in the context of the sentences they appear in. Tokens with similar roles, functions, or meanings are likely to have similar representations in the embedding space. We aim to determine whether this principle also holds for non-language tasks. To conduct the similarity analysis, we compute a square similarity matrix. Consider the hidden state matrix H for a particular layer, where each row represents the

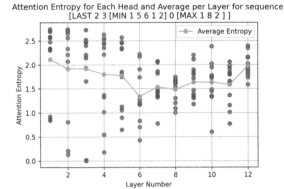

Fig. 10. Figure shows the entropy scores of each attention head in blue, as well as their layer-wise average in orange Notably, the lowest entropy values are predominantly found in layers 6 to 11. (Color figure online)

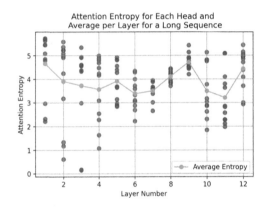

Fig. 11. Figure shows the entropy scores of each attention head in blue, as well as their layer-wise average in orange, for a long sequence. Notably, the lowest entropy values are predominantly found in layers 6, 10 and 11. (Color figure online)

hidden state for a token in the input sequence. The dot product with its transpose can be written as:

$$S = HH^\top \tag{2}$$

In this equation, S is the resulting square similarity matrix, and $H^\top$ represents the transpose of the hidden state matrix H. The element at position (i, j) in the matrix S corresponds to the similarity between the i-th and j-th token representations in the hidden state matrix H. Lastly, we utilize a heatmap to visualize this square matrix, illustrating the similarity between tokens. In the heatmaps, dark blue represents a high similarity between tokens, while the color gradient transitioning to light yellow signifies decreasing similarity between them.

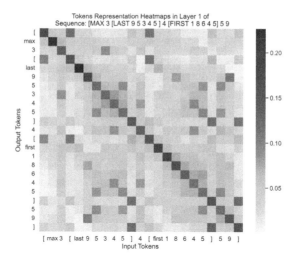

Fig. 12. Figure illustrates that in the initial layers (layer 1, as depicted in the figure), tokens representing the numbers exhibit similar representations.

In the initial layers, there is a strong similarity between numbers across the entire sequence, as depicted in Fig. 12. This is expected, as the early layers associate numbers with each other, deriving this property from the pre-trained embeddings. However, the intriguing result is that by the final layer, the model has learned to associate the tokens responsible for the prediction together. Referring back to Fig. 1 with step 2, where we show the last step before solving the problem, we can observe that it successfully correlates the essential tokens for the prediction, simplifying the sequence correctly. This analysis demonstrates that the model can solve the task hierarchically, revealing the relationship between these tokens, as illustrated in Fig. 13. Therefore, similar to how the model associates comparable roles or meanings in language tasks, it connects similar embeddings for tokens most crucial for answer prediction in this task.

The sequence shown in Fig. 13 is:

$$[\text{MAX} \quad 3 \; [\text{MIN} \; 0 \; 5 \; 3 \; 4 \; 5][\text{MIN} \; 1 \; 8 \; 6 \; 4 \; 5 \;] \; 5 \; 9 \;]$$

The simplified version after solving all of the sub-sequences with only the last operator to be solved should be:

$$[\text{MAX} \quad 3 \; 0 \; 1 \; 5 \; 9 \;]$$

Upon examining the similarity between these tokens, Fig. 13 evidently shows that they are most closely related to each other (including the sub-sequence operators). As a result, we claim that the model can solve the task in a manner similar to how a human would approach it, using a hierarchical strategy. We provide another example of this behavior in Fig. 14, where we observe that the input sequence has been simplified from:

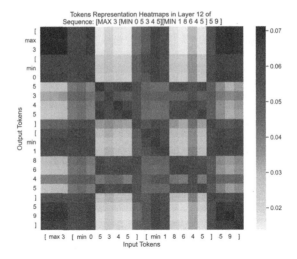

Fig. 13. Figure shows that at late layers (in this figure layer 12) the tokens that are similar to each other are the important tokens that are responsible for predicting the correct answer.

[MAX 3 [LAST 9 5 3 4 5] 4 [FIRST 1 8 6 4 5] 5 9]

to :

[MAX 3 5 4 1 5 9]

This is a common pattern that we see along many examples.

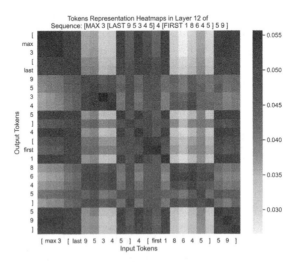

Fig. 14. Figure shows that at late layers (in this figure layer 12) the tokens that are similar to each other are the important tokens that are responsible for predicting the correct answer.

5 Generalization to Long Sequences

Based on the analyses and conclusions presented above, and considering that the model can capture these types of strategies to solve the ListOps problem, we expect the model, when trained on short sequences, to generalize to longer sequences. To determine whether the model can indeed generalize to longer sequences, we compare two additional settings to the original one, where we trained and tested on sequences of length 200–400. The first setting involves training on sequences of length 20–50 and testing on sequences of length 50–200, while the second entails testing on sequences of length 200–400.

Table 2 and 3 display the results of the fully fine-tuned BERT on the original ListOps and the modified ListOps, respectively. The findings indeed demonstrate the model's ability to generalize, particularly when trained on sequences of length 20–50 and tested on sequences of length 50–200 for both datasets. For example, the model achieves a 76.1% score on the modified ListOps dataset when trained on sequences of length 20–50 and tested on sequences of length 50–200, significantly surpassing the 10% random chance. The model's performance declines when tested on longer sequences, reaching 52.5%, but this score remains well above the 10% random chance. In conclusion, due to the strategy employed by the model, as explained in the previous analysis, the model can generalize and achieve satisfactory scores on test datasets that are substantially longer than the sequences it was trained on.

Table 2. Table shows the generalization results on longer sequences on the original ListOps dataset

Trained on sequence length of	Tested on sequence length of	Accuracy
200–400	200–400	61.6%
20–50	20–50	68.0%
20–50	50–200	47.2%
20–50	200–400	30.1%

Table 3. Table shows the generalization results on longer sequences on the modified ListOps dataset

Trained on sequence length of	Tested on sequence length of	Accuracy
200–400	200–400	95.1%
20–50	20–50	99.9%
20–50	50–200	76.1%
20–50	200–400	52.5%

6   Limitation of Attention Analysis

In this section, we examine the attention of a BERT model fine-tuned to predict the winner of a Tic Tac Toe game. This simple 2D game has a 3×3 dimension, which we flatten into a 1D sequence. The model achieves 100% accuracy on this game, demonstrating that it can easily predict the winner if a player ("x" or "o") completely fills a horizontal, vertical, or diagonal line. Through this experiment, we investigate whether the attention could generalize to a 2D input. The model perfectly attends to the correct token when the winner fills a horizontal line, as shown in Fig. 15, but struggles to attend to the correct tokens when the winner fills vertical or diagonal lines, as illustrated in Fig. 16. The difficulty in attending to the correct tokens for vertical and diagonal lines could be due to the way the 2D structure is flattened into a 1D sequence, making it more challenging for the model to recognize vertical and diagonal patterns, even in short sequences. This limitation is expected for a model like BERT, as it was trained on 1D language data and may not generalize well to 2D data structures. However, even though the model does not attend to the correct tokens that determine the game's winner when the lines are diagonal or vertical, the heatmaps reveal that it mostly attends to some tokens associated with the actual winner. This could suggest that the attention is present but not clearly depicted in the illustrations.

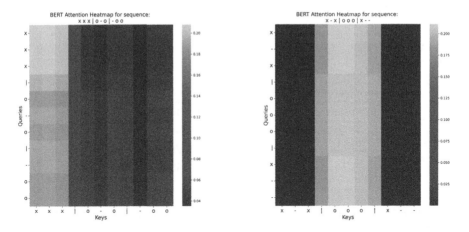

Fig. 15. Figure shows the ability of the model to attend to winner when the winner fills horizontal line

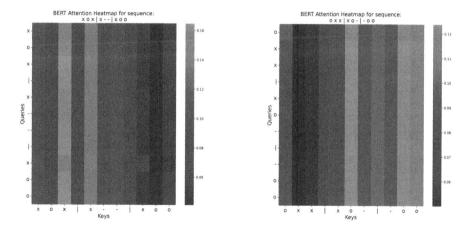

Fig. 16. Figure shows that the model cannot detect the tokens responsible for the win, but still attends to the winner

7 Conclusion and Outlook

In conclusion, this paper presents novel probing tasks to comprehend the steps that BERT model follows in solving non-language tasks. In contrast to vision and language tasks, where we lack an understanding of human processing, the carefully chosen tasks involve a hierarchical approach with straightforward steps. Our analysis includes token-to-token examination, through which we discover that specific layers have designated tasks. For example, layer 6 identifies subsequences within the entire sequence, while layer 10 simplifies the input sequence into a more straightforward sequence, similar to how humans might approach the problem. These observations are supported by entropy calculations for each layer, with layers 6 and 10 exhibiting lower scores, indicating their specialized tasks. These observations have led to the identification of an unconventional yet efficient fine-tuning approach, in which we only fine-tune the parameters of layer 10 of the model, resulting in comparatively good performance. Additionally, our representation analysis demonstrates that the model can assign similar embeddings to tokens crucial for accurately answering the sequence. Lastly, we highlight a limitation of the analysis, as attention mechanisms only partially succeed in identifying 2D patterns.

This paper could serve as a base for future work in this area, particularly concerning analyzing attention for non-language tasks, as these models are increasingly being employed for tasks beyond language processing. Additionally, we hope that this study inspires the development of novel fine-tuning techniques. We believe that this work could be expanded by examining more non-language tasks, where insights gained from the attention outputs could contribute to a deeper understanding of the underlying mechanisms in these models. Finally, conducting a psychological study to compare the methods various individuals use to solve the ListOps tasks with the demonstrated steps of the model's problem-solving approach would be interesting.

Acknowledgements. This work was funded by the Deutsche Forschungsgemeinschaft (DFG, German Research Foundation). The cluster used to train the models was also funded by the German Research Foundation (DFG) - 456666331.

References

1. Vaswani, A., et al.: Attention is all you need. In: Advances in Neural Information Processing Systems, vol. 30 (2017)
2. Devlin, J., et al.: BERT: pre-training of deep bidirectional trans- formers for language understanding. arXiv preprint arXiv:1810.04805 (2018)
3. Raffel, C., et al.: Exploring the limits of transfer learning with a unified text-to-text transformer. J. Mach. Learn. Res. **21**, 5485–5551 (2020). Article no. 140
4. Lewis, M., et al.: BART: denoising sequence-to-sequence pre-training for natural language generation, translation, and comprehension. arXiv preprint arXiv:1910.13461 (2019)
5. Radford, A., Narasimhan, K., Salimans, T., Sutskever, I.: Improving language understanding by generative pre-training (2018)
6. Dosovitskiy, A., et al.: An image is worth 16x16 words: transformers for image recognition at scale. arXiv preprint arXiv:2010.11929 (2020)
7. Dong, L., Xu, S., Xu, B.: Speech-transformer: a no-recurrence sequence-to-sequence model for speech recognition. In: 2018 IEEE International Conference on Acoustics, Speech and Signal Processing (ICASSP). IEEE (2018)
8. Jawahar, G., Sagot, B., Seddah, D.: What does BERT learn about the structure of language?. In: ACL 2019–57th Annual Meeting of the Association for Computational Linguistics (2019)
9. Kovaleva, O., et al.: Revealing the dark secrets of BERT. arXiv preprint arXiv:1908.08593 (2019)
10. Serrano, S., Smith, N.A.: Is attention interpretable?. arXiv preprint arXiv:1906.03731 (2019)
11. OpenAI. GPT-4 technical report. arXiv preprint arXiv: 2303.08774 (2023)
12. Jain, S., Wallace, B.C.: Attention is not explanation. arXiv preprint arXiv:1902.10186 (2019)
13. Tay, Y., et al.: Long range arena: a benchmark for efficient transformers. arXiv preprint arXiv:2011.04006 (2020)
14. Hoover, B., Strobelt, S., Gehrmann, S.: exBERT: a visual analysis tool to explore learned representations in transformers models. arXiv preprint arXiv:1910.05276 (2019)
15. Vig, J.: BertViz: a tool for visualizing multihead self-attention in the BERT model. In: Debugging Machine Learning Models, ICLR workshop (2019)
16. Goldberg, Y.: Assessing BERT's syntactic abilities. arXiv preprint arXiv:1901.05287 (2019)
17. Clark, K., et al.: What does BERT look at? an analysis of BERT's attention. arXiv preprint arXiv:1906.04341 (2019)
18. Wiegreffe, S., Pinter, Y.: Attention is not not explanation. arXiv preprint arXiv:1908.04626 (2019)
19. Piękos, P., Michalewski, H., Malinowski, M.: Measuring and improving BERT's mathematical abilities by predicting the order of reasoning. arXiv preprint arXiv:2106.03921 (2021)
20. Peng, S., et al.: MathBERT: a pre-trained model for mathematical formula understanding. arXiv preprint arXiv:2105.00377 (2021)

21. Lu, K., et al.: Pretrained transformers as universal computation engines. arXiv preprint arXiv:2103.05247 1 (2021)
22. Rajpurkar, P., Jia, R., Liang, P.: Know what you don't know: unanswerable questions for SQuAD. arXiv preprint arXiv:1806.03822 (2018)
23. Sun, C., Huang, L., Qiu, X.: Utilizing BERT for aspect-based sentiment analysis via constructing auxiliary sentence. arXiv preprint arXiv:1903.09588 (2019)
24. Wolf, T., et al.: HuggingFace's transformers: state-of-the-art natural language processing. arXiv preprint arXiv:1910.03771 (2020)
25. Nangia, N., Bowman, S.R.: ListOps: a diagnostic dataset for latent tree learning. arXiv preprint arXiv:1804.06028 (2018)
26. Nogueira, R., Jiang, Z., Lin, J.: Investigating the limitations of transformers with simple arithmetic tasks. arXiv preprint arXiv:2102.13019 (2021)

Evaluating Self-attention Interpretability Through Human-Grounded Experimental Protocol

Milan Bhan[1,2(✉)], Nina Achache[1], Victor Legrand[1], Annabelle Blangero[2,3], and Nicolas Chesneau[1]

[1] Ekimetrics, Paris, France
milan.bhan@ekimetrics.com
[2] Sorbonne University, Paris, France
[3] Aix-Marseille University, Aix-Marseille, France

Abstract. Attention mechanisms have played a crucial role in the development of complex architectures such as Transformers in natural language processing. However, Transformers remain hard to interpret and are considered as black-boxes. In this paper we assess how attention coefficients from Transformers help in providing classifier interpretability when properly aggregated. A fast and easy-to-implement way of aggregating attention is proposed to build local feature importance. A human-grounded experiment is conducted to evaluate and compare this approach to other usual interpretability methods. The experimental protocol relies on the capacity of an interpretability method to provide explanation in line with human reasoning. Experiment design includes measuring reaction times and correct response rates by human subjects. Attention performs comparably to usual interpretability methods and significantly better than a random baseline regarding average participant reaction time and accuracy. Moreover, data analysis highlights that high probability prediction induces great explanation relevance. This work shows how self-attention can be aggregated and used to explain Transformer classifiers. The low computational cost of attention compared to other interpretability methods and its availability by design within Transformer classifiers make it particularly beneficial. Finally, the quality of its explanation depends strongly on the certainty of the classifier's prediction related to it.

Keywords: Interpretability · NLP · XAI · Attention · Human-grounded ML

1 Introduction

The field of machine learning (ML) has recently witnessed great advances. ML algorithms have achieved high levels of performance in a wide variety of tasks due to their rapid development. Natural language processing (NLP) has also taken

L. Longo (Ed.): xAI 2023, CCIS 1903, pp. 26–46, 2023.
https://doi.org/10.1007/978-3-031-44070-0_2

advantage of recent breakthroughs in ML with the development and democratization of Transformer-type models [29]. Attention mechanism [3] is a crucial component in Transformer architecture, enabling models to focus on specific parts of the input text. The complexity of these new models led to an increasing difficulty in understanding and interpreting their predictions. The field of eXplainable Artificial Intelligence (XAI) has emerged to overcome this lack of transparency by developing methods of "interpretability" or "explainability" [18]. Such a gap needs to be filled in many areas ,e.g., health care [13] and finance [32]. Most commonly used interpretability methods are computationally greedy and based on strong hypothesis such as features' independence and linear approximation [21]. More specifically, attention interpretability from Transformers has been debated [7] and remains questionable. The diversity of interpretability methods raises the need for their comparison.

Human-grounded protocols have been proposed to experimentally address the assessment and the comparison of interpretability methods [5, 24, 25, 31]. These empirical approaches consist in asking humans to interact with a machine and to perform a specific task under the influence of interpretability methods. An XAI method will be considered as better than another should it yield to an improved human-making performance.

This paper aims at assessing how self-attention from Transformer classifiers can be used to build reliable local feature importance. Self-attention is aggregated in a specific way that we call CLaSsification-Attention (CLS-A) for convenience in the following. The main contributions of this paper are summarized as follows:

1. CLS-A, an easy-to-implement way of aggregating self-attention in Transformer classifiers is presented.
2. CLS-A is experimentally compared to other interpretability methods with a human-grounded protocol.
3. The dependency between prediction certainty and explanation reliability is highlighted.

In this paper we first introduce key notions of Transformers architecture and local feature importance. We then present CLS-A and the experimental protocol used to assess its interest compared to a baseline and other XAI approaches. Finally, we analyze the data produced by the three experiments.

2   Background and Related Work

This section introduces some key notions about Transformers architectures and XAI.

2.1   Background

Transformers, Attention and BERT. In NLP, Transformer-like models have achieved high levels of performance in a variety of tasks, such as text summarizing, question answering or named entity recognition. These models are particularly complex, with a number of parameters that can exceed the billion [23]. The Transformer architecture is based on multi-head self-attention mechanisms, aiming at making learning more efficient [3] by encoding the relations between words. The model attends to different parts of the input in parallel, using multiple self-attention heads. A self-attention head takes as input a triplet (Q, K, V) and outputs a representation as formalized in the following formula:

$$\texttt{Attention}(Q, K, V) = \texttt{softmax}(\frac{QK^T}{\sqrt{d_k}})V \tag{1}$$

where:

- Q (query) is a matrix that represents the input in which the attention mechanism focuses on.
- K (key) is a matrix that represents the different elements in the input that the attention mechanism can attend to.
- V (value) is a matrix that represents the output of the attention mechanism.
- d_k is the dimension of matrices Q and V and allows to stabilize the model during the training phase

Hence, each head has its own set of parameters, allowing the model to learn different types of attention patterns. The attentions resulting from each of the heads are then concatenated and projected on a dense layer.

Bidirectional Encoder Representations from Transformers (BERT) [11] is a stack of n encoders from the Transformer architecture. Each BERT layer contains h attention heads with its own set of weights, which have been learned during training. These weights determine how the model will attend to different parts of the input when making a prediction. In this way, words are related to each other even in the case of long-term dependency. BERT has been widely adopted and has achieved state-of-the-art performance on a variety of benchmarks.

One of the key features of BERT is its bidirectional nature. Unlike previous models that were only trained to look *before* or *after* a word, BERT is trained to look *before* and *after* a word at the same time. This allows BERT to understand the full context of a word and improve its performance on NLU tasks. Moreover, BERT has several advantages such as its scalability, its compatibility with parallelization and its ability to capture long-distance dependencies. The BERT *CLS* (for "classification") token is a special token added at the beginning of an input text. This token is used as a representation of the entire input sequence by the classifier to perform prediction. The final hidden state of the *CLS* token, which is a fixed-size vector, is typically used as the input to a classifier or other downstream task. This allows BERT to take into account information from the entire sequence when making a prediction by computing only one token.

Local Feature Importance. There are several ways to interpret black-box systems such as BERT models [15]. One of the main approaches consists in computing local feature importance [18]. When the model to explain is a classifier, contributions to the probability score of the predicted class are computed and assigned to input features. It can be done by considering ML models as black-boxes and explaining their predictions *ex post*, without referring to their inherent parameters. This kind of approach is called *post-hoc model-agnostic* [8]. Another way to compute local feature importance is to go through inherent model parameters [27,28], which can be significantly less computationally greedy. However, this requires access to the model parameters, which is not always the case. This kind of approaches is referred to as *post-hoc model-specific*. The large number of local feature importance methods can make it difficult to choose the most appropriate one.

Due to their flexibility and the plurality of data types on which they can be applied, Linear Interpretable Model-agnostic Explainer (LIME) [22] and SHapley Additive exPlanations (SHAP) [16] are the most frequently used interpretability methods in the industry [6]. LIME offers to explain a prediction locally using models that are interpretable by design such as sparse regressions. The algorithm artificially generates data points in a neighborhood around the instance to explain and fits an interpretable model on these new examples. The SHAP method is inspired by the Shapley values [26] from economics and game theory. It aims to distribute fairly the rewards from a set of games to all the players. Feature importance of a specific prediction is computed by associating the features of a model to the players to whom the gains are distributed.

2.2   Related Work

Substantial amount of linguistic and syntactic knowledge can be found in Transformer attention [10]. However, the interpretability of the attention coefficients is still an open question [7]. Several methods based on self-attention coefficients have been proposed to explain the predictions made by Transformer-type models, such as attention flow and attention roll-out [1]. These methods are based on complex aggregators to synthesize the information contained in the attention layers. Visualization tools allowing to dive in detail into self-attention have been developed as well [30]. Visualizing attention is the basis of saliency map approaches specific to Computer Vision for Vision Transformers [4,9]. If these approaches enable to compute local feature importance, the quality of the explanation produced is not rigorously assessed. This raises the question of the evaluation of interpretability.

One way to assess the interpretability of a given method is to compare it quantitatively [2] to common interpretable approaches such as SHAP. A given method would thus be considered interpretable if it strongly correlates with one target local feature importance method. One way to measure such correlation is to use Pearson or Kendall coefficients in order to compare feature importance rankings resulting from these interpretability methods. This approach has its limitations because it would imply that LIME and SHAP would be unique ground truths to replicate.

When no ground truths are available, a given method can be evaluated with function-grounded metrics [2]. *Faithfulness* measures the impact on the probability score by perturbing the features considered as important or unimportant by a specific method. The higher the faithfulness, the more relevant the interpretability method. Another measure called *stability* (or *robustness*) assesses the explanation sensitivity to changes in features or model parameters. Finally, *fidelity* measures how closely an explanation reflects the model prediction. If these approaches bring rich information about an interpretability method, they say nothing about the intelligibility of the resulting explanations to a human.

Human-grounded evaluation and experimental approaches can be alternatives to reach a rigorous science of interpretable machine learning [12]. Since local feature importance methods can have significant positive effect on human performance [24,31], these methods can also be compared by evaluating how they make human more effective during a specific annotation task [21]. Such experimental protocols obtain contrasted outcomes, resulting in a more positive effect of XAI assistance on text than tabular data [24]. In the context of NLP, this type of protocol consists in asking humans to perform text annotation under the influence of local feature importance [14,25]. The response time and the average accuracy are measured and compared between the different methods. This typology of experimental protocol has the advantage of quantifying the quality of an explanation, as long as the explanation is intended to support human decision.

Attention-based explanations in particular have been experimentally compared to LIME on a BERT model classifying genuine and deceptive hotel reviews [14]. In this work, attention is aggregated by averaging the attention coefficients over the whole 12 attention heads of the last BERT layer. This results in a higher human annotation performance with LIME compared to aggregated attention. The simplicity of this aggregation, however, does not enable one to conclude about the interest of using attention. Furthermore, attention-based explanations are not compared to a simple baseline, such as a random generator.

3   Methodology

We present an easy-to-implement way of aggregating attention from Transformer models that we call CLS-A. Then we define an experimental protocol inspired from the ones introduced in Sect. 2 that we apply on three different annotation tasks of binary classification. Finally we introduce the evaluation protocol with data description, linear and non linear modeling.

3.1   CLS-A

We introduce the way we aggregate Transformer self-attention to build a local feature importance metric. This approach can be used in every Transformer-like

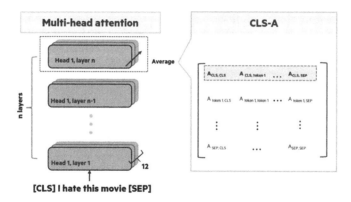

Fig. 1. Scheme of CLS-A. Average attention related to the *CLS* token is computed on the last attention layer.

classifier such as BERT, as long as the *CLS* token is used to perform classification. We use the attention coefficients related to the *CLS* token. We call context the distribution of attention between an input word and the rest of the sequence. This way, CLS-A represents the average context of the *CLS* token.

We focus on the last layer of the BERT architecture. Figure 1 shows the global process of the CLS-A computation from an initial text. Since this last layer contains h self-attention heads, the coefficients are aggregated by averaging to build a one-dimensional local feature importance explanation. The proximity of the attention head within a specific layer [10] justifies our choice of aggregating through the whole layer. This results in an average context of the classification token in the last layer of BERT. A weight is assigned to each word of the input text, representing its importance in the context that induced the prediction of the classifier. The interest of this approach lies in the focus on the relationship between the CLS token and its context.

Since the *CLS* token plays a central role in the computation of CLS-A, it is recommended that the BERT forward pass passes by the *CLS* token to perform its prediction. Therefore, the prediction has to be done by computing the embedding from the *CLS* token only. In the case where the BERT forward pass does not pass exclusively through the *CLS* token, a less satisfying alternative is to compute the average of all the coefficients of the attention heads (see Sect. 2).

3.2 Experimental Protocol

Motivated by the proven utility of experimental protocols to compare XAI methods [24,25,31], we ask participants to annotate one hundred texts in a binary classification task. Each text has some words colored with a more or less intense shade of blue (see in the screen in Fig. 2), based on an underlying interpretability method or a random generator. The higher the coefficient of the method, the stronger the highlighted blue shade. Accuracy and response time are measured to evaluate each method's ability to assist the participant in the annotation task. The higher the accuracy and the shorter the response time, the more relevant the method as it facilitates the human semantic processing of the text.

Setup and Instructions. All participants take part in the experiment in the same room and can be up to three at the same time. They are isolated in order to limit any other exogenous influence (visual, sound) and are placed in front of a computer as depicted in Fig. 2. An explanation of the protocol is displayed on the screen to put the participants in the right conditions. In order to perform the annotation task, participants are asked to press either one of two buttons corresponding to the two possible answers as shown in Fig. 2. The buttons correspond to keys on the keyboard of the computer used. Two colored stickers are stuck on the keys to help locate them. When a text is annotated (response given/key pressed), the next one is displayed on the screen.

Three classification tasks are evaluated. The first one (Experiment 1) is to evaluate the global sentiment of a movie review. The participant must choose between the "positive" and "negative" sentiment. The second and third (Experiment 2 and 3) are film genre evaluations. In Experiment 2, the task is to distinguish between action and drama films, in Experiment 3 between horror and comedy. The information given in the explanation of the protocol differs depending on the classification task. Participants annotating film genres are asked to respond quickly. Participants are also told that displayed colors can potentially be useful in the annotation task. Participants annotating movie review sentiments have no information about the colors displayed and no incentive to respond quickly.

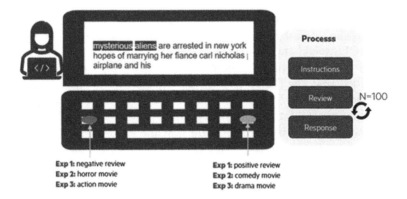

Fig. 2. Scheme of the experimental protocol. Each participant labels 100 different texts after reading the instructions. The participant has two possible answers, depending on the experiment he/she is participating in. The text is colored according to the interpretability method used to explain the classifier's prediction. The selected texts are all classified properly by the classifier.

Experiment Characteristics. All the 100 participants have a background in data science or statistics. None of the participants labels data as a profession. The first experiment involved 50 participants while the other two had 25 each. The participants were predominantly male: about 76% compared to 24% for women. They were between 22 and 40 years old and none of the subjects were cognitively impaired to our knowledge.

Every participant is asked to annotate 100 different texts in a binary classification task. The asked classification task remains the same during the whole experiment. A participant cannot see the same text twice during the experiment. Each text has its words colored in different shades of blue. This coloring is proportional to the coefficients chosen at random among a random baseline, SHAP, LIME and CLS-A built on the DistilBERT classifier attention. The random baseline assigns randomly a coefficient to each word. This way, participants are subjected to exogenous attentional orientation effects in order to compare the methods one-to-one. We show in Appendix, Table 6 the balanced distribution of the methods used to color the plotted texts. An example of the text displayed during the experiment is plotted in Fig. 2.

The classes of the various classification tasks are all equally represented among the displayed texts. We assess the contribution of interpretability methods under the assumption that the prediction of a model is correct. Therefore, the instances selected for the study were all correctly predicted. We wanted to look at the effect of the review length and the prediction probabilities in Experiments 2 and 3. The reviews corresponding to the sentiment analysis task contain between 32 and 50 words. The text sequence lengths of the other classification tasks vary between 19 and 145 words. The probability scores of belonging to the target class are highly polarized for the sentiment analysis and the horror/comedy classification while probability score is more uniformly distributed for the action/drama classification task. We assume that an interpretability method provides good explanations to the extent that it helps an annotator to go faster and be more efficient. An explanation will then be the object of a semantic congruence between the label to be predicted and the words highlighted. Therefore, the response time is precisely measured for each text and the correctness of the answers is assessed.

3.3 Implementation Details

The three classifiers analyzed during the three annotation tasks were based on a DistilBERT [23]. Each pre-trained DistilBERT was retrieved from Hugging Face[1]. A dense layer was added to perform the classification and fine-tune each model. The forward pass was defined as getting the embedding of the CLS token to perform the classification task. The library used to compile and fine-tune the models were Keras on the TensorFlow framework. Each model was trained with an initial learning rate of 10^{-5} and a reducing learning strategy when reaching a plateau. The number of epochs was for each model of 5 and the batch size was 32. The models were trained with a binary crossentropy loss and the Adam

---

[1] www.huggingface.co/.

optimizer. The first model was fine-tuned for sentiment analysis on the IMDB database [17]. The second and third one were fine-tuned to perform movie genre classification on a Kaggle dataset[2].

For each text, SHAP was computed with the `shap` library [16]. The Shapley values were computed in a permutation way. Finally, LIME was computed with the `lime` [22] library. The whole experiment was performed on the `psychopy` [20] framework on Python.

3.4 Data Analyses

In this section we define the followed methodology to analyze the data produced by the experimental protocol presented above. Each experiment produces $n \times 100$ answers, with n the number of participants, and 100 the number of plotted text samples during each experiment. The indicators of interest are the labeling time, which we call "reaction time", and whether or not the participant is wrong, which we call "accuracy". These variables of interest are then analyzed through their relationship with other characteristics such as features about the text (sequence length, probability score, trial number, relative position of impacting word) and the interpretability method used to color it.

Data Description. The descriptive analysis is first performed by calculating the average reaction time and the average accuracy. The one-tailed t-test is then used to compare the distributions of reaction times between interpretability methods and the random baseline in order to have statistically significant comparisons. This test is applied here to the average difference between each interpretability method and the random baseline, per participant, per experiment.

Linear Modeling. The impact of interpretability methods on reaction time is estimated with a linear regression by incorporating the effect of other explanatory variables. The random baseline is used for reference. Thus, the coefficients of the linear regression associated with the method used to color the text are expressed with respect to this baseline. For each experiment, one linear model is built per participant to explain its reaction time to the labeling task. The explanatory variables of the models for an experiment are the same for all participants. The mean value of the regression parameters and their distribution are then analyzed with the one-tailed t-test presented above.

Non-linear Modeling. Decision tree boosting algorithms enable to model complex and non-linear phenomena. We apply this type of algorithm to model the participant accuracy. This binary classification problem is addressed via Explainable Boosting Machine (EBM) [19]. EBM reaches performance levels equivalent

---

[2] www.kaggle.com/competitions/movie-genre-classification/overview.

to other boosting approaches based on decision trees, while decomposing its prediction into interpretable contributions of the explanatory variables. EBM is a generalized additive model (GAM) of the form:

$$g(\mathbb{E}[y]) = \beta_0 + \sum_i f_i(x_i) + \sum_{i,j,i \neq j} f_{i,j}(x_i, x_j) \qquad (2)$$

where:

- y is the variable indicating whether a participant has successfully completed its labeling
- g is the link function
- β_0 is the intercept
- f_i is the feature function of the variable x_i,
- $f_{i,j}$ is the pairwise interaction function of the two variables x_i and x_j

Table 1. Average reaction time and accuracy per experiment per method. The numbers in bold correspond to the best performance.

Metrics	Experiment	CLS-A (mean ± std)	LIME (mean ± std)	SHAP (mean ± std)	Random (mean ± std)
Reaction Time (s)	Exp 1	**10.3 ± 4.2**	10.6 ± 4.6	10.5 ± 4.5	11.0 ± 3.9
	Exp 2	9.0 ± 3.7	**8.3 ± 3.5**	8.4 ± 4.1	8.6 ± 3.3
	Exp 3	**11.02 ± 6.8**	11.3 ± 6.8	11.8 ± 5.9	12.3 ± 7.5
Accuracy (%)	Exp 1	**97.0 ± 5.8**	96.3 ± 3.9	95.5 ± 5.3	95.0 ± 5.5
	Exp 2	**80.6 ± 9.9**	79.4 ± 12.4	79.9 ± 9.1	79.8 ± 10.1
	Exp 3	**86.1 ± 9.5**	85.4 ± 9.3	81.3 ± 12.8	84.1 ± 8.9

A response curve represents the effect of a given explanatory variable by plotting the evolution of its contribution to the target variable. One model is fitted per method and per experiment to compare the response curves of the methods within a given experiment. Each model has to be trained with the same explanatory variables. Since the participants generally perform their annotation tasks accurately, the data are largely imbalanced. Sub-sampling is therefore performed to run the EBM on a balanced dataset with a balanced distribution between right and wrong answers. Since this sub-sampling induces sampling bias, this operation is run 50 times. Average response curves and standard deviations are finally calculated.

4   Results

In this section we compare CLS-A to LIME, SHAP and a random baseline following the methodology introduced in Sect. 3. We show that CLS-A improves both speed and accuracy of annotation in a statistically significant way compared to the random baseline. CLS-A, SHAP and LIME result in statistically similar response times and accuracy. Furthermore, we highlight the relationship between the quality of an explanation and the certainty of the classifier's prediction.

4.1   Data Description

The first experiment consisted of responses from 50 participants while the other two had 25 each. Table 1 relates the average reaction time and the average accuracy per experiment and per interpretability method. This shows that the average reaction time related to CLS-A is lower for experiments 1 and 3. Accuracy is also on average higher for participants who were exposed to CLS-A. The random baseline induces less accurate and slower responses overall.

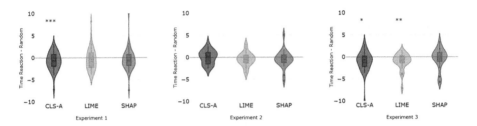

Fig. 3. Distribution of mean reaction time difference from random baseline by participant, by experiment. The results of the one-tailed t-test are represented with stars above the violin plots. With p as the p-value of the t-test, $*p < 5\%$, $**p < 1\%$, and $***p < 0.5\%$

We compare the distributions of the average response time of the CLS-A, LIME and SHAP methods in comparison to the random baseline. We perform this distribution comparison using the one-tailed t-test on the average difference between the XAI method and the baseline, per participant as presented in Sect. 3. Figure 3 plots the distribution of the average reaction time deviation from the random baseline with the results of the t-tests, by method and by experiment. The mean difference in reaction time between CLS-A and the random baseline is statistically significant in the first and third experiments. This difference is also statistically significant between LIME and the baseline in the third experiment.

Therefore, participants went faster on average in the text annotation task in Experiments 1 and 3 when they were exposed to CLS-A compared to the baseline. This difference from baseline is exclusive to CLS-A for Experiment 1, and shared with LIME for Experiment 3.

4.2   Linear Modeling

The target variable is reaction time and the explanatory variables (see Table 3 in Appendix A) are information about the assessed text on one hand and the interpretability method used to color it on the other. The performance metrics of the linear regressions on reaction times are presented in Table 2 Appendix A.

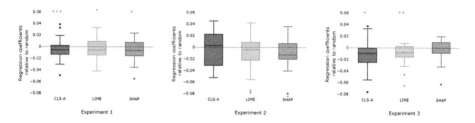

Fig. 4. Distribution of linear modeling on reaction times coefficients of each interpretability method variable with respect to the baseline. The results of the one-tailed t-test are represented with stars above the box plots. With p as the p-value of the one-tailed t-test, $*p < 5\%$, $**p < 1\%$, and $***p < 0.5\%$

Method Effect. Figure 4 shows the distributions of coefficients of linear regressions on reaction times associated with the interpretability method used to color the text. All coefficients are computed with respect to the random baseline.

The average linear regression coefficients on reaction times of CLS-A and LIME are significantly negative for Experiment 1 and 3. Average reaction time coefficient is negative for SHAP in Experiment 1. The results for the CLS-A method are broadly consistent with the previous exploratory analysis. Participants took less time on average to complete their annotation task on Experiment 1 and 3 when important words in the text were colored via the CLS-A method compared to the random baseline. However, the results differ for SHAP and LIME, and Experiment 2 does not show a statistically significant difference between these 3 methods compared to the random baseline.

Probability Score and Review Length Effects. We similarly assess the distributions of two more features in the linear regression model on reaction times, namely the probability of belonging to the target class, and the length of the review. The Fig. 5 represents the distribution of these coefficients, by experiment. The significance of the means of the distributions is assessed with a one-tailed paired t-test.

The sign of each of the two coefficients is consistent across all three experiments. The effect of the probability score variable on response time is negative on average, whereas the effect of the sequence length is positive. These impacts are statistically significant across all three experiments. Thus, all things being equal, the higher the probability score of belonging to the target class, the lower the reaction time. This highlights the relationship between the quality of an explanation and the certainty of a prediction from a time reaction perspective. In the same way, all things being equal, the annotation time increases with the length of the textual sequence processed.

To summarize, linear modeling highlights that CLS-A fosters quicker responses on average compared to the random baseline. Besides, the higher the prediction certainty, the lower the human reaction time.

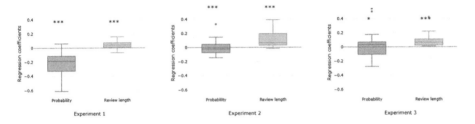

Fig. 5. Distribution of probability score and review length coefficients in linear modeling. The results of the one-tailed t-test are represented with stars above the box plots. Noting p as the p-value of the statistical test, the notations are as follows. $*p < 5\%$, $**p < 1\%$, and $***p < 0.5\%$

4.3   Non-linear Modeling

This section compares CLS-A and the random baseline through the prism of the participant's accuracy, which is modelled using non-linear Explainable Boosting Machines (EBM) introduced in Sect. 3. The explanatory variables used to explain participant's response to the experiment are presented in Appendix A, Table 3.

In this section we focus on the impact of the probability score and the reaction time on the annotation accuracy. Figure 6, 7 and 8 represent the EBM response curves of the probability score and the reaction time, by method, by experiment. These curves represent the contributions to the probability scores that the participant performs the correctly the annotation. The interval around the mean curve represented the standard deviation measured on 50 sampling iterations for a given model. For each of the analyzed variables, we focus on the comparison between CLS-A and the random baseline.

Sentiment Analysis. The first experiment emphasizes a higher target class probability score contribution for CLS-A compared to the random baseline in Fig. 6. The response curves tend to merge for the polarized probability scores and CLS-A falls below the baseline for the probability score distribution tail. Fast reactions induce higher accuracy contribution for CLS-A. Accuracy contribution tend to be the same for very long response times. Therefore, the interest of CLS-A compared to the random generator lies in the relatively low probabilities in the first experiment. Note however that the probability score distribution is very high in the first experiment, and covers very few non-polarized predictions. Moreover, the contribution of CLS-A is significant for fast predictions, and tends to vanish gradually.

Movie Genre Classification, Action vs. Drama. The second experiment has a more dispersed distribution of target class probability scores than the first experiment. The CLS-A response curve associated with the target class probability score variable is higher for polarized predictions as shown in Fig. 7. Then, the contribution of CLS-A compared to the baseline seems to be related to the certainty of the classifier prediction. The area in which the CLS-A response curve is higher corresponds to the majority of the probability score distribution of the target variable. Finally, the accuracy contributions of the reaction time variables are higher for CLS-A for short and very long responses. Finally and similarly to the first experiment, CLS-A has a strong impact to form rapid responses when labeling a high target class probability score text.

Movie Genre Classification, Horror vs. Comedy. The distribution of the target class probability score variable is less dispersed in the last experiment than in the second one. Figure 8 depicts a higher CLS-A response curve for high probability scores and falls below it at the distribution tail. Finally, the effect of CLS-A on the response time variable with respect to the baseline in experiment 3 is relatively similar to Experiment 2. Short and very long answers are more accurate with CLS-A compared to the random baseline.

To summarize, the analysis of the response curves highlights the non-linear relationships between the explanatory variables and the target variable. The interest of CLS-A is strong for high certainty prediction and less important or even non-existent for texts whose probability scores are low. This highlights a strong relationship between the quality of an explanation and the certainty of a prediction. Additional analysis in Appendix A Fig. 9, 10 and 11 and Table 5 generalize this link to SHAP and LIME.

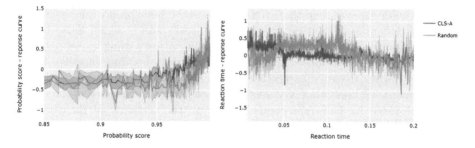

Fig. 6. Explainable boosting machine response curves of probability score and time reaction in the first experiment. The contribution of the probability score variable becomes positive at a lower probability threshold for CLS-A compared to the random generator. The contributions of the reaction time variables are positive for the fast reactions for the CLS-A method unlike the random generator.

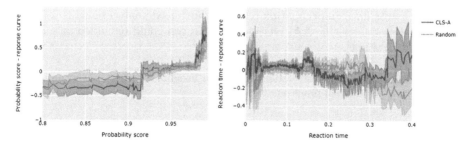

Fig. 7. Explainable boosting machine response curves of probability score and time reaction in the second experiment. The contribution of the probability score increases at a faster rate than the random generator. CLS-A favors more fast reactions.

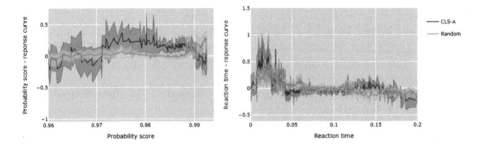

Fig. 8. Explainable boosting machine response curves of probability score and time reaction in the third experiment. The contribution of the probability score variable increases at a faster rate than the random generator and decreases for very high prediction probability score unlike the random generator. The contributions are slightly higher for fast response times for CLS-A.

5 Discussion and Conclusion

We applied an experimental protocol to compare a local feature importance method called CLS-A based on Transformer self-attention to SHAP, LIME and a random baseline. We found that CLS-A helps in the same proportions as SHAP and LIME to annotate text on three different tasks and is significantly better than a random baseline. This work adds to the literature aiming to evaluate the interpretability of attention coefficients in recent deep learning models. Attention is appropriate to explain attention-based classifiers in NLP when aggregated in the proper way. Like other XAI methods, however, the relevance of the explanations provided by CLS-A depends heavily on the certainty of their related prediction. The higher the probability score, the more relevant the explanation. As far as we know, this is the first time that the relationship between the quality of an explanation and the certainty of its associated prediction has come to light.

We believe that additional experimental studies analyzing texts with more distributed probability score would be enlightening. The link between prediction certainty and explanation relevance would be more precisely outlined. The results of our study must be evaluated considering that all the participants had a data science or statistics background. This may induce a bias in our results, insofar as the participants have an occupation requiring advanced analytical skills. Finally, other usual model-specific XAI methods comparison could be added in such an experiment (Table 4).

Acknowledgment. We thank Gariel Olympie for insights and methodology and Jean-Baptiste Gette for English proof reading.

Ethic statement. Each participant signed an informed consent form containing the project purpose and details and the intended use of the data they would generate. The data was anonymized and processed only by our team. The data produced is stored in a file in respect with the General Data Protection Regulation (GDPR) regulations in force. Participation in the study was fully voluntary. It was possible to stop performing the labeling tasks at any time. Consent form used is presented anonymized in Appendix A , Fig. 12 & 13. The authors of this paper do not represent any organization or institution whose activity is data labeling. This study was conducted for research purposes only.

A Appendix

Table 2. R-square of linear regression explaining participant reaction time

Metrics	Experiment	R^2
Reaction Time (s)	Exp 1	4.23e-1
	Exp 2	6.01e-1
	Exp 3	6.59e-1

Table 3. Linear regression and explainable boosting machine explanatory variables. The variables of the relative positions of the second and third most important words were used only for reaction time modeling in the first .

Task	Target variable	Model	Explanatory variables
Regression	Reaction time	Linear model	expected answer, probability score, review length, trial number, interpretability method, relative positions of 1st, 2nd and 3rd most impacting words
Classification	Accurate	Explainable Boosting Machine	reaction time, probability score, review length, trial number, interpretability method, relative position of 1st most impacting word

Table 4. Average EBM performance per experiment, per method.

Experiment	Method	Accuracy	Precision	F1-score	Recall
Exp 1	CLS-A	0.952	0.945	0.953	0.961
	LIME	0.992	0.991	0.992	0.993
	SHAP	0.961	0.955	0.961	0.976
	Random	0.982	0.988	0.982	0.976
Exp 2	CLS-A	0.889	0.894	0.888	0.884
	LIME	0.897	0.888	0.898	0.909
	SHAP	0.913	0.917	0.913	0.909
	Random	0.878	0.867	0.880	0.894
Exp 3	CLS-A	0.957	0.950	0.957	0.965
	LIME	0.946	0.943	0.946	0.949
	SHAP	0.920	0.916	0.920	0.925
	Random	0.920	0.921	0.920	0.919

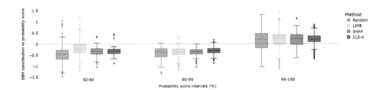

Fig. 9. Discretized EBM contributions of probability score in Experiment 1. High certainty prediction with probability higher than 95% have higher contributions.

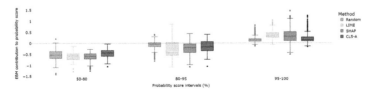

Fig. 10. Discretized EBM contributions of probability score in Experiment 2. High certainty prediction with probability higher than 95% have higher contributions.

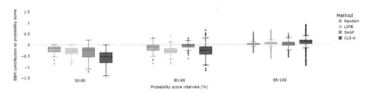

Fig. 11. Discretized EBM contributions of probability score in Experiment 3. High certainty prediction with probability higher than 95% have higher contributions.

Table 5. Average EBM contribution to probability score. High certainty predictions lead to higher contribution. Highest average contributions per probability interval are highlighted in bold.

Probability score interval	Method	Average EBM contribution to probability score		
		Experiment 1	Experiment 2	Experiment 3
50–80%	CLS-A	−0.34	**−0.46**	−0.59
	LIME	**−0.17**	−0.61	−0.30
	SHAP	−0.34	−0.60	−0.35
	RANDOM	−0.48	−0.53	**−0.21**
80–95%	CLS-A	**−0.32**	−0.16	−0.30
	LIME	−0.41	−0.30	−0.29
	SHAP	−0.38	−0.29	**−0.05**
	RANDOM	−0.40	**−0.08**	−0.15
95–100%	CLS-A	**0.19**	0.22	**0.10**
	LIME	0.18	**0.38**	0.05
	SHAP	0.17	0.31	0.02
	RANDOM	0.14	0.16	0.03

Table 6. Method distribution per participant per experiment.

Experiments	CLS-A (mean ± std)	LIME (mean ± std)	SHAP (mean ± std)	RANDOM (mean ± std)
Exp 1	25.5 ± 3.8	25.5 ± 3.6	24.5 ± 3.9	24.5 ± 4.2
Exp 2	25.6 ± 4.2	25.0 ± 4.1	24.0 ± 4.8	25.4 ± 4.1
Exp 3	23.0 ± 4.9	24.3 ± 5.6	27.4 ± 5.4	25.3 ± 5.9

INFORMED CONSENT FORM

Project Title : Evaluating self-attention interpretability through human-grounded experimental protocol

---

Research team : Omitted for anonymity

Research location : Omitted for anonymity

Project Presentation

Machine learning models for classification tasks on text are often black boxes. Today there are different methods to evaluate the factors (words) that were important for the decision of the algorithm. However the validity of these methods and their link with human semantics are not studied. The objective of this project is to establish the congruence between the results of different interpretability methods and human semantic analysis.

If you agree to participate in this study, we will ask you to read movie reviews and rate the category of the movie by pressing a key on the keyboard. The approximate duration of the experience is about fifteen minutes.

Your privacy rights

All the information collected during this experiment for the pursuit of the purposes set out in the previous paragraph will be processed by Omitted for anonymity, anonymously and will remain confidential. The legal basis for processing is your consent.

These will be kept in a computer file that complies with the applicable regulations in force (General Data Protection Regulations and Data Protection Act).

The data collected will be communicated only to the following recipients from the research team:

• Omitted for anonymity

The results obtained from the processing of this questionnaire may be the subject of scientific publications, but the identity of the participants will not be revealed, and no information that could reveal your identity will be disclosed.

The data is kept until the publication of an article or a maximum of 3 years.

Your rights to withdraw from this research at any time

Participation in this study is completely voluntary. Please note that even if you decide to complete this questionnaire, it is possible to stop completing it at any time, and as long as the final registration has not been made, none of your data will be processed.

You can access the data concerning you, rectify it, request its deletion or exercise your right to limit the processing of your data. You can withdraw your consent to the processing of your data at any time; you can also object to the processing of your data. Visit the cnil.fr website for more information on your rights.

To exercise these rights, you can contact Omitted for anonymity

If you believe, after contacting us, that your "Data Protection" rights are not respected, you can file a complaint with the CNIL.

Fig. 12. Consent form (1/2)

Diffusion

The results of this research may be published in scientific journals or be the subject of communications at scientific conferences.

You can ask questions about the research at any time by contacting Omitted for anonymity

Consent to participate

By checking the box below and **signing this consent form**, you certify that you have read and understood the above information and that you have been informed of your right to withdraw your consent or withdraw from this research at any time, without prejudice.

☐   *I have read and understood the above information and I voluntarily agree to participate in this research.*

Done at :   _____

On the :   _____

Name, First Name : _____

Signature :

Fig. 13. Consent form (2/2)

References

1. Abnar, S., Zuidema, W.H.: Quantifying attention flow in transformers. CoRR abs/2005.00928 (2020). https://arxiv.org/abs/2005.00928
2. Agarwal, C., et al.: Openxai: towards a transparent evaluation of model explanations (2023)
3. Bahdanau, D., Cho, K., Bengio, Y.: Neural machine translation by jointly learning to align and translate. CoRR abs/1409.0473 (2014)
4. Bastings, J., Filippova, K.: The elephant in the interpretability room: why use attention as explanation when we have saliency methods? In: Proceedings of the Third BlackboxNLP Workshop on Analyzing and Interpreting Neural Networks for NLP, pp. 149–155. Association for Computational Linguistics, Online (2020). https://doi.org/10.18653/v1/2020.blackboxnlp-1.14. https://aclanthology.org/2020.blackboxnlp-1.14
5. Bell, A., Solano-Kamaiko, I., Nov, O., Stoyanovich, J.: It's just not that simple: an empirical study of the accuracy-explainability trade-off in machine learning for public policy. In: 2022 ACM Conference on Fairness, Accountability, and Transparency, pp. 248–266. FAccT 2022, Association for Computing Machinery, New York, NY, USA (2022). https://doi.org/10.1145/3531146.3533090
6. Bhatt, U., et al.: Explainable machine learning in deployment. In: Proceedings of the 2020 Conference on Fairness, Accountability, and Transparency, pp. 648–657.

FAT* 2020, Association for Computing Machinery, New York, NY, USA (2020). https://doi.org/10.1145/3351095.3375624

7. Bibal, A., et al.: Is attention explanation? an introduction to the debate. In: Proceedings of the 60th Annual Meeting of the Association for Computational Linguistics (Volume 1: Long Papers), pp. 3889–3900. Association for Computational Linguistics, Dublin, Ireland (2022). https://doi.org/10.18653/v1/2022.acl-long.269. https://aclanthology.org/2022.acl-long.269

8. Carvalho, D.V., Pereira, E.M., Cardoso, J.S.: Machine learning interpretability: a survey on methods and metrics. Electronics **8**(8), 832 (2019). https://www.mdpi.com/2079-9292/8/8/832

9. Chefer, H., Gur, S., Wolf, L.: Transformer interpretability beyond attention visualization. CoRR abs/2012.09838 (2020). https://arxiv.org/abs/2012.09838

10. Clark, K., Khandelwal, U., Levy, O., Manning, C.D.: What does BERT look at? an analysis of BERT's attention. In: "Proceedings of the 2019 ACL Workshop BlackboxNLP: Analyzing and Interpreting Neural Networks for NLP", pp. 276–286. Association for Computational Linguistics, Florence, Italy (2019). https://doi.org/10.18653/v1/W19-4828. https://aclanthology.org/W19-4828

11. Devlin, J., Chang, M.W., Lee, K., Toutanova, K.: BERT: pre-training of deep bidirectional transformers for language understanding. Technical report arXiv:1810.04805, arXiv (2019), https://arxiv.org/abs/1810.04805, arXiv:1810.04805

12. Doshi-Velez, F., Kim, B.: Towards a rigorous science of interpretable machine learning (2017). https://doi.org/10.48550/ARXIV.1702.08608. https://arxiv.org/abs/1702.08608

13. Farah, L., Murris, J.M., Borget, I., Guilloux, A., Martelli, N.M., Katsahian, S.I.: Assessment of performance, interpretability, and explainability in artificial intelligence-based health technologies: what healthcare stakeholders need to know. Mayo Clinic Proc. Digital Health **1**(2), 120–138 (2023)

14. Lai, V., Liu, H., Tan, C.: "why is 'chicago' deceptive?" towards building model-driven tutorials for humans. In: Proceedings of the 2020 CHI Conference on Human Factors in Computing Systems. p. 1–13. CHI 2020, Association for Computing Machinery, New York, NY, USA (2020). https://doi.org/10.1145/3313831.3376873

15. Linardatos, P., Papastefanopoulos, V., Kotsiantis, S.: Explainable AI: a review of machine learning interpretability methods. Entropy **23**(1), 18 (2020)

16. Lundberg, S.M., Lee, S.I.: A unified approach to interpreting model predictions. In: Guyon, I., Luxburg, U.V., Bengio, S., Wallach, H., Fergus, R., Vishwanathan, S., Garnett, R. (eds.) Advances in Neural Information Processing Systems, vol. 30. Curran Associates, Inc. (2017). https://proceedings.neurips.cc/paper/2017/file/8a20a8621978632d76c43dfd28b67767-Paper.pdf

17. Maas, A.L., Daly, R.E., Pham, P.T., Huang, D., Ng, A.Y., Potts, C.: Learning word vectors for sentiment analysis. In: Proceedings of the 49th Annual Meeting of the Association for Computational Linguistics: Human Language Technologies, pp. 142–150. Association for Computational Linguistics, Portland, Oregon, USA (2011). https://aclanthology.org/P11-1015

18. Molnar, C.: Interpretable Machine Learning. Lulu.com (2020). google-Books-ID: jBm3DwAAQBAJ

19. Nori, H., Jenkins, S., Koch, P., Caruana, R.: Interpretml: a unified framework for machine learning interpretability. arXiv preprint arXiv:1909.09223 (2019)

20. Peirce, J., et al.: Psychopy2: experiments in behavior made easy. Behav. Res. Methods **51**(1), 195–203 (2019)

21. Poursabzi-Sangdeh, F., Goldstein, D.G., Hofman, J.M., Wortman Vaughan, J.W., Wallach, H.: Manipulating and measuring model interpretability. In: Proceedings of the 2021 CHI Conference on Human Factors in Computing Systems, pp. 1–52 (2021)
22. Ribeiro, M.T., Singh, S., Guestrin, C.: "why should i trust you?": explaining the predictions of any classifier. In: Proceedings of the 22nd ACM SIGKDD International Conference on Knowledge Discovery and Data Mining, pp. 1135–1144. KDD 2016, Association for Computing Machinery, New York, NY, USA (2016). https://doi.org/10.1145/2939672.2939778
23. Sanh, V., Debut, L., Chaumond, J., Wolf, T.: DistilBERT, a distilled version of BERT: smaller, faster, cheaper and lighter (2019)
24. Schemmer, M., Hemmer, P., Nitsche, M., Kühl, N., Vössing, M.: A meta-analysis of the utility of explainable artificial intelligence in human-AI decision-making. In: Proceedings of the 2022 AAAI/ACM Conference on AI, Ethics, and Society, pp. 617–626. AIES 2022, Association for Computing Machinery, New York, NY, USA (2022). https://doi.org/10.1145/3514094.3534128
25. Schmidt, P., Biessmann, F.: Quantifying interpretability and trust in machine learning systems (2019)
26. Shapley L.S.: A value for n-person games. Contrib. Theory Games II, Ann. Math. Stud. **28** (1953)
27. Shrikumar, A., Greenside, P., Kundaje, A.: Learning important features through propagating activation differences. In: Proceedings of the 34th International Conference on Machine Learning, vol. 70, pp. 3145–3153. ICML 2017, JMLR.org (2017)
28. Sundararajan, M., Taly, A., Yan, Q.: Axiomatic attribution for deep networks. In: Proceedings of the 34th International Conference on Machine Learning, vol. 70, pp. 3319–3328. ICML 2017, JMLR.org (2017)
29. Vaswani, A., et al.: Attention is all you need. In: Guyon, I., Luxburg, U.V., Bengio, S., Wallach, H., Fergus, R., Vishwanathan, S., Garnett, R. (eds.) Advances in Neural Information Processing Systems. vol. 30. Curran Associates, Inc. (2017). https://proceedings.neurips.cc/paper/2017/file/3f5ee243547dee91fbd053c1c4a845aa-Paper.pdf
30. Vig, J.: A multiscale visualization of attention in the transformer model. In: Proceedings of the 57th Annual Meeting of the Association for Computational Linguistics: System Demonstrations, pp. 37–42. Association for Computational Linguistics, Florence, Italy (2019). https://doi.org/10.18653/v1/P19-3007. https://www.aclweb.org/anthology/P19-3007
31. Wang, X., Yin, M.: Are explanations helpful? a comparative study of the effects of explanations in AI-assisted decision-making. In: 26th International Conference on Intelligent User Interfaces. p. 318–328. IUI 2021, Association for Computing Machinery, New York, NY, USA (2021). https://doi.org/10.1145/3397481.3450650
32. Weber, P., Carl, K.V., Hinz, O.: Applications of explainable artificial intelligence in finance-a systematic review of finance, information systems, and computer science literature. Manage. Rev. Q. 1–41 (2023)

Understanding Interpretability: Explainable AI Approaches for Hate Speech Classifiers

Sargam Yadav[(✉)] [ID], Abhishek Kaushik[(✉)] [ID], and Kevin McDaid [ID]

Dundalk Insitute of Technology, Dundalk, Ireland
d00263026@student.dkit.ie, {abhishek.kaushik,kevin.mcdaid}@dkit.ie

Abstract. Cyberbullying and hate speech are two of the most significant problems in today's cyberspace. Automated artificial intelligence models might be used to find and remove online hate speech, which would address a critical problem. A variety of explainable AI strategies are being developed to make model judgments and justifications intelligible to people as artificial intelligence continues to permeate numerous industries and make critical change. Our study focuses on mixed code languages (a mix of Hindi and English) and the Indian sub-continent. This language combination is extensively used in SARRAC nations. Three transformer-based models and one machine learning model was trained and fine-tuned on the modified HASOC-Identification of Conversational Hate-Speech in Code-Mixed Languages (ICHCL) data for hate speech classification. Several types of explainability techniques have been explored on the respective models, such as Local interpretable model-agnostic explanations (LIME), Shapley additive explanations (SHAP), and model attention, to analyze model behavior. The analysis suggests that better trained models and comparison of Explainable Artificial Intelligence (XAI) techniques would provide better insight.

Keywords: explainable artificial intelligence · hate speech · LIME · SHAP · sentiment analysis · Hinglish · Attention · Transformers · BERT

1 Introduction

Online hate speech is an unintended but severe consequence of the rise in usage of social media. The abuse can take several forms, such as cyberbullying [22], doxing, stealing private information [32], spreading misinformation [6], etc. Several companies are rushing to solve this problem through the use of automated classifiers, content moderators, and user reports. Certain governments are also in the process of criminalizing hate speech, as online harassment can often turn into real world hate crimes. In recent years, Machine learning (ML) and Deep Learning (DL) classifiers have become an increasingly popular solution to combat online hate speech [29]. The advancement of Natural Language Processing

L. Longo (Ed.): xAI 2023, CCIS 1903, pp. 47–70, 2023.
https://doi.org/10.1007/978-3-031-44070-0_3

(NLP) techniques, such as the introduction of Large Language Models (LLMs) has rapidly advanced the current-state-of-the art in hate speech classifiers [3]. However, even such advanced models have trouble with the fine-grained classification of the types and targets of abuse [20]. Also, it is generally not possible to understand the decision-making process and rationale of the models due to their black-box nature. Explainability Artificial Intelligence (XAI) is a branch of study that deals with handling the black box problem by introducing explainability to opaque models [19,23]. This can help improve models by making their decisions human-interpretable, allowing for error analysis, and making the model more trustworthy and dependable. Common explainability techniques include the Local-interpretable Model Agnostic Explanations (LIME) [23] and Shapely additive values (SHAP) [19]. Research on hate speech classifiers is still nascent for under-resourced and code-mixed languages [20,24,25]. Language-specific models and processing tools are scarce, making the process more difficult. In recent years, an effort has been made to stimulate research in the area through holding shared tasks [18,20] in several under-resourced languages.

In this paper, we have analysed 2 groups of models: ML, and Transformer-based language models on several categories of explainability algorithms such as LIME, SHAP, and model attention for IndicBERT [13], mBERT [8], and XLM-RoBERTa [7]. The models are fine-tuned on the cleaned version of the HASOC-ICHCL 2021 and 2022 datasets for hate speech detection. The explainability techniques are then applied and evaluated using human rationale. To our knowledge, no other studies have been performed to evaluate explainability methods on this cleaned code-mixed Hinglish data. Hinglish is a portmanteau of Hindi and English, and consists of terms from both English and Romanized Hindi [17].

The rest of the article is structured as follows: Sect. 2 describes the motivation of the study, states the research hypothesis, and formulates the research questions. Section 3 discusses the relevant literature in hate speech detection and XAI techniques. Section 4 outlines the experimental methodology used in the study. Section 5 discusses the empirical results of the experiments and evaluation of the explainability techniques. Section 6 provides a discussion of the research hypothesis and questions with respect to our result findings and previous studies. Section 7 provides a conclusion to the study.

2   Motivation

Online hate speech is a pertinent problem on online social forums. Automated systems that utilise machine learning and deep learning models have recently become popular to tackle the problem [28]. DL classifiers have performed exceptionally well in the task of hate speech detection. However, they still have trouble performing fine-grained classification to differentiate the types of hate speech [11,20]. For example, in HASOC 2020 [20], the highest macro-f1 score achieved for Subtask A (binary classification) in Hindi was 0.53, which is significantly higher than for Subtask B (fine-grained classification was 0.33. The criminalisation of hate speech is currently in the process of being legislated, which makes legal accountability of decisions made by automated systems a priority [12]. A major problem with deep learning and ML with complex architectures is the opaqueness and lack of rationale provided by the model. XAI techniques can open up the black box of deep learning models and provide insight into the model decisions and help us understand the model rationale. This increases trust in the model, reduces model bias, and provides human-interpretable explanations for model decisions. There have been very few studies exploring explainability for hate speech classifiers [1,14]. The motivation for this study is to analyse the implementation of explainability techniques of machine learning and deep learning models trained on code-mixed Hinglish. The findings of the study will indicate if XAI tools have help to make the hate speech classifiers more interpretable and trustworthy. We perform qualitative comparative analysis of XAI models on the same hate speech dataset in Hinglish and quantitative comparative analysis of ML and DL models on the low-resource Hinglish dataset. This work can serve as a basis for further experimentation on XAI techniques on low-resource languages.

Hypothesis: XAI techniques, such as LIME and SHAP, can be used to make hate speech classifiers trained on code-mixed Hinglish text more transparent and interpretable.

The research questions to investigate the hypothesis are as follows:

1. Do XAI techniques provide reasonable explanations for model decisions for the code-mixed language Hinglish?
2. Which category of XAI tools, attention-based, perturbation-based, or simplification-based provides better explanations for Hinglish?

3   Literature Review

In this section, we will discuss the relevant literature on hate speech classifiers using explainability tools.

Social media has become a breeding ground for intolerant behaviour towards certain marginalized groups in the form of hate speech. Several platforms have tackled this problem through the use of automated content moderators, which do not always perform well [29]. Keyword filtering has also proven ineffective for the removal of hateful content, as the context of a sentence helps to determine if it is considered hate speech [16]. A more viable approach to handling hate speech online is artificial intelligence models, which have been shown to perform well. It is difficult to understand why a model is performing a particular decision given a set of features. XAI is field of study that works towards making deep learning and ML models transparent and understandable to humans.

3.1   Code-Mixed Languages

Machine learning models were used by Kaur et al. [15] to conduct sentiment analysis on code-mixed Hinglish comments obtained from two YouTube cookery channels, Nisha Madhulika's and Kabita Kitchen. The sentiment classification was performed using three different vectorization techniques. Logistic regression combined with term frequency vectorizer yielded the highest accuracy scores of 74.01% and 75.37% for both datasets. Donthula and Kaushik [9] performed sentiment analysis to the aforementioned two cooking datasets using deep learning models. Count vectorizer with a multi-layer perceptron outperformed other models and achieved the highest accuracy rates of 98.48% and 98.53%.

Yadav et al. [31] used Bidirectional Encoder Representations from Transformers (BERT)-based on the same cookery datasets. Robustly Optimized BERT Pre-training Approach (RoBERTa) model and the Cross-lingual Language Model (XLM-RoBERTa) outperformed other models and attained the highest accuracy scores of 84.82% and 88.37% for the two datasets. An alternative approach was also tried where sentence level embeddings were calculated by taking the mean of all token embeddings in a sentence, and the resulting vector was passed as input to machine learning classifiers. The best accuracy of 76% was achieved using a Support vector machine (SVM) -Radial basis kernel (RBF) model for Kabita's dataset. For Nisha's dataset, Logistic regression outperformed all other models and achieved an accuracy of 72%. Yadav et al. [30] further experimented with Transformers by extracting contextualized embeddings from the last four hidden layers of mBERT and RoBERTa and feeding them into downstream machine learning classifiers. This approach seemed to perform better than simple fine-tuning, achieving the highest accuracy of 92.73% for Kabita Kitchen's channel and 87.42% for Nisha Madhulika's channel using embeddings from the second last and last layers of mBERT, respectively, and using a logistic regression classifier.

3.2   XAI

Recent studies in the area have made significant progress. Atanasova et al. [1] presented a list of diagnostic properties for different explainability techniques on text classification tasks using 3 neural network architectures: CNN, LSTM, and BERT. The explainability techniques evaluated were: Saliency, InputXGradient, Guided Backpropagation, Occlusion, Shapley Value Sampling, and LIME. The 3 datasets used for the study were e-SNLI [5], Movie Reviews [33], and Tweet Sentiment Extraction (TSE), and all consisted of human-annotated saliency explanations. Out of all explanation techniques, gradient-based techniques usually have the best performance for all 3 architectures. Out of all the non-gradient explainability methods, LIME performs the best.

Attanasio et al. [2] conducted a study to benchmark interpretability methods for a fine-tuned BERT misogyny classifier. The study explored four local post-hoc attribution methods, namely Gradients, Integrated Gradients, SHAP, and Sampling-And-Occlusion. Attention analysis was also performed and compared to the attributions. The AMI English and Italian datasets [10,11] were consisted for the study. For evaluation of the explainability methods, plausibility and faithfulness were considered as metrics. The analysis of the study suggests that SHAP and SOC scored high on plausibility and faithfulness criteria where as gradient and attention-based approaches did not provide plausible and faithful explanations on the respective datasets using the fine-tuned BERT models. Mathew et al. [21] introduce HateXplain, a benchmark dataset for hate speech detection in English. The dataset is labelled into the following three classes: hate, offensive, and normal. The target community of the hate speech and the rationale for classifying a statement as hate speech is also included in the dataset. State-of-the-art models were trained on the dataset and evaluated using empirical metrics and also explainability metrics, such as plausibility and faithfulness. The results show that models that score high on empirical metrics do not always perform well on explainability metrics.

Karim et al. [14] introduce DeepHateExplainer, a hate speech detection approach with explainability in the South-Asian language Bengali. The dataset was divided into the following hate categories: political, personal, geopolitical, and religious. Monolingual Bangla BERT-base, multilingual BERT cased/uncased, and XLM-RoBERTa were trained on the dataset. Sensitivity analysis and Layer-wise relevance propagation has been performed and the models have been further evaluated on comprehensiveness and sufficiency. Out of all the models XLM-RoBERTa performed the best on comprehensiveness and sufficiency. The study suggests that even though a model performs best on empirical metrics, it may not also perform best on faithfulness explainability metrics. Vijayaraghavan et al. [27] present a deep neural multi-modal network for the detection of hate speech by also capturing the socio-cultural comment of the speech and providing explanations for the results. Out of all the models tested, the best scores achieved were using the BiGRU+Char+Attn+FF model.

The studies suggest that hate speech classifiers are necessary to ensure a safe space online for everyone. However, models built to detect hate speech in code-mixed and under-resourced languages are fairly low. Also, explainability techniques have barely been explored in hate speech classifiers, considering their high potential for model improvement. To build on this, in this study, we compared the machine learning and deep learning models and apply XAI techniques to understand model behaviour in a code-switched low-resource language.

The literature suggests that machine learning classifiers perform well for filtering online hate speech. However, even though the models achieve high on accuracy, explainability must be considered so that they do not make biased decisions in real-world scenarios.

4 Methodology

In this section, we will discuss the methodology used in the study.

4.1 Dataset

The dataset used in this study is a combination of training sets from HASOC ICHCL 2021 [25] and 2022 [24]. The original datasets consisted of the entire context of the tweet, including the parent tweet, comments, and replies. Table 1 gives details about the original datasets, final altered dataset, and label counts. The dataset consists of two labels: Hate and Offensive (HOF), and Non Hate-Offensive (NOT). The cleaned dataset consists only of comments in English and Hinglish, and only self-contained sentences are kept in the final dataset. Also, only the standalone comment, tweet, or reply is taken instead of the entire statement. For example, a statement from the original dataset, is *'Rationality is against the country... Inke Dimag me bhi Gobar bhara hua hai.'* which translates to *'Rationality is against the country... They have cow dung in their brain.'* In this study, only the unique part of the entire statement, which is *'Inke Dimag me bhi Gobar bhara hua hai'*, is considered as a unique example. This was done to remove repetition, as machine learning models are statistical models and over-fitting may occur. One downside of this approach is that context is very important in determining hate speech, and the process removes some of the context from the raw tweet.

The original dataset has been further modified by removing all sentences that are not in mix-code Hinglish and English. Tweets with less than two words were removed. Pre-processing on the remaining tweets has been done by removing all non-English characters and emojis, user handles, hyperlinks, abundant white spaces and newlines, and English stopwords. Stemming has also been performed on the tweets. The final cleaned dataset consists of a total of 6000 comments, with 3000 instances of HOF and 3000 instances of NOT.

Table 1. Dataset Description and Count

Shared Task	HOF	NOT	Total
HASOC-2021	2841	2899	5740
HASOC-2022	1339	3575	4914
Total		4180	6474	10,654
After cleaning	3000	3000	**6000**

For example, Fig. 1 shows a statement in Hinglish taken from the dataset and translated into English [20].

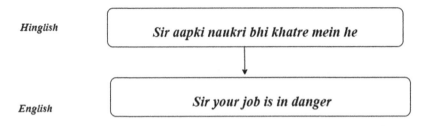

Fig. 1. Example of a Hinglish statement from the dataset with translation into English

4.2 Experiment

Data Preprocessing. Before training the model, certain preprocessing steps have been performed. ForXGBoost, Logistic Regression (LR) and Gradient Boosting(GB), stemming has been performed using Snowball stemmer. Also, the text has been converted to lower and stopwords have been removed. For BERT-based models [7,8], no additional pre-processing was performed on the cleaned dataset.

Feature Engineering. Features were extracted from the datasets depending on the type of model.

1. Machine learning models: For XGBoost, LR, and GB classifiers, Term frequency-inverse document frequency (TF-IDF) vectorizer has been used on the raw data to extract features. The maximum number of features was limited to 3000. This value was obtained through trial and error.
2. Transformer-based Models: The following three BERT-based models were used: Indic-BERT, multilingual BERT (mBERT), and XLM-RoBERTa. For mBERT, the 'bert-base-multilingual-cased' tokenizer was used, with all the sequences truncated and padded to 64. For XLM-RoBERTa, the 'xlm-roberta-base' tokenizer was used with the maximum sequence length of 64. For IndicBERT, the *'ai4bharat/indic-bert'* tokenizer was used with maximum sequence length of 64. This value was chosen due to memory limitations.

Model Training

1. Machine learning: Grid Search with 10 k-fold cross validation was used to train the models using the XGBoost library[1] and Sklearn [4]. Parameter tuning was performed for the following parameters: learning rate (0.01, 0.02, 0.03, 0.05, 0.1, 1.0) and max-depth in the range of 3 to 10 for XGBoost, C in a range of 0.0001 to 1000 in steps of x10 for LR, and learning rate = [1, 0.5, 0.25, 0.1, 0.05, 0.01], estimators = [320, 330, 340, 350, 360, 370, 380, 390], and max features = sqrt. These parameters were chosen after studying best practices and observing the affect of the parameters on model accuracy.
2. Transformer-based Models: XLM-RoBERTa, BERT, and IndicBERT were fine-tuned on the dataset using the HuggingFace library[2].
   For IndicBERT, fine-tuning was done using the following hyper-parameters: learning rate = 1e−05, train and eval batch size = 2, Adam optimizer with epsilon=1e−05, and 2 training epochs. For XLM-RoBERTa, fine tuning was done using the following hyper-parameters: learning rate = 1e−05, train and eval batch size = 2, Adam optimizer with epsilon=1e−05, and 3 training epochs. For mBERT, the following hyper-parameters were used to perform fine tuning: learning rate = 3e−5, train and eval batch size = 2, Adam optimizer with epsilon = 1e−05, and 2 training epochs. These parameters were obtained through trial and error of the fine-tuning process.

---

[1] https://xgboost.readthedocs.io/en/stable/.
[2] https://huggingface.co/.

Evaluation Metrics. Several commonly used evaluation criteria were used to evaluate model performance. These include accuracy, macro-F1 score, precision, and recall.

Explainability. LIME and SHAP are used for providing explanations to model decisions.

LIME [23] is a local post-hoc attribution approach to explainability. It attempts to approximate a linear model around a single data instance and provides an explanation around the data point. It is posthoc and model agnostic, which means that it is applied after model training and can be used for any model. The LIME python[3] library was used to implement the algorithm. Lundberg et al. [19] propose a unified approach to interpreting model predictions called SHAP. In this feature attribution method, Shap values are calculated, which attribute to a particular feature the change in the expected model behaviour when that feature is conditioned, thus providing the unique additive importance of that feature. The SHAP python[4] library was used to implement the algorithm.

BERT attention visualisations were generated using the BertViz[5] library [26]. BERT performs contextual learning through attention mechanisms. BERTViz helps us visualize how BERT learns complex relationships between words. The visualisation tool helps determine the complex relationship between tokens in sentence, and which tokens contribute the highest towards the classification.

5   Results and Analysis

In this section, we will discuss the results of the study and provide an analysis.

5.1   Empirical Results

Table 2. Model Results

Model	Accuracy	Precision	Recall	Macro-F1
XGBoost	64.61	0.6534	0.6461	0.6418
GBC	65.27	0.6548	0.6527	0.6516
LR	66	0.6602	0.66	0.6598
mBERT	65.83	0.6627	0.6611	0.6533
IndicBERT	**66.88**	**0.6720**	**0.6688**	**0.6673**
XLM-RoBERTa	66.11	0.6627	0.6611	0.6602

Table 2 displays the results of fine-tuning the 6 models. LR outperformed all machine learning models, with the highest scores were achieved when the value

---

[3] https://github.com/marcotcr/lime.
[4] https://github.com/slundberg/shap.
[5] https://github.com/jessevig/bertviz.

of C = 1. IndicBERT performs the best out of all models, with an accuracy of 66.88%, precision of 0.6720, recall of 0.6688, and macro-F1 score of 0.6673.

Figure 2 displays the confusion matrix for the best performing models. We wanted to examine the True Positives (TP) for the class 'HOF'. The best performing model, IndicBERT, has a total number of TPs equal to 541, which is the second lowest score out of all models. The highest number of TPs for class 'HOF' are produced by XGBoost, which performs the worst on accuracy out of all the models.

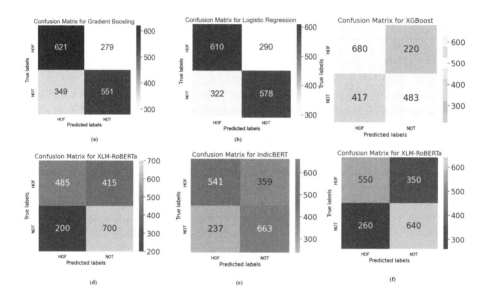

Fig. 2. Confusion matrix for all models

5.2 Statistical Testing

Statistical testing has been performed using one-way t-test. The null hypothesis assumes that none of the model results are better than the group average, which is 65.74. The alternative hypothesis is that at least one model performs better than the group average. The t-statistic obtained was 0.01802 with p-value = 0.9863. Thus, the null hypothesis failed to reject.

5.3 Explainability Evaluation

Machine Learning Models For machine learning classifiers, LIME and SHAP were used to generate model explanations.

Figure 3 displays a LIME explaination for a correct prediction made by the LR classifier. The statement *'Tum logo se secular hone ki umeed bhi toh kar rahe hain log yaha par'* in Hinglish translated to *'People here are expecting you people to become secular'*. The correct class and predicted class of the statement is 'HOF'. The model assigns weights to tokens such as 'rahe', 'log', and 'secular' for performing this classification. Figure 4 displays a LIME explanation for an incorrect prediction made by LR. The statement *'Koi sense hai iss baat ka yahan Aa jaate hain propaganda failane'* in Hinglish translates to *'Does this many any sense they come here to spread propaganda'*. The model has incorrectly predicted this statement as 'HOF' with a probability of 0.67, by assigning weights to tokens such as 'baat', 'ka', and 'propaganda'. It seems that tokens which related to politics, for example 'secular' and 'propaganda', contribute towards the classification into 'HOF'. Figure 5 displays a SHAP text plot generated for a single example from the dataset. The statament is *'BC they had no plan so big daddy came in to save small daddy otherwise image would have ruined understand this IMAGE That s what they all care we wish some white personality had twitted this time too then may be they would have taken steps early'*. The correct class of the statement is 'NOT'. A text plot shows the contribution of positive tokens (in red) and negative tokens (in blue) towards classification. Tokens such as 'otherwis' and 'taken' alter the base value towards the positive class. Figure 6 displays a SHAP waterfall plot for the aforementioned sentence. The waterfall plot again measures token contribution towards classification. For instance, the tokens 'taken' and 'otherwis' have the highest contribution in this statement.

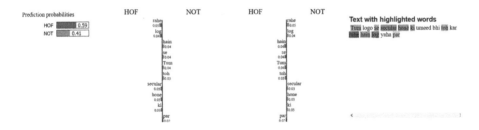

Fig. 3. LIME plot for correct prediction made by LR classifier

Figure 8 displays the LIME explaination for an incorrect prediction made by the GB classifier. The statement 'All are equal and humans Peace be with you' is incorrectly classifier as 'HOF', even though it depicts positive sentiment. The prediction probability of the correct class, 'NOT' is quite low (0.35). Tokens such as 'and' and 'you' contribute the highest towards the prediction. Figure 7 displays the LIME explaination for a correct prediction made by the GB classifier. The statement *'Tum logo se secular hone ki umeed bhi toh kar rahe hain log yaha par'* is correctly identified as 'HOF' again and the highest weight is assigned to 'secular' (0.06).

Figure 9 displays a SHAP text plot for the same statement used to generate explainations for LR classifier. Again we can see that tokens such as 'othersiwe' and 'taken' contribute the highest towards the class 'NOT'. Figure 10 displays a SHAP waterfall plot for the same statement. It displays how the SHAP value

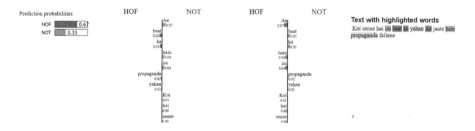

Fig. 4. LIME plot for wrong prediction made by LR classifier

Fig. 5. SHAP text plot for LR classifier

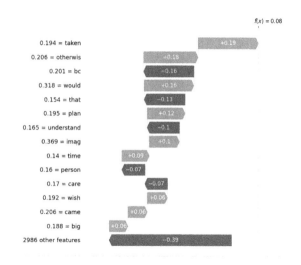

Fig. 6. SHAP waterfall plot for LR classifier

of each feature moves the model decision for the prior expectation to the final result.'Otherwis' and 'taken' have the highest positive impact of +0.37 and +0.27 on model decision respectively.

Figure 11 displays a LIME explaination for an incorrect predicition made by XGBoost. The statement 'All are equal and humans Peace be with you' has the correct label of 'NOT'. Tokens such as 'all' and 'are' are contributing negatively towards model decision. Figure 12 displays a LIME explaination for an incorrect predicition made by XGBoost. The statement *'Chup be teri ma ka*

Fig. 7. LIME plot for wrong prediction made by GB

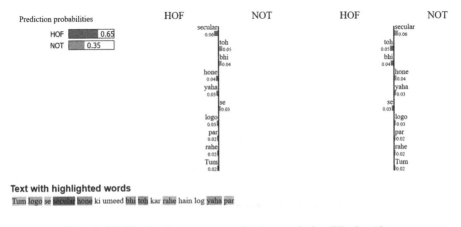

Fig. 8. LIME plot for correct prediction made by GB classifier

Fig. 9. SHAP text plot for GB classifier

bsda' translates to *'Shut up [expletive]'*, and the correct label is 'HOF'. Tokens such as 'chup' (shut up) and 'teri' (yours) are responsible for this classification according to LIME. Figure 13 displays a SHAP text plot for a prediction made by XGBoost. Model prediction is again mostly attributed to the 'otherwise' and 'taken' tokens. Figure 14 displays a SHAP waterfall plot for a prediction made by XGBoost. Unlike previous models, the highest attribution is of the token 'taken' (0.33) and 'otherwis' does not contribute much.

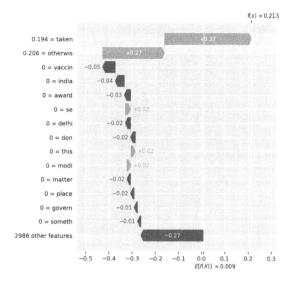

Fig. 10. SHAP waterfall plot for GB classifier

Fig. 11. LIME plot for wrong predicition made by XGBoost classifier

Fig. 12. LIME plot for correct prediction made by XGBoost classifier

Fig. 13. SHAP text plot for XGBoost classifier

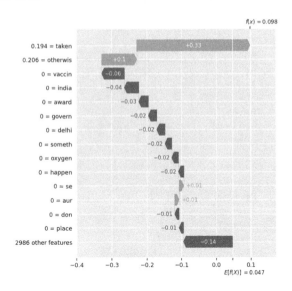

Fig. 14. SHAP waterfall plot for XGBoost classifier

Transformer-Based Models: For Transformer-based models, explainability has been explored using LIME [21], SHAP [14], and attention visualisations [26].

Figure 15 displays a LIME interpretation of an incorrect prediction made by mBERT. The correct class of the statement is 'NOT', but it has been classified as 'HOF'. Tokens such as 'propaganda' contribute the highest towards prediction of the label. Figure 16 displays a LIME interpretation of a correct prediction made by mBERT. The correct label of the statement 'All are equal and humans Peace be with you' is 'NOT', which was predicted with a high probability of 0.68. Tokens such as 'Peace', 'equal', and 'humans', which seem relevant to the class 'NOT'. Figure 17 displays the text plot for the mBERT model for the statement *'kya hua Bhai tumhe chance nhi mila kya kuch krne ka Apne aapko col kahte ho sharam kro thhodi'* which roughly translates to 'what happened did you not get the chance to do something you call yourself col have some shame'. The correct label of this statement is 'HOF'. The text plot of the statement displays attribution of subwords such as 'ky', 'a', etc. Figure 18 displays the SHAP waterfall plot for the aforementioned statement. Again, we observe the attribution of subwords such as 'aa' and 'a' towards model prediction. Figure 19 displays the LIME explaination for an incorrect prediction made by IndicBERT. The statement is predicted as 'HOF' has a high probability (0.79). Tokens such as 'Peace' and 'equal' are now contributing towards the 'HOF' class. Figure 20 displays the LIME explaination for a correct prediction made by IndicBERT. The statement 'Like you people have to be wash out from the planet' belongs to the class 'HOF'. LIME uses tokens such as 'planet' and 'have' to predict the 'HOF' label.

Fig. 15. LIME plot for wrong prediction made by mBERT classifier

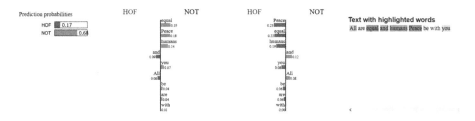

Fig. 16. LIME plot for correct prediction made by mBERT

Fig. 17. SHAP text plot for mBERT

Figure 21 displays the text plot for the same statement as mBERT. The features that attributed the most to model prediction are 'col', 'ap', and more. Figure 22 displays the waterfall plot for IndicBERT for the same statement. The waterfall plot shows that the tokens that impact model prediction negatively and positively.

Figure 23 displays a LIME explaination for an incorrect model prediction made by XLM-RoBERTa. The statement is incorrectly labeled as 'NOT' with a high probability of 0.76, due to the presence of words such 'par', 'secular', etc. Figure 24 displays the LIME explaination for a correct prediction made by the model. The statement is classified as 'HOF' with high confidence (0.93). Tokens such as 'sense' and 'propaganda' contribute the highest towards this label.

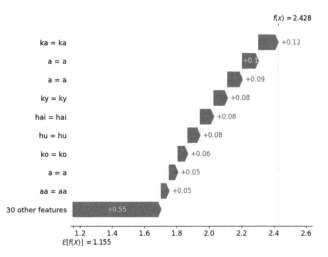

Fig. 18. SHAP waterfall plot for XGBoost classifier

Fig. 19. LIME plot for wrong prediction made by IndicBERT

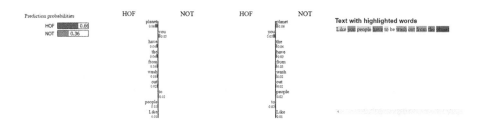

Fig. 20. LIME plot for correct prediction made by IndicBERT

Fig. 21. SHAP text plot for IndicBERT

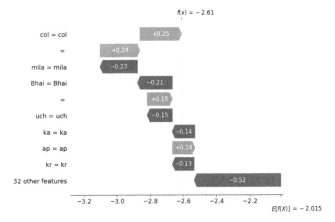

Fig. 22. SHAP waterfall plot for IndicBERT

Fig. 23. LIME plot for wrong prediction made by XLM-RoBERTa

Fig. 24. LIME plot for correct prediction made by XLM-RoBERTa

Figure 25 displays the SHAP text plot for an example from the dataset. More token attribution can be seen using XLM-RoBERTa. Tokens such as 'kya', 'chance', etc., contribute towards the class prediction. In Fig. 26, a waterfall plot depicting the token attributions of the statement is displayed. The token 'chance' provides the highest contribution towards the class prediction.

Fig. 25. SHAP text plot for XLM-RoBERTa

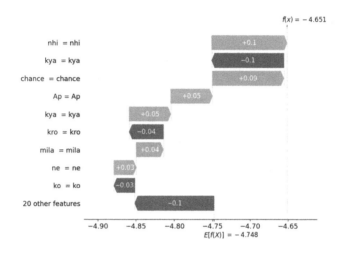

Fig. 26. SHAP waterfall plot for XLM-RoBERTa

The right side of Fig. 27 displays the attention view for mBERT model for the two statements from the dataset: *'Chup be teri ma ka bsda'* and *'Are moorkho koi kaam dhoondh lo'*, which translate to 'Shup up [expletive]' and 'Idiots find some work'. Both the statements have the true class of 'HOF'. In the figure, the lines point from the word to be updated to the word that is being attended it. The lines for higher attention weights are darker and lighter for lower attention weights. The separator token ([SEP]) and classification token ([CLS]) are also displayed. In the example, most of the attention is pointed from and to the [SEP] and [CLS] tokens. This means that the attention head is focusing more on the special tokens rather than other words in the two sentences.

Figure 28 displays the attention pattern for layer 6 and head 5 for the first of the aforementioned sentences. Again, for a single sentence, all the words have the highest attention weight towards the 2nd [SEP] token. The [CLS] token also attends to tokens 'ma', 'ka', 'b' with a significantly lower weight. The left side of Fig. 27 displays the attention view for the two aforementioned statements for the 11th attention head and 11th layer of the IndicBERT model. We can see that each word attends the most to the next word in the sequence. The two exceptions to these are the [CLS] and the 2nd [SEP] tokens, that attend to themselves. Figure 29 displays the attention view for the 1st sentences. Most of the words attend the highest to the [CLS] and [SEP] tokens. Some of the tokens such as 't', 'eri', and 'ma' assing some attention weight to their proceeding token.

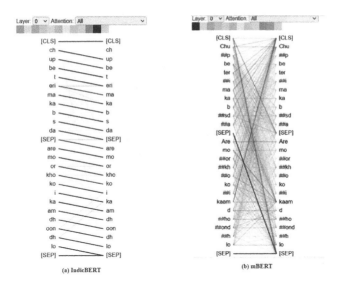

Fig. 27. Attention view of IndicBERT and mBERT using BertViz

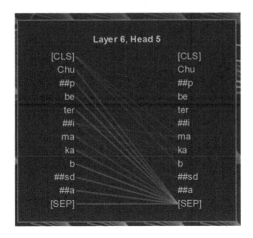

Fig. 28. Model view of mBERT using BertViz

It appears that the models are breaking up Hinglish tokens as these tokens do not exist in BERT's vocabulary. The model attempts to learn it by learning encodings of the subtoken.

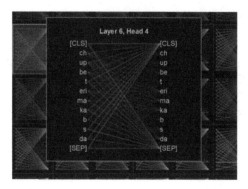

Fig. 29. Model view of IndicBERT using BertViz

6   Discussion

In this section, we will discuss the findings of the study with respect to our research questions.

1. Do XAI techniques provide reasonable explanations for model decisions for the code-mixed language Hinglish?

   In this study, we have implemented three machine learning models (Gradient boosting, LR, and XGBoost) and 3 Tranformer-based models (mBERT, IndicBERT, and XLM-RoBERTa). For the ML models, LIME and SHAP were used to introduce explainability to the model. For the 3 Transformer-based models, LIME, SHAP and attention visualisations for used to generate explanations. The XAI methods provide some insight into model behaviour, however, do not provide an extensive understanding of model behavior on this dataset. The Hinglish tokens were split up while being processed by the models. This may be due to the code-mixed nature of the dataset. Further studies should look into developing language-specific tools for Hinglish. This may also be due to the poor performance of the models. The model could have performed poorly because of the difficulty models face while classifying hate speech, the lack of context from the dataset (only unique text is consider), the small size of the dataset, unreliable class names in dataset due to removing context, etc. The presence of Hinglish tokens may have also impacted the results. The models used were mBERT, which was trained on a 100 languages excluding Hinglish, IndicBERT, which was trained on 12 major Indian languages excluding Hinglish, XLM-RoBERTa which is also not trained on Hinglish. Recent shared tasks and studied have shown that even the current SOTA models have trouble with fine-grained classification [11,20]. Further work should include examination of a different Hinglish dataset, different models, and XAI tools.
2. Which category of XAI tools, attention-based, perturbation-based, or simplification-based provides better explanations?

In this study, all three models as discussed above, gave relatively poor performance. The highest accuracy achieved was by IndicBERT of 67.44 %. For XGBoost, LIME and SHAP were used to generate explanations. For the transformer-based models, model explanations were generated through LIME, SHAP, and attention visualisation. LIME explanations generated for all six models suggest that although the model is sometimes using the presence of curse words to classify a statement as hateful, other classifications are not aligning with human rationales. The dataset has been altered to remove context, and thus must be not as robust. Out of all the three methods, LIME has provided some valuable insight into model bias and performance [21]. SHAP also successfully displayed some feature attributions for hate speech [2], however all explanation techniques are having trouble with code-switched Hinglish words. Further work is need by quantifying the performance of the XAI techniques for different models for comparison. Also, different approaches to explainability can be explored, such as in [21]. This study served as a preliminary examination of XAI for Hinglish.

In relation to the research hypothesis, we can see that XAI tools such as LIME, SHAP and Attention can be used to study model behaviour. This study was preliminary, but we did observe interesting patterns related to the contribution of certain tokens towards positive and negative classes. A deeper look should be taken using other XAI tools such as saliency scores, gradient-based approaches, etc. in near future.

7 Conclusion

This study was conducted to analyse the model rationales of hate speech classifiers using the following XAI techniques: LIME, SHAP, and attention. The models were fine-tuned on the HASOC 2021 and 2022 datasets and explanations were generated. The novelty of this study is that it was the first to propose the analysis of explainability approaches to hate speech classification for code-mixed Hinglish dataset. LIME mostly provided explanation rationales that align with human expectations. However, this may also be because the model is biased towards the presence of curse words and political words. The XAI techniques provide shallow insight into why the classifiers are predicting a statement as hateful. This could be because of the nature of the dataset, the code-mixed comments, improper labelling of the tweets, or the removal of context from the original HASOC ICHCL datasets. The future scope of this study involves studying XAI tools with a more robust dataset, which has human rationales for comparison. Other models must be trained on the dataset and integrated with interpretability components. Other explainability algorithms, such as gradient-based approaches, samples and occlusion, and layer-wise relevance propagation, must also be studied on hate speech classifiers.

References

1. Atanasova, P., Simonsen, J.G., Lioma, C., Augenstein, I.: A diagnostic study of explainability techniques for text classification. arXiv preprint arXiv:2009.13295 (2020)
2. Attanasio, G., Nozza, D., Pastor, E., Hovy, D.: Benchmarking post-hoc interpretability approaches for transformer-based misogyny detection. In: Proceedings of NLP Power! The First Workshop on Efficient Benchmarking in NLP, pp. 100–112 (2022)
3. Biradar, S., Saumya, S., et al.: Fighting hate speech from bilingual Hinglish speaker's perspective, a transformer-and translation-based approach. Soc. Netw. Anal. Min. **12**(1), 1–10 (2022)
4. Buitinck, L., et al.: API design for machine learning software: experiences from the scikit-learn project. In: ECML PKDD Workshop: Languages for Data Mining and Machine Learning, pp. 108–122 (2013)
5. Camburu, O.M., Rocktäschel, T., Lukasiewicz, T., Blunsom, P.: e-SNLI: natural language inference with natural language explanations. In: Advances in Neural Information Processing Systems, vol. 31 (2018)
6. Cheng, J., Bernstein, M., Danescu-Niculescu-Mizil, C., Leskovec, J.: Anyone can become a troll: causes of trolling behavior in online discussions. In: Proceedings of the 2017 ACM Conference on Computer Supported Cooperative Work and Social Computing, pp. 1217–1230 (2017)
7. Conneau, A., et al.: Unsupervised cross-lingual representation learning at scale. arXiv preprint arXiv:1911.02116 (2019)
8. Devlin, J., Chang, M.W., Lee, K., Toutanova, K.: Bert: Pre-training of deep bidirectional transformers for language understanding. arXiv preprint arXiv:1810.04805 (2018)
9. Donthula, S.K., Kaushik, A.: Man is what he eats: a research on Hinglish sentiments of Youtube cookery channels using deep learning. Int. J. Recent Technol. Eng. (IJRTE) **8**(2S11), 930–937 (2019)
10. Fersini, E., Nozza, D., Rosso, P., et al.: Overview of the evalita 2018 task on automatic misogyny identification (ami). In: EVALITA Evaluation of NLP and Speech Tools for Italian Proceedings of the Final Workshop 12–13 December 2018, Naples. Accademia University Press (2018)
11. Fersini, E., Nozza, D., Rosso, P., et al.: Ami@ evalita2020: automatic misogyny identification. In: Proceedings of the 7th Evaluation Campaign of Natural Language Processing and Speech Tools for Italian (EVALITA 2020). (seleziona...) (2020)
12. Hate crime: Law Commision united kingdom government. https://www.lawcom.gov.uk/project/hate-crime/. Accessed 02 Dec 2022
13. Kakwani, D., et al.: IndicNLPSuite: monolingual corpora, evaluation benchmarks and pre-trained multilingual language models for Indian languages. In: Findings of EMNLP (2020)
14. Karim, M.R., et al.: Deephateexplainer: explainable hate speech detection in under-resourced Bengali language. In: 2021 IEEE 8th International Conference on Data Science and Advanced Analytics (DSAA), pp. 1–10. IEEE (2021)
15. Kaur, G., Kaushik, A., Sharma, S.: Cooking is creating emotion: a study on Hinglish sentiments of Youtube cookery channels using semi-supervised approach. Big Data Cogn. Comput. **3**(3), 37 (2019)

16. Kokatnoor, S.A., Krishnan, B.: Twitter hate speech detection using stacked weighted ensemble (SWE) model. In: 2020 Fifth International Conference on Research in Computational Intelligence and Communication Networks (ICR-CICN), pp. 87–92. IEEE (2020)
17. Kothari, R., Snell, R.: Chutnefying English: The Phenomenon of Hinglish. Penguin Books India (2011)
18. Kumar, R., Ojha, A.K., Malmasi, S., Zampieri, M.: Evaluating aggression identification in social media. In: Proceedings of the Second Workshop on Trolling, Aggression and Cyberbullying, pp. 1–5 (2020)
19. Lundberg, S.M., Lee, S.I.: A unified approach to interpreting model predictions. In: Advances in Neural Information Processing Systems, vol. 30 (2017)
20. Mandl, T., Modha, S., Kumar, M.A., Chakravarthi, B.R.: Overview of the HASOC track at fire 2020: hate speech and offensive language identification in Tamil, Malayalam, Hindi, English and German. In: Forum for Information Retrieval Evaluation, pp. 29–32 (2020)
21. Mathew, B., Saha, P., Yimam, S.M., Biemann, C., Goyal, P., Mukherjee, A.: Hatexplain: a benchmark dataset for explainable hate speech detection. In: Proceedings of the AAAI Conference on Artificial Intelligence, vol. 35, pp. 14867–14875 (2021)
22. Moreno, M.A., Gower, A.D., Brittain, H., Vaillancourt, T.: Applying natural language processing to evaluate news media coverage of bullying and cyberbullying. Prev. Sci. **20**(8), 1274–1283 (2019)
23. Ribeiro, M.T., Singh, S., Guestrin, C.: "Why should i trust you?" explaining the predictions of any classifier. In: Proceedings of the 22nd ACM SIGKDD International Conference on Knowledge Discovery and Data Mining, pp. 1135–1144 (2016)
24. Satapara, S., et al.: Overview of the HASOC subtrack at fire 2022: hate speech and offensive content identification in English and Indo-Aryan languages. In: Proceedings of the 14th Annual Meeting of the Forum for Information Retrieval Evaluation, pp. 4–7 (2022)
25. Satapara, S., Modha, S., Mandl, T., Madhu, H., Majumder, P.: Overview of the HASOC subtrack at FIRE 2021: conversational hate speech detection in code-mixed language. Working Notes FIRE (2021)
26. Vig, J.: A multiscale visualization of attention in the transformer model. In: Proceedings of the 57th Annual Meeting of the Association for Computational Linguistics: System Demonstrations, pp. 37–42. Association for Computational Linguistics, Florence, Italy (2019). https://doi.org/10.18653/v1/P19-3007, https://www.aclweb.org/anthology/P19-3007
27. Vijayaraghavan, P., Larochelle, H., Roy, D.: Interpretable multi-modal hate speech detection. arXiv preprint arXiv:2103.01616 (2021)
28. Warner, W., Hirschberg, J.: Detecting hate speech on the world wide web. In: Proceedings of the Second Workshop on Language in Social Media, pp. 19–26 (2012)
29. Waseem, Z., Hovy, D.: Hateful symbols or hateful people? predictive features for hate speech detection on Twitter. In: Proceedings of the NAACL Student Research Workshop, pp. 88–93 (2016)
30. Yadav, S., Kaushik, A.: Contextualized embeddings from transformers for sentiment analysis on code-mixed Hinglish data: an expanded approach with explainable artificial intelligence. In: Anand Kumar, M., et al. (eds.) SPELLL 2022. Communications in Computer and Information Science, vol. 1802, pp. 99–119. Springer, Cham (2022). https://doi.org/10.1007/978-3-031-33231-9_7

31. Yadav, S., Kaushik, A., Sharma, S.: Cooking well, with love, is an art: transformers on Youtube Hinglish data. In: 2021 International Conference on Computational Performance Evaluation (ComPE), pp. 836–841. IEEE (2021)
32. Yang, C., Srinivasan, P.: Translating surveys to surveillance on social media: methodological challenges & solutions. In: Proceedings of the 2014 ACM Conference on Web Science, pp. 4–12 (2014)
33. Zaidan, O., Eisner, J., Piatko, C.: Using "annotator rationales" to improve machine learning for text categorization. In: Human Language Technologies 2007: The Conference of the North American Chapter of the Association for Computational Linguistics; Proceedings of the Main Conference, pp. 260–267 (2007)

From Black Boxes to Conversations: Incorporating XAI in a Conversational Agent

Van Bach Nguyen[1,2(✉)] [ID], Jörg Schlötterer[1,2,3] [ID], and Christin Seifert[1,2] [ID]

[1] University of Marburg, Marburg, Germany
{vanbach.nguyen,joerg.schloetterer,christin.seifert}@uni-marburg.de
[2] University of Duisburg-Essen, Duisburg, Germany
[3] University of Mannheim, Mannheim, Germany

Abstract. The goal of Explainable AI (XAI) is to design methods to provide insights into the reasoning process of black-box models, such as deep neural networks, in order to explain them to humans. Social science research states that such explanations should be conversational, similar to human-to-human explanations. In this work, we show how to incorporate XAI in a conversational agent, using a standard design for the agent comprising natural language understanding and generation components. We build upon an XAI question bank, which we extend by quality-controlled paraphrases, to understand the user's information needs. We further systematically survey the literature for suitable explanation methods that provide the information to answer those questions, and present a comprehensive list of suggestions. Our work is the first step towards truly natural conversations about machine learning models with an explanation agent. The comprehensive list of XAI questions and the corresponding explanation methods may support other researchers in providing the necessary information to address users' demands. To facilitate future work, we release our source code and data https://github.com/bach1292/XAGENT/.

Keywords: explainable artificial intelligence · XAI · conversational agents

1 Introduction

Deep neural networks [16] are the de-facto standard in machine learning-based artificial intelligence (AI) systems, having shown to outperform humans on many tasks (e.g., [30]). However, there is a trade-off between predictive performance and interpretability – while modern AI systems are highly powerful, they are also black-boxes by nature and their reasoning process is not interpretable anymore [19]. This tradeoff is addressed by the young, but rapidly growing research field of XAI [4].

L. Longo (Ed.): xAI 2023, CCIS 1903, pp. 71–96, 2023.
https://doi.org/10.1007/978-3-031-44070-0_4

```
X-Agent:  I recorded the profile: [Age 39, Workclass: State-gov, Education-num: 15,
Marital-status: Separated, Occupation: Other-service, Relationship: Not-in-family, Race:
White, Sex: Male, Capital-gain: 0, Capital-loss: 0, Hour-per-week: 20.0, Native-country:
England].
With this profile, the income will be <=50K.

User: Give me the reason for this prediction!
X-Agent:
```

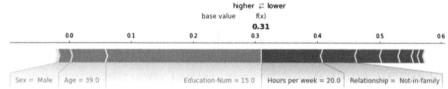

The above graph shows important features for this prediction. The red features increase the income, while the blue features decrease it.

```
User: Why is this profile predicted <=50K instead of >50K?
X-Agent:  There are multiple reasons for this result:
Age is too low and Workclass is not suitable.
If Age increases to at least 66.3 and Workclass changes to Self-emp-inc, this person's
predicted income will be more than 50K.
User: That's hard, how could I change only Occupation to get >50K prediction?
X-Agent:  The Occupation should be changed to Tech-support to get an income of more than 50K.
```

Fig. 1. XAI user questions are matched to reference questions. Answers are provided by a mapping of reference question to XAI methods along with additional explanations. The X-Agent explains the model's reasoning by feature importance scores of SHAP [28] and an explanation how to interpret them. (Color figure online)

While much progress has been made in XAI in terms of algorithmic development in recent years, this progress is not accessible to all stakeholders, in particular not to end users [25]. Miller [31] argues that human explanations are social conversations and, in order for XAI to be truly interpretable and valuable for all stakeholders, XAI needs to be conversational as well. These conversations are not restricted to natural language, but explanations could also be presented in a visual manner. The maxim is to provide explanations in a conversational manner, with interactions based on questions and answers. This maxim is explicitly expressed by practitioners [24]. While the need for conversational XAI has been recognized, fulfilling it remains an open challenge with solutions either limited to small, specific data sets and models [23] or mere collections of requirements for conversational XAI [47]. In this work, we develop methods to leverage a standard conversational agent architecture to conversational XAI. Building upon well-established conversational agent techniques allows us to focus on XAI-specific requirements, in order to cover a broad range of user questions, types of data, and types of models.

Our target group is users without machine learning knowledge who interact with the system. Following the taxonomy by Tomset et al. [45], users can be executors or operators, e.g., doctors making decisions based on the system's advice, or lenders using systems to assess applicant profiles. Figure 1 shows an example of a conversation between our prototype agent and a user asking to explain a prediction of a Random Forest model on the Adult dataset[1] (details on each individual interaction step, as well as a conversational scenario about a Convolutional Neural Network model on image data can be found in the Appendix, Sect. F.2).

We propose a systematic approach to enable XAI in a standard conversational agent architecture [6] (see Fig. 2 for an overview, full details in Sect. 3). First, we construct a question phrase bank data set based on the question bank of Liao et al. [25] to enable the agent to understand XAI questions. Second, based on a systematic literature survey of explanation methods, we establish a mapping between user intents, represented as reference questions in the question phrase bank, and XAI methods to answer user questions. Finally, a template-based natural language generation component creates the answers using the information from the selected XAI methods. Specifically, our contributions are:

- We present a systematic overview of methods to answer the information need implied in these questions and categorise questions by identifying which subsets require an XAI method for answering.
- We create a publicly available XAI question phrase bank for training and evaluating the natural language understanding component of the conversational agent based on the XAI question bank of Liao et al. [25].[2]
- We incorporate XAI in a standard conversational agent framework and present a prototype that can communicate about the internals of the machine learning model in natural language. (See Footnote 2)

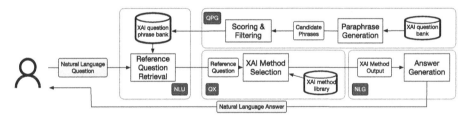

Fig. 2. Incorporating XAI in conversational agents: 1) Question-Phrase-Generation (QPG) uses a paraphrase generation model on the questions from the XAI question bank [25]. The generated candidates are scored by multiple annotators and ranked, resulting in the XAI question phrase bank. 2) In the Natural Language Understanding (NLU) component, the reference question for a user question is retrieved from the phrase bank. 3) The intent of the reference question defines the XAI method to be applied to the model in the Question-XAI method mapping component (QX). 4) A natural language generation (NLG) component converts the output of the XAI method (e.g., a table, graph, or number) with an answer in natural language. Omitted for overview: data sets are loaded and machine learning models are trained dynamically on user requests.

---

[1] https://archive.ics.uci.edu/ml/datasets/adult/.
[2] https://github.com/bach1292/XAGENT/.

2   Related Work

XAI is a highly active research field from the algorithmic perspective (see [2] for a recent survey). While the four key XAI surveys [1,4,15,19] focus on different perspectives, a common pattern in their taxonomies is the distinction between intrinsically interpretable models, i.e., the model itself constitutes the explanation, and posthoc explanations, i.e., methods explaining black-box models by, e.g., linear models approximating local decision boundaries [41]. Posthoc explanations can be further classified as model-specific, applicable only to certain types of models or model-agnostic, applicable to any machine learning model. We focus on model-agnostic posthoc explanations to be able to capture a broad range of machine learning tasks and models in the conversational agent. We derive posthoc explanation methods, which are suitable to answer specific XAI questions from the aforementioned surveys, and additionally from the suggested methods for each group of XAI questions in [25,26].

Recent research in conversational agents has gradually shifted to end-to-end approaches, based on fully data-driven systems [11]. However, the abundance of data is an ultimate prerequisite of such systems, and large data sets are not available for XAI yet. In contrast, the Genial Understander System (GUS) [6], which underlies most modern commercial digital assistants [22], requires only a small amount of data to build a conversational agent. Therefore, we focus on enabling XAI in this framework. Since public data sets are limited to a few domains [39] and not available for XAI, we create a question phrase corpus to fill this gap.

Research on Conversational XAI is still in its infancy, and agents are strongly limited in scope. Werner [47] presents a work-in-progress prototype of a rule-based XAI chatbot to iteratively elaborate requirements, accompanied by findings from literature and user studies. His prototype is limited to the classification of tabular data and a small set of pre-defined questions. Kuźba and Biecek's [23] goal is to collect the needs of users interacting with a conversational XAI agent, i.e., questions a human would ask. Their prototype is limited to a Random Forest, applied to the Titanic Dataset, and explanations addressing a few types of XAI questions, since the primary goal is the collection of interaction data. Contrary to the data-driven approach of Kuźba and Biecek, Liao et al. [25] construct an XAI question bank from literature review, expert reviews by XAI practitioners, and around 1000 min of interviews with 20 user experience and design practitioners working in multiple domains. This question bank contains 73 XAI questions in 10 categories (see Table 1, columns 2 and 3) and serves as the basis for our question phrase bank. While the aforementioned work collects users' needs and questions to (conversational) XAI, our goal is to automatically provide answers to the identified user questions. Developed at the same time, the conversational XAI agent by Slack et al. [43] is most similar to our work, in particular in using language models to identify users' intents and template-based answer generation. However, their focus is on open-ended natural language dialogues and hence their agent is limited to tabular data, whereas we focus on a broad coverage of XAI questions, including a multitude of data types and models.

3 System Overview

A standard conversational agent architecture [6] is generally composed of the following components: i) Natural Language Understanding (NLU) to, e.g., determine a user's intent(s), ii) a dialogue state tracker (DST) to maintain the current state and history of the dialogue, iii) a dialogue policy, deciding the system's next step, and iv) Natural Language Generation (NLG) to generate the system's output. We integrate XAI into this architecture and assume that an XAI question contains all relevant information to select a proper explanation method as a response (the extension to incomplete information is subject to future work). Hence, we omit the DST. This section outlines our approach to incorporate XAI into the remaining components.

The general architecture of our conversational XAI agent is depicted in Fig. 2. The NLU component is responsible for identifying the user's actual intent from a wide range of XAI utterances. To cope with this variety of utterances, we expand the XAI question bank [25] into an XAI question phrase bank. This phrase bank constitutes a training data set to identify user intents from a wide range of XAI utterances. We construct the extended question phrase bank from an initial set of XAI questions, paraphrase generation, and scoring. We describe the construction (QPG) in full detail in Sect. 4.1. Upon a user question, the NLU component retrieves the corresponding reference question from the question phrase bank. We explain this retrieval in Sect. 4.2. The intent of the reference question determines the XAI method to be applied to the model in the Question-XAI method mapping, which is our integration of XAI to the dialogue policy component (QX, see Sect. 5). The natural language generation (NLG) component [13, 40] enriches the output of the XAI method, e.g., SHAP, by natural language to form the final answer, e.g., explaining SHAP's output graph (see Sect. 6).

4 Understanding Questions

In this section, we first describe the construction of the question phrase bank, which helps the agent understand a broad set of XAI questions, and then describe how reference questions can be retrieved from this question phrase bank to implement the NLU component.

4.1 Question Phrase Bank (QPG)

Training the NLU component of a conversational XAI agent requires conversational data about XAI. However, such data does not exist. Therefore, we introduce an XAI question phrase bank as a data set to train and evaluate the NLU component. The phrase bank represents a broad variety of utterances of possible user questions to XAI systems and is publicly available. (See Footnote 2)

To create the phrase bank, we use a language model to generate paraphrase candidates for each reference question in the XAI question bank of Liao et al. [25]. Our goal is to capture a high variance of utterances in the phrase bank while retaining semantics of the reference questions in the initial question bank. The paraphrase candidates were manually scored for similarity by multiple annotators before we filter them by their scores (Fig. 2, QPG component, top right).

We use GPT-3 [7] and few-shot learning to generate paraphrase candidates of XAI questions[3] (for details and an example see Appendix A). During the paraphrase generation process, we discard any generated text that does not clearly constitute a paraphrased question (e.g., answers to questions, incomplete sentences). We generate at least 2 paraphrases per question, 4.2 on average, 20 at maximum, and 310 pairs of (question, paraphrase candidate) in total.

To assess the quality of the paraphrase candidates, we annotated all generated pairs manually by human-perceived similarity. We extended our paraphrase candidate set by 59 negative pairs, i.e., we sampled paraphrases from different, non-matching questions at random. Thus, our data set for annotation comprises 369 phrase pairs. Annotators were first introduced to the task, shown a simple example, and then asked to assess the similarity of phrase pairs on a 6-point Likert scale (1: very different, 6: very similar) [3]. We chose a scale with an even number of items to force respondents to select between either similar or different because a neutral element "halfway similar and halfway different" is neither meaningful nor can it be assessed. Seven participants, consisting of five males and two females, with a Master's or Ph.D. degree in computer science and a background in machine learning, took part in the annotation process.

We randomly assigned participants to one of 3 groups, one participant was assigned to all groups. Each group annotated approx. 125 phrase pairs, resulting in each pair having at least 2 annotations. In the final annotation scores, most of the paraphrases generated by GPT-3 have a score ≥ 4, while most of negatives pairs have a score < 4 supporting the high quality of GPT-3 paraphrases as well as human annotation. Further details on the scores can be found in the Appendix, Sect. B.

For our final XAI question phrase bank, we select all pairs of paraphrases with an average annotation score ≥ 4 (Likert score of 4 means *more similar than different*). Each paraphrase is linked to its reference question, and the reference question is a paraphrase of itself. The task of the NLU component is then to identify the reference question for a user question, based on the known paraphrases of the reference question.

---

[3] We use the Open AI API: https://openai.com/api/.

4.2   Reference Question Retrieval (NLU)

We preprocess a given user question to a standard format. We use a placeholder
<feature> to substitute all feature names from the data set. Similarly, labels
(classes) in user questions are replaced by the placeholder <class>. For example, on the Adult data set (See Footnote 1) (Fig. 1), the question *How could I
change only Occupation to get >50K?* is transformed to *How could I change only
<feature> to get <class>?*, in which, the *Occupation* is a feature and *>50K* is
a class in the Adult data set. We assume that feature and class names in user
questions match those in the data set (i.e., no typos or synonyms). We formulate
the matching of a user question to a reference question as a multi-class classification problem with class labels corresponding to reference questions in the
XAI question phrase bank (see Sect. 4.1). First, we generate sentence embeddings of the pre-processed user and reference questions with SimCSE [12] and
RoBERTa-large [27]. We then train a feedforward network with 1 hidden layer
and ReLU activation on the sentence embeddings to classify user questions into
one of the reference questions in the question phrase bank. The output of this
step is a reference question that reflects the intent of the user question. From the
classifier's output, we select the reference question with the highest probability.
If the probability is lower than a predefined threshold θ (no match), we consider
the question as an (yet) unknown variation (paraphrase) of a reference, save it
for later, and ask the user for an alternative phrasing of the question. We set
$\theta = 0.5$ in our experiments. We provide an evaluation of this matching approach
and a comparison to other approaches in Sect. 7.

In summary, given a user question, we substitute all feature names and class
names in the question with placeholders. Then, we use a pretrained model to
match the preprocessed question to one of the reference questions in the question
phrase bank, which we created using GPT-3 and human annotation.

5   Retrieving Answer Information

After matching user input to its corresponding reference question, the next step
is to obtain the relevant information to provide an answer. Previous work [25, 26]
suggested some XAI methods as responses for question groups, but it remains
unclear how to select the appropriate method for each specific question, i.e.,
how to design a simplified dialogue policy in a conversational XAI agent (QX
component in Fig. 2).

Table 1. Overview of XAI questions [25] with reference questions, number of paraphrases (**Phr.**), whether the question requires an XAI method (highlighted rows, see Sect. 5.2), and (optional) sources of information (Sect. 5.1). "n.a.": no method matches the selection criteria; **bold** indicates the final selected methods. Options are not always available, limited to certain types of data/models or provide only partial information.

ID	Category	Reference Question	Phr.	Method	Option
1	How	How are the parameters set?	6	Model Generation	ModelCards [32]
2	How	How does feature f impact its predictions?	4	**SHAP** [28], (LIME [41])	
3	How	How does it weigh different features?	7	**SHAP** [28], (LIME [41])	
4	How	How does the system make predictions?	4	n.a.	ProtoTree [35], ProtoPNet [8], ModelExtraction [5]
5	How	Is feature X used or not used for the predictions?	4	**SHAP** [28], (LIME [41])	
6	How	What are the top features it uses?	4	**SHAP** [28], (LIME [41])	
7	How	What are the top rules it uses?	4	n.a.	
8	How	What features does the system consider?	4	**SHAP** [28], (LIME [41])	
9	How	What is the system's overall logic?	4	n.a.	ProtoTree [35], ProtoPNet [8], ModelExtraction [5]
10	How	What kind of algorithm is used?	4	Model Generation	ModelCards [32]
11	How	What rules does it use?	4	n.a.	ProtoTree [35]
12, 13	How to be	How should this instance/feature change to get a different prediction?	7	**DICE** [34], **CFProto** [46] for 12	
14	How to be	What kind of instance gets a different prediction?	4	**DICE** [34], **CFProto** [46]	
15, 16	How to still	What are the necessary features present/ absent to guarantee this prediction?	6	n.a.	SHAP [28], (LIME [41])
17, 18	How to still	What is the highest/lowest feature one can have to still get the same prediction?	12	**Anchors** [42]	
19	How to still	What is the scope of change permitted to still get the same prediction?	4	**Anchors** [42]	

(continued)

Table 1. (*continued*)

ID	Category	Reference Question	Phr.	Method	Option
20	How to still	What kind of instance gets this prediction?	4	**Anchors** [42]	
21	Input	How much data like this is the system trained on?	4	Model Generation	ModelCards [32], DataSheets [14]
22, 23	Input	How were the ground-truth/labels produced?	8	Data Generation	DataSheets [14]
24, 25	Input	What are the biases/limitations of the data?	9	Data Generation	DataSheets [14]
26	Input	What data is the system not using?	5	Model Generation	ModelCards [32]
27	Input	What is the sample size?	3	Model Generation	ModelCards [32], DataSheets [14]
28	Input	What is the source of the data?	3	Data Generation	ModelCards [32], DataSheets [14]
29	Input	What kind of data does the system learn from?	5	Model Generation	ModelCards [32], DataSheets [14]
30	Output	How can I best utilize the output of the system?	4	Model Generation	ModelCards [32], DataSheets [14]
31	Output	How is the output used for other system component(s)?	4	System Context	
32	Output	What does the system output mean?	4	Data/Model Generation	ModelCards [32], DataSheets [14]
33	Output	What is the scope of the system's capability? Can it do [A]?	4	Model Generation	ModelCards [32]
34	Output	What kind of output does the system give?	3	Data/Model Generation	ModelCards [32], DataSheets [14]
35–37	Performance	How accurate/precise/reliable are the predictions?	12	Model Generation	ModelCards [32]
38	Performance	How often does the system make mistakes?	4	Model Generation	ModelCards [32]
39, 40	Performance	In what situations is the system likely to be correct/incorrect?	8	Model Generation	ModelCards [32]
41	Performance	Is the system's performance good enough for [A]?	2	System Context	
42	Performance	What are the limitations of the system?	2	Model Generation	ModelCards [32]

(*continued*)

Table 1. (*continued*)

ID	Category	Reference Question	Phr.	Method	Option
43	Performance	What kind of mistakes is the system likely to make?	5	Model Generation	ModelCards [32]
44	What if	What would the system predict for [a different instance]?	2	Prediction	
45, 46	What if	What would the system predict if feature(s) f of this instance change(s) to f'?	8	Prediction	
47–48	Why	Why/How is this instance given this prediction?	20	**SHAP** [28], (LIME [41])	
49	Why	What features of this instance lead to the system's prediction?	15	**SHAP** [28], (LIME [41])	
50	Why	Why are instance A and instance B given the same prediction?	4	**SHAP** [28], (LIME [41])	
51	Why not	How is this instance not predicted A?	4	**DICE** [34], **CFProto** [46]	
52	Why not	Why are instances A and B given different predictions?	8	**DICE** [34], **CFProto** [46]	
53	Why not	Why is this instance predicted P instead of Q?	11	**DICE** [34], **CFProto** [46]	
54	Others	How to improve the system?	4	External Knowledge	
55	Others	What are the results of other people using the system?	4	External Validation	
56	Others	What does [ML terminology] mean?	2	External Knowledge	
57–67	Others	How/What/Why will the system adapt/change/drift/improve over time?	35	External Validation	
68–70	Others	Why NOT using this data/feature/rule?	8	n.a.	
71–73	Others	Why using this data/feature/rule?	14	n.a.	

We analyzed all 73 reference questions in the XAI question phrase bank for their implied information need and identified methods to retrieve this information. Table 1 presents an overview of all questions. Specifically, we identified the questions that require an XAI method for extracting the answer information (highlighted rows), and not only require to access stored values, e.g. the size of the training data. Following the general definition of XAI by Arrieta et al. [4], we define an XAI method[4] as a method that produces details or reasons to make the AI's functioning clear or easy to understand. That is, an XAI method must have access to a model's internal reasoning or to a proxy that reveals this reasoning at least to some extent. For instance, the question *Why is this instance predicted P instead of Q?* requires a counterfactual explanation, identifying feature sets that – if changed – would change the model's prediction from P to the specified counterfactual class Q. On the other hand, the question *What would the system predict if feature [..] of this instance changed to f'*, with f' given as specific feature values, just requires to create a new test instance with the specific feature set and apply the trained (black-box) model on this new instance.

In the following, we first discuss the information needed for the 50 questions that do not require an XAI method, and outline how the information for the answer can be obtained. Second, we discuss the 23 XAI questions and present our criteria for analysing existing XAI methods and our final mapping from reference question to XAI-method for extracting the answer information.

5.1 Non XAI Specific Questions

Analysing the 50 questions in this category, we identified six subcategories w.r.t. information need. The categories are indicated in column "Method" in Table 1. Questions in the **data generation** subcategory require information about the data or the data generation process. They can either be directly answered by querying data set statistics or accessing an accompanying data sheet for the data set [14] if available. Examples of such questions are *What is the sample size?* or *How were the ground-truth labels produced?* Questions in the **model generation** subcategory can be answered by retrieving easily accessible information about the underlying machine learning model, such as hyperparameters set during training or evaluation results. If the model is equipped with a Model-Card [32], the information can be obtained from the latter. Example questions for this category are *How often does the system make mistakes?* and *What kind of algorithm is used?* ModelCards also contain information about biases, scope, and limitations of the machine learning model, thus containing information for other questions, such as *What is the scope of the systems ability?*. Questions in the **prediction** subcategory, such as *What would the system predict for [a different instance]?*, can simply be answered by applying the model on a newly generated test instance. Some questions require **external knowledge**, either additional information from humans or an additional external knowledge base and an information retrieval approach, to access the information. For example, the question *How to improve the system?* requires domain knowledge on

---

[4] By defining XAI methods, our goal is to distinguish between approaches that rely on models' internal reasoning and those that only involve simple actions such as retrieving information or making predictions using the model.

model optimization, a judgment of model performance in comparison with similar approaches, and, for instance, an estimate of whether additional training data are likely to improve performance. For the question *What does [ML terminology] mean?*, we envision a knowledge base or lexicon with Machine Learning terms that can be queried for the information. Questions in the **external validation** subcategory, such as *How will the system improve over time*, require additional evaluation during the system's lifetime and/or information from similar systems. The simplest and easily accessible information would be a binary indicator of whether the system is capable of online learning at all, but more details require elaborate experiments. **System context** questions ask for information about the integration of the machine learning model with other system components and their embedding in the application. E.g., the question *How is the output used for other system component(s)?* depends on the actual system deployment, and *Is the system good enough for [A]?* requires knowledge about the application context and its requirements.

5.2   XAI Questions

To identify suitable candidates able to provide the information for answering the 23 XAI questions remaining (highlighted rows in Table 1), we conducted a literature survey. Our sources were the four key XAI surveys [1,4,15,19], the methods referred to in the initial XAI question bank and the follow-up work by the same authors [25,26]. To further filter the candidate set for XAI methods to incorporate in conversational agents, we defined the following four criteria for our analysis, the latter three based on the categorization scheme of a recent survey [36], which identified 312 original papers, presenting a novel XAI technique in one of the major ML/AI conferences since 2014 until 2020:

Source Code: The paper should be accompanied by easy-to-use, publicly accessible source code in order to integrate the method into the conversational agent in a reasonable amount of time. This criterion significantly reduced the number of methods.

Model: We assessed the applicability of the XAI method to different types of models and favored approaches that are model agnostic [4] or at least can be applied to multiple types of models.

Data: We assessed the applicability of the XAI method to different types of input data. To enable efficient implementation of components that process the XAI method's raw output to generate a user-friendly natural language answer, possibly accompanied by visualizations, we favor methods that can be applied to multiple types of input data.

Problem: Explanation methods may be restricted to particular machine learning tasks, e.g., regression. We account for this restriction by including the category "type of problem" in our analysis. In this paper, we focus on explaining models for supervised machine learning, more specifically classification tasks.

We provide the detailed overview in the Appendix, Table 6 and focus on the finally selected methods in this section. Table 1 shows the selected methods (in **bold**) and their corresponding questions for which they provide the necessary information. We briefly describe the selected methods in the following:

SHAP [28] is a widely used method to quantify the importance of features for the prediction of a single instance. SHAP follows a game-theoretic approach to identify the contribution of each feature (player) in an additive setting. Quantitative feature importance values are relevant for answering questions w.r.t. feature contribution on the prediction (questions 2, 3, 5, 8, 48) as well as for top features (question 6). Furthermore, feature importance also can explain why/how the prediction is given (questions 47, 50). To answer question 49 *Why are instance A and instance B given the same prediction?*, we show one explanation per instance. SHAP can explain both, image and tabular data and the feature importance values have been shown to be consistent with human judgment. We, therefore, use SHAP to answer the questions that require feature importance information.

DICE [34] is an explanation method, focusing on counterfactual explanations for tabular data. Given an instance, DICE searches for the minimum feature changes required to get a different prediction, and therefore provides information to answer questions 12, 14, and 51–53. DICE can also identify required changes for a specific feature to change the prediction to a different target class and therefore provides the information for answering question 13: *How should this feature change to get a different prediction?*.[5] Similar to DICE, CFProto [46] is a counterfactual explanation method applicable to image data. However, the method does not allow to change single, specific features to obtain a target class, because features in image data are hard to define. Thus, we apply CFProto to gather information for answering questions 12, 14, and 51–53 on image data. Anchor [42] computes sufficient conditions for a prediction, so called anchors, such that as long as the anchor holds, changes to the remaining feature values of the instance do not matter. Therefore, it can be used to determine the boundaries of the prediction, which are suitable to answer questions 17–20.

In summary, to integrate XAI into the dialogue policy component, we systematically map XAI questions to XAI methods.

6   Generating Answers

XAI methods provide the core information to answer the corresponding questions, but they lack explanatory text in natural language for the end user. Presenting just the raw information in form of a table or importance values alongside feature names to end users is not always adequate. Instead, additional context, such as what the values represent or how to interpret them, is desirable. To address this problem, we incorporate a template-based natural language generation component. For each question, we define text templates (partially with dataset-specific vocabulary) containing placeholders for the information obtained

---

[5] Despite limitations of DICE in generating actionable counterfactual explanations [17], we include this method in our study due to its alignment with our predefined criteria and high overall quality [17,33].

from XAI methods. We combine this information with – or convert it to – textual explanations depending on the type of information generated by the XAI method. For images and graphs (e.g. SHAP's outputs), we add a textual explanation. For tabular format (e.g. DICE's outputs), we convert the table to natural language by extracting feature names and corresponding values. For example, in Fig. 1, the answer "The Occupation should be changed to Tech-support to get an income of more than 50K" is the combination of the template "The <feature> should be changed to <value> to get <class>" and the counterfactual information obtained from DICE [34].

In case of counterfactual explanations, relations need to be extracted in addition to feature names and values. For the counterfactual question 53 (*Why is this instance predicted P instead of Q?*), we extract and compare the relation between the given instance with class P and a counterfactual instance with the target class Q. In particular, for numerical features, we identify the relation between two values, whether the first is greater or smaller than the second. In the case of categorical/textual features, we check if a value is different from the other. We then use the corresponding templates for the extracted relations. For example, in Fig. 1, we identify 2 relations between the given instance (label ≤ *50K*) and its counterfactual (label *>50K*): the numerical feature "Age = 39" is smaller than "Age = 66.3" and the categorical feature "Workclass = State-gov" is different to "Workclass = Self-emp-inc". The corresponding templates are "<feature> is too low", and "<feature> is not suitable". The next sentence "If Age increases to at least 66.3 and Workclass changes to ..." also contains 2 different templates for these relations. Finally, we combine the templates with the XAI information to return the answers.

For questions that cannot be answered (either below the matching threshold or no available methods), we define a template asking users for an alternative phrasing or a different question.

7 Evaluation of NLU Component

In this section, we describe the evaluation of promising approaches to implement the natural language understanding (NLU) component, i.e., the mapping from user input to XAI questions as described in Sect. 4.2. Specifically, we compare traditional text classification to sentence embeddings.

7.1 Experimental Setup

We use the XAI question phrase bank as described in Sect. 4.1, i.e., the data set with reference questions and paraphrases after manual quality control. We use the reference question ID as a label and assign a common label to sets of questions with identical answers in the same category. For instance, question 2 *How does feature f impact its predictions?* and question 5 *Is feature f used or not used for the predictions?* both ask for (binary) feature contribution of one specific feature and can be answered with the feature importance information for feature f of an XAI method. After relabeling, the final data set contains 329

Table 2. Evaluation results for 3-fold cross-validation. Showing mean on the full data set ($std \leq 0.05$) and on the subset of XAI questions ($std \leq 0.09$) with (and without) training on paraphrases.

	All questions		XAI questions only	
	Accuracy	Macro F1	Accuracy	Macro F1
SVM + TF-IDF	0.61 ± 0.05 (0.55)	0.50 ± 0.04 (0.49)	0.67 ± 0.05 (0.62)	0.59 ± 0.06 (0.53)
RF + TF-IDF	0.57 ± 0.04 (0.39)	0.47 ± 0.05 (0.30)	0.68 ± 0.05 (0.53)	0.55 ± 0.06 (0.45)
SimCSE + Cosine	**0.72 ± 0.03** (0.61)	0.65 ± 0.05 (0.57)	0.83 ± 0.03 (0.58)	0.78 ± 0.06 (0.52)
SimCSE + NN	**0.72 ± 0.03** (0.55)	**0.67 ± 0.03** (0.45)	**0.85 ± 0.08** (0.67)	**0.83 ± 0.09** (0.61)

instances and 52 different labels (from 73 initial questions). Additionally, we also evaluate our models on the subset of XAI questions only, i.e., 23 questions whose rows are highlighted in gray in Table 1. This XAI-only set contains 111 instances and 14 labels.

We compare four different approaches using two different feature representation methods: classical TF-IDF weighting, and sentence embeddings extracted by SimCSE [12] (More details of representation methods can be found in the Appendix, Sect. C). On the TF-IDF vector space, we evaluate two classifiers commonly applied to text classification: Support Vector Machines (SVMs) with various kernels and Random Forests (RF). On the sentence embedding space (SimCSE), we compare a similarity-based approach to a supervised model. In the similarity-based approach, we rank reference questions by their cosine similarity to a user question. As a supervised model, we use a fully connected feedforward neural network (NN) with a single hidden layer of size 256, trained with cross-entropy loss. We employ grid-search for hyperparameter tuning with details available in the Appendix, Table 5.

We present the mean of micro- and macro-averaged F1 scores on 3-fold cross-validation. For multi-class classification, the micro-averaged F1 score is equal to accuracy. To further evaluate the importance of paraphrases, we compare all approaches without training on additional paraphrases. Specifically, for SVM, RF and SimCSE + NN, we train the models on only 73 reference questions (Table 1) and evaluate them on the generated paraphrases.

7.2   Results

Table 2 shows the evaluation results (more details can be found in Appendix, Sect. D). The supervised approach based on sentence embeddings (SimCSE + NN) outperforms the other approaches on both, the full data set and the XAI subset with an accuracy of 0.85 on the XAI subset. Both traditional text classification approaches (RF + TF-IDF and SVM + TF-IDF) are already outperformed by the unsupervised similarity-based approach on sentence embeddings (SimCSE + Cosine) and even more so by the supervised approach on sentence embeddings (SimCSE + NN), highlighting the efficiency of pre-trained models for natural language processing tasks. In addition, for all approaches, training with paraphrases yields significantly higher results than without paraphrases indicating the strong impact of the generated paraphrases.

8   Conclusion

Following the conversational style of human-to-human explanations, we leveraged a conversational agent to explain machine learning models. To capture the variance of questions that can be asked about the topic, we extended an XAI question bank with paraphrases. Each question-paraphrases set defines a specific information need, represented by a reference question. We presented a systematic analysis of methods that can address those information needs aiming at a sufficient, but small subset of all available XAI methods. Our XAI question phrase bank and XAI method collection can serve as guidance for the future development of conversational XAI agents. In future work, we plan to integrate a learning component for dialogue policies to make the system self-adaptable from interactions. Furthermore, it is essential to extensively evaluate the framework through human evaluation and diverse datasets, which we leave for future work.

Appendix

A   GPT-3 Paraphrase Prompting

We finetune the GPT-3 model with two instances for each reference question in the initial XAI question bank (2-shot). Each instance consists of the reference question and two paraphrases of this question. Subsequently, we prompt the model to generate paraphrases with a new question (see Fig. 3 for an example). We repeat the prompt multiple times for each reference question.

Step 1, Finetuning:
Question: *Why is this instance given the prediction?*
Paraphrase1: *Give me the reason for this result.*
Paraphrase2: *What is the reason for this prediction?*
Question: *What features does the system consider?*
Paraphrase1: *What attributes are used?*
Paraphrase2: *What features does the model use?*

Step 2, Prompting:
Question: *What is the sample size?*
GPT-3 output:
Paraphrase1: *How many did they sample?*
Paraphrase2: *How many items are considered in this result?*

Fig. 3. Example GPT-3 finetuning, prompt and output to generate XAI paraphrase candidates

B   Phrase Annotation Details

The distribution of annotation scores varies among each question category (see Fig. 4). In general, most of the score medians are above 4, indicating the good quality of GPT-3 in generating paraphrases. However, varying interquartile ranges suggest that GPT-3 generates better paraphrases in specific categories such as *How to be that* or *Why not*, and mixed paraphrases in others, such as *What if* or *Other*.

Figure 5 depicts the average annotator score per phrase pair. Phrase pairs are ranked by their score, separately for the 310 paraphrase pairs and 59 negative pairs. Most of the paraphrase pairs that were generated by GPT-3 have a score ≥ 4, and thus are perceived as being similar, indicating that GPT-3 generates high-quality paraphrases in general. Conversely, most negative pairs, which were sampled from different questions, have an average score < 4, supporting the quality of the human annotations. However, there are a few outliers of negative pairs which are annotated with a high similarity score. This is likely caused by our choice of negative phrases, sampled at random from a different question. These pairs may not be truly negative, as one question may be more general than the other or they can be interpreted in different ways (see Table 3 for examples). Furthermore, annotators disagree on ambiguous pairs and agree on unambiguous pairs (Table 4), further supporting the good quality of the dataset.

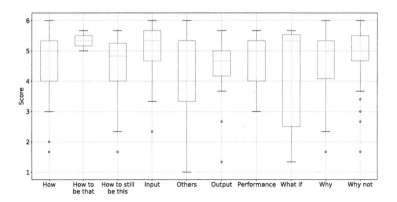

Fig. 4. Annotation score distribution for each question category.

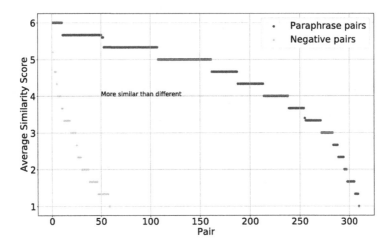

Fig. 5. Average human annotation score for all phrase pairs ranked by score. Negative pairs are paraphrases from different questions.

Table 3. Example negative pairs with average score > 4

Phrase A	Phrase B	Scores
How are the predictions made?	What kind of algorithm is used?	5, 5, 4
How should this Instance change to get a different prediction?	What should be the value of this feature in order to change the prediction?	5, 5, 4
What features of this instance lead to the system's prediction?	How was this instance given this value/category?	5, 5, 3

C   Representation Methods

We test two different feature representation methods: classical TF-IDF weighting, and sentence embeddings. For TF-IDF weighting, we follow a standard preprocessing pipeline: We select tokens of 2 or more alphanumeric characters (punctuation is ignored and always treated as a token separator) and stem the text using the Porter Stemmer [29] to obtain our token dictionary. Maximum and minimum DF thresholds are subject to hyperparameter optimization (see full list of hyperparameters in Table 5). We embed sentences (i.e., question instances) using SimCSE [12] to obtain an alternative feature representation to TF-IDF. We employ the pretrained RoBERTa-large model [27] as base model in SimCSE.

Table 4. Phrase pairs with highest agreement/disagreement between annotators (bold indicates the reference questions in the question bank)

Phrase A	Phrase B	Scores
Disagreement		
Why this instance has class P but Q does not?	**Why is this instance predicted P instead of Q?**	6, 4, 1
How much data like this is the system trained on?	Give me an instance which is similar to this.	5, 1, 1
How is this instance not predicted A?	How is the result B for this instance possible?	6, 1, 2
Agreement		
Which features does it take into account?	**What features does the system consider?**	6, 6, 6
What are the results of other people using the system?	What was the result when other people used the system?	5, 5, 5
What is the reason for this prediction?	Which features does the system use?	2, 2, 2

Table 5. Hyperparameters for Grid Search, **bold** indicates the chosen hyperparameters. For the other hyperparameters, we use default value in scikit-learn [38].

Model	Hyperparameter
TF-IDF	max_df = [1.0, **0.8**]; min_df = [0.1, 0.2, **1**]
SVM	kernel = ['linear', 'poly', **'rbf'**, 'sigmoid', 'precomputed']; C = [0.1, 1, 10, **100**, 1000]; gamma = [**0.1**, 1, 10, 100]; degree = [0, 1, 2, **3**]
RF	bootstrap = [**True**, False]; max_depth = [10, **None**]; min_samples_leaf = [1, **2**, 4]; min_samples_split = [**2**, 5, 10]; n_estimators = [10, **50**, 100]
NN	Epoch = [**50**, 100]; batch_size = **1**; learning_rate = [**4**, 6]

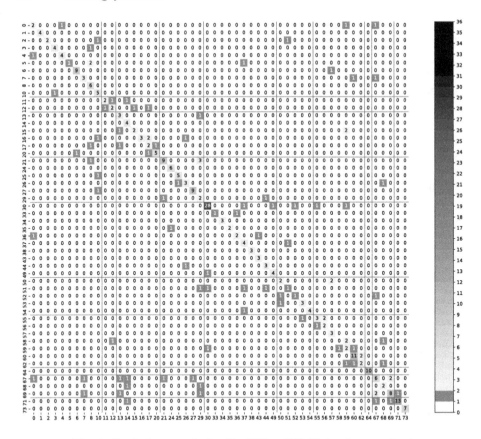

Fig. 6. Confusion matrix for SimCSE + NN (Color figure online)

D   Details on NLU Evaluation

Figure 6 shows the confusion matrix for SimCSE + NN's. The blue lines separate the questions in each category (see Table 1), and the diagonal contains number of the True Positive rate for each question. This prominent diagonal reflects the high accuracy of the approaches. The squares around the diagonal are subconfusion matrices between questions in the same group. The high number of gray color in these squares indicates that questions in the same category are harder to distinguish than questions in different category (note that the numbers on x and y axes indicate the merged labels, not IDs).

Table 6. XAI methods and selection criteria (Abbreviation: Cls = Classification, Reg = Regression, RL = Reinforcement Learning)

Method	Year	Reference Question	Code	Type of data	Model	Problem
GAM [20]	1990	2–9, 11, 47–50, 68–73		Tabular	Intrinsically interpretable	Cls, Reg
GoldenEye [21]	2014	5, 8	✓(in R)	Tabular	All	Cls
MFV [37]	2016	4	✓	Image	Neural Network	Cls
LIME [41]	2016	2, 3, 5, 6, 8, 47–50	✓	Tabular, Image, Text	All	Cls, Reg
Feature Tweaking [44]	2017	2, 3, 6, 12	✓	Tabular	Tree-based	Cls
Model Extraction [5]	2017	2–9, 11, 47–50, 68–73		Tabular	All	Cls, Reg, RL
SHAP [28]	2017	2, 3, 5, 6, 8, 47–50	✓	Tabular, Image, Text	All	Cls, Reg
ANCHOR [42]	2018	17–20	✓	Tabular, Text	All	Cls
Boolean rules [9]	2018	2–9, 11, 47–50, 68–73	✓	Tabular	Intrinsically interpretable	Cls
LORE [18]	2018	2, 3, 5, 6, 8, 47–50	✓	Tabular	All	Cls
CEM [10]	2018	12, 14, 51–53	✓	Image	Neural Network	Cls
ProtoPNet [8]	2019	2–9, 11, 47–50, 68–73	✓	Image	Neural Network	Cls
DICE [34]	2020	12–14, 51–53	✓	Tabular	All	Cls
CFProto [46]	2020	12, 14, 51–53	✓	Tabular, Image	All	Cls
ProtoTree [35]	2021	2–9, 11, 47–50, 68–73	✓	Image	Neural Network	Cls

E   XAI Method Overview

Table 6 shows the criteria, which are mentioned in Sect. 5.2 in the paper, to choose the proper XAI method for each XAI question.

F   Conversation Scenarios

F.1   Random Forest Classifier on Adult Data

In this section, we show an example conversation between a prototype implementation of our proposed framework and a user on tabular data (Adult dataset (See footnote 1)) with a Random Forest (RF) classifier.

The task on this data set is to predict whether the income exceeds $50.000/year (abbreviated 50K) based on census data. We train the classifier using the sklearn library and its standard parameter settings[6]. The mean accuracy of the classifier using 3-fold cross-validation is 0.85. For explanations, we retrain the RF classifier with the same parameter settings on the full data set. The data set and the classifier are loaded at the beginning of the conversation.

Figure 1 in the main body of the paper shows a conversation with the prototype agent (X-Agent). At the beginning of the conversation, the user provides information about her features by answering retrieval questions from the agent. These questions can be generated based on DataSheets [14] of the data set. We omit this part of the conversation in Fig. 1 and show how the X-Agent reacts to several questions about the model.

The first question is the request: *Give me the reason for this prediction!* The natural language understanding (NLU) component matches this question to the

---

[6] https://scikit-learn.org/stable/modules/generated/sklearn.ensemble.
RandomForestClassifier.html.

reference question *Why is this instance given this prediction?* in the question bank (question 47 in Table 1). The Question-XAI method mapping (QX) selects SHAP [28] as the XAI method to provide the information for the answer. The natural language generation (NLG) component combines SHAP's feature importance information with the predefined text "The above graph ..." to respond to the user question.

For the next question, *Why is this profile predicted ≤50K instead of >50K*, the labels *≤50K* and *>50K* are replaced by the token <class> before matching to reference question 53 in Table 2 (main body of the paper) *Why is this instance predicted P instead of Q?*. The QX component identifies DICE [34] as the explanation method for this reference question, and the information is translated into natural language. In detail, DICE returns a counterfactual instance with the desired target label (*>50K*), yielding two features (Age and Workclass) that need to change in order to obtain the desired prediction. The NLG component extracts the relations between feature values of the original instance (Age: 39, Workclass: State-gov) and counterfactual instance (Age: 66.3, Workclass: Self-emp-inc). In comparison to the counterfactual, Age of the original instance is lower and Workclass differs. These relations are converted and rendered as text in the final answer by the NLG component.

For the final question *That's hard, how could I change only Occupation to get >50K prediction?*, the words "Occupation" and ">50K" are substituted by tokens <feature> and <class> respectively. Then, the question is matched to reference question 13 (see Table 1) *How should this feature change to get a different prediction?*. DICE is again determined as the XAI method for providing the required information to answer this question. However, this question asks for a specific feature, i.e., constrains the search space of DICE for counterfactuals. Finally, the provided information is again translated to natural language.

F.2   Convolutional Neural Network on MNIST

We use the MNIST data set and a pre-trained convolutional neural network [46] to showcase a conversation on an image data set (see Fig. 7). First, the NLU component matches the first question *Why did you predict that?* to reference question 47 *Why is this instance given this prediction?* (see Table 1). Then, QX maps this question to SHAP [28] as the explanation technique. SHAP highlights the important parts on the image that lead to prediction 7. The NLG component adds an explanation in form of natural language text to the information provided by SHAP (the image). For the second question *How should this image change to get number 9 predicted?*, *number 9* is replaced by token <class>. NLU maps this processed question to reference question 12 (see Table 1). QX identifies CFProto [46] as the method to answer this question. CFProto outputs the modified image that is closer to number 9. Finally, NLG generates the explanation text along with the output of CFProto.

X-Agent: This is your input image.

My prediction for this image is number 7.
User: Why did you predict that?
X-Agent:

On the right image above, I highlight the important parts (red color) of the image that impact this prediction.
User: How should this image change to get number 9 prediction?
X-Agent:

Here you go! I just modified your image a bit to make it look like number 9.

Fig. 7. Conversation example to explain a Convolutional Neural Network on MNIST (Color figure online)

References

1. Adadi, A., Berrada, M.: Peeking inside the black-box: a survey on explainable artificial intelligence (XAI). IEEE Access **6**, 52138–52160 (2018). https://doi.org/10.1109/ACCESS.2018.2870052
2. Ali, S., et al.: Explainable Artificial Intelligence (XAI): what we know and what is left to attain Trustworthy Artificial Intelligence. Inf. Fusion **99**, 101805 (2023)
3. Amidei, J., Piwek, P., Willis, A.: The use of rating and Likert scales in Natural Language Generation human evaluation tasks: a review and some recommendations. In: INLG 2019. ACL (2019). https://doi.org/10.18653/v1/W19-8648. https://aclanthology.org/W19-8648
4. Barredo Arrieta, A., et al.: Explainable Artificial Intelligence (XAI): concepts, taxonomies, opportunities and challenges toward responsible AI. Inf. Fusion **58**, 82–115 (2020). https://doi.org/10.1016/j.inffus.2019.12.012. https://www.sciencedirect.com/science/article/pii/S1566253519308103
5. Bastani, O., Kim, C., Bastani, H.: Interpretability via model extraction. In: FAT/ML (2017)

6. Bobrow, D.G., Kaplan, R.M., Kay, M., Norman, D.A., Thompson, H., Winograd, T.: GUS, a frame-driven dialog system. Artif. Intell. **8**(2), 155–173 (1977). https://doi.org/10.1016/0004-3702(77)90018-2. https://www.sciencedirect.com/science/article/pii/0004370277900182
7. Brown, T., et al.: Language models are few-shot learners. In: NeurIPS, vol. 33, pp. 1877–1901 (2020)
8. Chen, C., Li, O., Tao, C., Barnett, A.J., Su, J., Rudin, C.: This looks like that: deep learning for interpretable image recognition. Curran Associates Inc. (2019)
9. Dash, S., Günlük, O., Wei, D.: Boolean decision rules via column generation. In: Proceedings of the 32nd International Conference on Neural Information Processing Systems, NIPS 2018, Red Hook, NY, USA, pp. 4660–4670. Curran Associates Inc. (2018)
10. Dhurandhar, A., et al.: Explanations based on the missing: towards contrastive explanations with pertinent negatives. In: Proceedings of the 32nd International Conference on Neural Information Processing Systems, NIPS 2018, Red Hook, NY, USA, pp. 590–601. Curran Associates Inc. (2018)
11. Gao, J., Galley, M., Li, L., et al.: Neural approaches to conversational AI. Found. Trends Inf. Retrieval **13**(2–3), 127–298 (2019)
12. Gao, T., Yao, X., Chen, D.: SimCSE: simple contrastive learning of sentence embeddings. In: EMNLP, pp. 6894–6910. ACL (2021). https://doi.org/10.18653/v1/2021.emnlp-main.552. https://aclanthology.org/2021.emnlp-main.552
13. Gatt, A., Krahmer, E.: Survey of the state of the art in natural language generation: core tasks, applications and evaluation. J. Artif. Intell. Res. **61**, 65–170 (2018)
14. Gebru, T., et al.: Datasheets for datasets. Commun. ACM **64**(12), 86–92 (2021). https://doi.org/10.1145/3458723
15. Gilpin, L.H., Bau, D., Yuan, B.Z., Bajwa, A., Specter, M., Kagal, L.: Explaining explanations: an overview of interpretability of machine learning. In: DSAA, pp. 80–89. IEEE (2018). https://doi.org/10.1109/DSAA.2018.00018
16. Goodfellow, I., Bengio, Y., Courville, A.: Deep Learning. MIT Press (2016). https://www.deeplearningbook.org
17. Guidotti, R.: Counterfactual explanations and how to find them: literature review and benchmarking. Data Min. Knowl. Disc. 1–55 (2022). https://doi.org/10.1007/s10618-022-00831-6
18. Guidotti, R., Monreale, A., Giannotti, F., Pedreschi, D., Ruggieri, S., Turini, F.: Factual and counterfactual explanations for black box decision making. IEEE Intell. Syst. **34**(6), 14–23 (2019). https://doi.org/10.1109/MIS.2019.2957223
19. Guidotti, R., Monreale, A., Ruggieri, S., Turini, F., Giannotti, F., Pedreschi, D.: A survey of methods for explaining black box models. ACM Comput. Surv. **51**(5), 93:1–93:42 (2018). https://doi.org/10.1145/3236009
20. Hastie, T., Tibshirani, R.: Generalized Additive Models. Chapman and Hall/CRC (1990)
21. Henelius, A., Puolamäki, K., Boström, H., Asker, L., Papapetrou, P.: A peek into the black box: exploring classifiers by randomization. Data Min. Knowl. Disc. **28**(5), 1503–1529 (2014). https://doi.org/10.1007/s10618-014-0368-8
22. Jurafsky, D., Martin, J.H.: Speech and Language Processing, 3rd edn. draft (2022)
23. Kuźba, M., Biecek, P.: What would you ask the machine learning model? Identification of user needs for model explanations based on human-model conversations. In: Koprinska, I., et al. (eds.) ECML PKDD 2020. CCIS, vol. 1323, pp. 447–459. Springer, Cham (2020). https://doi.org/10.1007/978-3-030-65965-3_30
24. Lakkaraju, H., Slack, D., Chen, Y., Tan, C., Singh, S.: Rethinking explainability as a dialogue: a practitioner's perspective (2022). arXiv:2202.01875

25. Liao, Q.V., Gruen, D., Miller, S.: Questioning the AI: informing design practices for explainable AI user experiences. In: Proceedings of the CHI Conference on Human Factors in Computing Systems, pp. 1–15. ACM, New York (2020). https://doi.org/10.1145/3313831.3376590

26. Liao, Q.V., Varshney, K.R.: Human-centered explainable AI (XAI): from algorithms to user experiences (2022). arXiv:2110.10790

27. Liu, Y., et al.: RoBERTa: a robustly optimized BERT pretraining approach (2019). arXiv:1907.11692

28. Lundberg, S.M., Lee, S.I.: A unified approach to interpreting model predictions. In: NeurIPS (2017)

29. Manning, C.D., Raghavan, P., Schütze, H.: Introduction to Information Retrieval. Cambridge University Press (2008). https://nlp.stanford.edu/IR-book/

30. McKinney, S.M., et al.: International evaluation of an AI system for breast cancer screening. Nature **577**(7788), 89–94 (2020)

31. Miller, T.: Explanation in artificial intelligence: insights from the social sciences. Artif. Intell. **267**, 1–38 (2019). https://doi.org/10.1016/j.artint.2018.07.007. https://www.sciencedirect.com/science/article/pii/S0004370218305988

32. Mitchell, M., et al.: Model cards for model reporting. In: FAT* 2019, pp. 220–229. ACM (2019). https://doi.org/10.1145/3287560.3287596

33. Moreira, C., Chou, Y.L., Hsieh, C., Ouyang, C., Jorge, J., Pereira, J.M.: Benchmarking counterfactual algorithms for XAI: from white box to black box (2022). https://doi.org/10.48550/arXiv.2203.02399. http://arxiv.org/abs/2203.02399. arXiv:2203.02399

34. Mothilal, R.K., Sharma, A., Tan, C.: Explaining machine learning classifiers through diverse counterfactual explanations. In: FAT* 2020. ACM (2020). https://doi.org/10.1145/3351095.3372850

35. Nauta, M., van Bree, R., Seifert, C.: Neural prototype trees for interpretable fine-grained image recognition. In: CVPR, pp. 14933–14943 (2021)

36. Nauta, M., et al.: From anecdotal evidence to quantitative evaluation methods: a systematic review on evaluating explainable AI. ACM Comput. Surv. **55**(13s), 1–42 (2023). https://doi.org/10.1145/3583558

37. Nguyen, A., Yosinski, J., Clune, J.: Multifaceted feature visualization: uncovering the different types of features learned by each neuron in deep neural networks (2016)

38. Pedregosa, F., et al.: Scikit-learn: machine learning in Python. J. Mach. Learn. Res. **12**, 2825–2830 (2011)

39. Rastogi, A., Zang, X., Sunkara, S., Gupta, R., Khaitan, P.: Towards scalable multi-domain conversational agents: the schema-guided dialogue dataset. In: AAAI, vol. 34, no. 05, pp. 8689–8696 (2020). https://doi.org/10.1609/aaai.v34i05.6394. https://ojs.aaai.org/index.php/AAAI/article/view/6394

40. Reiter, E., Dale, R.: Building applied natural language generation systems. Nat. Lang. Eng. **3**(1), 57–87 (1997)

41. Ribeiro, M.T., Singh, S., Guestrin, C.: "Why should i trust you?": explaining the predictions of any classifier. In: KDD 2016. ACM (2016). https://doi.org/10.1145/2939672.2939778

42. Ribeiro, M.T., Singh, S., Guestrin, C.: Anchors: high-precision model-agnostic explanations. In: AAAI, vol. 32, no. 1, pp. 1527–1535 (2018). https://ojs.aaai.org/index.php/AAAI/article/view/11491

43. Slack, D., Krishna, S., Lakkaraju, H., Singh, S.: TalkToModel: explaining machine learning models with interactive natural language conversations (2022). arXiv:2207.04154

44. Tolomei, G., Silvestri, F., Haines, A., Lalmas, M.: Interpretable predictions of tree-based ensembles via actionable feature tweaking. In: Proceedings of the 23rd ACM SIGKDD International Conference on Knowledge Discovery and Data Mining, KDD 2017, pp. 465–474. Association for Computing Machinery, New York (2017). https://doi.org/10.1145/3097983.3098039

45. Tomsett, R., Braines, D., Harborne, D., Preece, A., Chakraborty, S.: Interpretable to whom? A role-based model for analyzing interpretable machine learning systems. In: WHI 2018 (2018)

46. Van Looveren, A., Klaise, J.: Interpretable counterfactual explanations guided by prototypes. In: Oliver, N., Pérez-Cruz, F., Kramer, S., Read, J., Lozano, J.A. (eds.) ECML PKDD 2021. LNCS (LNAI), vol. 12976, pp. 650–665. Springer, Cham (2021). https://doi.org/10.1007/978-3-030-86520-7_40

47. Werner, C.: Explainable AI through rule-based interactive conversation. In: EDBT/ICDT Workshops (2020)

Toward Inclusive Online Environments: Counterfactual-Inspired XAI for Detecting and Interpreting Hateful and Offensive Tweets

Muhammad Deedahwar Mazhar Qureshi[1,2]([✉]) [iD], M. Atif Qureshi[1,2] [iD], and Wael Rashwan[1] [iD]

[1] eXplainable Analytics Group, Faculty of Business, Technological University Dublin, Dublin, Ireland
{D22124696,atif.qureshi,wael.rashwan}@tudublin.ie
[2] Centre for Research Training in Machine Learning (ML-Labs), Science Foundation Ireland, Dublin, Ireland

Abstract. The prevalence of hate speech and offensive language on social media platforms such as Twitter has significant consequences, ranging from psychological harm to the polarization of societies. Consequently, social media companies have implemented content moderation measures to curb harmful or discriminatory language. However, a lack of consistency and transparency hinders their ability to achieve desired outcomes. This article evaluates various ML models, including an ensemble, Explainable Boosting Machine (EBM), and Linear Support Vector Classifier (SVC), on a public dataset of 24,792 tweets by T. Davidson, categorizing tweets into three classes: hate, offensive, and neither. The top-performing model achieves a weighted F1-Score of 0.90. Furthermore, this article interprets the output of the best-performing model using LIME and SHAP, elucidating how specific words and phrases within a tweet contextually impact its classification. This analysis helps to shed light on the linguistic aspects of hate and offense. Additionally, we employ LIME to present a suggestive counterfactual approach, proposing no-hate alternatives for a tweet to further explain the influence of word choices in context. Limitations of the study include the potential for biased results due to dataset imbalance, which future research may address by exploring more balanced datasets or leveraging additional features. Ultimately, through these explanations, this work aims to promote digital literacy and foster an inclusive online environment that encourages informed and responsible use of digital technologies (A GitHub repository containing code, data, and pre-trained models is available at: https://github.com/DeedahwarMazhar/XAI-Counterfactual-Hate-Speech).

Keywords: Digital Literacy · LIME · SHAP · Counterfactual · Machine Learning · XAI

1   Introduction

In today's internet-driven global village, various social media platforms, such as Twitter, Reddit, Facebook, and Instagram, have emerged as popular forums for social connectivity. As people increasingly engage in these forums, they become fertile ground for hateful views that harm individuals and communities. The spread of such information damages a victim's mental health and well-being and can potentially incite violence against specific individuals and communities [52].

Twitter has gained popularity as a micro-blogging platform for social interaction, political influencing, marketing campaigns, and a space to express views. This also results in the dissemination of hateful trends. Various political factions have utilized Twitter for propaganda and personal attacks aimed at opposition members and marginalized communities. For instance, during the most recent Indian elections, certain political parties utilized Twitter as the primary platform for orchestrating systematic hate speech campaigns against minority groups, dissidents, and opposition members [42]. Additionally, both Gab and Twitter have seen an increase in 'fear speech', which is based on irrational fears of certain groups such as religious communities, immigrants, and racial groups [41]. Events such as Covid-19 [15] and GamerGate [43] have led to vulnerable groups, including Asians and women, experiencing significant hate speech, resulting in bullying, trolling, violence, and even incitement. Studies on internet hate speech [9], particularly racism from the critical race perspective, have highlighted how platform policies affect hate speech moderation [29].

Digital literacy is a significant concern with potential societal implications for both young individuals and adults. Young individuals, including teenagers and children, often have unrestricted access to social media, exposing them to harmful content. Similarly, adults who lack digital literacy skills may be susceptible to misinformation and manipulation online. A 2005 study revealed that nearly 20% of children aged 9–16 encountered online hate speech [25]. More recently, Harriman et al. in 2020 [16] found that 57% of participants aged 14–20 had witnessed online hate speech in the past two months. Similarly, Donaldson et al. [14] reported that among surveyed youth aged 16–20, one in four trolled people online, one in five violent messages, one in eight engaged in online harassment, and one in ten shared hate speech.

This lack of digital literacy among both young people and adults contributes to the normalization of harmful language on unmoderated platforms, posing risks to the well-being of vulnerable community members and perpetuating the spread of misinformation and other online threats. Bernsmann et al. [4] discuss the potential of ICT/Social media-based digital literacy in the context of social cohesion and active citizenship. The authors particularly discuss lifelong learning for disadvantaged members of society as well as people outside traditional education mechanisms, such as adults. The promotion of digital literacy amongst adults is also important due to their positions in roles of leadership and power. Lukasz Tomczyk [46] points out the lack of digital literacy among school teachers for various topics of digital life like health, safety, and online interactions.

Therefore, there is a pressing need to integrate digital literacy promotion for people of all ages for safe and inclusive online and offline environments.

Explainability and transparency are crucial issues in the context of hate speech. Many hate speech detection models exhibit bias towards specific slurs that are more frequently used against certain groups, leading to the inaccurate classification of hate speech. This has particularly negative impacts on African American individuals [10] and erodes trust between users and the algorithms in place [1]. Moreover, the lack of transparency, interpretability, and explainability of hate speech detection models hinders their integration into policies, which would otherwise promote the application of these models and enable non-technical stakeholders to fully understand the functioning of the models.

This paper aims to achieve the following objectives:

1. To compare the effectiveness of traditional machine learning techniques with the Explainable Boosting Machine (EBM) in hate and offensive speech detection.
2. To use XAI (Explainable Artificial Intelligence) techniques to enhance the interpretability of results and compare explanations generated by different explainers (LIME and SHAP) for hate and offensive speech detection.
3. To develop a counterfactual method that suggests alternative non-hateful and non-offensive tweets to the user, promoting digital literacy and raising awareness about inclusive online environments among social media users.

The remainder of this paper is structured as follows: *Related Work* reviews prior research on hate speech detection and explainable machine learning. *Methodology* details the dataset used, the feature engineering process, and the machine learning models employed. *Results and Discussion* presents the evaluation results and an analysis of the explainability methods used in the study. Finally, *Conclusion and Future Work* summarizes the findings of the study and outlines future research directions.

2   Related Work

Kwok and Wang [22] conducted an analysis of Twitter data, focusing on identifying racist tweets targeting black communities. They employed a Naive Bayes classifier and achieved a 76% accuracy score on binary classification. Waseem and Hovy [48] used character n-grams to classify racist and sexist tweets, obtaining an F1-score of 73.89%. T. Davidson [11] also used tweets and classified them into three classes (*Hate, Offensive* and *Neither*) and found that Logistic Regression was the best-performing model, achieving an F1-Score of 84%. Watanabe et al. [50] used both datasets used by Waseem and Davidson, testing them as both binary and non-binary classification problems, and reported a 78.4% accuracy on the Davidson [11] dataset. Ricardo Martins [28] employed NLP techniques with Support Vector Machine [17] and achieved 81% accuracy on the dataset presented by Davidson. Talat [49] used a multi-task approach to classify tweets using the Davidson dataset [11] and the Waseem and Hovy dataset [48]. The authors reported a weighted F-1 score of 0.89 on the dataset. Gibert et al. [12] presented a dataset from a white-supremacist site called Stormfront and proposed an LSTM [18] model for classifying the posts, achieving an F-1 score of 78%. More recently, Mozafari et al. [31] used BERT [13] encoding with deep learning architectures, including CNN [35], LSTM, and Multilayer Perceptrons, on both the Waseem and Davidson datasets, achieving an accuracy score of 88%. The use of Machine and Deep learning models for hate speech classification has been extensively studied; however, the black-box nature of these models presents challenges in their interpretability and understanding.

Recent developments in Explainable AI (XAI) have provided new opportunities to enhance the interpretability of machine learning models, particularly in natural language processing. Liu et al. [24] proposed an explainable NLP model for text classification in recommender systems. The authors proposed a numerical approach towards explainability with a rating system integrated with a Convolutional Variational Autoencoder (CVAE). Betty van Aken [47] employed an ensemble of deep learning architectures for toxicity classification on the Davidson dataset. The study reported an 80% F1-Score and performed an error analysis to explain the misclassification of important terms. David Noever [32] also presented an explainable model that focused on essential terms and their profanity in determining hate speech. Mosca et al. [30] applied an explainable deep learning approach to classify hate speech using the Davidson dataset. The study used SHAP values to explain phrases and also used contextual explanations for hate speech classification. The study achieved an 87.6% F-1 score.

Similarly, Maronikolakis et al. [27] used BERT to analyze the Davidson dataset and highlighted the biases of BERT in terms of gender/race-specific language. The authors achieved an F1-score of 88% and used LIME to provide explanations and interpretations. The paper draws attention to the inability of hate speech classifiers to accurately classify African-American English (AAE) and the linguistics bias against their cultural use of certain terms. Silva et al. [44] utilized the Explainable Boosting Machine (EBM) for text summarization with similar NLP applications and discussed its limitations in dealing with text data and vector embeddings. Arafah et al. [2] highlighted the role of digital literacy in mitigating social media hate speech. The authors reported that the lack of digital literacy leads to the consumption and the spread of problematic content that is often influenced by unconscious biases and passive prejudices. The growing adoption of explainable models is undoubtedly a positive development; however, the field still needs its integration with digital literacy objectives, and the absence of suggestive methods like counterfactuals, among others, represents a gap in the research.

Michael A Peters [36] emphasizes the importance of digital literacy in reducing the prevalence of hate speech on the internet. Similarly, Rad and Demeter [38] observe how exposure to hateful content as a non-participating bystander in online forums can normalize such behaviors and propose increased internet literacy and awareness as a solution. Cruft et al. [8] also highlight the need for a more inclusive moderation method for Twitter instead of outright censorship or a complete lack of moderation. Ortega-Sanchez et al. [34] also mention the importance of inclusive digital spaces on social media and their role in education as a road toward sustainable and inclusive democratic citizenship. Table 1 provides a comparison of the relevant literature. It is evident that the existing literature on hate speech analysis of social media, in general, and Twitter, in particular, has not extensively explored Explainable AI. Moreover, much of the existing work does not focus on advancing digital literacy, which has the potential to become an application of XAI in social media. In this context, this paper utilizes both LIME and SHAP to provide explanations for tweets and implements a counterfactual mechanism to suggest alternative phrases for hateful tweets. By incorporating the counterfactual approach, it becomes possible to take corrective measures on certain tweets that should be regulated from public forums due to their potential for harm while also educating users about the consequences, thereby advancing the cause of digital literacy.

Table 1. Comparison of relevant literature.

Work/Author	Multiple Classes	Non-Text Features	Explainability	Counterfactual
Davidson [11]	✓	✓		
Waseem [49]	✓	✓		
Kwok [22]		✓		
Mozafari [31]	✓	✓		
Betty Van Aken [47]	✓		✓	
Mosca [30]	✓	✓	✓	
This Paper	✓	✓	✓	✓

3   Methodology

3.1   Dataset

The Hate Speech and Offensive Language (HSOL) dataset, as presented by T. Davidson in 2017 [11], was utilized in this study. It comprises 24,792 tweets, each of which is annotated by three human annotators and labeled as *hate*, *offensive*, or *neither*. Of the total dataset, only 5.77% of the dataset (1,430 tweets) is labeled as *hate*, which is significantly lower than similar datasets, such as the one presented by Burnap and Williams [7], which had a higher percentage (11.6%) of hate speech, and Waseem and Hovy's dataset, which had 31% of *hate* tweets [48]. This may be due to the stricter criteria for hate speech in the HSOL dataset, which also includes an *offensive* category. The majority of tweets, 19,190, belong to the *offensive* category, while 4,163 tweets belong to the *neither* category. The tweets were preprocessed to generate features for the models to train on. The details about the dataset are presented in Table 2.

Table 2. Summary of the Dataset.

Class/Split	Training	Testing	Overall
Hate	1,266	164	1,430 (5.77%)
Offensive	17,285	1,905	19,190 (77.43%)
Neither	3,753	410	4,163 (16.80 %)
Total	22,304 (90%)	2,479 (10%)	24,783

3.2 Data Preprocessing and Feature Engineering

To begin, each tweet is vectorized using the term frequency-inverse document frequency (TF-IDF) vectorizer [39]. This combines two key concepts, term frequency (TF), which denotes the number of occurrences of a specific term within a tweet, and document frequency (DF), which represents the number of tweets containing that term in the dataset. Therefore, it is inferred that TF tells us the importance of any term within a tweet, whereas DF tells us how common that term is within the dataset. Furthermore, the product of inverse document frequency (IDF) and the term frequency (TF) is used as the weight for each term. Next, we use the Natural Language Toolkit for Python (NLTK) [5] to perform parts-of-speech (POS) tagging on each tweet, and the resulting tags are vectorized using the same TF-IDF vectorizer. The resultant weights are appended to the previously computed embeddings. Here, POS-tagging helps describe the sentence structure within the tweet and deal with any deficiencies based on contextual information within the sentence [51]. It enables the classifier to infer the structural semantics of the text data in addition to individual words.

Similarly, the sentiments expressed in the tweets are captured using Valence Aware Dictionary and Sentiment Reasoner (VADER) [19], which are classified into *positive*, *negative*, and *neutral* categories. Each lexical term (i.e., word, slang, emoticon) in the tweet is mapped to a predetermined dictionary and assigned a polarity score between -4 and $+4$. The sentiment score of each tweet is then obtained by taking the normalized sum of the polarity scores of all the terms. Each tweet is assigned a different sentiment score for each of the three categories, and these scores are appended to the previous vector. Furthermore, hashtags (#), mentions (@), URLs, words, and characters are counted for each tweet [3]. Finally, the readability of the tweets is scored using FRE (Flesch Reading Ease) and FKRA (Flesch Kincaid Reading Age) scores [20]. A high FRE score indicates high readability, while a lower FKRA score indicates higher readability. The combination of these features results in a total of 11,172 features. This process is shown in Fig. 1.

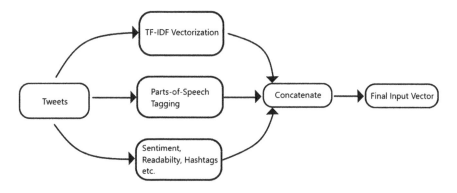

Fig. 1. Process Diagram for the Feature Engineering process.

3.3 Classification

Davidson et al. [11] employed Logistic Regression and LinearSVC for analyzing hate speech on tweet data. In contrast, other studies, including Gibert et al. [12], and Mozafari et al. [31], used deep learning techniques for classification. However, with recent advancements in XAI, the Explainable Boosting Machine (EBM) has gained attention as a reliable, interpretable, and effective method for analysis. In this study, the following models are utilized for classification:

1. An ensemble of various Logistic Regression Models and Deep Neural Networks (DNNs).
2. The AutoML winner model is the Linear Support Vector Classifier.
3. Explainable Boosting Machine (EBM) Classifier.

Ensemble Model. An ensemble model combines multiple models that use different architectures and hyperparameters to make predictions on data. The predictions from each model are then combined to produce a single output. A significant advantage of using such a model is that generalization errors made by individual models can be reduced. Our proposed ensemble consists of two types of models; Logistic Regression and Deep Neural Network. Logistic Regression is a simple but effective machine learning model that efficiently trains and makes quick inferences on unseen data. The model is trained with an L-1 penalty and a Regularization parameter (C value) of 0.5. The second type of architecture in the ensemble model is the Deep Neural Network (DNN), a complex network of fully connected layers that are more accurate but take longer to train and infer. The model has an output layer with three nodes and a Softmax activation function [6] to predict the probabilities of the input belonging to each class. The Adaptive Momentum Estimation (Adam) optimizer [21] is used to train the model with the Categorical Cross Entropy loss function.

The ensemble model comprises six models with different architectures and hyperparameters:

1. Logistic Regression with balanced class weights and complete feature set.
2. Logistic Regression with equal class weights and complete feature set.
3. Logistic Regression with balanced class weights and reduced feature set with Sci-Kit Learn Feature Selection.
4. Logistic Regression with equal class weights and reduced feature set.
5. Deep Neural Network with balanced class weights and complete feature set.
6. Deep Neural Network with balanced class weights and reduced feature set with Sci-Kit Learn Feature Selection.

The individual outputs from each model are aggregated and normalized. The class with the highest probability is then selected as the final output. The results are then explained using model-agnostic techniques such as LIME and SHAP.

AutoML Strategy. Automated Machine Learning (AutoML) is a set of tools designed to automate the optimization and tuning of machine learning models, thereby accelerating ML research. TPOT [23] is one such tool that leverages genetic programming to generate optimized pipelines for various ML tasks. In this study, preprocessed data is fed to the TPOT classifier with the *population size* set to 40 and the number of *generations* set to 4. This limits the extent of brute-force search across ML architectures[1]. The *generations* parameter controls the vertical scope while the *population* parameter controls the horizontal scope. Additionally, the TPOT classifier was configured to maximize the weighted F-1 score, given the class imbalance issue in the dataset.

Once the TPOT classifier is set up with the desired parameters, it generates a pipeline that includes the Maximum Absolute Scaling (MaxAbs) of the input data followed by a Linear Support Vector Classifier (LinearSVC). The scaler transforms the features to ensure the maximum value of the feature observed in the dataset becomes 1. At the same time, the model is optimized with a square-hinge loss function, *L-1* penalty, and a Regularization parameter (C value) of 0.5. Finally, the complete pipeline is trained on the training set.

Explainable Boosting Machine. To train the EBM model [33], it is necessary to preprocess the input data by reducing the number of features. This is due to the model's inability to process feature embeddings such as those obtained from TF-IDF vectorization [45]. The feature reduction step also makes EBM computationally efficient and accurate. A meta-transformer from Sci-Kit Learn is used to select the most important features based on their feature weights [37]. To prevent overfitting and ensure that the model does not prioritize the majority (Offensive) class, L1 regularization is implemented with balanced class weights. The advantage of using the EBM model is quick and accurate inference.

---

[1] we skipped NN models.

The explainability of EBM is limited by the transformation of the original features, which restricts the use of its in-built explanation mechanisms. EBM explanations are based on changing feature values, which works well for interpreting predictions for categorical data but not for features that are transformed into meta-features (such as PCA) or features that do not represent distinct values (such as Vector Embeddings) [45]. To address this limitation, model-agnostic approaches such as LIME and SHAP are used to explain model inference. A summary of how the proposed system is theoretically designed to work can be seen in Fig. 2.

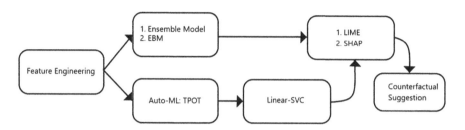

Fig. 2. System Diagram illustrating the entire process discussed in the paper.

4   Results and Discussion

4.1   Data Exploration

Before the performance of the models is evaluated, it is important to discuss how different classes of tweets (Hate, Offensive, Neither) relate to some of the features discussed in the previous section. Figures 3(a) and (b) illustrate the distribution of hashtags and mentions among the three classes. Figure 3(a) shows that the distribution of hashtags is similar across the classes. There is a minute difference here as the percentage of *hate* tweets containing no hashtags (almost 80%) is higher than the *offensive* and *neither* percentages (around 70% and 60% respectively). Similarly, Fig. 3(b) shows the distribution of mentions across the classes. While there is a small difference here as the percentage of *hate* tweets with at least one mention (around 70%) is higher than *offensive* and *neither* tweets, the difference is not big enough to play a deterministic role when it comes to inference.

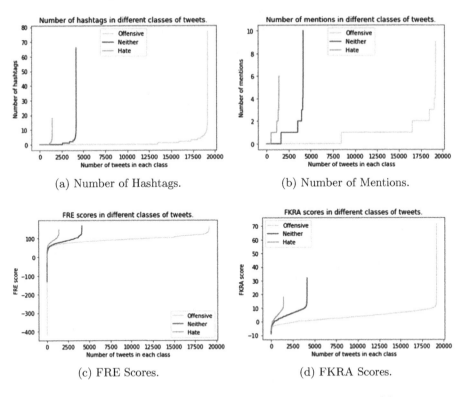

(a) Number of Hashtags.   (b) Number of Mentions.

(c) FRE Scores.   (d) FKRA Scores.

Fig. 3. Comparison of the Cumulative Distribution Function graphs of (a) the number of Hashtags, (b) the number of Mentions, (c) FRE scores, and (d) FKRA scores across tweets belonging to different classes.

Figures 3(c) and 3(d) present two readability metrics for tweets belonging to each of the three classes, namely FRE (Flesch Reading Ease) and FKRA (Flesch Kincaid Reading Age) scores. The complexity of the language used determines the readability of a tweet, whereas a more readable tweet contains less complex vocabulary and structure. A higher FRE score suggests higher readability, whereas a lower FKRA score suggests higher readability. The trend shows a lack of complexity in hateful or offensive tweets. The trend observed across the three classes is almost identical here, showing that readability is not directly related to any class.

4.2   Model Performance

Each model was first measured holistically on the complete testing dataset using accuracy as the metric. Then a more detailed analysis of its implementation across the three classes was carried out using precision, recall, and F1-score as the metric. Table 3 shows the models' overall performance and performance across different classes.

Table 3. Performance comparison of models. The metrics reported against each model are weighted averages for Precision, Recall, and F1-score.

Model/Class	Precision	Recall	F1-score	Accuracy
Linear SVC	**0.89**	**0.90**	**0.90**	**90%**
Hate	0.48	0.29	0.36	–
Offensive	0.94	0.95	0.94	–
Neither	0.84	0.90	0.87	–
Ensemble Model	**0.90**	**0.88**	**0.89**	**88%**
Hate	0.41	0.60	0.49	–
Offensive	0.97	0.89	0.93	–
Neither	0.81	0.95	0.87	–
EBM	**0.90**	**0.85**	**0.86**	**85%**
Hate	0.33	0.73	0.45	–
Offensive	0.98	0.84	0.90	–
Neither	0.79	0.93	0.86	–

The AutoML TPOT winner LinearSVC model, as outlined in Sect. 3.3, outperforms the ensemble and the EBM on the test set in terms of overall accuracy. However, given the imbalanced nature of the dataset, relying solely on accuracy as a metric may not provide a complete assessment of the models' performance. In particular, we are interested in the *Hate* class as our target label, which is the minority class in the dataset. While the LinearSVC model achieved the highest precision, the EBM exhibited a higher recall value. This indicates that the EBM was able to classify more hateful samples, whereas the LinearSVC model was better at preventing misclassifications from other classes (*Offensive* and *Neither*) into the *Hate* class. Furthermore, the LinearSVC model demonstrates better recall for the *Offensive* class compared to the EBM. Similarly, for the *Hate* class, there is a trade-off between precision and recall across the models. It is important to note that since the *Hate* class is a substantial minority, the weighted recall metric indicates that LinearSVC outperforms other models over-all. The ensemble model's performance lies in between both models regarding the weighted F1-score, precision, and recall. Figure 4 shows the confusion matrix for all three models, demonstrating the impact of class imbalance. Given the semantic relationship between the *Hate* and *Offensive* classes, with *Hate* being a subset of *Offensive*, misclassification between these two classes is distinct from misclassifying them as *Neither*. Across all models, Fig. 4 illustrates that misclas-sification of the *Hate* or *Offensive* class as *Neither* is considerably lower than misclassification between *Hate* and *Offensive*. This finding is reasonable as the *Hate* and *Offensive* classes are closely related to each other.

Table 3 shows that the LinearSVC model outperforms other models in terms of weighted F1-score. This metric is more appropriate for discerning performance due to the imbalanced nature of the dataset, which could otherwise impact the interpretation of the scores. Finally, Table 4 presents a comparison of the pro-posed models' weighted F1 scores with the state-of-the-art benchmarks. The results obtained by using Auto-ML pipeline to achieve comparable performance to more complex architectures highlight the potential of fine-tuning simpler mod-els to maximize their outputs. It is worth noting that several studies mentioned in the table do not emphasize or demonstrate the explainability of their models, and even those that do fail to connect it with ideas of digital literacy.

Table 4. Comparison of Relevant Literature

Model	Weighted F1-Score
van Aken [47]	0.80
Martins [28]	0.81
Davidson [11]	0.84
Mosca [30]	0.87
Maronikolakis [27]	0.88
Talat [49]	0.89
Mozafari [31]	0.89
This Paper	**0.90**

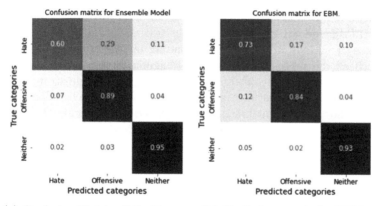

(a) Confusion Matrix of the Ensemble model.   (b) Confusion matrix for EBM.

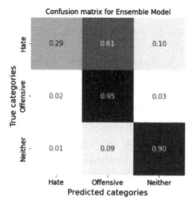

(c) Confusion matrix for LinearSVC.

Fig. 4. Comparison of the confusion matrices of (a) The ensemble model, (b) EBM, and (c) the LinearSVC model.

4.3 Explainability

LIME (Local Interpretable Model-Agnostic Explanation) [40] and SHAP (Shapeley Additive Explanation) [26] are applied to interpret the model outputs. These methods are model-agnostic, meaning they are not dependent on the model being explained. They use a probabilistic approach to assess the impact of various input components, taking the original tweet as input and viewing the predicted probabilities for each class as the output. We used LIME and SHAP in local connotations, meaning each prediction was individually explained without considering any other sample from the dataset. Furthermore, an individual may look at the explanations and understand how the prediction was made without requiring a precise technical understanding of the underlying model.

Figures 5 and 6 demonstrate the contextual nature of the explanations provided by LIME and SHAP for two distinct tweets. The figures reveal that the significance of various words varies depending on the tweet's contextual features, such as the presence of potentially significant phrases associated with hate speech, such as abuse and slurs. Figures 5(a) and 6(a) illustrate how LIME and SHAP provide explanations for a tweet that has been classified as hateful. The figures show the weight assigned to each term in the context of the tweet and how it contributes to the model's output. The term 'n**ger' is a racial slur commonly used to express hateful sentiments and has a significant impact on the predicted class. Other terms in the tweet, such as 'not' and 'At least,' are common words that do not have a significant influence on the model's prediction and, therefore, carry little weight in determining the predicted class[2]. Upon closer inspection of the LIME and SHAP explanations in Figs. 5 and 6, there is also a slight weight towards the *Offensive* class. It can be assumed that dropping the term 'n**ger' would result in an offensive prediction. However, when we substitute the term 'n**ger' with 'peanut', the weights associated with neighboring terms also change, and the tweet gets classified as *neither*, as can be seen in Figs. 5(b) and 6(b).

The explanations provided by LIME and SHAP in Figs. 5(a) and 6(a) demonstrate that hatefulness is not solely dependent on one word, although slur words have a high probability of being deemed hateful. The context in which a term is used also plays a crucial role. Thus, altering a word affects the interpretation of the surrounding terms. This is particularly relevant since the other words in the tweet do not carry any positive or negative connotations. Therefore, swapping out the term 'n**ger' with 'peanut' in Figs. 5(b) and 6(b) resulted in a change in the classification of the tweet from *Hate/Offensive* to *Neither*. On the contrary, using a substitution term like b**ch instead of *peanut* will lead to an *Offensive* classification. Therefore, including words such as 'n**ger', 'peanut', or 'b**ch' in a tweet can influence the classification of the tweet as *Hate, Offensive*, or *Neither*, as well as the interpretation of the surrounding terms. However, the explanations provided by LIME and SHAP differ in their attribution of importance to each term, particularly in instances where no term significantly affects the classification, as seen in Figs. 5 and 6. The term 'peanut' carries varying weights according to each interpreter, and the importance of surrounding words also varies. Nevertheless, in cases where hateful racial slurs such as 'n**ger' or offensive terms like 'b**ch' are present, the explanations provided by both LIME and SHAP are consistent, owing to the substantial influence of these terms on the classification result.

Unlike the Hateful tweet shown in Figs. 5(a) and 6(a), some tweets can be classified as hateful due to the combined contributions of multiple words. Unlike racial slurs like 'n**ger', such tweets depend more on the aggregation of terms. In such cases, it is possible to lower the *Hate* scores of the tweet by iteratively replacing such words with lesser offensive synonyms and ultimately suggesting the resultant tweet as an alternative to the user. The words that can be iteratively

---

[2] i.e., they mildly influence the not *Hate* class.

substituted generally carry a hate score ranging between 0.2 and 0.35. Intuitively, by replacing such words with lower-scoring alternatives, we can also reduce the hate score of the surrounding words. This process may continue iteratively until no word exists, with a hate score in the range of 0.2–0.35[3]. Figure 7 shows an example of this process, where the tweet is initially classified as hateful due to the strong contribution of the word 'kill' (0.47) and the smaller contribution of the word 'cracker' (0.22). In the first iteration, the word 'cracker' is replaced with a less hateful synonym, 'firecracker', significantly reducing the hate score but still keeping the tweet classified as hateful. Changing this word also reduces the hate score associated with 'kill' to 0.33. In the second iteration, the word 'kill' is replaced with the least hateful synonym obtained from a dictionary, resulting in a significant reduction in the hate score, and the tweet is now classified as 'Neither'. Integrating such processes is necessary for social media moderation to prevent outright censorship and ostracization of individuals and allow them to address their thoughts in a manner that minimizes the potential for harm while also promoting digital literacy around problematic content. This would foster an inclusive digital space where individuals with diverse political and social perspectives can safely engage with each other.

Figure 8 shows the LIME and SHAP explanations for five tweets each[4] that were correctly predicted by the model and belonged to different classes. The first two tweets fall under the *Hate* class, and both methods provide consistent explanations for these tweets. The primary contribution to the prediction is the racial slur, but the phrase "HATE BLACK PEOPLE" also plays a significant role. This indicates that the tweet would still be classified as 'Hate' even without the racial slur because the term 'HATE' amplifies the *Hate* score associated with 'BLACK' and 'PEOPLE' by changing their context towards something that could potentially be perceived as hateful.

On the other hand (see Fig. 8), when examining the last two tweets in the *Offensive* class, there is less agreement in the explanations provided by the two models. SHAP focuses heavily on the expletives used in the tweet, while the context of whether these expletives are directed at specific individuals/groups is not given as much consideration. In contrast, LIME places greater emphasis on the context in which the expletives are used, interpreting it better than SHAP. Conversely, with LIME, the focus on the context in which these expletives are used is greater. LIME's weights are distributed around words that build context rather than being concentrated solely on expletives. Finally, the example belonging to the *Neither* class shows similar trends to those observed in the *Offensive* class, with LIME showing a better understanding of the context of the words in the tweet, whereas SHAP's focus is more on individual words.

Figure 9 shows the situations where the models misclassify tweets, and the explanations may appear misleading. The figure shows two tweets meant to exhibit *Hate* but misclassified as *Neither*. In the first example, the model assigns

---

[3] or chosen threshold values.

[4] SHAP explanations require the string to be unified; therefore, all SHAP explanations have lowercase textual representation.

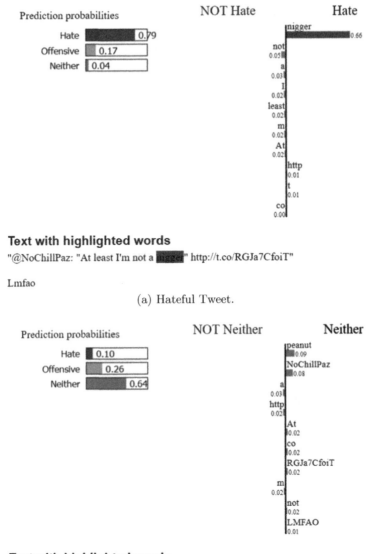

(a) Hateful Tweet.

(b) Neutral(*neither*) Tweet.

Fig. 5. Comparison of LIME explanations made for a tweet classified as (a) Hateful and (b) Offensive.

similar probabilities to both the *Hate* and *Neither* classes, with 0.45 and 0.47, respectively, i.e., a close call. Here, the first tweet contains complex words like "mongrels" and "ghettos", which the model deems uncommon in tweets and would not have much hateful context attached to them. Also, phrases like "say no

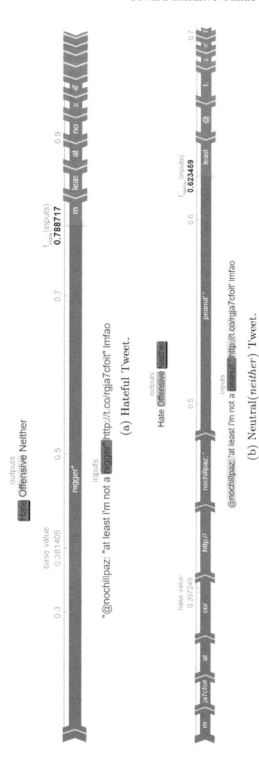

(a) Hateful Tweet.

(b) Neutral(*neither*) Tweet.

Fig. 6. Comparison of SHAP explanations made for a tweet classified as (a) Hateful and (b) Offensive.

Iteration	Tweet	Probability Scores		
0	"Let's ▮▮ cracker babies!". WTF did I just hear???????? WOW.	HATE:	0.73	
		OFFENSIVE:	0.08	
		NEITHER:	0.19	
1	"Let's ▮▮ firecracker babies!". WTF did I just hear???????? WOW.	HATE:	0.40	
		OFFENSIVE:	0.35	
		NEITHER:	0.26	
2	"Let's drink_down firecracker babies!". WTF did I just hear???????? WOW.	HATE:	0.09	
		OFFENSIVE:	0.36	
		NEITHER:	0.55	

Fig. 7. Progress of changing a hateful tweet to a neutral (*neither*) tweet

more" and "race" are typically found in hateful contexts and therefore contribute to the tweet's hate score. However, despite this, the model marginally misclassifies the tweet as non-hateful. The second tweet uses the hashtag "DTLA," which refers to "Downtown Los Angeles", an area in Los Angeles, California. This tweet was misclassified more significantly than the previous example. The term "non-Europeans" used in the tweet is not commonly found in hateful tweets (whereas terms referring to ethnicities, nationalities, or simply immigrants may alter the view). As a result, the use of this term contributes to the misclassification of the tweet as *Neither* instead of *Hate*.

To summarize, interpretability can be a valuable tool in improving hate speech moderation by clarifying the factors underlying the model's decision-making process. This can benefit non-technical individuals, such as policy-makers, in addressing issues related to hate speech targeting specific groups or ideas on online platforms. Additionally, replacing hateful or offensive language with alternative terms would promote safer and more inclusive online spaces without resorting to complete censorship. However, this requires obtaining the user's consent to allow the service provider, such as Twitter, to substitute processed tweets instead of filtering them out entirely while ensuring that the tweet's original meaning remains intact.

Nonetheless, implementing such a model in real-world situations entails several ethical considerations. Datasets in this domain often exhibit biases against particular genders and ethnicities that must be mitigated to create an inclusive virtual space for diverse individuals. Moreover, interpretability can promote digital literacy as a means to uphold the principles of free speech instead of resorting to viewpoint censorship. The practical implications of this system extend to the fair utilization of such technologies to ensure impartiality and the cultivation of a safe digital environment for all. By implementing explainable artificial intelligence (XAI) in social networks, it becomes possible to enhance users' digital literacy while upholding principles and policies of free speech.

CLASS	LIME
H	"@MarkRoundtreeJr: LMFAOOOO I HATE BLACK PEOPLE https://t.co/RNvD2nLCDR" This is why there's black people and niggers
	#California is full of white trash
N	RT @mayasolovely: As a woman you shouldn't complain about cleaning up your house. as a man you should always take the trash out...
O	RT @ShenikaRoberts: The shit you hear about me might be true or it might be faker than the bitch who told it to ya |#57361;
	#8220;@selfiequeenbri: cause I'm tired of you big bitches coming for us skinny girls
	SHAP
H	"@markroundtreejr: lmfaoooo i hate black people https://t.co/rnvd2nlcdr" this is why there's black people and niggers
	#california is full of white trash
N	@mayasolovely: as a woman you shouldn't complain about cleaning up your house. as a man you should always take the trash out
O	@shenikaroberts: the shit you hear about me might be true or it might be faker than the bitch who told it to ya &#57361
	#8220;@selfiequeenbri: cause i'm tired of you big bitches coming for us skinny girls

Fig. 8. LIME and SHAP explanations for *Hate* (H), *Offensive* (O), and *Neither* (N) tweet classes are as follows: LIME uses blue for target class words and green for other classes; SHAP uses red for target class words and blue for other classes.

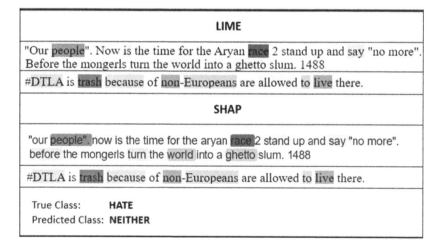

Fig. 9. LIME and SHAP Explanations of misclassified tweets.

5   Conclusion and Future Work

This study presented an explainable approach to enhance hate and offensive speech moderation in online environments. The use of machine learning models on Twitter content data has demonstrated the effectiveness of interpretability in enabling stakeholders to make informed decisions. Despite the limitations of EBM in explaining transformed features and the black-box nature of neural networks, the model-agnostic approach, such as LIME and SHAP, has been demonstrated as effective. The research also highlighted the scenarios where explanations from LIME and SHAP are similar and where they behave differently, providing insights into the interpretability of our approach. This study emphasizes the significance of transparency and interpretability in decision-making processes by utilizing the model-agnostic approach.

Furthermore, the study has shown the impact of highly hateful or offensive words, such as racial slurs and swears, on the context of tweets. Crucially, this study has proposed a counterfactual method to recommend alternative terms for the tweet to replace the problematic expression, such as racial slurs, which is a step toward promoting digital literacy. The transparent explanation of the model's decision-making mechanisms increases user trust and knowledge and enhances users' understanding of the tools used by social media platforms. As a result, this promotes the integration of such tools into policy-making environments, which increases non-technical stakeholders' confidence in understanding the systems, ultimately enabling them to make informed decisions. It is important to note that this paper aims not to undermine freedom of speech but to promote digital literacy. Also, the paper proposes the integration of interpretations and explanations into existing moderation methods, which could aid in furthering the cause of digital literacy for peaceful online global citizenship.

Collaborative efforts involving governments, tech companies, media, and individuals are crucial in countering harmful content. Public awareness campaigns, media literacy, and transparent moderation are ways to mitigate negative impacts and protect well-being. This research serves as a foundational block for further insights into content moderation and interpretability.

In the future, we intend to evaluate more datasets, improve the classification pipeline concerning the language, and deepen our understanding of interpretability and its association with digital literacy and digital platforms. Also, we intend to explore offerings of explainable artificial intelligence systems for policy-making frameworks. The improvement of counterfactual methods to avoid false suggestions is also a possible research direction. This research contributes to developing a more inclusive online environment, promoting digital literacy, and enhancing content moderation techniques, and we intend to continue further development along these lines.

Acknowledgements. This publication has emanated from research conducted with the financial support of Science Foundation Ireland under Grant number 18/CRT/6183. For Open Access, the author has applied a CC BY public copyright license to any Author Accepted Manuscript version arising from this submission.

References

1. Alkiviadou, N.: Hate speech on social media networks: towards a regulatory framework? Inf. Commun. Technol. Law **28**, 19–35 (1 2019). https://doi.org/10.1080/13600834.2018.1494417, https://www.tandfonline.com/doi/full/10.1080/13600834.2018.1494417

2. Arafah, B., Hasyim, M.: Social media as a gateway to information: digital literacy on current issues in social media. Webology **19**(1), 2491–2503 (2022)

3. Bauwelinck, N., Lefever, E.: Measuring the impact of sentiment for hate speech detection on twitter. In: Proceedings of HUSO, pp. 17–22 (2019)

4. Bernsmann, S., Croll, J.: Lowering the threshold to libraries with social media: the approach of "digital literacy 2.0", a project funded in the EU lifelong learning programme. Libr. Rev. **62**, 53–58 (2013)

5. Bird, S., Klein, E., Loper, E.: Natural Language Processing with Python: Analyzing Text with the Natural Language Toolkit. O'Reilly Media, Inc. (2009)

6. Bridle, J.: Training stochastic model recognition algorithms as networks can lead to maximum mutual information estimation of parameters. In: Advances in Neural Information Processing Systems, vol. 2 (1989)

7. Burnap, P., Williams, M.L.: Cyber hate speech on twitter: an application of machine classification and statistical modeling for policy and decision making. Policy Internet **7**(2), 223–242 (2015)

8. Cruft, R., Ashton, N.A.: Social media regulation: why we must ensure it is democratic and inclusive. Conversation **27**, 2022 (2022)

9. Daniels, J.: Race and racism in internet studies: a review and critique. New Media Soc. **15**, 695–719 (2013). https://doi.org/10.1177/1461444812462849, https://journals.sagepub.com/doi/10.1177/1461444812462849

10. Davidson, T., Bhattacharya, D., Weber, I.: Racial bias in hate speech and abusive language detection datasets. arXiv preprint arXiv:1905.12516 (2019)

11. Davidson, T., Warmsley, D., Macy, M., Weber, I.: Automated hate speech detection and the problem of offensive language. In: Proceedings of the International AAAI Conference on Web and Social Media, vol. 11, pp. 512–515 (2017)

12. De Gibert, O., Perez, N., García-Pablos, A., Cuadros, M.: Hate speech dataset from a white supremacy forum. arXiv preprint arXiv:1809.04444 (2018)

13. Devlin, J., Chang, M.W., Lee, K., Toutanova, K.: BERT: pre-training of deep bidirectional transformers for language understanding. arXiv preprint arXiv:1810.04805 (2018)

14. Donaldson, S., Davidson, J., Aiken, M.: Safer technology, safer users: the UK as a world-leader in safety tech (2020)

15. Fan, L., Yu, H., Yin, Z.: Stigmatization in social media: Documenting and analyzing hate speech for COVID-19 on twitter. Proc. Assoc. Inf. Sci. Technol. **57**, e313 (2020). https://doi.org/10.1002/pra2.313, https://onlinelibrary.wiley.com/doi/10.1002/pra2.313

16. Harriman, N., Shortland, N., Su, M., Cote, T., Testa, M.A., Savoia, E.: Youth exposure to hate in the online space: an exploratory analysis. Int. J. Environ. Res. Public Health **17**(22), 8531 (2020)

17. Hearst, M.A., Dumais, S.T., Osuna, E., Platt, J., Scholkopf, B.: Support vector machines. IEEE Intell. Syst. Appl. **13**(4), 18–28 (1998)

18. Hochreiter, S., Schmidhuber, J.: Long short-term memory. Neural Comput. **9**(8), 1735–1780 (1997)

19. Hutto, C.: Valence aware dictionary and sentiment reasoner (2018)

20. Kincaid, J.P., Fishburne, R.P., Jr., Rogers, R.L., Chissom, B.S.: Derivation of new readability formulas (automated readability index, fog count and flesch reading ease formula) for navy enlisted personnel. Technical report, Naval Technical Training Command Millington TN Research Branch (1975)
21. Kingma, D.P., Ba, J.: Adam: a method for stochastic optimization. arXiv preprint arXiv:1412.6980 (2014)
22. Kwok, I., Wang, Y.: Locate the hate: detecting tweets against blacks. In: Proceedings of the AAAI Conference on Artificial Intelligence, vol. 27, pp. 1621–1622 (2013). https://doi.org/10.1609/aaai.v27i1.8539
23. Le, T.T., Fu, W., Moore, J.H.: Scaling tree-based automated machine learning to biomedical big data with a feature set selector. Bioinformatics **36**(1), 250–256 (2020)
24. Liu, H., Yin, Q., Wang, W.Y.: Towards explainable NLP: a generative explanation framework for text classification. arXiv preprint arXiv:1811.00196 (2018)
25. Livingstone, S., Bober, M.: UK children go online: final report of key project findings (2005)
26. Lundberg, S.M., Allen, P.G., Lee, S.I.: A unified approach to interpreting model predictions. https://github.com/slundberg/shap
27. Maronikolakis, A., Baader, P., Schütze, H.: Analyzing hate speech data along racial, gender and intersectional axes. arXiv preprint arXiv:2205.06621 (2022)
28. Martins, R., Gomes, M., Almeida, J.J., Novais, P., Henriques, P.: Hate speech classification in social media using emotional analysis. In: 2018 7th Brazilian Conference on Intelligent Systems (BRACIS), pp. 61–66 (2018). https://doi.org/10.1109/BRACIS.2018.00019
29. Matamoros-Fernández, A., Farkas, J.: Racism, hate speech, and social media: a systematic review and critique. Telev. New Media **22**, 205–224 (2021). https://doi.org/10.1177/1527476420982230, https://journals.sagepub.com/doi/10.1177/1527476420982230
30. Mosca, E., Wich, M., Groh, G.: Understanding and interpreting the impact of user context in hate speech detection. In: Proceedings of the Ninth International Workshop on Natural Language Processing for Social Media, pp. 91–102 (2021)
31. Mozafari, M., Farahbakhsh, R., Crespi, N.: Hate speech detection and racial bias mitigation in social media based on BERT model. PLoS ONE **15**(8), e0237861 (2020)
32. Noever, D.: Machine learning suites for online toxicity detection. arXiv preprint arXiv:1810.01869 (2018)
33. Nori, H., Jenkins, S., Koch, P., Caruana, R.: InterpretML: a unified framework for machine learning interpretability (2019)
34. Ortega-Sánchez, D., Blanch, J.P., Quintana, J.I., Cal, E.S.D.l., de la Fuente-Anuncibay, R.: Hate speech, emotions, and gender identities: a study of social narratives on twitter with trainee teachers. Int. J. Environ. Res. Public Health **18**(8), 4055 (2021)
35. O'Shea, K., Nash, R.: An introduction to convolutional neural networks. arXiv preprint arXiv:1511.08458 (2015)
36. Peters, M.A.: Limiting the capacity for hate: hate speech, hate groups and the philosophy of hate (2022)
37. Pilnenskiy, N., Smetannikov, I.: Feature selection algorithms as one of the python data analytical tools. Future Internet **12**(3), 54 (2020)
38. Rad, D., Demeter, E.: A moderated mediation effect of online time spent on internet content awareness, perceived online hate speech and helping attitudes disposal of bystanders. Postmodern Openings **11**(2 Supl 1), 107–124 (2020)

39. Ramos, J., et al.: Using TF-IDF to determine word relevance in document queries. In: Proceedings of the first Instructional Conference on Machine Learning, vol. 242, pp. 29–48. Citeseer (2003)
40. Ribeiro, M.T., Singh, S., Guestrin, C.: "Why should i trust you?" Explaining the predictions of any classifier, vol. 13–17-August-2016, pp. 1135–1144. Association for Computing Machinery (2016). https://doi.org/10.1145/2939672.2939778
41. Saha, P., et al.: On the rise of fear speech in online social media. Proc. Natl. Acad. Sci. **120** (2023). https://doi.org/10.1073/pnas.2212270120, https://pnas.org/doi/10.1073/pnas.2212270120
42. Saha, P., Mathew, B., Garimella, K., Mukherjee, A.: "Short is the road that leads from fear to hate": fear speech in Indian WhatsApp groups, pp. 1110–1121. ACM (2021). https://doi.org/10.1145/3442381.3450137
43. Shepherd, T., Harvey, A., Jordan, T., Srauy, S., Miltner, K.: Histories of hating. Soc. Media + Soc. **1**, 205630511560399 (2015). https://doi.org/10.1177/2056305115603997, https://journals.sagepub.com/doi/10.1177/2056305115603997
44. da Silva, V., Papa, J.P., da Costa, K.A.: Extractive text summarization using generalized additive models with interactions for sentence selection, pp. 737–745. SCITEPRESS - Science and Technology Publications (12 2023). https://doi.org/10.5220/0011664100003417, https://www.scitepress.org/DigitalLibrary/Link.aspx?doi=10.5220/0011664100003417
45. da Silva, V.C., Papa, J.P., da Costa, K.A.P.: Extractive text summarization using generalized additive models with interactions for sentence selection. arXiv preprint arXiv:2212.10707 (2022)
46. Tomczyk, Ł: Skills in the area of digital safety as a key component of digital literacy among teachers. Educ. Inf. Technol. **25**(1), 471–486 (2020)
47. Van Aken, B., Risch, J., Krestel, R., Löser, A.: Challenges for toxic comment classification: an in-depth error analysis. arXiv preprint arXiv:1809.07572 (2018)
48. Waseem, Z., Hovy, D.: Hateful symbols or hateful people? Predictive features for hate speech detection on twitter. In: Proceedings of the NAACL Student Research Workshop, pp. 88–93 (2016)
49. Waseem, Z., Thorne, J., Bingel, J.: Bridging the gaps: multi task learning for domain transfer of hate speech detection. Online Harassment 29–55 (2018)
50. Watanabe, H., Bouazizi, M., Ohtsuki, T.: Hate speech on twitter: a pragmatic approach to collect hateful and offensive expressions and perform hate speech detection. IEEE Access **6**, 13825–13835 (2018). https://doi.org/10.1109/ACCESS.2018.2806394
51. Xu, R.: POS weighted TF-IDF algorithm and its application for an MOOC search engine. In: 2014 International Conference on Audio, Language and Image Processing, pp. 868–873. IEEE (2014)
52. Yong, C.: Does freedom of speech include hate speech? Res. Publica **17**, 385–403 (2011). https://doi.org/10.1007/s11158-011-9158-y, https://link.springer.com/10.1007/s11158-011-9158-y

Causal-Based Spatio-Temporal Graph Neural Networks for Industrial Internet of Things Multivariate Time Series Forecasting

Amir Miraki[1]([✉]) [iD], Austėja Dapkutė[2], Vytautas Šiožinys[2], Martynas Jonaitis[2], and Reza Arghandeh[1] [iD]

[1] Western Norway University of Applied Sciences, Bergen, Norway
{amir.miraki,reza.arghandeh}@hvl.no
[2] Company JSC Energy Advices, Kaunas, Lithuania
{austeja,vytautas.siozinys,martynas.jonaitis}@energyadvice.lt

Abstract. Spatio-temporal data forecasting is a challenging task, especially in the context of the Internet of Things (IoT), due to the complicated spatial dependencies and dynamic trends of temporal patterns between different sensors. Existing frameworks for spatio-temporal data forecasting often rely on pre-defined spatial adjacency graphs based on prior knowledge for modeling spatial features. However, these methods may not effectively capture the hidden connections between components of complex industrial systems. To overcome this challenge, this paper proposes a new approach called Causal-based Spatio-Temporal Graph Neural Networks (CSTGNN) for multivariate time series forecasting. The CSTGNN model uses a causality graph to discover hidden relationships between sensors and comprises three main modules: causality graph, temporal convolution, and graph neural network, to handle spatio-temporal data features effectively. Experimental results on industrial datasets demonstrate that the proposed method outperforms existing baselines and achieves state-of-the-art performance. The proposed approach offers a promising solution for accurate and interpretable spatio-temporal data forecasting.

Keywords: Spatio-Temporal · Causal Inference · Graph Neural Network

1 Introduction

Internet of Things (IoT), Digital Twins, and Industry 4.0 are advanced technological systems that rely on the collection and analysis of sensor-based, time-series data. Approximately 35.8 billion IoT devices were estimated to be in use worldwide in 2021, with future projections estimating that this number will reach 55.7 billion by 2025 [1]. The utilization of smart sensors and time-series

© The Author(s), under exclusive license to Springer Nature Switzerland AG 2023
L. Longo (Ed.): xAI 2023, CCIS 1903, pp. 120–130, 2023.
https://doi.org/10.1007/978-3-031-44070-0_6

data enables industrial systems to gain valuable insights into performance trends, maintenance needs, automation, and optimization [2].

Mining and monitoring of sequential data over time from sensors has received considerable attention over the past few decades [3]. Despite this, in recent years, the emphasis has shifted from utilizing this data to making predictions [4]. By analyzing historical time series data, it is possible to develop models and algorithms that can predict future process outcomes [5]. Predictive analytics for time series data in industrial IoT provides early anomaly detection, efficient maintenance and optimized production processes [6]. The methods of time series prediction can generally be classified into two categories: statistical methods and machine learning methods. Statistical methods such as ARIMA [7], exponential smoothing [8], and autoregressive [9] models are used to predict time series data from industrial sensors. Despite the effectiveness of these methods, they do have limitations such as being less effective with complex and noisy environment.

Machine learning models have recently enhanced the predictive capabilities of time series and solved these limitations in complex and noisy data [10]. Commonly used machine learning models for predicting time series data in industrial IoT applications include Support Vector Regression (SVR) [11], Random Forests (RF) [12], Convolutional Neural Networks (CNNs) [13], Recurrent Neural Networks (RNNs) [14] and Long Short-Term Memory (LSTM) [15]. In all these statistical and machine learning models, the objective is to discover the pattern of historical data and use that pattern to make predictions. Most real-world systems do not have completely independent sensors, and they are dependent on each other. Therefore, it is not sufficient to rely solely on historical data. In the context of spatio-temporal data [16], it is convenient to consider data both spatially and temporally and be able to consider the relationship between variables. All mentioned statistical and machine learning models are not applicable to spatio-temporal data when irregular spatial features are considered.

Graph Neural Networks (GNNs), which can represent irregular data, are used to model and analyse complex networks [17]. The use of GNNs for forecasting spatio-temporal data has become increasingly popular in recent years [18–20]. Despite the fact that these models have satisfactory results when it comes to predicting time series data, they have a problem concerning interpretation. To be considered trustworthy, machine learning based systems must meet several key requirements, including transparency, technical robustness, and safety [21]. ML methods and systems must be transparent and explainable in order to succeed [22,23].

In this paper, we propose an innovative **C**ausal-based **S**patio-**T**emporal **G**raph **N**eural **N**etworks(CSTGNN) for multivariate time Series forecasting combining GNNs with causality in order to improve performance and interpretability. Inspired by the works in causal inference in recent years [24,25], we use causality to build graphs form time series data that represent the relationships between variables and the graph used in GNN is causal graph. Knowing the concealed connections between sensors would enable us to identify the impacted area of the system during an anomaly or problem in maintenance, leading to improved decision-making. This study's significant contributions are as follows:

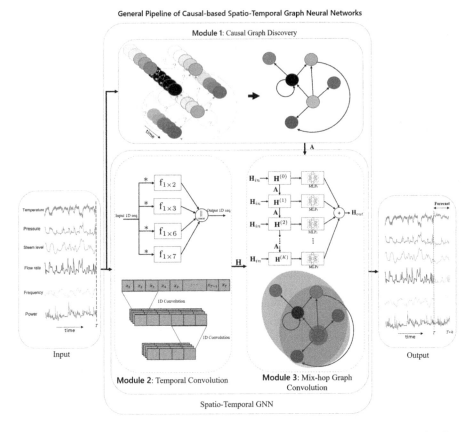

Fig. 1. Pipeline of the proposed approach. Module 1 constructs causality graphs that reveal hidden relationships between variables. In module 2, time features are extracted using dilated convolution on the time series. Module 3 performs the prediction model by applying the GNN to the data and considering the causality graph.

- We propose a framework that incorporates both temporal and spatial features to provide accurate predictions of multivariate time series data. There are various objectives and advantages of utilizing causal relationships between sensors within this framework: i) performance improvement for GNN structure by establishing meaningful neighborhoods for each node based on causal relationships. ii) Due to the causality module, we are able to reduce the parameters of the model as well as make the graph sparser, both of which contribute to a reduction of computational complexity. iii) We have both the prediction results and the causality graph of the system, which together enhance the interpretability of both the model and the system under investigation.
- Extensive experiment are carried out on real-world industrial IoT data from biomass boiler system, which verify that our model has robust and accurate

forecasting performance compared to the existing baselines. To the best of our knowledge, this study represents the pioneering effort in employing a spatio-temporal Graph Neural Network model, which incorporates causality to enhance the interpretability of a complex industrial system, for the purpose of predicting time series data.

2   Causal-Based Spatio-Temporal Graph Neural Networks

Figure 1 illustrates the proposed model's general framework, which comprises three modules: causal graph (CG), time convolution (TC), and graph neural network(GNN). The following sections provide details on these three major modules.

2.1   Causal Graph

Graphical models are a popular way to understand large and complex datasets. In particular, with the growing need for interpretable models and causal insights into underlying processes, directed acyclic graphs (DAGs) have been shown to be promising in a wide variety of applications. In this study, causality graph can be derived only from observed data. The formulation is as follows:

Given a data matrix $\mathbf{X} \in \mathbb{R}^{T \times N}$ consisting of T observations of vector $X = (X_1, \cdots, X_N)$ and a (discrete) space of DAGs denoted by $\mathbb{D}$, where $\mathcal{G} = (\mathcal{V}, \mathcal{E})$ is a DAG with d nodes, our objective is to learn DAG $\mathcal{G} \in \mathbb{D}$ that models the joint distribution $\mathbb{P}(X)$ [26]. To accomplish this, we adopt a structural equation model (SEM) for X that is defined by an adjacency matrix $\mathbf{A} \in \mathbb{R}^{N \times N}$. With considering the vectors of adjacency matrix $\mathbf{A} = [A_1, \cdots, A_N]$ we can define SEM by $X_j = A_j^T X + z_j$ or in general form based on parent variable $\mathbb{E}(X_j \mid X_{pa}(X_j)) = f(A_j^T X)$, so we can model the conditional distribution of Xj given its parents. The general problem we are attempting to solve to determine the adjacency matrix is as follows:

$$\min_{\mathbf{A} \in \mathbb{R}^{N \times N}} F(\mathbf{A})$$
$$\text{s.t}\quad G(\mathbf{A}) \in \mathbb{D}. \tag{1}$$

We use least-squares (LS) loss $\ell(\mathbf{A}; \mathbf{X})$ and ℓ_1-regularization $\|\mathbf{A}\|_1 = \|\text{vec}(\mathbf{A})\|_1$ to define score function as $F(\mathbf{A}) = \ell(\mathbf{A}; \mathbf{X}) + \lambda \|\mathbf{A}\|_1 = \frac{1}{2N} \|\mathbf{A} - \mathbf{X}\mathbf{A}\|_F^2 + \lambda \|\mathbf{A}\|_1$. By utilizing gradient-based numerical methods and the continuous optimization approach presented in [27], we can efficiently solve optimization problem (1) and identify a DAG that represents the inter-dependencies between variables.

2.2   Temporal Convolution

Temporal convolution refers to the operation on time series data, where a window (filter) of fixed size is slid over the input sequence to extract temporal patterns.

Our proposed method uses dilated convolution [28] instead of the conventional convolution method. In the context of one-dimensional time series data with a size of T ($X \in \mathbb{R}^T$) and a filter of size K ($f_{1 \times K} \in \mathbb{R}^K$), dilated convolution define as follows:

$$X * f_{1 \times K}(t) = \sum_{s=0}^{K-1} f_{1 \times K}(s) X(t - d \times s), \qquad (2)$$

where d is the dilation factor. When dealing with time series data, recurring patterns such as daily, weekly, or hourly cycles are often present, and cannot be accurately captured by a single filter. To address this, multiple filters with different lengths are commonly employed for temporal convolution to capture all relevant features [29]. To this end, we draw on previous research and utilize filters with lengths of 2, 3, 6 and 7 in our method. The resulting outputs of these filters are concatenated, and the convolution output can be represented as $\widetilde{X} = \text{concat}(X * f_{1 \times 2}, X * f_{1 \times 3}, X * f_{1 \times 6}, X * f_{1 \times 7})$, where X is one-dimensional time series input and $\widetilde{X}$ is output of convolution with four different size filters and concatenation. Figure 1 (module 2) illustrates the concept of time convolution discussed in this section.

2.3   Graph Neural Network

The primary concept of GNN involves the integration of the data associated with each node in a graph and the data related to its neighboring nodes, with the goal of utilizing the interdependence of nodes and spatial inter-connections. Instead of using basic graph convolution techniques [30], our approach involves implementing mix-hop propagation. Mix-hop propagation graph convolution is an extension of traditional graph convolution operation. Mixing coefficients are used to combine the hidden states of neighboring nodes across multiple layers in order to capture higher-order relationships. This technique is illustrated in Fig. 1 (module 3) and incorporates deeper fusion of information between nodes and their neighboring nodes [31]. Mix-hop propagation is defined as follows:

$$\mathbf{H}_{out} = \sum_{i=0}^{K} \mathbf{H}^{(i)} \mathbf{W}^{(i)} \qquad (3)$$

where K is the depth of propagation, $\mathbf{W}^{(i)}$ are learnable parameters in multilayer perceptron (MLP) and propagation using graph adjacency matrix is $\mathbf{H}^{(i)} = \beta \mathbf{H}_{in} + (1 - \beta) \widetilde{\mathbf{A}} \mathbf{H}^{(i-1)}$ where β is a hyper parameter, $\mathbf{H}_{in}$ represents the input features from previous layer, normalized adjacency $\widetilde{\mathbf{A}} = \widetilde{\mathbf{D}}^{-1}(\mathbf{A} + \mathbf{I})$ and $\widetilde{\mathbf{D}}_{ii} = 1 + \sum_{j=1}^{N} \mathbf{A}_{ij}$ [32].

3   Experimental Results and Discussion

We conducted experiments using the biomass boiler as a real-world industrial process dataset to evaluate the predictive accuracy of the CSTGNN. The boiler is designed to burn waste wood and produce steam for industrial purposes. We monitor all parts of the process with multivariate sensors to ensure that it is operating as intended. Illustrated in Fig. 2 is the diagram of this complex system.

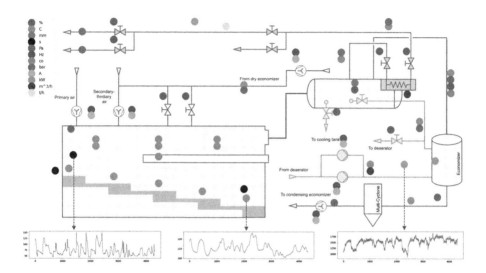

Fig. 2. Diagram of the biomass boiler system. Sensors are displayed as nodes; each color represents a different type of sensor. In addition, time series data are shown for some sensors over a 3-day period.

3.1 Data Set Description

Data has been collected from 62 sensors embedded in biomass boiler over a period of one month from 2022.12.12 to 2023.01.11. The sample rate for all sensors is one minute. In total, we have 43200 samples for each sensor. In this complex industrial system, there are 12 different types of sensors, each measuring a different parameter. A list of these sensors and their units and measurements is shown in Table 1.

3.2 Experimental Settings

We split the datasets into a training set (60%), validation set (20%), and test set (20%). Models are trained independently to predict the target future step (horizon) 10, 15, and 20. The number of training epochs is 30. In order to train the model, we used the Adam optimizer with a learning rate of 0.001, an L2 regularization penalty of 0.0001, and a gradient clip of 5. Additionally, we used a mix-hop propagation layer with a depth of 2.

Table 1. List of the various types of sensors in the biomass boiler system, along with their units and measurements.

Unit	Unit	Measured values
%	Percentage	Valve opening percentage
C	Celcius	Temperature
mm	millimetre	Steam drum level
s	second	Time period
Pa	Pascal	Pressure
Hz	Hertz	Frequency setting of fans
Co	ppm	Carbon monoxide level
bar	bar	Pressure in bars
A	Amper	Electric current
kW	Kilowatt	Thermal power
m^3/h	Cubic meters per hour	Volumetric mass flow rate
t/h	tonnes per hour	Mass flow rate

3.3 Baseline Methods

In this study, we compare CSTGNN with the following models:

- LSTM: Long Short-Term Memory is a recurrent neural network architecture that is capable of capturing long-term dependencies in sequential data, making it suitable for time series prediction [15].
- STGCN: Spatiotemporal Graph Convolutional Networks that integrate graph convolution into a 1D convolutional layer [18].
- MTGNN: Multivariate Time Series Graph Neural Network is capable of learning spatial and temporal features, during the training phase [32].

3.4 Comparison Results

As shown in Table 2, we have compared the performance of our proposed method CSTGNN with baseline methods LSTM [15], STGCN [18], and MTGNN [32]. The forecast was conducted over three horizons of 10, 15 and 20 min (h = 10, 15,

Table 2. Performance comparison for multivariate time series forecasting.

	Horizon 10			Horizon 15			Horizon 20		
	MAE	RMSE	MAPE	MAE	RMSE	MAPE	MAE	RMSE	MAPE
LSTM [15]	36.62	111.73	12.67%	35.03	112.07	12.43%	35.66	117.27	12.84%
STGCN [18]	17.44	66.71	7,26%	19.57	73.92	6.88%	21.01	78.66	8.07%
MTGNN [32]	11.66	46.41	4.50%	16.28	59.75	6.39%	18.36	66.38	6.38%
CSTGNN	**11.38**	**46.31**	**3.86%**	**14.62**	**57.48**	**5.00%**	**16.96**	**64.48**	**5.59%**

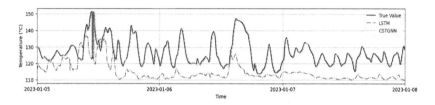

Fig. 3. Time series forecasting comparison results for 3 days in January 2023.

20) and three metrics (MAE, MAE, and MAPE) were calculated. The LSTM method examines only temporal features, and hidden dependencies between sensors are generally not taken into account. It is evident from the poor results obtained from this method that the sensor effects on each other and graph modeling are key factors. By using GNNs, STGCN uses a predefined graph based on the distance between sensors to achieve better results than LSTM. MTGNN learn the graph and provide better results, but they do not reveal anything about the system or process being studied. CSTGNN offers superior results to all other models because it includes causality graphs and adds physical awareness to the process.

In Fig. 3, the prediction results for temperature sensor illustrated for three consecutive days from 2023.01.05 to 2023.01.08 using two LSTM and CSTGNN methods. Clearly, the use of GNN based on the causality graph is much more effective at predicting than using only temporal data.

3.5   Interpretability

The theoretical foundations for the causal graph inference module enable CST-GNN to be highly interpretable. A causality graph is extracted from the time series data in this module. Directed edges from node i to node j demonstrate that sensor i is influencing sensor j. Figure 4 shows the graphs extracted using two methods CSTGNN and MTGNN which have significantly better predictions than the others. Figure 4a illustrates the graph learned by MTGNN method and Fig. 4b illustrates the causality graph discovered using the proposed method.

An important discovery has been made concerning the inter-sensor edges among multiple sensors. Specifically, the two temperature sensors inside the burner have been examined, and their corresponding graphs have been presented. The edge labeled with number 1 in Fig. 4a indicates that the temperature of the burner affects the input fuel measured by the black sensor, whereas it should have been the other way around, rendering the edge inaccurate. Additionally, edge 2 demonstrated in Fig. 4a indicate that the output steam affects the temperature in the burner. However, it is clear that the opposite is true, i.e., the higher the temperature inside the burner, the more steam is produced and exits the system. In addition to the density problem, we conclude that the graph learned by the MTGNN method is difficult to interpret and does not provide useful insights for improving industrial processes.

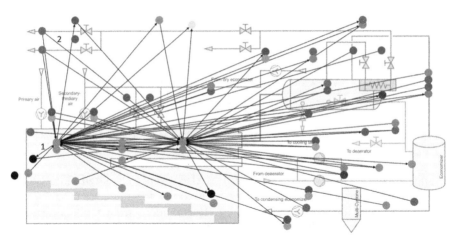

(a) Learned graph by MTGNN method for two temperature target sensors.

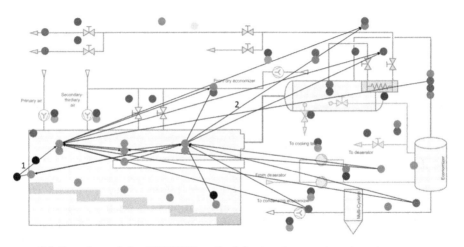

(b) Causal graph by CSTGNN method for two temperature target sensors.

Fig. 4. Visualization of the learned graph for MTGNN method and the inferred causal graph for proposed CSTGNN method.

Discovering and interpreting causal relationships is crucial to industrial processes and leads to critical decisions. The more accurately we understand how one part of a process interacts with other parts, the better and more effective we may be in controlling the process during anomalies or instabilities. In Fig. 4b, edge number 1 demonstrates correctly that fuel input influences burner temperature, and edge number 2 indicates that higher temperatures produce more steam. Despite the fact that some edges in this graph are easy to interpret, not all connections are so straightforward since the industrial process tested in this study is more complex and requires further investigation and practical testing.

4   Conclusion

In this paper, we have presented the Causal-based Spatio-Temporal Graph Neural Networks (CSTGNN) model. CSTGNN effectively addresses complex spatial dependencies and dynamic temporal trends. This framework leverages a causality graph to discover hidden connections between system components. Proposed model consists of three main modules including causality graph, temporal convolutions, and graph neural networks to handle the spatio-temporal data characteristics in the most effective way. Experimental results demonstrate CSTGNN outperforms existing baselines and achieves state-of-the-art accuracy and interpretability on industrial IoT datasets.

Acknowledgements. This work is partly funded by the EEA and Norway Grants under the "Development of an innovative complex predictive maintenance system (EA-Predictive)" project. The authors confirm contribution to the paper as follows: study conception, design, algorithms and implementations: A. Miraki and R. Arghandeh; providing data (through EA-SAS platform: www.easas.net) and data related insights: A. Dapkutė, V. Šiožinys and M. Jonaitis. All authors reviewed the results and approved the final version of the manuscript.

References

1. International data corporation (IDC). Worldwide internet of things forecast, 2021–2025 (2021)
2. Kalsoom, T., et al.: Impact of IoT on manufacturing industry 4.0: a new triangular systematic review. Sustainability **13**(22), 12506 (2021)
3. Esling, P., Agon, C.: Time-series data mining. ACM Comput. Surv. (CSUR) **45**(1), 1–34 (2012)
4. Mushtaq, M.F., Akram, U., Aamir, M., Ali, H., Zulqarnain, M.: Neural network techniques for time series prediction: a review. JOIV: Int. J. Inform. Vis. **3**(3), 314–320 (2019)
5. Montgomery, D.C., Jennings, C.L., Kulahci, M.: Introduction to Time Series Analysis and Forecasting. Wiley, Hoboken (2015)
6. Blázquez-García, A., Conde, A., Mori, U., Lozano, J.A.: A review on outlier/anomaly detection in time series data. ACM Comput. Surv. (CSUR) **54**(3), 1–33 (2021)
7. Contreras, J., Espinola, R., Nogales, F.J., Conejo, A.J.: Arima models to predict next-day electricity prices. IEEE Trans. Power Syst. **18**(3), 1014–1020 (2003)
8. Gardner Jr., E.S.: Exponential smoothing: the state of the art. J. Forecast. **4**(1), 1–28 (1985)
9. Lewis, R., Reinsel, G.C.: Prediction of multivariate time series by autoregressive model fitting. J. Multivar. Anal. **16**(3), 393–411 (1985)
10. Masini, R.P., Medeiros, M.C., Mendes, E.F.: Machine learning advances for time series forecasting. J. Econ. Surv. **37**(1), 76–111 (2023)
11. Yang, H., Huang, K., King, I., Lyu, M.R.: Localized support vector regression for time series prediction. Neurocomputing **72**(10–12), 2659–2669 (2009)
12. Dudek, G.: Short-term load forecasting using random forests. In: Filev, D., et al. (eds.) IS 2014. AISC, vol. 323, pp. 821–828. Springer, Cham (2015). https://doi.org/10.1007/978-3-319-11310-4_71

13. Koprinska, I., Wu, D., Wang, Z.: Convolutional neural networks for energy time series forecasting. In: 2018 International Joint Conference on Neural Networks (IJCNN), pp. 1–8. IEEE (2018)
14. Connor, J.T., Martin, R.D., Atlas, L.E.: Recurrent neural networks and robust time series prediction. IEEE Trans. Neural Netw. **5**(2), 240–254 (1994)
15. Hochreiter, S., Schmidhuber, J.: Long short-term memory. Neural Comput. **9**(8), 1735–1780 (1997)
16. Cressie, N., Wikle, C.K.: Statistics for Spatio-Temporal Data. Wiley, Hoboken (2015)
17. Wu, Z., Pan, S., Chen, F., Long, G., Zhang, C., Philip, S.Y.: A comprehensive survey on graph neural networks. IEEE Trans. Neural Netw. Learn. Syst. **32**(1), 4–24 (2020)
18. Yu, B., Yin, H., Zhu, Z.: Spatio-temporal graph convolutional networks: a deep learning framework for traffic forecasting. arXiv preprint arXiv:1709.04875 (2017)
19. Cao, D., et al.: Spectral temporal graph neural network for multivariate time-series forecasting. Adv. Neural. Inf. Process. Syst. **33**, 17766–17778 (2020)
20. Bui, K.-H.N., Cho, J., Yi, H.: Spatial-temporal graph neural network for traffic forecasting: an overview and open research issues. Appl. Intell. **52**(3), 2763–2774 (2022)
21. Ethics guidelines for trustworthy AI, high level expert group on artificial intelligence set up by the EU commission (2019). https://digital-strategy.ec.europa.eu/en/library/ethics-guidelines-trustworthy-ai
22. Gunning, D., Stefik, M., Choi, J., Miller, T., Stumpf, S., Yang, G.-Z.: XAI-explainable artificial intelligence. Sci. Robot. **4**(37), eaay7120 (2019)
23. Gade, K., Geyik, S.C., Kenthapadi, K., Mithal, V., Taly, A.: Explainable AI in industry. In: Proceedings of the 25th ACM SIGKDD International Conference on Knowledge Discovery & Data Mining, pp. 3203–3204 (2019)
24. Schölkopf, B.: Causality for machine learning. In: Probabilistic and Causal Inference: The Works of Judea Pearl, pp. 765–804 (2022)
25. Pearl, J.: Causality. Cambridge University Press, Cambridge (2009)
26. Spirtes, P., Glymour, C.N., Scheines, R., Heckerman, D.: Causation, Prediction, and Search. MIT Press, Cambridge (2000)
27. Zheng, X., Aragam, B., Ravikumar, P.K., Xing, E.P.: DAGs with NO TEARS: continuous optimization for structure learning. Adv. Neural Inf. Process. Syst. **31** (2018)
28. Yu, F., Koltun, V.: Multi-scale context aggregation by dilated convolutions. arXiv preprint arXiv:1511.07122 (2015)
29. Szegedy, C., et al.: Going deeper with convolutions. In: Proceedings of the IEEE Conference on Computer Vision and Pattern Recognition, pp. 1–9 (2015)
30. Kipf, T.N., Welling, M.: Semi-supervised classification with graph convolutional networks. arXiv preprint arXiv:1609.02907 (2016)
31. Abu-El-Haija, S., et al.: MixHop: higher-order graph convolutional architectures via sparsified neighborhood mixing. In: International Conference on Machine Learning, pp. 21–29. PMLR (2019)
32. Wu, Z., Pan, S., Long, G., Jiang, J., Chang, X., Zhang, C.: Connecting the dots: multivariate time series forecasting with graph neural networks. In: Proceedings of the 26th ACM SIGKDD International Conference on Knowledge Discovery & Data Mining, pp. 753–763 (2020)

Investigating the Effect of Pre-processing Methods on Model Decision-Making in EEG-Based Person Identification

Carlos Gómez Tapia$^{(\boxtimes)}$ (iD), Bojan Bozic (iD), and Luca Longo (iD)

Artificial Intelligence and Cognitive Load Research Lab, Applied Intelligence Research Centre, School of Computer Science, Technological University Dublin, Dublin, Ireland
`carlos.g.tapia@myTUDublin.ie`, {`bojan.bozic,luca.longo`}`@tudublin.ie`

Abstract. Electroencephalography (EEG) data has emerged as a promising modality for biometric applications, offering unique and secure personal identification and authentication methods. This research comprehensively compared EEG data pre-processing techniques, focusing on biometric applications. In tandem with this, the study illuminates the pivotal role of Explainable Artificial Intelligence (XAI) in enhancing the transparency and interpretability of machine learning models. Notably, integrating XAI methodologies contributes significantly to the evolution of more precise, reliable, and ethically sound machine learning systems. An outstanding test accuracy exceeding 99% was observed within the biometric system, corroborating the Graph Neural Network (GNN) model's ability to distinguish between individuals. However: high accuracy does not unequivocally signify that models have extracted meaningful features from the EEG data. Despite impressive test accuracy, a fundamental need remains for an in-depth comprehension of the models. Attributions proffer initial insights into the decision-making process. Still, they did not allow us to determine why specific channels are more contributory than others and whether the models have discerned genuine cognitive processing discrepancies. Nevertheless, deploying explainability techniques has amplified system-wide interpretability and revealed that models learned to identify noise patterns to distinguish between individuals. Applying XAI techniques and fostering interdisciplinary partnerships that blend the domain expertise from neuroscience and machine learning is necessary to interpret attributions further and illuminate the models' decision-making processes.

Keywords: Electroencephalography · eXplainable Artificial Intelligence · Deep Learning · Signal processing · attribution xAI methods · Graph-Neural Network · Biometrics · signal-to-noise ratio

1 Introduction

The human brain has been the subject of intense study and fascination for centuries. One of the primary tools used to explore this complex organ is electroencephalography (EEG), a non-invasive technique that records electrical activity

L. Longo (Ed.): xAI 2023, CCIS 1903, pp. 131–152, 2023.
https://doi.org/10.1007/978-3-031-44070-0_7

in the brain. EEG data has played a pivotal role in furthering our understanding of the human brain, enabling researchers and clinicians to investigate brain function, diagnose neurological disorders, and develop innovative treatments. Electroencephalography was first introduced in 1924 by German psychiatrist Hans Berger [6], who discovered that the brain's electrical activity could be measured using electrodes placed on the scalp. Since then, EEG technology has evolved significantly, resulting in more sophisticated equipment and analysis techniques, opening new avenues for research and applications [18, 29, 30].

EEG data is composed of time-varying voltage measurements that represent the activity of thousands of neurons in the cerebral cortex. These voltage fluctuations generate distinct patterns, called brain waves, that can be categorized into various frequency bands: delta, theta, alpha, beta, and gamma. Each frequency band is associated with specific cognitive processes, emotional states, and levels of consciousness, providing invaluable information about the brain's functioning. The non-invasive nature of EEG renders it a desirable method for studying brain activity, as it presents minimal risk to the participant and allows for conducting the study in a wide range of settings. EEG's excellent temporal resolution also enables researchers to examine rapid neural processes occurring on a millisecond scale. This high temporal resolution proves advantageous when investigating the temporal dynamics of cognitive functions, such as attention, memory, and perception. In recent years, advancements in computational power and signal-processing techniques have expanded the scope of EEG applications. Researchers can now analyze large-scale brain networks, decode neural signals for brain-computer interfaces, and even predict cognitive decline in ageing populations. Moreover, EEG data has been instrumental in developing innovative therapies for conditions such as epilepsy [27], depression [21], and attention deficit hyperactivity disorder (ADHD) [15].

Biometric technologies have become increasingly prevalent in recent years, driven by the need for secure and efficient personal identification and authentication methods. Traditional biometric techniques rely on physiological traits, such as fingerprints, facial features, and iris patterns, which are unique to each individual. However, these methods can be susceptible to forgery and may not provide sufficient security in some contexts [5]. Consequently, researchers have turned their attention to alternative biometric modalities, with EEG data emerging as a promising candidate for biometric applications [20]. EEG-based biometrics offer unique advantages over traditional biometric techniques like iris or fingerprint scanning. Like fingerprints and irises, each individual's brainwave patterns are unique, contributing to precise identification [8, 17]. The brain's electrical activity is inherently unique to each individual, resulting from the complex interplay of genetics, experiences, and cognitive processes. This individual variability translates into distinct EEG patterns that can be harnessed for identification. EEG data collection is non-intrusive, making it difficult to acquire someone's EEG data without their awareness or consent, thereby enhancing security [17]. Mimicking or forging EEG patterns is challenging, providing a robust safeguard against fraud and identity theft [8]. EEG signals are dynamic, changing with a person's mental state, thus offering additional security against replication attempts. Certain EEG biometric systems measure responses to specific stimuli, which are nearly impossible to duplicate, offering another layer of protection. Moreover, while traditional biometrics often require a one-time authentication, EEG has the potential to provide continuous or periodic authentication, augmenting security throughout an entire session [12]. Nevertheless, the implementation of EEG-based biometrics is more complex than traditional methods due to the intricacies of data acquisition, processing requirements, the need for specialized equipment, and its generally more intrusive nature.

We aim to compare various pre-processing methods for EEG data in biometric applications. A meticulous evaluation of pre-processing techniques is necessary to ensure that the model accurately learns the genuine differences in cognitive processing rather than less valuable features, such as discrepancies in voltage amplitudes caused by improperly placed electrodes. By doing so, we can identify the most effective methods to eliminate confounding factors and enhance the reliability of the extracted features, ultimately leading to the development of more accurate and robust EEG-based biometric systems. Furthermore, Explainable Artificial Intelligence (XAI) methods can prove instrumental in achieving this objective. Attribution-based methods assign importance values, or 'attributions', to inputs, which can elucidate the significance of specific features (like particular EEG channels or frequency bands) in distinguishing individuals. Moreover, XAI models can shed light on the internal workings of complex machine learning models used in EEG biometrics, improving transparency and fostering trust in the system. Understanding the decision-making process helps researchers spot and rectify biases or mistakes, contributing to more accurate and reliable biometric systems. For these experiments, a Graph Neural Network (GNN) was chosen as a learning approach given its high interpretability and performance when learning from raw EEG data [11], and Integrated Gradients as the explainability method, due to its consistency, completeness, and broad applicability to any differentiable model, including complex deep learning architectures.

This research is devoted to answering the following question: How does comparing two different pre-processing methods for EEG data affect the signal-to-noise ratio (SNR), model performance in biometric applications, and model attributions as revealed by XAI methods.

The structure of this manuscript is as follows: Sect. 2 comprises a brief literature review. Section 3 describes the different hypotheses and the methods employed to test them. Section 4 includes the results, and finally, Sect. 5 interprets the results obtained.

2   Related Work

EEG has become crucial for investigating cognitive processes, diagnosing neurological disorders, and developing brain-computer interfaces. In this context, signal pre-processing techniques and the role of Explainable AI (XAI) have emerged as key research areas, given their impact on the performance and interpretability of EEG-based systems. Pre-processing EEG data is a critical step in the analysis process, as it directly impacts the data quality used for subsequent analysis or modelling. The presence of artefacts such as eye blinks, muscle movements and line noise can severely contaminate the EEG signal, thereby affecting the interpretability and reliability of the results [31]. A standard pre-processing pipeline typically consists of down-sampling, filtering, artefact removal and re-referencing. The raw EEG signal is filtered using notch filters to remove high-frequency noise and low-frequency drifts, respectively. Various techniques can be employed to remove artefacts from the EEG signal, including independent component analysis (ICA) [10], principal component analysis (PCA) [13], and regression-based methods [37].

Researchers have applied the aftermentioned methods to EEG to remove the noise while maintaining the signals for several decades. In recent years new methods for isolating the signals have been proposed. These methods are often referred to as pipelines, given they are composed of several individual steps applied iteratively over the original signal. Although the stages vary from method to method, the final goal is the same. Remove the unwanted noise while preserving the characteristics of the original signal. FASTER (Fully Automated Statistical Thresholding for EEG artefact Rejection) is one of the pipelines [19]. FASTER is an EEG pre-processing method developed to automate the process of identifying and removing artefacts in EEG data. It combines data-driven statistical techniques with conventional EEG analysis methods to improve signal quality and facilitate a more accurate interpretation of the data. Another example of a modern EEG pre-processing pipeline is the PREP (Pipeline for EEG pre-processing) [7]. The PREP pipeline is a standardized and automated pre-processing pipeline that addresses several common issues in EEG pre-processing. The main steps of the PREP pipeline include Line noise removal: The pipeline removes line noise (e.g., 50 or 60 Hz) using a multi-taper regression method. This step mitigates the impact of electrical interference from power lines and other electronic devices on the EEG data. Robust reference estimation: The pipeline computes a robust average reference by iteratively detecting and interpolating bad channels based on their correlation with other channels and their deviation from a robust reference signal estimate. Bad channel detection and interpolation: Bad channels are identified based on their correlation with other channels, deviation from the reference signal, and abnormal spectral properties. Once detected, these channels are interpolated using spherical spline interpolation to ensure the quality and consistency of the data. Re-referencing: The cleaned and interpolated data is re-referenced to the robust average reference computed earlier in the pipeline. The PREP pipeline has been shown to improve the consistency and comparability of results across studies by providing a standardized pre-processing approach. However, it is essential to consider that the choice of pre-processing techniques, whether using the standard pipeline or the PREP pipeline, can significantly impact the signal quality and model performance.

Signal-to-noise ratio (SNR) is a measure used to quantify the desired signal level compared to the background noise. It is typically expressed in decibels (dB) and is used to evaluate the quality of a signal. A higher SNR indicates a clearer and less noisy signal. The ratio is determined by comparing the power or amplitude of the signal to that of the noise, which may include any unwanted interference or distortion. A higher SNR indicates that the signal is stronger and clearer than the noise, resulting in better quality and performance. Conversely, a lower SNR means that the noise is more prominent and may interfere with the clarity or accuracy of the signal. SNR can be calculated using Eq. 1, where SNR (dB) represents the signal-to-noise ratio in decibels (dB), P_{signal} represents the power of the desired signal and P_{noise} represents the power of the noise present in the system. In the context of EEG data, the signal represents the underlying neural activity, while the noise represents unwanted artefacts, such as muscle activity, eye movements, or external electrical interference. By computing the SNR for pre-processed EEG data, we can assess the effectiveness of the pre-processing techniques in enhancing the signal quality and reducing the impact of noise. Available literature for SNR used to measure EEG signal quality is very scarce.

$$\text{SNR (dB)} = 10 \cdot \log_{10} \left(\frac{P_{\text{signal}}}{P_{\text{noise}}} \right) \qquad (1)$$

The growing interest in Graph Neural Network (GNN) architectures has impacted EEG-based applications, demonstrating their effectiveness in domains with elements and relationships. Examples of such applications include traffic flow prediction, point cloud classification, and text classification [9,25,38]. One advantage of these systems is their ability to implicitly represent relationships between elements, making them potentially valuable for explainability purposes [22,32–34]. However, the use of graphs in EEG-based applications remains relatively unexplored. For instance, [39] applied a Graph Convolutional Network model for EEG-based emotion recognition and achieved results comparable to non-graph-based methods. Meanwhile, [36] utilized a graph to map brain functional connectivity for Participant Classification without relying on message-passing Graph Neural Networks. Their approach involved creating brain connectivity networks using multi-channel settings, node centrality, and global network metrics to compute graph node features. They demonstrated that the generated networks exhibited significant inter-individual distinctiveness, making them suitable for biometric applications.

In recent years, electroencephalography (EEG) has gained attention as a viable modality for biometric applications due to its unique characteristics, such as non-invasiveness, low cost, and the ability to provide real-time measurements of brain activity [17]. Numerous studies have demonstrated the potential of EEG data for personal identification and authentication, leveraging the inherent variability in individual brain activity patterns [1,35]. While these studies have shown promising results, gaps in the literature need to be addressed to advance the field. One significant gap is the lack of consensus on the most effective pre-processing techniques for improving the quality of EEG data [26]. Another gap in the literature is the interpretability of the models employed in EEG-based biometric systems. As machine learning algorithms become more complex, there is a growing need for Explainable Artificial Intelligence (XAI) methods to provide transparency and understandability in the models' decision-making processes [2]. Another critical challenge in AI systems is the dataset shift problem [23], which occurs when the training data distribution differs from the real-world data distribution encountered during deployment. Dataset shifts can arise due to various factors, such as changes in data collection techniques, biases in data sampling, or evolving user preferences. These shifts can significantly impact the performance and reliability of AI models in practical applications. However, XAI methods offer promising solutions to mitigate the dataset shift problem [3]. By providing interpretability and transparency, XAI methods enable the identification of data distribution discrepancies and model behavior changes. Moreover, XAI methods enhance the trustworthiness and accountability of AI systems by enabling users to understand the model's decision-making process, fostering user acceptance and facilitating system refinement. Although some studies have explored using XAI techniques in EEG-based applications, more research is needed to establish their effectiveness in elucidating the models' predictions and attributions. By addressing these gaps in the literature and integrating domain knowledge from multiple disciplines, researchers can contribute to developing more accurate, reliable, and ethically sound EEG-based biometric systems, facilitating their widespread adoption across various applications. LIME (Local Interpretable Model-Agnostic Explanations) [24], SHAP (SHapley Additive exPlanations) [16], and Integrated Gradients (IG) [28] are all methods used for interpreting machine learning models, but they operate differently. LIME creates local linear approximations to explain model predictions around a specific instance, which is useful for interpreting any model but may not perform well for complex, non-linear models. Based on cooperative game theory, SHAP assigns each feature an importance value for a particular prediction. It guarantees consistency and local accuracy, offering more robust and extensive explanations than LIME, but computation can be intensive. On the other hand, IG attributes a neural network's prediction to its input features by integrating gradients along a path from a baseline to the instance. It provides fine-grained attributions, being particularly useful for deep learning models, and is generally more robust and comprehensive than LIME.

3   Design

We aim to address three critical research questions about electroencephalogram (EEG) data in the context of biometric applications. Firstly, we seek to investigate the differences in signal-to-noise ratio (SNR) resulting from using two distinct pre-processing methods. Secondly, the article will examine how the performance of biometric models varies when implementing these two pre-processing techniques on the EEG data. Lastly, we will explore the comparative attributions of the model, as determined by explainable artificial intelligence (XAI) methodologies, when using the two aforementioned pre-processing methods. Sections 3.1 and 3.2 explain the chosen dataset, the pre-processing techniques applied to it and how SNR was computed for each signal. Section 3.3 details the biometric problem and the training procedure for the Graph Neural Network model, and finally 3.4 explains how attributions for the trained models were computed.

3.1   Dataset Acquisition

The DEAP (Dataset for Emotion Analysis using Physiological Signals) dataset is a publicly available[1], multimodal dataset designed for the analysis of human affective states, particularly emotions [14]. The dataset contains EEG and peripheral physiological signals collected from 32 participants while they were watching 40 one-minute-long excerpts of music videos. These music videos were specifically chosen to elicit various emotional responses from the participants. The DEAP dataset comprises EEG data collected from 32 electrodes, sampled at a rate of 512 Hz and positioned in accordance with the International 10–20 system. The dataset includes data from 4 electrooculography (EOG) electrodes and 4 electromyography (EMG) electrodes.

3.2   Pre-processing Methods

In this study, we aim to analyze the impact of two different pre-processing algorithms on the DEAP dataset for the purpose of creating a biometric system: the STANDARD and PREP methods. Both methods involve cleaning and preparing the physiological data for further analysis. The STANDARD pre-processing method begins by sub-sampling the raw data into one-minute segments where the video stimuli happen. Next, the EEG channels are reordered to follow the Geneva order, a standardized channel ordering convention that facilitates data comparison and reproducibility across studies. To increase processing speeds and reduce computational requirements, the data is then downsampled to 128 Hz. Following these initial steps, the data is further processed by applying a band-pass filter between 4 Hz and 45 Hz. This filtering process removes unwanted frequencies, such as low-frequency drifts and high-frequency noise, while preserving the relevant frequency bands associated with cognitive processing. The EEG data is then re-referenced to an average reference, which enhances the signal-to-noise ratio. Finally, Independent Component Analysis (ICA) uses the EOG channels to identify and remove unwanted components, such as eye blinks, muscle activity, and other noise sources. The resulting data is divided into 1-second long non-overlapping windows, which are used as input for subsequent modelling. The PREP method follows the same steps as the STANDARD method, with the additional implementation of the PREP pipeline. A more detailed description of the PREP pipeline can be seen in Sect. 2. The PREP addresses various issues commonly encountered in EEG data analysis, such as noisy channels, non-stationary signals, and inconsistent referencing schemes. By this pipeline, the PREP method aims to further enhance the data quality and improve the performance of the biometric systems. Figure 1 shows a sample from each pre-processing method.

---
[1] https://www.eecs.qmul.ac.uk/mmv/datasets/deap/.

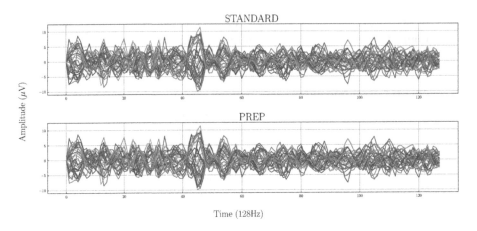

Fig. 1. First sample in the dataset after applying STANDARD and PREP pre-processing methods. Contains 1 s of data at 128 Hz for 32 electrodes. Measured in microvolts.

We used an indirect method to estimate the signal-to-noise ratio (SNR), given the separate signal and noise components are unavailable and no reference signal is provided. This approach leverages the coefficient of variation (CV) as a proxy for estimating the SNR under certain assumptions about the underlying signal and noise distributions. SNR can be estimated as the ratio of the squared mean to the standard deviation. Equation 2 shows how to estimate SNR in decibels using values taken from the sample. N represents the total number of values in the sample, x_n is the value at point n, and s represents the standard deviation of the sampled signal.

$$\text{SNR (dB)} = 10 \cdot \log_{10}\left(\frac{\frac{1}{N}\sum_{n=0}^{N} x_n^2}{s}\right) \tag{2}$$

To evaluate the signal quality, we analyzed both pre-processed versions of the entire signal dataset (40 participants * 40 min each) using the SNR equation (Eq. 2). One SNR value was obtained per channel and participant, and then the mean SNR for a particular pre-processing method was calculated. Results can be seen in Sect. 4.1.

Hypothesis 1 (H1): If the PREP pre-processing pipeline is applied to data sampled from the DEAP dataset, then the signal-to-noise ratio (SNR) will be significantly higher than the SNR for the same data without the PREP pipeline applied.

We expect the PREP pipeline to improve the signal-to-noise ratio, enhancing the quality of EEG data for biometric applications. The PREP pipeline is expected to outperform its counterpart due to its robust artefact removal and advanced techniques for handling noisy and corrupted channels, contributing to isolating the neural signal more effectively from background noise.

3.3 Modelling

Person identification biometrics refers to using unique biological or behavioural characteristics to recognize or verify an individual's identity. Biometric systems rely on measurable and distinctive features specific to each person. In the context of EEG-based person identification biometrics, the focus is on using an individual's unique brainwave patterns to establish their identity. The DEAP dataset is composed of 40 one-minute recordings per participant. After the pre-processing step, we divide these recordings into non-overlapping windows of a fixed duration (1 s). The goal of the biometric system is to be presented with an input window and be able to predict which participant the sample was taken from. More formally, The objective is to estimate a parametric function f_σ that associates an input matrix X with a vector of predicted probabilities p, containing one entry per known participant (N = 32). Here, p_i signifies the probability of the input features being attributed to the subject with ID i. Can be represented as:

$$f_\sigma(X \in \mathbb{R}^{n \times d}) \to p_s \in [0,1]^p \tag{3}$$

where n denotes the number of EEG channels used, d represents the number of data points per channel (128 for 1 s at 128 Hz), and p corresponds to the total number of participants. After windowing, the dataset consists of 76,800 samples (32 participants * 40 videos per participant * 60 windows per video). We used 50% of the data for training the model, 25% for validation, and allocated the remaining 25% for testing. We sampled windows randomly using a seed to ensure reproducibility and maintained an equal number of examples for each class. Before modelling, all data underwent Z-score normalization across subjects and channels. This normalization process involved substituting each value in the dataset with its corresponding Z-score. We calculated Z-scores for each individual channel and electrode, ensuring that outlier channels and subjects did not affect the resulting normalized signal.

Graph Neural Network. A graph $G = \{V, E\}$ is defined as a finite set of nodes V along with a set of edges E determining the connections between said nodes. Graph Neural Networks (GNNs) comprise a set of learning techniques which aim at learning efficiently from graphs. GNNs use Graph Convolutional layers to spread information along edges via the message-passing algorithm, which iteratively updates the values of each node according to nodes in their vicinity $N(v) \in V$. To represent the data as a graph, we model each electrode as an individual node, with the vector of data points recorded for each electrode as node features. Connections between nodes are defined based on Euclidean distances between electrodes. Nodes close to each other will have an edge connecting them, whereas nodes far apart will not. This representation assumes electrodes closer to each other will have a relation between them and aims at capturing these spatial dependencies (see [39]). Figure 2 depicts the different connections among close-together electrodes and the graph's adjacency matrix A.

A   B

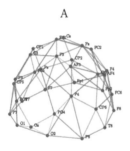 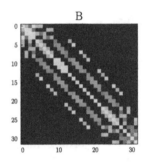

Fig. 2. A) Electrode positions in 3D along with edges connecting the 20% of electrodes that are closer together. B) Adjacency matrix for the graph. Shared among participants.

The model architecture consists of two SAGEConv layers, each followed by a ReLU activation function, a dropout layer ($p = 0.25$) and a BatchNorm layer to reduce overfitting. The convolutional graph layers transform the input features for each node from a 128-long vector containing 1 s of data at 128 Hz to a latent space representation of size 512. After the graph convolution, each node gets added a positional encoding value, concatenating node id to the latent space representation of the node. These features are then fed through a shared feature aggregator, consisting of a shared linear layer that shrinks the node vector size from 513 down to 8. The feature aggregator condenses the information in each node and reduces the computational complexity of the overall model. Finally, all the reduced versions of the node features are concatenated and fed through the final classifier. The GNN starts by processing the input data through graph convolutional layers, which help capture the relationships between nodes in the graph. After each layer, the model applies normalization and dropout techniques to improve stability and prevent overfitting. The GNN incorporates positional information about the nodes in the graph, which can help the model better understand the underlying structure of the data. After processing the data through the graph convolutional layers, the model aggregates the node features and passes them through a series of fully connected layers. These layers help the model make its final predictions or classifications. Utilizing a 10-fold cross-validation method, the training procedure was carried out with a chosen batch size of 256. The Adam optimizer was implemented, featuring a learning rate of 0.0001. Before commencing the training, the dataset underwent shuffling. Training continued until no additional reduction in validation loss was detected. The entire process was executed using PyTorch and PyTorch Geometric, with each model requiring around 5 min of training time on a GTX 3080 GPU.

Hypothesis 2 (H2): If a model is trained on two versions of the same data, one of them processed through the PREP pre-processing pipeline and the other one not, then the model that used the PREP data will have a significant higher accuracy than the opposing model.

3.4   XAI Methods

The final step in the analysis is understanding what the model is learning. DL models are often referred to as 'black boxes' given the difficulty of understanding the predictions of these models. We know that models can accurately identify participants for this specific dataset, even when using half of the dataset as unseen testing data. To gain insight into this problem, we employ the Integrated Gradients algorithm. The main idea behind Integrated Gradients is to compute the gradients of the model's output concerning its input features along a straight path from a baseline input to the given input. The baseline input is usually minimal or insignificant to the model's output. The gradients obtained for each input feature are then integrated along the path to determine their contribution to the output. We used a vector of zeros as a baseline. The integrated gradient method interpolates between the baseline and the input. It creates a series of inputs along a straight path from the baseline input to the original input by linear interpolation. IG computes the gradients of the model's output concerning the input features for each interpolated input to capture how the output changes for small changes in input features. The final step is to integrate the gradients from the baseline to the original input. The integrated gradients for each input feature represent their importance or contribution to the model's output. By applying Integrated Gradients to the GNN, we can gain insights into which features are important for the model's predictions and better understand the model's behaviour and decision-making process.

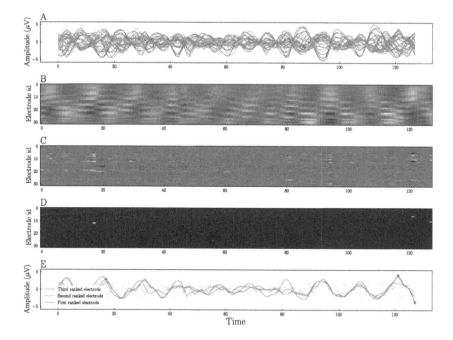

Fig. 3. A&B) Individual test sample, plotted two different ways. C) Attributions for that particular test sample. D) Three most important values within this attribution. E) Original sample with points with maximum attributions represented in red, purple and green. (Color figure online)

The complete steps to calculate attributions for a given example can be seen under Fig. 3. Attributions are computed on correctly labelled samples from the test set. The Integrated gradients algorithm computes the weight of the output concerning the input. A rank-based system is introduced to compare attributions for all of the available samples from the test set. The three most prevalent electrodes from a specific sample are saved. The idea is that attributions should differ for each case and not be particular to an individual electrode. The higher the variance in attributions, the more useful features the model is learning. We assume that if all predictions from a model happen because of a single electrode, it is not because the model learns unique traits from each person in processing information but because the model learns to identify noisy channels.

Hypothesis 3 (H3): If attributions are computed for all test cases for similar models trained with the same data, one of them processed through the PREP pre-processing pipeline and the other one not then the model that used the PREP data will have significantly higher variance in the distribution of electrodes chosen for making the predictions than the opposing model.

The model trained on the EEG data pre-processed by the method with a higher signal-to-noise ratio will exhibit more consistent and meaningful attributions, indicated by a higher variance in the distribution of electrodes, in turn demonstrating better learning of the genuine differences in cognitive processing.

4   Results and Discussion

4.1   Signal to Noise Ratio Results

Our results revealed that the signal-to-noise ratio for both pre-processing methods was almost identical, indicating that the overall quality of the signals was similar. However, we observed a slightly lower standard deviation in the SNR values for the PREP pre-processing pipeline. This reduced variation suggests that the PREP method may provide a more consistent signal quality across different channels and subjects. Overall the signal-to-noise ratio for the STANDARD pre-processing pipeline was $6.95 \pm 1.56dB$ compared to $6.84 \pm 1.40dB$ obtained by the PREP pipeline. To help readers visualize these findings, we have included a figure displaying the signal-to-noise ratio for each channel and subject in both the STANDARD and PREP pre-processed data (Fig. 4).

The objective of this block of the study was to test H1 (Sect. 3.2, page 138). Contrary to our expectations, our results revealed that the SNR of the data pre-processed using the PREP pipeline was not significantly different from that of the data pre-processed using the standard pipeline. Our analysis showed that the SNR values obtained from the EEG data pre-processed using the PREP pipeline were comparable to those obtained from the data pre-processed using the standard pipeline. This result was unexpected, as the PREP pipeline is known for

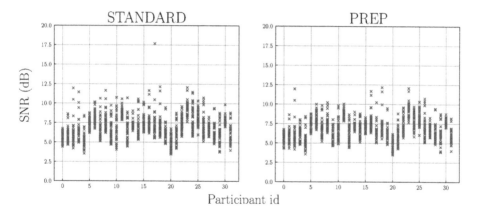

Fig. 4. Signal to noise ratio (dB) as computed per channel and participant for both pre-processing methods being analyzed.

its advanced artefact removal techniques and robust handling of noisy and corrupted channels, ideally leading to a higher SNR and improved data quality. Our results did not provide conclusive evidence to support Hypothesis 1. The expected improvement in SNR with the use of the PREP pre-processing pipeline was not observed, and the SNR values for both pre-processing methods were found to be similar. This unexpected outcome raises questions about the effectiveness of the PREP pipeline in enhancing the quality of EEG data for biometric applications. It suggests that further investigation is needed to better understand the underlying reasons for this observation. Future research could explore factors that might have contributed to the lack of improvement in SNR with the PREP pipeline, such as the specific characteristics of the EEG data used in this study, the influence of individual differences between subjects, or potential limitations in implementing the pre-processing techniques. Additionally, alternative pre-processing methods or combining multiple pre-processing techniques could be investigated to identify the most effective approach for improving the SNR and data quality in EEG-based biometric applications.

4.2   Model Evaluation

The results for the two models were very similar as well. The models using the PREP pipeline obtained an average test set accuracy of 99.37% vs the 99.58% obtained by the models that did not include PREP as a pre-processing step. Confusion matrices for both approaches can be seen under Fig. 5

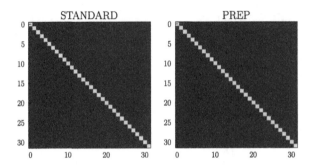

Fig. 5. Confusion matrices for models trained with both pre-processing methods

The objective of this block of the study was to test H2 (Sect. 3.3, page 140). Our results showed that the models trained with both versions of the data achieved accuracies close to 100%, indicating no difference in performance between the PREP and standard pipelines. This result was somewhat expected, as we knew that the models could learn from different noise patterns for each participant. However, we initially anticipated that the models trained with the PREP pipeline would learn more useful, participant-specific features due to the improved data quality and enhanced signal-to-noise ratio. Our results did not provide conclusive evidence to support Hypothesis 2. The expected improvement in model performance using the PREP pre-processing pipeline was not observed, as both models achieved close to 100% accuracy. This equal performance across pre-processing methods raises questions about the effectiveness of the PREP pipeline in facilitating the learning of more useful features for person identification from EEG data. These results lead us to also reject H2. The fact that both models achieved perfect accuracy suggests that the GNN model was able to learn from the noise in the data, which might have masked the potential benefits of the improved data quality provided by the PREP pipeline. Future research could focus on methods to mitigate the impact of noise on model learning, such as employing advanced denoising techniques or incorporating domain knowledge into the model architecture. Other performance metrics beyond accuracy could be used to better evaluate and compare the models' ability to learn meaningful features from the EEG data pre-processed using different pipelines.

4.3   XAI Methods

In this section, we analyze the attributions generated using the integrated gradients method and highlight the gaps in understanding the models' decision-making process, emphasizing the need for further research. In our preparatory research work, we found that when training biometric models from EEG data using a single dataset, the performance of the models was outstanding, surpassing 99% test set accuracy in most cases. However, the transferability of the models to other datasets still needs to be explored. We employed the integrated gradients method to extract the features the models used to differentiate so accurately

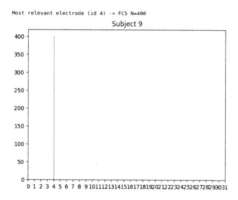

Fig. 6. Attributions extracted from a GNN model trained with un-normalized data pre-processed using the STANDARD pipeline. Attributions show a single electrode (FC5) being the most important for all test set samples for subject number 9 (N = 400)

amongst participants. One of the first results from our preliminary work, shown under Fig. 6, depicts how an individual electrode (FC5) was responsible for all correct predictions for subject number 9. More specifically, this figure represents the electrode that had the most impact on the prediction for all test cases for a particular subject (subject 9). The x-axis represents the 32 available electrodes, and the y-axis represents the number of times that specific electrode was the most important, which in this case, was electrode number 4 (FC5) for all test samples, indicating the model could perform predictions based on this channel alone. This is potentially caused due to channel 4 being noisy. The model understands that a sample with a very noisy FC5 channel belongs to subject 9, and this assumption is correct.

We theorised that the model was learning to differentiate subject nine due to extreme amplitudes in an individual electrode (FC5) and not because it was learning to identify unique patterns in cognitive processing. The DEAP dataset consists of 40 videos recorded in a single session. One misplaced electrode could happen for various reasons, such as too much gel between the electrode and the scalp. It could lead to extreme amplitudes for a participant for all recordings at a specific channel (because the eeg headset was not removed between trials), and the biometric models are learning to identify these misplaced electrodes instead of more valuable, transferable features. To put it simply, the model would know that a sample belonged to subject nine because the amplitude of the signal for the FC5 electrode for that given sample would be significantly more prominent than in the recordings from other participants, and these differences in amplitudes were not caused because the subject produced a different signal for that channel but instead due to a misplaced electrode when the original recordings happened.

To alleviate the aforementioned issue and align with the findings presented in [4], we employed z-score normalization across channels and subjects. We took each channel from each subject and applied z-score normalization for that particular channel. This normalization step should ensure that absolute amplitude is not considered anymore, but instead, the data the model trains on is the signal's amplitude relative to itself. Figure 7 shows an example of a sample when the z-score normalization is applied and when it is not. Consequently, the models are encouraged to focus on learning meaningful, participant-specific features, which can lead to better generalization. Our results show that when normalization is applied, the GNN models do not exhibit the same reliance on noise distribution for making correct predictions (see Fig. 9).

As explained, our goal was to apply the PREP pre-processing pipeline on top of the STANDARD one to identify the misplaced electrodes and interpolate their data with signals from all other 'good' electrodes around them. We relied on the attributions to know which pre-processing pipeline led the model to learn more informative features. We hypothesised that higher variance in the ranked attributions would imply the model relied not on an individual channel but instead on a combination of channels, demonstrating learning features other than noise patterns from individual electrodes.

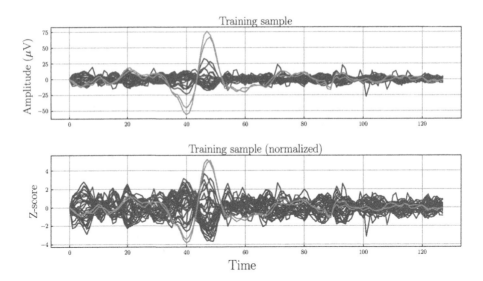

Fig. 7. Un-normalized vs normalized STANDARD data. 'Fp1' and 'AF3' channels are marked in red. Models trained with non-normalized data would learn to identify subjects based on extreme amplitudes at specific noisy channels. (Color figure online)

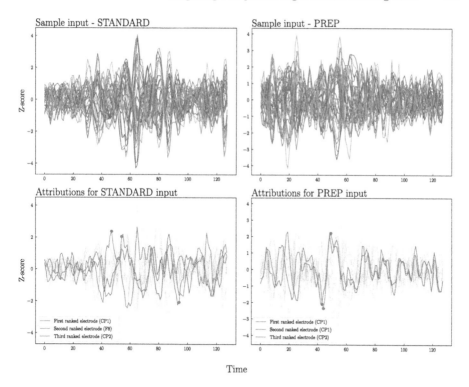

Fig. 8. Sample attributions for a test case belonging to subject 29. Predictions for models trained with data using both pre-processing methods are correct, but attributions differ.

When analyzing the attributions produced by models trained with both versions of the data, we found that models produced similar patterns. Figure 8 shows a test sample for subject 29, where electrode CP1 had the most weight onto the final (correct) prediction for both models. However, models trained with PREP data did not consider electrode F8, potentially because it was removed as part of the PREP pre-processing pipeline. These attribution patterns suggested the models were no longer relying on individual electrodes but instead on a combination of electrodes. Each test case ranked a different electrode as their most important one, as opposed to un-normalized data where there was a single electrode causing all of the predictions.

Finally, we analyzed the complete distribution of attributions for both pre-processing versions of the data (Appendix A & B), where we expected to see a difference in the variance of the attributions. We hypothesized that the models would make predictions using a combination of electrodes by removing the noisy channels employing the PREP pipeline. However, this did not happen. Both distributions for attributions produced by the models look similar and are not significantly different. Correct predictions for most subjects generally rely on a combination of electrodes. However, there are still some cases (e.g. Figure 9 subject 24) where most predictions rely on a single electrode. There are some cases (e.g. Figure 9 subject 24) where, contrary to our expectations, applying the PREP pipeline did not mitigate this issue.

These results lead us to deny the third and final hypothesis H3(section 3.4, page 142). First, models were trained using different data, but both versions had a similar signal-to-noise ratio. We would expect the PREP data to perform better and produce attributions with higher electrode variance, but this was not the case.

5   Conclusion

In this study, we investigated the impact of the PREP pipeline on the quality of EEG data employing Graph Neural Networks and XAI methods in the context of person identification. We tested three hypotheses, all refuted by our results: The PREP pre-processing pipeline did not significantly improve the signal-to-noise ratio, contrary to our expectations. Model performance, measured by accuracy, was not significantly better when using the EEG data pre-processed with the PREP pipeline, as both models achieved close to 100% test accuracy. Finally, when analysed using XAI methods, the model trained on the EEG data pre-processed by the PREP pipeline did not exhibit more consistent and meaningful attributions.

These unexpected results highlight the problem's complexity and the challenges in understanding the relationship between EEG data pre-processing and the interpretability of model attributions. Our results indicate that GNN models can correctly identify individuals from EEG data, relying on noisy channels caused by improperly placed electrodes. This reliance on noise distribution can be mitigated by applying normalisation techniques, encouraging the models to focus on learning meaningful features. Additionally, we prove that the PREP pipeline did not significantly affect the quality of the features learnt by the models as indicated by the SNR. Despite these findings, our understanding of the models' decision-making process and the PREP pipeline's effect on the data quality is limited. The motivation for performing these experiments came from removing the outlier channels from the data so that the models could not focus on these outliers and instead identify more useful features. However, it is unclear whether the PREP pipeline had this desired effect. It is apparent that, after normalisation, the models do not rely on individual electrodes to make their predictions but instead on a combination of electrodes; however, it is unclear why particular channels are chosen over others by the models to make their decisions. Our findings highlight the importance of XAI methods when training DL models and call for further research to address the gaps in knowledge and improve our understanding of the role of pre-processing in EEG-based biometric applications.

Some potential avenues for future work include: 1) Investigating alternative pre-processing methods or combinations of multiple pre-processing techniques to identify the most effective approach for improving the signal-to-noise ratio and data quality in EEG-based biometric applications. 2) Utilizing multiple datasets where subjects perform different tasks under different conditions so the effect of improperly placed electrodes is mitigated. 3) Exploring advanced denoising techniques or incorporating domain knowledge into the model architecture to mitigate the impact of noise on model learning, enabling a better evaluation of the benefits of different pre-processing pipelines. 4) Employing more sophisticated XAI techniques to provide clearer insights into the models' decision-making process and better understand the relationship between pre-processing and attributions in the context of personal identification from EEG data. Furthermore, there is a need for interdisciplinary collaboration between researchers in the fields of machine learning, signal processing, and neuroscience. By working together, these experts can combine their domain-specific knowledge to better understand the attributions generated by the models and elucidate the models' decision-making process. Ultimately designing more robust and interpretable architectures. Such collaborative efforts can advance the state of the art and pave the way for more effective and reliable EEG data biometric applications.

Acknowledgment. This publication has emanated from research supported partly by a grant from SFI Centre for Research Training in Machine Learning at Technological University Dublin under Grant number 18/CRT/6183. For the purpose of OpenAccess, the author has applied a CC BY public copyright licence to any Author Accepted Manuscript version arising from this submission.

A   Ranked Attributions STANDARD

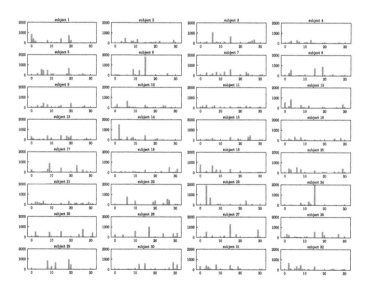

Fig. 9. Ranked attributions for all test cases from a model trained using the STANDARD pre-processing pipeline

B   Ranked Attributions PREP

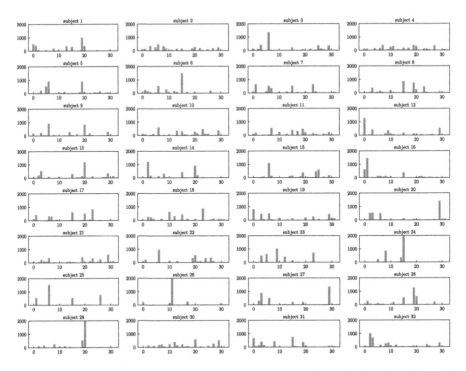

Fig. 10. Ranked attributions for all test cases from a model trained using the PREP pre-processing pipeline

References

1. Anokhin, A., et al.: A genetic study of the human low-voltage electroencephalogram. Hum. Genet. **90**(1–2), 99–112 (1992)
2. Antoniadi, A.M., et al.: Current challenges and future opportunities for XAI in machine learning-based clinical decision support systems: a systematic review. Appl. Sci. **11**(11), 5088 (2021)
3. Apicella, A., Isgrò, F., Pollastro, A., Prevete, R.: Toward the application of XAI methods in EEG-based systems. In: Proceedings of the 3rd Italian Workshop on Explainable Artificial Intelligence co-located with 21th International Conference of the Italian Association for Artificial Intelligence(AIxIA 2022), Udine, Italy, 28 November – 3 December 2022. CEUR Workshop Proceedings, vol. 3277, pp. 1–15. CEUR-WS.org (2022)
4. Apicella, A., Isgrò, F., Pollastro, A., Prevete, R.: On the effects of data normalization for domain adaptation on EEG data. Eng. Appl. Artif. Intell. **123**, 106205 (2023)

5. Ballard, L., Lopresti, D., Monrose, F.: Forgery quality and its implications for behavioral biometric security. IEEE Trans. Syst. Man Cybernet. Part B (Cybernetics) **37**(5), 1107–1118 (2007)

6. Berger, H.: Über das elektroenkephalogramm des menschen. Arch. Psychiatr. Nervenkr. **87**(1), 527–570 (1929)

7. Bigdely-Shamlo, N., Mullen, T., Kothe, C., Su, K.M., Robbins, K.A.: The prep pipeline: standardized preprocessing for large-scale EEG analysis. Front. Neuroinform. **9**, 16 (2015)

8. Campisi, P., La Rocca, D.: Brain waves for automatic biometric-based user recognition. IEEE Trans. Inf. Forensics Secur. **9**(5), 782–800 (2014)

9. Cui, Z., Henrickson, K., Ke, R., Wang, Y.: Traffic graph convolutional recurrent neural network: a deep learning framework for network-scale traffic learning and forecasting. IEEE Trans. Intell. Transp. Syst. **21**(11), 4883–4894 (2019)

10. Delorme, A., Makeig, S.: EEGLAB: an open source toolbox for analysis of single-trial EEG dynamics including independent component analysis. J. Neurosci. Methods **134**(1), 9–21 (2004)

11. Gómez-Tapia, C., Bozic, B., Longo, L.: On the minimal amount of EEG data required for learning distinctive human features for task-dependent biometric applications. Front. Neuroinform. **16**, 844667 (2022)

12. Ehatisham-ul Haq, M., Azam, M.A., Naeem, U., Amin, Y., Loo, J.: Continuous authentication of smartphone users based on activity pattern recognition using passive mobile sensing. J. Netw. Comput. Appl. **109**, 24–35 (2018)

13. Jung, T.P., et al.: Removing electroencephalographic artifacts: comparison between ICA and PCA. In: Neural Networks for Signal Processing VIII. Proceedings of the 1998 IEEE Signal Processing Society Workshop (Cat. No. 98TH8378), pp. 63–72. IEEE (1998)

14. Koelstra, S., et al.: DEAP: a database for emotion analysis; using physiological signals. IEEE Trans. Affect. Comput. **3**(1), 18–31 (2011)

15. Lenartowicz, A., Loo, S.K.: Use of EEG to diagnose ADHD. Curr. Psychiatry Rep. **16**, 1–11 (2014)

16. Lundberg, S.M., Lee, S.I.: A unified approach to interpreting model predictions. In: Advances in Neural Information Processing Systems, vol. 30 (2017)

17. Marcel, S., Millán, J.D.R.: Person authentication using brainwaves (EEG) and maximum a posteriori model adaptation. IEEE Trans. Pattern Anal. Mach. Intell. **29**(4), 743–752 (2007)

18. Nidal, K., Malik, A.S.: EEG/ERP Analysis: Methods and Applications. CRC Press, Boca Raton (2014)

19. Nolan, H., Whelan, R., Reilly, R.B.: Faster: fully automated statistical thresholding for EEG artifact rejection. J. Neurosci. Methods **192**(1), 152–162 (2010)

20. Paranjape, R., Mahovsky, J., Benedicenti, L., Koles, Z.: The electroencephalogram as a biometric. In: Canadian Conference on Electrical and Computer Engineering 2001. Conference Proceedings (Cat. No. 01TH8555), vol. 2, pp. 1363–1366. IEEE (2001)

21. Pollock, V.E., Schneider, L.S.: Quantitative, waking EEG research on depression. Biol. Psychiat. **27**(7), 757–780 (1990)

22. Pope, P.E., Kolouri, S., Rostami, M., Martin, C.E., Hoffmann, H.: Explainability methods for graph convolutional neural networks. In: 2019 IEEE/CVF Conference on Computer Vision and Pattern Recognition (CVPR), pp. 10764–10773. IEEE Computer Society, Los Alamitos, CA, USA (2019). https://doi.org/10.1109/CVPR.2019.01103

23. Quinonero-Candela, J., Sugiyama, M., Schwaighofer, A., Lawrence, N.D.: Dataset Shift in Machine Learning. MIT Press, Cambridge (2008)
24. Ribeiro, M.T., Singh, S., Guestrin, C.: "Why should i trust you?" explaining the predictions of any classifier. In: Proceedings of the 22nd ACM SIGKDD International Conference on Knowledge Discovery and Data Mining, pp. 1135–1144 (2016)
25. Shi, W., Rajkumar, R.: Point-GNN: graph neural network for 3D object detection in a point cloud. In: Proceedings of the IEEE/CVF Conference on Computer Vision and Pattern Recognition, pp. 1711–1719. Pittsburgh, PA 15213 (2020)
26. Shoka, A., Dessouky, M., El-Sherbeny, A., El-Sayed, A.: Literature review on EEG preprocessing, feature extraction, and classifications techniques. Menoufia J. Electron. Eng. Res **28**(1), 292–299 (2019)
27. Smith, S.J.: EEG in the diagnosis, classification, and management of patients with epilepsy. J. Neurol. Neurosurg. Psychiatry **76**(suppl 2), ii2-ii7 (2005)
28. Sundararajan, M., Taly, A., Yan, Q.: Axiomatic attribution for deep networks. In: International Conference on Machine Learning, pp. 3319–3328. PMLR (2017)
29. Thompson, T., Steffert, T., Ros, T., Leach, J., Gruzelier, J.: EEG applications for sport and performance. Methods **45**(4), 279–288 (2008)
30. Tong, S., Thankor, N.V.: Quantitative EEG analysis methods and clinical applications. Artech House, Norwood (2009)
31. Urigüen, J.A., Garcia-Zapirain, B.: EEG artifact removal–state-of-the-art and guidelines. J. Neural Eng. **12**(3), 031001 (2015)
32. Vilone, G., Longo, L.: Explainable artificial intelligence: a systematic review. arXiv preprint arXiv:2006.00093 (2020). https://doi.org/10.48550/arXiv.2006.00093
33. Vilone, G., Longo, L.: Classification of explainable artificial intelligence methods through their output formats. Mach. Learn. Knowl. Extr. **3**(3), 615–661 (2021)
34. Vilone, G., Longo, L.: Notions of explainability and evaluation approaches for explainable artificial intelligence. Inf. Fusion **76**, 89–106 (2021)
35. Vogel, F.: The genetic basis of the normal human electroencephalogram (EEG). Humangenetik **10**(2), 91–114 (1970)
36. Wang, M., Hu, J., Abbass, H.A.: BrainPrint: EEG biometric identification based on analyzing brain connectivity graphs. Pattern Recogn. **105**, 107381 (2020)
37. Woestenburg, J., Verbaten, M., Slangen, J.: The removal of the eye-movement artifact from the EEG by regression analysis in the frequency domain. Biol. Psychol. **16**(1–2), 127–147 (1983)
38. Yao, L., Mao, C., Luo, Y.: Graph convolutional networks for text classification. In: Proceedings of the AAAI Conference on Artificial Intelligence, vol. 33, pp. 7370–7377. Northwestern University, Chicago, IL (2019)
39. Zhong, P., Wang, D., Miao, C.: EEG-based emotion recognition using regularized graph neural networks. IEEE Trans. Affect. Comput. **13**(3), 1290–1301 (2020)

State Graph Based Explanation Approach for Black-Box Time Series Model

Yiran Huang$^{(\boxtimes)}$ (ID), Chaofan Li (ID), Hansen Lu, Till Riedel (ID),
and Michael Beigl (ID)

Telecooperation Office, Karlsruhe Institute of Technology, Karlsruhe, Germany
{yhuang,li,lu,riedel,michael}@teco.edu

Abstract. In recent years, there has been a growing trend in the utilization of Artificial Intelligence (AI) technology to construct human-centered systems that are based on implicit time series information, ranging from contextual recommendations on smartwatches to human activity recognition on production workshop. Despite the advantages of these systems, the opaqueness and unpredictability of these systems for users has elicited concerns. To mitigate these issues, time-series explanation methods have been proposed. However, existing methods only focus on the segment importance of the instance to be explained and ignore its chronological nature. In this paper, we propose a novel explanation method named State-graph Based eXplanable Artificial Intelligent (SBXAI), which exhibits the sequential relationship between time periods through directed circular graphs while emphasizing the importance of each time period in an instance. Our proposed method was evaluated on 20 time-series datasets, and the results showed that the explanations provided by SBXAI are consistent with the behavior of the AI model in making predictions.

Keywords: Explanable Artificial Intelligent · Time Series · hidden markov model

1 Introduction

With the rapid development of the always-on network technology and micro-/nano-electromechanical systems, the use of live sensor information presents an increasingly important role in human-centered Artificial Intelligent (AI) system in our daily life. Schilit [19] already described in 1994 the different types of implicit interactions with computer systems stemming from such contextual information, which since then has led to a wide range of context-aware recommender systems from context-aware advertising to adjusting music playlists based on the user behaviors [13].

Y. Huang and C. Li—These authors contributed equally to this work.

Typical examples of devices enabling such implicit interactions are smartwatches and mobile phones equipped with numerous sensors. These devices collect time-series data on daily human activities and provide relevant recommendations based on the insight derived from the collected data. However, since the models used by these devices are becoming increasingly complex, it is becoming more challenging to explain the underlying logic behind these recommendations. Therefore, there is a requirement for explanatory methods for time-series AI models, more precisely, for methods that clarify how AI models process the sequential relationships inherent in the data to derive a context-based recommendation.

To this day, explainability research has gained much attention and progress in the computer vision domain [25]. However, the unique characteristics of time series data, which are the foundation for many context-aware information retrieval models, make it challenging to directly apply these advancements to time-series explanations. There are several reasons for this, with the two most notable being: *(i)* for humans, images often possess inherent semantics, whereas time-series data is incomprehensible without domain knowledge, *(ii)* the features of the image data are typically related to the values and their numerical differences, while the features of time series data are usually characterized by the values and their chronological order.

Several methodologies have emerged for interpreting time series models in recent years. Approaches [3,16] evaluate the significance of input data by introducing perturbations. Schlegel et al. [21] adapts the LIME approach to the time series domain, utilizing six distinct segmentation methods and elucidating the target model through the training of local models with the generated segmentations. Doddaiah et al. [6] broadens this method to encompass multi-class forecasting issues. Guidotti et al. [9] utilizes rules created within the latent space and employs mean squared error (MSE)-based Shapelets to identify the segments that exert influence on the model's predictions. While these approaches offer model explanation, they are restricted to the importance of input segments. This constraint appears incongruous with the prediction foundations inherent to most time series models. For instance, in predicting a head nod using data from a gravitational acceleration sensor affixed to the head, the assessment should encompass the entire sequence of acceleration increasing in the direction of gravity, returning to zero, increasing in the opposite direction, and returning to zero once more. Although the value at a given moment might exhibit a linear correlation with the predicted outcome, it cannot be deemed a comprehensive explanation for the predicted result.

To this end, we proposed a novel time series explanation method named the State-graph Based eXplanation Artificial Intelligent (SBXAI). This method utilizes Bayesian optimization to aggregate data that are adjacent to each other in the given example to create multiple, more understandable data units (state). Furthermore, it applies Directed Circular Graphs (DCG) to visualize the sequential relationships between states and used it to explain the model decision.

Our contributions can be summarized as *(i)* We applied DCG to explain the decision of an AI model, which demonstrates how the sequential relationship within the given example determines the decision made by the AI model. To the best of our knowledge, this is the first approach to explain a time-series model in terms of chronological order. *(ii)* We utilized the Bayesian optimization algorithm to group adjacent data, creating states that are more understandable by humans. *(iii)* We provided scalable algorithm architecture in GitHub[1], which facilitates the subsequent research and development.

2   Related Works

Theissler et al. [25] divided the existing time series explanation methods into three main categories: Time Points-Based Explanations, Subsequences-Based Explanations, and Instance-Based Explanations. Among them, Time Points-Based Explanations usually assign a weight for each time point in the input time series data, reflecting how much the value at this time point contributes to the final decisions of the model [11,15,20,27]. Subsequences-Based Explanations explain the model by figuring out the input sub-segments most representative of the model's decisions. Such sub-segments could either be real-valued sub-sequences directly extracted from the raw time series [2,14,22] or discretized representations obtained through an aggregate algorithm [17,18,26]. Instance-Based Explanations, on the other hand, rely on the whole time series instance to show the reasons why the model makes a judgment, such as features extracted from the entire time series instance [7,23], the most exemplifying examples of a particular classification made by the model [8,24], counter-examples that lead to changes in classification through minimal modification [5,12], etc.

It is not difficult to see that Time Points-Based Explanations and Subsequences-Based Explanations have difficulty showing the effect of chronological order when presenting explanations. On the other hand, Instance-Based Explanations are based on implicit assumptions, e.g., the feature or exemplifying examples they found are themselves explainable. And this assumption, as stated earlier, is not always true. Time-series data (especially longer or with more complex trends ones) are often difficult to understand, sometimes even for experts with domain knowledge.

3   Methodology

The preceding discourse led to the inspiration that a successful explanation method for time series models should prioritize the following two elements: *(i)* the ability to effectively analyze and visually demonstrate the impact of the chronological order of the input value on the model prediction, *(ii)* the avoidance of presenting overly length time series segments that are difficult for humans to

---

[1] https://github.com/HuangYiran/sbxai.

understand and single value that contains little information. The proposed explanation method is constructed based on these two principles, and its structure is depicted in Fig. 1(a). The framework consists of three modules: the Segment & Clustering Module, the Perturbation Module, and the Explanation Module.

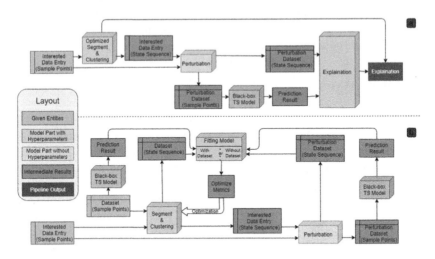

Fig. 1. (a) Description of the Whole Model Pipeline. (b) Details of the Hyperparameter Optimization Procedure for the Segment & Clustering Module.

3.1   Segment & Clustering Module

The Segment & Clustering Module is responsible for dividing all the time series from given data into small segments and categorizing them according to their similarity. This module aims to summarize the to-be-explained time series input (hereinafter referred to as Interested Data Entry x_I) into a series of clustered segments (hereinafter referred to as states) s_I that are easily understandable to humans.

To be more precisely, x_I is a time series input with length m (Eq. 1):

$$x_I = \{t_1, t_2, ..., t_m\} \tag{1}$$

After the processing of the Segment & Clustering Module, it will be transformed into a sequence of states s_I with length n, and each state has the same length J (Eq. 2):

$$s_I = \{g_1, g_2, ..., g_n\}, \quad n = \lceil m/J \rceil \tag{2}$$

in which the value of each state g_i is worked out from a clustering algorithm $G(e \mid K, T)$, in which e is the to-be-clustered segment, K is the number of clusters, and T is all the available Segments (Eq. 3):

$$g_i = G([t_{i*J+1}, ..., t_{(i+1)*J}] \mid K, T) \tag{3}$$

It's obvious that the module includes two essential hyperparameters, namely the length of the segment J and the number of clusters K. The proper setting of these two hyperparameters could be searched using Bayesian optimization. The basic idea is proper segmentation and clustering of the data shouldn't damage the information in the time series. So we train a Fitting Model $F(s)$, which takes the sequences of states as input and predicts the output of the to-be-explained Black-box Model. The better the Fitting Model performs, the better the Segment & Clustering Module works (Eq. 4).

$$\hat{K}, \hat{J} = \arg\max_{K,J} \sum_s ACC(F(s)) \tag{4}$$

The Fitting Model needs enough data to train, however, this is not ensured for some of the scenarios that demand the time series Black-box explanation. As shown in Fig. 1(b), two processes are presented to solve the problem.

The process that feeds data from the left side of the Fitting Model pertains to the scenario where the original dataset used to train the Black-box model is available during the explanation stage. For example, the model's trainer wants to get an explanation of the misclassified samples, to optimize the accuracy of the trained model further or to enhance its robustness against adversarial attacks. In this case, we don't need to worry about the data amount. We use all data entries in the given dataset to get T, as well as to train the Fitting Model.

The process that feeds data from the right side of the Fitting Model pertains to the scenario where the original dataset used to train the Black-box model is not available during the explanation stage. For example, when users of a Black-box model have concerns regarding the output. In this case, we process the x_I through the Segment & Clustering Module to obtain the state sequence representation of this entry s_I. Then we randomly shuffle s_I, for each random shuffle we also note down the corresponding original sample point representation of it. By this we get two perturbation datasets: the state sequence perturbation dataset and the sample points perturbation dataset. The state sequence perturbation dataset will be used as the input of the Fitting Model, and the sample points perturbation dataset will be input into the to-be-explained Black-box Model to get the label for the Fitting model.

3.2   Perturbation Module

The task of the perturbation module is to shuffle the s_I obtained from the previous module (Segment & Clustering Module) to get a perturbation dataset. At the same time, with the help of the one-to-one correspondence between the state and the original data, the sample points representation of the shuffled s_I can also be easily obtained. Thus, we could get the prediction of the Black-box model to the perturbation dataset. These two will serve as inputs to the next module.

3.3   Explanation Module

As the output of the previous module, we performed various chronological perturbations to the Interested Data Entry and obtained the prediction results of the Black-box model for these perturbations. By analyzing the response of the Black-box model to different perturbations, we can explain the behavior of the Black-box model. In this module, we fit an explainable model to the behavior of the Black-box model. Thus, the explanation of the fitted model can be used to explain the Black-box model.

In our study, we choose Hidden Markov Model (HMM) as the explainable model because its visualization is straightforward and clear. Taking an instance from 'AllgesturewiimoteY' dataset 'Pick-up' Class[2] and a Long Short Term Memory (LSTM) black box as an example, the final presented explanation consists of three parts. The first is the representation state generated by the Segment & Clustering Module (see Fig. 2(c)). Each state describes the center of a cluster. It represents a simple trend of data change, thus making it easy to understand. For example, state 0 here indicates maintaining stabilization, while states 1 and 3 distinguish between sinking and rising. Each state consists of multiple single values, and its complexity is determined by the length of the state. The second part of the explanation pertains to the importance of different features. This importance is obtained at the state level by using an existing counterfactual-based explanation method TS-MULE [21] and indicated through the length superimposed on the state transition curve of the Interested Data Entry, as shown in Fig. 2(b). The explanation identifies the initial segment of the instance (state 1) as crucial and assigns different importance values to it. The final part of the explanation centers on the significance of various state transitions, which is demonstrated by the transitions graph of the Hidden Markov Model (HMM) presented in Fig. 2(a). In this graph, each node represents a state, and each edge represents a transition, with each edge corresponding to a value that describes the importance of the corresponding transition. In this specific example, the edge from state 3 to state 1 is assigned a value of 1, whereas the value from state 1 to itself is 0.8. Notably, there is no edge from state 3 to itself, indicating that the corresponding value is 0. This leads us to conclude that the classification of this example is based on the sensor value being maintained in a stable state for an extended duration following a downward trend.

Figure 3 presents a visual depiction of TS-MULE [21]'s explanation of the selected instance. TS-MULE elucidates the instance through the significance of the original signal segment, represented by the color overlay on the value transition curve of the Interested Data Entry. As revealed in the Fig. 3, TS-MULE ascribes the classification of the given instance as a "pickup" primarily to the segment where the sensor value exhibits a decreasing trend, with the degree of importance commensurate with the degree of decrease.

In comparison to the SBXAI method, we found that: *(i)* Although TS-MULE assigns significance to each individual segment, the segments considered impor-

---

[2] It is performed when the user picks up the control device from its neutral motionless position and takes hold of it in a no particular predefined way [10].

tant vary widely. The manner in which these segments contribute to the prediction remains unclear. Conversely, SBXAI employs states derived from clustering techniques to characterize each segment, which is represented by a cluster kernel that outlines a prevalent trend among the respective clusters. For instance, the segments TS-MULE deems essential align with the state that delineates a descending trend, providing greater comprehensibility than the initial segments. *(ii)* Decisions in time series generally rely on value trends rather than the magnitude of discrete values, as exemplified by the process of "pickup" encompassing the progression from increasing to maintaining stabilization. TS-MULE solely emphasizes the significance of individual segments (in our example case sinking) while disregarding the sequential relationship between distinct segments (e.g., transitioning from sinking to maintaining stabilization). This alteration in the trend is distinctly observable within the state transition diagram pertaining to the SBXAI approach. *(iii)* TS-MULE argues that only the decreasing part of the values is relevant to the decision-making, without considering the stable part. This contradicts the class description.

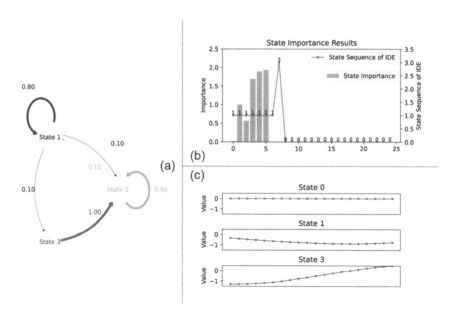

Fig. 2. (a) Transitions graph of HMM, showing the importance of different state transitions. (b) The state sequence of the interested data entry (IDE) and the background color showing the feature importance. (c) The Correspondence between the state and the cluster core. The x-coordinates in Figures (b), (c) both represent timestamp.

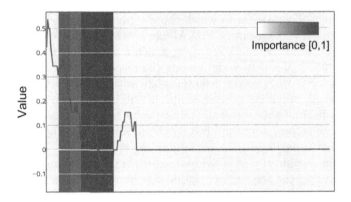

Fig. 3. Explanation for the example data entry given the TS-MULE, which 1) only contains the feature importance, 2) only shows the original data instead of summarizing the characteristic of the trend.

4   Experiments and Evaluation

In the preceding section, we demonstrated the manner in which SBXAI explains a given instance. In this section, we empirically validate the reliability of the generated explanation (how accurately the explanation found by the proposed method fits the Black-box model's behavior toward the prediction).

Given a dataset, we randomly sample items from the dataset and explain them with the selected methods. Then we modify the item according to the explanation. Suppose the Black-box prediction changed after the modification. We record the modification as a success. For each dataset, we repeat this process 100 times to get an average attack success rate (ASR), which indicates the importance of the rules broken by the modification. The performance of the following modification methods are compared: *(i)* replace the value of a random position in the item with the least important state found by the proposed method in the given item (Random-Fe); *(ii)* exchange the position of random two states in the given sequence (Random-Seq); *(iii)* remove important feature found by TS-MULE [21] with the proposed Segment Module (TS-MULE-Fe); *(iv)* exchange the position of the state pair considered to be the most important by the proposed method (SBXAI-Seq). For example, given state sequence [abcba], the proposed method found out that the sequence relationship 'ab' is important to identify the class of the item. We exchange the position of the states and transform the original sequence to [bacba]. We try to emphasize the meaning of the successful attack by limiting the strength of the applied modification. During the experiment, we utilize the Hyperopt [1] package to do the optimization and set its hyperparameter max_iter to 100 and the optimization algorithm to 'tpe.suggest'.

For the reliability of the results, we conducted experiments on the UCR datasets [4] with various numbers of classes and sequence lengths. The Black-box model used in the experiment is constructed with Long Short Term Memory

Table 1. Attack Success Rate (ASR) of different modification methods.

Dataset	Number Class	Sequence Length	Random-Fe	Random-Seq	Fe	SBXAI-Seq
AllGestureWiimote	10	vary	10	7	86	89
Car	4	577	16	10	63	68
YoGA	2	426	19	12	76	81
ShapesAll	60	512	13	17	50	72
PigAirwayPressure	50	2000	3	9	18	95
Mallat	8	1024	10	5	98	88
InlineSkate	7	1882	20	17	42	85
CricketY	12	300	11	16	69	83
RefrigerationDevices	3	720	11	10	46	64
MixedShapesRegularTrain	5	1024	3	2	37	65
BirdChicken	2	512	13	28	79	89
WordSynonyms	25	270	12	12	57	64
DodgerLoopGame	2	288	0	20	42	72
FreezerRegularTrain	2	301	16	15	45	96
EthanolLevel	4	1751	11	8	96	100
LargeKitchenAppliances	3	720	6	8	56	72
FiftyWords	50	270	8	17	74	75
ArrowHead	3	251	16	20	74	84
EOGHorizontalSignal	12	1250	18	14	70	80
ACSF1	10	1460	0	1	17	90

layers. To the best of our knowledge, no heuristic method employing sequential relations has been used to explain black-box models. Therefore, we did not compare the proposed method with other sequential-based explanatory methods in the experiment. The search space and the Black-box models are presented in https://github.com/HuangYiran/sbxai.

As summarized in Table 1, the element found by the two different modification methods, TS-MULE-Fe and SBXAI-Seq, have a substantial impact on the Black-box prediction. The average attack success rate for modifying the state order is 79.9%, while that for eliminating important status is 60.4%. These results suggest that the explanation generated by the proposed method is reasonable. And we can conclude that the prediction of a time series depends not only on its states, but also on the sequential relationship between them. For time series data, sequential changes between states have a more pronounced effect on decisions than the removal of individual states. In addition, we find that some models are strongly influenced by the sequential relationship and are almost unaffected by the individual states, e.g., 'PigAirwayPressure'. This is likely because the states considered important appear multiple times in the same item. Besides, no significant correlation was found between the attack success rate, number of classes, and sequence length.

5   Conclusion

In this paper, we propose a method to explain the time series Black-box model in terms of sequential relations and experimentally demonstrate the correctness of the explanation obtained by this method. However, there is still room for improvement, both in experiments and in the further development of the algorithm. For example, all the Black-box models have the same structure in the experiment. The impact of the proposed method on models of different architectures should be verified. Besides, we believe that further improvements could be made to the algorithms by enlarging the search space, e.g., adding more segmentation and clustering methods.

Acknowledgements. This work was partially funded by the Ministry of Science, Research and the Arts Baden-Wuerttemberg as part of the SDSC-BW, by the German Ministry for Research as well as by Education as part of SDI-S (Grant 01IS22095A) and by Helmholtz European Partnership for Technological Advancement (HEPTA).

References

1. Bergstra, J., Yamins, D., Cox, D.D., et al.: Hyperopt: a python library for optimizing the hyperparameters of machine learning algorithms (2013)
2. Cho, S., Chang, W., Lee, G., Choi, J.: Interpreting internal activation patterns in deep temporal neural networks by finding prototypes. In: Proceedings of the 27th ACM SIGKDD Conference on Knowledge Discovery & Data Mining, pp. 158–166 (2021)
3. Crabbé, J., Van Der Schaar, M.: Explaining time series predictions with dynamic masks. In: International Conference on Machine Learning, pp. 2166–2177. PMLR (2021)
4. Dau, H.A., et al.: The UCR time series archive. IEEE/CAA J. Automatica Sinica **6**(6), 1293–1305 (2019)
5. Delaney, E., Greene, D., Keane, M.T.: Instance-based counterfactual explanations for time series classification. In: Sánchez-Ruiz, A.A., Floyd, M.W. (eds.) ICCBR 2021. LNCS (LNAI), vol. 12877, pp. 32–47. Springer, Cham (2021). https://doi.org/10.1007/978-3-030-86957-1_3
6. Doddaiah, R., Parvataraju, P., Rundensteiner, E., Hartvigsen, T.: Explaining deep multi-class time series classifiers (2023)
7. Gay, D., Guigourès, R., Boullé, M., Clérot, F.: Feature extraction over multiple representations for time series classification. In: Appice, A., Ceci, M., Loglisci, C., Manco, G., Masciari, E., Ras, Z.W. (eds.) NFMCP 2013. LNCS (LNAI), vol. 8399, pp. 18–34. Springer, Cham (2014). https://doi.org/10.1007/978-3-319-08407-7_2
8. Gee, A.H., Garcia-Olano, D., Ghosh, J., Paydarfar, D.: Explaining deep classification of time-series data with learned prototypes. In: CEUR Workshop Proceedings, vol. 2429, p. 15. NIH Public Access (2019)
9. Guidotti, R., Monreale, A., Spinnato, F., Pedreschi, D., Giannotti, F.: Explaining any time series classifier. In: 2020 IEEE Second International Conference on Cognitive Machine Intelligence (CogMI), pp. 167–176. IEEE (2020)
10. Guna, J., Humar, I., Pogačnik, M.: Intuitive gesture based user identification system. In: 2012 35th International Conference on Telecommunications and Signal Processing (TSP), pp. 629–633. IEEE (2012)

11. Huang, Y., et al.: McXai: local model-agnostic explanation as two games. arXiv preprint arXiv:2201.01044 (2022)
12. Karlsson, I., Rebane, J., Papapetrou, P., Gionis, A.: Locally and globally explainable time series tweaking. Knowl. Inf. Syst. **62**(5), 1671–1700 (2020). https://doi.org/10.1007/s10115-019-01389-4
13. Lozano Murciego, Á., Jiménez-Bravo, D.M., Valera Román, A., De Paz Santana, J.F., Moreno-García, M.N.: Context-aware recommender systems in the music domain: a systematic literature review. Electronics **10**(13), 1555 (2021)
14. Mercier, D., Dengel, A., Ahmed, S.: PatchX: explaining deep models by intelligible pattern patches for time-series classification. In: 2021 International Joint Conference on Neural Networks (IJCNN), pp. 1–8. IEEE (2021)
15. Munir, M., Siddiqui, S.A., Küsters, F., Mercier, D., Dengel, A., Ahmed, S.: TSXplain: demystification of DNN decisions for time-series using natural language and statistical features. In: Tetko, I.V., Kůrková, V., Karpov, P., Theis, F. (eds.) ICANN 2019. LNCS, vol. 11731, pp. 426–439. Springer, Cham (2019). https://doi.org/10.1007/978-3-030-30493-5_43
16. Parvatharaju, P.S., Doddaiah, R., Hartvigsen, T., Rundensteiner, E.A.: Learning saliency maps to explain deep time series classifiers. In: Proceedings of the 30th ACM International Conference on Information & Knowledge Management, pp. 1406–1415 (2021)
17. Patri, O.P., Panangadan, A.V., Chelmis, C., Prasanna, V.K.: Extracting discriminative features for event-based electricity disaggregation. In: 2014 IEEE Conference on Technologies for Sustainability (SusTech), pp. 232–238. IEEE (2014)
18. Rakthanmanon, T., Keogh, E.: Fast shapelets: a scalable algorithm for discovering time series shapelets. In: Proceedings of the 2013 SIAM International Conference on Data Mining, pp. 668–676. SIAM (2013)
19. Schilit, B., Adams, N., Want, R.: Context-aware computing applications. In: 1994 First Workshop on Mobile Computing Systems and Applications, pp. 85–90. IEEE (1994)
20. Schlegel, U., Arnout, H., El-Assady, M., Oelke, D., Keim, D.A.: Towards a rigorous evaluation of XAI methods on time series. In: 2019 IEEE/CVF International Conference on Computer Vision Workshop (ICCVW), pp. 4197–4201. IEEE (2019)
21. Schlegel, U., Vo, D.L., Keim, D.A., Seebacher, D.: TS-MULE: local interpretable model-agnostic explanations for time series forecast models. In: Kamp, M., et al. (eds.) ECML PKDD 2021, Part I. CCIS, vol. 1524, pp. 5–14. Springer, Cham (2022). https://doi.org/10.1007/978-3-030-93736-2_1
22. Senin, P., Malinchik, S.: SAX-VSM: interpretable time series classification using SAX and vector space model. In: 2013 IEEE 13th International Conference on Data Mining, pp. 1175–1180. IEEE (2013)
23. Shalaeva, V., Alkhoury, S., Marinescu, J., Amblard, C., Bisson, G.: Multi-operator decision trees for explainable time-series classification. In: Medina, J., et al. (eds.) IPMU 2018. CCIS, vol. 853, pp. 86–99. Springer, Cham (2018). https://doi.org/10.1007/978-3-319-91473-2_8
24. Tang, W., Liu, L., Long, G.: Interpretable time-series classification on few-shot samples. In: 2020 International Joint Conference on Neural Networks (IJCNN), pp. 1–8. IEEE (2020)
25. Theissler, A., Spinnato, F., Schlegel, U., Guidotti, R.: Explainable AI for time series classification: a review, taxonomy and research directions. IEEE Access **10**, 100700–100724 (2022)

26. Ye, L., Keogh, E.: Time series shapelets: a new primitive for data mining. In: Proceedings of the 15th ACM SIGKDD International Conference on Knowledge Discovery and Data Mining, pp. 947–956 (2009)
27. Zhou, L., Ma, C., Shi, X., Zhang, D., Li, W., Wu, L.: Salience-CAM: visual explanations from convolutional neural networks via salience score. In: 2021 International Joint Conference on Neural Networks (IJCNN), pp. 1–8. IEEE (2021)

A Deep Dive into Perturbations as Evaluation Technique for Time Series XAI

Udo Schlegel[(✉)] and Daniel A. Keim

University of Konstanz, Universitätsstraße 10, 78464 Konstanz, Germany
{u.schlegel,daniel.keim}@uni-konstanz.de

Abstract. Explainable Artificial Intelligence (XAI) has gained significant attention recently as the demand for transparency and interpretability of machine learning models has increased. In particular, XAI for time series data has become increasingly important in finance, healthcare, and climate science. However, evaluating the quality of explanations, such as attributions provided by XAI techniques, remains challenging. This paper provides an in-depth analysis of using perturbations to evaluate attributions extracted from time series models. A perturbation analysis involves systematically modifying the input data and evaluating the impact on the attributions generated by the XAI method. We apply this approach to several state-of-the-art XAI techniques and evaluate their performance on three time series classification datasets. Our results demonstrate that the perturbation analysis approach can effectively evaluate the quality of attributions and provide insights into the strengths and limitations of XAI techniques. Such an approach can guide the selection of XAI methods for time series data, e.g., focusing on return time rather than precision, and facilitate the development of more reliable and interpretable machine learning models for time series analysis.

Keywords: Explainable AI · XAI Evaluation · XAI for Time Series

1 Introduction

Artificial intelligence (AI) has become an integral part of our daily lives, from the personalized advertisement we receive on social media to conversational AI (chatbots) answering questions of users and customers using deep neural networks. However, as the complexity of deep neural network models increases, so does the difficulty in understanding how they get to their decisions [7]. A lack of interpretability can lead to severe consequences in critical domains such as finance, healthcare, and transportation, including financial losses, medical errors, and even loss of life by providing wrong decisions if complex models are deployed [16]. One promising approach to addressing such issues is through the usage of explainable artificial intelligence (XAI), which seeks to provide insights into the inner workings of complex models and the factors that drive

L. Longo (Ed.): xAI 2023, CCIS 1903, pp. 165–180, 2023.
https://doi.org/10.1007/978-3-031-44070-0_9

their decision-making [7]. One particular area of interest is time series data, which is characterized by the sequential nature of its observations and the inter-dependencies between them, as more sensors generate a massive amount of data and more tasks are tackled by complex models [25].

In recent years, a growing body of research has focused on developing XAI techniques tailored explicitly for time series data [25]. These techniques often rely on the concept of attributions, which aim to identify the contributions of individual features and time points to the overall prediction made by a model [25]. By providing insights into which parts of the input data are most relevant to the output, attributions can help users understand the reasoning behind the model's decision-making process [18]. However, the evaluation of such attributions is not trivial [19]. To address the challenge of evaluating the quality of explanations for time series data, perturbation analysis has emerged as a promising evaluation technique [17,22]. Perturbation analysis involves systematically modifying the input data and assessing the impact on the attributions generated by XAI methods [19]. By perturbing the input data, it is possible to evaluate the robustness of the explanations provided by XAI methods [25]. However, the effectiveness of perturbation analysis for evaluating the quality of attributions for time series data has not been extensively studied [19].

In this paper, we apply attribution techniques from various fields to a convolution neural network trained on time series classification data to evaluate and inspect the generated attributions in detail using perturbations, which involves systematically altering the input data and observing the effect on the model's output. We investigate the performance of attribution techniques compared to each other based on the perturbation analysis result and explore the perturbation changes based on these attributions to gain insights into the model. Through such an analysis, we can identify spurious correlations and shortcuts in the complex models and thus enable developers to potentially improve models by debugging datasets. We show that our convolution neural network trained on time series classification learned certain shortcuts to achieve state-of-the-art performances. Based on these experiments and results, we provide guidelines for the application of attribution techniques for time series classification and release our evaluation framework to investigate other attribution techniques.

Thus, we contribute: (1) an in-depth analysis of attribution techniques on time series classification for deep learning models using a perturbation analysis, (2) insights into convolution neural networks trained on time series based on the generated attributions, (3) guidelines and a framework for applying attribution techniques for time series models with a perturbation analysis card for reporting. We first look into related work, and then we introduce the perturbation analysis methodology and the experiment setup we use for our deep dive. Here we also propose perturbation analysis cards as a guideline to report the results of an evaluation. Next, we present our results and discuss the impact of our conclusions for attribution techniques applied to time series. Lastly, in future work, we motivate new measures for the evaluation of attributions on time series data.

Results and source code of the experiments is online available at: https://github.com/visual-xai-for-time-series/time-series-xai-perturbation-analysis.

2   Related Work

Explainable AI (XAI) accelerated through several surveys [1,7] and techniques, e.g., LIME [15] and SHAP [12] in the last few years. Especially, attributions are prevalent in the image domain as heatmap explanations are easy to understand for users [10]. Some theoretical works dig into the backgrounds of why models learn certain shortcuts to solve tasks [6] and thus enable further explanations for decisions. However, evaluating explanations is still a slowly growing area with limited work toward benchmarking different techniques against each other [8]. Further, shortcuts or spurious correlations are not trivial to detect in explanations and need an in-depth analysis to be able to identify these [29].

Some works started to collect possible evaluation techniques [14] and categorized these into five measurements: mental model, explanation usefulness and satisfaction, user trust and reliance, human-AI task performance, and computational measures. The first few measures focus on evaluating with or in cooperation with humans and are thus heavily influenced by human factors. The computational measures exclude human factors and focus on purely automatic evaluation of explanations. In this work, we inspect the computational measures and, more precisely, the explainer fidelity of the attribution technique on the model to show how the attributions fit the model.

XAI for time series classification (TSC), on the one hand, incorporates previously proposed explanation techniques from other fields and introduces the time dependence into some of the techniques [25]. Theissler et al. [25] categorize possible explanations for TSC into time point, subsequence, and instance explanations. All these operate on a different level of the time series and are thus unique in their explanation and evaluation. In this work, we tackle time point explanations and, to be more precise, attributions to highlight and explore shortcuts and spurious correlations. As Schlegel et al. [17] and others [13,22,25] demonstrated, attributions techniques such as LIME [15], SHAP [12], LRP [4], GradCAM [21], Integrated Gradients [24], and more [20], produce working attributions on time series to extract explanations from a model. However, in most cases, only purely computational measures are applied to the attributions, which are not further inspected, e.g., Mercier et al. [13] to gain deeper insights.

Schlegel et al. [17] started by using a perturbation analysis on attribution techniques applied to TSC using various perturbation functions to highlight that techniques for images and text are also working on time series. Based on such preliminary experiments, they enhanced their approach with additional perturbation functions to showcase deeper insights into the fidelity evaluation [19]. Mercier et al. [13] enhanced these perturbations with further measures from the image domain, such as (in)fidelity and sensitivity [27]. Simic et al. [22] extended the proposed methods by Schlegel et al. [19] with out-of-distribution detecting functions and gave guidelines for the selection of attribution techniques and the size of the window for the perturbation. Turbe et al. [26] enhance previous approaches with another metric to improve the comparison of the attribution techniques and the ability to demonstrate their fidelity towards the model. However, all of these approaches do not look into the attributions and the produced values to investigate further into the techniques behind the attributions and the models. Thus, an in-depth analysis is needed to investigate the attributions generated for time series classification models.

3   Perturbation Analysis

We use the perturbation analysis approach by Schlegel et al. [19] to generate attributions, verify, and compare them using the proposed perturbation function strategies [17,22]. We extend the comparison by calculating the Euclidean and cosine distance between the original and the perturbed time series instance and the Euclidean and cosine distance between the original attributions of the dataset and the attributions of the perturbed instances of the dataset. Collecting these results can help us have a more in-depth analysis of the attribution techniques and reveal relations between attributions and models. However, we first need to establish the general perturbation analysis.

Let $D = (X, Y)$ be a time series classification dataset with X as the time series samples and Y as the time series labels. $X = \{ts_1, ts_2, ..., ts_n\}$ contains n time series samples with m time points for each sample represented as $ts = \{tp_1, tp_2, ..., tp_m\}$, where tp_1 is the value for the ith time point of ts. $Y = \{l_1, l_2, ..., l_n\}$ contains n labels one label for each time series sample. Let $M(ts, \theta) = y'$ be a time series classification model which predicts a label y' based on a time series input ts and has the parameters θ. Let $A(X, M, \theta)$ be an XAI technique for generating attributions for the time series data. The original attributions for X generated by A can be represented as $A(X, M, \theta) = \{a_1, a_2, ..., a_m\}$, where a_i is the attribution score for the ith time point of X, M the time series classification model for which the attributions are calculated, and θ the parameters of the attribution technique.

To perform perturbation analysis, we introduce a perturbation function g that modifies X in a controlled manner. Specifically, we define a perturbed time series dataset X' as:

$$X' = g(X, A, \xi) \tag{1}$$

Our perturbation function g modifies the dataset X based on the attributions A and a threshold ξ. The value for the modification can be changed and depends on the selected function g, e.g., exchange to zero. The threshold ξ can be set to a value by hand or some other function, e.g., using the 90-percentile of the attributions so that the attributions, e.g., a_i the ith element, above the threshold, will be modified to the previously set value, e.g., zero. Figure 1 demonstrates the approach with zero perturbations on attributions with high values.

The original X and the perturbed dataset X' get predicted with the model M to get $M(X) = Y'$ and $M(X') = Y''$. Based on Schlegel et al. [19], we incorporate a quality metric qm, e.g., accuracy, to compare the performance of the model M with the original X and the perturbed dataset X'. For the time series classification, we assume that the qm decreases after the original data changes, and thus the labels are not fitting anymore [17]. We further assume

Fig. 1. Starting from a time series ts, we use a selected attribution technique A to get attributions. Based on the attributions, we use a selected perturbation function g to set highly relevant time points, e.g., to zero. Further information in Schlegel et al. [19].

a suiting attribution technique decreases the performance more heavily as the most relevant parts of the input data get perturbed [8]. Thus, we assume:

$$qm(Y', Y) \leq qm(Y'', Y) \tag{2}$$

However, in some cases, the scores are very similar [13,17], and a deeper investigation into the attributions is necessary to find similarities or dissimilarities in the relevances of the techniques. Thus, we do not only compare the quality metrics but also focus on the distances between the original X and the perturbed X' datasets. We apply the Euclidean and cosine distances to the datasets as these are common distance functions for time series [2] to collect the changes of the perturbation function g. We define the Euclidean distance as:

$$Euc(X, X') = \sqrt{\sum_{i=1}^{n} (ts_i - ts_i')^2} \tag{3}$$

where $X = ts_1, ts_2, ..., ts_n$ and $X' = ts_1', ts_2', ..., ts_n'$ are the two time series being compared. And we define the cosine distance as:

$$Cos(X, X') = 1 - \frac{\sum_{i=1}^{n} ts_i \times ts_i'}{\sqrt{\sum_{i=1}^{n} ts_i^2} \times \sqrt{\sum_{i=1}^{n} ts_i'^2}} \tag{4}$$

where $X = ts_1, ts_2, ..., ts_n$ and $X' = ts_1', ts_2', ..., ts_n'$ are the two time series being compared. These changes enable us to compare the attributions not only on a performance level but on a raw level directly on the data.

4   Experiments with Perturbation Analysis

For our analysis, we look into the time series that changed and those that did not change during the perturbation analysis. We especially want to understand the attribution distributions to investigate the attribution techniques responsible for fitting explanations, with high fidelity [14], on the models. Fitting explanations in our assumptions are techniques that change the prediction of more samples in a perturbation analysis [13,17,19]. However, a general measure and metric for evaluating explanations are essential, but another factor is the attributions, as these can also hide information or present spurious correlations [29]. E.g., the question of how attributions are distributed over the techniques arises.

To answer such questions and others, we use the changes from Y (old prediction) to Y' (new prediction) to look into the samples that changed their prediction and those that do not change. We especially want to know when a change in the prediction happened, e.g., after how many removals based on the attributions and the perturbation strategy. Thus, we look at the prediction changes from one class to the other. E.g., in a binary classification with the assumption from above, the predictions change from one to the other class to demonstrate that the attributions highlight relevant time points for the model. Thus, we slowly perturb more and more values from the time series until there is a change in prediction. We use the percentile values (99, 98, ..., 25) as a threshold for the perturbation and record when the change happens. Further, we collect the skewness of the attributions of the changed and unchanged predictions. With such an exploration of the distributions of the attributions, we enable to inspect patterns inside of the attributions generated by different techniques. Also, the distributions of the skewness enable to have another factor for the comparison of the attribution techniques. Lastly, we do not only collect the skewness but also the Euclidean and the cosine distances of the original sample to the perturbed instance with regard to the changed and unchanged predictions. All these different collected statistics and properties can help us to identify various findings, insights, and correlations in the attribution techniques as we collect as much data from our perturbation analysis as possible.

Summary – Overall, we have the following dimensions we want to experiment on: a) attribution techniques, b) perturbation strategy. We collect and analyze the following properties: a) mean of the raw data samples of the changed and unchanged predictions; b) skewness of attributions based on the changed and unchanged predictions after the perturbation; c) new class distributions of the changed and unchanged predictions after the perturbation; d) amount of relevant attributions needed to perturb an instance to another class prediction. Figure 2 presents the collected properties using a perturbation analysis card with various statistics aggregated and visualized for easier analysis. We created these perturbation cards for all the experiments.

Hypotheses –   After we established our experiment setup, we generated hypotheses around the results of the experiment on the basis of other work. Based on the preliminary experiments by Schlegel et al. [17], we generated the hypothesis that SHAP or SHAP derivatives will lead to the best results for the TSC task. Based on the results of Simic et al. [22], we will further look into the other attributions and double-check the results of Schlegel et al. [17] and the SHAP results even if SHAP results are less consistent [22]. Based on Simic et al. [22], we further look into the different perturbation strategies as we hypothesize that using one strategy is not enough to find a suitable attribution technique. Based on Geirhos et al. [6], we want also to check if there are patterns in the data the attributions show as relevant to find shortcuts the model learned to classify the data. E.g., using certain maximum or minimum values to separate one class from the other in a binary classification problem.

Perturbation Analysis Card – The perturbation analysis card is our proposed approach to reporting the results of our perturbation analysis strategies and techniques. Figure 2 shows such a perturbation analysis card with meta information (S), bar charts about the switch from one class to another (C), bar charts for the distribution of distances (D), statistics about the attributions (A), and a line plot visualization about the raw time series data (R).

Starting on top, Fig. 2(S), a short introduction presents a description of the dataset, the attribution technique, and the perturbation strategy. Right under the description, a stacked vertical bar chart shows a short glimpse of how good or bad the overall perturbation was. A good perturbation with an attribution technique presents just a lot of blue in this bar chart, while a bad perturbation shows a lot of orange in the visualization. Next to it, the exact numbers of the changed and unchanged samples are shown so that comparable numbers enhance the fast glance with other cards.

Figure 2(C) gives a detailed view of the perturbation and the changes there. The bar chart on the left visualizes the classes of the changed and unchanged predictions. For the changed prediction, the visualization also further presents the classes before and after the perturbation. Such visualization can help to identify spurious correlations as a model could, for instance, learn one feature of one class for the prediction. The bar chart on the right at (C) shows the number of perturbed values needed to change the prediction. The fewer changes needed, the better the attribution can identify relevant values.

In Fig. 2(D), the histogram of the distances between the perturbed and the original instances are shown. On top of (D), the Euclidean distances, and on the bottom of (D), the cosine distance can help to find clusters of needed changes for the perturbation of the samples by revealing a trend towards a certain distance range. Also, the distances can be used to compare the individual attribution techniques against each other. A smaller distance range, together with a lower number of perturbed values, presents a more focused technique.

Figure 2(A) visualizes more statistical information about the attributions. The plot on top of (A) shows the skewness of the attributions of the samples of the dataset. On the bottom, the means of the attributions are visualized. Through these, a general trend of the changed and unchanged samples and their attributions can be seen. Especially, outliers are interesting as a starting point for deeper analysis with other methods and visualizations.

Lastly, in Fig. 2(R), the time series time point means of the changed and unchanged samples can be inspected. So, for every time point in the time series, the mean of it over the subset (changed or unchanged) of the whole dataset is calculated and visualized. Thus, in the case of, e.g., FordA, with a standardization of the dataset, the samples slowly converge to zero. The visualization enables to spot large differences between the changed and unchanged samples.

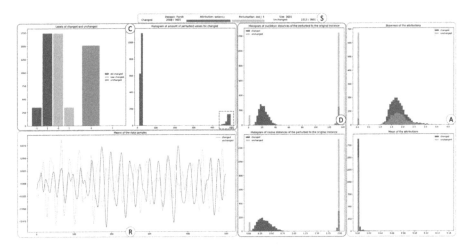

Fig. 2. Perturbation analysis card for the FordA dataset: the top description (S) contains general statistics for the card, starting with the dataset, the attribution technique, and the perturbation strategy. Beneath are the statistics for the amount of changed and unchanged sample predictions encoded as a progress bar and with numbers. The plots in (C) give a more detailed insight into the class changes after the perturbation. The left plot presents the amount of changed and unchanged samples for each class and also visualizes the class change for changed predictions. The right plot shows the number of perturbed values when a change in prediction happens. In (D), the distances of the original to the perturbed instance are shown. The top presents the Euclidean distance between the pairs, and the bottom shows the cosine distance. (A) presents the skew (top) and mean (bottom) of the attributions for the changed and unchanged sample predictions. In (R), the mean of every value at a specific time point is visualized for the changed and unchanged samples. (Color figure online)

5   Results and Discussion

Our current experiment setup evolves around an in-depth analysis of the attributions of seven attribution techniques (Saliency, IntegratedGradients, DeepLift, Occlusion, GradientShap, DeepLiftShap, KernelShap) based on the implementations in Captum[1]. We incorporate 16 perturbation strategies, two based on Simic et al. [22], six based on Schlegel et al. [19], and eight extensions we describe later. We implemented nine single time point perturbations (zero, mean, inverse, dataset mean, dataset max, dataset min, OOD high, OOD low, random between min and max) and seven subsequence perturbations (zero, subsequence mean, dataset mean, inverse, OOD high, OOD low, random between min and max). The subsequence length is fixed to ten percent of the length of the data.

We focus on the UCR benchmark datasets [5] and take three of the most extensive datasets (FordA, FordB, ElectricDevices) to investigate data characteristics. However, our approach can be applied to any time series classification

---

[1] Captum is a Pytorch-based XAI module for Python: https://captum.ai/.

dataset. The FordA and FordB are sensor data with a length of 500 and provide an anomaly detection binary classification task. FordA has 3601 samples in the training set and 1320 in the test set. FordB has 3636 samples in the training set and 810 in the test set. The ElectricDevices dataset is shorter, with only 96 time points. However, the dataset has 8926 training samples and 7711 test samples.

We investigate two architectures of convolutional neural networks. The first architecture tackles the FordA and FordB datasets. The model consists of three 1D convolutional layers with a kernel size of three and increases the channels from one to 10 to 50 to 100. A max-pooling of three after the convolutional layer decreases the size again. A ReLu activation function activates the neuron. Afterward, a fully connected layer with 100 neurons and a ReLu function uses the feature maps from the convolutional layers to process the data further. And lastly, another fully connected layer with two neurons classifies the data with a softmax activation on top. We train the model with a batch size of 120 and the Adam optimizer [11]. The second architecture is trained on the ElectricDevices data and introduces a residual from the input to the fully connected layers. The original input gets downsampled using a 1D convolution with kernel size seven for the residual addition right before the fully connected layers.

We train our models using the cross-entropy loss for multi-label classification on the datasets for 500 epochs. Our models achieve for FordA an accuracy of 0.99 for the training set and 0.89 for the test set, demonstrating overfitting to the training data. Our models achieve for FordB an accuracy of 0.99 for the training set and 0.70 for the test set, demonstrating overfitting to the training data. Our models achieve for ElectricDevices an accuracy of 0.94 for the training set and 0.64 for the test set, demonstrating overfitting to the training data. As Ismail Fawaz et al. [9] showed, even our simple models are not too far from the state-of-the-art with other more sophisticated models. However, as we want to analyze our model, we look into the attributions of the training data, and thus our overfitting is a nice bonus to investigate spurious correlations and shortcuts [6].

Results – First, we start with the FordA dataset; next, we will present the FordB results, and lastly, the ElectricDevices dataset. FordA demonstrates interesting results regarding the attribution techniques and the perturbation strategies. The best working strategies are setting the perturbed value to an out-of-distribution low [26] on a subsequence [19] as you can see in Fig. 6. Especially, the saliency method [23] achieves the best result regarding the flip of predictions by flipping 2088 of 3601 samples, as also seen in Fig. 2. However, the KernelSHAP method [12] comes close to the flip with just 39 less with 2049 flips. Also, as seen in Fig. 2 on the plot on the right, the perturbation strategy out-of-distribution low changes the class quite late with a lot of perturbed values. Such an effect is unwanted in many cases as the model is, so to say, attacked by an adversarial attack outside of the distribution of the original data. In some cases, we can use such a method to test the model on data shifts, as, for example, the attributions can shift heavily. However, for our focus on the model itself, such an adversarial attack is interesting but does not show internal decision makings for the dataset we are interested in.

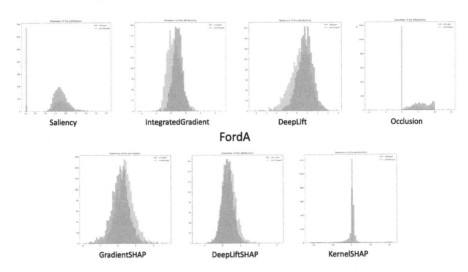

Fig. 3. Skewness distribution of the attribution techniques on the FordA dataset. Clear differences in the distributions of the attributions are visible. Further, the differences between changed and unchanged sample predictions and their attributions in the distributions are observable and show two different patterns in the techniques.

However, we also notice that the perturbation strategy heavily influences the best working method. If we switch, for example, to a perturbation to zero, we see Occlusion [28] as the winner in Fig. 6. Such a change in the best working technique demonstrates that the perturbation analysis just with one strategy is not enough to compare attribution techniques. We need multiple strategies to decide on one technique. However, we can also further take a deeper look into the attributions themselves. Focusing on the different skewness of the attributions and their distributions as seen in Fig. 3, we can already see some trends toward techniques enabling an easier inspection of the method and how well the method performs for the perturbation analysis. Especially, KernelSHAP in Fig. 3 demonstrates a nice pattern with two nearly not overlapping distributions. Such a nice distribution can help us to decide on one attribution technique.

The model for the FordB dataset is a bit worse than for the FordA dataset, which leads, in most cases, to worse performance in the perturbation analysis [22]. However, again the KernelSHAP and Saliency generate good working attributions for the change in the prediction for the perturbation to zero strategy. For this dataset, KernelSHAP achieves to change of 3472 from 3636 samples as seen in Fig. 7. Especially interesting is the distribution of the skewness of the attributions. A more in detail analysis of these two peaks could lead to further insights into the model and the attributions, but such an analysis needs another visualization, e.g., projecting the attributions in a scatter plot. However, if we further inspect our corresponding model card in Fig. 4, we can see that on the plot on the right, the change happens if a lot of values are removed from the original sample. Such a result is also observable in the other perturbation cards for

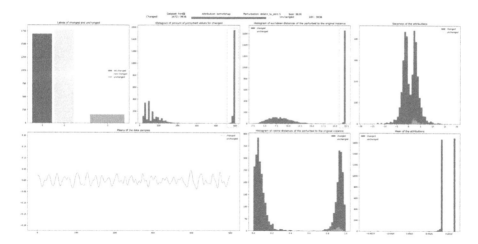

Fig. 4. Perturbation analysis card for the FordB dataset. The visualizations show a very distinct pattern. For the means of the raw samples (R), the few unchanged samples compose quite a diverse pattern, while the changed ones go to zero based on their standardization. However, the plot on the top (C) with the orange marker presents a pattern we do not want to have in a perturbation analysis, as it shows that we need to perturb a lot of data to achieve a change in prediction. (Color figure online)

the other techniques. In our study, we have identified a possible shortcut [6] that our model has learned from the training data. We speculate that the shortcut consists of a certain range or specific time points which need to be in a certain range of values to be classified as one class or the other class, and if we destroy this property, we change the prediction. So, our model learns a static version or range for one class and classifies everything else into the other class. Such a model does have more in common with an outlier detector than with a wanted classifier. Thus, we identified a shortcut of the model to be able to improve the classification without using all available features [6].

The ElectricDevices dataset is harder for the model as we do not only have a binary classification problem but seven classes the model needs to separate. However, as before, not even the state-of-the-art performance is as accurate as possible [9], which leads to worse attributions and a more diverse perturbation analysis result. Again, KernelSHAP performs best with a change of 8906 from 8926 samples with the values perturbed to the global max as seen in the perturbation card of Fig. 5. However, also IntegratedGradients [24] works well, but only with another perturbation strategy, namely changing the perturbed value to the global mean of the dataset. The dataset demonstrates quite nicely that the attribution techniques need different perturbation strategies to reveal the models' internal decision-making. Some of the techniques focus on different features the model learned as the ranking of the best-performing attribution techniques based on the perturbation analysis changes from strategy to strategy for this dataset. Additionally, when we delve into the labels of the changed and

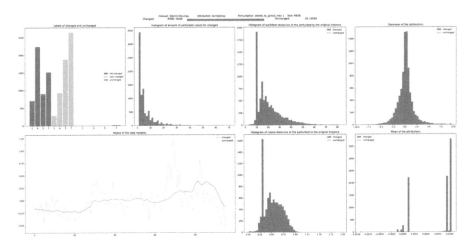

Fig. 5. Perturbation analysis card for the ElectircDevices dataset. The skewness distribution is quite interesting as it nearly presents a Gaussian distribution, with the mean being more sparse and quite focused on only three large pillars.

unchanged predictions, we notice that various attribution methods alter different labels in the perturbation. For example, KernelSHAP seems to modify every class besides seven, whereas Saliency influences classes other than five and six. However, unlike the previous FordB dataset, we do not see an unwanted perturbation pattern in the amount of perturbed values visualization. Such an effect presents that the attribution techniques are more suitable for the dataset and model than for the FordB model.

Summary – As we have seen in our results (Fig. 6, Fig. 7, Fig. 8), KernelSHAP performs quite well but takes a lot of time to calculate the attributions. Due to the sampling-based approach of KernelSHAP, the attributions are not deterministic and can vary from multiple computational runs. Further, in many cases, Saliency (or Vanilla Gradient multiplied by the Input) works surprisingly well and is only sometimes improved by additional extensions on top, such as IntegratedGradients. Thus, Saliency provides a promising variant for future experiments and techniques on top of it. So, if the attribution (explanation) is time-critical, Saliency is a well-suited method. If it is not time-critical, KernelSHAP provides the best-working attributions based on our experiments. Our collected data has even more insights and findings using the proposed perturbation analysis cards, which we look forward to analyzing and publishing with the code. The published source code can be used as a framework to experiment on more datasets, and the perturbation analysis cards can be used to report the results. The GitHub repository can be explored with more perturbation analysis cards and JSON data for the collected results of our experiments.

FordA / 3601	Saliency	IntegratedGradients	DeepLIFT	Occlusion	GradientSHAP	DeepLIFTSHAP	KernelSHAP
Zero	1744	1746	1743	<u>2029</u>	1746	1744	1743
Inverse	1744	1743	1743	1639	1743	1743	1743
Local Mean	1744	1746	1743	<u>2029</u>	1746	1744	1743
Global Mean	1744	1746	1743	<u>2028</u>	1746	1744	1743
Global Max	1743	1743	1743	1624	1743	1743	1743
Global Min	1743	1743	1743	1594	1744	1743	1743
OOD Low	1743	1743	1743	1636	1743	1744	1743
OOD High	1744	1743	1743	1606	1743	1743	1743
Random	1744	1744	1743	1641	1743	1744	1743
Zero Sub	1743	1789	1756	1807	1749	1754	1743
Inverse Sub	1823	1745	1748	1628	1749	1752	1852
Local Mean Sub	1743	1789	1756	1807	1749	1754	1743
Global Mean Sub	1743	1789	1756	1810	1748	1754	1743
OOD Low Sub	<u>**2088**</u>	1768	1804	1639	1876	1870	<u>**2049**</u>
OOD High Sub	1997	1760	1776	1445	1835	1815	1985
Random Sub	1796	1787	1774	1625	1780	1793	1771

Fig. 6. Changed samples from the perturbation analysis for the FordA dataset. The higher, the better. Saliency and KernelSHAP as winners, with Occlusion behind.

FordB / 3636	Saliency	IntegratedGradients	DeepLIFT	Occlusion	GradientSHAP	DeepLIFTSHAP	KernelSHAP
Zero	1777	1777	1777	1614	1777	1777	1777
Inverse	1777	1777	1777	1445	1777	1777	1777
Local Mean	1777	1777	1777	1614	1777	1777	1777
Global Mean	1778	1777	1777	1614	1777	1777	1777
Global Max	1777	1777	1777	1444	1777	1777	1777
Global Min	1777	1777	1777	1416	1777	1777	1777
OOD Low	1777	1777	1777	1531	1777	1777	1777
OOD High	1777	1741	1729	1066	1776	1759	1777
Random	1777	1777	1777	1411	1777	1777	1777
Zero Sub	<u>3425</u>	2903	2558	1557	2535	2328	<u>3472</u>
Inverse Sub	1851	1802	1796	1424	1804	1790	1855
Local Mean Sub	<u>3425</u>	2903	2558	1557	2535	2328	<u>3472</u>
Global Mean Sub	3387	2846	2505	1554	2478	2285	<u>3440</u>
OOD Low Sub	2132	2047	2002	1548	2046	1984	2136
OOD High Sub	1904	1039	1009	461	1719	1306	1919
Random Sub	1815	1810	1801	1421	1809	1793	1822

Fig. 7. Changed samples from the perturbation analysis for the FordB dataset. The higher, the better. KernelSHAP is the winner, and Saliency is behind.

ElectricDevices / 8926	Saliency	IntegratedGradients	DeepLIFT	Occlusion	GradientSHAP	DeepLIFTSHAP	KernelSHAP
Zero	7227	8566	8782	5249	8100	7959	7944
Inverse	7263	8632	8596	5281	8461	8486	8159
Local Mean	7227	8566	8782	5249	8100	7959	7944
Global Mean	7823	8495	8734	5185	8228	8118	8219
Global Max	8627	8844	8884	5606	8861	8591	8906
Global Min	6636	6968	7129	5337	6791	6675	6719
OOD Low	8261	7926	7955	5581	8096	7791	7893
OOD High	6563	5669	6067	4070	6152	5815	6194
Random	7531	7930	8032	5313	7789	7672	7728
Zero Sub	8502	8786	8829	5162	8628	8799	8433
Inverse Sub	6743	7067	6781	4907	6971	6892	6944
Local Mean Sub	8502	8786	8829	5162	8628	8799	8433
Global Mean Sub	8451	8874	8865	5182	8749	8831	8687
OOD Low Sub	7742	7283	7089	5317	7455	7383	7367
OOD High Sub	6034	5416	5553	3760	5718	5718	5943
Random Sub	7601	7751	7707	5254	7786	7608	7826

Fig. 8. Changed samples from the perturbation analysis for the FordB dataset. The higher, the better. KernelSHAP is the winner, and DeepLIFT and IntegratedGradients are behind on different perturbation strategies.

6   Conclusion and Future Work

After reviewing related work, we presented an in-depth analysis of perturbation strategies for attributions on time series. With the analysis, we dug into a CNN trained on time series classification to investigate attributions, perturbation strategies, and shortcuts the network learned. We presented our results in perturbation analysis cards to enable users to analyze the results in detail by inspecting the aggregated data in visualizations and comparing them easily with other techniques based on the provided cards. We identified SHAP as a suitable method to generate working attributions in all experimented datasets. Other gradient-based methods also work quite well but do not perform as well as, e.g., KernelSHAP. However, depending on the perturbation strategy, the best working attribution technique changes quite drastically also for some techniques. We advise not only focusing on a single strategy but to using multiple strategies and aggregating the results of these, and looking at the distribution of the skewness to enhance the comparability. In our experiments, we also found a shortcut or spurious correlation for the FordB dataset, which our model learned to classify one class and to classify everything else as the other class.

Future Work − We want to extend the experiment to other attribution techniques and compare the results with the already collected experiment results. Also, we want to compare the attributions even in more detail by, e.g., aggregating the attributions and comparing them on a higher level to find matching patterns. Different trends and subsequences are further patterns to analyze to gain knowledge into the attribution techniques. With such an approach, we also want to include the *local Lipschitz estimate* [3] to rank consistent attributions higher. Last, we want to extend the *Perturbation Effect Size* [22] and use our gained knowledge to combine perturbation strategies, switching predictions, and distances to generate a measure to evaluate attributions on time series classification models more robust and fully automatically to make it easier for users to decide which attributions to use for explanations. We also want to enhance our perturbation analysis cards further to be more easily readable and comfortable for non-experts to be able to gain insights at a single glance.

Acknowledgment. This work has been partially supported by the Federal Ministry of Education and Research (BMBF) in VIKING (13N16242).

References

1. Adadi, A., Berrada, M.: Peeking inside the black-box: a survey on explainable artificial intelligence (XAI). IEEE Access **6**, 52138–52160 (2018)
2. Aghabozorgi, S., Shirkhorshidi, A.S., Wah, T.Y.: Time-series clustering-a decade review. Inf. Syst. **53**, 16–38 (2015)
3. Alvarez-Melis, D., Jaakkola, T.S.: On the robustness of interpretability methods. arXiv preprint arXiv:1806.08049 (2018)
4. Bach, S., Binder, A., Montavon, G., Klauschen, F., Müller, K.R., Samek, W.: On pixel-wise explanations for non-linear classifier decisions by layer-wise relevance propagation. PLoS ONE **10**(7), e0130140 (2015)
5. Dau, H.A., et al.: The UCR time series archive. IEEE/CAA J. Automatica Sinica **6**(6), 1293–1305 (2019)
6. Geirhos, R., et al.: Shortcut learning in deep neural networks. Nat. Mach. Intell. **2**(11), 665–673 (2020)
7. Guidotti, R., Monreale, A., Ruggieri, S., Turini, F., Giannotti, F., Pedreschi, D.: A survey of methods for explaining black box models. ACM Comput. Surv. (CSUR) **51**(5), 1–42 (2018)
8. Hooker, S., Erhan, D., Kindermans, P.J., Kim, B.: A benchmark for interpretability methods in deep neural networks. In: Wallach, H., Larochelle, H., Beygelzimer, A., d'Alché-Buc, F., Fox, E., Garnett, R. (eds.) Advances in Neural Information Processing Systems, vol. 32. Curran Associates, Inc. (2019)
9. Ismail Fawaz, H., Forestier, G., Weber, J., Idoumghar, L., Muller, P.A.: Deep learning for time series classification: a review. Data Min. Knowl. Disc. **33**(4), 917–963 (2019). https://doi.org/10.1007/s10618-019-00619-1
10. Jeyakumar, J.V., Noor, J., Cheng, Y.H., Garcia, L., Srivastava, M.: How can i explain this to you? An empirical study of deep neural network explanation methods. In: Advances in Neural Information Processing Systems, vol. 33 (2020)
11. Kingma, D.P., Ba, J.: Adam: a method for stochastic optimization. arXiv preprint arXiv:1412.6980 (2014)
12. Lundberg, S., Lee, S.I.: A unified approach to interpreting model predictions. In: Advances in Neural Information Processing Systems (2017)
13. Mercier, D., Bhatt, J., Dengel, A., Ahmed, S.: Time to focus: a comprehensive benchmark using time series attribution methods. arXiv preprint arXiv:2202.03759 (2022)

14. Mohseni, S., Zarei, N., Ragan, E.D.: A multidisciplinary survey and framework for design and evaluation of explainable AI systems. ACM Trans. Interact. Intell. Syst. (TIIS) **11**(3–4), 1–45 (2021)

15. Ribeiro, M.T., Singh, S., Guestrin, C.: "Why should i trust you?" Explaining the predictions of any classifier. In: International Conference on Knowledge Discovery and Data Mining (2016)

16. Rudin, C.: Stop explaining black box machine learning models for high stakes decisions and use interpretable models instead. Nat. Mach. Intell. **1**(5), 206–215 (2019)

17. Schlegel, U., Arnout, H., El-Assady, M., Oelke, D., Keim, D.A.: Towards a rigorous evaluation of XAI methods on time series. In: ICCV Workshop on Interpreting and Explaining Visual Artificial Intelligence Models (2019)

18. Schlegel, U., Keim, D.A.: Time series model attribution visualizations as explanations. In: TREX: Workshop on TRust and EXpertise in Visual Analytics (2021)

19. Schlegel, U., Oelke, D., Keim, D.A., El-Assady, M.: An empirical study of explainable AI techniques on deep learning models for time series tasks. In: Pre-Registration Workshop NeurIPS (2020)

20. Schlegel, U., Vo, D.L., Keim, D.A., Seebacher, D.: TS-MULE: local interpretable model-agnostic explanations for time series forecast models. In: Kamp, M., et al. (eds.) ECML PKDD 2021. CCIS, vol. 1524, pp. 5–14. Springer, Cham (2021). https://doi.org/10.1007/978-3-030-93736-2_1

21. Selvaraju, R.R., Cogswell, M., Das, A., Vedantam, R., Parikh, D., Batra, D.: Grad-CAM: visual explanations from deep networks via gradient-based localization. In: International Conference on Computer Vision (2017)

22. Šimić, I., Sabol, V., Veas, E.: Perturbation effect: a metric to counter misleading validation of feature attribution. In: Proceedings of the 31st ACM International Conference on Information & Knowledge Management, pp. 1798–1807 (2022)

23. Simonyan, K., Vedaldi, A., Zisserman, A.: Deep inside convolutional networks: visualising image classification models and saliency maps. In: Proceedings of the International Conference on Learning Representations (ICLR) (2014)

24. Sundararajan, M., Taly, A., Yan, Q.: Axiomatic attribution for deep networks. In: International Conference on Machine Learning. JMLR.org (2017)

25. Theissler, A., Spinnato, F., Schlegel, U., Guidotti, R.: Explainable AI for time series classification: a review, taxonomy and research directions. IEEE Access **10**, 100700–100724 (2022)

26. Turbé, H., Bjelogrlic, M., Lovis, C., Mengaldo, G.: InterpretTime: a new approach for the systematic evaluation of neural-network interpretability in time series classification. arXiv preprint arXiv:2202.05656 (2022)

27. Yeh, C.K., Hsieh, C.Y., Suggala, A., Inouye, D.I., Ravikumar, P.K.: On the (in)fidelity and sensitivity of explanations. In: Advances in Neural Information Processing Systems, vol. 32 (2019)

28. Zeiler, M.D., Fergus, R.: Visualizing and understanding convolutional networks. In: Fleet, D., Pajdla, T., Schiele, B., Tuytelaars, T. (eds.) ECCV 2014. LNCS, vol. 8689, pp. 818–833. Springer, Cham (2014). https://doi.org/10.1007/978-3-319-10590-1_53

29. Zhou, Y., Booth, S., Ribeiro, M.T., Shah, J.: Do feature attribution methods correctly attribute features? In: AAAI Conference on Artificial Intelligence (2022)

Human-Centered Explanations and xAI for Trustworthy and Responsible AI

Towards a Comprehensive Human-Centred Evaluation Framework for Explainable AI

Ivania Donoso-Guzmán[1,2]([✉]) [iD], Jeroen Ooge[1] [iD], Denis Parra[2] [iD], and Katrien Verbert[1] [iD]

[1] Department of Computer Science, KU Leuven, Leuven, Belgium
`indonoso@uc.cl`
[2] Department of Computer Science, Pontificia Universidad Católica de Chile, Santiago, Chile

Abstract. While research on explainable AI (XAI) is booming and explanation techniques have proven promising in many application domains, standardised human-centred evaluation procedures are still missing. In addition, current evaluation procedures do not assess XAI methods holistically in the sense that they do not treat explanations' effects on humans as a complex user experience. To tackle this challenge, we propose to adapt the User-Centric Evaluation Framework used in recommender systems: we integrate explanation aspects, summarise explanation properties, indicate relations between them, and categorise metrics that measure these properties. With this comprehensive evaluation framework, we hope to contribute to the human-centred standardisation of XAI evaluation.

Keywords: XAI Evaluation · Human-centred evaluation · Evaluation framework

1 Introduction

Explainable AI (XAI) is advancing fast: between 2017 and 2021 alone, the number of XAI papers increased eight-fold [39] and researchers have proposed XAI methods for virtually all existing media types and families of AI models. However, it is still unclear to what extent explanations are effective in practice [34] because full-fledged standardised evaluation procedures are missing. This is partly due to lacking consensus on which explanation properties should be assessed and which measurements should be used [8,34,35,39,49].

To better assess XAI methods, researchers have tried to disentangle explanation's characteristics into simple measurable properties such as completeness [5,39,49], novelty [8,30,32,43], and interactivity [21,39,49]. However, there is little evidence on how these properties relate to explanations being appropriate in real scenarios [29]. In addition, while many researchers stress the importance of context, we are unaware of XAI evaluation methods that treat explanations'

L. Longo (Ed.): xAI 2023, CCIS 1903, pp. 183–204, 2023.
https://doi.org/10.1007/978-3-031-44070-0_10

effects on humans as a **complex user experience** involving factors such as user perception and system interaction.

To evaluate explanations holistically, we are working towards a human-centred evaluation framework for XAI, which extends pioneering work on developing and evaluating user experience [25] and explanations [46] for recommender systems. We categorise explanation properties according to this framework and indicate their relations reported in the literature. Additionally, we present the *explanation elements* that help to classify metrics to simplify the choice of measurements. This adapted user-centric framework will allow researchers and practitioners to evaluate explanations of AI-based systems and potentially increase deployment of such systems in their respective domains [34,36].

The contributions of this paper are three-fold: first, we present an extensive analysis of existing definitions of explanation properties and methods, as well as their interrelationships. Our analysis aligns different properties and methods as defined by different research communities. Second, based on this analysis, we define a human-centred evaluation framework for XAI that presents an integrative approach and combines user-centric evaluation and functional metrics. Third, we present an example of the use of this framework.

2   Background and Related Work

2.1   Human-Centred Explainable AI

The XAI area of research has been led mostly by the AI community, even though it is a multidisciplinary area of research. For this reason, XAI methods have been criticised for being developed with the AI researchers' intuition of what constitutes a good explanation [35]. In particular, the design and evaluation of XAI methods are often conducted without considering the final users' needs and their cognitive processes [29].

More recently, the HCI community started proposing ideas for tackling the XAI design, considering how the users reason about explanations: Wang et al. [51] proposed a framework to design explanations based on how humans reason; Chen et al. [10] characterised how explanations affect human understanding of task decision boundary, model decision boundary and model error; Most recently, Chen et al. [12] conducted a study to investigate the decision-making process users follow when faced with AI predictions and their explanations.

Another line of work has been understanding the wants and needs of different shareholders and ensuring they are considered in the design. Mohseni et al. [36] categorised the goals of target user groups and developed design guidelines to iteratively design and evaluate Explainable AI systems; Suresh et al. [44] proposed a framework to characterise users with two multidimensional criteria: knowledge and interpretability needs, that together help to understand the system's users; Langer et al. [26] review the main types of users of XAI systems and their wants and needs, to propose a model for designing XAI systems according to these desiderata; Liao et al. [28] proposed a question-driven design process to fulfil the Explainable AI user's needs; Rong et al. [41] analysed human-based XAI evaluations and provided guidelines for conducting user studies in the area.

Overall, these studies have emphasised the importance of users' characteristics and the tasks they perform during the design phase of XAI experiences. Although it has been stated as an important aspect of the final adoption of XAI systems [36,41], to the best of our knowledge, evaluation procedures that capture the complexity of the human-AI interaction have not yet been proposed. We contribute by adapting a widely accepted procedure in recommender systems to evaluate explanations generated by XAI methods holistically.

2.2 Evaluating Explanations

Even though AI/ML models have standard evaluation metrics, there is still no consensus on the strategy to evaluate XAI methods. Doshi-Velez et al. [18] proposed the first standardisation of XAI evaluation. According to their work, the evaluation could be performed in three levels: application-grounded, with real tasks and users; human-grounded, with real users and proxy tasks; and functionality-grounded, with proxy tasks and no users. Currently, application or human-grounded approaches have been criticized for their lack of rigour [22,23], and for using proxy tasks [6].

To conduct functionally-grounded evaluations, i.e. proxy tasks and no users, some studies have focused on grouping concepts and defining properties [5,8,34,49] and their corresponding metrics [39]. These works aggregate existing literature that defines properties or presents metrics to assess them. The proposed properties try to measure the quality of the explanations without context so that they can be used in functionality-grounded evaluation. Similarly, Hoffman et al. [20] proposed to evaluate explanations using the 'goodness criteria' that assess the explanation quality without context. Most recently, Agarwal et al. [2] presented a framework to benchmark different XAI methods using automatic metrics. Still, it is limited to particular methods and only works with specific datasets created for the benchmark.

Little work has been conducted to present the connections between these properties. Most papers state that trade-offs exist [8,30,34,39], but they have not quantified them. To the best of our knowledge, only the study by Balog et al. [4] uncovered conflicting relationships between some of the proposed properties, but they did not evaluate XAI-generated explanations.

Given the number of properties to evaluate, selecting the aspects to consider in the evaluation is becoming an important topic. According to Liao et al. [30], this selection depends on the tasks the system has to support because the user accomplishment of these tasks determines the overall system's success. Knijnenburg et al. [25] indicate the selection is made according to theoretical models, i.e., it results from previous studies or from the hypothesis that is tested. Recently, Liao et al. [30] presented a study that connects tasks with evaluation criteria to provide general guidelines for the field. In this study, experts and end-users selected the most appropriate properties to evaluate diverse XAI tasks. They found that XAI tasks obtained different property rankings regardless of the application domain (loan application, medical diagnosis, among others).

Our work builds upon these previous studies by proposing a unified framework that integrates previously proposed definitions and measurements by making the relations between them explicit and grounded in previous work. Additionally, we analysed measurement procedures and classified them by which explanation element they measure according to Miller's definition of explanation [35], which declares that explanations are composed of a cognitive process, a product and a social process. This new criteria to classify measurements provides researchers and practitioners with a new understanding of how to measure properties of explanations.

2.3   User Centric Evaluation of Recommender Systems

The User Centric Evaluation Framework for recommender systems in Fig. 1 was proposed by Knijnenburg et al. [25] to explain how users experience the interaction with a recommendation system and to predict how users behave under similar circumstances. This framework has six *conceptual components* encompassing different *constructs* that can be measured during a user study. For example, the conceptual component *Subjective system aspects* groups constructs such as *Perceived recommendation quality* or *Interaction adequacy*, while *User experience* contains *Choice difficulty* and *Choice satisfaction* among others. The constructs and the causal relations between them found with Structural Equation Modelling (SEM) [24] help explain how different aspects of the experience affect each other and influence the outcomes.

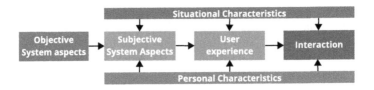

Fig. 1. The User-Centric Evaluation Framework by Knijnenburg et al. [25]. Each box represents a *conceptual component* that groups related *constructs*.

This evaluation framework has been used and appreciated in recommender systems because of its capacity to provide relations between different user experience aspects. By capturing the causal relations between different measurements, researchers can not only report and compare these measurements but also explain why differences do or do not occur. This provides a better understanding of what makes a system more adapted to the users and, ultimately, predicts whether it will be successful and why.

In this work, we expand this successful framework for XAI evaluation. We believe our comprehensive work sheds light on which explanation aspects are more important and relevant to users and their circumstances. Furthermore, since the framework provides causal relations between different properties, we believe it can provide better guidelines for XAI design.

3   Methods

To adapt the user-centric evaluation framework by Knijnenburg et al. [25], we analysed current literature on the topic with a grounded theory approach. This section describes how we collected papers and categorised them along two axes (conceptual components and explanation elements), to build the foundation for our XAI framework.

3.1   Paper Collection

Finding relevant literature on XAI evaluation requires searching several research disciplines. Evaluation, in particular, has been published in several types of venues (workshops, posters, surveys), presenting concrete methods and execution procedures but also proposals and blue-sky ideas. To include as much relevant literature as possible, we consulted Google Scholar with this query:

```
intitle:properties OR intitle:evaluation OR intitle:metrics
OR intitle:property OR intitle:metric
("explainable" OR "interpretable")
("artificial intelligence" OR "machine learning" OR XAI OR AI)
```

The search was conducted at the end of October 2022 and was limited to the years 2017 and onwards because Doshi-Velez et al. [18] then proposed one of the first XAI evaluation procedures. This query returned approximately 5970 results. As a first step, only the titles were reviewed to check whether the result was related to AI or XAI. We checked all result pages until the first page where no papers related to XAI or AI appeared. This occurred on page 25, similar to the results of Vilone et al. [49]. This first screening yielded 80 research works.

These works were analysed by looking at the abstract and, in doubt, at the full paper. The aim of this second screening was to remove duplicate works and keep only works that describe properties, relations between them and measurements. The exclusion criteria were the following:

- The research did not use or propose properties or measurements for XAI explanations.
- The study considered only non-XAI-generated explanations.
- The research compared different XAI methods using different metrics, but said metrics were not grounded on explanation quality aspects.
- The evaluation of the explanations was performed with a ground truth explanation.
- The search result was a master's or PhD thesis, and one or more papers were already published based on the same research, making it redundant.

After this screening process, only 19 results were kept. From their references, other related papers were found. We also included [46] because it is a comprehensive review of the evaluation of explanations in the context of recommender systems. The final number of papers included was 29.

3.2 Classification Axis 1: Conceptual Components

A Grounded Theory [9] approach was followed to analyse the collected works in three steps: Initial Coding, aimed at finding quotes that related to properties of explanation; Focused Coding, which consisted of labelling the passages according to a set of concepts; and finally Axial Coding, which connects and groups the different concepts.

The Initial Coding step was conducted with NVivo. Definitions of explanation properties, definitions of metrics to measure aspects of explanations, and relations between properties were searched for. Some of the papers had definitions of properties based on multiple previous works. In those cases, we kept the summarised definition and did not look for primary sources. In contrast, if the definition made in the survey paper did not fully explain metrics, we added the primary source to the group of papers.

The Focused Coding Step consisted of labelling the different definitions with the most appropriate concept, independently of the name the authors had coined. This iterative process aimed to group the definitions that point to the same desiderata of an explanation while avoiding overlapping concepts. The definition of each property was created at this step. In addition, passages that described a procedure to measure the property were marked as such. The procedure to analyse those quotations is described in Sect. 3.3.

The Axial Coding phase was conducted by first collecting the relations that were described in the selected papers. After these relations were captured, new relations that emerged from the definitions were investigated and added to the model. Additionally, relations were added based on evidence of other papers the researchers were aware of.

Finally, each of the found properties was matched to a conceptual component as defined in Knijnenburg's framework [25]. Our analysis yielded very few and general properties for the situational and personal characteristics components, so it was decided to leave those properties out of the current analysis. During this phase, it was noted that some properties belonged to a new category that captured the abstract quality of the explanation. This idea aligns with the nature of XAI methods: the original framework was made for recommender systems, i.e., an AI model that selects objects, but XAI methods **generate** an object. To evaluate the quality of generated objects, it was decided to add the conceptual component *Explanation Aspects* (see Fig. 3), which groups properties that evaluate the explanation quality.

3.3 Classification Axis 2: Explanation Elements

Previous analysis of properties had classified measurement and metrics depending on their user dependency [5], the nature of the procedure (objective, subjective) [16,21] or according to umbrella properties [38,39]. However, during the analysis of the conceptual components and the properties of explanations, it was found that similar properties are often named differently because of the ways in which they are measured. For example, Carvalho et al. [8] defined two similar

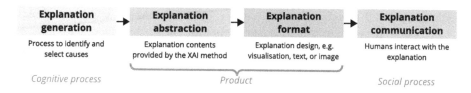

Fig. 2. The four elements of explanations. We use the same ideas as [35] but changed the names of the elements. Additionally, we further divide the explanation product into *abstraction* and *format*.

concepts that were applied in two types of evaluation. They used the name *Representativeness* for the evaluation without users and the concept *General and probable* for evaluation with user studies, even though both refer to the number of instances that can be explained with the same causes. We argue this inconsistency occurs because explanations are made of different elements. Miller [35] states that *explanations* are both processes and products: the *Cognitive process* selects a subset of the causes; the *Product* is the resulting outcome; and the *Social process* consists of transferring the knowledge from explainer to explainee.

With these ideas in mind, a focused coding was conducted only of the passages marked as describing a procedure to measure a property. Each passage was labelled as *generation, product* or *communication*. It was found that many metrics that were labelled *product* were very format dependent: for example, BLEU (BiLingual Evaluation Understudy) [14], which evaluates machine-translation quality, cannot be applied to visual-based explanations, but Covariate Homogeneity [39] could be applied to both text and visual-based explanations. For this reason, the metrics under the *product* label were further categorised between *abstraction* and *format*. Figure 2 displays the new definitions and the relation to Miller's definitions.

This categorisation allows classifying measurement procedures under three criteria: property they measure, element of explanation and type of procedure (questionnaire, metrics, etc.). Different measurements can be applied to evaluate the properties along the four explanation elements. Some properties can only be assessed by measuring one element, while others can be measured in more than one. These new criteria are explained and justified in Sect. 4.3.

4 A User-Centric Evaluation Framework for XAI

This section presents an adapted version of the *User-Centric Evaluation Framework*. To describe it, we use the following terminology: **conceptual components** group **explanation properties**, which in turn can be measured with **measurements**. While each measurement applies to only one **explanation element**, a single property can be measured by several measurements.

This section is organised as follows: in Sect. 4.1, the choice of properties for each conceptual component is justified and explained, and the properties are defined; then, in Sect. 4.2, the connections between properties are presented;

finally in Sect. 4.3 the classification criteria for measurements is presented and justified, as well as the existing measurements for each property.

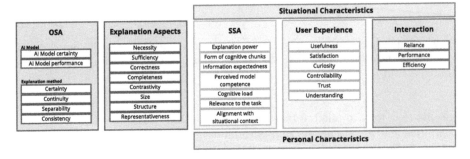

Fig. 3. The User-Centric Evaluation Framework by Knijnenburg et al. [25] extended with a new conceptual component: *Explanation Aspects*. Each conceptual component displays its properties. The box of Objective system aspects (OSA) marks the properties that apply to the AI model and the ones that apply to the XAI method.

4.1   Explanation Properties

Objective System Aspects. Objective systems aspects (OSAs) are 'the aspects of the system that are currently being evaluated' [25]. It was found from the analysis that characteristics from the particular instance of the XAI method and AI model can affect the explanation. For instance, the AI model performance will affect the level of Trust users can achieve. Making these characteristics explicit in the framework can help to understand the specific aspects of the XAI method and AI model that affect the user experience.

The analysis yielded six properties: AI model performance, AI model certainty, Certainty, Continuity, Separability and Consistency. The first two properties measure the AI model, and the last four are applied to the XAI method. Continuity was described in several works as the desired 'smoothness' of the XAI function. In the beginning, Separability and Continuity were one concept, but it was noted that providing similar explanations to similar instances does not guarantee that different instances will get different explanations. Consistency evaluates the randomness of the XAI method: if different runs of the XAI method algorithm return different functions, the model will be highly inconsistent.

AI model certainty and XAI method certainty were complicated properties. Uncertainty quantification is a very active field of research within AI, and several approximation methods have been proposed. However, the problem is still being investigated due to its high computational cost [1]. Papers' definitions for these concepts emphasised the fact that the models needed to tell the users when to trust their outputs. For this reason, we decided to keep them, even though there are no proven ways to compute them yet.

Explanation Aspects. The Explanation aspects component was added to the original framework (see Sect. 3.2). This component groups the properties that measure the quality of the generated explanation. These concepts have been generally associated with Functionality-Grounded evaluation because these properties can be measured with metrics at the abstraction level, that is, without the need for users.

From the analysis, eight properties were found. Necessity, Sufficiency and Contrastivity specifically measure the quality of the selected causes. Their goal is to evaluate whether the reasons the XAI method is providing clearly inform the prediction that was made. Correctness and Completeness are analogous to precision and recall in AI performance metrics. Correctness describes whether the XAI method selected the causes that the AI model used to make a prediction. For explanations generated using the AI model parameters, such as linear regression, the correctness will always be high. Explanations generated by surrogate models will have lower correctness. Completeness quantifies if all the causes that the model used to generate the prediction are present in the explanation. Representativeness determines whether the explanations are unique to each instance or they generalise over multiple instances. This property helps to estimate the Cognitive Load the users will face when using the system. Size and Structure evaluate the explanations' length and organisation, which affects how easy it will be for users to understand them.

Subjective System Aspects. Subjective System Aspects (SSA) are "users' perceptions of the Objective System Aspects" [25]. These properties provide evidence that the users perceive the Objective System Aspects. In this modified framework, they help to establish whether the users perceive the OSAs and the Explanation Aspects. Additionally, this component helps us to understand the pertinence of the generated explanations to the users' situational context. These properties are mostly measured at the communication level, but some of them have measures at the abstraction and format level that can be used as proxies of the real value.

The analysis yielded seven properties for this component. Explanation power measures the perceived quality of the selected causes. Explanations with high power provide valuable justifications for the AI model behaviour. Form of cognitive chunks estimates the semantics of the information provided by the explanation. This concept was coined by Doshi-Velez et al. [18] and it has been widely used in the XAI domain. Information expectedness measures whether the explanation provides new knowledge to the user. The analysed works used three concepts for this notion: plausibility, coherence with prior knowledge/beliefs, and novelty. We decided to keep these notions under one umbrella term because we found that they are part of the same scale (see Fig. 4). The relation of each concept with information expectedness is the following:

- Plausibility [5,8,38]: if the information is expected, the user will think it is plausible. However, the contrary does not necessarily holds. The information can be new but still plausible in the user's mind.

- Coherence with prior knowledge/beliefs [8,39,43]: the information provided by the explanation should have some level of connection to the user's background. If that relation does not exist, it will be hard for the user to understand the explanation.
- Novelty [8,30,32,35,43]: explanations should focus on abnormal causes [35] and provide information the user does not expect to increase her engagement with the system. However, if the reasons are too unexpected, the user will probably dismiss them and ignore the system.

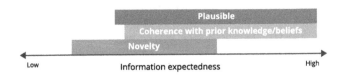

Fig. 4. Relation between plausibility, coherence with prior knowledge/beliefs and Novelty with Information Expectedness. Each bar represents the amount of new information that according to the concepts relates to user acceptance.

Perceived model competence evaluates whether the user thinks the AI model can perform as expected. The Cognitive load measures the cognitive effort the user makes to understand the explanations.

The last two properties measure the fit between the explanation and the situational context. Relevance to the task measures whether the explanation provides insights that help to perform the task better. An explanation has to be relevant to be useful for the task the user has to perform; otherwise, she will not exploit it. For example, in a medical context, this would measure whether the explanations are actionable in the patient's state. Alignment with situational context evaluates whether the provided explanation is appropriate for the usage context. For instance, a complex visualisation cannot be used correctly in a time-constrained context.

Table 1. Table of all explanation properties and their definitions based on the reviewed literature.

Property	Definition	References
Objective system aspects		
AI Model performance	The accomplishment level the AI model has with respect to the task for which it was trained.	
AI Model certainty	The confidence the AI model has in its prediction.	[8,30,39,49]
Certainty	The confidence the XAI method has in the explanation.	[5,8,20,30,39,46]
Continuity	The function should provide similar explanations for similar instances.	[8,16,20,21,34]
Separability	The XAI method should return different explanations for different instances	[8]
Consistency	The degree to which different runs of the XAI method yield similar XAI functions.	[5,8,21,30,32,39, 47,49]

(*continued*)

Table 1. (*continued*)

Property	Definition	References
Explanation aspects		
Necessity	Measures whether the explanation method selected the causes that are responsible for the prediction. If the necessary causes change, then the prediction will also change	[8,30,35,39]
Sufficiency	Measures whether the explanation method did not select causes that do not affect the prediction. If non-selected causes change, the prediction would still hold, and thus the explanation should not change	[35]
Correctness	Quantifies the extent to which the selected causes are correct with respect to the model reasoning	[8,30,34,39,43,49]
Completeness	Quantifies if all the causes that the model used to generate the prediction are present in the explanation	[8,30,34,39,49]
Contrastivity	Measures whether the explanation contains reasons that highlight differences with respect to other possible outcomes. Low contrastivity will provide the same reasons for instances in which the model predicts different classes	[8,35,39]
Size	Refers to the amount of information present in the explanation	[8,18,30,34,39,49]
Structure	The information should be displayed in a way that allows the users to understand the hierarchy of the information quickly	[8,21,34,39,43,46, 47,49]
Representativeness	An explanation is representative if it holds for many distinct but similar instances	[8,16,43,49]
Subjective system aspects		
Explanation power	Measures whether the selected causes make the user understand the reasons the model considered when making a decision	[8,30,49,52]
Form of cognitive chunks	Refers to the semantics and structure of the pieces of information the user will receive	[8,18,39,49]
Information expectedness	Level of surprise of the information revealed by the explanation	[5,8,21,30,32,35, 37–39,43,47,49]
Perceived model competence	Measures the user's impression of the model competence for the task at hand	[11]
Cognitive Load	Refers to the cognitive effort the user has to do to achieve the task	[8,30,49]
Relevance to the task	Level of explanation usefulness to the user's task	[21,30,35,38,39,47, 49,52]
Alignment with situational context	Level of appropriateness of the explanation to the usage context	[8,21,30,43,47]
User experience		
Curiosity	Measures whether the user is intrinsically motivated to understand the explanation. If the user is curious, she will be more attentive to the task and, therefore, more engaged with the system	[20,21,49]
Satisfaction	Refers to the level of fulfilment the user gets while interacting with the system. This satisfaction is always measured at the communication level because it is for the users to decide whether they feel good about the overall system interaction	[20,21,46,49,52]
Trust	We use the definition by Tintarev et al. [46]: "perceived confidence in a system's competence"	[3,11,20,21,30,46, 47,52]
Understanding	Refers to the ability of the user to interpret the system's output correctly. The user fails to understand when she cannot interpret or incorrectly interprets the system's explanation and prediction. This involves the creation of the user's mental model and how that aligns with the system's functionality	[8,20,21,32,34,49, 52]
Usefulness	Measures whether the explanation helps the user to achieve a certain goal	[5,46,49,52]
Controllability	Measures whether the user perceives she has some level of control over the system. This could manifest as the ability to reverse actions, correct the system, filter or zoom the explanation, or ask questions to clarify the explanation or prediction	[20,21,30,39,43,46, 49]
Interaction		
Efficiency	Measures the speed at which a task can be performed	[46,49]
Performance	Measures how well the user can do the task while using the system (prediction+explanations)	[20,21,32]
Reliance	Measures whether the user is willing to provide control to the machine for the given task	[20,21,46,49]

User Experience. The User experience factors evaluate what the user encounters when interacting with the system [25]. The analysis did not find surprising aspects because all but Curiosity, have been studied in recommender systems. The aspects found are Satisfaction, Trust, Understanding, Usefulness, Controllability and Curiosity. This last one was highlighted as extremely relevant in the case of explanations because the search for an explanation is modulated by the user's curiosity [21]. Moreover, the motivation to ask or explore an explanation is determined by the user's curiosity [20].

Interaction. Interaction factors measure aspects related to the possible adoption of the system. Three properties were found to be relevant: Efficiency, Performance and Reliance. Efficiency measures how fast the user can perform the task. Performance evaluates the level of achievement the user reaches while using the system. Finally, Reliance measures to which extent the user is willing to provide control to the AI model to perform the task.

4.2 Relations Between Properties

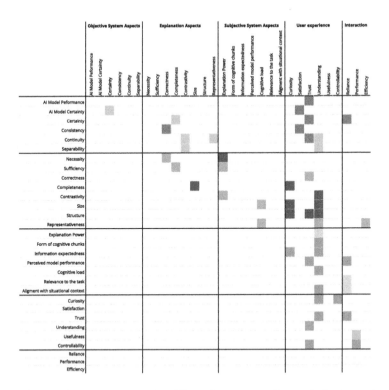

Fig. 5. Relations between properties. The relations are directed: horizontal properties are the source, and vertical properties receive the effect. High saturation squares indicate that the relationship has been described in the literature, and low saturation squares indicate the relation was inferred from the definitions.

Explanation properties are related to each other in intricate ways [25]. As stated in Sect. 3.2, by scanning past research, we identified such relationships and linked the properties in our framework as described in the literature; for instance, explanation size affects user curiosity [20]. In this way, we mapped out relations proposed in the literature and relations inferred from the properties' definitions. Table 1 describes the relations found for each property and Fig. 5 displays a visual summary of the interactions. These relations help theorise the expected causal effects between the properties. In practical terms, they serve as hypotheses for the Structural Equation Model.

Table 2. Relations between properties. Relations with no reference means that it was inferred from the definitions

Explanation Property	Relations with other properties
Objective system aspects	
Model performance	The performance of the AI will affect the level of Trust the users can achieve [17,46]
Model certainty	If the AI model is uncertain of the predictions, the XAI method will have more difficulties obtaining consistent explanations, which will affect the XAI method's certainty. This confidence will also affect the satisfaction with the system because, as Tintarev et al. [46] explains, a user might be more forgiving if the system admits it is not confident about a prediction
Certainty	If the explanation shows its limitations, the user may not relay or trust the system [20,30]. Low certainty will affect the correctness of the explanation
Continuity	Higher continuity increases the understanding of the model because the similarity of explanations helps to learn from the model. It also helps to produce contrastive and representative explanations. Ultimately, high continuity can also increase Trust [47]
Separability	Higher separability increases the understanding of the model and the contrastivity of the explanations
Consistency	Low consistency may decrease user satisfaction [21] and correctness [30]
Explanation Aspects	
Necessity	Affects the explanation power [30]. Additionally, if the necessary causes are selected, then the correctness will be high
Sufficiency	Affects the explanation power. Moreover, if the sufficient causes are selected the completeness of the explanation will increase
Correctness	An explanation with high correctness will faithfully reflect the decision process of the AI model. This could increase Trust in the explanation and AI model
Completeness	The explanation size is related to completeness: the bigger the explanation, the more complete it will be [8,30]. However, bigger explanations might decrease curiosity [21]
Contrastivity	High contrastivity will increase the explanation power. Additionally, this property will affect understanding because the people expect explanations to be contrastive [35]
Size	The amount of information affects curiosity in an inverted U-shaped pattern: little or excessive information reduces curiosity [21]. The size of the explanation also affects how easily a user can understand the explanation [30,34]. This last effect could be mediated by the Cognitive Load
Structure	The design of the information that will be shown affects its trustworthiness [46], curiosity [21] and ultimately how easy they can be understood [34,43]
Representativeness	This property affects understanding, cognitive load and efficiency because the user can understand an explanation more quickly if it is similar to those she has seen before

(continued)

Table 2. (*continued*)

Explanation Property	Relations with other properties
Subjective System Aspects	
Explanation power	The quality of the selected causes will help increase understanding
Form of cognitive chunks	It affects understanding because this property measures how interpretable are the information pieces the user receives [8]
Information expectedness	If the information is coherent with the user's beliefs, they will be more likely to understand it [43]. However, if the information does not add anything new to their existing knowledge, they are less likely to be curious [43]
Perceived model competence	When the users perceive the AI model can perform, they are more likely to trust it and eventually to rely on it [11]
Cognitive Load	An explanation with low cognitive load will be easier to understand [30]
Relevance to the task	If the explanations help the development of the task, the user is more likely to rely on the AI advice
Alignment with situational context	Trust in the system is context-dependent. If the system is aligned with the situation the user has to perform, she will be more likely to trust it [20]. Additionally, this could build up until the user starts to rely on the AI agent
User experience	
Curiosity	Mental model formation, which is the final goal of understanding, is modulated by Curiosity [21]. Additionally, Curiosity encourages users to explore and interact with the system [21]
Satisfaction	
Trust	Reliance is an outcome of appropriate trust [11,20,21,46]. Mental model formation is also modulated by Trust in the system [21]
Understanding	If users cannot understand the behaviour, Trust will be lost [21]
Usefulness	If the user finds the explanations helpful, they are more likely to increase the user performance with the system
Controllability	The possibility of interaction increases Trust in the system [46]. Good interaction with the system can increase the performance of the users [21]

4.3   Measurements

As explained in Sect. 3.3, we classified measurements of properties with three criteria: property they measure, explanation element in which they are applied

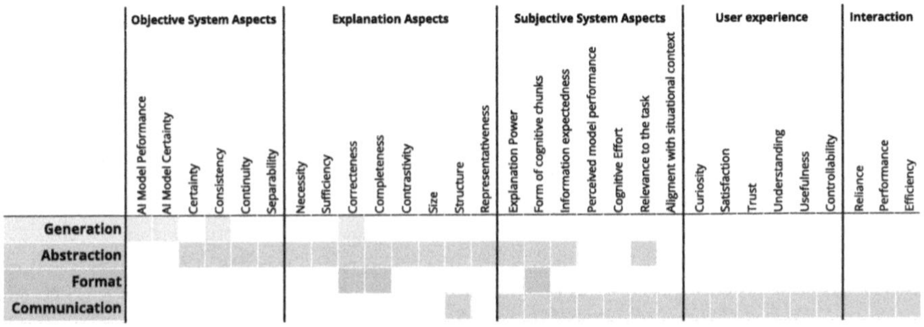

Fig. 6. Existence of a measurement procedure for each property in each explanation element. Each coloured rectangle indicates that a measurement has been defined for the tuple (property, explanation element)

and type of procedure. The explanations elements allow us to capture the complexity of the explanations: they are not simply an object we show to users; a model has generated them and then transformed them to be shown to users in a specific situational context. The four elements are:

- **Generation element**. Refers to the process that was conducted to select the causes that will be displayed in the explanation for a specific object. The measures of this element are applied to the XAI function and AI model. They check the function's parameters to obtain indicators.
- **Abstraction element**. Represents the selected causes of the explanation without considering the format in which they will be displayed. For example, for feature importance, this could be a table with the features and their corresponding importance values. Measurements that are applied at this level look at the data that was selected by the XAI method as an explanation.
- **Format element**. Refers to the manner in which the causes will be presented to the user. This could be as example-based, text, visualisation, etc. In this study, few measurements were found to be applicable at this level. However, each specific media type has its own measurements that could be modified to be applied. For instance, for visual explanations, the data-ink ratio could be applied to analyse whether the most important features use more ink in the visualisation.
- **Communication element**. It refers to the process of interacting with the formatted explanation. During this process, information can be captured as interaction measurements, as well as self-reported information.

In Fig. 6, a coloured square is present if at least one measurement exists for that (property, element) tuple. It is noted that the User Experience and Interaction conceptual components are only measured at the communication level, i.e. only when the explanation is displayed to users. What stands out in this figure is the number of measurements at the abstraction level for the Subjective System Aspects component. In Knijnenburg's framework [25], these aspects were recommended to be measured with self-reporting questionnaires. However, our analysis found that for some of them, metrics have been proposed at the Abstraction element, which means that some computational metric is applied to the abstract explanation to obtain a value.

The main advantage of decoupling the properties from the ways to measure them is that it allows researchers to select measurements considering the study constraints. For instance, if the study is conducted with users that do not have much time to answer questionnaires, and the researchers want to measure *Explanation power* , *Form of cognitive chunks* , *Curiosity* and

Understanding , they may choose to measure the first two properties at the abstract level of the explanation and the last two at the communication level with questionnaires. In this way, they do not overwhelm the users with questions but still measure the required properties.

As pointed out before, we also classified the measurements by the type of procedure. In this analysis, only procedures that produce a quantitative value were considered. This means that qualitative interviews were not considered, nor were experiment tasks. The four types are:

- **Quantitative interviews**: closed-ended questions, usually in Likert scale.
- **Computational metrics**: mathematical functions that are applied to the explanations or XAI methods.
- **Behaviour metrics**: indicators of user behaviour and interaction with a system. For example, the number of interactions within the system and the time to complete a task.
- **Objective Body Measurements**: measurements taken from the user body. The most common is eye-tracking.

Table 3. Measurements of properties

Explanation Property	Measurement
Generation	
AI Model performance	Measured by the model type appropriate metrics: accuracy, f-score, precision, recall and others
AI Model certainty	This property can be measured for each individual prediction and the global model. If it is measured globally, it should be measured over a dataset similar to the data the real system will face [16]
Consistency	Implementation invariance: check whether the XAI function parameters are the same after different runs of the XAI method creation [8,49]
Correctness	Translucency [8]
Abstraction	
Certainty	Confidence Accuracy [39]
Continuity	Connectedness [39] also in [7,19,37,38,42,49]; Stability for Slight Variations [39]; Fidelity for Slight Variations [39]
Separability	Separability [8]
Consistency	Stability of explanation: check whether the explanations for a single object change for different instances of the XAI method [8,16]
Necessity	Responsability of an outcome [35]; Sparsity and Sparsity rate [38]; Deletion Check [27,39]
Sufficiency	Count whether the AI model prediction changes when the non-selected causes change [35]
Correctness	Model Parameter Randomization Check, Explanation Randomization, White Box Check, Controlled Synthetic Data Check, Predictive Performance [39]; Fidelity [16,39,43]; Alignment between AI model features and explanation features [27,48]
Completeness	Preservation Check [39]; Completeness [16,37]; Recall [48]
Contrastivity	Data Randomization, Target Sensitivity, Target Discriminativeness [39]; Sensitivity [49]
Size	Total size or sparsity [39]
Structure	Incremental Deletion [16,39]; Covariate Regularity [16,39]; Chronology [43]; Single Deletion [39]
Representativeness	Explanation support (number of instances to which the explanation applies over the number of instances) [8,16,43,49]
Explanation power	Sensitivity Axiom [8]
Form of cognitive chunks	Covariate Homogeneity [39]
Information expectedness	Alignment with Domain Knowledge [39]
Relevance to the task	Pragmatism [16,38,39]; Attribute costs [49]

(*continued*)

Table 3. (*continued*)

Explanation Property	Measurement
Format	
Correctness	Percentage of invalid rules [49]
Completeness	Rules redundancy [49]
Form of cognitive chunks	BLEU and METEOR [49]; Perceptual Realism [39]
Communication	
Structure	Questionnaire [11,49]
Explanation power	Questionnaire [50]
Form of cognitive chunks	Perceived Homogeneity [39]
Information expectedness	Questionnaire [50]
Perceived model competence	Questionnaire [3]
Cognitive Load	NASA TLX [21]
Relevance to the task	Questionnaire [50]
Alignment with situational context	Goodness explanation [20]
Curiosity	Curiosity Checklist [20]; Eye Movement Pattern [21]
Satisfaction	Explanation Satisfaction Scale [20]; Eye Movement Pattern [21]; Loyalty [46]; Questionnaire [3]
Trust	Trust Scale [20]; Questionnaire [3,11,40,50]
Understanding	Questionnaires [3,46,50]
Helpfulness	Questionnaires [46,50]; Evaluate user action before and after explanation [46]
Controllability	Concept-level feedback Satisfaction Ratio [13]; The extent to which a user can produce certain outcomes [20]
Efficiency	Interaction time and number of interactions to perform a task [46]
Performance	Performance metrics with respect to the primary goal [20]
Reliance	Questionnaires [3,11]; Willingness to accept AI agent advice [21]

The metrics for each (property, element) are listed in Table 3. This table was built under the following rules:

- Several measurements have been defined in multiple works. To avoid naming all of them in the tables, we built upon existing work by using the name proposed by Nauta et al. [39] to summarise metrics every time a similar metric was defined in another work. This new work was added as a reference under the same name.
- Some procedures were not described with a specific name in the paper. In those cases, an explanatory sentence was used to name them.
- If asking questions was proposed as a procedure, but no measurement model or questions were provided, the measurement was not considered.
- For a given property, questions proposed in different papers were joined together under the *Questionnaire* term.

5   Illustrative Example

In this section, we provide an illustrative example of how our framework can be used. Researchers have an AI model that predicts whether a patient will be readmitted to the emergency department within 30 days. *SHAP* [33] is used to determine the *feature importance* on a patient level and this information is then visualised in a *force plot* [33]. Finally, medical staff *analyses* the prediction and visual explanation to decide whether they discharge a patient.

In this context, assessing the explanation requires several steps. First, researchers have to decide which properties to measure. This is a decision support system, so according to [30], the most relevant properties would be *Trust*, *Controllability*, and *Understanding*. The researchers conjecture that *Reliance* and *Performance* will be good indicators of adoption. Second, they have to select explanation properties that relate to these five properties. Following the theoretical causal relations in Table 1 and Fig. 5, such properties are:

- *AI Model performance*, *Certainty*, *Continuity*
- *Size*, *Structure*, *Representativeness*
- *Form of cognitive chunks*, *Information expectedness*, *Cognitive load*, *Perceived model competence*, *Alignment with situational context*
- *Curiosity*

Finally, to assess all selected properties, researchers pick appropriate metrics from Table 2. The metrics' scores applied to the elements *abstraction* and *format* are averaged over the single explanations, and the questionnaires are applied at the end of the experience. This data is then analysed using structural equation modelling.

6   Conclusion and Future Work

In this work, we have presented a user-centric evaluation framework for XAI inspired by research on recommender systems allowing researchers to conduct systematic user experience evaluations in the context of XAI-based systems. Our proposal integrates the current state of the art in XAI evaluation but also allows to easily incorporate new properties or metrics that might become relevant for new applications. By decoupling the aspects of explanations and the procedures to measure them, this framework provides researchers with more tools to choose what and how to measure, and why it is necessary to do it, with the ultimate goal of evaluating the user experience under these new XAI scenarios.

For future work, we plan to validate the framework with user studies. We aim at validating metrics, properties, as well as mediation and causal effects between them. Additionally, we could include experimental designs that compare different explanations, for instance, by comparing the user experience under two different visualisations for explanations generated with SHAP. Furthermore, we did not analyse how specific situational and personal characteristics affect the properties. This area has been explored [15, 31, 45], but more work is needed to connect those findings to explanation properties. Another area of improvement is proposing a standardised report of results to increase fair comparison with previous studies. Lastly, there is no comprehensive survey on the maturity of each of the measurements and on the relations between the properties. Such a survey would help researchers and practitioners to understand the maturity of each property and measurement to help them plan their studies based on current evidence.

Acknowledgements. This work was partially funded by ANID Chile, Millennium Science Initiative Program, codes ICN2021_004 (iHealth) and ICN17_002 (IMFD), by Basal Funds for Center of Excellence FB210017 (CENIA), the Research Foundation Flanders (FWO, grant G0A3319N) and KU Leuven (grant C14/21/072). In addition, we thank Fondecyt grant 1231724. The research of Ivania Donoso-Guzmán was supported by the doctoral scholarship of ANID Chile.

References

1. Abdar, M., et al.: A review of uncertainty quantification in deep learning: techniques, applications and challenges. Inf. Fusion **76**, 243–297 (2021). https://doi.org/10.1016/j.inffus.2021.05.008
2. Agarwal, C., et al.: OpenXAI: towards a transparent evaluation of model explanations (2022). https://doi.org/10.48550/arxiv.2206.11104. https://arxiv.org/abs/2206.11104v2
3. Ashoori, M., Weisz, J.D.: In AI we trust? Factors that influence trustworthiness of AI-infused decision-making processes (2019). http://arxiv.org/abs/1912.02675
4. Balog, K., Radlinski, F.: Measuring recommendation explanation quality. In: Proceedings of the 43rd International ACM SIGIR Conference on Research and Development in Information Retrieval, pp. 329–338. ACM, New York (2020). https://doi.org/10.1145/3397271.3401032. https://dl.acm.org/doi/10.1145/3397271.3401032
5. Beckh, K., Müller, S., Rüping, S.: A quantitative human-grounded evaluation process for explainable machine learning. Technical report (2022). http://ceur-ws.org
6. Buçinca, Z., Lin, P., Gajos, K.Z., Glassman, E.L.: Proxy tasks and subjective measures can be misleading in evaluating explainable AI systems. In: International Conference on Intelligent User Interfaces, Proceedings IUI, pp. 454–464 (2020). https://doi.org/10.1145/3377325.3377498
7. Carlevaro, A., Lenatti, M., Paglialonga, A., Mongelli, M.: Counterfactual building and evaluation via eXplainable support vector data description. IEEE Access **10**, 60849–60861 (2022). https://doi.org/10.1109/ACCESS.2022.3180026
8. Carvalho, D.V., Pereira, E.M., Cardoso, J.S.: Machine learning interpretability: a survey on methods and metrics. Electronics **8**(8), 832 (2019). https://doi.org/10.3390/electronics8080832. https://www.mdpi.com/2079-9292/8/8/832
9. Charmaz, K.: Constructing Grounded Theory: A Practical Guide Through Qualitative Analysis. No. 4, 2nd edn. Sage, London (2014)
10. Chen, C., Feng, S., Sharma, A., Tan, C.: Machine explanations and human understanding (2022). http://arxiv.org/abs/2202.04092
11. Chen, L., Kong, H., Pu, P.: Trust building in recommender agents. Technical report (2005). https://www.researchgate.net/publication/229020498

12. Chen, V., Liao, Q.V., Vaughan, J.W., Bansal, G.: Understanding the role of human intuition on reliance in human-AI decision-making with explanations (2023). http://arxiv.org/abs/2301.07255
13. Chen, Z., et al.: Towards explainable conversational recommendation. Technical report (2020). https://concept.research.microsoft.com/
14. Clinciu, M.A., Eshghi, A., Hastie, H.: A study of automatic metrics for the evaluation of natural language explanations. In: Proceedings of the 16th Conference of the European Chapter of the Association for Computational Linguistics: Main Volume, Stroudsburg, PA, USA, pp. 2376–2387. Association for Computational Linguistics (2021). https://doi.org/10.18653/v1/2021.eacl-main.202. https://aclanthology.org/2021.eacl-main.202
15. Conati, C., Barral, O., Putnam, V., Rieger, L.: Toward personalized XAI: a case study in intelligent tutoring systems. Artif. Intell. **298**, 103503 (2021). https://doi.org/10.1016/J.ARTINT.2021.103503
16. Coroama, L., Groza, A.: Evaluation metrics in explainable artificial intelligence (XAI). In: Guarda, T., Portela, F., Augusto, M.F. (eds.) ARTIIS 2022. CCIS, vol. 1675, pp. 401–413. Springer, Cham (2022). https://doi.org/10.1007/978-3-031-20319-0_30
17. Dominguez, V., Donoso-Guzmán, I., Messina, P., Parra, D.: The effect of explanations and algorithmic accuracy on visual recommender systems of artistic images. In: International Conference on Intelligent User Interfaces, Proceedings IUI, vol. Part F1476 (2019). https://doi.org/10.1145/3301275.3302274
18. Doshi-Velez, F., Kim, B.: Towards a rigorous science of interpretable machine learning. Arxiv, pp. 1–13 (2017). http://arxiv.org/abs/1702.08608
19. Ge, Y., et al.: Counterfactual evaluation for explainable AI (2021). http://arxiv.org/abs/2109.01962
20. Hoffman, R.R., Mueller, S.T., Klein, G., Litman, J.: Metrics for explainable AI: challenges and prospects, pp. 1–50 (2018). http://arxiv.org/abs/1812.04608
21. Hsiao, J.H.W., Ngai, H.H.T., Qiu, L., Yang, Y., Cao, C.C.: Roadmap of designing cognitive metrics for explainable artificial intelligence (XAI) (2021). https://doi.org/10.48550/arxiv.2108.01737. http://arxiv.org/abs/2108.01737v1
22. Johs, A.J., Agosto, D.E., Weber, R.O.: Qualitative investigation in explainable artificial intelligence: a bit more insight from social science. In: Association for the Advancement of Artificial Intelligence (2020). http://arxiv.org/abs/2011.07130
23. Johs, A.J., Agosto, D.E., Weber, R.O.: Explainable artificial intelligence and social science: further insights for qualitative investigation. Appl. AI Lett. **3**(1), e64 (2022). https://doi.org/10.1002/ail2.64
24. Kline, R.B.: Principles and Practice of Structural Equation Modeling, 5th edn. Guilford Publications (2023)
25. Knijnenburg, B.P., Willemsen, M.C.: Evaluating recommender systems with user experiments. In: Ricci, F., Rokach, L., Shapira, B. (eds.) Recommender Systems Handbook, pp. 309–352. Springer, Boston (2015). https://doi.org/10.1007/978-1-4899-7637-6_9
26. Langer, M., et al.: What do we want from Explainable Artificial Intelligence (XAI)? - A stakeholder perspective on XAI and a conceptual model guiding interdisciplinary XAI research. Artif. Intell. **296**, 103473 (2021). https://doi.org/10.1016/J.ARTINT.2021.103473
27. Li, Y., Zhou, J., Verma, S., Chen, F.: A survey of explainable graph neural networks: taxonomy and evaluation metrics (2022). http://arxiv.org/abs/2207.12599

28. Liao, Q.V., Pribić, M., Han, J., Miller, S., Sow, D.: Question-driven design process for explainable AI user experiences **1**(1), 1–23 (2021). http://arxiv.org/abs/2104.03483

29. Liao, Q.V., Varshney, K.R.: Human-centered explainable AI (XAI): from algorithms to user experiences (2021). http://arxiv.org/abs/2110.10790

30. Liao, Q.V., Zhang, Y., Luss, R., Doshi-Velez, F., Dhurandhar, A.: Connecting algorithmic research and usage contexts: a perspective of contextualized evaluation for explainable AI. In: Proceedings of the AAAI Conference on Human Computation and Crowdsourcing, vol. 10, no. 1, pp. 147–159 (2022). https://doi.org/10.1609/hcomp.v10i1.21995. https://ojs.aaai.org/index.php/HCOMP/article/view/21995

31. Lim, B.Y., Dey, A.K., Avrahami, D.: Why and why not explanations improve the intelligibility of context-aware intelligent systems. In: Conference on Human Factors in Computing Systems - Proceedings, pp. 2119–2128 (2009). https://doi.org/10.1145/1518701.1519023. https://dl.acm.org/doi/10.1145/1518701.1519023

32. Löfström, H., Hammar, K., Johansson, U.: A meta survey of quality evaluation criteria in explanation methods (2022). http://arxiv.org/abs/2203.13929

33. Lundberg, S.M., et al.: Explainable machine-learning predictions for the prevention of hypoxaemia during surgery. Nat. Biomed. Eng. **2**(10), 749–760 (2018). https://doi.org/10.1038/s41551-018-0304-0

34. Markus, A.F., Kors, J.A., Rijnbeek, P.R.: The role of explainability in creating trustworthy artificial intelligence for health care: a comprehensive survey of the terminology, design choices, and evaluation strategies. J. Biomed. Inform. **113**, 103655 (2020). https://doi.org/10.1016/j.jbi.2020.103655. http://arxiv.org/abs/2007.15911

35. Miller, T.: Explanation in artificial intelligence: insights from the social sciences. Artif. Intell. **267**, 1–38 (2019). https://doi.org/10.1016/j.artint.2018.07.007. https://linkinghub.elsevier.com/retrieve/pii/S0004370218305988

36. Mohseni, S., Zarei, N., Ragan, E.D.: A multidisciplinary survey and framework for design and evaluation of explainable AI systems. ACM Trans. Interact. Intell. Syst. **1**(3–4), 1–45 (2021). https://doi.org/10.1145/3387166. http://arxiv.org/abs/1811.11839

37. Moraffah, R., Karami, M., Guo, R., Raglin, A., Liu, H.: Causal interpretability for machine learning-problems, methods and evaluation. Technical report

38. Moreira, C., Chou, Y.L., Hsieh, C., Ouyang, C., Jorge, J., Pereira, J.M.: Benchmarking counterfactual algorithms for XAI: from white box to black box (2022). http://arxiv.org/abs/2203.02399

39. Nauta, M., et al.: From anecdotal evidence to quantitative evaluation methods: a systematic review on evaluating explainable AI (2022). http://arxiv.org/abs/2201.08164

40. Pu, P., Chen, L.: Trust-inspiring explanation interfaces for recommender systems. Knowl.-Based Syst. **20**(6), 542–556 (2007). https://doi.org/10.1016/j.knosys.2007.04.004

41. Rong, Y., et al.: Towards human-centered explainable AI: user studies for model explanations (2022). http://arxiv.org/abs/2210.11584

42. Singh, V., Cyras, K., Inam, R.: Explainability metrics and properties for counterfactual explanation methods. In: Calvaresi, D., Najjar, A., Winikoff, M., Främling, K. (eds.) EXTRAAMAS 2022. LNAI, vol. 13283, pp. 155–172. Springer, Cham (2022). https://doi.org/10.1007/978-3-031-15565-9_10

43. Sokol, K., Flach, P.: Explainability fact sheets: a framework for systematic assessment of explainable approaches. In: FAT* 2020 - Proceedings of the 2020 Con-

ference on Fairness, Accountability, and Transparency, pp. 56–67. Association for Computing Machinery, Inc. (2020). https://doi.org/10.1145/3351095.3372870

44. Suresh, H., Gomez, S.R., Nam, K.K., Satyanarayan, A.: Beyond expertise and roles: a framework to characterize the stakeholders of interpretable machine learning and their needs. In: Proceedings of the 2021 CHI Conference on Human Factors in Computing Systems, vol. 16, pp. 1–16. ACM, New York (2021). https://doi.org/10.1145/3411764.3445088. https://dl.acm.org/doi/10.1145/3411764.3445088

45. Szymanski, M., Abeele, V.V., Verbert, K.: Explaining health recommendations to lay users: the dos and don'ts. Technical report (2022). http://ceur-ws.org

46. Tintarev, N., Masthoff, J.: Explaining recommendations: design and evaluation. In: Ricci, F., Rokach, L., Shapira, B. (eds.) Recommender Systems Handbook, pp. 353–382. Springer, Boston (2015). https://doi.org/10.1007/978-1-4899-7637-6_10

47. Tonekaboni, S., Joshi, S., McCradden, M.D., Goldenberg, A.: What clinicians want: contextualizing explainable machine learning for clinical end use. In: Proceedings of Machine Learning Research (2019). http://arxiv.org/abs/1905.05134

48. Velmurugan, M., Ouyang, C., Moreira, C., Sindhgatta, R.: Developing a fidelity evaluation approach for interpretable machine learning (2021). http://arxiv.org/abs/2106.08492

49. Vilone, G., Longo, L.: Notions of explainability and evaluation approaches for explainable artificial intelligence. Inf. Fusion **76**, 89–106 (2021). https://doi.org/10.1016/J.INFFUS.2021.05.009

50. Vilone, G., Longo, L.: A novel human-centred evaluation approach and an argument-based method for explainable artificial intelligence. In: Maglogiannis, I., Iliadis, L., Macintyre, J., Cortez, P. (eds.) AIAI 2022. IFIPAICT, vol. 646, pp. 447–460. Springer, Cham (2022). https://doi.org/10.1007/978-3-031-08333-4_36

51. Wang, D., Yang, Q., Abdul, A., Lim, B.Y.: Designing theory-driven user-centric explainable AI. In: Conference on Human Factors in Computing Systems - Proceedings. Association for Computing Machinery (2019). https://doi.org/10.1145/3290605.3300831

52. Wanner, J., Herm, L.V., Heinrich, K., Janiesch, C.: A social evaluation of the perceived goodness of explainability in machine learning. J. Bus. Anal. **5**(1), 29–50 (2022). https://doi.org/10.1080/2573234X.2021.1952913

Development of a Human-Centred Psychometric Test for the Evaluation of Explanations Produced by XAI Methods

Giulia Vilone[1,2](✉) and Luca Longo[1,2]

[1] The Artificial Intelligence and Cognitive Load Research Lab, Technological
University Dublin, Dublin, Ireland
luca.longo@tudublin.ie
[2] The Applied Intelligence Research Center, School of Computer Science,
Technological University Dublin, Dublin, Ireland
giulia.vilone@tudublin.ie

Abstract. One goal of Explainable Artificial Intelligence (XAI) is to interpret and explain the inferential process of data-driven machine-learned models to make it comprehensible for humans. To reach it, it is necessary to have a reliable tool to collect the opinions of human users about the explanations generated by XAI methods of trained complex models. Psychometrics can be defined as the science behind psychological assessment. It studies the theory and techniques for measuring latent constructs such as intelligence, introversion, and conscientiousness. The knowledge developed in psychometrics was exploited to develop and evaluate a novel questionnaire for reliably evaluating the explanations produced by XAI methods. Explainability is a multi-faceted concept. Thus, it was necessary to create a set of questions to assess various facets and return a comprehensive, reliable measurement of explainability. The questionnaire development process was divided into two phases. First, a pilot study was designed and carried out to test the first version of the questionnaire. The results of this study were exploited to create a second, refined version of the questionnaire. The questionnaire was evaluated by assessing 1) its internal structure with the Exploratory Factor Analysis to analyse the interrelationships between the questionnaire's items, 2) its reliability with the Cronbach alpha tests, and 3) its construct validity by comparing the distribution of the questionnaire's answers with a set of quantitative metrics. Results showed that the questionnaire is promising as it was deemed a valid and reliable tool for evaluating XAI methods.

Keywords: Explainable Artificial Intelligence · Human-centred evaluation · Psychometrics

1 Introduction

XAI aims to develop methods and techniques to make the inferential process of Machine Learning (ML) models understandable by humans. As discussed in

L. Longo (Ed.): xAI 2023, CCIS 1903, pp. 205–232, 2023.
https://doi.org/10.1007/978-3-031-44070-0_11

[24], scholars have proposed many XAI methods to try to meet the requests for transparency and explainability made by the users of ML models. Since the early 2000s, research studies have been conducted on the comprehensibility of the knowledge extracted with data-driven models and techniques belonging to different areas of Artificial intelligence (AI), such as Knowledge Discovery and Data Mining [19]. More recently, scholars have analysed the role of humans in XAI by creating and testing valid and reliable instruments to gather the opinion of both human experts and the lay public about the explanations obtained from these XAI methods [7,8]. This study aims to fill this gap by creating a questionnaire to evaluate the explanations produced by any XAI methods with a reliable, human-centred approach. The questionnaire development process was carried out in the pilot and refined stages. The pilot stage focused on testing the validity and reliability of the first version of the questionnaire and collecting feedback from humans about it. The data collected in this phase were analysed to uncover any limitations in the structure of the questionnaire and the wording of its questions. The outcome informed the creation of a refined version of the questionnaire that aimed to overcome the questionnaire's shortcomings uncovered by the pilot study. The refined questionnaire was tested over six groups of human participants, interacting with argument-based and decision-tree explanations of deep neural networks trained on three datasets.

The remainder of this manuscript is organised as follows. Section 2 summarises the questionnaires developed by scholars to assess the quality of rule-based explanations with a human-in-the-loop approach and the knowledge developed in psychometrics relevant to this study. Section 3 describes the development of a psychometric evaluation instrument for XAI and designing a primary research experiment. Section 5 discusses the findings of this experiment and its limitations, whereas its contribution to the existing body of knowledge and future research directions are suggested in Sect. 6.

2   Related Work

As explainability is a multi-faceted and multi-field construct, developing a questionnaire for its comprehensive assessment requires expertise from fields other than XAI, in particular psychometrics. The scientific literature on XAI was reviewed to study how researchers have tested one or multiple XAI methods with a human-in-the-loop approach, which aspects of explainability were examined and, consequentially, the type and wording of the questions asked in the experiments and their findings. The knowledge developed in psychometrics was exploited to ensure that the questionnaire is a valid and reliable evaluation instrument.

2.1   Human-Centred Evaluation for XAI

Explanations can be considered effective when they help end-users build a complete and correct mental representation of the inferential process of a given model. The scientific articles focused on testing XAI methods with a human-in-the-loop approach followed a process shown in a diagrammatic way in Fig. 1. The human participants in these experiments were of two kinds:

1. people randomly picked out from the lay public and without any prior technical/domain knowledge who were asked to interact with one or more explanatory tools and give feedback by filling out questionnaires;
2. domain experts were asked to give informed opinions on machine-generated explanations and verify their consistency with the domain knowledge.

Fig. 1. Diagrammatic view of the general process followed by human-centred evaluation approaches, retrieved from [24].

Human-centred evaluation approaches can also be clustered into two broad categories, depending on the nature of the questions. Qualitative studies use open-ended questions to achieve deeper insights, whereas quantitative studies are based on close-ended questions that can be easily analysed statistically. As the envisioned questionnaire is based on close-ended questions for testing rule-based explanations, this section focuses on the subset of the latter studies proposing quantitative approaches for this explanation type. The explanations of a model trained to accept or reject loan applications, consisting of IF-THEN rules shown as a Decision Tree (DT), were assessed in [13]. Participants were asked to predict the model's outcome on a new loan application by answering a few yes/no questions like "Does the model accept all the people age above 60?" and rate, for each question, their degree of confidence in the answer from 1 (Totally not confident) to 5 (Very confident). The authors also computed answer accuracy, measured as the percentage of correct answers and the time in seconds spent answering the questions. In another experiment [15,16], participants were invited to interact with a model predicting if a person is doing physical exercise or is at rest based on the body temperature and the pace. They were shown with examples of inputs and outputs accompanied by graphical (DTs) and textual explanations of the model's logic. Half of the participants saw why explanations, such as "Output classified as Not Exercising because Body Temperature <37 and Pace <3" whereas the other half saw why not explanations, such as "Output not classified as Exercising because not Body Temperature >37". Then, participants had to answer a mix of open and closed 7-point Likert scale questions designed to check their understanding by asking how the system works and collect their feedback on explanations' understandability, trust and usefulness. The System Causability Scale is a questionnaire containing ten 5-point Likert questions (from strongly disagree to strongly agree) to assess the usability of user interfaces presenting explanations of an ML model [12]. Similarly, the System Usability Scale, consisting of a ten 5-point Likert-item questionnaire, was proposed in [2] to collect participants' feedback on the persuasiveness of automatically generated explanations. The influence of explanations over end-users' capacity to develop a mental representation of a model's inferential process was investigated in [10,11]. Findings showed that users of simulation-based training systems with virtual players prefer short explanations over long ones. The length of an explanation is defined by the number of its elements that can be a goal or an event of the training program. This was tested by showing four explanation alternatives of different lengths (with either one or two elements), in the form of DTs, for each action of the virtual players and asked to indicate which alternative they considered the most useful for increasing their understanding.

2.2 Psychometrics

Psychometrics can be defined as the science behind psychological assessment [22] as it studies the theory and techniques for measuring latent psychological constructs that cannot be directly observed, such as intelligence, introversion, and conscientiousness, in any knowledge field. For example, psychometrics was exploited to create questionnaires to assess the satisfaction of type-1 diabetes patients with injected versus inhaled insulin [1], or the social skills of young immigrants moving to Spain to identify the services required to integrate into Spanish society [23]. The construction and validation of psychometric instruments follow five principles [5,22]: content validity, construct validity, internal structure, reliability and face validity of the instrument.

Content Validity assesses the match between a psychometric instrument's actual and expected content [6]. In this study, content validity means ensuring the novel questionnaire covers all important facets of explainability by answering questions based on relevant notions related to the concept of explainability. A previous analysis [24] identified 36 notions of explainability that contribute to the effectiveness of an explanation and can be considered candidates to form the basis of the questionnaire if it must satisfy the requirement of content validity. Although, not all these notions are relevant to construct the questionnaire under development. This questionnaire aims to be a generic tool for assessing the quality of rule-based explanations produced by any XAI methods. This means that the notions must be measurable by a human being, including a non-expert in the domain, without conducting complex analyses or calculations. The notions must be considered relevant to any application of every XAI method and cover distinct aspects of explainability. For example, comprehensibility, interpretability, transparency, and understandability are similar concepts; thus, only one should be used in the questionnaire to avoid asking multiple indistinguishable questions that might confuse the respondents. This reduces the list of suitable notions from 36 to 12 (see Table 1).

Table 1. Definition of the notions related to the concept of explainability

Notion	Description & Reference
Actionability	The capacity of a learning algorithm to transfer new knowledge to end-users
Causality	The capacity of an XAI method to clarify the relationship between input and output
Comprehensibility	The quality of the language used by an XAI method
Cognitive relief	The degree to which an explanation decreases the "surprise value", which measures the cognitive dissonance between the explanandum and the user's beliefs
Efficiency	The capacity of an XAI method to support faster user decision-making
Explicitness	The capacity of an XAI method to provide immediate and understandable explanations
Intelligibility	The capacity to be apprehended by the intellect alone
Interestingness	The capacity of an XAI method to facilitate the discovery of novel knowledge and to engage user's attention
Informativeness	The capacity of an XAI method to provide useful information to end-users
Mental Fit	The ability for a human to grasp and evaluate a model
Security	The reliability of a model to perform to a safe standard across all reasonable contexts
Simplification	The capacity to reduce the number of the considered variables to a set of principal ones
Stability	The consistency of an XAI method to provide similar explanations for similar/neighbouring inputs

Construct validity assesses the match between an instrument's actual versus expected associations with other external variables. For example, the Rosenberg Self-Esteem scale (RSE) was created to assess a person's global self-esteem [21]. Theoretically, RSE, to be considered valid, should have a positive correlation with variables quantifying happiness and social motivation and a negative correlation with variables assessing depression and insecurity. As shown in a previous publication [25], a rule-based explanation should be perceived as more intuitive and understandable when it is positively correlated with the metrics of completeness, correctness, fidelity, robustness, and the fraction of classes and negatively correlated with the remaining metrics (the number of rules, average rule length, and fraction overlap).

The *internal structure* assesses the match between a psychometric instrument's actual and theorised structure. The theorised structure refers to the relationship between the questions/items to determine whether or not items are strongly correlated. The instrument's actual and theorised internal structures must match for validity. For example, the actual structure of the questionnaire to measure the social skills of young immigrants was designed to cover six fundamental factors to assess these skills, consisting of the capacity to 1) say no and cut toxic relationships, 2) to self-express in social situations, 3) to defend one's rights, 4) to express anger or disagreement, 5) to make requests to others, and 6) to initiate constructive relationships with people of the opposite sex [23]. Similarly, [17] developed a 31-item psychometric instrument to assess if a person was addicted to the internet by adding these items together to create a single score. So, the expectation was that all the items were highly related. In this study, the items are derived from the selected 12 notions of explainability that are expected to be somehow related. However, the literature does not state anything about these relationships. Still, the expectation is that the questionnaire's items could be combined in a few, but not just a single, factors because explainability is a multifaceted concept.

The fourth principle, *reliability*, refers to the overall consistency of an instrument. The questionnaire is reliable if it returns the same result under consistent conditions [22]. For example, a highly-reliable personality test must always return the same result as long as the person's personality has not changed. Approaches for quantifying reliability include test-retest reliability, parallel-forms reliability, and Cronbach's alpha (α) [22]. In this study, the questionnaire's reliability was assessed with Cronbach's α approach, designed to measure the internal consistency of a psychometric instrument. Cronbach's α ranges from 0 (completely unrelated items) to 1 (identical items). Generally, a psychometric instrument measuring psychological traits is considered reliable when its Cronbach's α is 0.7 or higher. In contrast, a value of 0.8 or higher is recommended for instruments measuring an ability. A shortcoming of Cronbach's α is that it can be inflated by including the same items multiple times.

The fifth principle, *face validity*, corresponds to the degree to which non-experts think the instrument measures the construct under analysis [6]. This is a fundamental requirement for any psychometric instrument because if people do not believe in its validity, they might not take the experiment seriously or respond honestly. For example, applicants to a job might expect to be asked in an aptitude test questions about their problem-solving and social skills. In contrast, questions about their family history or personal life might be answered in such a way as to make them appear socially desirable.

3   Survey Development

The questionnaire was tested on two XAI methods generating rule-based explanations. The first method returns argument-based representations of the inferential process of a trained ML model. These explanations aim to enhance their explainability by employing principles and techniques from computational argumentation. The second XAI method generates rule-based explanations that can be graphically visualised as Decision Trees (DTs). Due to the constraints on the manuscript's length, it is impossible to describe the processes followed by the two XAI methods to generate these two rule-based explanations. However, both processes are described in detail in previous scientific publications, such as [26]. The ML models consisted of feed-forward neural networks with two fully-connected hidden layers trained on three datasets: Airline passenger satisfaction, E-commerce shipping data, and Spam. The choice of these datasets was based on the following inclusion criteria:

– The size of these datasets varies significantly regarding the number of independent variables and samples.
– The datasets differ in the portion of numerical versus categorical variables.
– The reported data describe a real-world phenomenon or problem that does not require any technical knowledge to be understood and has been experienced by most people. Millions take a flight daily, use an email account with a spam filter, and purchase products on e-commerce websites.

The first two criteria allow for evaluating the explainability of the two rule-based explanations on datasets with different complexity levels. The E-commerce Shipping Data dataset is the simplest as it has a few samples ($\sim$11,000) and independent variables (11). The Spam dataset is small in terms of sample size. Still, it has many independent variables (57), representing a middle case. The Airline Passenger Satisfaction dataset is the most complex, containing more than 130,000 samples and 22 independent variables. The third criterion reduces the risk that the participants cannot assess the degree of explainability of the proposed explanations because they do not have the right level of competency in a specific subject to understand the problem or phenomenon at hand. For instance, people might find it hard to judge the rules extracted from data about a medical condition, such as diabetes, if unfamiliar with it. The participants must not spend too much time figuring out the phenomenon described by the data and the trained model. They must focus on the explanations to understand the logic followed by the model to reach its predictions.

3.1   Pilot Survey

A pilot study was run over the first version of the questionnaire to check if it is a valid and reliable instrument. The questionnaire was split into two sections: 1) background information (Table 2) and 2) evaluation of the XAI method (Table 3).

Table 2. Background information section of the pilot questionnaire.

Measured property	Question	Response options
Spam filter	What code is displayed under the "Take the survey" button? (This question is to confirm that you are a human and to prevent spam submissions)	[Free-text box]
Age	What is your age?	18–24; 25–34; 35–44; 45–54; 55–64; 65 and older
Education	What is the highest level of education you have completed?	Secondary/High school education; Bachelor's degree; Master's degree; Doctorate degree; Other
First language	Is English your first language?	Yes; No
Experience in ML	How would you quantify your experience with artificial intelligence technologies/ machine learning techniques?	Less than a year; One year but less than two years; Two years but less than three years; Three years but less than four years; Four years or more
Industry background knowledge	How would you describe your knowledge of the industry?	Very poor; Poor; Neutral; Good; Very good
Feedback	Do you have any suggestions on how to improve the survey?	[Free-text box]

The first question of the background information section asks participants to type in a unique numeric code displayed on the experiment's interface to avoid collecting multiple responses from a participant and answers from bots. Then, there are five questions to gather participants' age, education level, whether English is the participant's first language, and the participants' knowledge of AI/ML technologies and the industry referred to by the dataset. These items could be potentially confounding variables with the explainability of XAI methods. For instance, participants with AI and industry knowledge could find the rules in the XAI frameworks easier to interpret, whilst their fluency in English might affect how they interpret the questions in the second section. Lastly, the last question at the end of the questionnaire asks for open-text feedback about the questionnaire to make further improvements to its final version. The section about evaluating an XAI method consists of 24 questions derived from the 12 relevant notions related to explainability. Each notion is converted into two Likert-style questions about the XAI method under analysis by applying three standard practices described by [22]:

Table 3. Section of the pilot questionnaire about evaluating an XAI method.

#	Measured property	Question	Response options
1	Actionability	I have learned something from the explanatory method	Strongly disagree; Disagree; Neither agree nor disagree; Agree; Strongly agree; Don't understand the statement
2	Actionability rev.	I have learned nothing from the explanatory method	Same as previous question
3	Causality	The relationship between the input data and the predictions is clear	Same as previous question
4	Causality rev.	The relationship between the input data and the predictions is vague	Same as previous question
5	Cognitive relief	No rules in the proposed explanation return surprising predictions	Same as previous question
6	Cognitive relief rev.	Some rules in the proposed explanation return unexpected predictions	Same as previous question
7	Comprehensibility	The structure of the explanatory method is clear	Same as previous question
8	Comprehensibility rev.	The structure of the explanatory method is not clear	Same as previous question
9	Efficiency	I was able to understand the explanatory method very quickly	Same as previous question
10	Efficiency rev.	It took me a long time to understand the explanatory method	Same as previous question
11	Explicitness	The explanatory method is understandable	Same as previous question
12	Explicitness rev.	The explanatory method is incomprehensible	Same as previous question
13	Informativeness	The explanatory method provides useful information	Same as previous question
14	Informativeness rev.	The exploratory method is not informative	Same as previous question
15	Intelligibility	I did not need support to understand the explanatory method e.g. books, internet search, another person	Same as previous question
16	Intelligibility rev.	I needed support to understand the explanatory method e.g. books, internet search, another person	Same as previous question
17	Interestingness	The explanatory method is engaging	Same as previous question
18	Interestingness rev.	The explanatory method is not interesting	Same as previous question
19	Mental fit	The explanatory method allows me to understand the logic of the machine learning model used to generate the predictions	Same as previous question
20	Mental fit rev.	The explanatory method does not allow me to understand the logic of the machine learning model used to generate the predictions	Same as previous question
21	Security	Thanks to the explanatory method, I believe that the model will return accurate predictions for all reasonable inputs	Same as previous question
22	Security rev.	The explanatory method makes me mistrust the model	Same as previous question
23	Simplification	The explanatory method includes the most relevant variables	Same as previous question
24	Simplification rev.	The explanatory method does not include the most relevant variables	Same as previous question

1. Questions should be as unambiguous as possible. This was achieved using simple, consistent language and short questions (12 words or less).
2. The Likert scale must contain enough response options to enable participants to express themselves freely, but not so many that the differences between options would be too subtle and, therefore, meaningless. It was assumed that a five-point Likert scale would suffice to get a holistic view of participants' opinions. Hence, each question has five options ranging from "Strongly agree" to "Strongly disagree", plus a sixth option ("Don't understand the statement") in case the participants did not understand the question.
3. The questionnaire must include at least 20 questions to maintain reliability because it was expected to remove half of the questions from its final version.

Besides following these standard practices, the questionnaire must consider response bias, which is the tendency for participants to respond inaccurately or falsely to questionnaires. Common types of response biases are acquiescence, social desirability, random responding, indecisiveness, and item order bias [6,18,22]. *Acquiescence* occurs when participants agree or disagree with any statement, regardless of the subject. It is usually caused by participants getting distracted while filling out the questionnaire and not understanding the questions or the material in general. To avoid this bias, the questionnaire contains two questions for each notion of explainability: one question is positively phrased (for example, "the explanation is understandable"), the other negatively ("the explanation is not understandable"). *Social desirability* is the tendency for participants to answer questions to make them appear socially desirable. This bias was minimised by informing participants that their answers would be anonymised and by phrasing questions neutrally. The participants are not the subject of the questions ("I took a long time to understand the explanation"); questions are instead phrased to have the XAI method as their subject ("The XAI method requires a long time to be understood"). *Random responding* happens when participants answer the questions randomly because fatigued or bored. As the questionnaire was hosted online, avoiding creating a long questionnaire was the only way to minimise this bias. Lastly, *item order bias* is the tendency for participants to answer the questions differently depending on their order in the questionnaire. This bias occurs when the context and/or content of previous questions affects the responses to later ones. For example, respondents poll described in [20] were more likely to favour giving same-sex couples the same rights as married couples when they were first asked if they would allow same-sex couples to get married (45% versus 37% in favour without the previous context). Item order bias was minimised by randomising the order of the questions for each respondent by exploiting the shuffle question order functionality of the survey tool used in the experiment (Google Form). This does not eliminate the bias at the individual level, but it reduces it when the responses are aggregated and used for statistical purposes.

3.2 Refined Survey

The responses obtained from the pilot stage were exploited to improve the questionnaire's final format by selecting the most reliable questions and rephrasing those perceived as confusing. This was done by using a combination of three different approaches. First, any questions that some participants responded with "Don't understand the statement" was rephrased. Second, the questions were modified so that the subject of the question was the XAI method instead of the participant. Only the questions related to the notions of efficiency and intelligibility were affected by this issue. The questions about actionability ("I have learned something from the explanatory method" and "I have learned nothing from the explanatory method") were kept unchanged, as any rephrasing attempts sounded more confusing and dull to the authors. Third, the questions were edited by accounting for participant feedback from the final open-text question to enhance face validity. By looking at the final open-text question, the common feedback was that participants were annoyed to respond to two almost identical questions, just rephrased positively or negatively. This means they do not see the value in having two questions for each notion of explainability. Based on this feedback, half of the questions in the second session (one per notion) are removed while maintaining a balance of positively and negatively phrased questions to counteract acquiescence. One last modification regards the question related to the industry background knowledge. The refined survey was carried out on three datasets, so this question must be worded differently. In the experiments based on the Airline Passenger Satisfaction and E-commerce Shipping Data datasets, this question became "How would you describe your knowledge of the airline/e-commerce industry?" with 5-level Likert scale answer options. In contrast, it was rephrased as "Are you familiar with the notion of spam in emails and anti-spam filters?" with Yes/No answer options for the Spam dataset. The resulting questionnaire is shown in Table 4.

Table 4. Refined questionnaire.

#	Measured property	Question	Response options
	Background information		
	Spam filter	What code is displayed under the "Take the survey" button? (This question is to confirm that you are a human and to prevent spam submissions)	[Free-text box]
	Age	What is your age?	18-24; 25-34; 35-44; 45-54; 55-64; 65 and older
	Education	What is the highest level of education you have completed?	Secondary/High school education; Bachelor's degree; Master's degree; Doctorate degree; Other
	First language	Is English your first language?	Yes; No
	Experience in ML	How would you quantify your experience with artificial intelligence technologies/machine learning techniques?	Less than a year; One year but less than two years; Two years but less than three years; Three years but less than four years; Four years or more
	Industry background knowledge	How would you describe your knowledge of the industry?	Very poor; Poor; Neutral; Good; Very good
	Evaluation of XAI method		
1	Actionability	I have learned something from the explanatory method	Strongly disagree; Disagree; Neither agree nor disagree; Agree; Strongly agree; Don't understand the statement
2	Causality reversed	The relationship between the input data and the predictions is vague	Same as previous question
3	Cognitive relief	No rules in the explanatory method return surprising predictions	Same as previous question
4	Comprehensibility rev.	The structure of the explanatory method is not clear	Same as previous question
5	Efficiency rev.	It took me a long time to understand the explanatory method	Same as previous question
6	Explicitness rev.	The explanatory method is incomprehensible	Same as previous question
7	Informativeness	The explanatory method provides useful information	Same as previous question
8	Intelligibility rev.	External support was required to understand the explanatory method e.g., books, internet search, another person	Same as previous question
9	Interestingness rev.	The explanatory method is not interesting	Same as previous question
10	Mental fit	The explanatory method allows me to understand the logic of the machine learning model used to generate the predictions	Same as previous question
11	Security	Thanks to the explanatory method, I believe that the model will return accurate predictions for all reasonable inputs	Same as previous question
12	Simplification	The explanatory method only includes the most relevant variables from the data	Same as previous question
	Feedback	Do you have any suggestions on how to improve the survey?	[Free-text box]

4   Questionnaire Evaluation

The questionnaire's evaluation requires assessing its reliability and validity. Reliability was assessed using Cronbach's alpha, as is commonly done in modern psychometrics [22]. This involved calculating Cronbach's alpha for the overall questionnaire and its factors. To calculate this metric, each Likert-scale response is decoded with the following scores: Strongly disagree = 1; Disagree = 2; Neither agree nor disagree = 3; Agree = 4; Strongly agree = 5. The negatively phrased questions must be scored in the opposite direction because agreeing with them means the framework is less explainable. Therefore, the reverse-phrased Likert-scale questions are decoded as Strongly disagree = 5; Disagree = 4; Neither agree nor disagree = 3; Agree = 2; Strongly agree = 1. Validity was established by measuring its construct validity (Does the questionnaire behave consistently with the objective, quantitative metrics for explainability?). This was conducted by calculating the mean explainability score (meaning the average value of the decoded answers to questions 1–12) for each XAI framework and checking if they relate to a set of objective metrics. In that case, the XAI framework with a higher mean score should score higher in the metrics for completeness, correctness, fidelity, robustness, and the fraction of classes and lower in the metrics for the number of rules, average rule length, and fraction overlap.

The structure of the refined questionnaire was evaluated with Exploratory Factor Analysis (EFA), a statistical technique to analyse the interrelationships between questionnaire items and identify a set of underlying latent constructs that cannot be directly measured but affect a battery of measured variables. EFA is used when researchers do not have any explicit *a priori* hypotheses to guide the probing of the data underlying structure [4], as is the case with explainability. The scientific literature does not indicate the interrelationships between the various notions of explainability [24]. EFA is based on the assumption that any variable may be associated with any other variables. Data must pass three tests to validate this assumption. First, the strength of the correlation between variables is examined by using Bartlett's sphericity test. This test compares the correlation matrix of the questionnaire's items to an identity matrix with no correlations to assess if there is a statistically significant difference between them. The correlation matrix was generated using Spearman's rank correlation coefficients as Likert data is inherently non-normal. The alternative hypothesis of Bartlett's test states that the variables are not orthogonal, meaning that the correlation matrix diverges significantly from the identity matrix. In this case, the variables are correlated and, therefore, suitable for EFA. The alternative hypothesis can be accepted when the p-value of the test is lower than the significance level, which is typically 0.05, but in this experiment it equals the conservative level of 0.01. The second step checks if there is any multicollinearity between the items. Multicollinearity occurs when two or more variables are strongly related, and one variable can be accurately predicted from the values of the other(s). One way to check for multicollinearity is to calculate the determinant of the correlation matrix, and a determinant different from zero indicates no multicollinearity. Finally, the third step uses the Kaiser-Meyer-Olkin Measure of Sampling Adequacy (KMO-MSA) to check if the items are suitable for a data dimension reduction technique. KMO-MSA quantifies the proportion of variance among variables that might be common variance or, in other words, how much variance in the questionnaire's items is caused by underlying factors. According to [14], if the overall KMO-MSA for the questionnaire is greater than 0.5, then the items are suitable for EFA. Any items with a KMO score lower than 0.5 must be removed [3,9].

EFA consists of a fitting procedure to identify the number of latent factors to be extracted from the questionnaire and estimate their *loadings*, corresponding to the regression coefficients between the items and the latent factors that measure the influence of a factor on an item. Principal Axis Factoring (PAF) is a non-parametric EFA approach that extracts those factors through an iterative process. It starts from the items' correlation matrix, where the 1 s are replaced with the commonalities of the measured items. Commonalities are initially estimated as the square multiple regression coefficients of one item concerning the other items. Then, the eigenvalues and eigenvectors are calculated to estimate the loadings associated with the latent factors. The eigenvalues represent the variance explained by each factor and are used to create a scree plot (see Sect. 5) that helps determine the optimal number of factors using the "elbow" method. A scree plot displays the eigenvalues from largest to smallest in a downward curve, and the "elbow" of the graph is where their values seem to level off. EFA also involves interpreting what the factors represent. This was achieved by repeating PAF using the recommended number of factors from the first step and applying the direct olbimin rotation. Direct olbimin rotation is an oblique rotation technique used when the factors are expected to be related. It aids in interpreting factors by maximising the loading of an item onto one factor and minimising it on other factors. The goal of direct oblimin rotation is to rotate the axes (or dimensions) determined by the chosen factors until the pattern of loadings becomes easier to interpret or more pronounced.

5   Results

The pilot and the refined studies were designed to adhere to the General Data Protection Regulation (GDPR) (EU) 2016/679. They had been approved by the Research Ethics and Integrity Committee of Technological University Dublin before their inception. Participants were sourced from staff and students in the Computer Science department at Technological University Dublin, ADAPT Research Centre for AI-Driven Digital Content Technology members, and authors' acquaintances, colleagues and connections on LinkedIn. The experiments began by emailing participants a link to the hosting website. Upon entering the website, participants had to provide informed consent before being presented with the XAI method to be evaluated.

5.1 Pilot Study

The pilot study was conducted on the rulesets automatically extracted from the ANN trained on the Airline Passenger Satisfaction dataset. Each participant tested one of the two XAI methods, the first returning an argument-based explanation of the trained ANN and the second showing a DT. Then, each participant had to answer a Google Forms questionnaire to evaluate the framework's explainability. As shown in Fig. 2, the DT displayed each rule as a path from the tree's root to a leaf. Each node on the path represented a rule's antecedent, which defined a range of values on an input variable, such as "Age is greater than 20 (years)", and each edge is an outcome of the previous node ("True" or "False"). The leaves represented the model's predictions, which indicated whether the passenger was satisfied or dissatisfied with their flight. The second XAI method was an argumentation graph shown in Fig. 2 where a node represented a rule and an edge corresponded to a conflict between two rules. Conflicts occur when two rules applied to the same input instance reach different conclusions. For example, two rules with conflicting information are "IF the flight serves food, THEN the passenger will be satisfied" and "IF the food served on the flight is bad, THEN the passenger will be dissatisfied".

The pilot study was carried out between the end of 2021 and the beginning of 2022, when Ireland was experiencing a surge of COVID-19 cases, so the only way to contact people was via online tools. This harmed the response rate. As a result, only 39 people completed the survey, of which 19 were presented with the decision tree and 20 with the argument graph. Most participants were 25–34 and 35–44 years old with a Master's or Doctorate and 4+ years of experience with AI technologies but with limited airline industry knowledge; 23 participants were not native English speakers. Figure 3 presents the distribution of the answers given by the participants to the Likert scale questions. Some participants responded that they did not understand the statement of some questions. These questions were rephrased in the refined survey to make them more understandable.

Cronbach's Alpha test was calculated for each XAI method to check the reliability of the questionnaire explainability (Table 3). The alpha coefficients were 88% for the DT and 92% for the argumentation graph, suggesting that the two surveys had high reliability. Then, the Spearman-rank correlation coefficients were computed for each pair of the 24 Likert-scale questions to check that two notions of explainability, expected to be theoretically related, are indeed related. In particular, two questions assessing the same notion but worded positively and negatively should be strongly correlated with direct correlation, as the five levels of the Likert scale of the negatively phrased questions were scored in the opposite direction of the positively phrased questions. As noticeable from the correlation matrices in Fig. 4, most of these pairs are directly correlated in both surveys. However, some pairs that should be correlated, such as questions 3 and 4 related to causality, are not. This unexpected result reinforced the necessity to revise the questionnaire. The next step of the questionnaire evaluation was to carry out an EFA based on the assumption that any independent variable may be

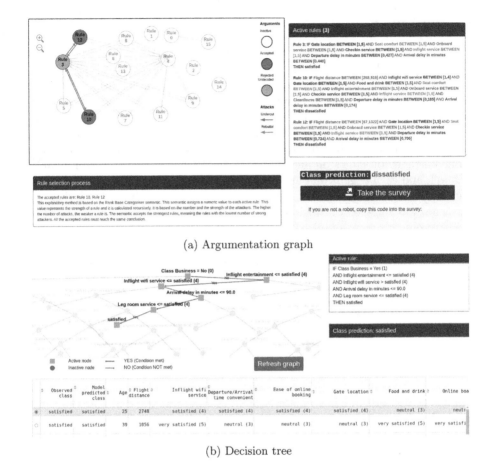

(a) Argumentation graph

(b) Decision tree

Fig. 2. Screenshots of the graphical representations of the rules in the two alternative XAI methods embedded in the online platform used for the pilot and refined surveys (see also [27]).

associated with any other variables. One test to verify this assumption involves the calculation of the determinant of the correlation matrices to check if there is any multicollinearity between any pair of them. The determinant must be different from zero to indicate no multicollinearity. However, the determinants of the correlation matrices related to the argumentation graph and the DT are, respectively, 7.4508e−20 and 1.0509e−20. Both these values can be considered, with a good approximation, equal to 0. As this test failed and it was not possible to support the EFA's basic assumption, no further analyses were carried out on the validity of the pilot questionnaire.

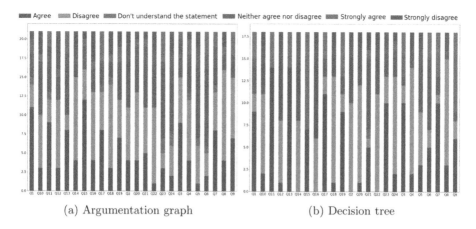

(a) Argumentation graph   (b) Decision tree

Fig. 3. Distributions of the answers of the questionnaire assessing the degree of explainability of the (a) argument-based and (b) decision-tree XAI methods.

5.2   Refined Questionnaire

The refined survey was carried out in two phases. The first phase was based on the XAI methods generated over the Airline Passenger Satisfaction dataset during the second half of 2022 to ensure that the pilot survey's shortcomings were overcome and that there was an improvement in the reliability and validity of the answers. In the second phase, carried out during the first months of 2023, the participants were presented with either an argumentation graph or a DT containing the rules extracted from either the E-commerce Shipping Data or the Spam datasets. The scope was to collect substantial evidence about the validity and reliability of the refined questionnaire. Neither the COVID-19 lockdown nor any other health-related restrictions policies were in place in those two periods, which could prevent an in-person survey. However, it was decided to keep it online as, due to time limitations, this was the quickest way to contact the largest number of people and gather as many participants as possible. Furthermore, an online survey reduces the risk of response biases as the participants do not meet the researchers and are not affected by their expectations of the survey's outcome. Overall, 89 people answered the refined questionnaire. 24 participants were presented with one of the two frameworks related to the E-commerce Shipping Data, 23 the Spam, and 42 the Airline Passenger Satisfaction datasets. The participants' demographic and background information is provided in Fig. 5. As in the pilot study, most participants have a bachelor's or higher degree and at least three years of experience in AI/ML, whilst the numbers of native and non-native English speakers are pretty even.

As done in the pilot study, Cronbach's Alpha test was computed to assess the reliability of the refined questionnaire. The test was applied first to the entire distribution of answers, regardless of the dataset and the framework presented to the participants, and then to the distributions of the answers split by XAI method, dataset, and both (see Fig. 6). Almost all Cronbach's alpha scores are

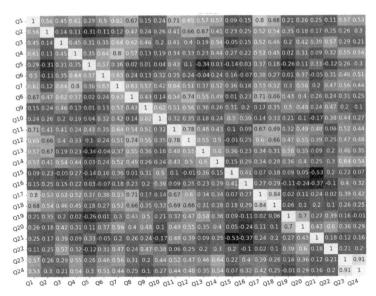

(a) Argumentation graph

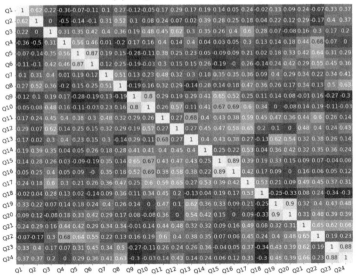

(b) Decision tree

Fig. 4. Correlation matrices of the 24 Likert-scale questions assessing the degree of explainability of the (a)argument-based and (b)decision-tree XAI methods.

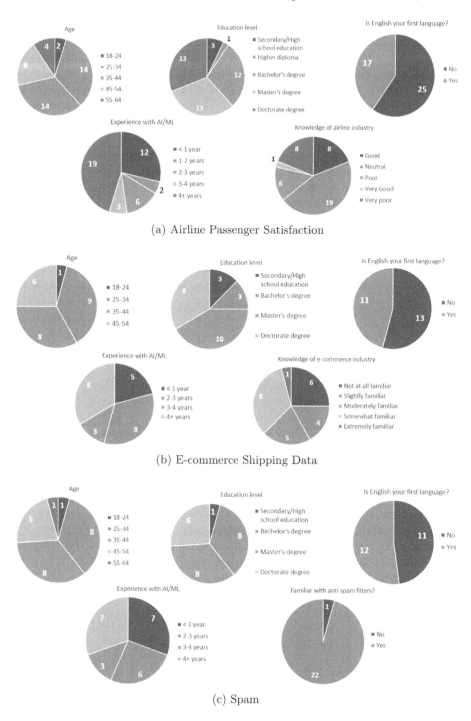

(a) Airline Passenger Satisfaction

(b) E-commerce Shipping Data

(c) Spam

Fig. 5. Distributions of the responses given by participants of the refined study to the questions related to their demographic and knowledge background, split by dataset.

greater than the threshold 0.7, confirming that the refined surveys are reliable, as expected (see Table 5). The only exception is the answers related to the argumentation graph generated over the Spam dataset. However, this is possibly due to the small number of participants presented with this specific case. So, overall it was possible to conclude that the survey had high reliability.

Table 5. Cronbach's alpha scores of the refined survey.

Dataset	XAI method	Cronbach's alpha
All datasets	Both	77.14%
All datasets	Argumentation graph	75.13%
All datasets	Decision tree	79.07%
Airline Passenger Satisfaction	Both	78.26%
Airline Passenger Satisfaction	Argumentation graph	76.85%
Airline Passenger Satisfaction	Decision tree	79.33%
E-commerce Shipping Data	Both	80.46%
E-commerce Shipping Data	Argumentation graph	81.62%
E-commerce Shipping Data	Decision tree	77.68%
Spam	Both	70.69%
Spam	Argumentation graph	52.73%
Spam	Decision tree	73.87%

Before performing the EFA, the EFA's basic assumption had to be verified (see Sect. 4). Bartlett's test of sphericity checks whether or not the observed variables intercorrelate at all using the observed correlation matrix against the identity matrix. One should not use a factor analysis if the test is statistically insignificant. The Bartlett's test p-values are reported in Table 6. The p-values are all below the typical tolerance level of 5% (but also below the more restrictive tolerance level of 1%). The test showed a statistically significant difference between the correlation matrices of the questionnaire's answer distribution data and an identity matrix, indicating that the questionnaire observed variables were correlated. Table 6 also reports the determinants of the correlation matrices. Most are greater than zero, indicating no multicollinearity among the questionnaire's observed variables. However, the determinants related to the distributions of the answers split XAI method and dataset related to the E-commerce Shipping Data and Spam datasets can be rounded to zero with a good approximation. Thus, there is the risk of multicollinearity between the observed variables of these two datasets. However, this might be due to the limited number of participants who tested the two XAI methods on these two datasets, as this issue does not occur for the Airline Passenger Satisfaction dataset analysed by a higher number of people. Therefore, it was decided to carry out the next steps of the EFA while bearing in mind that its assumption could not be fully proved.

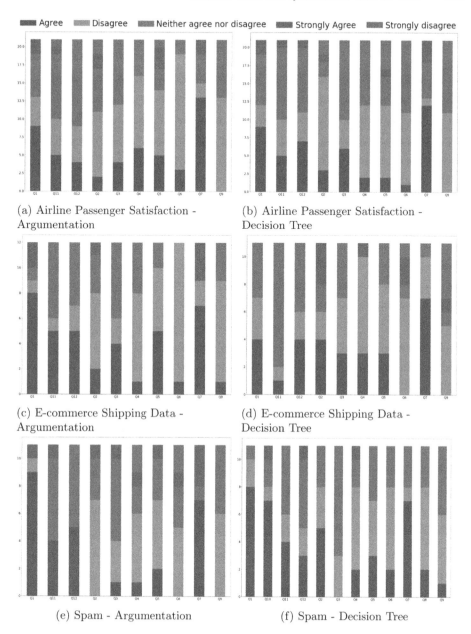

(a) Airline Passenger Satisfaction - Argumentation

(b) Airline Passenger Satisfaction - Decision Tree

(c) E-commerce Shipping Data - Argumentation

(d) E-commerce Shipping Data - Decision Tree

(e) Spam - Argumentation

(f) Spam - Decision Tree

Fig. 6. Distribution of the answers given to the Likert-scale questions by the participants to the online survey related to the argument-based and the DT-based XAI methods showing the rules extracted from the ANN trained on the three datasets.

Table 6. P-values of Bartlett's test of sphericity and determinants of the correlation matrices of the distributions of the answers given the refined survey.

Dataset	XAI method	Bartlett's p-values	Determ.
All datasets	Both	5.0048e−29	0.0218
All datasets	Argumentation graph	8.6657e−09	0.0152
All datasets	Decision tree	2.1289e−14	0.004
Airline Passenger Satisfaction	Both	4.0649e−09	0.011
Airline Passenger Satisfaction	Argumentation graph	0.008	0.0027
Airline Passenger Satisfaction	Decision tree	3.515e−05	0.0002
E-commerce Shipping Data	Both	4.2413e−05	0.0012
E-commerce Shipping Data	Argumentation graph	0.0014	−5.24e−11
E-commerce Shipping Data	Decision tree	0.0004	−1.04e−13
Spam	Both	4.1398e−06	0.0002
Spam	Argumentation graph	0.0048	−1.21e−11
Spam	Decision tree	0.0041	−1.12e−12

The KMO-MSA measures the adequacy of each observed variable for factor analysis by estimating the proportion of variance among all the observed variables that might be common variance. The lower the proportion, the higher the KMO-MSA value, and the more suited the data is to factor analysis. The KMO-MSA values for the questionnaire observed variables are shown in the third column of Table 7. The overall value of KMO-MSA for the refined questionnaire was 0.8, which is considered meritorious, according to [14]. In contrast, the KMO values calculated for each XAI method separately are 0.75 (argumentation graph) and 0.73 (DT), which can be considered middling. The value of KMO-MSA drops when the three datasets are analysed separately. As the scientific literature suggests, KMO-MSA values less than 0.5 indicate the sampling is inadequate for factor analysis. The Spam and the E-commerce Shipping Data datasets do not meet this threshold. By examining the KMO-MSA values of each Likert-scale question, it was possible to notice that question number 3, which measures cognitive relief, received KMO-MSA values below 0.5 except when calculated over the distribution of answers related to the argumentation graph across all three datasets. So, it was removed, and the KMO-MSA values were recalculated, and they are presented in the last columns of Table 7. Generally, the KMO-MSA values improved by removing the third question. They were all above the 0.5 threshold, with the two exceptions of the KMO-MSA related to the E-commerce Shipping Data when the two XAI methods were analysed separately. As done with the analysis of the determinant of the correlation matrices, it was decided to remove the third question and perform the final step, which consisted of the Principle-Axis Factoring approach, on all the observed variables excluded cognitive relief (as it is the variable measure by question 3).

Table 7. KMO Measure of Sampling Adequacy values calculated over the distributions of the answers given to the Likert scale questions, grouped by dataset and XAI method, with and without the answers to the third question.

Dataset	XAI method	KMO-MSA	
		With Q.3	Without Q.3
All datasets	Both	0.8	0.83
All datasets	Argumentation graph	0.75	0.75
All datasets	Decision tree	0.74	0.76
Airline Passenger Satisfaction	Both	0.72	0.77
Airline Passenger Satisfaction	Argumentation graph	0.57	0.57
Airline Passenger Satisfaction	Decision tree	0.53	0.63
E-commerce Shipping Data	Both	0.68	0.73
E-commerce Shipping Data	Argumentation graph	0.37	0.23
E-commerce Shipping Data	Decision tree	0.33	0.31
Spam	Both	0.41	0.52
Spam	Argumentation graph	0.49	0.55
Spam	Decision tree	0.31	0.39

Principle-Axis Factoring (PAF) was performed using all the questionnaire data except the item related to cognitive relief grouped by dataset and XAI method. The eigenvalues of this factor analysis are plotted on the scree plot shown in Fig. 7. All the scree plots tend to level off after the third eigenvalue, suggesting that the internal structure of the questionnaire could contain three factors. This met the expectation that assessing explainability as a single factor is impossible. Explainability is a multifaceted concept resulting from a combination of different factors, spanning from syntactic simplicity to causality, comprehensibility and interestingness, just to name a few. However, the results obtained by PAF showed that the questionnaire's items are related to each other. It is possible to reduce them to three latent constructs that theoretically capture the internal structure of explainability well.

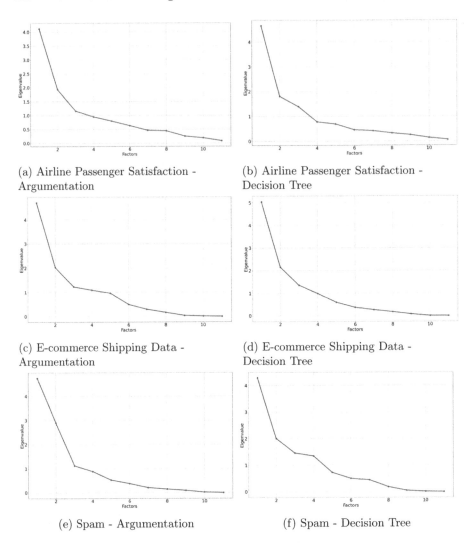

(a) Airline Passenger Satisfaction - Argumentation

(b) Airline Passenger Satisfaction - Decision Tree

(c) E-commerce Shipping Data - Argumentation

(d) E-commerce Shipping Data - Decision Tree

(e) Spam - Argumentation

(f) Spam - Decision Tree

Fig. 7. Scree plots of the eigenvalues computed over the answers given to the Likert-scale questions by the participants to the online survey related to the argument-based and the DT-based XAI methods showing the rules extracted from the ANN trained on the three datasets.

6 Conclusions

In summary, results showed that the proposed questionnaire is a reliable and valid instrument for collecting human feedback about machine-generated rule-based explanations. The questionnaire assesses the impact on explainability of 12 characteristics associated with 12 notions related to explainability that could not be measured quantitatively, such as the level of informativeness of these explanations. The questionnaire proved reliable for assessing two different XAI methods, meaning that the questions consistently elicited the same answers each time they were asked in the same situation repeatedly. Then, an EFA was carried out to assess the questionnaire's internal structure and identify the underlying relationships between the 12 measured characteristics. The outcome was that the question related to cognitive relief could be discarded as its KMO-MSA values were below the acceptability threshold of 0.5 across the three datasets. This means that only the other 11 notions proved to be somehow related to explainability. The PAF, a statistical technique used to extract common factors from a set of observed variables, showed that the internal structure of this questionnaire consisted of three common factors. This confirms the expectation that explainability is a multifaceted construct that cannot be summarised with a single measure. However, these conclusions must be drawn carefully as the questionnaire was answered by a limited number of participants over three variations of two XAI methods. Overall, the final explainability questionnaire has many strengths. Firstly, it is a short, 12-item questionnaire that can be easily and quickly administered online or in person without any guidance from the researchers, and it does not require the user to be an expert in the application domain of the dataset or AI. Secondly, it provides researchers with an objective instrument to assess and compare all XAI methods applied to models induced with any existing learning algorithms by highlighting their strengths and weaknesses in terms of explainability. However, along with its strengths, the questionnaire has limitations due to its design and the experiment's methodology. Firstly, the questionnaire examines explainability using only Likert-scale items. It does not ask any knowledge-based questions to measure the user's understanding of the system in an unbiased way. Secondly, the experiment only assessed two XAI methods, so the relationships between the items could be specific to DTs and argumentation graphs rather than the structure of explainability as a general concept. Lastly, due to lack of time and difficulty finding participants, the experiment only had 89 participants split over three variations of the two XAI methods in the refined stage so that no definite conclusions could be made about the questionnaire (Table 8).

Table 8. Factors with the highest commonality value (in absolute terms) and the commonality value for each refined questionnaire question, grouped by dataset and XAI method.

	Question	Strongest correlated factor (Commonality value)					
		Airline		E-commerce		Spam	
#	Measured property	Arg. Graph	DT	Arg. Graph	DT	Arg. Graph	DT
1	Actionability	3 (0.91)	2 (0.98)	1 (0.51)	1 (1.00)	1 (0.71)	1 (1.00)
2	Causality rev.	2 (0.58)	1 (0.77)	1 (0.82)	1 (0.6)	1 (0.66)	2 (0.6)
4	Comprehensibility rev.	1 (0.72)	1 (0.58)	2 (0.7)	1 (0.51)	1 (0.98)	1 (0.54)
5	Efficiency rev.	1 (0.71)	1 (0.74)	1 (0.31)	1 (0.39)	1(0.92)	1 (0.58)
6	Explicitness rev.	1 (0.71)	1 (0.73)	2 (0.99)	2 (0.6)	1 (0.73)	2 (0.53)
7	Informativeness	1 (0.31)	1 (0.7)	1 (0.71)	1 (0.9)	2 (0.865)	1 (0.72)
8	Intelligibility rev.	1 (0.51)	1 (0.69)	3 (1.00)	2 (0.81)	2 (0.27)	3 (0.261)
9	Interestingness rev.	3 (0.44)	1 (0.62)	1 (0.82)	3 (0.78)	2 (1.00)	2 (0.77)
10	Mental fit	3 (0.53)	1 (0.72)	1 (0.72)	1 (0.84)	2 (0.57)	3 (0.67)
11	Security	2 (0.59)	1 (0.34)	2 (0.42)	2 (0.75)	2 (0.4)	3 (0.56)
12	Simplification	3 (0.76)	1 (0.87)	3 (-0.43)	1 (-0.77)	3 (0.88)	3 (-0.84)
	Cumulative variance	49.1%	61.9%	60.7%	68.4%	69.9%	56.6%

Future work will extend this research in various directions. The questionnaire's universal character will be tested further by applying it to explanations of models induced with other learning algorithms, such as support vector machines, over datasets with different types of input data, like texts and images. Knowledge-based questions could be added to the questionnaire to incorporate an unbiased way of measuring the user's understanding of the XAI framework. The audience of the online survey could be widened by using other tools to find participants, such as crowd-sourcing platforms like Amazon Mechanical Turk, and by translating questions into different languages to improve accessibility.

References

1. Cappelleri, J.C., Gerber, R.A., Kourides, I.A., Gelfand, R.A.: Development and factor analysis of a questionnaire to measure patient satisfaction with injected and inhaled insulin for type 1 diabetes. Diabetes Care **23**(12), 1799–1803 (2000)
2. Dragoni, M., Donadello, I., Eccher, C.: Explainable AI meets persuasiveness: translating reasoning results into behavioral change advice. Artif. Intell. Med. 101840 (2020). https://doi.org/10.1016/j.artmed.2020.101840
3. Field, A., Miles, J., Field, Z.: Discovering Statistics Using R. Sage Publications, Ltd., Great Britain (2012)
4. Finch, J.F., West, S.G.: The investigation of personality structure: statistical models. J. Res. Pers. **31**(4), 439–485 (1997)
5. Fung, G., Sandilya, S., Rao, R.B.: Rule extraction from linear support vector machines. In: Proceedings of the Eleventh ACM SIGKDD International Conference on Knowledge Discovery in Data Mining, pp. 32–40. ACM, Chicago (2005). https://doi.org/10.1145/1081870.1081878

6. Furr, R.M.: Psychometrics: An Introduction. SAGE publications (2021)
7. Gunning, D., Aha, D.: DARPA's explainable artificial intelligence (XAI) program. AI Mag. **40**(2), 44–58 (2019)
8. Gunning, D., Vorm, E., Wang, Y., Turek, M.: DARPA's explainable AI (XAI) program: a retrospective. Authorea Preprints (2021)
9. Hair, J., Black, W., Babin, B., Anderson, R.: Multivariate Data Analysis: Pearson New International Edition PDF eBook. Pearson Education (2013)
10. Harbers, M., van den Bosch, K., Meyer, J.J.: Design and evaluation of explainable BDI agents. In: 2010 IEEE/WIC/ACM International Conference on Web Intelligence and Intelligent Agent Technology, vol. 2, pp. 125–132. IEEE, Toronto (2010). https://doi.org/10.1109/wi-iat.2010.115
11. Harbers, M., Broekens, J., Van Den Bosch, K., Meyer, J.J.: Guidelines for developing explainable cognitive models. In: Proceedings of ICCM, pp. 85–90. Citeseer, Berlin (2010)
12. Holzinger, A., Carrington, A., Müller, H.: Measuring the quality of explanations: the system causability scale (SCS): comparing human and machine explanations. KI-Künstliche Intell. **34**(2), 193–198 (2020). https://doi.org/10.1007/s13218-020-00636-z
13. Huysmans, J., Dejaeger, K., Mues, C., Vanthienen, J., Baesens, B.: An empirical evaluation of the comprehensibility of decision table, tree and rule based predictive models. Decis. Support Syst. **51**(1), 141–154 (2011). https://doi.org/10.1016/j.dss.2010.12.003
14. Kaiser, H.F., Rice, J.: Little jiffy, mark IV. Educ. Psychol. Measur. **34**(1), 111–117 (1974). https://doi.org/10.1177/001316447403400115
15. Lim, B.Y., Dey, A.K.: Assessing demand for intelligibility in context-aware applications. In: Proceedings of the 11th International Conference on Ubiquitous Computing, pp. 195–204. ACM, Orlando (2009). https://doi.org/10.1145/1620545.1620576
16. Lim, B.Y., Dey, A.K., Avrahami, D.: Why and why not explanations improve the intelligibility of context-aware intelligent systems. In: Proceedings of the SIGCHI Conference on Human Factors in Computing Systems, pp. 2119–2128. ACM, Boston (2009). https://doi.org/10.1145/1518701.1519023
17. Nichols, L.A., Nicki, R.: Development of a psychometrically sound internet addiction scale: a preliminary step. Psychol. Addict. Behav. **18**(4), 381 (2004)
18. Oldendick, R.W.: Question order effects. In: Encyclopedia of Survey Research Methods, pp. 664–665. Sage Publications Inc., California (2008). https://doi.org/10.4135/9781412963947
19. Pazzani, M.J.: Knowledge discovery from data? IEEE Intell. Syst. Their Appl. **15**(2), 10–12 (2000)
20. Pew Research Centre: Religious beliefs underpin opposition to homosexuality (2003). https://www.pewresearch.org/religion/2003/11/18/religious-beliefs-underpin-opposition-to-homosexuality/. Accessed 23 Dec 2022
21. Robins, R.W., Hendin, H.M., Trzesniewski, K.H.: Measuring global self-esteem: construct validation of a single-item measure and the Rosenberg self-esteem scale. Pers. Soc. Psychol. Bull. **27**(2), 151–161 (2001). https://doi.org/10.1177/0146167201272002
22. Rust, J., Kosinski, M., Stillwell, D.: Modern Psychometrics: The Science of Psychological Assessment, 4th edn. Routledge (2020). https://doi.org/10.4324/9781315637686
23. Tomé-Fernández, M., Fernández-Leyva, C., Olmedo-Moreno, E.M.: Exploratory and confirmatory factor analysis of the social skills scale for young immigrants. Sustainability **12**(17), 6897 (2020). https://doi.org/10.3390/su12176897

24. Vilone, G., Longo, L.: Notions of explainability and evaluation approaches for explainable artificial intelligence. Inf. Fusion **76**, 89–106 (2021). https://doi.org/10.1016/j.inffus.2021.05.009

25. Vilone, G., Longo, L.: A quantitative evaluation of global, rule-based explanations of post-hoc, model agnostic methods. Front. Artif. Intell. **4**, 717899 (2021)

26. Vilone, G., Longo, L.: A global model-agnostic XAI method for the automatic formation of an abstract argumentation framework and its objective evaluation. In: 1st International Workshop on Argumentation for eXplainable AI Co-located with 9th International Conference on Computational Models of Argument (COMMA 2022), p. 2119. CEUR Workshop Proceedings (2022)

27. Vilone, G., Longo, L.: A novel human-centred evaluation approach and an argument-based method for explainable artificial intelligence. In: Maglogiannis, I., Iliadis, L., Macintyre, J., Cortez, P. (eds.) AIAI 2022, Part I. IFIP Advances in Information and Communication Technology, vol. 646, pp. 447–460. Springer, Cham (2022). https://doi.org/10.1007/978-3-031-08333-4_36

Concept Distillation in Graph Neural Networks

Lucie Charlotte Magister[1]([✉]) [ID], Pietro Barbiero[1,2] [ID], Dmitry Kazhdan[1] [ID],
Federico Siciliano[3] [ID], Gabriele Ciravegna[4] [ID], Fabrizio Silvestri[3] [ID],
Mateja Jamnik[1] [ID], and Pietro Liò[1] [ID]

[1] University of Cambridge, Cambridge CB3 0FD, UK
{lcm67,pb737,dk525,mj201,pl219}@cam.ac.uk
[2] Universitá della Svizzera Italiana, 6900 Lugano, Switzerland
barbiero@tutanota.com
[3] University of Rome, La Sapienza, 00185 Rome, Italy
{federico.siciliano,fabrizio.silvestri}@uniroma1.it
[4] Politecnico di Torino, 10129 Turin, Italy
gabriele.ciravegna@polito.it

Abstract. The opaque reasoning of Graph Neural Networks induces
a lack of human trust. Existing graph network explainers attempt to
address this issue by providing post-hoc explanations, however, they fail
to make the model itself more interpretable. To fill this gap, we introduce the Concept Distillation Module, the first differentiable concept-
distillation approach for graph networks. The proposed approach is a
layer that can be plugged into any graph network to make it explainable
by design, by first distilling graph concepts from the latent space and then
using these to solve the task. Our results demonstrate that this approach
allows graph networks to: (i) attain model accuracy comparable with
their equivalent vanilla versions, (ii) distill meaningful concepts achieving 4.8% higher concept completeness and 36.5% lower purity scores on
average, (iii) provide high-quality concept-based logic explanations for
their prediction, and (iv) support effective interventions at test time:
these can increase human trust as well as improve model performance.

Keywords: Explainability · Concepts · Graph Neural Networks

1 Introduction

Human trust in machine learning requires high task performance alongside interpretable decision making [33]. For this reason, the opaqueness of Graph Neural Networks (GNNs, [32])—despite their state-of-the-art performance [6,10,30,
34]—raises ethical [11,25] and legal [12,36] concerns. As their practical deployment is now under question, interpreting GNN reasoning has become a major
concern in the field [31,39].

L.C. Magister and P. Barbiero—Equal Contribution.

© The Author(s), under exclusive license to Springer Nature Switzerland AG 2023
L. Longo (Ed.): xAI 2023, CCIS 1903, pp. 233–255, 2023.
https://doi.org/10.1007/978-3-031-44070-0_12

Early explainability methods for GNNs produce local, low-level post-hoc explanations [26,35,39], which exhibit the same unreliability as analogous methods for convolutional networks [1,16,23]. In contrast, concept-based explainability overcomes the brittleness of low-level explanations by providing robust global explanations in form of human-understandable concepts [22], i.e., interpretable high-level units of information [17,24]. In relational learning, the Graph Concept Explainer (GCExplainer, [27]) pioneered concept-based explainability for GNNs by extracting global subgraph-based concepts, such as a "house-shaped" structure, from the latent space of a trained model. This way users can check whether the extracted concepts are meaningful [17], whether they are coherent across samples [27], and whether they contain sufficient information to solve a target task [38]. However, as any post-hoc approach, GCExplainer does not encourage the GNN to make interpretable predictions using the extracted concepts [31]. At best, post-hoc techniques can correctly describe what models learn [31], but they cannot make the GNN itself more interpretable. Therefore, the opaque reasoning of GNNs remains an open problem.

To fill this knowledge gap, we propose the Concept Distillation Module (CDM, Fig. 1), the first concept-based end-to-end differentiable approach which makes graph networks **explainable by design**. It achieves this by first distilling a set of concepts present in the GNN's latent space and then using these to solve the task at hand. Our module can be introduced in any GNN architecture. We will refer to the resulting family of architectures as "Concept Graph Networks", or CGNs. We experimentally show that CGNs: (i) attain better or competitive task accuracy w.r.t. their equivalent vanilla GNN, (ii) distill coherent human-understandable concepts from the latent space and obtain high scores in all the key concept-based explainability metrics, i.e., purity and completeness, (iii) can provide simple and accurate logic explanations based on discovered concepts, (iv) allow effective interventions at concept level: these can increase human trust and significantly improve model performance.

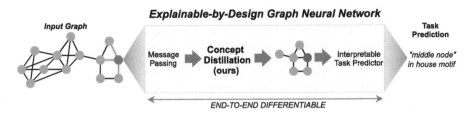

Fig. 1. The proposed Concept Distillation Module makes graph networks explainable-by-design by discovering a set of concepts and using these to solve the task with an interpretable classifier.

2   Background and Related Work

2.1   Graph Neural Networks

Graph Neural Networks (GNNs, [32]) are differentiable models designed to process relational data in the form of graphs. A graph can be defined as a tuple $G = (V, E)$ which comprises nodes $V = \{1, \ldots, n\}$, the entities of a domain, and edges $E \subseteq \{1, \ldots, n\} \times \{1, \ldots, n\}$, the relations between pairs of nodes. Nodes (or edges) can be endowed with features $\mathbf{x}_i \in \mathbb{R}^d$, representing d characteristics of each entity (or relation), and with l ground truth task labels $y_i \in Y \subseteq \{0, 1\}^l$. A typical GNN g learns a set of node embeddings $\mathbf{h}_i$ with a scheme known as message passing [18]. Specifically, message passing aggregates for each node $i \in V$ local information shared by its neighboring nodes $N_i = \{k : (k, i) \in E\}$:

$$\mathbf{h}_i = \sum_{k \in N_i} g(\mathbf{m}_{ik}, \mathbf{x}_i) \qquad \mathbf{m}_{ik} = \phi(\mathbf{x}_i, \mathbf{x}_k) \tag{1}$$

where $\mathbf{m}_{ik}$ is the aggregate of the feature vectors $\mathbf{x}_i$ and $\mathbf{x}_k$ of nodes i and k, respectively, computed using a permutation invariant function ϕ. A readout function $f : H \to Y$ then processes the node embeddings to predict node labels $\hat{y}$. GNNs are trained via stochastic gradient descent minimizing the cross entropy loss between $\hat{y}_i$ and ground-truth y_i.

2.2   Graph Concept Explainer

The Graph Concept Explainer (GCExplainer, [27]) is the first concept-based approach for interpreting GNNs. Following methods successfully applied in vision [17], GCExplainer is an unsupervised approach for post-hoc discovery of global concepts. It achieves this by applying k-Means clustering [14] on the node embeddings $\mathbf{h}_i$ of a trained GNN. [27] argue that each of the k clusters possibly represents a learnt concept according to human perception, as already suggested by [40] and [38]. Using this clustering, GCExplainer then assigns a concept label $\hat{c}_i \in \hat{C} \subseteq \{0, 1\}^k$ to each sample. Finally, it represents each concept using the five samples closest to each cluster centroid, where each sample is visualized as a subgraph with the corresponding node and its p-hop neighbors. This visualization technique is aligned with the reasoning of GNNs, as it takes into account how the information flows via message passing. For example, after three layers of message passing, each node can receive at most information from its 3-hop neighbors.

2.3   Trust Through Concepts and Interventions

Predicting tasks as a function of learnt concepts makes the decision process of deep learning models more interpretable [24,33]. In fact, learning intermediate concepts allows models to provide concept-based explanations for their predictions [16] which can take the form of simple logic statements [9]. In addition, [24] show how learning intermediate concepts allows human experts to rectify mispredicted concepts through test-time interventions, improving model performance and engendering human trust [33].

2.4   Related Work

State of the Art Graph Explainers. GNNExplainer [39] represents the first seminal work on GNN explainability. It maximizes the mutual information between GNN predictions and the distribution of possible subgraphs for explanations. By focusing on individual predictions, the method is limited to explaining one instance at a time corresponding to a localized view of the data distribution. To get a full picture, [39] suggest to perform subgraph matching on a substantial number of instances. However, this is not scalable as subgraph matching is NP-Hard [39]. In an attempt to alleviate this issue, the Parameterised Graph Explainer (PGExplainer, [26]) and the Probabilistic Graphical Model Explainer (PGM-Explainer, [35]) parametrize the process of generating explanations using deep neural networks to provide multi-instance explanations. However, all these methods remain fundamentally limited in their locality as they cannot explain a class of samples in its entirety. In contrast, GCExplainer [27] fills the gap of global explainability for GNNs using concept-based explanations. Similarly, the concurrent work of [3] propose a global and differentiable explainer for GNNs, however, it is post-hoc as it is applied to a trained GNN. While these existing techniques begin to address the lack of insight into the computations of GNNs, they are all post-hoc methods whose goal is to explain a trained GNN, not to make it more interpretable. The proposed method instead aims at filling this knowledge gap by making GNNs explainable by design. The Prototype Graph Neural Network (ProtGNN, [41]) learns prototypical graph patterns that can be used for classification. While ProtGNN has a similar aim of producing an interpretable model as opposed to post-hoc explanations, it is not concept-based. In contrast our method is concept-based and increases the interpretability of the model.

Concept-Based Explainability. From a broader perspective, our work borrows ideas from supervised and unsupervised concept-based methods. These methods have been explored in various ways for other neural networks, such as convolutional neural networks [2,8,17,20,24] and recurrent architectures [19]. From supervised concept-based methods, our approach inherits the ability to perform effective human interventions at concept level extending Concept Bottleneck Models [24] to graphs. As for unsupervised methods, our approach mainly draws from the Automatic Concept Extraction algorithm (ACE, [16]). The algorithm extracts visual concepts by performing k-Means clustering [14] on image segments in the activation space of a convolutional network. The ACE approach is based on the observation that the learned activation space is similar to human perceptual judgement [40]. This was the main motivation behind GCExplainer, as well as our approach. However, in contrast to ACE and GCExplainer, we embed the clustering step within the network architecture, making GNNs explainable by design. While our work proposes clustering within the GNN, similar to [21], we focus on the interpretability aspect achieved via this clustering.

3   Concept Distillation in Graph Neural Networks

We propose the *Concept Distillation Module* (CDM), a differentiable approach which makes GNNs explainable by design. In fact, CDM empowers GNNs through a more interpretable decision making process. It achieves this by first distilling a set of concepts present in the latent space and then using these to solve a classification task. Note that these concepts are inherent to the GNN, and CDM only filters them from the latent space. Thus, they do not improve classification accuracy but make classification more interpretable. Our approach can be integrated in any GNN architecture. We will refer to the resulting family of architectures as Concept Graph Networks (CGNs). As in GCExplainer, humans can visualize CGN concepts to check whether they are meaningful and coherent. Yet, in contrast to GCExplainer, CGNs allow effective interventions at concept level, allowing human experts to improve model performance. CDM integrates a differentiable concept distillation layer to extract node-level and graph-level concepts with an interpretable task predictor providing logic-based explanations.

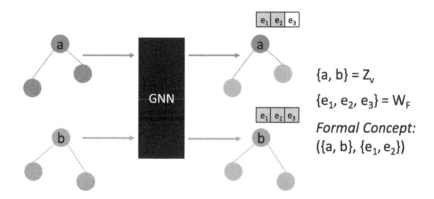

Fig. 2. Formal Concepts in Graph Neural Networks.

3.1   Formal Concepts in Graph Neural Networks

Our work relies on concepts being inherently present in the latent space of GNNs, which can be shown using formal concept analysis based on the theory of complete lattices [15]. We provide a short formal definition of concepts, but refer the reader to [15] for a complete overview. Let us first define a formal context K as $K := (Z, W, I)$, where I is the relation between the objects Z and the attributes W. We denote the relation I of an object z with an attribute w as zIw. For a subset of objects $A \subseteq Z$, we can define the set of associated attributes $A' := \{w \in W | zIw \ \forall \ z \in A\}$. In the same manner, we can define a subset of attributes $B \subseteq W$ via a subset of objects $B' := \{z \in Z | zIw \ \forall \ w \in B\}$. This allows to represent a formal concept of the context K as a pair (A, B), where

$A' = B$ and $B' = A$, as the relation I allows us to map from objects to attributes and vice versa. This also achieves a hierarchical ordering, where an ordered set of all concepts in a context is $\underline{\mathcal{B}}(Z, W, I)$, the concept lattice of the context.

In the setting of GNNs, we can apply the theory of concept lattices in the following way. Let the nodes of a graph or set of graphs be our set of objects Z_v. Let the feature vectors found when aggregating across a node's neighborhood be our set of attributes W_f. This set of attributes is dependent on the number of GNN layers, which leads to more distant neighbors being taken into account. Let the relation I_e associate our objects Z_v with the feature attributes W_f. Given this definition, it becomes evident that concepts are inherently present in the latent space of GNNs. Let us illustrate this with an example, visualized in Fig. 2. Assume a GNN with a single layer, which means that W_f will be the feature vectors found when aggregating a node's feature vector with those of all of its neighbors. Each node, representative of an object in Z_v (a and b in Fig. 2), is associated with a feature vector, representative of an attribute in W_f (e_1, e_2 and e_3 in Fig. 2). Then nodes with similar features and neighborhoods will map to the same set of attributes and can be formally represented as a concept $((\{a, b\}, \{e_1, e_2\})$ in Fig. 2). Moreover, this implies that nodes forming a concept will be clustered in the activation space, which we exploit in the concept distillation step of CDM.

3.2   Concept Distillation

The first CDM step consists of extracting node-level clusters corresponding to concepts from the GNN's latent space. This is based on the observation that the arrangement of the activation space shows similarities to human perceptual judgement [40], as shown by GCExplainer [27] for GNNs, and the application of concept lattice theory [15]. However, in contrast to GCExplainer, in CDM this step is differentiable and integrated in the network architecture, allowing gradients to optimize clusters in GNN embeddings. Specifically, we implement this differentiable clustering using a normalized softmax activation on the node-level embeddings $\mathbf{h}_i$, associating each node with one cluster/concept. This operation returns for each node a fuzzy encoding $\mathbf{q}_i \in [0, 1]^s$:

$$\tilde{\mathbf{q}}_i = \frac{\exp(\mathbf{h}_i)}{\sum_{u=1}^{s} \exp(\mathbf{h}_{iu})}, \qquad \mathbf{q}_i = \frac{\tilde{\mathbf{q}}_i}{\max_i \tilde{\mathbf{q}}_i + \epsilon} \tag{2}$$

where s is the size of the encoding vector. CDM then clusters nodes considering the similarity of their fuzzy encodings $\mathbf{q}_i$. Specifically, CDM groups the samples together depending on their Booleanized encoding $\mathbf{r}_i \in \{0, 1\}^s$:

$$\mathbf{r}_{iu} = \begin{cases} 1 & \text{if } \mathbf{q}_{iu} \geq \tau \\ 0 & \text{otherwise} \end{cases} \tag{3}$$

where $\tau \in [0, 1]$ is conventionally set to 0.5. In particular, two samples a and b belong to the same cluster if and only if their encodings $\mathbf{r}_a$ and $\mathbf{r}_b$ match. For example, consider the two node embeddings $\mathbf{h}_a = [-1.2, 2.3]$ and $\mathbf{h}_b = [2.2, 1.8]$. For these inputs, the normalized softmax would return the fuzzy encodings $\mathbf{q}_a = [0.029, 0.971]$ and $\mathbf{q}_b = [0.599, 0.401]$, respectively. As their Booleanizations $\mathbf{r}_a = [0, 1]$ and $\mathbf{r}_b = [1, 0]$ do not match, we can then conclude that the two nodes belong to different clusters. Notice how our concept encoding is theoretically justified via concept lattices and is highly efficient, as it allows to learn up to 2^s different concepts on GNN embeddings $\mathbf{h}_i$ of size s. This way the GNN can dynamically find the optimal number of concepts/clusters, thus relieving users from this burden. In fact, users just need to choose an upper bound to the number of concepts s rather than an exact value, as when using k-Means like in GCExplainer. In order to account for graph classification, the concept encodings for a graph are pooled before being passed to the interpretable model predicting the task, as explained in the next paragraph.

3.3   Interpretable Predictions

The second CDM step consists of using the distilled concepts to make interpretable predictions for downstream tasks. In particular, the presence of concepts enables pairing GNNs with existing concept-based methods which are explainable by design, such as Logic Explained Networks (LENs, [9]). LENs are neural models providing simple concept-based logic explanations for their predictions. Specifically, LENs can provide class-level explanations which makes our approach the first at providing unique global explanations for GNNs. Given the formal definition of concepts, they naturally lend themselves as propositions for the logic explanations produced by LENs. CDM uses a LEN as the readout function f for the classification, applying it on top of concept representations $\mathbf{q}_i$. For graph classification tasks, the input data is composed of a set of t graphs $G^j \in \{(V^j, E^j)\}_{j=1}^t$, where each graph is associated with a task label $y^j \in Y$. In this setting, GNN-based models predict a single label for each graph G^j by pooling its node-level encodings $\mathbf{q}_i^j$ to aggregate over multiple concepts:

$$\hat{y}_i = \text{LEN}_{\text{node}}(\mathbf{q}_i), \qquad \hat{y}^j = \text{LEN}_{\text{graph}}\left(\frac{1}{n_j} \sum_{i=1}^{n_j} \mathbf{q}_i^j \right) \qquad (4)$$

where n_j is the number of nodes associated with graph j. In our implementation, we use the entropy-based layer to implement LENs [5]) as it can provide high classification accuracy with high-quality logic explanations. This entropy-based layer implements a sparse attention layer designed to work on top of concept activations. The attention mechanism allows the model to focus on a small subset of concepts to solve each task. It also introduces a parsimony principle in the architecture corresponding to an intuitive human cognitive bias [28]. This parsimony principle allows the extraction of simple logic explanations from the network, thus making these models explainable by design.

3.4 Concept-Based and Logic-Based Explanations

The proposed method provides two types of explanations: concept-based and logic-based explanations. Global concept-based explanations can be extracted in a similar manner as in GCExplainer: a concept for a node or graph is extracted by finding the cluster with which a node's embedding is associated, and visualising the samples closest to the cluster centroid. The logic-based formula provided per class broadens the explanation scope, as it indicates which neurons of the concept encoding q_i are activated and representative of a class. This provides a more comprehensive explanation since a class can be associated with multiple concepts.

3.5 Concept Interventions

As in Concept Bottleneck Models [24], our approach supports human interaction at concept level. In fact, in contrast to existing post-hoc methods, an explainable-by-design approach creates an explicit concept layer which can positively react to test-time human interventions. For instance, consider a misclassified node with concept encoding $q_a = [0.21, 0.93]$. Assume that the vast majority of nodes with the binary encoding $r_{grid\_node} = [0, 1]$ are nodes of a grid-like structure, which allows a human to label this cluster as "grid nodes". Now, a human expert can inspect the neighborhood of the misclassified node and realize that this node belongs to a circle-like structure and not to a grid structure. As the binary encoding for the concept "circle nodes" is $r_{circle\_node} = [1, 1]$, the user can easily apply an intervention to correct the misclassified concept by changing its encoding to $q_a := [1, 1]$. Such an update allows the interpretable readout function to act on information related to the corrected concept, thus improving the original model prediction.

4 Experiments

In our experiments we focus on the following research questions:

- **Task Accuracy and Completeness**—What is the impact of our approach on the generalization error of a GNN? Is the identified concept set complete w.r.t. the task?
- **Concept Interpretability**—Are the unsupervised concepts identified by our model meaningful? Do they match ground truths or human expectations?
- **Explanation Performance**—Are concepts pure and coherent? Are the logic explanations provided accurate and simple enough to be interpretable?

With these questions in mind, we hypothesize that our approach can: (i) obtain similar task accuracy w.r.t. a standard GNN; (ii) extract the ground truth graph concepts aligned with human expectations, and (iii) identify pure concepts as well as simple and accurate logic explanations.

4.1   Metrics

In our evaluation, we measure model performance and interpretability based on five metrics. We measure model performance via *classification accuracy* to compare the generalization error of CGNs w.r.t. their equivalent vanilla GNNs. To evaluate model interpretability, we compute *concept completeness* [38], which assesses whether the concepts discovered are sufficient to describe the downstream task. Following [38], we use a decision tree [7] to predict the task labels given the concept encoding associated with each input instance. We also examine concept coherence via *concept purity* [27]. Following [27], we measure concept purity by considering the graph edit distance of samples' neighborhoods within each cluster/concept. Having checked concept quality, we evaluate logic explanations in terms of their accuracy and complexity. We calculate the *accuracy of logic explanations* using the learnt logic formulas for classifying test samples based on their concept encoding as done by [9]. This mirrors the computation of concept completeness, however, instead of a decision tree, we use the learnt logic formulas for classification. Lastly, we evaluate the *complexity of logic explanations* by measuring the number of terms in logic rules [9]. We compute all metrics on test sets across five random weight initializations and report their means and 95% confidence intervals using the t-distribution. We do not measure classical explainability metrics, such as sensitivity and sparsity [42], as they apply to explainers of models rather than explainable-by-design networks themselves.

4.2   Datasets

We perform the experiments on the same set of datasets as the Graph Neural Network Explainer (GNNExplainer, [39]), as subsequent research establishes them as benchmarks [26,27,35].

Node Classification. We use five synthetic node classification datasets put forward by [39], which have a ground truth motif encoded. A ground truth motif is a subgraph, which a successful explainability technique should recognize. The first dataset is BA-Shapes, which consists of a single graph where the base structure is a Barabási-Albert (BA) graph [4] of width 300, which has 80 house motifs and 70 random edges attached to it. The dataset has 4 classes, with the goal of discriminating between a node being part of the base graph or the top, middle or bottom of a house structure. The second dataset is BA-Community, generated by the union of two BA-Shapes graphs. Here, the task is to classify a node into 8 classes, which represent graph membership and the structural role of the node as in BA-Shapes. The third dataset is BA-Grid, which is a BA graph of width 300 with 80 3-by-3 grids attached to it. The goal is to classify whether a node is part of the base graph of a grid structure. The fourth dataset is Tree-Cycles, formed by a binary tree of depth 8 with 60 cycle structures of 6 nodes attached to it. The task is to classify between a node belonging to the tree or cycle structure. Lastly, the fifth dataset is Tree-grid, which consists of a binary tree of depth 8, which has 80 3-by-3 grid structures attached. The classification task is the same, asking to discriminate between a node being part of the tree or grid structure.

4.3 Graph Classification

We also include two real-world datasets to evaluate model performance on less structured data and on graph classification tasks. The first dataset is Mutagenicity [29], which is a collection of graphs representing mutagenic and non-mutagenic molecules. The task is to identify a molecule as mutagenic or non-mutagenic. The second dataset is Reddit-Binary [29], which is a collection of graphs representing Reddit discussion threads where nodes represent users and edges represent interactions. A challenge in evaluating these datasets is that there are no ground truth motifs. However, [39] suggests the ring structure and nitrogen dioxide compound in Mutagenicity, and the star-like structure in Reddit-Binary as desirable motifs to be recovered. Figure 1 provides further statistics on the datasets, such as the graph size and number of classes.

Table 1. An overview of key markers of the datasets.

Dataset	Classification Problem	Number of Graphs	Graph Size	Number of Features	Number of Classes
BA-Shapes	Node	1	700	1	4
BA-Community	Node	1	1400	1	8
BA-Grid	Node	1	1020	1	2
Tree-Cycles	Node	1	871	1	2
Tree-Grid	Node	1	1231	1	2
Mutagenicity	Graph	4337	30.32 (on average)	14	2
Reddit-Binary	Graph	2000	429.63 (on average)	1	2

4.4 Baselines and Setup

To address our research questions, we compare our approach against an equivalent convolutional vanilla GNN explained by GCExplainer. Specifically, we perform a quantitative evaluation by comparing the averages and confidence intervals obtained for each metric. We perform a qualitative evaluation by comparing the concepts extracted and whether they recover the desired motifs. Notice that we do not focus on other post-hoc explainability methods, such as GNNExplainer [39], PGExplainer [26] or PGM-Explainer [35], as to the best of our knowledge GCExplainer is the only explainability method providing global concept-based explanations for GNNs. We do later provide a brief comparison of the proposed method with GNNExplainer and ProtGNN [41] for completeness.

For each of the datasets, we use 80% of the data for training and 20% for testing. The examples in each split vary across seeds due to the different random intitialization. We select the models' hyperparameters, such as the number of hidden units and learning rate, using a grid search. To ensure fairness in our results, we use the same architecture capacity and hyperparameters for our model as well as for its vanilla counterpart. We initialize the hyperparameters of GCExplainer to the values determined experimentally by [27].

5 Results

5.1 Concept Graph Networks are as Accurate as Vanilla GNNs (Table 2)

Our results show that CDM allows GNNs to achieve better or comparable task accuracy w.r.t. equivalent GNN architectures. Specifically, our approach outperforms vanilla GNNs on the Tree-Cycle dataset, having a higher test accuracy (plus ~8% on average) and less variance across different parameter initializations. We hypothesize that this effect is due to more stable and pure concepts being learnt thanks to CDM, as we will see later when discussing the concept purity scores. We do not observe any significant negative effect of using CDM on the generalization error of GNNs.

Table 2. Model accuracy for the Concept-based Graph Network (CGN) and an equivalent vanilla GNN.

	Model Accuracy (%)	
	CGN	Vanilla GNN
BA-Shapes	**98.11 (97.04, 99.18)**	98.02 (96.40, 99.65)
BA-Community	85.67 (81.38, 89.95)	**87.50 (85.56, 89.45)**
BA-Grid	99.51 (98.75, 100.00)	**99.71 (99.38, 100.00)**
Tree-Cycle	**94.97 (92.50, 97.44)**	86.26 (58.58, 100.00)
Tree-Grid	**95.17 (93.59, 96.75)**	94.54 (93.61, 95.46)
Mutagenicity	**82.40 (81.31, 83.48)**	82.35 (81.64, 83.06)
Reddit-Binary	90.55 (87.95, 93.15)	**91.20 (88.82, 93.58)**

5.2 The Concept Distillation Module Discovers Complete Concepts (Table 3)

Our experiments show that overall CDM discovers a more complete set of concepts w.r.t. the concept set extracted by GCExplainer on equivalent GNN architectures. This is particularly emphasized in the Tree-Grid, BA-Shapes and BA-Community datasets, where CDM significantly outperforms GCExplainer by up to ~13%. For the other datasets, the proposed approach matches the concept completeness scores of GCExplainer. The completeness scores on the BA-Grid and Mutagenicity datasets are only slightly lower, however, within the margins of the confidence interval. In absolute terms, CDM discovers highly complete sets of concepts with completeness scores close to the model accuracy for the synthetic datasets.

Table 3. Concept completeness and purity for the Concept-based Graph Network (CGN) and an equivalent vanilla GNN.

	Concept Completeness (%)		Concept Purity	
	CGN	Vanilla GNN	CGN	Vanilla GNN
BA-Shapes	**98.11 (96.85, 99.36)**	93.69 (86.21, 100.00)	**0.00 (0.00, 0.00)**	0.00 (0.00, 0.00)
BA-Community	**83.10 (78.90, 87.29)**	75.74 (72.85, 78.64)	1.70 (0.43, 3.83)	**1.60 (0.49, 2.71)**
BA-Grid	99.61 (98.80, 100.00)	**99.71 (99.38, 100.00)**	0.20 (0.00, 0.76)	2.40 (0.00, 6.48)
Tree-Cycle	**91.98 (83.71, 100.00)**	91.16 (84.47, 97.86)	**0.00 (0.00, 0.00)**	0.60 (0.00, 2.27)
Tree-Grid	**91.37 (84.58, 98.16)**	78.48 (76.17, 80.79)	**0.00 (0.00, 0.00)**	0.00 (0.00, 0.00)
Mutagenicity	63.40 (58.84, 67.96)	**63.95 (60.14, 67.77)**	1.00 (0.00, 3.78)	**0.60 (0.00, 2.27)**
Reddit-Binary	**75.91 (61.16, 90.66)**	73.10 (58.44, 87.75)	0.40 (0.00, 1.51)	**0.00 (0.00, 0.00)**

Ablation Study on the Size of the Concept Embedding Size. In order to verify the effectiveness and robustness of our approach, we perform an ablation study on the concept embedding size s. More specifically, we control the upper bound of the size of the concept lattice while observing the concept completeness score for different values of s. We conduct this ablation study on the BA-Shapes dataset using the values 2, 6, 10, 12 and 14 for s. Table 4 summarises the results obtained. We observe that the completeness score is stable for different values of $s \sim 10$.

Table 4. The concept completeness score for a CDM trained on the BA-Shapes dataset for different concept embedding sizes.

Concept Embedding Size s	Concept Completeness (%)
2	70.35 (44.26, 96.44)
6	94.09 (89.83, 98.35)
10	**98.11 (96.85, 99.36)**
12	97.57 (96.48, 98.60)
14	97.58 (95.48, 99.67)

5.3 The Concept Distillation Module Identifies Meaningful Concepts (Table 5)

CDM discovers high-quality concepts, which are meaningful to humans. Similar to GCExplainer, our results demonstrate that CDM can discover concepts corresponding to the ground truth motifs embedded in the toy datasets. For example, our approach recovers the "house motif" in BA-Shapes. Moreover, CDM proposes plausible concepts for the real-world datasets where ground truth motifs are lacking. In this case, the extracted concepts match the desirable motifs suggested by [39], corresponding to ring structures and the nitrogen dioxide compound in Mutagenicity, and a star-like structure in Reddit-Binary. As we use the same visualization technique as GCExplainer the merit of our contribution lies in the discovery of a more descriptive set of concepts, which includes rare and fine-grained concepts.

Table 5. The Concept Distillation Module detects meaningful concepts matching the expected ground truth. Blue nodes are the instances being explained, while orange nodes represent their p-hop neighbors. Similar motifs are identified by GCExplainer.

	BA-Shapes	BA-Grid	Tree-Grid	Tree-Cycle	BA-Community	Mutagenicity	Reddit-Binary
Ground Truth							
Extracted Concept							

Table 6. The Concept Distillation Module detects concepts more fine-grained than the simple ground truth motif encoded, as well as rare motifs. Blue nodes are the instances being explained, while orange nodes represent their p-hop neighbors. Notably, GCExplainer gives no indication of rare concepts.

Ground Truth	Fine-Grained Concepts		Rare Concepts	

5.4 The Concept Distillation Module Identifies Rare and Fine-Grained Concepts (Table 6)

CDM discovers more fine-grained concepts than just the "house motif" suggested by GNNExplainer, as it can differentiate whether a middle or bottom node is on the far or near side of the edge attaching to the BA graph. This matches the quality of concepts extracted by GCExplainer. In contrast to GCExplainer, CDM also identifies rare concepts. Rare motifs are present in toy datasets through the insertion of random edges. As the proposed approach can find the optimal number of clusters/concepts dynamically, clusters of a very small size possibly represent rare motifs. To check the presence of rare concepts, we visualize the p-hop neighbors of nodes found in small clusters. For example, CDM identifies a rare concept represented as a "house" structure attached to the BA graph via the top node of the house in the BA-Shapes dataset. This represents a rare concept as it is generated by the insertion of a random edge. We confirm this observations on other toy datasets, such as BA-Community and Tree-Cycle, where motifs with random edges are clearly identified. We have not identified rare concepts in BA-Grid or Tree-Grid, which may be attributed to the random edges being distributed within the base graph, which has a less definite structure. Due to the lack of expert knowledge, we cannot confirm whether the rare motifs found in Mutagenicity and Reddit-Binary align with human expectations.

5.5 The Concept Distillation Module Identifies Pure Concepts (Table 3)

CDM discovers high-quality concepts, which are coherent across samples, as measured by concept purity. Our approach discovers concepts with nearly optimal purity scores on toy datasets, with a graph edit distance close to zero. For these datasets, CDM provides either better or comparable purity scores when compared to GCExplainer. CDM provides slightly worse purity scores in both the Mutagenicity and Reddit-Binary datasets. However, also in this case the absolute purity of CDM is almost optimal.

5.6 The Concept Distillation Module Provides Accurate Logic Explanations (Table 7, Table 8)

LEN allows CDM to provide simple and accurate logic explanations for task predictions. The accuracy of the logic explanations extracted reaches at least 90% for the BA-Shapes, BA-Grid and Tree-Cycle datasets, indicating that CDM derives a precise description of the model decision process. Relating the accuracy of explanations back to the model accuracy, we observe that the explanation accuracy is bounded by task performance, as already noticed by [9]. This explains the slightly lower logic explanation accuracy on the real-world datasets, which can be ascribed to the absence of definite ground-truth concepts and to the task being more complex. Besides being accurate, logic explanations are very short, with a complexity below 4 terms. In conjunction with the explanation accuracy, this means that CDM finds a small set of predicates which accurately describes the most relevant concepts for each class.

Table 7. Accuracy and complexity of logic explanations found using the Concept Distillation Module. Accuracy is computed using logic formulas to classify samples based on their concept encoding. Complexity measures the minterms in logic formulas.

	Logic Explanation Accuracy (%)	Logic Explanation Complexity
BA-Shapes	96.56 (92.17, 100.95)	3.10 (2.75, 3.45)
BA-Community	81.43 (78.20, 84.66)	3.85 (3.09, 4.61)
BA-Grid	99.61 (98.86, 100.36)	1.30 (0.74, 1.86)
Tree-Cycle	90.49 (78.43, 102.55)	1.90 (1.22, 2.58)
Tree-Grid	89.66 (82.71, 96.62)	2.20 (1.07, 3.33)
Mutagenicity	59.94 (44.99, 74.90)	2.60 (0.88, 4.32)
Reddit-Binary	71.84 (54.10, 89.59)	1.60 (1.08, 2.12)

5.7 The Concept Distillation Module Supports Human Interventions (Fig. 3)

Supporting human interventions is one of the main benefits of more interpretable architectures that learn tasks as a function of concepts. In contrast to vanilla GNNs, CDM enables interventions at concept-level, which allows human experts to correct mispredicted concepts. Similarly to Concept Bottleneck Models [24],

Table 8. An example of a concept-based logic explanations discovered by the Concept Distillation Module per dataset. Blue nodes are the instances being explained, while orange nodes represent their p-hop neighbors. For Mutagenicity the color of each node represents a different chemical element. The logic formulae describe how the presence of concepts can be used to infer task labels. For example, the first logic rule states that the task label "middle nodes in house motifs" ($y = 2$) can be inferred from the concepts: "middle node with attaching edge on the near side" or "middle node with attaching edge on the far side".

Dataset	Concept-based Logic Explanation	Ground Turth Concepts
BA-Shapes	$y = 2 \leftarrow$ ... OR ...	*Node in house motif*
BA-Grid	$y = 1 \leftarrow$ ...	*Node in grid motif*
Tree-Grid	$y = 1 \leftarrow$ ... OR ...	*Node in grid motif*
Tree-Cycle	$y = 1 \leftarrow$ ... OR ... OR ...	*Node in circle motif*
BA-Community	$y = 3 \leftarrow$ ... OR ... OR ...	*Node in house motif*
Reddit-Binary	$y = $ "Q/A" $\leftarrow$ ... OR ...	*Star motifs*
Mutagenicity	$y = $ "mutagenic" $\leftarrow$ ...	*Ring motifs or NO_2*

our results show that correcting concept assignments significantly improves the model test accuracy to over 98% for the synthetic datasets, achieving 100% test accuracy on BA-Grid and BA-Shapes. We also observe an increase in task accuracy in BA-Community, however, the increase is much more gradual. Most notably, in both real-world datasets CDMs allow GNNs to improve their task accuracy by up to $\sim+10\%$ with less than 10 interventions.

5.8   Ablation Study on Tau

In order to verify our choice of tau ($\tau = 0.5$), we run an ablation study. We adapt the value for tau in 0.1 intervals and calculate results for the BA-Shapes and BA-Community datasets in line with our previous evaluation. We collect the completeness score and number of clusters found, as these metrics are most indicative of the effect on the explanation scope provided. Table 9 summarises the results. The optimal value for tau varies across the three datasets. Going by the completeness score, the optimal values are 0.6 and 0.8 for BA-Shapes, BA-Community, respectively. However, based on the number of clusters found, which can indicate a more rare set of concepts being found, the optimal values for tau would be 0.1 and 0.9 respectively. It can be argued that concept completeness is a better indicator, as it directly correlates the concept to the prediction of the output label, nevertheless, it easily glosses over rare concepts. This trade-off must be considered, wherefore, it can be argued that choosing tau at 0.5 is a robust and conventional parameter setting, as differences in results are minute. Nevertheless, for optimal results tau should be finetuned, as it is dependent on the dataset.

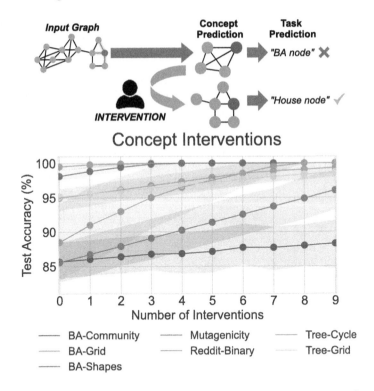

Fig. 3. The Concept Distillation Module supports interventions at concept-level, allowing human experts to correct mispredicted concepts, increasing human trust in the model [33]. This interaction significantly improves task performance, achieving almost 100% accuracy on synthetic datasets.

Table 9. The concept completeness score and number of clusters discovered when varying the value of tau.

Tau	BA-Shapes		BA-Community	
	Completeness (%)	Number of Clusters	Completeness (%)	Number of Clusters
0.1	48.04 (42.64, 53.44)	**24.80 (20.38, 29.22)**	59.18 (53.99, 64.37)	50.00 (31.33, 68.67)
0.2	55.07 (49.64, 60.50)	22.60 (20.03, 25.17)	59.54 (52.37, 66.72)	60.00 (32.00, 89.00)
0.3	58.39 (51.61, 65.17)	21.80 (19.76, 23.84)	62.24 (51.86, 72.62)	68.20 (35.17, 101.23)
0.4	58.83 (53.55, 64.12)	20.80 (18.25, 23.34)	62.58 (52.21, 72.95)	81.60 (34.31, 128.89)
0.5	59.59 (55.01, 64.17)	21.40 (19.98, 22.82)	62.17 (49.49, 74.86)	86.80 (36.54, 137.06)
0.6	**60.40 (56.82, 63.97)**	20.60 (17.13, 24.07)	62.64 (49.54, 75.73)	85.20 (35.51, 134.89)
0.7	59.18 (50.00, 68.36)	21.40 (15.41, 27.39)	63.56 (49.03, 78.09)	88.00 (37.55, 138.45)
0.8	58.89 (47.68, 70.09)	20.00 (13.98, 26.02)	**63.89 (49.25, 78.53)**	80.40 (29.86, 130.94)
0.9	54.83 (44.62, 65.04)	21.00 (15.18, 26.82)	58.42 (43.88, 72.97)	**97.20 (33.88, 160.52)**

5.9 Qualitative Comparison to GNNExplainer and GCExplainer

We perform a qualitative comparison of the explanations produced using CDM, GCExplainer [27] and GNNExplainer [39]. We limit ourselves to a qualitative

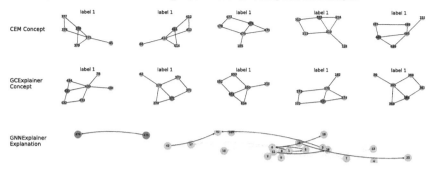

Fig. 4. Concept-based explanations produced using the Concept Distillation Module and GCExplainer, as well as the explanation produced by GNNExplainer for a node in the BA-Shapes dataset. In the explanations, the blue nodes are the nodes clustered together, while the orange nodes are the p-hop neighborhood. GNNExplainer has its own coloring, where the purple nodes are node part of the middle of the house and the turquoise nodes are part of the BA base graph. (Color figure online)

comparison against GCExplainer here, as we have already performed a quantitative comparison above. We compare the explanations produced by CDM against those of GNNExplainer, as GNNExplainer is the most prominent explainer for GNN, forming seminal work. However, we do not perform a quantitative evaluation against GNNExplainer, as the explanations are not concept-based and thus are evaluated in a different manner. For this reason, we refrain from also evaluating against other comparable explainers, such as PGExplainer [26] and PGM-Explainer [35]. We select GNNExplainer over these explainers as it is the seminal work in the field. GCExplainer and GNNExplainer are applied on the vanilla GNN. We focus on an evaluation of the BA-Shapes and BA-Community datasets, as the ground truth motifs to be extracted are known for these datasets.

BA-Shapes (Fig. 4). Figure 4 shows the explanations provides by CDM, GCExplainer and GNNExplainer for a node, which is part of the middle of a house. Both CDM and GCExplainer successfully identify the house structure, which is the motif that should be recovered. CDM performs slightly better than GCExplainer, as it does not include a concept with a random edge. In contrast, the explanation provided by GNNExplainer does not visualise the house structure in full. Only the middle nodes of the house are visualised (purple), as well as a large part of the BA graph (turquoise). It can be argued that the explanations provided by CDM and GCExplainer are more intuitive, however, GNNExplainer highlights important edges.

We struggle to reproduce the quality of explanations presented by [39] for GNNExplainer. We first adapted the threshold to observe an effect on the explanations, however, this only impacted the visualisation of the important edges. We fix the threshold at 0.8 after this. We then examined the implementation of GNNExplainer used. To ensure that the quality of explanations is not the fault of

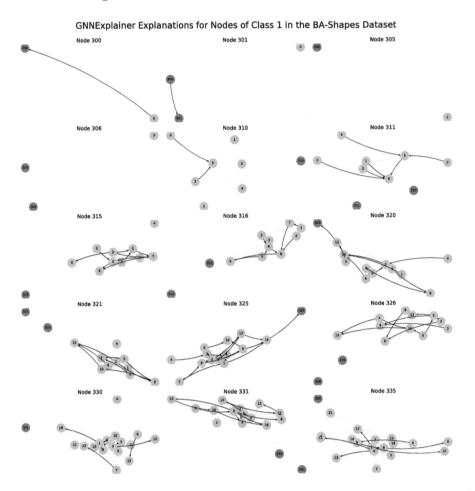

Fig. 5. A selection of explanations produced using GNNExplainer for nodes of class 1. The purple nodes are nodes part of the middle of the house, while the turquoise ones are part of the BA base graph.

the PyTorch Geometric [13] implementation of GNNExplainer, we also used the implementation provided by the Deep Graph Library [37]. After obtaining similar results, we exhaustively visualize the explanations for class 1. We present a selection in Fig. 5. In summary, we fail to produce the house motif using GNNExplainer, as the explanations provided mostly emphasize the importance of the BA base graph.

BA-Community (Fig. 6). Lastly, we compare the explanations for a node in the BA-Community dataset (Fig. 6). Similar to our previous observations, both CDM and GCExplainer successfully identify the house structure. More importantly, they both identify the existence of random edges to explain the node. In contrast, the explanation provided by GNNExplainer is more elusive,

Explanations for Node 434 in the BA_Community Dataset found using different Techniques

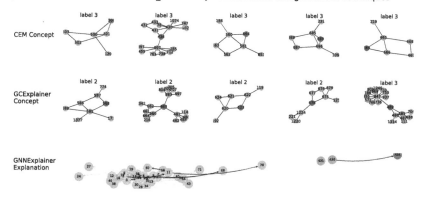

Fig. 6. Concept-based explanations produced using the Concept Distillation Module and GCExplainer, as well as the explanation produced by GNNExplainer for a node in the BA-Community dataset. In the explanations, the blue nodes are the nodes clustered together, while the orange nodes are the p-hop neighborhood. GNNExplainer has its own coloring, where the purple node is the 'top' node in the house, the blue nodes are the 'middle' of the house and the turquoise nodes are part of the BA base graph. (Color figure online)

highlighting mostly the BA base structure. In conclusion, it can be stated that the concept representations for CDM and GCExplainer are almost identical, which can be attributed to the same visualisation technique being used. However, we refer the reader back to the quantitative evaluation in the results section, which highlights the strengths of CDM over GCExplainer.

5.10   Quantitative Comparison to ProtGNN

While ProtGNN citezhang2022protgnn is not concept-based, it has a similar aim of producing an interpretable model as opposed to post-hoc explanation. We compare CDM to ProtGNN via classification accuracy on a synthetic node-classification dataset and real-world graph classification dataset, as [41] do not explain how the quality of their explanations should be evaluated. We perform the evaluation on ProtGNN+, which uses a novel conditional subgraph sampling module for improved efficiency and interpretability. CDM outperforms Prot-GNN+ on the BA-Shapes dataset, achieving an accuracy of 98.11% (97.04%, 99.18%) in comparison to 96.94% (95.38%, 98.51%). In contrast, CDM and Prot-GNN+ achieve similar accuracy on the Mutagenicity dataset with 82.4% (81.3%, 83.5%) and 81.7% (75.4%, 88.1%), respectively. We note that we only compute the results for Mutagenicity for 2 seeds, as training ProtGNN took significantly longer than training CDM, requiring 12 h for 500 epochs on the same hardware.

There are significant architectural differences between CDM and ProtGNN. Firstly, ProtGNN requires to define the number of class prototypes, while CDM only requires to define an upper bound via the concept embedding size s. Moreover, CDM allows to extract fine-grained subgraphs and the ability for human intervention. Moreover, ProtGNN does not provide formal explanations, which can be evaluated quantitatively. Lastly, we found that ProtGNN runs significantly slower than CDM, though some issues my be alleviated via optimising the implementation.

6   Discussion

6.1   Concept Graph Networks are Accurate and Self-explaining

In summary, our results demonstrate that CDM makes GNNs explainable by design without impairing their task performance. Our approach extracts high-quality concept-based and logic explanations. Our experiments show that the extracted concepts are pure, meaningful and interpretable, while task-specific logic explanations are simple and accurate. We also demonstrate that CDM supports human interventions at concept level, which is one of the main advantages of explainable-by-design architectures.

6.2   Strengths and Limitations

The main limitation of our work is the association of only one concept per sample. However, this also applies to GCExplainer, as well as to state-of-the-art unsupervised explainability methods for convolutional networks, such as ACE [17]. The second main limitation pertains the p-hop neighborhood visualization technique inherited from GCExplainer. Visualizing a concept by simply exploring the p-hop neighborhood may include nodes which are not relevant for identifying a concept. More specifically, the concept visualization technique could be improved by performing largest common subgraph matching across the samples representing a concept. However, such an approach would be extremely expensive in terms of computations even for small graphs and it would not scale for large concepts. In terms of novelties, the proposed approach is the first of its kind in terms of making GNNs explainable by design. Secondly, the approach allows to find the optimal number of concepts dynamically. While the size of the embedding space must still be defined, this size is just an upper bound, alleviating the user from the burden of tuning this hyperparameter as in other explainability methods, such as GCExplainer or ACE. This dynamic adaptation often produces a high number of clusters/concepts. While a higher number of concepts may appear redundant and be more complex to reason about, the extracted concepts accurately describe the dataset, as indicated by the high concept completeness scores and rare concepts found. Moreover, logic-based formulas allow to filter through the concepts relevant for each class. We note, however, that as stronger interpretable models are deployed, there are risks of societal harm which we must be vigilant to avoid.

7   Conclusion

In this work, we address the lack of human trust in GNNs caused by their opaque reasoning. To this aim, we propose the Concept Distillation Module which makes GNNs explainable by design. We demonstrate that the proposed method allows to discover and extract high-quality concept-based explanations. The proposed approach makes GNNs explainable by design without a reduction in performance, while also allowing for human intervention. Human intervention allows to alleviate dataset biases, further increasing trust in the model. The increased understanding of the model's working through the proposed approach fosters an increase in trust and may open up the possibility to use GNNs in more high-stake scenarios.

Acknowledgements. This work was partially supported by projects FAIR (PE0000013) and SERICS (PE00000014) under the MUR National Recovery and Resilience Plan funded by the European Union - NextGenerationEU and by ERC Starting Grant No. 802554 (SPECGEO) and PRIN 2020 project n.2020TA3K9N "LEGO.AI". Supported also by the ERC Advanced Grant 788893 AMDROMA, EC H2020RIA project "SoBigData++" (871042), PNRR MUR project IR0000013-SoBigData.it.

References

1. Adebayo, J., Gilmer, J., Muelly, M., Goodfellow, I., Hardt, M., Kim, B.: Sanity checks for saliency maps. In: Advances in Neural Information Processing Systems, vol. 31 (2018)
2. Alvarez Melis, D., Jaakkola, T.: Towards robust interpretability with self-explaining neural networks. In: Advances in Neural Information Processing Systems, vol. 31 (2018)
3. Azzolin, S., Longa, A., Barbiero, P., Lio, P., Passerini, A.: Global explainability of GNNs via logic combination of learned concepts. In: The First Learning on Graphs Conference (2022)
4. Barabási, A.L., Albert, R.: Emergence of scaling in random networks. Science **286**(5439), 509–512 (1999)
5. Barbiero, P., Ciravegna, G., Giannini, F., Lió, P., Gori, M., Melacci, S.: Entropy-based logic explanations of neural networks. In: Proceedings of the AAAI Conference on Artificial Intelligence, vol. 36, pp. 6046–6054 (2022)
6. Battaglia, P., Pascanu, R., Lai, M., Jimenez Rezende, D., et al.: Interaction networks for learning about objects, relations and physics. In: Advances in Neural Information Processing Systems, vol. 29 (2016)
7. Breiman, L., Friedman, J., Olshen, R., Stone, C.: Classification and Regression Trees. Wadsworth (1984)
8. Chen, Z., Bei, Y., Rudin, C.: Concept whitening for interpretable image recognition. Nat. Mach. Intell. **2**(12), 772–782 (2020)
9. Ciravegna, G., Barbiero, P., Giannini, F., Gori, M., Lió, P., Maggini, M., Melacci, S.: Logic explained networks. Artif. Intell. **314**, 103822 (2023)
10. Davies, A., et al.: Advancing mathematics by guiding human intuition with AI. Nature **600**(7887), 70–74 (2021)

11. Durán, J.M., Jongsma, K.R.: Who is afraid of black box algorithms? On the epistemological and ethical basis of trust in medical AI. J. Med. Ethics **47**(5), 329–335 (2021)
12. EUGDPR: GDPR. General data protection regulation (2017)
13. Fey, M., Lenssen, J.E.: Fast graph representation learning with PyTorch Geometric. In: ICLR Workshop on Representation Learning on Graphs and Manifolds (2019)
14. Forgy, E.W.: Cluster analysis of multivariate data: efficiency versus interpretability of classifications. Biometrics **21**, 768–769 (1965)
15. Ganter, B., Wille, R.: Formal Concept Analysis: Mathematical Foundations. Springer, Heidelberg (2012)
16. Ghorbani, A., Abid, A., Zou, J.: Interpretation of neural networks is fragile. In: Proceedings of the AAAI Conference on Artificial Intelligence, vol. 33, pp. 3681–3688 (2019)
17. Ghorbani, A., Wexler, J., Zou, J.Y., Kim, B.: Towards automatic concept-based explanations. In: Advances in Neural Information Processing Systems, vol. 32 (2019)
18. Gilmer, J., Schoenholz, S.S., Riley, P.F., Vinyals, O., Dahl, G.E.: Neural message passing for quantum chemistry. In: International Conference on Machine Learning, pp. 1263–1272. PMLR (2017)
19. Kazhdan, D., Dimanov, B., Jamnik, M., Liò, P.: MEME: generating RNN model explanations via model extraction. arXiv preprint arXiv:2012.06954 (2020)
20. Kazhdan, D., Dimanov, B., Jamnik, M., Liò, P., Weller, A.: Now you see me (CME): concept-based model extraction. arXiv preprint arXiv:2010.13233 (2020)
21. Khasahmadi, A.H., Hassani, K., Moradi, P., Lee, L., Morris, Q.: Memory-based graph networks. In: International Conference on Learning Representations (2020)
22. Kim, B., et al.: Interpretability beyond feature attribution: quantitative testing with concept activation vectors (TCAV). In: International Conference on Machine Learning, pp. 2668–2677. PMLR (2018)
23. Kindermans, P.-J., et al.: The (un)reliability of saliency methods. In: Samek, W., Montavon, G., Vedaldi, A., Hansen, L.K., Müller, K.-R. (eds.) Explainable AI: Interpreting, Explaining and Visualizing Deep Learning. LNCS (LNAI), vol. 11700, pp. 267–280. Springer, Cham (2019). https://doi.org/10.1007/978-3-030-28954-6_14
24. Koh, P.W., Nguyen, T., Tang, Y.S., Mussmann, S., Pierson, E., Kim, B., Liang, P.: Concept bottleneck models. In: International Conference on Machine Learning, pp. 5338–5348. PMLR (2020)
25. Lo Piano, S.: Ethical principles in machine learning and artificial intelligence: cases from the field and possible ways forward. Humanit. Soc. Sci. Commun. **7**(1), 1–7 (2020)
26. Luo, D., Cheng, W., Xu, D., Yu, W., Zong, B., Chen, H., Zhang, X.: Parameterized explainer for graph neural network. In: Advances in Neural Information Processing Systems, vol. 33, pp. 19620–19631 (2020)
27. Magister, L.C., Kazhdan, D., Singh, V., Liò, P.: GCExplainer: human-in-the-loop concept-based explanations for graph neural networks. arXiv preprint arXiv:2107.11889 (2021)
28. Miller, G.A.: The magical number seven, plus or minus two: some limits on our capacity for processing information. Psychol. Rev. **63**, 81–97 (1956)
29. Morris, C., Kriege, N.M., Bause, F., Kersting, K., Mutzel, P., Neumann, M.: TUDataset: a collection of benchmark datasets for learning with graphs. arXiv preprint arXiv:2007.08663 (2020)

30. Pal, A., Eksombatchai, C., Zhou, Y., Zhao, B., Rosenberg, C., Leskovec, J.: Pinner-Sage: multi-modal user embedding framework for recommendations at pinterest. In: Proceedings of the 26th ACM SIGKDD International Conference on Knowledge Discovery & Data Mining, pp. 2311–2320 (2020)
31. Rudin, C.: Stop explaining black box machine learning models for high stakes decisions and use interpretable models instead. Nat. Mach. Intell. **1**(5), 206–215 (2019)
32. Scarselli, F., Gori, M., Tsoi, A.C., Hagenbuchner, M., Monfardini, G.: The graph neural network model. IEEE Trans. Neural Networks **20**(1), 61–80 (2008)
33. Shen, M.W.: Trust in AI: interpretability is not necessary or sufficient, while black-box interaction is necessary and sufficient. arXiv preprint arXiv:2202.05302 (2022)
34. Stokes, J.M., et al.: A deep learning approach to antibiotic discovery. Cell **180**(4), 688–702 (2020)
35. Vu, M., Thai, M.T.: PGM-explainer: probabilistic graphical model explanations for graph neural networks. In: Advances in Neural Information Processing Systems, vol. 33, pp. 12225–12235 (2020)
36. Wachter, S., Mittelstadt, B., Russell, C.: Counterfactual explanations without opening the black box: automated decisions and the GDPR. Harv. JL Tech. **31**, 841 (2017)
37. Wang, M.Y.: Deep graph library: Towards efficient and scalable deep learning on graphs. In: ICLR Workshop on Representation Learning on Graphs and Manifolds (2019)
38. Yeh, C.K., Kim, B., Arik, S., Li, C.L., Pfister, T., Ravikumar, P.: On completeness-aware concept-based explanations in deep neural networks. In: Advances in Neural Information Processing Systems, vol. 33, pp. 20554–20565 (2020)
39. Ying, Z., Bourgeois, D., You, J., Zitnik, M., Leskovec, J.: GNNExplainer: generating explanations for graph neural networks. In: Advances in Neural Information Processing Systems, vol. 32 (2019)
40. Zhang, R., Isola, P., Efros, A.A., Shechtman, E., Wang, O.: The unreasonable effectiveness of deep features as a perceptual metric. In: Proceedings of the IEEE Conference on Computer Vision and Pattern Recognition, pp. 586–595 (2018)
41. Zhang, Z., Liu, Q., Wang, H., Lu, C., Lee, C.: ProtGNN: towards self-explaining graph neural networks. In: Proceedings of the AAAI Conference on Artificial Intelligence, vol. 36, pp. 9127–9135 (2022)
42. Zhou, J., Gandomi, A.H., Chen, F., Holzinger, A.: Evaluating the quality of machine learning explanations: a survey on methods and metrics. Electronics **10**(5), 593 (2021)

Adding Why to What? Analyses of an Everyday Explanation

Lutz Terfloth[(⊠)] [iD], Michael Schaffer [iD], Heike M. Buhl [iD],
and Carsten Schulte [iD]

Paderborn University, Paderborn, Germany
{lutz.terfloth,michael.schaffer,heike.buhl,
carsten.schulte}@uni-paderborn.de

Abstract. In XAI it is important to consider that, in contrast to explanations for professional audiences, one cannot assume common expertise when explaining for laypeople. But such explanations between humans vary greatly, making it difficult to research commonalities across explanations. We used the dual nature theory, a techno-philosophical approach, to cope with these challenges. According to it, onan explain, for example, an XAI's decision by addressing its dual nature: by focusing on the Architecture (e.g., the logic of its algorithms) or the Relevance (e.g., the severity of a decision, the implications of a recommendation). We investigated 20 explanations of games using the theory as an analytical framework. We elaborate how we used the theory to quickly structure and compare explanations of technological artifacts. We supplement results from analyzing the explanation contents with results from a video recall to explore how Explainers (EX) justified their explanation. We found that EX were focusing on the physical aspects of the game first (Architecture) and only later on aspects of the Relevance. Reasoning in the video recalls indicated that EX regarded the focus on the Architecture as important for structuring the explanation initially by explaining the basic components before focusing on more complex, intangible aspects. EX justified shifting between addressing the two sides by explanation goals, emerging misunderstandings, and the knowledge needs of the explainee. We discovered several commonalities that inspire future research questions which, if further generalizable, provide first ideas for the construction of synthetic explanations.

Keywords: Analysis of Human Explanations · Naturalistic Explanations · Qualitative Analysis · Technological Artifacts

1 Introduction

Enabling laypeople to "effectively understand, trust, and manage" [16] AI applications requires XAI systems that provide *understandable explanations*. In a similar sense, the General Data Protection Regulation (GDPR) calls for "meaningful explanations of the logic involved" in the context of automated decision-making,

L. Longo (Ed.): xAI 2023, CCIS 1903, pp. 256–279, 2023.
https://doi.org/10.1007/978-3-031-44070-0_13

too. However, in many instances, experts rely on a notion of what constitutes an explanation for the implementation [48]. We see potential in adhering to an empirically grounded conceptualization of explanations instead. If an XAI system could mimic how explanations evolve in naturalistic, everyday settings, it could be used to make an AI's output more understandable, especially for laypeople unfamiliar with the technology.

Over the years, plenty of research has been done on explanations [13,34]. For XAI, researching everyday explanations offers large potential for understanding how both parties of an explanation engage interactively; for a "Social Design of AI Systems" in which the explainer and explainee are put in focus [38]. But little research focused on explanations of technological artifacts in particular, even though important in the context of explaining and understanding such artifacts [37]. One central idea can be found across different sources: Technological artifacts are human-made objects engineered to serve as means to certain ends. Therefore, explaining technological artifacts can be done addressing the two sides of their dual nature [22,47]. Whenever, for example, engineers explain their inventions in texts, they are explaining aspects about the physical properties (e.g., the shape, the algorithms, or the logic – its Architecture) of the artifact in alignment with its functional capabilities (e.g., how it serves as a means to an end; its Relevance). In the context of XAI, in which synthetic explanations are constructed by technological artifacts, and based on decisions by technological artifacts, the peculiarities of their dual nature cannot be neglected. We believe, the theory provides a rich background for researching everyday explanations of technological artifacts.

Many scholars agree that knowledge about the dual nature of a technological artifact is relevant for understanding it, yet are undecided whether both sides are equally important or whether one side may be the precursor for the other [42,45]. However, to date, no study investigates specifically if and how the dual nature is addressed in naturalistic everyday explanations of technological artifacts. Thus, how the dual nature is addressed in explanations, which of the two sides are explained first, more frequently, or whether one or the other should be addressed in more detail or omitted completely, is not empirically investigated yet. An empirically grounded conceptualization of how technological artifacts are naturally explained in a verbal, interactive settings would be a useful prerequisite for many research areas, but especially for XAI and education in general. It could provide a foundation for formulating recommendations on whether and which of the artifact's properties should be referred to within a (synthetic) explanation, and thus improve the understandability and interpretability of XAI systems.

This paper is a step towards addressing these shortcomings and investigating how the content of naturalistic explanations evolves and is justified by the explainers (EX). It presents results from a study of dyadic explanatory dialogues in which a technological artifact, the board game *Quarto!*, is explained in a naturalistic setting. The contribution of this paper is twofold. First, we elaborate on the theoretical foundation used for an empirical study, after which we present results from that study. The paper consists of two parts: In the Sections Background and Study, we provide a brief introduction to the theoretical foundation of the research and connect it to the research questions of the paper, and elaborate how and why we use the dual nature theory as a framework. In the Method, Results and Discussion sections, the study, data acquisition and analysis are elaborated after which the results are presented and discussed.

2 Background

Considerable research attention has been directed towards the conceptualization of explanations from different perspectives and disciplines. A philosophical standpoint sheds light on quality characteristics of explanations and tries to identify factors that contribute to sound and satisfying explanations [11,40]. Social psychology examines why and when individuals explain [11,15,18,30]. Explanations can cover a vast array of topics and ideas, but regardless of content diversity, explanations in their composition are shaped by causal and logical factors [40], too. Cognitive sciences are investigating important elements of explanations, the process of explanation generation and which cognitive processes succumb to explanatory processes [11,27].

During extemporaneous explanations, EX are facing various challenges to give meaningful, and complete and precise explanations that are well-structured [39]. Structuring explanations requires organization of knowledge [39]. Therefore, explaining is a cognitive process, that is highly constructive [9,17] and utilizes existing domain knowledge [27], that is part of mental representations [9,20]. Thus, EX need to decide, over the course of explanations, which aspects of a domain they want to explain and especially at what point of time, for example by monitoring the explainee (EE) [26].

These challenges an EX faces makes researching such naturalistic explanations challenging as well as necessary, if the goal is to provide recommendations for XAI systems. To circumvent some of these challenges, shared properties of explananda are interesting. The content of an explanation is influenced by the explanandum (the subject of explanation), more precisely the EX's mental representation of that explanandum, and the knowledge needs of the Explainee (EE) regarding that explanandum [3,10]. Whenever the explanandum is a technological artifact, one can refer to its dual nature, following a techno-philosophical theory [22,46]. According to the dual nature theory, an explanation of a technological artifact – an object engineered to be a means to an end – can be formulated by addressing two properties [21]. On the one hand, a structural mode of description, "makes use of concepts from physical laws and theories and is free of any reference to the function of the object" and addresses the Architecture of the artifact [22,43]. On the other hand, the functional/teleological mode of description is a way in which "[w]ith regard to its function, a technological object is described in an intentional (teleological) way" [22] and addresses the Relevance of the artifact.

Interestingly, in the context of this dual nature theory, the idea of an engineer's ability to "bridge the gap" [23] between the two sides of the dual nature resulting from their deep understanding of the artifact is discussed. Not only, but especially because of this, the dual nature theory found application within the computing education community [43], as well as in the technology education community in the context of understanding technological artifacts [8]. It guided a development of an analytical framework to investigate pupil's understanding of programmed technical solutions (PTS), especially concerning their ability to open the black boxes [7]. The results indicated that both sides of their dual nature need to be understood to have a more profound understanding of a PTS: "[t]hus, these key elements are important to consider in pedagogical practice to promote learning regarding PTS." [7]. The theory served as a theoretical foundation for a program comprehension model, too [42]. On a more abstract level, comparable ideas were referred to using different foci and terms, but similar ideas in the context of program comprehension: "mechanisms" vs. "explanations" [45], and "text base" vs. "situation model" [36]. [1] investigated how children discuss a machine they got to know while visiting a museum, concerning which prompt resulted in the children addressing either the mechanisms or the components when asked questions about the machine. In summary, the main ideas of the dual nature theory have a rich history not only within and outside the computing community, but in the context of making sense of technological artifacts in general.

Whether the dual nature theory is useful for the analysis of explanation content whenever a technological artifact is explained, still needs investigation. We call the sides of the dual nature, the *Architecture* (roughly: what it is, what components are) and *Relevance* (roughly: why and what it and its components are for) of the artifact. Our conceptualization of the two sides is as follows: one can, for example, (1) explain how a navigation system works on the level of data, or the logic of the algorithms (i.e., addressing the Architecture), or by explaining (2) how one may use it for relaxed journey across foreign countries (i.e., addressing the Relevance). But there is uncertainty how the dual nature of the technological artifact influences the structure and evolution of an explanation, and whether these sides can be clearly identified within naturalistic explanations. This paper aims at answering three questions:

- (RQ1) How is the dual nature of the explanandum expressed in the utterances in the explanations?
- (RQ2) What are common patterns regarding sequences of utterances about the dual nature across the explanations?
- (RQ3) How do EX justify their choice of explanation content regarding which side of the dual nature was addressed?

3   Method

Given our overarching objective to analyze how EX address the sides of the dual nature in their explanations, we conducted a study in which a dyad of people engaged in a naturalistic explanation scenario. To acquire comparable explanations, a study design that allowed to control certain variables that would not be controllable with a more complex explanandum and in the field, was developed. Even though the naturalness of the explanations in the field would be higher, at this early stage of researching the phenomenon a certain uniformity is preferred. Researchers and research assistants adhered to a predefined study guideline. The study was conducted at Paderborn University as well as Bielefeld University in Germany. This study is part of a larger, more complex study consisting of five different phases: (1) pretesting, (2) explaining, (3) video recall, (4) playing and (5) post testing. This paper focuses on the analysis of phase 2 and 3 (explanation phase and video recall). We recorded the dyads during the explanation. To observe the explanations from another room, we placed a webcam for live-streaming, too. Prior to the explanation, every participant filled out a questionnaire for sociodemographic details. After the explanation (phase 2), we conducted a video recall to assess the EX underlying thinking and reasoning during the explanations based on questions of a structured interview. The analyses of the content of the explanations, and the justifications mentioned in the video recalls, is guided by the dual nature theory as an analytical framework.

3.1 Participants and Recruitment

For the recruitment, we relied primarily on onsite recruiting via handing out flyers on campus, hanging posters, and hearsay. We compensated all participants monetarily (10 per hour of participation). Participants signed up voluntarily for the study. All studies included COVID-19 safety measures and obtaining written informed consent before the studies. Communication with participants was based on boilerplate to ensure that all participants had the same information and instructions. We divided a total of 48 participants into two groups: Explainers and Explainees (24 dyads). Interaction between EE and EX before the study was prevented as much as possible by meeting and picking them up independently of each other on the day of the study. Through mail communication, we instructed the group of EX to make themselves familiar with the explanandum. They had the option to either pick up a physical copy of the game from our lab or use an online version of the game. EE received only directions to, and the location of the study. Exclusion criteria were (1) prior knowledge of the game *Quarto!* (for EE), (2) non-C2 level language skills (for both EE and EX), or (3) prior participation and knowledge about the overarching research endeavor. Four dyads were excluded from the corpus due to a language barrier, two instances in which the EE had prior knowledge of the game, and one instance in which the game was mistakenly present during explanation. The final sample of video data consists of 20 lab studies in which 20 EX explained the game to 20 EE (18 female, 19 male, 1 non-binary)[1]. Age ranged from 18 to 39 (M=24.92, SD=4.42). 36 participants had an academic background. 35 reported to be students (e.g., engineering, education, economics, law, computer science, media sciences, linguistics), 2 were full-time employees. Out of 19 EX, 7 reported to have explained the game to someone else before the study. EX reported to have between 0 and 18 rounds of gameplay experience (M=5.46, SD=5,18). 10 EX reported to have experience in explanations (e.g., tutoring). The studies were planned to take 2 to 3 h for

---

[1] 3 participants provided no information and are therefore not included in the descriptive statistics.

all assessments. Phase 2 (explanation) varied from 02:23 mm:ss to 16:17 mm:ss (M=07:24, SD= 03:22).

3.2   The Explanandum: *Quarto!*

The explanandum of the study is the strategical, two-player board game *Quarto!*. *Quarto!* is a game developed by Swiss mathematician Blaise Müller. It demands deductive reasoning and thinking, similar to chess. At any moments during the game, all information is openly available to every player. The game is made up of 16 pieces and a board consisting of 4×4 squares. Each of the 16 pieces one places on the board, is unique and differs in at least one of the following traits: size (tall or short), shade (light or dark), shape (round or square), and solidity (solid or hollow). The goal of the game is similar to Connect Four: connect a row, column, or diagonal of four pieces that share *at least one trait*. Contrary to the way Connect Four is played, players do not choose which piece they place themselves, but instead choose the piece the opponents have to place in their next move. After the opponent places the piece handed to them, they choose a piece, that the other person has to play. Turn-by-turn, the game continues until either a *Quarto!* is called, and a person wins, or all squares are occupied and the game ends in a draw.

We chose a game and specifically *Quarto!* as the explanandum for several reasons. As our interdisciplinary team strives to triangulate the results from different approaches to get a rich perspective of the phenomenon of natural explanations of technological artifacts, certain tradeoffs were inevitable. Explaining games is a common, social practice, making it an accessible domain for a large variety of participants. The occasion to explain a game creates a setting for natural explanations and lessens any perceived pressure or exam-like atmosphere. Regarding participant acquisition, one can learn the game quickly, whereas mastering the game can be considered challenging. As *Quarto!* provides strategical depth, it allows for some sort of variance in the explanations. Yet, the scope of what one may explain is narrow enough to make the explanations comparable.

Games, being invented by humans, share the main characteristics of technological artifacts. We believe, games exhibit their dual nature quite well in the context of explanations: One has to explain the pieces, board and rules, hence the Architecture but one also needs to explain how these things go together and create an interesting game in which two players struggle to win. Comparable to chess, for example, one could explain how certain moves can be interpreted as offensive or defensive. In theoretical terms, the explanation also needs to elaborate how one follows their intentions within the game and thus address the game's Relevance. In summary, providing an explanation that results in a deep understanding of a game does not only require explaining its components and rules (knowing what, Architecture), but also explaining why certain aspects of the game are important to consider during gameplay (knowing why; Relevance). This is comparable to understanding XAI explanations.

The decision for the absence of the game had different reasons. Regarding the theoretical framework for the analysis, we expected having the game on hand would limit utterances that address the Architecture of the game (e.g., about the different shapes of the pieces). Thus, the EX needs to decide which detail requires explanation, allowing us to perceive strategies that EX use to, for example, generalize such details. As gestures are linked to or results of cognitive processes, a gesture analysis offers additional insights to get an even more detailed understanding of what happens during explanations at later stages of the project [31,32]. As a consequence, the table between the participants needs to be free of any objects to not influence their gestures (e.g., participants could hold on to pieces of the game).

3.3   Procedure

The study was conducted by researchers and research assistants from an interdisciplinary background (linguistics, psychology, and computing education). After participants arrived, they were welcomed, and, for the sociodemographic questionnaire, led into two different rooms independently of each other. During the study, all communication between researchers and participants was based on boilerplate, too. In phase 2, the explanations were recorded from three different camera angles: a view of the table, a medium-shot of the EE upper body, and a medium-shot of the EX upper body.

After EE and EX filled out the questionnaires for sociodemographic details, they were instructed about the next phase. The EX's instruction was: "In the next room, please explain the game to the person opposite you in such a way, that the person would have a chance to win the game"[2]. The EE's instruction was, "[i]n a moment, a person will enter the room and explain a board game to you. Please participate actively in the explanation" before the EX entered the room[3].

In phase 2, the EX explains the board game *Quarto!* to the EE sitting vis-á-vis at a table. During the explanation, the game is *not* present due to reasons given in Sect. 3.2. After the instruction, the EX entered the room of the EE, sat down opposite of the EE and a researcher gave a starting signal, left the room, and the explanation phase started.

For the video recall, we observed the explanation via livestream and took notes of important scenes during the explanation. We used an identification scheme for the ad hoc selection of scenes to be used in the video recall. Criteria for selection were: substantial contributions, self- and other initiated repairs, turn taking, misunderstandings and questions that assessed understanding and knowledge of the EE. After the explanation ended (phase 2), we quickly started the video recall with the EX to investigate the EX's thoughts regarding specific points in the explanation [14], especially to discover reasons for addressing either of the two sides of the dual nature in their explanations.

---

[2] Original: "In dem nächsten Raum erklären Sie bitte dem Gegenüber das Spiel so gut, dass Ihr Gegenüber eine Chance hätte, das Spiel zu gewinnen".

[3] Original: "Im nächsten Raum ist eine Person, die Ihnen ein Spiel erklärt, bitte nehmen Sie aktiv an der Erklärung teil".

For the video recall with the EX, we used a semi-structured interview which included questions about explanation content, explaining intention, explanation quality, the assumed EE's understanding of the game, and perceived knowledge needs of the EE. During the video recall, a researcher watched the videotaped explanation with the EX from start to end, and stopped at the previously selected scenes. This served as a stimulus to enable the EX to give detailed insights into certain sequences of interaction, their interpretation of a particular moment [14] by allowing participants to not solely rely on memory when trying to answer the questions [28]. Questions were answered before information has been transferred from short- to long-term memory to avoid conflation of experiences and conjoined memories [29] by starting phase 3 as quickly as possible. The whole video call procedure was standardized.

3.4   Analyses

This paper puts the focus on the analysis of the explanation of the game, especially on what was said and why regarding the dual nature of the explanandum. An analysis of the explanations content provides the "what was said at a certain time". That analysis is, in a second step, supported by an analysis of the video recall to support the interpretation by investigating the underlying reasoning. The video recall data provides the EX justifications, and helps to understand the development of the explanation regarding the reasons for utterances addressing Architecture and Relevance at certain times.

Explanation Content Analysis. The explanations recorded in phase 2 served as the foundation for this analysis. Student assistants and colleagues from linguistics transcribed all recordings of the explanations according to the second complexity level (basic transcript) of the GAT2 transcription system [44]. The GAT2 transcription system level 2 segments the spoken text into intonational units. The length of the transcripts was between 118 and 653 intonational units (M=332, SD=146). In the final transcript, an intonational unit represented one line in the transcript.

We used qualitative content analysis [24, p. 70] to analyze the transcripts. The code system consisted of two deductive code categories: (1) utterances addressing the Architecture, and (2) utterances addressing the Relevance of the explanandum. We developed a coding manual over the course of multiple pilot studies during which the first and second coder (first author and a student assistant) discussed their coded segments in data sessions, and refined the coding manual. All transcripts were double coded using the final version of the manual. All coded segments were additionally labeled to represent whether the utterance was by the EX or EE. Inter-rater and intra-rater reliability were calculated using MaxQDA, which reports the Brennan and Prediger Kappa [2]. Across all transcripts, the inter-rater reliability between both coders was "Almost Perfect" (k=0.80) [25, p. 165]. The intra-rater reliability was calculated for both coders who coded four transcripts twice three weeks apart (k=0.91). The performance of the coding manual is satisfactory for the aim of the study. Overall, the content of the segments coded with the two code categories align with the theoretical ideas, and thus we were able to identify which sequences of the explanations contained utterances addressing the Architecture or Relevance reliably.

Table 1. Overview of the Code Categories used for the Analysis of the Explanations' Content

Code	Examples
Utterances addressing Architecture (UA)	EX h and they will then be ALTernately- put onto this BOARD, (P01, Pos. 55–56)
	if I would STARt now i would have to hand YOU one [a piece] (VP22, Pos. 213–214)
	and these PIECES have FOUR properties they are either uhm TALL or SMALL (VP06, Pos. 27–30)
Utterances addressing Relevance (UR)	EX SO what makes this game interestING is that uhm if YOU plAced one [piece] then YOU decide which piece your opPOnent places next (VP02, Pos. 204–208)

A total of 878 segments were coded across all transcripts (605 utterances addressing the Architecture, and 273 utterances addressing the Relevance of *Quarto!*). On average, 56% (SD=10,37%) of the transcripts were coded, while 44% (SD= 10,12%) received no code. This is mainly due to the transcription system which makes use of spaces and special characters to include additional information (e.g., pauses, breathing, overlaps). Another reason is that most explanations contained some small talk which was not part of the explanation. Out of 605 coded segments, 2,62% received both codes, as either one or the other category was possible due to different plausible interpretations. Examples for that were transcripts starting with an example ("the GA:ME / is a varIANT / of coNNECT four" (VP11, Pos. 5–7)[4]), or areas in which a shift from Architecture to Relevance occurred within one intonational phrase and thus both codes needed to be applied. In general, the content of each segment corresponded well (98%) to one of the code categories, thus allowing us to consistently identify whenever the Architecture or Relevance were addressed during an explanation. For an overview of the contents of each code category, see Table 1.

For the analyses, we used MaxQDA for coding, reliability calculations and the majority of qualitative work, and Python in subsequent steps, especially for visualizations and calculations, to investigate patterns regarding combination of sequences of the two code categories. For these visualizations, all transcripts were standardized in length. The starting point was always the first line in the transcript, that was coded. The end was the last line which received a code. For the standardization, all transcripts are divided into 100 sections with equal length and labeled regarding the codes used in each of the 100 sections, similar

---

[4] All examples we use from the transcripts of this paper were carefully translated from the German original to English by the first and second author of this paper.

to how MaxQDA realizes this feature[5]. We used these visualizations to identify specific points of interests in the corpora of explanations (e.g., switches from Architecture to Relevance, EE remarks regarding Relevance after a long phase of utterances about Architecture by the EX and vice versa). These points of interest served as a guide for the selection of video recalls we analyzed in the next section, which are used to underpin the analysis of the content of explanations.

Video Recall. To investigate the justification for the content of the explanations as perceived by the EX we analyzed the interview questions from the video recall. The video recall consisted of a larger variety of questions. Only questions regarding the EX's explaining intention, as well as the EX's perceived knowledge needs of the EE are analyzed. To achieve this, a student assistant transcribed the data from ten video recalls using standard orthography [35].

Material was coded using a deductive category system to categorize reasons for explanation content in consideration of the dual nature theory, and to categorize the reasons into two subordinated code categories: Knowledge Needs of the EE, and Explaining Intention of EX (see Table 2). Depending on whether a statement of the EX provided reasons for addressing "Architecture" or "Relevance" in their explanations, either the perceived knowledge needs of the EE or the explaining intention of the EX were coded with the corresponding sub-category. Statements which could not clearly be assigned to Architecture or Relevance were collected under a main category (Reasons for Explanation Content). The questions for the semi-structured interview guideline were derived from literature. We formulated the questions so that the explaining intention of the EX (why the EX wanted to explain specific aspects in certain situations irrespective of the situation, or the EE), as well as the knowledge needs of the EE as perceived by the EX, were focused on in the answers. We considered both of these aspects as important factors for the contents of explanations [10, 18, 26, 39].

We coded the material using a coding manual that we developed beforehand. The length of units of coding was flexible, ranging from at least one phrase to sometimes several sentences. Most important was that the unit encapsulated one specific reason stated by the EX (EX's explaining intention, or EE's knowledge needs). If multiple reasons were mentioned within a one answer to a question, each reason was assigned to a separate unit of coding [41]. All video recall transcripts were coded twice, and intra-rater reliability was "substantial" ($k = 0.72$)[25, p. 165], which is satisfactory as the data were complex. Only ten video recalls are part of this analysis, as the final solution for the video recall was not fully developed until the second half of data collection, especially due to finding a reliable technical solution.

---

[5] If, for example, one section contained three lines of transcripts, one addressing the Architecture and two addressing the Relevance, the visualization represented this by drawing a rectangle which is to 1/3 colored according to the code Architecture and 2/3 colored according to the code Relevance in order of their occurrence in the transcripts. In other words, there is no large loss of precision in the visualizations as a result of the standardization of length.

4   Results

Table 2. Category System to code the reasoning for explanation content stated by EX during the video recall

Code Category	Subcategory
Architecture	
	Knowledge Needs of EE
	Explaining Intention of EX
Relevance	
	Knowledge Needs of EE
	Explaining Intention of EX

We start this section by presenting results from the analysis of the content of the explanations. Afterward, to underpin the commonalities we found across the explanations, we support the findings with the results from the analysis of the video recalls.

Explanation Content. The investigation of RQ1 (How is the dual nature of the explanandum expressed in the utterances of the explanation?) is based on a qualitative content analysis. As an analytical framework, the techno philosophical theory of the dual nature provided two deductive code categories, which we used for coding the corpus.

Except for the EX in VP23, all EE and EX addressed both sides of the dual nature in the corpus (see Fig. 1). In general, the content of the coded segments within each category aligned well with the ideas of the dual nature theory. When the Architecture of *Quarto!* was addressed, EX and EE alike, used, for example, causal reasoning to address certain rules, described how the rules of the game result in a certain sequence in which each of the two players has to act, or described the physical makeup of different parts of the game. Whenever they addressed the aspects of Relevance of *Quarto!*, they shifted to teleological aspects, for example, that the complexity rises continuously throughout the game ("that means the MORE pieces are put onto the board (0.7) / the MORE you need to thInk / because there are MULTiple rows containing three pieces", VP25, Pos. 174–176), strategical recommendations ("a:nd it is a: stra_strategical GAME / because if a fiew pieces are PLACed / then YOU are able to see / which PIECE / would be GOOD / to hand to me / such that i would not WIN / that means you also have to thiNK a little" VP16, Pos. 75–82), and emotional aspects for example how it is especially annoying to personally hand the piece to the opponent who may win using that piece in their next move ("EX (0.3) the frus-TRATing bit about the game is that / that ONESELF is always the reason / for loSING / because one HANDS OVER (.) a piece" VP18, Pos. 372–375). A summary of the contents of the two categories, as well as examples from the transcripts, is provided in Table 1.

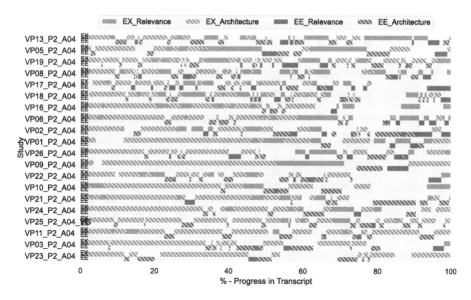

Fig. 1. Visualization of explanation content across studies. All transcripts standardized in length. Start- and endpoint are the first and last coded segments in the transcripts. Sorted by utterances addressing Architecture (least to most; EX = Explainer, and EE = Explainee)

Architecture Addressed More Frequently: Both EX and EE addressed each side of the dual nature in their explanations, but the balance of which side was focused on shifted throughout the explanations. While some EX (e.g., VP23, VP03) were focusing almost exclusively on aspects of the Architecture, other EX addressed aspects of the Relevance of *Quarto!* more often (e.g., VP13, VP05). The amount of talk EX

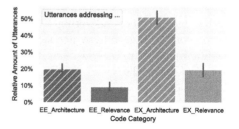

Fig. 2. Average code distribution across studies

and EE spent addressing each of the sides varied quite a lot across dyads, but on average, the Architecture was addressed more frequently than the Relevance for EX and EE (see Fig. 2).

Architecture First – Laying out the Tools? In the context of RQ2, we were especially interested in whether we would find any patterns across explanations regarding *when* and *in which configurations* the sides of the dual nature were addressed. A comparative visualization of all transcripts of the corpus grouped by utterances by EE and EX and colored according to which side of the dual nature was focused on throughout the transcripts, see Fig. 1. As indicated by the visualization, utterances addressing the Architecture were uttered more frequently overall. Especially in the early stages of the explanations, the aspects

268   L. Terfloth et al.

of the Architecture were addressed more frequently than in the middle and last third (cf. Figure 3).

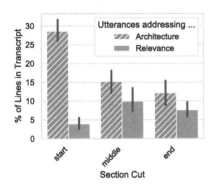

Fig. 3. Comparison of the percentage of lines in the transcripts addressing the two code categories by speaker sectioned in thirds.

Figure 3 provides additional evidence that EX referred to aspects of the Architecture in the first third of their explanation more often than in other parts of the explanation. In the explanations, the content of the first third, especially EX, seemed to address important components and pieces of the game, which they often referred to later in their explanations. We describe this phenomenon as *Laying out the Tools*. In the later stages of the explanation, the utterances are more balanced regarding the side they address. In the second third of the explanations, utterances addressing Relevance were more prominent than in the first or last third. But utterances about the Architecture were dominating the explanations across all dyads. Interestingly, when the dyads decided that the EE should share their understanding – that happened rather frequently at the end of the transcripts – the EE's reiteration addressed mainly aspects of the Architecture, too.

Video Recall. For answering RQ3 (How do EX justify their choice of explanation content regarding which side of the dual nature was addressed?) we used qualitative content analysis, too. Based on the results from Sect. 4, we selected 20 scenes from the video recalls: ten scenes focusing on the beginning of the explanation, and ten scenes after the content shifted from Architecture to Relevance.

Reasons for Architecture First. Reasons for addressing Architecture at the beginning of an explanation were found in the EX's explaining intention, i.e., what are the needs of the EX regarding the explanation content, and to a lesser degree in the EX reaction to EE's knowledge needs. From a total of 28 reasons stated by EX for explaining content addressed to Architecture, 26 were rooted in the explaining intention of the EX irrespective of the EE. No EX mentioned the need to address aspects of the Relevance at the beginning. In two instances (VP10, VP13), the EE expressed knowledge needs at the beginning of the explanation. Yet interestingly, the EX did not justify the explanation content by a desire to address these knowledge needs (Fig. 4).

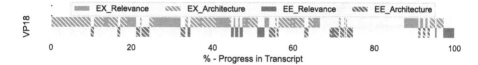

Fig. 4. Combination of analyses of explanation content, and EX' justification for the example of VP18. The EX addressed the Architecture in roughly the first 15% and justified it using the following reasoning: "starting/ at first I thought it was important to know the components of the game before saying how (...) the game progresses" (VP18, VR1, Pos. 5)

The reasons for focusing on the Architecture at the beginning (cf. *Laying out the tools*) as stated by the EX were manifold. Most EX regarded it as important that the explanation has a certain structure, meaning that some aspects were believed to be prerequisites that need to be explained, before explaining further details. Two EX stated, for example, that explaining game components and their physical characteristics was a requirement to be able to explain the goal of the game (VP10, VP18). In VP06, the EX reported: "In the beginning I wanted to explain the course of the game swiftly before explaining in-depth" (VP06, VR1, Pos. 3). Another reason for explaining Architecture first was found in the EX's wish to create an image of the game that the EE can imagine, and therefore explained game components and their appearance first. With a similar intention, one EX made a comparison to chess and described the game board as a smaller chessboard (VP21). In VP 24 the EX stated: "I just wanted to create a picture of the game so that he knows [...] what kind of game it is." (VP24, VR1, Pos. 4).

Even though the EX primarily addressed Architecture in the beginning and thus Relevance is not addressed in the explanations, we found indicators that Relevance might already be part of an explanation. We found cases, in which Relevance is not expressed verbally, yet considerations of the Relevance had an impact on the structure of the explanation (e.g., VP13, VP17). One EX explained the different pieces and their similarities in detail and justified it by addressing the Relevance in the interview stating: "Because that's what the goal of the game actually means to me. To find these similarities." (VP17, VR1, Pos. 5). This addresses the Relevance by implying that getting four in a row is *not* important, but instead finding the similarities on the board is.

In summary, reasons for addressing the Architecture in the beginning were rooted predominantly in the EX's explaining intention and covered, for example, structuring the explanation, as well as pictographic descriptions of main aspects.

Reasons for shifting to Relevance after addressing the Architecture: Reasons for shifting in later stages of the explanation were rooted in both the EX's explaining intention and the perceived knowledge needs of the EE. In total, 17 reasons in the 10 scenes included reasons for addressing the Relevance, whereof nine were related to knowledge needs of the EE and 8 were related to the explaining intention of the EX.

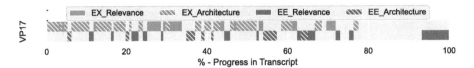

Fig. 5. Combination of analyses of explanation content, and EX's justification in VP17. The EX shifted from Architecture to Relevance between 20% and 40% of the explanations progress, and justified it using the following reasoning: "My counterpart wanted to know why or what the rationale is for the fact that one decides for the opponent [which piece to play]. Who then could have won the game using that piece. Which he would have handed to me [and thus I can win instead]." (VP17, VR3, Pos. 7)

There were three main reasons for addressing the Relevance rooted in the knowledge needs of EE, ranging from the desire to be able to assess the game's degree of complexity (VP6, VP24), to certain aspects that are important to consider when trying to build a row of four (VP25), and the expressed wish to learn more about the game's strategies (VP13). The EX's explaining intention, resulted in explanation content that was addressed towards Relevance, too (e.g., VP10, VP18, VP26). The EX of VP26 referred to gameplay experience: "It was about the exchange of my experience, it is not about knowledge, but about experience and about situations experienced during a round or the game." (VP26, VR 5, Pos. 9). There were instances within the explanations for which the reasons could not be categorized to EE knowledge needs or EX explaining intention. In these cases, the reasons for addressing the Relevance in the explanation emerged from the interaction between both EX and EE. Sometimes, for example, questions were posed by the EE that addressed the Architecture and the EX replied by addressing the Architecture while integrating information regarding the Relevance as well (VP21, VP22). In VP21, the EE asked what the end of the game looks like and the EX answered the question by referring to the Architecture, but also addressed to Relevance by mentioning the difficulty of keeping an eye on every game detail as the game progresses (VP21). Another example of how shifts to Relevance occur within an explanation is found in VP17, where the EX was explaining content addressed towards Architecture, specifically that players have to choose pieces for the opponent. The EE struggled to find the rationale for this, especially as it would mean that one would have to hand the winning piece to the opponent, too, and by doing that forced a shift to Relevance in the explanation (see Fig. 5).

The reasons for explanation content after shifting from Architecture to Relevance can be highlighted as highly diverse and for now, it can be said that reasons are rooted in EE's knowledge needs, the EX' explaining intention, and in questions emerging from the interaction between both EX and EE during the explanation.

5 Discussion

This paper investigated how the content of a naturalistic explanation of the board game *Quarto!* evolves, and how this evolution of content is justified by the EX. Regarding potentials for XAI research, we believe that researching how explanations of technological artifacts evolve naturally is an important prerequisite for formulating recommendations on how to construct synthetic explanations. One of the aims of this study was to investigate how the dual nature of the explanandum is addressed in the utterances of the explanations (RQ1). Existing literature was very sparse regarding this question. The objective of the content analysis was to categorize utterances reliably into the two code categories: Architecture and Relevance. Throughout all explanations, both sides of the dual nature were addressed to a varying degree. Answering RQ2 (what are common patterns regarding sequences of utterances about the dual nature across the explanations?) resulted in a deeper understanding of when which side was addressed more frequently. We found that in most explanations, aspects of the game's Architecture were addressed in the first third of the explanation, and only in the middle and last third, aspects of the Relevance were addressed more frequently. Based on these findings, RQ3 (How do EX justify their choice of explanation content regarding which side of the dual nature was addressed?) helped to gain better insights to the reasons why EX explained predominantly the Architecture at the beginning of explanations, and how shifts from Architecture to Relevance were justified by the EX. We found that at the beginning of an explanation, especially the explaining intention of the EX, is the reason for explaining content addressed towards Architecture. In later stages, shifts from addressing Architecture to addressing Relevance were justified by the EX's explaining intention, the perceived knowledge needs of the EE, and their interactive sequences of EX and EE throughout the explanation.

The study design worked as anticipated. All dyads engaged quickly into the explanation after getting the start signal. The EX explained intuitively, and EE frequently asked questions or shared their confusion. Our observation is that all dyads were interested in a successful explanation, and motivated to continue the explanation, until they thought they had finished. The comparability across explanations was satisfactory, as the time and content did not deviate too much and dyads kept their focus on explaining in such a way, that the EE would be able to win the game, too. Thus, instruction worked as well. Our overarching motivation is that finding certain patterns would provide insights useful for future research on other explananda to, eventually decide, for example, whether certain patterns are generalizable and maybe even a useful scheme for synthetic explanations, too.

As stated earlier, we believe, the theory provides a rich background for research on everyday explanations of technological artifacts and offers potentials for XAI research, too. Based on our findings, we still believe that. It could provide a foundation for formulating recommendations on whether and which of the artifacts properties should be referred to within a (synthetic) explanation. In our study, EX tended to put more effort into explaining aspects that address the

Architecture than the Relevance. In the case of *Quarto!*, the questions of which side of the dual nature is more important or whether one is a precursor for the other (cf. Sect. 2) can thus be answered: Explaining the Architecture first before diving into what EX considered to be more complex details of the Relevance of the game, seemed to be a natural way to approach an explanation in the context of *Quarto!*. Regarding what we saw in the explanations, we would interpret it as a verbal realization of *laying out the tools*, by addressing the bits of Architecture which the EX can refer to in later stages of the explanation to connect aspects of the Architecture of *Quarto!* to aspects of its Relevance. Thus, we believe that, especially looking at the fairly large percentage of utterances addressing the Relevance with the justifications that the EX stated in the video recalls, provide a solid foundation for the claim that **both** sides can be considered important in the case of *Quarto!*. Whether and how these findings are generalizable, especially for more complex artifacts, is still an open research question.

The question of (RQ3) how do EX justify their choice of explanation content regarding which side of the dual nature was addressed, brought further insights into the reasons why the EX addressed either the Architecture or Relevance. The EX provided a broad range of reasons for explaining aspects addressed to Architecture and Relevance at different stages of the explanation. The variety of different reasons indicate, that deciding on which aspects to explain is a process in which the EX has to consider a large variety of factors, not only concerning their intention but also guided by what they intend to explain. At the beginning of the explanations, EX dominated the explanation and the reasons for addressing the Architecture are usually rooted in the EX's explaining intention. Therefore, the first part of the explanation follows the explanation goal and plan of the EX without further consideration of the specific needs of the EE, albeit important for understanding [5, 26]. EX mentioned reasons like explaining physical components and their characteristics and appearance first as a preparation for providing more details later in the explanation, especially in regard to shifting to Relevance. At times, the shift from Architecture to Relevance did not occur suddenly, but emerged gradually in the context of the interaction of both participants. In these instances, even though the explaining intention of the EX was still apparent, the knowledge needs of EE became more evident. Reasons for that were not mentioned, but could potentially be out of general interest or due to identifying certain misunderstandings [10]. Aspects that were addressed to Relevance were seldom part of the first third of the explanations. Yet, our analyses of the video recall showed that in some instances, EX structured their explanations with aspects of the Relevance in mind. They interpreted these bits of information as highly important for their explanation. This might be an indicator that Relevance is (1) an important part of an explanation and (2) even though verbally the Relevance is not yet addressed in the explanation, it still guides the choice of which aspects of the Architecture are addressed at the start.

The theoretical background puts focus on the characteristics of technological artifacts, but empirical investigations only addressed more technical, text-based explanations (e.g., patents) [37]. As texts are very different from extemporaneous explaining, we were surprised how clearly, and easily distinguishable Architecture and Relevance were addressed within the explanations of *Quarto!*. In the cognitive sciences, the theory of people taking different stances to explain things may be useful for explaining this phenomenon [12,19]. Two stances seem to be connected to addressing the sides of the dual nature. Whereas in the context of the dual nature theory, the question was raised whether one side is a precursor or more important, the cognitive sciences spent time researching how explanations from different stances result in different understanding. If (and only if!) these stances would be connected to addressing either the Architecture or the Relevance, our findings *may* support the hypothesis, that by categorizing utterances into either of the two code categories of the dual nature, in the case of *Quarto!*, we identified areas in which these stances were observable. If this was the case, interestingly, our dyads shifted between stances fairly quickly and multiple times throughout one explanation.

Potentials for XAI Research. We are convinced that researching how explanations of technological artifacts evolve naturally is an important prerequisite for formulating recommendations for the construction of synthetic explanations. The limitations of popular notions of explanations in XAI elaborated in [38] provide a good rationale for why research such as this is required for *real explanations* in XAI: understanding human-to-human (H-H) explanations and their co-constructive nature offers large potential for insights on what exactly is important for human understanding in explanations of artifacts. It is needed to establish a foundation of knowledge for formulating, for example, recommendations on whether and which of the artifacts properties should be referred to within a synthetic explanation and, for example, how that is related to certain knowledge needs or explaining intentions of EE and EX. Our findings, and our methodology, provide valuable tools for future research, too. To close this thought, we share an insight that surprised us in our studies: We did not anticipate the pattern that utterances about the Architecture were more present in the first third of the explanations. Instead, our intuition was guided by the idea of providing a source of motivation to create an atmosphere that is attractive, regularly referred to as good practice in teaching and education [4]. We intuitively expected that the EX would focus on the Relevance of *Quarto!* at the start of the explanations, to provide a source to stimulate the EE's motivation (e.g., by giving reasons why the game is exciting or fun to play). Yet, the opposite happened. Even if just anecdotal, we believe it provides an important learning: Simply sticking to popular beliefs or plausibility for constructing synthetic explanations already skips important steps. Instead, taking these steps in the shape of research on naturalistic, everyday H-H explanations of artifacts are an important prerequisite for the field and thus for *real* XAI.

Quality Standards. We adhered to a variety of recommendations [24,33]. We documented the different stages of codings from initial codings until the final codings of the transcripts, especially for being able to reconstruct the interrater data sessions in which the codings were discussed between the two coders and adjusted accordingly. Inter-rater and intra-rater reliability was examined for the analysis of the explanation content, intra-rater reliability was assessed for the video recalls. Additionally, three independent coders unfamiliar with the theoretical background used the coding manual for the explanation content analysis and coded three transcripts. We compared the results to our codings using intercoder reliability tests (k=0.53). All reliability measures were good (see Sect. 3.4). Parts of the final codings were discussed within and outside the research project (peer debriefing). Earlier results were presented and discussed during a research retreat of the Transregional Collaborative Research Centre TRR 318 "Constructing Explainability". To prevent false conclusions, and for a deeper understanding of the practical implications of the study design, all researchers involved in this publication were present during at least a quarter of the studies (experiencing the study). We triangulated the results from the content analysis with EX justifications stated in the video recalls to underpin, contrast or contradict our interpretations.

5.1 Limitations and Future Work

We found two commonalities across the explanations we analyzed. First, the majority of time was spent addressing the Architecture, especially in the first third of the explanation. Only later, the content was more balanced between utterances addressing the Architecture and Relevance. Whether this applies for other technological artifacts, too, is still an open research question that this study cannot answer. We believe that, especially if artifacts were more complex, describing the most important aspects of the Architecture at the beginning would maybe not be possible as (1) the amount of information could simply not be remembered (i.e., too much information) and (2) the amount of information would require explanations that would be far too long to be interesting for XAI. But, our insights open up new research opportunities and questions:

- Is *laying out the tools* a generally reasonable strategy when explaining technological artifacts? Do circumstances exist, in which it would make more sense to start with addressing the Relevance?
- How much focus on the Relevance is needed (and when) to provide a *good* explanation?
- What explanation strategies are used to start the explanation, if the explanandum is a very complicated, technological artifact (i.e., what are other strategies opposed to *laying out the tools*)?
- How is the level of understanding of the EE related to certain patterns or the ratio between the utterances addressing the two sides in the explanations?
- How is the EE ability to competently play the game connected to knowledge about both sides conveyed in the content of the explanations?

Based on our results, we now are in a position in which we claim that using the dual nature theory as an analytical tool to structure the content of explanations of technical artifacts is a worthwhile, and a viable approach. Coding the content of the explanations is quick, and the structure provided by the codes allows quick insights into how the explanation was carried out. Based on this, further analyses can be carried out which ultimately may help for recommendations for the construction of synthetic explanations, too. In the theoretical background elaborated in Sect.2, we addressed how different researchers have different perceptions regarding this question, yet more empirical support for the claims is needed. Our ongoing research will address such questions of which explanations, regarding their structure of addressing the dual nature of *Quarto!*, are better, that is, result in a deeper understanding of the EE. Currently, we are in the process of developing an instrument for such an assessment.

One remark that is necessary is, that in the case of games, the need for knowing the Architecture of the game is inherently clear. For example, if one does not know the shapes of the pieces in *Quarto!*, one would not be able to play it competently. Especially in the case of digital artifacts, this is not necessarily needed[6]. Therefore, if researching explanations of digital artifacts, another layer of complexity is added, which most likely also influences how easy it is to distinguish which side of the dual nature is addressed. Yet, as a first step, by investigating an example in which the need to understand the Architecture is so prominent, we gained insights that could be fundamental for a deeper understanding of explanations of more complex, and especially digital artifacts.

To further support, contrast or contradict our results, our study design could be changed in a way in which one participant is previously trained to influence the explanation by drawing the attention to either the Architecture or the Relevance, for example by instructing them to have certain knowledge needs (e.g., you want to program the game afterward vs. you want to know whether the game is a suitable present for a friend). Controlling that variable is promising to get a better understanding if one side may also be omitted completely or if it would always emerge naturally, regardless of what was instructed before.

The video recall method has some limitations, for example, the anxiousness of the participants, self-censorship and reduced visual hints through fixed perspective and technical format [6]. We addressed this by creating an atmosphere in the lab that reduced factors leading to stress or anxiety in the participants and gave room for self-exploration. By using this introspective method, we were able to better identify the reasons for explaining specific aspects of the game.

In some instances, the EX verbally remarked that they were surprised about the absence of the game during phase 2. Thus, the absence of the game is a potential factor influencing the beginning of the explanations quite drastically. But, as elaborated in 3.2, we believe this circumstance to be the norm rather than the exception, as it created a black box scenario. Yet, this factor needs to be addressed in future research. However, due to the low number of instances, we believe it to have only a minor effect on the naturalness of the explanations.

---

[6] Research areas such as user experience and interface design are a good example in this regard. Put very briefly and naively, they are interested in circumventing the need to understand the Architecture by providing enough Relevance to be able to use things competently.

5.2 Conclusion

In the case of natural explanations of the board game *Quarto!*, EX referred to a carefully selected set of information about the Architecture of the game in the first third of the explanation. Their rational was that such information (the *What*) is a prerequisite for information that they considered to be more complex (the *why*). They did this to make the more complex content of the explanation more accessible for the EE later in their explanations. At later stages of the explanations, the reasons for shifting from addressing the Architecture (the *what*) to addressing the Relevance (the *why*) were rooted in a larger variety of reasons, one of them being that they slowly emerged from the interaction between EX and EE. Our findings are a first step towards a more general understanding of extemporaneous explanations of technological artifacts, especially regarding when and how the two sides of the dual nature are addressed in explanations. Other researchers suggested that such an approach is not only viable, but necessary for the development of XIA systems which can explain *naturally* and thus for a broad audience [38]. A better conceptualization of these naturalistic explanations of technological artifacts can provide crucial insights into how XAI can explain its decision more naturally. Especially if certain patterns – such as adding why to what – are generalizable and thus could be embedded in an interactive explanation system, this could improve the interpretability of decisions, and ultimately support the agency of a large variety of people interacting with XAI.

Acknowledgements

This research was funded by the Deutsche Forschungsgemeinschaft (DFG, German Research Foundation): TRR 318/1 2021 - 438445824. We thank Vivien Lohmer and Friederike Kern for their input during discussions, as well as for creating the transcripts. We thank all research assistants for their support during coding, data acquisition and data analysis.

Ethics Statement

This study was approved by the Paderborn University Ethics Board. All participants participated voluntarily and provided written informed consent before the studies. The studies were conducted in concordance with local COVID-19 policies.

References

1. Attisano, E., Nancekivell, S.E., Denison, S.: Components and mechanisms: how children talk about machines in museum exhibits. Front. Psychol. **12**, 1737 (2021). https://doi.org/10.3389/fpsyg.2021.636601
2. Brennan, R.L., Prediger, D.J.: Coefficient kappa: some uses, misuses, and alternatives. Educ. Psychol. Measur. **41**(3), 687–699 (1981). https://doi.org/10.1177/001316448104100307
3. Brennan, S.E., Hanna, J.E.: Partner-specific adaptation in dialog. Top. Cogn. Sci. **1**(2), 274–291 (2009). https://doi.org/10.1111/j.1756-8765.2009.01019.x
4. Brophy, J.E.: Motivating Students to Learn. 3rd edn. Routledge, New York (2010). https://doi.org/10.4324/9780203858318
5. Buhl, H.M.: Partner orientation and speaker's knowledge as conflicting parameters in language production. J. Psycholinguist. Res. **30**(6), 549–567 (2001). https://doi.org/10.1023/A:1014217421749
6. Calderhead, J.: Stimulated recall: a method for research on teaching. Br. J. Educ. Psychol. **51**(2), 211–217 (1981). https://doi.org/10.1111/j.2044-8279.1981.tb02474.x
7. Cederqvist, A.M.: Pupils' ways of understanding programmed technological solutions when analysing structure and function. Educ. Inf. Technol. **25**(2), 1039–1065 (2020). https://doi.org/10.1007/s10639-019-10006-4
8. Cederqvist, A.M.: Seeing the parts, understanding the whole - A technology education perspective on teaching and learning in processes of analysing and designing programmed technological solutions. University of Gothenburg (2021)
9. Chi, M.T.H.: Self-explaining: the dual processes of generating inference and repairing mental models. In: Advances in Instructional Psychology: Educational Design and Cognitive Science, vol. 5, pp. 161–238. Lawrence Erlbaum Associates Publishers, Mahwah, NJ, US (2000)
10. Chi, M.T.H., Siler, S.A., Jeong, H.: Can tutors monitor students' understanding accurately? Cogn. Instr. **22**(3), 363–387 (2004). https://doi.org/10.1207/s1532690xci2203_4
11. Chin-Parker, S., Bradner, A.: A contrastive account of explanation generation. Psychon. Bull. Rev. **24**(5), 1387–1397 (2017). https://doi.org/10.3758/s13423-017-1349-x
12. Dennett, D.C.: The Intentional Stance. MIT Press, Cambridge (1987)
13. El-Assady, M., et al.: Towards XAI: structuring the processes of explanations. In: Proceedings of the ACM Workshop on Human-Centered Machine Learning, Glasgow, UK (2019)
14. Fox-Turnbull, W.: Autophotography. In: Benson, C., Lunt, J. (eds.) International Handbook of Primary Technology Education: Reviewing the Past Twenty Years, pp. 195–209. International Technology Education Studies, SensePublishers, Rotterdam (2011). https://doi.org/10.1007/978-94-6091-546-8_16
15. Gilbert, J.K., Boulter, C., Rutherford, M.: Models in explanations, Part 1: horses for courses? Int. J. Sci. Educ. **20**(1), 83–97 (1998). https://doi.org/10.1080/0950069980200106
16. Gunning, D., Stefik, M., Choi, J., Miller, T., Stumpf, S., Yang, G.Z.: XAI-explainable artificial intelligence. Sci. Robot. **4**(37), eaay7120 (2019). https://doi.org/10.1126/scirobotics.aay7120
17. Hale, C.R., Barsalou, L.W.: Explanation content and construction during system learning and troubleshooting. J. Learn. Sci. **4**(4), 385–436 (1995). https://doi.org/10.1207/s15327809jls0404.2

18. Heider, F.: The Psychology of Interpersonal Relations. John Wiley & Sons Inc, Hoboken (1958). https://doi.org/10.1037/10628-000
19. Keil, F.C.: The birth and nurturance of concepts by domains: the origins of concepts of living things. In: Mapping the Mind: Domain Specificity in Cognition and Culture, pp. 234–254. Cambridge University Press, New York, NY, US (1994). https://doi.org/10.1017/CBO9780511752902.010
20. Keil, F.C.: Explanation and understanding. Annu. Rev. Psychol. **57**(1), 227–254 (2006). https://doi.org/10.1146/annurev.psych.57.102904.190100
21. Kroes, P., Meijers, A.W.M.: The dual nature of technical artifacts?: presentation of a new research programme. Techné **6**(2), 4–8 (2002)
22. Kroes, P.: technological explanations. Phil. Tech. **3**(3), 124–134 (1998). https://doi.org/10.5840/techne19983325
23. Kroes, P.: Design methodology and the nature of technical artefacts. Des. Stud. **23**(3), 287–302 (2002). https://doi.org/10.1016/S0142-694X(01)00039-4
24. Kuckartz, U.: Qualitative Text Analysis: A Guide to Methods. Practice and Using Software, SAGE (2014)
25. Landis, J.R., Koch, G.G.: The measurement of observer agreement for categorical data. Biometrics **33**(1), 159–174 (1977). https://doi.org/10.2307/2529310
26. Levelt, W.J.M., Le Page, R.B., Longuet-Higgins, H.C., Longuet-Higgins, H.C., Lyons, J., Broadbent, D.E.: The speaker's linearization problem. Philos. Trans. Royal Soc. London. B, Biol. Sci. **295**(1077), 305–315 (1981). https://doi.org/10.1098/rstb.1981.0142
27. Lombrozo, T., Carey, S.: Functional explanation and the function of explanation. Cognition **99**(2), 167–204 (2006). https://doi.org/10.1016/j.cognition.2004.12.009
28. Lyle, J.: Stimulated recall: a report on its use in naturalistic research. Br. Edu. Res. J. **29**(6), 861–878 (2003). https://doi.org/10.1080/0141192032000137349
29. Mackey, A., Gass, S.M.: Second language research: methodology and design. Methodology and design, Lawrence Erlbaum Associates Publishers, Mahwah, NJ, US, Second Language Research (2005)
30. Malle, B.F.: How the Mind Explains Behavior: Folk Explanations, Meaning, and Social Interaction. MIT Press, Cambridge (2004). https://direct.mit.edu/books/book/2642/How-the-Mind-Explains-BehaviorFolk-Explanations
31. McNeill, D.: Hand and Mind: What Gestures Reveal About Thought. University of Chicago Press, Chicago (1992)
32. McNeill, D.: Gesture and Thought. The University of Chicago Press, Chicago (2008). oCLC: 781253715
33. Miles, M.B., Huberman, A.M., Saldaña, J.: Qualitative Data Analysis: A Methods Sourcebook. 3rd edn. SAGE Publications Inc, Thousand Oaks (2014)
34. Miller, T.: Explanation in artificial intelligence: insights from the social sciences. Artif. Intell. **267**, 1–38 (2019). https://doi.org/10.1016/j.artint.2018.07.007
35. O'Connell, D.C., Kowal, S.: Transcription systems for spoken discourse. In: The Pragmatics of Interaction, pp. 240–254 (2009)
36. Pennington, N.: Stimulus structures and mental representations in expert comprehension of computer programs. Cogn. Psychol. **19**(3), 295–341 (1987). https://doi.org/10.1016/0010-0285(87)90007-7
37. de Ridder, J.: Mechanistic artefact explanation. Stud. Hist. Philos. Sci. Part A **37**(1), 81–96 (2006). https://doi.org/10.1016/j.shpsa.2005.12.009
38. Rohlfing, K.J., et al.: Explanation as a social practice: toward a conceptual framework for the social design of AI systems. IEEE Trans. Cogn. Develop. Syst. **13**(3), 717–728 (2021). https://doi.org/10.1109/TCDS.2020.3044366

39. Roscoe, R.D.: Self-monitoring and knowledge-building in learning by teaching. Instr. Sci. **42**(3), 327–351 (2014). https://doi.org/10.1007/s11251-013-9283-4
40. Salmon, W.C.: Four Decades of Scientific Explanation. University of Pittsburgh Press, Pittsburgh (1990)
41. Schreier, M.: Qualitative Content Analysis in Practice. SAGE, Los Angeles (2012)
42. Schulte, C.: Block model - an educational model of program comprehension as a tool for a scholarly approach to teaching. In: Proceeding of the Fourth international Workshop on Computing Education Research, pp. 149–160. ICER 2008, ACM, Sydney, Australia (2008). https://doi.org/10.1145/1404520.1404535
43. Schulte, C.: Duality reconstruction - teaching digital artifacts from a socio-technical perspective. In: In: Mittermeir, R.T., Sysło, M.M. (eds.) Informatics Education - Supporting Computational Thinking. ISSEP 2008. Lecture Notes in Computer Science, vol. 5090, pp. 110–121. Springer, (2008). https://doi.org/10.1007/978-3-540-69924-8.10
44. Selting, M., et al.: Gesprächsanalytisches Transkriptionssystem (GAT 2). Gesprächsforsch **10**, 152–183 (2009)
45. Soloway, E.: Learning to program = learning to construct mechanisms and explanations. Commun. ACM **29**(9), 850–858 (1986). https://doi.org/10.1145/6592.6594
46. Vermaas, P., Kroes, P., van de Poel, I., Franssen, M., Houkes, W.: A philosophy of technology: from technical artefacts to sociotechnical systems. Synth. Lect. Eng. Technol. Soc. **6**(1), 1–134 (2011). https://doi.org/10.2200/S00321ED1V01Y201012ETS014
47. Vermaas, P.E., Houkes, W.: Technical functions: a drawbridge between the intentional and structural natures of technical artefacts. Stud. Hist. Philos. Sci. Part A **37**(1), 5–18 (2006). https://doi.org/10.1016/j.shpsa.2005.12.002
48. van der Waa, J., Nieuwburg, E., Cremers, A., Neerincx, M.: Evaluating XAI: a comparison of rule-based and example-based explanations. Artif. Intell. **291**, 103404 (2021). https://doi.org/10.1016/j.artint.2020.103404

For Better or Worse: The Impact of Counterfactual Explanations' Directionality on User Behavior in xAI

Ulrike Kuhl[1,2]([✉]) [ID], André Artelt[2] [ID], and Barbara Hammer[2] [ID]

[1] Research Institute for Cognition and Robotics (CoR-Lab), Bielefeld University, Bielefeld, Germany
[2] Faculty of Technology, Machine Learning Group, Bielefeld University, Bielefeld, Germany
{ukuhl,aartelt,bhammer}@techfak.uni-bielefeld.de
https://www.uni-bielefeld.de/zwe/cor-lab/,
https://hammer-lab.techfak.uni-bielefeld.de/doku.php

Abstract. Counterfactual explanations (CFEs) are a popular approach in explainable artificial intelligence (xAI), highlighting changes to input data necessary for altering a model's output. A CFE can either describe a scenario that is better than the factual state (*upward* CFE), or a scenario that is worse than the factual state (*downward* CFE). However, potential benefits and drawbacks of the directionality of CFEs for user behavior in xAI remain unclear. The current user study (N = 161) compares the impact of CFE directionality on behavior and experience of participants tasked to extract new knowledge from an automated system based on model predictions and CFEs. Results suggest that *upward* CFEs provide a significant performance advantage over other forms of counterfactual feedback. Moreover, the study highlights potential benefits of *mixed* CFEs improving user performance compared to *downward* CFEs or no explanations. In line with the performance results, users' explicit knowledge of the system is statistically higher after receiving *upward* CFEs compared to *downward* comparisons. These findings imply that the alignment between explanation and task at hand, the so-called regulatory fit, may play a crucial role in determining the effectiveness of model explanations, informing future research directions in (xAI). To ensure reproducible research, the entire code, underlying models and user data of this study is openly available: https://github.com/ukuhl/DirectionalAlienZoo

Keywords: Human-centric explainable AI · Counterfactual explanations · User study

This research was supported by research training group Dataninja (Trustworthy AI for Seamless Problem Solving: Next Generation Intelligence Joins Robust Data Analysis) funded by the German federal state of North Rhine-Westphalia, and by the European Research Council (ERC) under the ERC Synergy Grant Water-Futures (Grant agreement No. 951424).

L. Longo (Ed.): xAI 2023, CCIS 1903, pp. 280–300, 2023.
https://doi.org/10.1007/978-3-031-44070-0_14

1   Introduction

The question of how to provide users with understandable, usable, and trustworthy explanations for machine learning (ML) decisions is at the heart of explainable artificial intelligence (xAI). A popular variant within the community are counterfactual explanations (CFEs), drawing out "what-if" scenarios that highlight necessary perturbations of the input data to change a model's output [60]. Recent years have brought a notable uptick of studies investigating various aspects of CFEs for ML. Prior work focuses, inter alia, on their robustness [2], impact on user trust and satisfaction [61,62], and usability as a function of algorithmic properties [21] (see [56] for an extensive review of the research landscape).

One key defining characteristic of counterfactual statements is their directionality: *upward* counterfactuals describe scenarios that are superior to the factual state (i.e. , how it would have been better), while *downward* counterfactuals refer to more negative alternatives to the factual state (i.e. , how it would have been worse) [28].

There is general agreement among cognitive and social psychologists that *upward* counterfactuals serve a preparatory role, increasing motivation and guiding future action [8,64]. The role of *downward* counterfactuals, however, seems to be more complex. A common argument points towards a predominantly affective role, inducing a sense of relief about the factual state by emphasizing how a scenario could have been worse [46]. However, alternative empirical evidence suggests that *downward* counterfactuals may act as a wake-up call by drawing attention towards the possibility of worse outcomes, thus increasing motivation to take action [30].

In xAI, the impact of CFE directionality remains even more ambiguous, given that counterfactuals used to explain a model are not spontaneously generated by humans, but automatically computed as actionable feedback deepening users' understanding. CFE user studies commonly investigate CFEs that flip a binary outcome class [9,10,43,61,62]. While these outcomes may have qualitative implications within their respective task domains (e.g. , being under vs. over the legal blood alcohol limit to drive [9,61,62], chemicals being safe vs. unsafe [9], grass growth levels on a farm being high vs. low [10]), the directionality of provided explanations is often outside the respective research focus. Thus, this aspect has not yet been extensively studied in xAI, and preliminary data available presents inconsistencies.

For instance, [43] report *downward* CFEs for positive decisions to be less popular compared to importance rankings, and find no differences between rankings and *upward* CFEs in terms of user preference. In contrast, [9] suggest a behavioral impact of explanations that establish a *downward* comparison to the factual state on personal decision-making. Following this reasoning, *downward* CFEs may potentially serve as better actionable feedback.

Given these sparse and inconsistent accounts, it is unclear whether one type of CFEs is more effective than the other in improving user performance in tasks that require model interpretation. Therefore, the current study systematically compares the impact of CFE directionality for ML predictions on user behavior. Specifically, we perform a user study that requires participants to extract new knowledge from an automated system given model predictions and corresponding CFEs. On top of groups exclusively receiving *upward* and *downward* CFEs, we provide a third group of users with both types in a *mixed* condition. We find it conceivable that collective information on better and worse outcomes may grant a more complete understanding of the causal relationships between actions and outcomes, effectively informing future decision-making. We investigate how CFEs of either type impact users' objective performance, explicit knowledge of the system, and subjective experience, compared to each other and a no-explanation *control* condition.

2   Related Work

In contrast to using inherently interpretable models such as rule sets or decision trees, establishing explainability for opaque models like support vector machines or neural networks is a challenging endeavor. Proposed approaches include feature importance methods providing insights into the relevance and influence of input features on model predictions [27,47], rule extraction techniques distilling interpretable decision rules from complex models [40], and prototype-based explanations leveraging representative instances to explain model behavior [52].

In this broader xAI landscape, CFEs take a prominent role given an emerging user-centric focus on explainability [31]. CFEs facilitate human comprehension by explicitly revealing the necessary changes in input data to influence the model's output [60]. In this way, CFEs provide explanations for instances where the model's predictions deviate from the desired outcomes, allowing users to understand the factors that contribute to the model's decision-making process. Their particular appeal lies in their intrinsically contrastive format, bearing a strong resemblance to human cognitive reasoning. Indeed, individuals routinely engage in counterfactual thinking [14,45]. During this process, one not only retains the representation of actual facts, but also simulates an alternative scenario of how the reality might have differed [8]. This distinct characteristic positions CFEs as a valuable addition to the xAI toolkit, promising to provide users with actionable insights for decision-making and understanding model behavior for a given decision.

How humans reason from counterfactuals has been a prominent research topic in cognitive psychology studies [16,25,49], producing relevant implications for the use of CFEs in xAI applications [7]. Human-generated counterfactuals typically change only a limited set of features, preferably undoing recent and controllable events to create hypothetical scenarios that are strongly aligned with the individual's personal world knowledge and beliefs [7,12]. The current literature encompasses various computational approaches for generating CFEs [1,53], reflecting the continuing development within the field of counterfactual explanation generation. To yield explanations that closely resemble human counterfactual thought [31], generation approaches have placed emphasis on producing

CFEs that are sparse [32], stay close to the original input (with variations in terms of the distance measures, [18,20]), focus on controllable (and thus actionable) features [18,54], and may even diversify the generated solutions to meet end-user's needs [32].

Still, gaps in understanding in how far certain aspects of CFEs may facilitate or hinder a user's understanding when they are used in xAI remain. Just recently, [61] demonstrated that human users more readily understand explanations relying on categorical features in contrast to continuous ones, a distinction not typically taken into account by CFE generation approaches. In a similar vein, the current work investigates the potential impact of CFE directionality on user behavior, a fundamental property commonly not addressed in xAI. *Upward* counterfactuals (i.e. , how it would have been better) are typically generated following negative events [28]. In this way, they may provide a clear roadmap for future improvement and action [7]. Indeed, imagining "better-worlds" broadly leads to performance improvements in various tasks and settings as a driving force for learning from past mistakes [13,36,44,64]. When individuals engage in *upward* counterfactual thinking, their motivational orientation towards improvement aligns with the counterfactual focus on a hypothetical "better world", thus inducing regulatory fit [15]. The positive affect associated with regulatory fit may enhance motivation, persistence, and goal-directed behavior, leading to an increased likelihood of taking action to bridge the gap between the current and desired states [33].

Downward counterfactuals, in contrast, refer to imagining more negative alternatives to the factual state (i.e. , how it would have been worse) [28]. This downward comparison may have different functional implications, and research indeed reveals a complex pattern. On the one hand, *downward* counterfactual thinking is frequently associated with affective regulation, eliciting relief [46] and reducing regret [38]. Through this positive affective role of inducing a feeling of "I'm better off than I could have been", it seems to serve a self-enhancement function leading to more favorable self-perception [63]. In this way, *downward* counterfactual thinking may lead to a sense of complacency, reducing the motivation to act [30]. On the other hand, putting one's attentional focus on an objectively worse counterfactual possibility may induce negative affect, which may in turn serve as a motivator by signaling that the present condition is inadequate and requires action [30]. Thus, by focusing on mistakes and missed opportunities, *downward* counterfactuals may potentially highlight areas for improvement. Despite these indications for fundamental differences in how humans reason with *upward* and *downward* counterfactuals, this crucial aspect of CFEs' effectiveness and usability received little attention in xAI research so far. An extensive literature review revealed only two previous papers partially addressing this issue.

First, [43] conducted a study examining the effectiveness of feature rankings and CFEs in two everyday contexts: online advertising and loan applications. Specifically, their second experiment focuses on the directionality of explanations, with a particular emphasis on providing *upward* CFEs following negative outcomes and *downward* CFEs following positive outcomes. Participants made trade-off decisions between the two explanation modes, thus indicating their preferences for either feature rankings or CFEs. The results present a notable contrast to the prevailing preference for CFEs within the xAI community. Surprisingly, users show a higher preference for feature rankings over *downward* CFEs when faced with positive outcomes. This suggests that users found feature rankings more favorable in such scenarios. In the case of negative decisions, users exhibit no significant difference in terms of preference between the explanation formats, selecting *upward* CFEs as frequently as feature rankings. It is important to note, however, that such an assessment of user preference does not specifically allow drawing conclusions about relative usability differences of the explanation formats. Usability and user preference are two distinct aspects when evaluating the effectiveness of a system; aspects that – while being associated to some extent – often do not align [37]. Users may exhibit a subjective preference for systems or explanations, irrespective of the measurable impact on performance [24,59].

More recently, [9] exposed participants to a model's input, its decision, and either counterfactual or causal explanations, framed as a software application built to aid decision-making. Depending on the experimental group, the domain presented to a participant encompassed either a familiar scenario (i.e. , blood alcohol level and driving limit), or an unfamiliar one (i.e. , chemical safety). After rating the perceived helpfulness of the explanation presented, participants reached personal decisions whether they would be prepared to drive/handle an unknown chemical for a series of cases where they only saw the model input (Experiment 2 of [9]). Intriguingly, the personal decisions aligned better with model predictions when the preceding explanations would specifically establish a downward comparison. While this may shed a favorable light on *downward* CFEs for guiding personal action, it is unclear to which extent the familiarization phase framed as judging the helpfulness of a software application carried over to the subsequent decision-making phase. Furthermore, the reported beneficial effect of explanations that establish a downward comparison presents an incidental finding, as the actual focus of the study was on effects related to domain familiarity.

In light of these inconclusive preliminary findings, we aim to take a first step towards a systematic investigation of their directionality impacts CFEs' usability as actionable feedback in xAI. Specifically, we ask whether novice users tasked to gain new information from an unknown system in an abstract domain [22] benefit more from receiving *upward*, *downward*, or *mixed* CFE feedback. By examining the effects of directionality, we aim to shed light on a nuance of CFEs that has yet to be explored, contributing to a more comprehensive understanding of their effectiveness and applicability in xAI.

3   Methods

To assess the impact of directionality of CFEs in xAI on user behavior, we employ the game-inspired Alien Zoo framework [22]. Consequently, our study assesses the efficacy of *upward*, *downward*, and *mixed* CFEs in acquiring new knowledge from an automated system in a low-knowledge domain, specifically targeting novice users. The Ethics Committee of Bielefeld University, Germany, approved this study.

3.1 Participants

We determined the required sample size for the current study by running an *a-priori* power analysis, using openly-available empirical data from an earlier empirical study based on the same experimental paradigm [22]. These exemplary data provided us with realistic estimates for fixed and random effects to be expected in the current study. The power analysis (R package mixedpower v.0.1.0 [23]) indicated that 40 participants per group were required to achieve a power of $> 85\%$ (medium effect size with alpha$< .05$).

161 Participants were recruited in April 2023 using *Prolific Academic*[1], and assigned to one of four between-participant conditions in a fixed order: *upward* CFEs (n = 40), *downward* CFEs (n = 40), *mixed CFEs* (i.e. , receiving one *downward* and one *upward* CFEs in each feedback round, n = 41), and a no-explanation *control* group (n = 40). We restricted access to the study to native English speakers from the United States, Australia, Canada, New Zealand, Ireland, and the United Kingdom, who did not previously participate in studies with the given experimental framework. Before participating, users provided informed consent through electronic click wrap agreement.

All participants received a base pay of GBP£4 for participation. The three top performers in each condition received a bonus payment of GBP£1. Together with the experimental instructions, participants were informed about a potential monetary bonus to increase compliance with the task [3].

To ensure sufficient data quality, we applied several exclusion criteria prior to analysis. Specifically, a participant's responses were removed when they failed more than one attention check (n = 3). No participant displayed monotonous response patterns despite poor performance during the game, indicating high effort. Data from 158 participants contributed to the final game analysis (Table reftab:Participants).

Note that for a number of users, logging of survey responses failed due to technical difficulties (n = 8). Further, we excluded users from the subsequent survey analysis if they answered with positive or negative valence only, indicating low-effort entries (n = 4). Consequently, the survey analysis was based on a subset of 146 users from the game phase.

3.2 Experimental Procedure

A detailed account of procedure and design choices underlying the experimental framework is given in [22].

---

[1] https://www.prolific.co/.

Table 1. Demographic information of participants.

| | Before quality assurance measures ($N = 161$) | | | | | |
	control	upward	downward	mixed	H value[a]	p value
N	40	40	40	41		
Gender[b,c]	20f/20m	20f/20m	20f/20m	20f/19m/1nb	0.018	.999
Age (Mdn)[b,d]	35–44y	35–44y	25–34y	25–34y	5.091	.165
	After quality assurance measures ($N = 158$)					
	control	upward	downward	mixed	H value[a]	p value
N	40	39	38	41		
Gender[b,c]	20f/20m	20f/19m	19f/19m	20f/19m/1nb	0.214	.975
Age (Mdn)[b,d]	35–44y	35–44y	25–34y	25–34y	7.388	.061

[a] non-parametric Kruskal-Wallis H test
[b] note that one participant did not disclose age or gender information
[c] f = female, m = male, nb = non-binary/gender non-conforming
[d] Mdn = median age (options: 18–24y, 25–34y, 35–44y, 45–54y, 55–64y, 65y and over).

In short, users who agree to participate are directed to a web server to complete a short online game. As part of the game, participants feed a group of aliens iteratively over several trials, choosing combinations of different plants as food for their aliens. During every feeding choice, users may select up to 6 instances of each of five plants represented by leaf symbols of identical shape but different color (see Fig. 1A for an exemplary decision scene). Each player starts out with an initial pack size of 20 aliens. Tasked to find the best plant combination that makes the alien pack grow instead of declining, top players generating the highest number of aliens per experimental group received an additional monetary bonus.

To facilitate the learning process of what plants make an effective alien diet, participants receive feedback in the form of CFEs after every even trial. The feedback depends on the respective participant's condition (*upward* = "Your result would have been BETTER if you had selected:"; *downward* = "Your result would have been WORSE if you had selected:"; *mixed* = "Your result would have been BETTER/WORSE if you had selected:"; *control* = no explanation beyond an overview of past choices). Figure 1B depicts an exemplary feedback scene for a participant in the *upward* group. The game phase consists of 12 trials (i.e. , 12 feeding choices), with two attention checks assessing user's attentiveness after trials 3 and 7.

Following the game phase, a survey assessed users' subjective judgments of presented feedback via a modified version of the system causability scale (SCS, [17]). On top of two items assessing explicit knowledge of feature relevance for task success, this scale measures the extent to which an xAI system provides clear and understandable explanations for its decisions. Users rate the quality of explanations based on factors such as completeness, consistency, relevance, and comprehensibility on a five-point Likert scale. Finally, we collected demographic information on participants' age and gender, before users received a link to access full debriefing information.

3.3 Prediction of New Alien Number and Generation of CFE Feedback

During the game, an underlying ML model trained on simulated plant-growth-rate data determines changes in alien number. In each trial, the participant's feeding choice is passed on to a decision tree regression model [50] to predict a change rate for the current pack size (-10 to $+10$ aliens per decision, capped not to go below 2). Here, we use the model and training data from a previous study relying on the same experimental framework (maximal tree depth of 5 with Gini splitting rule of CART [6]; see Experiment 2 from [22]). This prior work demonstrated the feasibility of the experimental framework when comparing *upward* CFE feedback to a no-explanation *control* condition, promising to yield similarly meaningful insights into potential effects driven by different types of CFEs. In addition, the choice to rely on freely-available material that was previously published provided us with exemplary data distributions to obtain realistic estimates for fixed and random effects for the *a priori* power analysis.

The corresponding training data entails a dependency between two features (plant 2 and plant 4, respectively) and the output variable. Specifically, the growth rate scales linearly with values 1 to 5 for plant 2, iff plant 4 has a value of 1 or 2. To prevent users from applying a simple 'the more, the better' approach, the dependence between growth rate and the value 6 of plant 2 was disrupted.

Together with each prediction, we also compute a CFE presenting an alternative plant combination that differs minimally from the current input via optimization [60]. In our implementation, a CFE $x_{\text{cf}} \in \mathbb{R}^d$ of an ML model $h : \mathbb{R}^d \to \{Y\}$ is realized as solving:

$$\underset{x_{\text{cf}} \in \mathbb{R}^d}{\arg\min} \; \ell\left(h(x_{\text{cf}}), y'\right) + C \cdot \theta(x_{\text{cf}}, x) \tag{1}$$

where $x \in \mathbb{R}^d$ denotes the original input, the regularization $\theta(\cdot)$ penalizes deviations from the original input x (weighted by a regularization strength $C > 0$), $y' \in \{Y\}$ denotes the requested output/behavior of the model $h(\cdot)$ under the counterfactual x_{cf}, and $\ell(\cdot)$ denotes a loss function penalizing deviations from the requested prediction. Thus, returned CFEs correspond to minimal perturbations to the model's input that alter the final prediction to a desired outcome. Given the regularization term $\theta(\cdot)$, generated CFEs based on this definition remain as similar to the original input x as possible.

Depending on the participant's condition, computed CFEs either increase (*upward* condition, and odd trials of the *mixed* condition) or decrease (*downward* condition, and even trials of the *mixed* condition) the current growth rate prediction by a few decimal points. After two trials, participants receive these CFEs as feedback to further improve their performance in the game (see Fig. 1B).

(A)

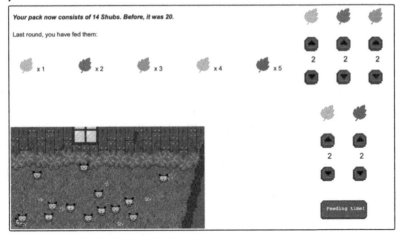

(B)

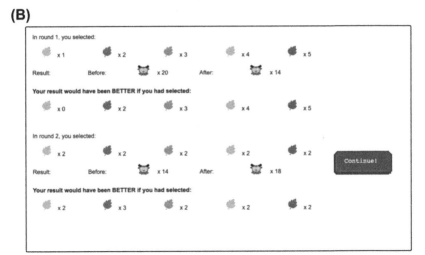

Fig. 1. Exemplary scenes from the Alien Zoo game. To improve visibility for this paper, font size in selected images was increased. **(A)** Example of a typical decision scene. Users are provided with a summary of their last choice, together with the previous and current pack size (note that the aliens are called 'Shubs' in the experimental scenario). Moreover, the page shows a padlock with animated aliens to visualize the current pack size. The right side of the screen shows the plant types alongside upward and downward arrow buttons. Note that plant counters are set to 0 at the beginning of each new decision trial, the image above already shows the next selection (all plants set to 2). **(B)** Example of a feedback scene for participants in the *upward* CFE condition, displaying user decision from the last two rounds, respective impact on alien number, and computed CFE. Note that type of feedback varied depending on experimental group.

3.4   Statistical Analysis

We use R-4.1.1 [41] for all statistical analyses, with experimental condition (*control, upward, downward, mixed*) as independent variable. Given our longitudinal design, we employ linear mixed models for data analysis to effectively address the correlations that arise from multiple measurements taken from each participant [11,35]. We investigate systematic differences between experimental groups over the 12 feeding trials (R package: lme4 v.4_1.1-27.1) [4], with alien pack size over trials as dependent variable, fixed effects of group, trial number and their interaction, and a by-subjects random intercept. We compared model fits using the analysis of variance function (stats package, base R). Effect sizes are reported as η_p^2 (R package: effectsize v.0.5) [5]. Pairwise estimated marginal means analysis followed-up significant main effects or interactions, Bonferroni corrected to account for multiple comparisons. We report respective effect sizes in terms of Cohen's d.

We analyze survey data based on item type. Missing values (i.e., users responding "I do not know." for items assessing explicit knowledge, or "I prefer not to answer." for items assessing subjective experience) were removed prior to the survey analysis.

The first two items of the survey evaluate the user's explicit knowledge of feature relevance for successful task completion. Our goal is to determine a comprehensive measure of user knowledge through rewards and penalties for correct and incorrect responses, respectively. To achieve this, we calculate the number of plants correctly identified per participant (i.e. , the number of matches between ground truth and user input).

The remaining items were adapted from the SCS, a rating scale that allows users to evaluate the extent to which an xAI system's explanations are clear, transparent, and understandable [17]. Based on their responses to these items, we compute an adapted SCS score for each participant to assess their subjective experience with the game.

Statistically, we investigate potential group differences concerning matches between user input and ground truth, Likert-style survey responses, age, and gender information using the non-parametric Kruskal-Wallis H test (R package: rstatix v.0.7.0) [19], with effect sizes given as η^2.

Significant effects revealed via the Kruskal-Wallis H test are followed-up by running pairwise comparisons between group levels, Bonferroni corrected for multiple testing.

4   Results

Overall, the results show group effects both in terms of performance during the game, and user's explicit knowledge of relevant and irrelevant features. However, we do not detect statistically significant differences when evaluating participants' subjective experience.

4.1 Game Performance

We evaluate users' game data to investigate whether naive users benefit comparably from different types of CFEs when tasked to extract knowledge in an unfamiliar domain. Specifically, we compare the number of aliens produced over time for participants receiving either *upward* CFEs, *downward* CFEs, *mixed* CFEs, or no CFEs (*control*) in the Alien Zoo iterative learning task.

Figure 2A depicts the development of average pack size over trials. All participants depict a positive learning trajectory, but with strikingly different slopes for different groups. The performance curves suggest that the mean number of generated aliens over trials varies as a function of experimental condition, with users receiving no explanations showing the least, and users receiving *upward* CFE feedback exhibiting the strongest performance increase. The corresponding linear mixed effects model revealed a significant interaction between trial number and group ($F(33,1694) = 13.114$, $p < .001$, $\eta_p^2 = 0.203$), confirming this observation.

Follow-up analyses reveal an intriguing pattern of distinctive group differences (see Figs. 2B-F).

The trajectories of the *control* and the *upward* group diverge significantly from trial 4 onward ($t(300) \geq -2.660$, $p \leq .0494$, $d \geq -1.066$), with participants in the *upward* group clearly outperforming *control* participants (Fig. 2B). This pattern also holds when comparing the *upward* group with the two remaining conditions. Trajectories of the *upward* and the *downward* group diverge significantly from trial 7 onward ($t(300) \geq 3.016$, $p \leq .0167$, $d \geq 1.224$; Fig. 2C). Statistical differences between the *upward* and the *mixed* groups emerge starting at trial 8 ($t(300) \geq 2.851$, $p \leq .0280$, $d \geq 1.135$; Fig. 2D).

While performing less efficient as participants in the *upward* group, participants in the *mixed* condition also achieve statistically higher scores in the last 5 trials compared to *control* participants ($t(300) \geq -2.891$, $p \leq .0247$, $d \geq -1.144$; Fig. 2E), and in the last 2 trials compared to *downward* participants ($t(300) \geq -3.121$, $p \leq .0119$, $d \geq -1.251$; Fig. 2F). Only trajectories of participants in the *control* and *downward* conditions do not show any statistically meaningful differences.

This interaction is complemented by a significant main effect of trial number ($F(11,1694) = 95.573$, $p < .001$, $\eta_p^2 = 0.380$), and group ($F(3,154) = 11.423$, $p < .001$, $\eta_p^2 = 0.180$).

4.2 Assessing User's Explicit Knowledge

The first two items of the survey phase assess participants' explicit knowledge of feature relevance for task completion. Across the two items, a participant could potentially reach 10 correct decisions by matching up their responses with the ground truth perfectly. In terms of mean number of matches between ground truth and user judgments, participants in the *control* condition matched highest ($M = 6.700 \pm 0.548$ *SE*), followed by participants in the *upward* ($M = 6.615 \pm 0.261$ *SE*), *mixed* ($M = 6.000 \pm 0.342$ *SE*), and *downward* condition

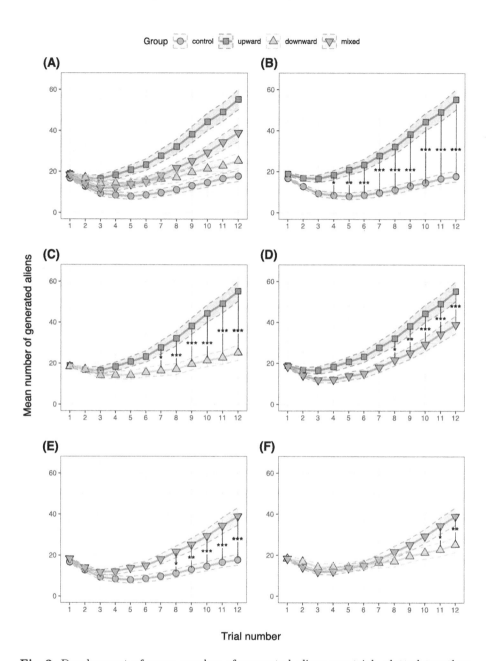

Fig. 2. Development of mean number of generated aliens per trial, plotted together for all groups (**A**), and pairwise for those groups showing significant differences in the analysis following-up the significant interaction (**B-F**). Shaded areas denote the standard error of the mean. Asterisks denote statistical significance with $p < .05$ (*), $p < .01$ (**), and $p < .001$ (***), respectively.

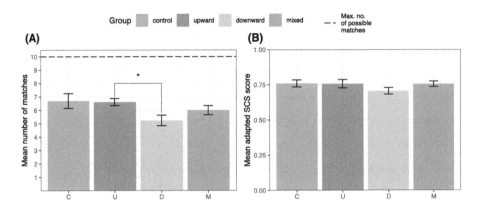

Fig. 3. (A) Mean number of matches between user input and ground truth in first two items of survey, assessing whether participants can correctly identify plants that are relevant and irrelevant for task success. The dashed line shows the maximally attainable number of matches (i.e. , user responses perfectly aligned with ground truth). Error bars denote the standard error of the mean. The asterisk denotes statistical significance with $p < 0.05$ (*). **(B)** Mean adapted SCS scores across groups. Error bars denote the standard error of the mean.

$(M = 5.241 \pm 0.390\ SE$; Fig. 3A). The corresponding statistical analysis reveals a significant effect of group $(H(3) = 10.9,\ p = .012,\ \eta^2 = 0.077)$. Follow-up pairwise comparisons show that participants in the *upward* match significantly higher than participants in the *downward* condition $(p = .028)$.

4.3   Assessing User's Subjective Experience

A modified version of the SCS informs whether participants perceive provided explanations as clear, understandable, and usable. As shown in Fig. 3B, participants in the *control* $(M = 0.760 \pm 0.025\ SE)$, *upward* $(M = 0.756 \pm 0.029\ SE)$, and *mixed* $(M = 0.754 \pm 0.019\ SE)$ conditions achieve very similar scores, while the mean SCS score of *downward* participants is slightly lower $(M = 0.705 \pm 0.023\ SE)$. There is no statistically significant effect of group in terms of SCS scores $(H(3) = 5.36,\ p = .147,\ \eta^2 = 0.017)$.

5   Discussion

The current study investigates the impact of directionality of CFEs for xAI on objective task performance, explicit knowledge, and subjective experience of novice users during an iterative learning paradigm in an unfamiliar domain.

The results suggest that participants benefit most from receiving *upward* CFE feedback (i.e. , informing them what choices would have been better), outperforming participants in all other conditions (Fig. 2). Consequently, we replicate prior work showing that *upward* CFEs induce a significant performance advantage over a no-explanation *control* [22] in the employed experimental framework, and extend previous insights by the aspect of directionality. In the current experimental setting, *upward* counterfactuals may have provided novice users with interpretable and clear pathways for actions that improve future behavior [7]. This is in line with previous psychological research demonstrating that reflecting upon "better worlds" may serve as a driving force for learning and adapting behavior [13,36,44,64]. Given the current task, the striking positive impact of *upward* CFEs is in line with the psychological concept of regulatory fit, as describing how a choice would have been better matches the motivational orientation to improve one's feeding choices [15]. Previous work in various domains suggests that such a feeling of fit induces more effective and satisfying performance, as well as greater persistence and motivation to continue the task [15,26,33]. A similar mechanism may be in effect in the current setting.

Intriguingly, participants who receive *mixed* CFE feedback also achieve statistically higher scores compared to *control* and *downward* groups, specifically towards later trials. Considering that *downward* CFEs do not improve user performance compared to providing no explanations at all (*control*), we may suspect that users in the *mixed* condition benefit from receiving feedback that partially possesses regulatory fit.

A previous study suggests a beneficial effect of explanations that establish a downward comparison [9]. However, other research shows that *downward* CFEs are relatively more disliked compared to feature rankings in terms of user preference [43]. Intriguingly, participants receiving *downward* CFEs in the current work do not show statistically meaningful differences in terms of task performance compared to participants receiving no explanations at all. While the current discrepancy of the *downward* group from the performance of the two other CFE groups is striking, it merits only cautious interpretation generally devoted to null effects. On the one hand, *downward* CFE feedback may have simply induced complacency that impeded participants' motivation to act, knowing that there still was a worse route they could have taken [30,44]. On the other hand, the current scenario may have been inadequate to unleash the negative affect necessary to stimulate action through the presented *downward* comparisons. Unsuccessfully feeding aliens had only limited personal consequences for participants, potentially keeping the level of perceived regret following a sub-optimal decision comparatively low. Consequently, the beneficial impact of *downward* CFEs in terms of regret minimization could not be observed [38]. A future study could investigate this possibility more closely via an adapted design that involves increased personal costs, thereby implementing a penalty for poor decision-making and a higher chance of inducing regret.

In terms of explicit knowledge, participants in the *upward* condition identified relevant and irrelevant input features more readily than in the *downward* condition, in line with the performance advantage for *upward* CFEs. This suggests that – in tasks requiring users to extract new information from a system – *upward* CFEs may be the better option for enhancing user's explicit knowledge.

A curious detail meriting comment, however, concerns the comparably high performance in terms of explicit knowledge by *control* users that do not receive explanations at all. This may be explained by the relatively high proportion of *control* participants indicating that they "do not know" for items assessing explicit knowledge, thus being discarded from this analysis. The remaining data may represent *control* individuals who are the most knowledgeable and confident in their responses.

In terms of objectively quantifiable measures, our study found tangible behavioral group differences, in stark contrast to user responses concerning the subjective usability of explanations provided. This observation is consistent with the literature on the mismatch between these two measures [21,61], and further highlights the need to carefully consider both subjective and objective measures when evaluating . (xAI) approaches.

5.1   Limitations

In order to provide a comprehensive evaluation of the current findings, it is important to acknowledge and address limitations inherent in this study.

Given the experimental Alien Zoo framework, the results are obtained in relation to a very specific context and with a specific task, diverging from many real-life domains. Today, we are already witnessing the significant impact of AI-based decision-making systems across a wide range of domains, including but not limited to health care [42], the legal system [34], and human resource management [58]. We carefully considered the trade-offs involved in selecting a specific context. Ultimately, the primary objective of investigating the usability and impact of counterfactual directionality on user behavior and experience, motivated the choice for a single and quite abstract domain (i.e. , feeding aliens). This set-up allowed us to maintain a high level of control over experimental variables to isolate effects driven by directionality of CFEs, while minimizing confounding variables that could arise from varying contexts. Importantly, participants could engage with the counterfactual explanations and extract new knowledge from the automated system without being influenced by pre-existing domain knowledge. Thus, the current approach facilitated a more detailed analysis of how CFE directionality specifically affects the task at hand and the extraction of new knowledge from an automated system. Uncovering these specific dynamics within a well-defined context provides a first step, laying out the foundation for future work. Results await validation across various domains, tasks, and user populations, to contribute to a more comprehensive understanding of the broader applicability and usefulness of CFEs across different scenarios.

Similarly, the current work does not cover different approaches for generating the CFEs. As outlined in Eq. 1, we follow an optimization approach to generate minimal adjustments to the model's input that – depending on experimental condition – either increase or decrease the predicted growth rate. This approach is based on the initial definition of CFE generation for ML [60] and various methods expand on the idea of using optimization principles for generating CFEs [29,32,51]. Alternative approaches generate counterfactual instances based on, e.g. , reinforcement learning [48,57] or conditional generative adversarial networks [55,65]. It is quite conceivable that the respective method for generating counterfactual explanations could indeed influence the final results. Different methods may introduce variations in the characteristics, interpretability, and quality of the explanations. Therefore, we have taken great care to select an optimization-based approach that aligns with established practices in the field.

A further potential confound of the design may be that it favors early discovery of an effective strategy, resulting in better performance over the duration of the experiment as the performance measure (number of generated aliens) accumulates over time. Finally, the current study neglects to account for individual user characteristics. It may be that anxiety-prone individuals respond more strongly to *downward* CFE feedback, given altered emotional and probabilistic appraisal of *upward* counterfactual thinking in individuals with high levels of trait anxiety [39]. Thus, further research is necessary to obtain a more comprehensive understanding of the role of directionality of CFEs in xAI.

5.2   Contribution to Knowledge for xAI

The findings presented in this study have significant implications for the field of explainable and trustworthy artificial intelligence. CFEs have emerged as a popular approach in xAI, as they provide insights into the changes required in input data to influence a model's output. This study specifically focuses on the directionality of CFEs, distinguishing between *upward* counterfactuals (describing scenarios better than the factual state) and *downward* counterfactuals (describing scenarios worse than the factual state).

Our results demonstrate the importance of CFE directionality in shaping behavior and experience of novice users when interacting with an unknown automated system in an unfamiliar domain to extract new knowledge. The findings indicate that *upward* CFEs offer a significant performance advantage over other forms of counterfactual feedback in the given explanation context. Specifically, users were able to extract new knowledge more effectively and demonstrated higher explicit knowledge of the system when provided with *upward* CFEs compared to *downward* CFEs.

These findings point towards critical role of regulatory fit in determining the effectiveness of model explanations [33]. Regulatory fit refers to the alignment between an explanation and the task at hand. In the context of xAI, this implies that the directionality of CFEs should be carefully considered to ensure they are relevant and meaningful to the users' objectives and cognitive processes. By providing explanations that align with users' goals and expectations, xAI systems can enhance user performance and improve their understanding of the underlying models [31].

The impact of these findings on xAI as a sub-field of artificial intelligence is substantial. xAI aims to bridge the gap between black-box models and human comprehension, enabling users to trust, interpret, and interact with automated systems more effectively. By identifying the advantages of *upward* CFEs and the potential benefits of *mixed* CFEs, this study contributes to the development of more effective and user-centric explainability techniques. Understanding the directionality of CFEs provides valuable insights into how explanations can be tailored to meet users' needs and improve their decision-making processes.

Furthermore, these findings have broader implications for the wider xAI community. Researchers and practitioners in xAI can leverage this knowledge to design better explainable systems. They can incorporate the directionality of CFEs into the design of xAI interfaces, ensuring that explanations are presented in a way that maximizes user understanding and performance. Additionally, these findings highlight the importance of user-centric evaluation methodologies in xAI research, as they provide valuable insights into the impact of explanations on user behavior and knowledge acquisition.

5.3   Conclusion

The canonical example illustrating the concept of counterfactuals in xAI is an *upward* CFE: "If you had done X, your loan would have been approved." The current results, suggesting that *upward* CFEs are most effective for guiding decision-making, may explain why this example is considered to be an inherently intuitive prototype. Further, the results of this study provide renewed evidence for the importance of considering not only algorithmic aspects of explainability approaches, but also their effectiveness during hands-on human-system interaction. Specifically, they give reason to assume that regulatory fit, i.e. , the alignment between an explanation and the task at hand, may act as a potentially crucial factor in determining the effectiveness of model explanations.

References

1. Artelt, A., Hammer, B.: On the computation of counterfactual explanations-a survey. arXiv preprint arXiv:1911.07749 (2019)
2. Artelt, A., et al.: Evaluating robustness of counterfactual explanations. In: 2021 IEEE Symposium Series on Computational Intelligence (SSCI), pp. 01–09. IEEE (2021). https://doi.org/10.1109/SSCI50451.2021.9660058
3. Bansal, G., Nushi, B., Kamar, E., Weld, D.S., Lasecki, W.S., Horvitz, E.: Updates in human-AI teams: understanding and addressing the performance/compatibility tradeoff. In: Proceedings of the AAAI Conference on Artificial Intelligence, vol. 33, pp. 2429–2437 (2019). https://doi.org/10.1609/aaai.v33i01.33012429
4. Bates, D., Mächler, M., Bolker, B., Walker, S.: Fitting linear mixed-effects models using lme4. J. Stat. Softw. **67**(1) (2015). https://doi.org/10.18637/jss.v067.i01
5. Ben-Shachar, M., Lüdecke, D., Makowski, D.: effectsize: estimation of effect size indices and standardized parameters. J. Open Source Softw. **5**(56), 2815 (2020). https://doi.org/10.21105/joss.02815
6. Breiman, L., Friedman, J.H., Olshen, R.A., Stone, C.J.: Classification and Regression Trees. 1st edn. Routledge, London (1984). https://doi.org/10.1201/9781315139470

7. Byrne, R.M.: Counterfactuals in explainable artificial intelligence (xAI): evidence from human reasoning. In: Proceedings of the Twenty-Eighth International Joint Conference on Artificial Intelligence, IJCAI-19, pp. 6276–6282. International Joint Conferences on Artificial Intelligence Organization (2019). https://doi.org/10. 24963/ijcai.2019/876

8. Byrne, R.M.: Counterfactual thought. Annu. Rev. Psychol. **67**, 135–157 (2016). https://doi.org/10.1146/annurev-psych-122414-033249

9. Celar, L., Byrne, R.M.: How people reason with counterfactual and causal explanations for artificial intelligence decisions in familiar and unfamiliar domains. Mem. Cogn. **51**, 1481–1496 (2023). https://doi.org/10.3758/s13421-023-01407-5

10. Dai, X., Keane, M.T., Shalloo, L., Ruelle, E., Byrne, R.M.: Counterfactual explanations for prediction and diagnosis in xAI. In: Proceedings of the 2022 AAAI/ACM Conference on AI, Ethics, and Society, pp. 215–226 (2022). https://doi.org/10. 1145/3514094.3534144

11. Detry, M.A., Ma, Y.: Analyzing repeated measurements using mixed models. JAMA **315**(4), 407 (2016). https://doi.org/10.1001/jama.2015.19394

12. Dyczewski, E.A., Markman, K.D.: General attainability beliefs moderate the motivational effects of counterfactual thinking. J. Exp. Soc. Psychol. **48**(5), 1217–1220 (2012). https://doi.org/10.1016/j.jesp.2012.04.016

13. Epstude, K., Roese, N.J.: The functional theory of counterfactual thinking. Pers. Soc. Psychol. Rev. **12**(2), 168–192 (2008)

14. Goldinger, S.D., Kleider, H.M., Azuma, T., Beike, D.R.: Blaming the victim under memory load. Psychol. Sci. **14**(1), 81–85 (2003). https://doi.org/10.1111/1467-9280.01423

15. Higgins, E.T.: Making a good decision: value from fit. Am. Psychol. **55**(11), 1217 (2000). https://doi.org/10.1037/0003-066X.55.11.1217

16. Hilton, D.J., Slugoski, B.R.: Knowledge-based causal attribution: the abnormal conditions focus model. Psychol. Rev. **93**(1), 75–88 (1986). https://doi.org/10. 1037/0033-295X.93.1.75

17. Holzinger, A., Carrington, A., Müller, H.: Measuring the quality of explanations: the system causability scale (SCS): comparing human and machine explanations. KI - Künstliche Intelligenz **34**(2), 193–198 (2020). https://doi.org/10.1007/s13218-020-00636-z

18. Karimi, A.H., Barthe, G., Balle, B., Valera, I.: Model-agnostic counterfactual explanations for consequential decisions. In: International Conference on Artificial Intelligence and Statistics, pp. 895–905. PMLR (2020)

19. Kassambara, A.: rstatix: pipe-friendly framework for basic statistical tests (2021). https://CRAN.R-project.org/package=rstatix. r package version 0.7.0

20. Keane, M.T., Smyth, B.: Good counterfactuals and where to find them: a case-based technique for generating counterfactuals for explainable AI (XAI). In: Watson, I., Weber, R. (eds.) ICCBR 2020. LNCS (LNAI), vol. 12311, pp. 163–178. Springer, Cham (2020). https://doi.org/10.1007/978-3-030-58342-2_11

21. Kuhl, U., Artelt, A., Hammer, B.: Keep your friends close and your counterfactuals closer: improved learning from closest rather than plausible counterfactual explanations in an abstract setting. In: 2022 ACM Conference on Fairness, Accountability, and Transparency, pp. 2125–2137 (2022). https://doi.org/10.1145/3531146. 3534630

22. Kuhl, U., Artelt, A., Hammer, B.: Let's go to the alien zoo: introducing an experimental framework to study usability of counterfactual explanations for machine learning. Front. Comput. Sci. **5**, 20 (2023). https://doi.org/10.3389/fcomp.2023. 1087929

23. Kumle, L., Võ, M.L.H., Draschkow, D.: Estimating power in (generalized) linear mixed models: an open introduction and tutorial in r. Behav. Res. Meth. **53**(6), 2528–2543 (2021). https://doi.org/10.3758/s13428-021-01546-0

24. Lage, I., et al.: Human evaluation of models built for interpretability. In: Proceedings of the AAAI Conference on Human Computation and Crowdsourcing, vol. 7, pp. 59–67 (2019). https://doi.org/10.1609/hcomp.v7i1.5280

25. Lombrozo, T.: Explanation and abductive inference. In: Holyoak, K.J., Morrison, R.G. (eds.) The Oxford Handbook of Thinking and Reasoning, pp. 260–276. Oxford University Press, Oxford, UK (2012). https://doi.org/10.1093/oxfordhb/9780199734689.013.0014

26. Ludolph, R., Schulz, P.J.: Does regulatory fit lead to more effective health communication? A systematic review. Soc. Sci. Med. **128**, 142–150 (2015). https://doi.org/10.1016/j.socscimed.2015.01.021

27. Lundberg, S.M., Lee, S.I.: A unified approach to interpreting model predictions. In: Advances in Neural Information Processing Systems, vol. 30 (2017)

28. Markman, K.D., Gavanski, I., Sherman, S.J., McMullen, M.N.: The mental simulation of better and worse possible worlds. J. Exp. Soc. Psychol. **29**(1), 87–109 (1993). https://doi.org/10.1006/jesp.1993.1005

29. Mc Grath, R., et al.: Interpretable credit application predictions with counterfactual explanations. In: NIPS 2018-Workshop on Challenges and Opportunities for AI in Financial Services: the Impact of Fairness, Explainability, Accuracy, and Privacy (2018)

30. McMullen, M.N., Markman, K.D.: Downward counterfactuals and motivation: the wake-up call and the Pangloss effect. Pers. Soc. Psychol. Bull. **26**(5), 575–584 (2000). https://doi.org/10.1177/0146167200267005

31. Miller, T.: Explanation in artificial intelligence: insights from the social sciences. Artif. Intell. **267**, 1–38 (2019). https://doi.org/10.1016/j.artint.2018.07.007

32. Mothilal, R.K., Sharma, A., Tan, C.: Explaining machine learning classifiers through diverse counterfactual explanations. In: Proceedings of the 2020 Conference on Fairness, Accountability, and Transparency, pp. 607–617 (2020). https://doi.org/10.1145/3351095.3372850

33. Motyka, S., et al.: Regulatory fit: a meta-analytic synthesis. J. Consum. Psychol. **24**(3), 394–410 (2014). https://doi.org/10.1016/j.jcps.2013.11.004

34. Mowbray, A., Chung, P., Greenleaf, G.: Utilizing AI in the legal assistance sector. In: LegalAIIA@ ICAIL, pp. 12–18 (2019)

35. Muth, C., Bales, K.L., Hinde, K., Maninger, N., Mendoza, S.P., Ferrer, E.: Alternative models for small samples in psychological research: applying linear mixed effects models and generalized estimating equations to repeated measures data. Educ. Psychol. Measur. **76**(1), 64–87 (2016). https://doi.org/10.1177/0013164415580432

36. Myers, A.L., McCrea, S.M., Tyser, M.P.: The role of thought-content and mood in the preparative benefits of upward counterfactual thinking. Motiv. Emot. **38**, 166–182 (2014). https://doi.org/10.1007/s11031-013-9362-5

37. Nielsen, J., Levy, J.: Measuring usability: preference vs. performance. Commun. CM **37**(4), 66–75 (1994). https://doi.org/10.1145/175276.175282

38. Parikh, N., De Brigard, F., LaBar, K.S.: The efficacy of downward counterfactual thinking for regulating emotional memories in anxious individuals. Front. Psychol. **12**, 712066 (2022). https://doi.org/10.3389/fpsyg.2021.712066

39. Parikh, N., LaBar, K.S., De Brigard, F.: Phenomenology of counterfactual thinking is dampened in anxious individuals. Cogn. Emot. **34**(8), 1737–1745 (2020). https://doi.org/10.1080/02699931.2020.1802230

40. Qiao, L., Wang, W., Lin, B.: Learning accurate and interpretable decision rule sets from neural networks. In: Proceedings of the AAAI Conference on Artificial Intelligence, vol. 35, pp. 4303–4311 (2021). https://doi.org/10.1609/aaai.v35i5.16555
41. R Core Team: R: A Language and Environment for Statistical Computing. R Foundation for Statistical Computing, Vienna, Austria (2021). https://www.R-project.org/
42. Rajpurkar, P., Chen, E., Banerjee, O., Topol, E.J.: Ai in health and medicine. Nat. Med. **28**(1), 31–38 (2022). https://doi.org/10.1038/s41591-021-01614-0
43. Ramon, Y., Vermeire, T., Toubia, O., Martens, D., Evgeniou, T.: Understanding consumer preferences for explanations generated by xAI algorithms. arXiv preprint arXiv:2107.02624 (2021)
44. Roese, N.J.: The functional basis of counterfactual thinking. J. Pers. Soc. Psychol. **66**(5), 805 (1994). https://doi.org/10.1037/0022-3514.66.5.805
45. Roese, N.J.: Counterfactual thinking. Psychol. Bull. **121**(1), 133–148 (1997). https://doi.org/10.1037/0033-2909.121.1.133
46. Roese, N.J., Olson, J.M.: Functions of counterfactual thinking. In: What Might Have Been: The Social Psychology of Counterfactual Thinking, pp. 169–197. Erlbaum (1995)
47. Rozemberczki, B.,et al.: The Shapley value in machine learning. In: The 31st International Joint Conference on Artificial Intelligence and the 25th European Conference on Artificial Intelligence (2022). https://doi.org/10.24963/ijcai.2022/778
48. Samoilescu, R.F., Van Looveren, A., Klaise, J.: Model-agnostic and scalable counterfactual explanations via reinforcement learning. arXiv preprint arXiv:2106.02597 (2021)
49. Sanna, L.J., Turley, K.J.: Antecedents to spontaneous counterfactual thinking: effects of expectancy violation and outcome valence. Pers. Soc. Psychol. Bull. **22**(9), 906–919 (1996). https://doi.org/10.1177/0146167296229005
50. Shalev-Shwartz, S., Ben-David, S.: Understanding Machine Learning: From Theory to Algorithms. Cambridge University Press, New York (2014)
51. Sharma, S., Henderson, J., Ghosh, J.: CERTIFAI: counterfactual explanations for robustness, transparency, interpretability, and fairness of artificial intelligence models. arXiv preprint arXiv:1905.07857 (2019)
52. Shin, Y.M., Kim, S.W., Yoon, E.B., Shin, W.Y.: Prototype-based explanations for graph neural networks. In: Proceedings of the AAAI Conference on Artificial Intelligence, vol. 36, pp. 13047–13048 (2022). https://doi.org/10.1609/aaai.v36i11.21660
53. Stepin, I., Alonso, J.M., Catala, A., Pereira-Fariña, M.: A survey of contrastive and counterfactual explanation generation methods for explainable artificial intelligence. IEEE Access **9**, 11974–12001 (2021). https://doi.org/10.1109/ACCESS.2021.3051315
54. Ustun, B., Spangher, A., Liu, Y.: Actionable recourse in linear classification. In: Proceedings of the Conference on Fairness, Accountability, and Transparency, pp. 10–19 (2019). https://doi.org/10.1145/3287560.3287566
55. Van Looveren, A., Klaise, J., Vacanti, G., Cobb, O.: Conditional generative models for counterfactual explanations. arXiv preprint arXiv:2101.10123 (2021)
56. Verma, S., Boonsanong, V., Hoang, M., Hines, K.E., Dickerson, J.P., Shah, C.: Counterfactual explanations and algorithmic recourses for machine learning: a review. arXiv preprint arXiv:2010.10596 (2020)
57. Verma, S., Hines, K., Dickerson, J.P.: Amortized generation of sequential algorithmic recourses for black-box models. In: Proceedings of the AAAI Conference on

Artificial Intelligence, vol. 36, pp. 8512–8519 (2022). https://doi.org/10.1609/aaai.v36i8.20828

58. Votto, A.M., Valecha, R., Najafirad, P., Rao, H.R.: Artificial intelligence in tactical human resource management: a systematic literature review. Int. J. Inf. Manage. Data Insights **1**(2), 100047 (2021). https://doi.org/10.1016/j.jjimei.2021.100047

59. van der Waa, J., Nieuwburg, E., Cremers, A., Neerincx, M.: Evaluating xAI: a comparison of rule-based and example-based explanations. Artif. Intell. **291**, 103404 (2021). https://doi.org/10.1016/j.artint.2020.103404

60. Wachter, S., Mittelstadt, B., Russell, C.: Counterfactual explanations without opening the black box: automated decisions and the GDPR. Harv. JL Tech. **31**, 841 (2017)

61. Warren, G., Byrne, R.M., Keane, M.T.: Categorical and continuous features in counterfactual explanations of AI systems. In: Proceedings of the 28th International Conference on Intelligent User Interfaces, pp. 171–187 (2023)

62. Warren, G., Keane, M.T., Byrne, R.M.: Features of explainability: how users understand counterfactual and causal explanations for categorical and continuous features in xAI. In: IJCAI-ECAI 2022 Workshop: Cognitive Aspects of Knowledge Representation (2022). https://ceur-ws.org/Vol-3251/paper1.pdf

63. White, K., Lehman, D.R.: Looking on the bright side: downward counterfactual thinking in response to negative life events. Pers. Soc. Psychol. Bull. **31**(10), 1413–1424 (2005). https://doi.org/10.1177/0146167205276064

64. Wong, E.M.: Narrating near-histories: the effects of counterfactual communication on motivation and performance. Manage. Organ. Hist. **2**(4), 351–370 (2007). https://doi.org/10.1177/1744935907086119

65. Yang, F., Alva, S.S., Chen, J., Hu, X.: Model-based counterfactual synthesizer for interpretation. In: Proceedings of the 27th ACM SIGKDD Conference on Knowledge Discovery & Data Mining, pp. 1964–1974 (2021). https://doi.org/10.1145/3447548.3467333

The Importance of Distrust in AI

Tobias M. Peters[1]([⊠]) and Roel W. Visser[2]([⊠])

[1] Cognitive Psychology, Paderborn University, 33098 Paderborn, Germany
tobias.peters@uni-paderborn.de
[2] CITEC - Cognitive Interaction Technology, Bielefeld University,
33619 Bielefeld, Germany
rvisser@techfak.uni-bielefeld.de

Abstract. In recent years the use of Artificial Intelligence (AI) has become increasingly prevalent in a growing number of fields. As AI systems are being adopted in more high-stakes areas such as medicine and finance, ensuring that they are trustworthy is of increasing importance. A concern that is prominently addressed by the development and application of explainability methods, which are purported to increase trust from its users and wider society. While an increase in trust may be desirable, an analysis of literature from different research fields shows that an exclusive focus on increasing trust may not be warranted. Something which is well exemplified by the recent development in AI chatbots, which while highly coherent tend to make up facts. In this contribution, we investigate the concepts of trust, trustworthiness, and user reliance.

In order to foster appropriate reliance on AI we need to prevent both disuse of these systems as well as overtrust. From our analysis of research on interpersonal trust, trust in automation, and trust in (X)AI, we identify the potential merit of the distinction between trust and distrust (in AI). We propose that alongside trust a healthy amount of distrust is of additional value for mitigating disuse and overtrust. We argue that by considering and evaluating both trust and distrust, we can ensure that users can rely appropriately on trustworthy AI, which can both be useful as well as fallible.

Keywords: XAI · Psychology · Appropriate Trust · Distrust · Reliance · Trustworthy AI

1 Introduction

Intelligent systems and decision making supported by Artificial Intelligence (AI) are becoming ever more present and relevant within our everyday lives. Especially their use in high-stakes applications like medical diagnosis, credit scoring, and parole and bail decisions have led to concerns about the AI models [49].

We gratefully acknowledge funding from the Deutsche Forschungsgemeinschaft (DFG, German Research Foundation) for grant TRR 318/1 2021 - 438445824.
T. M. Peters and R. W. Visser—These authors contributed equally to this work and share first authorship.

This includes concerns about the AI's transparency, interpretability, and fairness [1,16,42]. These objectives are acknowledged and further enforced in legislation by the EU's General Data Protection Regulation (GDPR, Art. 15), in which citizens are granted the right to be provided with meaningful information about the logic involved in automated decision making.

While contemporary AI methods are becoming increasingly accurate and sophisticated, they often remain opaque and may, and most likely will, produce errors. For instance, recent development in generative AI chatbots have highlighted that there remains a risk in relying on AI. While the current transformer-based large language models (LLMs) are very good at generating highly convincing and coherent texts, they are known to make up facts and can be inaccurate to the extent of fabricating entire quotes and references [24]. While it may be appropriate to use such models in certain low-stakes applications, their inherent fallibility is more problematic in, say, a medical setting.

These developments and different concerns have lead to increased research interest into making AI systems more trustworthy and reliable. One prominent way to address these growing concerns and new objectives is for modern (black-box) AI methods to be able to explain their outputs [1], leading to a surge in the development of explainable AI (XAI) over the last years for a host of different applications, domains, and data types [1,16,50]. Additionally, a number of different guidelines have been set out to ensure the trustworthiness of AI (for an overview see [57]), the main objective being that ensuring the trustworthiness of AI should help increase user trust. Likewise, in the literature explainability is often explicitly considered as a means to increase user trust [28].

In this contribution, we take a closer look at the connection between user trust and trustworthiness and explainability and its limitations with respect to insights from psychology. Currently, such insights are often incorporated only superficially or founded more on common-sense reasoning on trust. As even the best-performing models are prone to errors, we argue not to focus exclusively on increasing trust, but rather on establishing an appropriate level of reliance from the user on the AI with a **healthy amount of critical reflection, or distrust**, along with a **sufficient level of trust**. In the following, we investigate why not only increasing trust but also taking into account the importance of distrust is relevant for appropriate reliance on AI, preventing both the disuse as well as overtrust of such systems. For this, in the next sections we give an overview of literature related to automation, AI, human-computer interaction, and Psychology, in order to establish the relation between and importance of trust, distrust, reliance, and trustworthiness of AI. Some things which are of primary concern in the employment of XAI.

2   Trusting an AI?

Trustworthy AI is defined according to a number of design objectives that AI should conform to in order to be trustworthy to its users and to wider society [1]. An example of these are those formulated in the Ethics Guidelines for Trustworthy AI [20]. The exact definition of which design objectives should be taken into account and which concerns should be addressed depends, for example, on who the concerning party is (e.g. the European commission in place of wider society) or to whom it is addressed to (e.g. end users vs machine learning engineers) [1,42]. Of these objectives transparency, accountability, and interpretability are the most important ones in the context of trust and XAI [1,16,42].

2.1 Explainability and Trust

The development of explainable AI methods is currently one of the most prominent ways of working on means for addressing these concerns and fulfilling such regulations [30,59]. It is focused on developing ways to make AI both (more) interpretable and transparent, thereby ensuring that both its users and wider society can trust that an AI will work in a way that is intended, expected, and desirable [1]. A multitude of XAI studies implicitly or explicitly assume explainability to facilitate trust [12,28]. In their summary of current XAI studies concerned with user trust, [28] call this the explainability-trust hypothesis. In contrast, results of empirical investigations into the observed relation between explanations and trust are summarized by [28] as mixed and inconclusive. These results range from positive relations to no effect up to negative relations, which calls the validity of the explainability-trust hypothesis into question. Similarly, [12] have serious doubts about the usefulness of explainability methods in fostering trust in the case of medical AI applications, and note that the relation between the explainability of AI and trust are far from being clarified.

One potential reason, which [28] also entertain, of why explanations could fail to foster trust is that explanations can actually reveal problems of the system that may have otherwise gone unnoticed, which could lead a user not to trust the AI. To reveal problems of an AI is a function of explanations that is also targeted in the paper on the LIME algorithm, one of the first popular XAI methods which has been used for deep models [48]. According to [48] explanations are not only helpful for deciding when one should trust a prediction, but also beneficial in identifying when not to trust one. Thereby, they differentiate between the explanation's utility for trusting and not trusting, demonstrating the latter in an example where an explanation reveals a wrong causal relation underlying an automated decision. Yet, when generally discussing the benefit of explanations, [48] argue that "[...] explaining predictions is an important aspect in getting humans to trust and use machine learning effectively, if the explanations are faithful and intelligible". With the conditional part of the sentence they acknowledge the possibility of explanations to indicate erroneous predictions, but still mainly focus on convincing a human to trust. This sets the focus on the utility of explanations to identify correct predictions, while the utility of explanation to identify wrong predictions falls short.

This pattern can be found across much XAI literature that discusses user trust. When authors speak in broad terms, they connect explanations to the facilitation of trust, which represents the explainability-trust hypothesis as discussed above. Thereby, the explanation's utility to indicate correct predictions is discussed because only in this case a facilitation of trust is desired. However, when authors describe the actual utilities of explanation methods, another utility of explanations is also identified, e.g., not trusting predictions [48], critical reflection [9], or enabling distrust [23]. To clarify the aim of these different utilities, some XAI research employs the terms disuse and overtrust [23,42]. Before we discuss both utilities of explanations and their connection to disuse and overtrust in more detail in Sect. 2.3, it is first necessary to disentangle the terms trust and trustworthiness (Sect. 2.2).

This necessity partially stems from the fact that trust is a typical objective of XAI, but often in papers concerning the development of XAI methods no proper definitions of trust are given [2,17,48]. E.g., [48] only separate trusting a prediction and trusting a model without explicating what is meant by trusting. Comparably, [12] observed that the dynamics between trust and explainability are far from being clarified, which they primarily attribute to the lack of precise definitions of the two. A summary of important terms in the AI context, which we discuss in the following, is provided in Table 1.

Setting trust as a goal of explainability without providing information on what trust encompasses can lead to different problems. Firstly, in empirical investigations, cooperation or confidence might be easily mistaken for trust (see Sect. 3). Secondly, without drawing from previous work on trust and their definitions, trust in the (X)AI context runs the risk of falling back into the state of a conceptual confusion regarding the meaning of trust [34] that earlier work on trust aimed to overcome. Furthermore, basing trust in (X)AI research on the already established definitions of trust, the desired outcome, i.e. trust, becomes more standardized. This can improve the comparability between different studies, which then can allow researchers to make more general assumption about improvements of AI and their effect on trust. In addition, the process of evaluating potential effects of explainability on trust may profit as well.

2.2   Trustworthiness and Trust

When looking at literature related to (X)AI, **it is important to make a clear distinction between trust and trustworthiness**. Trust can be defined as an attitude that a stakeholder has towards a system [28], while trustworthiness is a property of the system that justifies to trust the system [59]. One complication in the current literature, is that these concepts are not always clearly defined. In some cases trust – the attitude of a user – and trustworthiness – the property of the system – are not clearly differentiated, or rather used interchangeably. For example, [3] describe trustworthiness as the confidence that a model will act as intended when facing a given problem, which is a fitting description of trust. The differentiation is critical, because there are further factors apart from the system's trustworthiness that also influence trust [59].

According to research on trust between humans (so-called trustor and trustee), trustworthiness is characterized by the trustee's ability, i.e. competence or expertise in the relevant context, the trustee's benevolence towards the trustor, and the trustee's integrity towards principles that the trustor finds

Table 1. Definitions of important terms in the AI context.

Term	Definition
Trustworthy AI	Descriptive term for a desired form of AI
Reliance	A human decision or action that considers the decision or recommendation of an AI
Trustworthiness	Property of an AI, which leads an interactor to trust the system. Property of an AI, which justifies to place trust in it [59]
Trust	The willingness of a person to rely on AI in a situation that involves risk and uncertainty. "Trust is an attitude a stakeholder holds towards a system" [28]
Appropriate Trust	"User's ability to know when to, and when not to, trust the system's recommendations and decisions" [17]

acceptable [37]. Furthermore, a high level of these three factors of trustworthiness does not necessarily lead to trust, and trust can also occur in situations where lesser degrees of trustworthiness are present [37].

For example, a meta-analysis [27] identified the expertise and personality traits of a person interacting with AI as significant predictors for trust in AI. Moreover, cultural differences, such as individualism and power relations within a culture, can influence a person's propensity to trust automation [6,7]. Other factors influencing trust in automation may be the type of technology (e.g. using a DNN (deep neural network) blackbox model [2] or decision tree [63]), the complexity of the task (e.g. tasks of varying cognitive load [26,62]), and perceived risk (e.g. using AI in a medical application [5]) [51].

For these reasons, trust is influenced, but not determined by the trustworthiness of the system. Even the most trustworthy model will not be trusted in every case by every person. Vice versa, persons may – and often do – trust an untrustworthy model.

2.3 Disuse, Overtrust, and Reliance in AI

In the previous sections, we have discussed the use of trustworthy AI and explainability methods in preventing both disuse of AI systems as well as users overtrusting a useful yet imperfect AI. Additionally, we have looked at the apparent connection between the objective of trust in AI, trustworthy AI, and explainability methods. In order to make a connection between trust and the concerns of disuse and overtrust, in this part we draw a connection between concerns of trust in AI and other (earlier) forms of automation [21,32]. While some issues and concerns may be specific to the AI context [15], the general concerns surrounding user reliance in technology have been a recurring theme over the last decades [29]. In the following, both work on trust in AI and trust in automation is considered.

AI systems can be regarded as a subcategory of automation, and overarchingly we will refer to both as trust in a(n automated) system.

In the field of trust in automation the prevention of disuse and overtrust has been targeted by **ensuring appropriate trust** or calibrated trust. [39] as well as [40] define appropriate trust as the alignment between perceived and actual performance of an automated system. This relates to a user's ability to recognize when the system is correct or incorrect and adjust their reliance on it accordingly. Within their model for trust calibration in human-robot teams, [61] define calibrated trust as given when a team member's perception of trustworthiness of another team member matches the actual trustworthiness of that team member. If this is not given, either 'undertrust', which leads to disuse, or 'overtrust' can occur [45, 61].

The aim of trust calibration by [61] is to assure a healthy level of trust and to avoid unhealthy trust relationships. Thereto, they establish a process of trust calibration which accompanies collaboration by establishing and continuously recalibrating trust between the team members. To prevent people from overtrusting, so-called, trust dampening methods are to be applied. According to the authors, these methods are especially worthwhile in interactions with machines and robots, as humans have a tendency to expect too much from automation [61]. The authors recommend to present exemplary failures, performance history, likelihood alarms, or provide information about the system's limitations. Moreover, they make the connection to the expanding field of XAI arguing that explanation activities can help with calibrating trust.

Reliance in the AI context can be understood as a human decision or action that considers the decision or recommendation of an AI. Trust is an attitude that benefits the decision to rely, as it has a critical role for human reliance on automation [21]. So, beneath the desideratum of increased appropriate trust lies the desideratum of increased appropriate reliance. To rely appropriately, one would consider correct decisions or recommendations of an AI and would disregard false ones. Trust does not lead to this because trust is not only influenced by the correctness, i.e. the performance of an AI. According to [21], the performance of an automated system is similar to the trustee's ability in interpersonal trust, and the process and purpose of an automated system are analogous to benevolence and integrity. On top of that and as mentioned before, trust is not fully determined by trustworthiness.

In other words, current improvements in automated systems, like XAI methods, are regarded as beneficial for **appropriate reliance** by preventing disuse and overtrust. Ideally, appropriate reliance should be achieved by fostering appropriate trust. Implied by the appropriateness of trust is that neither blind trust leading to overtrust, nor blind distrust leading to disuse is wanted. Several phrasing of this underlying notion of appropriate trust can be observed across the literature, which often entail trust and terms that can be summarized under distrust (see Fig. 1).

Yet, how can such an appropriate trust, its influencing factors, and the relation to appropriate reliance be conceptualized? More recent trust research highlights a distinction that might be of interest here. Several researchers provided evidence that trust and distrust are two related, yet separate dimensions [4, 19, 33, 60]. We assume that this separation of trust and distrust might help solving the conceptual issue and propose that **we need an understanding of appropriate trust and healthy distrust**. The psychological underpinnings of our hypothesis will be detailed in the next sections.

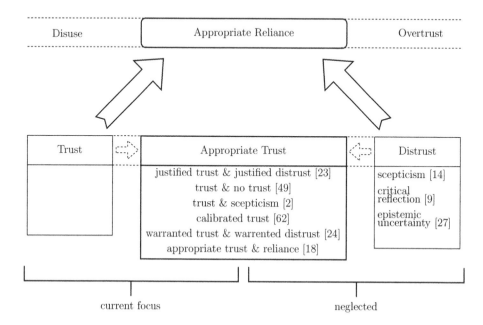

Fig. 1. Desideratum of appropriate trust in AI and the relation of trust and distrust to appropriate reliance with the goal of preventing both disuse and overtrust.

3   What is Trust?

Early, influential work on trust by sociologist [35] defines trust as a mechanism for reducing the complexity of social interactions. Within social interactions, multiple goals and motives can be present, and multiple interpretation are possible with varying truth. According to the author, to decide which interpretation to follow and how to act upon them, this complexity needs to be reduced. By trusting, a person engages in the interaction as if only certain interpretations are possible (e.g., taking things at face value), and thus rendering the interaction less complex [35]. In analogy, trust is also important in human-AI interactions, because of the involved risk caused by the complexity and non-determinism of AI [15]. Similarly, [21] argue that trust is not only important to interpersonal relations but can also be defining for the way people interact with technology.

The typical conceptualisation of trust within (X)AI research regards trust as one end of a single dimension with distrust being the opposing end. The

Integrative Model of Organizational Trust by [37], which elaborates this conceptualisation, is a prominent basis for trust in AI and automation [56]. [37] define trust as "[...] the willingness of a party to be vulnerable to the actions of another party based on the expectation that the other will perform a particular action important to the trustor, irrespective of the ability to monitor or control that other party" [37]. Based on this definition, they differentiate between factors that contribute to trust, trust itself, the role of risk, and the outcomes of trust.

The extent of a person's willingness to trust is influenced by the trustor's propensity to trust and the trustor's perception of the trustworthiness of the trustee. To separate trust from related constructs [37] highlight the importance of risk and vulnerability for trust. They argue that, if a situation does not involve a form of vulnerability to the trustor, cooperation can occur without trust. Similarly, if a trustor does not recognize and assume any risk, the trustor is in a situation of confidence and not of trust. Thus, trust serves the purpose of reducing complexity in an interaction, and for trust to be present, a form of vulnerability and risk is required.

Trust in a system and trust defined by [37] share that they influence the willingness to rely and the situational requirements of risk and vulnerability for them to be of importance. According to [43] users used automated systems they trust but not those they do not trust. [31] state that operators did not use automation systems if their trust in them was less than their own self-confidence.

Drawing from [37], definitions of trust in automation also consider the necessity of uncertainty (i.e., risk) [21,32] and vulnerability [29,32]. Trust in automated systems "plays a leading role in determining the willingness of humans to rely on automated systems in situations characterized by uncertainty" [21], and is defined as "[...] the attitude that an agent will help achieve an individual's goals in a situation characterized by uncertainty and vulnerability" [32].

Returning to the desired appropriate reliance via appropriate trust (Sect. 2.3) and combining it with the discussed insights on trust in automated systems, which drew from [37], we see a problem. To reiterate, the desideratum is to prevent either the case in which a person relies on the AI, even though it was wrong (overtrust), or the case, where a person does not rely on the AI, even though it was correct (disuse). Fostering trust, i.e., increasing the willingness to rely, mitigates the problem of disuse. However, for mitigating overtrust, not an absence of the willingness to rely, but the ability to identify reasons not to rely is needed. Trust in Mayer et al.'s model does not entail this, as they define trust "[...] irrespective of the ability to monitor or control that other party". Mayer et al.'s influential work on trust demonstrates the difference between trust and trustworthiness, but for the mitigation of overtrust, their model does not provide a basis to proceed. For our proposition to resolve this, not only trust but also distrust is needed.

4   The Importance of Distrust

Distrust is often connotated negatively [33,60] and sometimes explicitly considered something to be avoided [13,54], or at least implied to be avoided when focusing the sole strengthening of trust. Yet considering the imperfection of contemporary ML models, distrust towards erroneous predictions and towards explanations that indicate them is not to be avoided, but fostered. Otherwise, a neglect of distrust remains, which is serious because it renders potential positive consequences of distrust invisible.

In a study by [41] the disposition to distrust predicted high-risk perceptions better than the disposition to trust did. For their study context of online expert advice sites they suggest that future research should study dispositional trust and also dispositional distrust. Psychological studies also point to the benefit of considering distrust by identifying positive consequences of distrust. Distrust or suspicion led, for example, to an increase of creativity [36] or a reduction of the correspondence bias [11]. Moreover, a series of studies by [47] showed an increase of memory performance in their distrust condition as opposed to a trust or control condition. [60] identified a potential of distrust to improve critical reflection and innovation in the context of working in an organisational setting.

Looking at potential underlying mechanisms of distrust, Mayo's [38] review introduces a so-called distrust mindset as an explanation for the positive effects of distrust. The distrust mindset leads to an activation incongruent and alternative associations, which aligns very well with the increase of creativity, reflection, and innovation. According to [47], trust triggers a perception focus on similarities that makes it harder to remember single entities. Distrust shifts the perception focus towards differences and, therefore, increases memory performance. Interestingly, in one of their studies [47] observe a higher acceptance of misinformation in a trust condition, underlining the potential problem of the current trust focus in the (X)AI context and the danger of overtrust.

A conceptual example of how trust and distrust can be targeted is provided by [22] in their work on measuring trust in XAI. They advocate that people experience a mixture of justified and unjustified trust, as well as justified and unjustified mistrust. Ideally, the user would develop the ability to trust the machine in certain task, goals, and problems, and also to appropriately mistrust[1] the machine in other tasks, goals, and problems. This ideal scenario requires them to be able to decide when to trust or to correctly distrust, when scepticism is warranted. In sum, although often connotated negatively, distrust also has positive consequences and its own merits separate from those of trust.

5   Distrust as a Separate Dimension

While distrust is often regarded as the opposite of trust, the concept of a one-dimensional view of trust and distrust is being questioned and not widely accepted [18,33,52,53]. In the two-dimensional approach, by definition, low trust is not the same as high distrust, and low distrust is not equal to high trust [33]. This allows the coexistence of trust and distrust. Among others, trust is characterized by hope, faith, or assurance, and distrust by scepticism, fear, suspicion

---

[1] Mistrust is used as a synonym for distrust in this paper.

or vigilance [4,8,33]. [33] exemplify the separation of trust and distrust by contrasting low trust with high distrust. The authors regard expectations of beneficial actions being absent or present as antecedent to trust, and expectations of harmful actions being absent or present as antecedent to distrust. If the former is absent, low trust is expressed by a lack of hope, faith, and confidence. If the later is present, high distrust is expressed by vigilance, skepticism, and wariness. The combination of high trust and high distrust is described by the authors with a relationship in which opportunities are pursued while risks and vulnerabilities are continually monitored.

When reviewing research that draws from two-dimensional approaches, concepts and terms like critical trust, trust but verify, and healthy distrust are used [33,46,60]. These align well with the problem of mitigating overtrust, yet little consideration of the two-dimensional view on trust and distrust can be found when trust is considered in the technology context.

One, at least partial, reason for this is found in the field of organisational psychology. [60] discusses the trajectory of the conceptual debate about trust and distrust within the organizational context. He describes that most of the earlier work on trust falls into the category of the one-dimensional approaches. From the mid 80 s onward, doubt increased towards the one-dimensional approach, which was considered too simplistic [60]. Yet, efforts to resolve this debate and empirically test it remain scarce, while work on the two-dimensional approach mostly reproduces common-sense assumptions instead of providing empirical evidence [60].

Furthermore, [60] points out that only the concept trust has a good theoretical background and is well researched. Distrust remains in the state of conceptual debate and is given little research attention. As a consequence, even in the field of organizational psychology, in which the conceptual critique towards the one-dimensional approach is the most visible, applied work still relies mostly on the model by Mayer et al. [60]. As highly influential work on trust in automation [21,32] also draws from [37]'s model, which then was taken as a starting point in the context of trust in XAI [57], these fields inherited the focus on trust and the neglect of distrust.

Regardless of evidence for the two-dimensional conceptualisation, uni-dimensional scales are the common form to evaluate trust in automation [29]. Of those, the Checklist for Trust between People and Automation [25] is the most frequently used one [29]. This checklist measures trust and distrust as polar opposites along a single dimension. Five of the 12 items (statements rated by the user) measure distrust. In practice, these items are often reverse-scored and summed with the trust items to form one trust score, which was also suggested by the original authors of the scale [55]. A critical validation attempt of this scale by [55] compared a one-factor model (indicating the polar opposites along a single dimension) and a two-factor model. This factor analysis provided evidence for the conceptualization of trust and distrust as separate, yet related constructs [55]. Thus, reverse scoring distrust items to then form a sum score with the trust items entails a problematic entanglement of the two factors identified by [55] and disregards the incremental insight by measuring trust and distrust individually.

The merit of considering trust and distrust as separate dimension has been identified across different sub-fields of human-technology interaction [4, 10, 19, 29, 41, 44, 58]. A difference between dispositional trust and dispositional distrust was observed in the context of online expert advice [41], and trust and distrust co-existed as distinct construct in the context of online banking [4] and online shopping [44]. A study on website design showed that trust and distrust are affected by different antecedents, and the performance of a trust-aware recommender system was improved by not only predicting trust but also distrust [10]. [58] investigated work-related information systems and also identified trust and distrust as related yet separate influences on different outcome variables.

Some authors [10, 44, 58] emphasize that they are, to the best of their knowledge, the first to consider not only trust but also distrust in their field. Additionally, with a distance of two decades [19] and [29] both argue in favour for considering trust and distrust in the technology. This indicates a lack of generalization on the conceptualisation of trust and distrust in context of technology. The impression arises that within individual sub-fields at different points in time, the potential merit of considering trust and distrust is identified, and only some first steps are taken towards it. Some of the studies that take these first steps still only partially separate trust and distrust, which may hinder generalization.

For instance, [4, 10] make the distinction between trust and distrust only on a superficial level because they relate trust and distrust to the same antecedents [4, 10] and consequences [4]. Therefore, they do not fully acknowledge Lewicki et al.'s proposition [33] of different antecedents and consequences of trust and distrust. In both cases, the authors themselves suggest addressing these limitations in future research. [10] suggest to predict trust and distrust from different antecedents. [4] entertain the degree of monitoring as plausible outcome for distrust instead of the intention to use, which they had used as an outcome for both trust and distrust.

6 Conclusion

To summarize, a focus on trust and the neglect of distrust is evident in research about trust in (X)AI, trust in automation, and in trust research in organizational psychology. Some examples of considering both trust and distrust can be identified in different sub-fields about interaction with technology. The underlying idea of these studies, that trust does not suffice, is strengthened by the examples of positive consequences of distrust.

The notion of appropriate trust in current (X)AI research also acknowledges that trust alone does not suffice. However, by aiming for appropriate trust, a crucial ambiguity remains, because stating that it is not appropriate to trust allows for two interpretations: either that one does not trust, or that one distrusts. The same distinction has to be made when returning to the problems of disuse and overtrust. By increasing trust, the problem of disuse can be mitigated, as the willingness to rely increases. While it may be true that a lower willingness to rely, a lower trust, would decrease the likelihood of overtrust, there would only be less reliance overall. To this point, to mitigate overtrust, reliance should be prevented if, and only if, it would be wrong to rely. To conceptualize this distinction we regard distrust as relevant. Thus, **we propose the consideration and evaluation of both trust and distrust to achieve appropriate reliance in AI by mitigating both disuse and overtrust**. We consider our proposition to be in line with the underlying motivation of appropriate trust (see Fig. 1).

However, the term and work on it is often too keen on trust and disregards the critical review of distrust. The aim of our proposition is to ensure trust plus a healthy amount of distrust. Being inherently imperfect, contemporary AI will benefit from healthy distrust, as this entails a more conscientious usage of AI. With healthy distrust, a user would have a warranted critical stance towards the AI's outputs without being outright distrustful towards using the AI at all.

For instance, current AI chatbots generate plausible sounding and highly convincing texts. A situation in which overtrust is arguably a more prominent issue than disuse. Developing or implementing methods to support the identification of possibly wrong outputs would be a sensible approach to mitigate overtrust. Ideally, such methods would foster the user's wariness towards and the user's monitoring of the system, i.e. characteristics of distrust. If these envisioned methods were to only be evaluated by measuring trust, different results would be plausible. On the one hand, a decrease in trust could be observed. On the other hand, observing no change in trust or even an increase in trust, despite errors being identified more easily, would also be plausible. Firstly, the trust measurement may not change because only characteristics of distrust would be affected by the methods sketched above. Secondly, trust may increase if the user considered the output as correct regardless of the supported ability to monitor. This should occur by giving the user the opportunity to distrust. The user would have better ability to examine the output and could verify his trust, resulting in a stronger willingness to rely. Such potential impacts of distrust will not be directly noticed when only measuring trust. In these hypothetical scenarios additionally evaluating distrust would provide more insights into the user's attitude when interacting with AI.

Generally, evaluating both trust and distrust could help to clarify the mixed and inconclusive results in empirical research on the explainability-trust hypothesis (Sect. 2.1). As explanations have the two utilities of identifying both correct as well as wrong outputs, explanations may influence both the user's trust and distrust. To conclude, in the aim of appropriate reliance on trustworthy (X)AI both trust and distrust should be considered. Distrust may not only be of interest to solve conceptual problems but could also be of interest for AI regulation. Regulations towards trustworthy AI could not only aim to ensure that users and stakeholders can trust an AI but could also ensure that AI can be distrusted when warranted.

7   Open Questions and Future Work

The conceptualisation of distrust in AI and the empirical identification of its antecedents and consequences still needs further empirical research. Aspects that constitute healthy distrust have to be identified as well. To progress this, future work should not only separate trust and distrust on a superficial level, but also investigate whether and which individual antecedents and consequences of trust and distrust are relevant. Studies on trust and distrust in the (X)AI context need to continue to draw from the established work on (dis)trust without intermixing it with common-sense reasoning on trust and distrust.

Furthermore, for researchers to be able to appropriately compare what effects different (X)AI methods, design, and systems have on user trust and distrust standardized ways of measuring them as separate dimensions have to be created and validated. With overcoming such conceptual and methodological issues, the two-dimensional concept of trust and distrust can be validated more convincingly. Thereby the lack of generalization can be addressed and an improved starting point for further research on both trust and distrust can be established.

References

1. Arrieta, A., et al.: Explainable artificial intelligence (XAI): concepts, taxonomies, opportunities and challenges toward responsible AI (2020). https://www.sciencedirect.com/science/article/abs/pii/S1566253519308103
2. Bansal, G., et al.: Does the whole exceed its parts? The effect of AI explanations on complementary team performance. In: Proceedings of the 2021 CHI Conference on Human Factors in Computing Systems, ACM, New York (2021). https://doi.org/10.1145/3411764.3445717
3. Barredo Arrieta, A., et al.: Explainable artificial intelligence (XAI): concepts, taxonomies, opportunities and challenges toward responsible AI. Inf. Fusion **58**, 82–115 (2020). https://doi.org/10.1016/j.inffus.2019.12.012. ISSN 1566-2535
4. Benamati, J., Serva, M.A., Fuller, M.A.: Are trust and distrust distinct constructs? An empirical study of the effects of trust and distrust among online banking users. In: Proceedings of the 39th Annual Hawaii International Conference on System Sciences (HICSS 2006). IEEE (2006). https://doi.org/10.1109/hicss.2006.63
5. Bussone, A., Stumpf, S., O'Sullivan, D.: The role of explanations on trust and reliance in clinical decision support systems. In: 2015 International Conference on Healthcare Informatics, pp. 160–169 (2015). https://doi.org/10.1109/ICHI.2015.26
6. Chien, S.Y., Lewis, M., Hergeth, S., Semnani-Azad, Z., Sycara, K.: Cross-country validation of a cultural scale in measuring trust in automation. In: Proceedings of the Human Factors and Ergonomics Society Annual Meeting, vol. 59, no. 1, pp. 686–690 (2015). https://doi.org/10.1177/1541931215591149
7. Chien, S.Y., Lewis, M., Sycara, K.: Influence of cultural factors in dynamic trust in automation. In: 2016 IEEE International Conference on Systems, Man, and Cybernetics, SMC 2016, 9–12 October 2016, Budapest, Hungary. IEEE (2016). https://ieeexplore.ieee.org/abstract/document/7844677
8. Cho, J.: The mechanism of trust and distrust formation and their relational outcomes. J. Retail. **82**(1), 25–35 (2006). https://doi.org/10.1016/j.jretai.2005.11.002. ISSN 0022-4359

9. Ehsan, U., Riedl, M.O.: Human-centered explainable AI: towards a reflective sociotechnical approach. In: Stephanidis, C., Kurosu, M., Degen, H., Reinerman-Jones, L. (eds.) HCII 2020. LNCS, vol. 12424, pp. 449–466. Springer, Cham (2020). https://doi.org/10.1007/978-3-030-60117-1_33

10. Fang, H., Guo, G., Zhang, J.: Multi-faceted trust and distrust prediction for recommender systems. Decis. Support Syst. **71**, 37–47 (2015). https://doi.org/10.1016/j.dss.2015.01.005. ISSN 0167-9236

11. Fein, S.: Effects of suspicion on attributional thinking and the correspondence bias. J. Pers. Soc. Psychol. **70**(6), 1164–1184 (1996). https://doi.org/10.1037/0022-3514.70.6.1164

12. Ferrario, A., Loi, M.: How explainability contributes to trust in AI. In: 2022 ACM Conference on Fairness, Accountability, and Transparency, pp. 1457–1466 (2022)

13. Frison, A.K., et al.: In UX we trust. In: Brewster, S. (ed.) Proceedings of the 2019 CHI Conference on Human Factors in Computing Systems, pp. 1–13. ACM Digital Library, Association for Computing Machinery, New York (2019). https://doi.org/10.1145/3290605.3300374. ISBN 9781450359702

14. Gaube, S., et al.: Do as AI say: susceptibility in deployment of clinical decision-aids. NPJ Digi. Med. **4**(1), 31 (2021)

15. Glikson, E., Woolley, A.W.: Human trust in artificial intelligence: review of empirical research. Acad. Manag. Ann. **14**(2), 627–660 (2020). https://doi.org/10.5465/annals.2018.0057

16. Guidotti, R., Monreale, A., Ruggieri, S., Turini, F., Giannotti, F., Pedreschi, D.: A survey of methods for explaining black box models. ACM Comput. Surv. **51**(5), 1–42 (2019). https://doi.org/10.1145/3236009

17. Gunning, D., Aha, D.: DARPA's explainable artificial intelligence (XAI) program. AI Mag. **40**(2), 44–58 (2019). https://doi.org/10.1609/aimag.v40i2.2850

18. Guo, S.L., Lumineau, F., Lewicki, R.J.: Revisiting the foundations of organizational distrust. Found. Trends Manage. **1**(1), 1–88 (2017). https://doi.org/10.1561/3400000001. ISSN 2475-6946

19. Harrison McKnight, D., Chervany, N.L.: Trust and distrust definitions: one bite at a time. In: Falcone, R., Singh, M., Tan, Y.-H. (eds.) Trust in Cyber-societies. LNCS (LNAI), vol. 2246, pp. 27–54. Springer, Heidelberg (2001). https://doi.org/10.1007/3-540-45547-7_3

20. HLEG, A.: Ethics guidelines for trustworthy AI (2019). https://digital-strategy.ec.europa.eu/en/library/ethics-guidelines-trustworthy-ai

21. Hoff, K.A., Bashir, M.: Trust in automation: integrating empirical evidence on factors that influence trust. Hum. Factors **57**(3), 407–434 (2015). https://doi.org/10.1177/0018720814547570

22. Hoffman, R., Mueller, S.T., Klein, G., Litman, J.: Measuring trust in the XAI context. Technical report, DARPA Explainable AI Program (2018). https://doi.org/10.31234/osf.io/e3kv9

23. Jacovi, A., Marasović, A., Miller, T., Goldberg, Y.: Formalizing trust in artificial intelligence. In: Proceedings of the 2021 ACM Conference on Fairness, Accountability, and Transparency, pp. 624–635, ACM Digital Library, Association for Computing Machinery, New York (2021). https://doi.org/10.1145/3442188.3445923. ISBN 9781450383097

24. Ji, Z., et al.: Survey of hallucination in natural language generation. ACM Comput. Surv. **55**(12) (2023). https://doi.org/10.1145/3571730. ISSN 0360-0300

25. Jian, J.Y., Bisantz, A.M., Drury, C.G.: Foundations for an empirically determined scale of trust in automated systems. Int. J. Cogn. Ergon. **4**(1), 53–71 (2000). https://doi.org/10.1207/S15327566IJCE0401_04

26. Jiang, J., Kahai, S., Yang, M.: Who needs explanation and when? juggling explainable AI and user epistemic uncertainty. Int. J. Hum.-Comput. Stud. **165**, 102839 (2022). https://doi.org/10.1016/j.ijhcs.2022.102839. ISSN 1071-5819
27. Kaplan, A.D., Kessler, T.T., Brill, J.C., Hancock, P.: Trust in artificial intelligence: meta-analytic findings. Hum. Factors **65**(2), 337–359 (2023)
28. Kastner, L., Langer, M., Lazar, V., Schomacker, A., Speith, T., Sterz, S.: On the relation of trust and explainability: why to engineer for trustworthiness. In: Proceedings, 29th IEEE International Requirements Engineering Conference Workshops: REW 2021: 20–24 September 2021, Online Event, pp. 169–175, IEEE Computer Society, Conference Publishing Services, Los Alamitos (2021). https://doi.org/10.1109/REW53955.2021.00031. ISBN 978-1-6654-1898-0
29. Kohn, S.C., de Visser, E.J., Wiese, E., Lee, Y.C., Shaw, T.H.: Measurement of trust in automation: a narrative review and reference guide. Front. Psychol. **12**, 604977 (2021). https://doi.org/10.3389/fpsyg.2021.604977. ISSN 1664-1078
30. Langer, M., et al.: What do we want from explainable artificial intelligence (XAI)?- a stakeholder perspective on XAI and a conceptual model guiding interdisciplinary XAI research. Artif. Intell. **296**, 103473 (2021)
31. Lee, J.D., Moray, N.: Trust, self-confidence, and operators' adaptation to automation. Int. J. Hum.-Comput. Stud. **40**(1), 153–184 (1994). https://doi.org/10.1006/ijhc.1994.1007. ISSN 1071-5819
32. Lee, J.D., See, K.A.: Trust in automation: designing for appropriate reliance. Hum. Factors **46**(1), 50–80 (2004). https://journals.sagepub.com/doi/abs/10.1518/hfes.46.1.50_30392
33. Lewicki, R.J., McAllister, D.J., Bies, R.J.: Trust and distrust: new relationships and realities. Acad. Manage. Rev. **23**(3), 438–458 (1998). https://doi.org/10.5465/amr.1998.926620. ISSN 0363-7425
34. Lewis, J.D., Weigert, A.: Trust as a social reality. Soc. Forces **63**(4), 967–985 (1985)
35. Luhmann, N.: Vertrauen: ein Mechanismus der Reduktion sozialer Komplexität. UTB: 2185, Stuttgart: Lucius & Lucius, 4. aufl., nachdr. edn. (2009). ISBN 9783825221850
36. Mayer, J., Mussweiler, T.: Suspicious spirits, flexible minds: when distrust enhances creativity. J. Pers. Soc. Psychol. **101**(6), 1262–1277 (2011). https://doi.org/10.1037/a0024407. ISSN 1939-1315
37. Mayer, R.C., Davis, J.H., Schoorman, F.D.: An integrative model of organizational trust. Acad. Manage. Rev. **20**(3), 709–734 (1995). https://doi.org/10.5465/amr.1995.9508080335. ISSN 0363-7425
38. Mayo, R.: Cognition is a matter of trust: Distrust tunes cognitive processes. Eur. Rev. Soc. Psychol. **26**(1), 283–327 (2015). https://doi.org/10.1080/10463283.2015.1117249
39. McBride, M., Morgan, S.: Trust calibration for automated decision aids. Institute for Homeland Security Solutions, pp. 1–11 (2010)
40. McGuirl, J.M., Sarter, N.B.: Supporting trust calibration and the effective use of decision aids by presenting dynamic system confidence information. Hum. Factors **48**(4), 656–665 (2006)
41. McKnight, D.H., Kacmar, C.J., Choudhury, V.: Dispositional trust and distrust distinctions in predicting high- and low-risk internet expert advice site perceptions. e-Serv. J. **3**(2), 35 (2004). https://doi.org/10.2979/esj.2004.3.2.35. ISSN 1528-8226
42. Mohseni, S., Zarei, N., Ragan, E.D.: A multidisciplinary survey and framework for design and evaluation of explainable AI systems. ACM Trans. Interact. Intell. Syst. **11**(3–4) (2021). https://doi.org/10.1145/3387166. ISSN 2160-6455

43. Muir, B.M., Moray, N.: Trust in automation. Part II. Experimental studies of trust and human intervention in a process control simulation. Ergonomics **39**(3), 429–460 (1996)

44. Ou, C.X., Sia, C.L.: Consumer trust and distrust: an issue of website design. Int. J. Hum.-Comput. Stud. **68**(12), 913–934 (2010). https://doi.org/10.1016/j.ijhcs.2010.08.003. ISSN 1071-5819

45. Parasuraman, R., Riley, V.: Humans and automation: use, misuse, disuse, abuse. Hum. Factors **39**(2), 230–253 (1997). https://doi.org/10.1518/001872097778543886

46. Poortinga, W., Pidgeon, N.F.: Exploring the dimensionality of trust in risk regulation. Risk Anal. Off. Publ. Soc. Risk Anal. **23**(5), 961–972 (2003). https://doi.org/10.1111/1539-6924.00373

47. Posten, A.C., Gino, F.: How trust and distrust shape perception and memory. J. Pers. Soc. Psychol. **121**(1), 43–58 (2021). https://doi.org/10.1037/pspa0000269. ISSN 1939-1315

48. Ribeiro, M.T., Singh, S., Guestrin, C.: "Why should i trust you?" Explaining the predictions of any classifier. In: Proceedings of the 22nd ACM SIGKDD International Conference on Knowledge Discovery and Data Mining, pp. 1135–1144 (2016)

49. Rudin, C.: Stop explaining black box machine learning models for high stakes decisions and use interpretable models instead. Nat. Mach. Intell. **1**(5), 206–215 (2019)

50. Samek, W., Montavon, G., Lapuschkin, S., Anders, C.J., Müller, K.R.: Explaining deep neural networks and beyond: a review of methods and applications. Proc. IEEE **109**(3), 247–278 (2021). https://doi.org/10.1109/JPROC.2021.3060483

51. Schaefer, K.E., Chen, J.Y.C., Szalma, J.L., Hancock, P.A.: A meta-analysis of factors influencing the development of trust in automation. Hum. Factors J. Hum. Factors Ergon. Soc. **58**(3), 377–400 (2016). https://doi.org/10.1177/0018720816634228

52. Schoorman, F.D., Mayer, R.C., Davis, J.H.: An integrative model of organizational trust: past, present, and future. Acad. Manage. Rev. **32**(2), 344–354 (2007). https://doi.org/10.5465/amr.2007.24348410. ISSN 0363-7425

53. Schweer, M., Vaske, C., Vaske, A.K.: Zur Funktionalität und Dysfunktionalität von Misstrauen in virtuellen Organisationen (2009). https://dl.gi.de/handle/20.500.12116/35191

54. Seckler, M., Heinz, S., Forde, S., Tuch, A.N., Opwis, K.: Trust and distrust on the web: user experiences and website characteristics. Comput. Hum. Behav. **45**, 39–50 (2015). https://doi.org/10.1016/j.chb.2014.11.064. ISSN 0747-5632

55. Spain, R.D., Bustamante, E.A., Bliss, J.P.: Towards an empirically developed scale for system trust: take two. In: Proceedings of the Human Factors and Ergonomics Society Annual Meeting, vol. 52, no. 19, pp. 1335–1339 (2008). https://doi.org/10.1177/154193120805201907

56. Stanton, B., Jensen, T.: Trust and artificial intelligence (2021). https://doi.org/10.6028/nist.ir.8332-draft

57. Thiebes, S., Lins, S., Sunyaev, A.: Trustworthy artificial intelligence. Electron. Mark. **31**(2), 447–464 (2021). https://doi.org/10.1007/s12525-020-00441-4. ISSN 1422-8890

58. Thielsch, M.T., Meeßen, S.M., Hertel, G.: Trust and distrust in information systems at the workplace. PeerJ **6**, e5483 (2018). https://doi.org/10.7717/peerj.5483. ISSN 2167-8359

59. Toreini, E., Aitken, M., Coopamootoo, K., Elliott, K., Zelaya, C.G., Van Moorsel, A.: The relationship between trust in AI and trustworthy machine learning technologies. In: Proceedings of the 2020 Conference on Fairness, Accountability, and Transparency, pp. 272–283 (2020)

60. Vaske, C.: Misstrauen und Vertrauen. Universität Vechta (2016)

61. de Visser, E.J., et al.: Towards a theory of longitudinal trust calibration in human-robot teams. Int. J. Soc. Robot. **12**(2), 459–478 (2020). https://doi.org/10.1007/s12369-019-00596-x. ISSN 1875-4805

62. Wang, X., Yin, M.: Effects of explanations in AI-assisted decision making: principles and comparisons. ACM Trans. Interact. Intell. Syst. (2022). https://doi.org/10.1145/3519266

63. Zhang, Y., Liao, Q.V., Bellamy, R.K.E.: Effect of confidence and explanation on accuracy and trust calibration in AI-assisted decision making. In: Proceedings of the 2020 Conference on Fairness, Accountability, and Transparency. ACM (2020). https://doi.org/10.1145/3351095.3372852

Weighted Mutual Information for Out-Of-Distribution Detection

Giacomo De Bernardi[1,2(✉)], Sara Narteni[1] (ID), Enrico Cambiaso[1] (ID),
Marco Muselli[1,3], and Maurizio Mongelli[1]

[1] CNR-IEIIT, Corso F.M. Perrone 24, 16152 Genoa, Italy
{giacomo.debernardi,sara.narteni,enrico.cambiaso,
marco.muselli,maurizio.mongelli}@ieiit.cnr.it
[2] DITEN Department, Universitá degli studi di Genova, 16145 Genova, Italy
[3] Rulex Innovation Labs, Rulex Inc., 16122 Genoa, Italy

Abstract. Out-of-distribution detection has become an important theme in machine learning (ML) field, since the recognition of unseen data either "similar" or not (in- or out-of-distribution) to the ones the ML system has been trained on may lead to potentially fatal consequences. Operational data compliance with the training data has to be verified by the data analyst, who must also understand, in operation, if the autonomous decision-making is still safe or not. In this paper, we study an out-of-distribution (OoD) detection approach based on a rule-based eXplainable Artificial Intelligence (XAI) model. Specifically, the method relies on an innovative metric, i.e., the weighted mutual information, able to capture the different way decision rules are used in case of in- and OoD data.

Keywords: Out-of-distribution detection · eXplainable AI · mutual information · open data

1 Introduction

Nowadays out-of-distribution detection (ODD) is an important theme in ML, consisting in a comparison between the training and working conditions of a model. In case of divergence, the autonomous system should trigger an alert because the model may no longer be as performing as it was during the training stage (even if generalization is still acceptable[1]).

The problem constitutes a fundamental challenge in the field of Safe AI, which means individuating all the conditions under which autonomous decisions may lead to hazards. The impact of the ODD is then to make AI systems aware of this, thus understanding under which conditions the model may operate without

---

[1] Generalization bounds, see, e.g., [17], quantify the gap that exists between the empirical risk, calculated on the data actually available (on which the model is trained) and the theoretical risk, calculated on the distribution of probability that represents the data; this probability distribution is unknown in closed-form and, in the ODD context, represents the "in-distribution".

L. Longo (Ed.): xAI 2023, CCIS 1903, pp. 318–331, 2023.
https://doi.org/10.1007/978-3-031-44070-0_16

dangerous effects to humans and/or the environment. In this context, recently, standards were introduced in different fields, such as avionics [5,6], automotive ([9,22] and ISO/IEC) or medical informatics [2], stating the guidelines to identify all the operating conditions that can have an impact on safety. OoD can actually occur with different degrees of severity, as depicted through colored bars in Fig. 1 from EASA. First, the in-distribution is realized when the system working conditions are the same seen during training, which is referred to as nominal work domain and depicted through the green bar. When data start to diverge from such a distribution, several levels of OoD can be identified, as well as their relationship with the possible degradation of the underlying machine learning algorithm functioning. Starting from the lower risk level, the yellow bar reflects a situation where the model is still able to perform accurately enough; orange color bar indicates an OoD level in which a failure of the autonomous decision is observed, but the consequences on the system are not dangerous (the surrounding conditions of the environment are still compatible with safe actuations); finally, red bars express a high probability of the autonomous system to encounter dangerous conditions (if guided by the autonomous function). Including all the mentioned severity levels is thus essential in testing autonomous safety-critical systems and the ODD is therefore necessary to properly acknowledge the different zones. In particular, the study of the OoD according to distributional assumption-free and OoD-agnostic methods is an open research problem and is still little investigated[2].

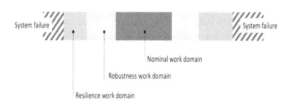

Fig. 1. Illustration of the work domains as reported in [6]. From central green bar to side yellow/orange/red bars, the nominal domain shifts and the severity of the OoD increases in parallel. (Color figure online)

1.1 Related Work

Most of the existing solutions to address the problem of the ODD are based on strong distributional assumptions of the feature space [13] or assume the knowledge of the in- and out-of-distribution probability density functions (pdf)

---

[2] Distributional assumption-free means no closed-form expressions of in- and out-probability distributions are considered. OoD-agnostic means no information about ODD conditions is considered. Another important issue, which is related with the assumption of probabilistic Gaussian or mixed-Gaussian functions, is to avoid calculating the covariance matrix from data, which can be numerically unstable.

[1], although this is not always true in practice. Moreover, several statistic tests often fail to estimate the real distribution of training data (data are not enough and the pdf are too coarse). Some methods, widely used across OoD detection are the Maximum Softmax Probability [10] which is one of the simplest but strong OOD detection method, being based on the tendency of maximum softmax probability to reach higher values in presence of out-of-distribution samples. Another approach, the OoD detector in neural networks (ODIN, [14]), is based on the observation that using temperature scaling and adding small perturbations to the input can separate the softmax score distributions between in and out. Energy-based OoD Detection [16] uses energy scores to better distinguish in and out than the traditional approach of softmax scores. Other important benchmarks are: model-based methods [3,8,25] and threshold-based methods [11,15,26]; label shift in deep learning is also considered in [7]. Our method is part of distributional assumption-free hypothesis models, as the work proposed in [24], but with the advantage of the eXplainability on its foundation.

1.2   Contribution

In this paper, we propose a distributional assumption-free method based on the evaluation of the histogram generated by the frequency of validation of a rule-based model by the data themselves. The histogram defined during the training phase constitutes a fingerprint to be verified at runtime. If the data at runtime generate a histogram "significantly different" from the training one, it means that the data are OoD. The purpose of the proposed approach is thus to quantify such a difference by introducing weighted mutual information $W\mu I$, i.e., a modification of mutual information able to consider the structure of the rule-based model. Also, unlike other approaches like K-NN [24] or Neural Networks distance [4], where a single metric is used for the ODD, we here infer the OoD through multiple metrics, namely $W\mu I$ and more traditional vector norms. This offers support to the tests mentioned by EASA, since the proposed method measures incremental cases of departure from in-distribution.

2   Logic Learning Machine

The rule-based model adopted in our work is called Logic Learning Machine (LLM), an efficient implementation of Switching Neural Networks [20], developed and available in Rulex software platform[3]. However, we remark that the methods for OoD detection presented in the paper can be easily extended to any other kind of rule-based model, such as decision tree or tree ensembles like random forests or Skope-Rules[4].

Given some input data, the LLM provides a classification model represented by ruleset $\mathcal{R} = \{r_k\}_{k=1,...,N_r}$, with each rule r_k expressed through the following structure: **if** $<premise>$ **then** $<consequence>$. The $<premise>$ is made up

---

[3] https://www.rulex.ai.
[4] https://github.com/scikit-learn-contrib/skope-rules.

of the logical conjunction (AND) of conditions on the input features and the $<consequence>$ constitutes the output of the classification rule.

Rule generation process occurs in three steps. First, a discretization and binarization of the feature space is performed by using the inverse-only-one coding. The resulting binary strings are then concatenated into a single large string representing the considered samples. Shadow clustering is then used to build logical structures, called implicants, which are finally transformed into simple conditions and combined into a collection of intelligible rules [21].

Covering $C(r_k)$ and error $E(r_k)$ metrics can be computed to evaluate the performance of each rule, being defined as:

$$C(r_k) = \frac{TP(r_k)}{TP(r_k) + FN(r_k)}, \qquad E(r_k) = \frac{FP(r_k)}{TN(r_k) + FP(r_k)} \qquad (1)$$

where $TP(r_k)$ and $FP(r_k)$ are the number of samples that, respectively, correctly and wrongly verify rule r_k; $TN(r_k)$ and $FN(r_k)$ are the number of samples that, respectively, correctly and wrongly do *not* verify the rule. The covering is also proportional to the relevance of the rule, therefore the larger it is, the higher is the probability that the rule is valid on new unseen samples. On the contrary, the error $E(r_k)$ measures how much wrongly covered is the rule and its maximum value is usually fixed as a model hyper-parameter (by default, it is of 5%).

3   Rule-Based ODD

3.1   Notation and List of Acronyms

TR	Training set
OP	Operational set
tr_i	i-th training subset
op_i	i-th operational subset
n_s	number of data samples in a split
N_r	Number of rules
N_{tr}	Number of training splits
N_{op}	Number of operational splits
$\mathcal{R}_{tr}$	Training reference ruleset
r_i	i-th rule
h_i^j	j-th hit for the i-th rule
l_p	l_p norm
μI	Mutual information
$W\mu I$	Weighted mutual information
H	Entropy

3.2   Rule Hits Histograms

Given a training dataset TR, we train the LLM on it and define a reference ruleset $\mathcal{R}_{tr}$. Also, we consider to split TR and the operational set OP into N_{tr} and N_{op} portions, called splits, respectively, thus obtaining $N_h = N_{tr} + N_{op}$ total splits. Let also n_s be the number of data samples present in a single split. For each split, samples[5] may (or not) verify each rule in $\mathcal{R}_{tr}$ a certain amount of times. We denote this number as the *number of hits* for the considered rule. Therefore we derive N_h vectors, considering this value scaled by the split size n_s:

$$\mathbf{h}^j = \{h_i^j\}, \quad h_i^j \in [0,1], \quad i = 1, \dots, N_r, \quad j = 1, \dots, N_h \qquad (2)$$

Each vector $\mathbf{h}^j$ can be thought as a histogram.

3.3   Data Splits and Metrics

The N_{tr} splits, available in training for the dataset $TR = \{tr_1, \dots, tr_{N_{tr}}\}$, become the reference for building the in-distribution histograms, as per Eq. 2. As anticipated, they represent the numbers of hits obtained by testing the rules in $\mathcal{R}_{tr}$ on each considered split. Regarding the operational setting, we consider $N_{op} = 1$, which is a suitable scenario when operational data are scarcely available, besides allowing to simplify the calculations.

The metrics driving ODD are the weighted mutual information $W\mu I$ and both l_1 and l_2 norms. For all metrics, the idea is to compare values computed in operation with the ranges achieved in training (*baseline*). An ODD occurs whenever the value in operation falls outside the baseline. The reason behind the choice of $W\mu I$ with respect to the classical μI is clearly explained in Sect. 7.

3.4   Weighted Mutual Information

In this Section, we present the algorithm to define Weighted mutual information, first for defining a baseline on the training domain and then to perform the OOD while being at operational.

Table 1. Training numbers of hits table. Each column refers to a training split $tr_i \in TR$ and each row to a rule $r_i \in \mathcal{R}_{tr}$.

	tr_1	....	$tr_{N_{tr}}$
r_1	$h_1^{tr_1}$	...	$h_1^{tr_{N_{tr}}}$
r_2	$h_2^{tr_1}$	...	$h_2^{tr_{N_{tr}}}$
...	...	...	...
...	...	...	...
r_{N_r}	$h_{N_r}^{tr_1}$		$h_{N_r}^{tr_{N_{tr}}}$

---

[5] Samples can satisfy multiple rules and there may be operational samples satisfying none of the rules.

In the training settings, as to Eq. 2, the matrix-like structure shown in Table 1 arises, where each column refers to a training split, each row represents a rule and the values are the numbers of hits obtained when rules are applied on the splits.

Based on that table, training baselines for weighted mutual information, as well as for l_1 and l_2 norms, are computed as described in Algorithm 1.

Algorithm 1: Weighted Mutual Information and Norms at Training Stage

---

$i, j = 1, \ldots, N_{tr}, \ i \neq j$

Input: Table 1

Output: Training baselines $W\mu I_{base}$ and $l_p{}^{base}$

1a. Define the weight associated with tr_i and tr_j, $\alpha_{i,j} \in (0,1)$, $\forall i, \forall j$:
$$\alpha_{i,j} = \frac{1}{N_r} \sum_{r=1}^{N_r} (|h_r^{tr_i} - h_r^{tr_j}|)$$

1b. Compute the weighted entropies $H(tr_i)$, $H(tr_j)$, $H(tr_i, tr_j)$, $\forall i, \forall j$:
$$H(tr_i) = -\sum_{r=1}^{N_r} [\alpha_{i,j} P(h_r^{tr_i}) \cdot log(\alpha_{i,j} P(h_r^{tr_i}))]$$
$$H(tr_j) = -\sum_{r=1}^{N_r} [\alpha_{i,j} P(h_r^{tr_j}) \cdot log(\alpha_{i,j} P(h_r^{tr_j}))]$$
$$H(tr_i, tr_j) = -\sum_{r=1}^{N_r} [\alpha_{i,j} P(h_r^{tr_i}, h_r^{tr_j}) \cdot log(\alpha_{i,j} P(h_r^{tr_i}, h_r^{tr_j}))]$$

2. Compute the weighted mutual information $(W\mu I)$:
$$W\mu I(tr_i, tr_j) = [H(tr_i) + H(tr_j) - H(tr_i, tr_j)], \forall i, \forall j$$

3. Compute the baseline $W\mu I_{base}$:
$$W\mu I_{base} \doteq [\min_{i,j}(W\mu I(tr_i, tr_j)), \max_{i,j}(W\mu I(tr_i, tr_j))]$$

4. Compute l_p $(p=1,2)$ norms:
$$l_p(tr_i, tr_j) = \left[\sum_{r=1}^{N_r} (|h_r^{tr_i} - h_r^{tr_j}|)^p \right]^{\frac{1}{p}}, \forall i, \forall j$$

5. Compute the baseline $l_p{}^{base}$ $(p=1,2)$:
$$l_p^{base} \doteq [\min_{i,j}(l_p(tr_i, tr_j)), \max_{i,j}(l_p(tr_i, tr_j))]$$

Similarly, considering the operational setting we can build the training-operational matrix as in Table 2.

Table 2. Training-operational number of hits table with $N_{op} = 1$. Columns refers to the training splits $tr_i \in TR$ and the operational split op_1, each row to a rule $r_i \in \mathcal{R}_{tr}$.

	tr_1	....	$tr_{N_{tr}}$	op_1
r_1	$h_1^{tr_1}$	...	$h_1^{tr_{N_{tr}}}$	$h_1^{op_1}$
r_2	$h_2^{tr_1}$	...	$h_2^{tr_{N_{tr}}}$	$h_2^{op_1}$
...	...	...	...	...
...	...	...	...	...
r_{N_r}	$h_{N_r}^{tr_1}$		$h_{N_r}^{tr_{N_{tr}}}$	$h_{N_r}^{op_1}$

Weighted mutual information and norms are then computed and compared to the training baselines, as described in Algorithm 2.

Algorithm 2: Weighted Mutual Information and Norms at Operational Stage

---

$i = 1, \ldots, N_{tr}, \ p = 1, 2$
Input: Table 2; baseline ranges $W\mu I_{base}$ and $l_p{}^{base}$
Output: ODD through $W\mu I$ and l_p

---

1. Compute the weighted entropies $H(tr_i)$, $H(op_1)$ and $H(tr_i, op_1)$ as done in the **Algorithm 1** (steps 1a-1b) $\forall i$
2. Compute the weighted mutual information $(W\mu I)$:
$$W\mu I(tr_i, op_1) = [H(tr_i) + H(op_1) - H(tr_i, op_1)], \quad \forall i$$
3. Compute l_p norms:
$$l_p(tr_i, op_1) = \left[\sum_{r=1}^{N_r}(|h_r^{tr_i} - h_r^{op_1}|)^p\right]^{\frac{1}{p}}, \forall i$$

4.OoD detection:

IF $W\mu I(tr_i, op_1) \notin W\mu I_{base}$ *for the majority of i* THEN flag is *on*
IF $l_p(tr_i, op_1) \notin l_p{}^{base}$ *for the majority of i* THEN flag is *on*
IF *{at least one flag is on}* THEN op_1 is OoD

---

4 Platooning Case Study

The OoD detection methodologies proposed in this work have been tested on a case study addressing collision avoidance in vehicle platooning [18], which is one of the most celebrated applications in autonomous driving. A group of vehicles is interconnected via wireless, based on the Cooperative Adaptive Cruise Control [23]. The behavior of the platooning system is synthesised by the physical quantities pointed out in Table 3. The physical quantities correspond to the features of the problem, which identify potential collisions in advance after a sudden brake.

Figure 2 shows speed (left) and reciprocal distance (right) of three vehicles when braking force changes from 1000 N (no collision) to 1300 N (collision). We consider two datasets: the first one (LOW), is obtained by fixing an upper bound on the communication delay, i.e., $d \leq 0.4$ s; conversely, the second one (HIGH) is characterized by $d > 0.4$ s. LOW is chosen as the training domain (tr_{LOW}, in-distribution) and the reference ruleset is denoted with $\mathcal{R}_{tr_{LOW}}$; HIGH dataset constitutes the operational domain instead. A typical ODD problem is thus posed (between LOW and HIGH) as d has a significant impact on performance.

Table 3. Platooning features.

Symbol	Description
N	Number of vehicles
$F0$	Braking force applied by the leader
PER	Probability of packet loss
$d0$	Initial mutual distance between vehicles
$v0$	Initial speed
d	Communication delay in the inter-connection of vehicles

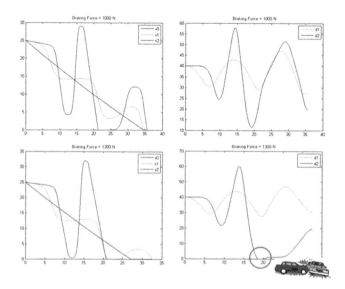

Fig. 2. Trend of the initial speed $v0$ (left) and initial mutual distance $d0$ (right) between three cars, when a different braking force $F0$ is applied. Image from [19].

The ODD has here a safety preserving role as it recognizes if the delay in operation is larger than the one in training. However, the algorithms are unaware that delay is the key to discriminating the datasets and they understand the ODD through the operational hits on $\mathcal{R}_{tr_{LOW}}$.

5   Results

In this Section, we show the results of the proposed approach for the platooning case study. The first row of Tables 4 and 5 reports the baseline ranges of the norms and mutual information metrics, respectively, which constitute the reference to infer possible OoD in operation. An even partial overlap between ranges in training and operation leads to a missed detection, i.e., a false negative (FN).

A false positive (FP) consists of a wrong ODD for a training (in-distribution) bunch of samples.

The operational sample (column) of Table 2 constitutes a FN in case no OoD is declared; a sample (column) of Table 1 constitutes a FP in case OoD is declared. Tables are built as follows. Each column refers to a bunch of $n_s = 500$ samples, with values reflecting the number of hits for the reference ruleset. We consider $N_{tr} = 50$ and $N_{op} = 1$ in Table 2. The total repetitions of the experiments for computing FNR and FPR is 2500. Example code and data for the experiments are available at the following link: https://github.com/giacomo97cnr/Rule-based-ODD.

As pointed out from Tables 4 and 5, good performance is registered for both $W\mu I$ and norms while μI runs worse.

Table 4. Algorithms 1 and 2: platooning. Norms.

Couples	l_1	FNR (l_1)	FPR (l_1)	l_2	FNR (l_2)	FPR (l_2)
$tr_{LOW} - tr_{LOW}$	[0.02, 0.12]		0%	[0.01, 0.04]		0%
$tr_{LOW} - op_{HIGH}$	[3.80, 3.90]	0%		[1.37, 1.39]	0%	

Table 5. Algorithms 1 and 2: platooning. μI and $W\mu I$.

Couples	μI	FNR (μI)	$W\mu I$	FNR ($W\mu I$)	FPR ($W\mu I$)
$tr_{LOW} - tr_{LOW}$	[0.87,2.73]		[0.02,0.06]		0%
$tr_{LOW} - op_{HIGH}$	[0.04,0.97]	8%	[0.51,0.73]	0%	

6   Groupwise in Operation

6.1   Incremental Technique

The method collects a bunch of operational data before processing and classifying them as in or out of distribution. For this reason, it falls in the category of groupwise methods [12]. Differently from pointwise, groupwise confirms a type of situation (in or out), without relying on a single point that could be a spike in a steady trend. The collection phase in operation does not imply that one would wait for new n_s samples to register a new split and to provide the ODD. Splits are generated continuously, as soon as new samples are collected. Like in incremental techniques, once a new sample is available, a new (operational) bunch of n_s samples is built, by adding the new sample and by disregarding the most far away point in the past (of n_s positions). In turn, the bunch leads to the split collection, by computing the inherent hits on the ruleset. The process assumes a sample-by-sample incremental time window, over which the following operations are performed. A new data bunch is firstly registered, a new split is calculated and a new ODD is then derived.

6.2   Incremental Groupwise in Operation

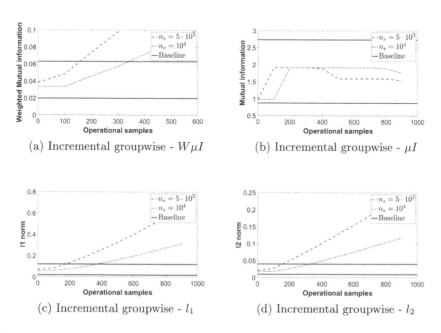

(a) Incremental groupwise - $W\mu I$

(b) Incremental groupwise - μI

(c) Incremental groupwise - l_1

(d) Incremental groupwise - l_2

Fig. 3. Trends of the metrics when operational data arrive sample-by-sample, in an incremental way.

The following experiments highlight the ODD when replacing in-distribution data with out-of, in a sample-by-sample incremental way. The analysis is relevant to the tracking of the OoD drift with both precision and measurement of distributions proximity. Every figure in the following contains the baseline derived at design time; the curves represent the behaviours of the metrics in operation. Increasing time windows with $n_s = 5 \cdot 10^3$ and $n_s = 10^4$ samples are used to emphasize the speed of the drift inference over time. The time size of the windows depends on the time granularity of the arrival of the points in operation; for this reason, the x-axis is not time, but it refers to the progressive identifier of the operational samples. The drift starts at time zero, that means the first operational sample derives from the OoD and previous points (of the window) are compliant with training conditions. As soon as the window collects more data (over the last n_s points), it senses more information about the OoD. As to the $W\mu I$ metric, the results confirm that the shorter the window, the faster the detection. On the other hand, the μI metric experiences a noise that can have different meanings as detailed later on. In the case of platooning $W\mu I$ and both l_p norms ($p = 1, 2$) (Fig. 3a, Fig. 3c and Fig. 3d) need at least 150 samples to exit the baseline with $n_s = 5 \cdot 10^3$ and twice as many samples with $n_s = 10^4$; so these metrics match the ODD and are coherent with previous results (Table 4), while μI is stuck in the baseline (Fig. 3b).

7   Rationale of Mutual Information Modification

When comparing two histograms, mutual information (μI) is useful to identify their dependence but it does not capture the differences among their values. Suppose we get these three histograms A, B and C (Table 6)

Table 6. Example of $W\mu I$ against μI

	A	B	C
r_1	0.156	0.171	0.314
r_2	0.172	0.186	0.329
r_3	0.328	0.314	0.171
r_4	0.349	0.329	0.186

According to μI, histograms A and B are dependent in the same measure as A and C are; but B and C are completely different (they have same values but in different positions). Since each row of the tr and op histograms corresponds to a rule, using μI may have a detrimental effect as the rule hits contain the information peculiar to the OoD. Introducing weights we can overcome this disadvantage both capturing the dependence and the differences between values. The correction consists of weighting the probabilities (used in entropy calculations) through the average of hits differences in each rule/row; this leads to $\alpha_{i,j}$ quantities in Algorithm 1. In the case of weighted mutual information the more the vectors are dependent and similar, the more $W\mu I$ goes towards zero. In the specific case of platooning situations in which similar values of training and operational were discovered in different positions were over 300 times (Table 7).

Table 7. Example of a training and an operational histogram in platooning; some values are roughly the same, but in different positions: r_7–r_6; r_9–r_{13}; r_{11}–r_8; r_{13}–r_3 (evidenced by the colors in the table).

	tr	op
r_1	0.1666	0
r_2	0.1689	0
r_3	0.1495	0.2535
r_4	0.1423	0.7914
r_5	0.1382	0.2379
r_6	0.0598	0.0999
r_7	0.0903	0.1918
r_8	0.0845	0.4262
r_9	0.0499	0
r_{10}	0.0303	1
r_{11}	0.4210	0
r_{12}	0.3383	0.0443
r_{13}	0.2516	0.0498
r_{14}	0.1117	0
r_{15}	0.0860	0.0171
r_{16}	0.717	0.0444

8   Conclusion

The paper introduced an innovative technique for the detection of out-of-distribution based on explainable AI. The approach has been validated through measures of proximity between in and out of distribution and it is corroborated by a real-world scenario. Future extensions comprise further testing on image datasets, including alternative ways to infer in-distribution behaviour.

Acknowledgements. This work was supported in part by REXASI-PRO H-EU project, call HORIZON-CL4-2021-HUMAN-01-01, Grant agreement ID: 101070028. The work was also supported by Future Artificial Intelligence Research (FAIR) project, Recovery and Resilience Plan ("Piano Nazionale di Ripresa e Resilienza"), Spoke 3 - Resilient AI. G. De Bernardi PhD is partially funded by Collins Aerospace.

References

1. Bitterwolf, J., Meinke, A., Augustin, M., Hein, M.: Breaking down out-of-distribution detection: many methods based on OOD training data estimate a combination of the same core quantities. In: International Conference on Machine Learning, pp. 2041–2074. PMLR (2022)

2. Cabitza, F., Campagner, A.: The need to separate the wheat from the chaff in medical informatics: introducing a comprehensive checklist for the (self)-assessment of medical AI studies. Int. J. Med. Inform. **153**, 104510 (2021)
3. DeVries, T., Taylor, G.W.: Learning confidence for out-of-distribution detection in neural networks (2018)
4. Dinh, T.Q., et al.: Performing group difference testing on graph structured data from GANs: analysis and applications in neuroimaging. IEEE Trans. Pattern Anal. Mach. Intell. **44**(2), 877–889 (2022). https://doi.org/10.1109/TPAMI.2020.3013433
5. Concepts of design assurance for neural networks codann. Standard, European Union Aviation Safety Angency, Daedalean, AG, March 2020. https://www.easa.europa.eu/sites/default/files/dfu/EASA-DDLN-Concepts-of-Design-Assurance-for-Neural-Networks-CoDANN.pdf
6. Easa concept paper: First usable guidance for level 1 machine learning applications, a deliverable of the easa ai roadmap. Standard, European Union Aviation Safety Angency, Daedalean, AG, April 2021. https://www.easa.europa.eu/easa-concept-paper-first-usable-guidance-level-1-machine-learning-applications-proposed-issue-01pdf
7. Guarrera, M., Jin, B., Lin, T.W., Zuluaga, M.A., Chen, Y., Sangiovanni-Vincentelli, A.: Class-wise thresholding for robust out-of-distribution detection. In: 2022 IEEE/CVF Conference on Computer Vision and Pattern Recognition Workshops (CVPRW), pp. 2836–2845 (2022). https://doi.org/10.1109/CVPRW56347.2022.00321
8. Guénais, T., Vamvourellis, D., Yacoby, Y., Doshi-Velez, F., Pan, W.: BaCOUn: Bayesian classifers with out-of-distribution uncertainty. arXiv preprint arXiv:2007.06096 (2020)
9. Heidecker, F., et al.: An application-driven conceptualization of corner cases for perception in highly automated driving. In: 2021 IEEE Intelligent Vehicles Symposium (IV), pp. 644–651 (2021). https://doi.org/10.1109/IV48863.2021.9575933
10. Hendrycks, D., Gimpel, K.: A baseline for detecting misclassified and out-of-distribution examples in neural networks. arXiv preprint arXiv:1610.02136 (2016)
11. Hsu, Y.C., Shen, Y., Jin, H., Kira, Z.: Generalized ODIN: detecting out-of-distribution image without learning from out-of-distribution data. In: 2020 IEEE/CVF Conference on Computer Vision and Pattern Recognition (CVPR), pp. 10948–10957 (2020). https://doi.org/10.1109/CVPR42600.2020.01096
12. Jiang, D., Sun, S., Yu, Y.: Revisiting flow generative models for out-of-distribution detection. In: International Conference on Learning Representations (2022). https://openreview.net/forum?id=6y2KBh-0Fd9
13. Lee, K., Lee, K., Lee, H., Shin, J.: A simple unified framework for detecting out-of-distribution samples and adversarial attacks. In: Bengio, S., Wallach, H., Larochelle, H., Grauman, K., Cesa-Bianchi, N., Garnett, R. (eds.) Advances in Neural Information Processing Systems, vol. 31. Curran Associates, Inc. (2018). https://proceedings.neurips.cc/paper_files/paper/2018/file/abdeb6f575ac5c6676b747bca8d09cc2-Paper.pdf
14. Liang, S., Li, Y., Srikant, R.: Principled detection of out-of-distribution examples in neural networks. corr abs/1706.02690 (2017). arXiv preprint arXiv:1706.02690 (2017)
15. Liang, S., Li, Y., Srikant, R.: Enhancing the reliability of out-of-distribution image detection in neural networks (2020)
16. Liu, W., Wang, X., Owens, J., Li, Y.: Energy-based out-of-distribution detection. Adv. Neural Inf. Process. Syst. **33**, 21464–21475 (2020)

17. Mirasierra, V., Mammarella, M., Dabbene, F., Alamo, T.: Prediction error quantification through probabilistic scaling. IEEE Control Syst. Lett. **6**, 1118–1123 (2022). https://doi.org/10.1109/LCSYS.2021.3087361
18. Mongelli, M.: Design of countermeasure to packet falsification in vehicle platooning by explainable artificial intelligence. Comput. Commun. **179**, 166–174 (2021)
19. Mongelli, M., Ferrari, E., Muselli, M., Fermi, A.: Performance validation of vehicle platooning through intelligible analytics. IET Cyber-Phys. Syst. Theory Appl. **4**(2), 120–127 (2019)
20. Muselli, M.: Switching neural networks: a new connectionist model for classification, January 2005. https://doi.org/10.1007/11731177_4
21. Parodi, S., Manneschi, C., Verda, D., Ferrari, E., Muselli, M.: Logic learning machine and standard supervised methods for hodgkins lymphoma prognosis using gene expression data and clinical variables. Health Inform. J. **24** (2016). https://doi.org/10.1177/1460458216655188
22. Road vehicles safety of the intended functionality pd iso pas 21448:2019. Standard, International Organization for Standardization, Geneva, CH, March 2019
23. Shladover, S.E., Nowakowski, C., Lu, X.Y., Ferlis, R.: Cooperative adaptive cruise control: definitions and operating concepts. Transp. Res. Rec. **2489**(1), 145–152 (2015)
24. Sun, Y., Ming, Y., Zhu, X., Li, Y.: Out-of-distribution detection with deep nearest neighbors. arXiv preprint arXiv:2204.06507 (2022)
25. Vernekar, S., Gaurav, A., Abdelzad, V., Denouden, T., Salay, R., Czarnecki, K.: Out-of-distribution detection in classifiers via generation (2019)
26. Zhou, K., Yang, Y., Qiao, Y., Xiang, T.: Mixstyle neural networks for domain generalization and adaptation (2021)

Leveraging Group Contrastive Explanations for Handling Fairness

Alessandro Castelnovo[1,2]([✉]), Nicole Inverardi[1], Lorenzo Malandri[3,4],
Fabio Mercorio[3,4], Mario Mezzanzanica[3,4], and Andrea Seveso[3,4]

[1] Data Science and Artificial Intelligence, Intesa Sanpaolo S.p.A., Milan, Italy
`a.castelnovo5@campus.unimib.it`
[2] Department of Informatics, Systems and Communication, University of
Milan-Bicocca, Milan, Italy
[3] Department of Statistics and Quantitative Methods, University of Milan-Bicocca,
Milan, Italy
[4] CRISP Research Centre crispresearch.eu, University of Milano Bicocca,
Milan, Italy

Abstract. With the increasing adoption of Artificial Intelligence (AI)
for decision-making processes by companies, developing systems that
behave fairly and do not discriminate against specific groups of people becomes crucial. Reaching this objective requires a multidisciplinary
approach that includes domain experts, data scientists, philosophers, and
legal experts, to ensure complete accountability for algorithmic decisions.
In such a context, Explainable AI (XAI) plays a key role in enabling professionals from different backgrounds to comprehend the functioning of
automatized decision-making processes and, consequently, being able to
identify the presence of fairness issues. This paper presents FairX, an
innovative approach that uses Group-Contrastive (G-contrast) explanations to estimate whether different decision criteria apply among distinct population subgroups. FairX provides actionable insights through
a comprehensive explanation of the decision-making process, enabling
businesses to: detect the presence of direct discrimination on the target
variable and choose the most appropriate fairness framework.

Keywords: XAI · Fairness · Contrastive Explanation · Direct
discrimination

1 Introduction

The adoption of Artificial intelligence (AI) in decision-making processes is
expanding across various sectors, including banking [11,41], online advertising [48], public health [52], criminal justice [17,19], and recruitment [3,38,39].
Although AI can support companies and institutions in making optimal and
data-based decisions, it could as well raise relevant ethical, legal, and technical
issues. One of the biggest challenges is guaranteeing that the (partially or fully)

L. Longo (Ed.): xAI 2023, CCIS 1903, pp. 332–345, 2023.
https://doi.org/10.1007/978-3-031-44070-0_17

automatised decision-making process is fair. The definition of fairness itself is a complex and multifaceted question that requires careful consideration of various factors, including philosophical assumptions, social norms and legal requirements. In addition, fairness is a highly contextual concept and also depends on the available data.

As is often the case when the crux of the matter is ethical, the notion of fairness cannot be conceived in a definitive and univocal way. Different understandings of bias and fairness depend on the belief system assumed beforehand. It is important to introduce the concept of worldviews as it provides a framework for understanding the diverse perspectives and ethical beliefs that influence fairness decisions [21,24]. More specifically, [21] define two extreme cases: What You See Is What You Get (WYSIWYG), and We are All Equal (WAE). By defining three different metric spaces, these two worldviews can be distinguished because of how they consider the relationship between them. The first domain, called Construct Space (CS), contains all of a person's unobservable but realised characteristics, such as intellectual capacities. The second space is the Observable Space (OS) which comprehends all the quantified features that attempt to capture the unobservable characteristics, for example, with an IQ measurement. The third realm is the Decision Space (DS) which describes all the decisions computed by the decision-makers (or the algorithms) starting from the data provided by OS. In the WYSIWYG worldview, CS and OS must be considered equal, and any eventual difference between them is irrelevant to the fairness of the corresponding choice in DS. Conversely, the WAE belief system does not envisage any equality between CS and OS and states that individuals are all equal in CS. Therefore, in this perspective, any distortion detectable between the two domains must be interpreted as caused by a biased observation method corresponding to an unfair mapping. If the assumptions of WYSIWYG are accepted, a fair decision-making process is ensured as soon as the mapping between OS and DS is fair. Contrarily, according to WAE, the decision-making process must take into account that any difference among persons is due to an unfair mapping between OS and CS (this distortion is called measurement bias [24]) and consequently to guarantee that the AI system behaves fairly those biases must be appropriately mitigated.

The law also addresses two extreme concepts. Indeed, the legal perspective typically evaluates the fairness of a decision-making process using two distinct notions: disparate treatment [23] and disparate impact [55]. A decision-making process suffers from disparate impact if its outcomes disproportionately hurt (or benefit) groups with certain sensitive attribute values, such as females or foreigners, and it produces disparate treatment if its decisions are (partly) based on the sensitive attribute itself [57]. Moreover, decisions based on protected attributes can result in accusations of direct discrimination [22].

The complex nature of fairness and the corresponding moral and legal perspectives results in many possible fairness metrics in the literature [12,20,45,51]. The notions of individual and group fairness are commonly embraced [8]. Individual fairness establishes that "similar individuals receive similar decisions", regardless of their sensitive attributes [18]. It aims to guarantee that similar individuals are not treated unfairly due to arbitrary or irrelevant factors, such as belonging to a certain gender or nationality. On the other hand, group fairness focuses on avoiding systematic biases against certain groups, ensuring that different groups receive similar portions of outcomes (independence) or similar portions of errors (separation and sufficiency) [13]. Numerous research studies have demonstrated that using sensitive features in model training causes violations of individual and group fairness [57] and is essentially to blame for introducing direct discrimination.

Motivation. Once the different definitions of fairness are acknowledged, companies need to decide which definition is more appropriate for each context of applications of AI systems so that they can be held accountable. This choice is necessary because, under certain conditions, the different conceptions of fairness are mutually incompatible [4]. Deciding which notion of fairness is more appropriate and understanding whether an AI system behaves fairly in decision-making requires extensive contextual understanding and domain knowledge [58].

Many companies have adopted guidelines [11,27,31,43,44] and checklists [1, 30,53] to respond to this challenge and to be able to identify the more suitable fairness framework for each application domain. In supervised Machine Learning, an important question to answer to decide on the proper concept of fairness is about the reliability of the target variable that the model has to replicate. In particular, it is fundamental to understand if that target variable quantified in the OS is objective, i.e. faithfully represents the real phenomenon (contained in CS) that the AI system aims to reproduce, or may already be distorted by some form of bias (see, e.g. [11,31]).

For example, considering a hypothetical situation in which it is known that the target variable is distorted by direct discrimination, the WYSIWYG moral framework would be hardly acceptable and, consequently, the implementation of target-based mitigation strategies. On the other hand, adopting WAE in such a context would make it possible not to blindly rely on the data contained in the OS and to implement mitigation measures so that the decision-making process is more congruent with the real phenomenon. Unfortunately, a concrete and sure understanding of whether the target variable is reliable or contains some form of bias remains a major issue, especially if it results from a human decision.

Contribution. In this work, we introduce FairX, a new approach that aims to support the choice of which worldview to assume when addressing fairness in developing an AI system through global contrastive explanations. Specifically, we extend the functionality of the ContrXT [33,34] tool to detect different patterns in treating different population subgroups before developing machine learning classifiers. FairX, our extension of ContrXT, enables users to recognize discriminatory behaviours, which is of utmost importance in ensuring fairness in machine learning systems.

By detecting direct discrimination on the target variable, we provide actionable insights to developers and decision-makers, allowing them to properly decide which worldview - WAE, WYSIWYG and nuances in between - may be more appropriate to assume when an AI system operates in a specific context. This work represents one of the first attempts to link XAI with moral frameworks with which the ethical-philosophical literature formalises and structures the matter of fairness.

2   Related Works

Both fairness and explainability are relevant ethical issues that, if appropriately addressed, can help promote the trust of users in AI-supported decision-making and building "Responsible AI" [58].

Previous research has found that explanations of AI systems' outcomes allow humans to interpret how they function and provide an interface for humans in the loop to identify and tackle potential issues [9,32], including the ones related to fairness [25]. [46] investigated the role of Fairness, Accountability, and Transparency (FAT) in AI-supported decision-making processes. The authors showed that FAT issues are multi-functionally related and that user attitudes about FAT depend on the context in which it takes place and based on who is looking at it. [14] and [7] proposed explainability methods for fairness evaluation based on the Shapley value framework [29].

In [36], the authors introduce FairShades, a model-agnostic approach for auditing the outcomes of abusive language detection systems combining explainability and fairness evaluation to identify unintended biases and sensitive categories towards which models are most discriminatory. FairShades goal is pursued through the auditing of meaningful counterfactuals [16] generated within the CheckList framework [42]. The proposed fairness explanations attribute a model's overall unfairness to individual input features, even though the model does not directly operate on protected attributes. [54] argued that effective regulation to ensure fairness requires AI systems to be transparent. While explainability is one of the approaches to acquire transparency, explainability requires that an AI system provides a human-understandable explanation of why any given decision was reached in terms of the training data, the decision function, and the rules for that decision.

Our work investigates fairness by exploiting contrastive explanations [28]. The idea behind contrastive explanations is that people usually explain the reason for an event in relation to - or in contrast to - another event that did not happen, rather than explaining the causes of the occurred event [40]. This means a human explanation is more likely to answer a question like "Why P rather than Q?" instead of "Why P?" even though Q is often implicit in the context. This is called contrastive explanation. However, people usually expect to see a specific event happen while another occurs, making the observed event the fact and the expected event the foil [50]. ContrXT [33] inspires our approach, which follows this principle. ContrXT (Contrastive eXplainer for Text/Tabular classifier) is an approach that traces the decision criteria of a black box text classifier by encoding the changes in the decision logic through Binary Decision Diagrams. Then it provides global, model-agnostic, Time-Contrastive (T-contrast) explanations, estimating why the model has modified its behaviour over time. In our extension, instead of comparing the behaviour of two text classifiers, we compare the decision patterns between different sensitive groups. Recently, ContrXT has been extended to deal with numerical variables and to perform model contrastive explanations as well [35].

3   Problem Formulation and Proposed Approach

Direct discrimination refers to treating somebody unfavourably because of their membership to a particular group, characterized by sensitive attributes, such as race or gender [22]. In mathematical terms, when a target variable Y depends on relevant attributes for the problem X and sensitive attributes S, i.e. $Y = f(X, S)$. In this case, two individuals a and b, with the same relevant attributes $(X_a = X_b)$, but belonging to different sensitive groups $(S_a \neq S_b)$, could results in different target variable $(Y_a \neq Y_b)$. Indirect discrimination arises when Y depends only on the relevant attributes X, but for some reason, X is not independent of S, i.e. $Y = f(X)$ with $X \not\perp S$. In this case, a and b in the previous example would have the same target variable $(Y_a = Y_b)$.

Still, since the relevant attributes X used by the decision-making process are not distributed in the same way between sensitive groups (e.g. males have, on average, higher salaries than females), the percentage of positive decisions varies among sensitive groups $(P(Y = 1|S = 1) \neq P(Y = 1|S \neq 1))$. Although both situations result in a non-independence between Y and S, indirect discrimination under certain conditions could be tolerable, i.e. assuming a WYSIWYG worldview, while direct discrimination is never acceptable. Moreover, training a machine learning model on Y without using S is insufficient for removing the effects of direct discrimination because of the latent effect of S on X.

We assume that we are in a common situation in creating a decision-making system, i.e., in our OS, we have a target variable correlated with sensitive attributes without knowing whether it results from direct or indirect discrimination. We must decide the fairness framework to follow upon which we will be held accountable. FairX, based on the available data, helps to understand whether a decision is based on sensitive attributes and consequently recommends the more suitable moral worldview to assume.

FairX is composed of 3 steps: (i) trace, (ii) g-contrast explanation and (iii) worldview recommendation (see Fig. 1).

In the **trace** step, a decision tree is trained within each class of the sensitive feature $i \in S$, using the features relevant to the problem X_i, to learn how to reproduce the target variable Y_i. At the end of this phase, a set j of decision rules DR_{ij} for each sensitive group is encoded via a global surrogate GS_i that mimics their real decision-making process. A decision rule is a series of minimum requirements, such as $income > z$ & $guarantees > g$, that lead to a positive decision.

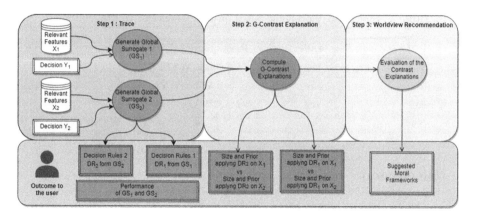

Fig. 1. Graphical overview of how FairX works with a sensitive feature S with two classes.

In the **G-contrast explanation** step, FairX first applies the decision rules DR_{ij} of each surrogate GS_i on each set of relevant features X_i to obtain their size (the number of instances that respect the decision rule from GS_i) and prior (the percentage of instance that respect the decision rule from GS_i and have a positive decision). For example, suppose that the sensitive attribute is composed of two classes: female ($i = 1$) and male ($i = 2$), and one of the decision rules learned by training the decision tree on X_1 and Y_1 is, as before, *income* $> z$ & *guarantees* $> g$. FairX applies this decision rule both on X_1 and X_2 to calculate how many females and how many males respect the rule (size) and how many females and how many males respecting the rule have a positive outcome (prior). Subsequently, every decision rule's size and prior are contrasted among sensitive groups. Suppose the size of the same decision rule differs between two groups. In that case, it indicates that the distributions of X are different between sensitive groups. It could signify direct discrimination if different groups have different priors for the same decision rule. In the FairX outcome, the surrogates' performances are reported to allow the user to evaluate the reliability of these conclusions.

Finally, in the **worldview recommendation** step, the moral framework to assume for the subsequent choice of the proper fairness metric is evaluated. It can be compared to the other frameworks according to a trade-off logic. The goal here is to provide decision-makers with a trustworthy and understandable outcome aligned with the results of the G-contrast explanation for supporting the hypothesis underlying worldviews. Table 1 summarises the characteristics required for decision rules to be shown to support a specific worldview. In our approach, the user may specify the threshold at which he considers the difference in prior significant.

Table 1. Suggested Worldview based on the G-contrastive explanation.

Differences in Size	Differences in Prior	Suggested Worldview
Yes	Yes	not WYSIWYG
Yes	No	WYSIWYG
No	Yes	WAE
No	No	Heaven: WAE = WYSIWYG

4 Discussion

On the G-contrast Step in the Landscape of Fairness Metrics. The prior comparison in the G-contrast step regarding fairness metrics can be seen as a form of stronger conditional demographic parity. Demographic parity (DP) is a group fairness metric strictly linked to independence. The independence criterion states that decisions should be independent of any sensitive attribute. Another version of the independence criteria is conditional demographic parity (CDP), where decisions should be independent of any sensitive attribute *given* a specific population class. For example, if a man and a woman have a certain rating level, we want them to have the same chance of getting the loan. Following [13], CDP compared to DP is one step further towards a more individual notion of fairness.

Our approach checks if the decisions are independent of any sensitive attribute *given* a specific decision rule, taking another step towards individual fairness. It could be argued why not directly use individual fairness metrics. In literature, individual fairness metrics aim to ensure that *similar people should receive similar outcomes*. This principle compares single individuals rather than focusing on groups sharing certain characteristics. The first attempt to deal with a form of individual fairness was presented in [18], where this concept is introduced as a Lipschitz condition on the map f from the feature space to the model space:

$$dist_Y(\hat{y}_i, \hat{y}_j) < L \times dist_{\widetilde{X}}(\widetilde{x}_i, \widetilde{x}_j), \tag{1}$$

where $dist_Y$ and $dist_{\widetilde{X}}$ denote suitable distances in the target and feature space, respectively, L is a constant. The main drawback of this definition lies in the ambiguous concept of "similar individuals". Indeed, defining a suitable distance metric $dist_{\widetilde{X}}$ on feature space to embody the concept of similarity on ethical grounds alone is almost as difficult as defining fairness in the first place. In addition, assigning equal importance to all the features in X space is inconsistent with the objective function of the classification model.

Our proposal provides a reasonable and easily understandable explanation of potential discrimination since it is computed following relevant patterns that synthesize the underline decision-making process.

On the Worldview Recommendation Step from a Philosophical Perspective. Finding a pattern that results in different proportions of favourable outcomes between population subgroups, i.e. different prior in Table 1 may indicate that the sensitive attribute was used to make the decision, i.e. that there is direct discrimination, or that other relevant information not present in the available data was used to make the decision. Both conclusions represent evidence of distortion between OS and CS; consequently, fairness metrics that rely on the WYSIWYG worldview are hardly justifiable. For this reason, WYSIWYG is hardly preferable when there are differences in prior.

WAE is the most appropriate moral framework when there are no differences between the relevant attributes among different sensitive groups, i.e. same size in Table 1. When there are differences in size, we are addressing the most complex situations because other forms of bias may also be present (see, e.g. [37]). In this case, businesses often favour WYSIWYG when proving that the target variable is reliable [11,43]. However, there may be cases where WAE is followed for strategic reasons [14,26] or because of strong moral beliefs that WAE in the potential space (see [24] for details).

On the Links Between Worldviews and Fairness Metrics. The complex nature of biases and the corresponding moral perspectives results in many possible fairness metrics [45,49]. According to recent literature, fairness definitions can be broadly categorised into three groups: *disparate impact (DI)*, *disparate mistreatment (DM)*, and *disparate treatment (DT)* [10,56].

A decision-making process suffers from *DI* if it gives a disproportionate share of favourable outcomes to subgroups of the population characterised by certain sensitive attributes. In these cases, the distortion is typically due to a dependence of the decision-making process on some sensitive variables and ends up differentiating between privileged and unprivileged groups. The most popular fairness metrics used to measure independence are *demographic parity (DP*, also called *statistical parity)* and *conditional demographic parity (CDP)*—both of which are discussed above. DI is usually enforced to mitigate fairness when the target variable Y is deemed unreliable or if differences in outcome probability between groups are unjustifiable [2,15]. These measures are compatible with a WAE worldview.

A decision-making process suffers from *DM* if its accuracy (or error rate) differs for subgroups of the population characterised by sensitive features. The concept of *DM* can be further divided into *separation* (sometimes referred to as *equalised odds*), and *sufficiency* (also called *conditional use accuracy equality* or *calibration by groups* if enforced over the entire range of predicted scores) [4]. *Separation* prescribe a conditioning on the outcome Y and requires *true positive rate (TPR) parity* (also known as *equality of opportunity, false negative error rate balance,* or *equal recall)* and *false positive rate (FPR) parity* (also known as *false positive error rate balance* or *predictive equality)*. Compared to *DP, TPR parity* and *FPR parity* require equal decision rates across all subgroups of S that have the same label Y. *Sufficiency* conditions on the decision D and requires *positive predictive value (PPV) parity* (also known as *predictive parity,* the *outcome test,* or *equal precision)* and *false omission rate (FOR) parity*. *PPV parity* requires individuals that are assigned a positive decision $D = 1$ (a negative decision $D = 0$

in the case of *FOR parity*) to be equally likely to belong to the positive class $Y = 1$ across S. *DM* criterion are typically adopted when is possible to claim that *"the fairness optimal classifier is perfectly fair only if the accuracy optimal classifier is perfectly accurate"* [47], and the goal is not to introduce or amplify already existing distortions between groups. These measures are compatible with a WYSIWYG worldview.

The *DT* concept is inextricably linked to the previously discussed individual fairness principle. The simplest way to represent *DT* is to define similar individuals as couples belonging to different groups with respect to sensitive features but with the same values for all the other features. In this approach, the outcome for each observation is required not to change when the sensitive attribute is flipped. This concept is usually referred to as *Fairness Through Unawareness (FTU)* or *blindness* [51], and is expressed as the *requirement to avoid explicitly employing protected attributes when making decisions*—though, alternative conceptualisations of *individual fairness* exist. These metrics are not a priori compatible with either WAE or WYSIWYG, but with both worldviews depending on the moral assumptions made about the origin and cause of the similarity of relevant features between individuals of groups differentiated by sensitive attributes. In fact, if the difference that exists between relevant features - which, according to the principle of individual fairness, justifies different outputs - is believed to be caused by different possibilities of realising one's abilities (distortion between PS and CS), then it means that a WAE worldview has been assumed, and so DT may be enforced. On the other hand, if such a difference between relevant features is believed to be a real difference in realised individual capabilities - not due to different social contexts, i.e. historical biases - then it means that a WYSIWYG worldview has been assumed and, having implicit confidence in what emerges in OS, the different outcomes for individuals belonging to different groups may be considered a justifiable source of inequality.

5   Experiments on Synthetic Dataset

We showcase an initial application of FairX to two synthetic cases generated using `Bias On Demand` [5]. `Bias On Demand` is an open-source toolkit [6] that generates synthetic datasets that contain various types of bias.

In particular, we generate (*a*) a dataset with *historical bias* on a relevant input feature R and; (*b*) a dataset with *measurement bias* on the target variable Y[1]. The first can be seen as a case of indirect discrimination, while the second as a case of direct discrimination. Both datasets correlate A and Y, as shown in Fig. 2a and 2b, making it difficult to distinguish between the two biases without prior knowledge of the process that generated them.

---

[1] Compared to the notation in previous chapters, $X = (R, Q)$, $S = A$ and $Y = Y$. Historical bias is generated using $l_{hr} = 1.5$. Measurement bias is generated using $l_{my} = 1.5$. For further detail on the data generation framework, see github.com/rcrupiISP/ISParity and [5].

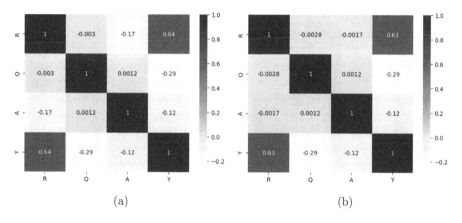

Fig. 2. (a) Correlation Matrix on the Dataset with Historical Bias. (b) Correlation Matrix on the Dataset with Measurement Bias.

Our experiment aims to demonstrate that with FairX it is possible to distinguish the two cases and therefore be able to decide the proper worldview to adopt in these two cases. We set the difference in prior to being significant when greater than 5%.

a) Results with historical bias on Y. Since the sensitive feature A is binary, two decision trees are trained in the Trace step. The first, trained when $A = 0$, has learned six decision rules with 85.2% *accuracy* and 85.6% *F1*, while the second, trained when $A = 1$, has learned five decision rules with 86.8% *accuracy* and 86.9% *F1*. In the G-contrast explanation step, the rules are contrasted between groups of A by observing the difference in priors. Figure 3 summarises these differences. Finally, since the differences are all between -5 and 5, the Worldview recommendation step suggests following a WYSIWYG worldview.

b) Results with measurement bias on Y. The trace step is analogous to the case with historical bias, with a similar number of decision rules learned and performance achieved. What changes are the results in the G-contrast explanation step: Fig. 3 shows that all of the decision rules have differences in prior greater than 5%, and three decision rules have a deviation up to 30%. As a consequence, the worldview recommendation step suggests that it is preferable to enforce a WAE worldview.

The FairX recommendation in both cases results to be consistent with the nature of the types of bias present in the datasets. Indeed, as clarified by [21], measurement bias is a distortion between CS and OS that is recognised by a WAE worldview since it assumes equality among groups in CS and requires mitigating any differences in CS in the name of fairness between individuals in PS. On the other hand, historical biases impact CS, which is then fairly reported in OS, and therefore, if a WYSIWYG worldview is assumed, structural differences between individuals are legitimate sources of inequality.

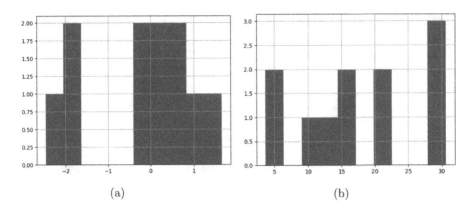

Fig. 3. (a) Frequency of the difference in prior of each decision rule between groups of A with Historical Bias. (b) Frequency of the difference in prior of each decision rule between groups of A with Measurement Bias.

6   Conclusion and Future Outlook

Several areas for future research could enhance the impact and applicability of our approach. We plan to employ FairX to benchmark datasets from various domains, such as healthcare, banking and criminal justice, to evaluate the effectiveness of our approach in different contexts. This will help us to identify potential limitations or trade-offs in our approach and determine how widely it can be generalized. Second, we will conduct user studies to evaluate the impact of our approach on end-users perceptions of fairness and trust in XAI models. This will involve recruiting participants from diverse backgrounds and evaluating their experiences with our approach in a realistic setting. We will use their feedback to refine our approach and identify new outcomes for supporting the recommendations of worldviews. Finally, we will design and release in open source the code and a visual user interface for interacting with FairX in an efficient and intuitive way.

References

1. Agarwal, A., Agarwal, H.: A seven-layer model with checklists for standardising fairness assessment throughout the AI lifecycle. AI Ethics 1–16 (2023)
2. Aghaei, S., Azizi, M.J., Vayanos, P.: Learning optimal and fair decision trees for non-discriminative decision-making. In: Proceedings of the AAAI Conference on Artificial Intelligence, vol. 33, pp. 1418–1426 (2019)
3. Alimonda, N., Castelnovo, A., Crupi, R., Mercorio, F., Mezzanzanica, M.: Preserving utility in fair top-k ranking with intersectional bias. In: Boratto, L., Faralli, S., Marras, M., Stilo, G. (eds.) BIAS 2023. CCIS, vol. 1840, pp. 59–73. Springer, Cham (2023). https://doi.org/10.1007/978-3-031-37249-0_5
4. Barocas, S., Hardt, M., Narayanan, A.: Fairness and Machine Learning. fairmlbook.org (2019). http://www.fairmlbook.org

5. Baumann, J., Castelnovo, A., Crupi, R., Inverardi, N., Regoli, D.: Bias on demand: a modelling framework that generates synthetic data with bias. In: Proceedings of the 2023 ACM Conference on Fairness, Accountability, and Transparency, pp. 1002–1013 (2023)

6. Baumann, J., Castelnovo, A., Crupi, R., Inverardi, N., Regoli, D.: An open-source toolkit to generate biased datasets (2023)

7. Begley, T., Schwedes, T., Frye, C., Feige, I.: Explainability for fair machine learning. arXiv preprint arXiv:2010.07389 (2020)

8. Binns, R.: On the apparent conflict between individual and group fairness. In: Proceedings of the 2020 Conference on Fairness, Accountability, and Transparency, pp. 514–524 (2020)

9. Cambria, E., Malandri, L., Mercorio, F., Mezzanzanica, M., Nobani, N.: A survey on XAI and natural language explanations. Inf. Process. Manag. **60**(1), 103111 (2023)

10. Castelnovo, A., Cosentini, A., Malandri, L., Mercorio, F., Mezzanzanica, M.: FFTree: a flexible tree to handle multiple fairness criteria. Inf. Process. Manag. **59**(6), 103099 (2022)

11. Castelnovo, A., et al.: Befair: addressing fairness in the banking sector. In: 2020 IEEE International Conference on Big Data (Big Data), pp. 3652–3661. IEEE (2020)

12. Castelnovo, A., Crupi, R., Greco, G., Regoli, D., Penco, I.G., Cosentini, A.C.: The zoo of fairness metrics in machine learning (2021)

13. Castelnovo, A., Crupi, R., Greco, G., Regoli, D., Penco, I.G., Cosentini, A.C.: A clarification of the nuances in the fairness metrics landscape. Sci. Rep. **12**(1), 4209 (2022)

14. Castelnovo, A., Malandri, L., Mercorio, F., Mezzanzanica, M., Cosentini, A.: Towards fairness through time. In: Kamp, M., et al. (eds.) ECML PKDD 2021. CCIS, vol. 1524, pp. 647–663. Springer, Cham (2022). https://doi.org/10.1007/978-3-030-93736-2_46

15. Corbett-Davies, S., Goel, S.: The measure and mismeasure of fairness: a critical review of fair machine learning. arXiv preprint arXiv:1808.00023 (2018)

16. Crupi, R., Castelnovo, A., Regoli, D., San Miguel Gonzalez, B.: Counterfactual explanations as interventions in latent space. Data Mining Knowl. Discov. 1–37 (2022)

17. Dieterich, W., Mendoza, C., Brennan, T.: Compas risk scales: demonstrating accuracy equity and predictive parity. Northpointe Inc. (2016)

18. Dwork, C., Hardt, M., Pitassi, T., Reingold, O., Zemel, R.: Fairness through awareness. In: TCSC, pp. 214–226 (2012)

19. Flores, A.W., Bechtel, K., Lowenkamp, C.T.: False positives, false negatives, and false analyses: a rejoinder to machine bias: there's software used across the country to predict future criminals. and it's biased against blacks. Fed. Probat. **80**, 38 (2016)

20. Franklin, J.S., Bhanot, K., Ghalwash, M., Bennett, K.P., McCusker, J., McGuinness, D.L.: An ontology for fairness metrics. In: Proceedings of the 2022 AAAI/ACM Conference on AI, Ethics, and Society, pp. 265–275 (2022)

21. Friedler, S.A., Scheidegger, C., Venkatasubramanian, S.: The (im) possibility of fairness: different value systems require different mechanisms for fair decision making. Commun. ACM **64**(4), 136–143 (2021)

22. Grabowicz, P., Perello, N., Mishra, A.: Marrying fairness and explainability in supervised learning. In: 2022 ACM FAccT, pp. 1905–1916 (2022)

23. Green, T.K.: The future of systemic disparate treatment law. Berkeley J. Emp. Lab. L. **32**, 395 (2011)
24. Hertweck, C., Heitz, C., Loi, M.: On the moral justification of statistical parity. In: Proceedings of the 2021 ACM FAccT, pp. 747–757 (2021)
25. Hilton, D.J.: Conversational processes and causal explanation. Psychol. Bull. **107**(1), 65 (1990)
26. Hu, L., Immorlica, N., Vaughan, J.W.: The disparate effects of strategic manipulation. In: Proceedings of the Conference on Fairness, Accountability, and Transparency, pp. 259–268 (2019)
27. Jobin, A., Ienca, M., Vayena, E.: The global landscape of AI ethics guidelines. Nat. Mach. Intell. **1**(9), 389–399 (2019)
28. Lipton, P.: Contrastive explanation. R. Inst. Philos. Suppl. **27**, 247–266 (1990)
29. Lundberg, S.M., Lee, S.I.: A unified approach to interpreting model predictions. In: Advances in Neural Information Processing Systems, vol. 30 (2017)
30. Madaio, M.A., Stark, L., Wortman Vaughan, J., Wallach, H.: Co-designing checklists to understand organizational challenges and opportunities around fairness in AI. In: 2020 CHI Conference on HFCS, pp. 1–14 (2020)
31. Makhlouf, K., Zhioua, S., Palamidessi, C.: On the applicability of machine learning fairness notions. ACM SIGKDD **23**(1), 14–23 (2021)
32. Malandri, L., Mercorio, F., Mezzanzanica, M., Nobani, N.: Convxai: a system for multimodal interaction with any black-box explainer. Cogn. Comput. **15**(2), 613–644 (2023)
33. Malandri, L., Mercorio, F., Mezzanzanica, M., Nobani, N., Seveso, A.: Contrxt: generating contrastive explanations from any text classifier. Inf. Fusion **81**, 103–115 (2022)
34. Malandri, L., Mercorio, F., Mezzanzanica, M., Nobani, N., Seveso, A.: The good, the bad, and the explainer: a tool for contrastive explanations of text classifiers. In: Raedt, L.D. (ed.) Proceedings of the Thirty-First International Joint Conference on Artificial Intelligence, IJCAI 2022, Vienna, Austria, 23–29 July 2022, pp. 5936–5939. ijcai.org (2022). https://doi.org/10.24963/ijcai.2022/858
35. Malandri, L., Mercorio, F., Mezzanzanica, M., Seveso, A.: Model-contrastive explanations through symbolic reasoning. Decis. Support Syst. 114040 (2023). https://doi.org/10.1016/j.dss.2023.114040. https://doi.org/www.sciencedirect.com/science/article/pii/S016792362300115X
36. Manerba, M.M., Guidotti, R.: Fairshades: fairness auditing via explainability in abusive language detection systems. In: 2021 IEEE Third International Conference on Cognitive Machine Intelligence (CogMI), pp. 34–43. IEEE (2021)
37. Mehrabi, N., Morstatter, F., Saxena, N., Lerman, K., Galstyan, A.: A survey on bias and fairness in machine learning. ACM Comput. Surv. (CSUR) **54**(6), 1–35 (2021)
38. Miller, C.C.: Can an algorithm hire better than a human. The New York Times, vol. 25 (2015)
39. Miller, C.C.: When algorithms discriminate. The New York Times, vol. 9 (2015)
40. Miller, T.: Explanation in artificial intelligence: insights from the social sciences. Artif. Intell. **267**, 1–38 (2019)
41. Mukerjee, A., Biswas, R., Deb, K., Mathur, A.P.: Multi-objective evolutionary algorithms for the risk-return trade-off in bank loan management. Int. Trans. Oper. Res. **9**(5), 583–597 (2002)
42. Ribeiro, M.T., Wu, T., Guestrin, C., Singh, S.: Beyond accuracy: behavioral testing of NLP models with checklist. arXiv preprint arXiv:2005.04118 (2020)

43. Ruf, B., Detyniecki, M.: Towards the right kind of fairness in AI. arXiv preprint arXiv:2102.08453 (2021)

44. Ryan, M., Stahl, B.C.: Artificial intelligence ethics guidelines for developers and users: clarifying their content and normative implications. J. Inf. Commun. Ethics Soc. **19**(1), 61–86 (2020)

45. Saxena, N.A.: Perceptions of fairness. In: Proceedings of the 2019 AAAI/ACM Conference on AI, Ethics, and Society, pp. 537–538 (2019)

46. Shin, D., Park, Y.J.: Role of fairness, accountability, and transparency in algorithmic affordance. Comput. Hum. Behav. **98**, 277–284 (2019)

47. Speicher, T., et al.: A unified approach to quantifying algorithmic unfairness: measuring individual & group unfairness via inequality indices. In: Proceedings of the 24th ACM SIGKDD International Conference on Knowledge Discovery & Data Mining, pp. 2239–2248 (2018)

48. Sweeney, L.: Discrimination in online ad delivery. Commun. ACM **56**(5), 44–54 (2013)

49. Tadmor, C.T., Hong, Y.Y., Chao, M.M., Wiruchnipawan, F., Wang, W.: Multicultural experiences reduce intergroup bias through epistemic unfreezing. J. Pers. Soc. Psychol. **103**(5), 750 (2012)

50. Van Bouwel, J., Weber, E.: Remote causes, bad explanations? J. Theory Soc. Behav. **32**(4), 437–449 (2002)

51. Verma, S., Rubin, J.: Fairness definitions explained. In: 2018 IEEE/ACM International Workshop on Software Fairness (FairWare), pp. 1–7. IEEE (2018)

52. Wahl, B., Cossy-Gantner, A., Germann, S., Schwalbe, N.R.: Artificial intelligence (AI) and global health: how can AI contribute to health in resource-poor settings? BMJ Glob. Health **3**(4), e000798 (2018)

53. Wang, H.E., et al.: A bias evaluation checklist for predictive models and its pilot application for 30-day hospital readmission models. J. Am. Med. Inform. Assoc. **29**(8), 1323–1333 (2022)

54. Warner, R., Sloan, R.H.: Making artificial intelligence transparent: fairness and the problem of proxy variables. CJE **40**(1), 23–39 (2021)

55. Willborn, S.L.: The disparate impact model of discrimination: theory and limits. Am. UL Rev. **34**, 799 (1984)

56. Zafar, M.B., Valera, I., Gomez-Rodriguez, M., Gummadi, K.P.: Fairness constraints: a flexible approach for fair classification. J. Mach. Learn. Res. **20**(1), 2737–2778 (2019)

57. Zafar, M.B., Valera, I., Rogriguez, M.G., Gummadi, K.P.: Fairness constraints: mechanisms for fair classification. In: Artificial Intelligence and Statistics, pp. 962–970. PMLR (2017)

58. Zhou, J., Chen, F., Holzinger, A.: Towards explainability for AI fairness. In: Holzinger, A., Goebel, R., Fong, R., Moon, T., Müller, K.R., Samek, W. (eds.) xxAI 2020. LNCS, vol. 13200, pp. 375–386. Springer, Cham (2022). https://doi.org/10.1007/978-3-031-04083-2_18

LUCID–GAN: Conditional Generative Models to Locate Unfairness

Andres Algaba[1]([✉]), Carmen Mazijn[1], Carina Prunkl[2], Jan Danckaert[1], and Vincent Ginis[1,3]

[1] Vrije Universiteit Brussel, Pleinlaan 2, 1000 Brussels, Belgium
{andres.algaba,carmen.mazijn,jan.danckaert,vincent.ginis}@vub.be
[2] Oxford University, Wellington Square, Oxford OX1 2JD, UK
carina.prunkl@philosophy.ox.ac.uk
[3] Harvard University, 150 Western Ave, Boston, USA

Abstract. Most group fairness notions detect unethical biases by computing statistical parity metrics on a model's output. However, this approach suffers from several shortcomings, such as philosophical disagreement, mutual incompatibility, and lack of interpretability. These shortcomings have spurred the research on complementary bias detection methods that offer additional transparency into the sources of discrimination and are agnostic towards an a priori decision on the definition of fairness and choice of protected features. A recent proposal in this direction is LUCID (Locating Unfairness through Canonical Inverse Design), where canonical sets are generated by performing gradient descent on the input space, revealing a model's desired input given a preferred output. This information about the model's mechanisms, i.e., which feature values are essential to obtain specific outputs, allows exposing potential unethical biases in its internal logic. Here, we present LUCID–GAN, which generates canonical inputs via a conditional generative model instead of gradient–based inverse design. LUCID–GAN has several benefits, including that it applies to non–differentiable models, ensures that canonical sets consist of realistic inputs, and allows to assess proxy and intersectional discrimination. We empirically evaluate LUCID–GAN on the UCI Adult and COMPAS data sets and show that it allows for detecting unethical biases in black–box models without requiring access to the training data (Code is available at https://github.com/Integrated-Intelligence-Lab/canonical_sets).

Keywords: algorithmic fairness · bias detection · discrimination · generative models

We thank Arne Vanhoyweghen, Brecht Verbeken, and Bert Verbruggen for stimulating discussions and feedback on earlier drafts of this work. This project benefited from financial support from Innoviris. Any remaining errors or shortcomings are those of the authors.

L. Longo (Ed.): xAI 2023, CCIS 1903, pp. 346–367, 2023.
https://doi.org/10.1007/978-3-031-44070-0_18

1   Introduction

The increasing use of Artificial Intelligence (AI) algorithms in (semi–)automated decision–making processes has raised concerns about harmful and discriminatory decision patterns observed in contexts such as healthcare [30,43], education [34], and hiring [12,46]. In these cases, the algorithmic decisions discriminate against people based on (legally) protected features, including gender, age, and ethnicity [32]. Often, the very detection of discrimination is difficult because protected characteristics are encoded in so–called proxies. Proxy discrimination is especially prevalent in the era of big data, where algorithms can reconstruct many protected features from non–protected data [7]. In this paper, we address this challenge by developing a fairness evaluation method that reveals an algorithm's desired feature values for a given outcome. Our method exposes proxies that embed potential unethical biases and enhances transparency in the algorithm's decision–making process.

Algorithmic discrimination can be direct or indirect [6]. Indirect discrimination focuses on the impact of a given decision on a protected group. Within US law, this is often labeled "disparate impact". While algorithmic decision–making tools have been shown to frequently put members of particular social groups at a disadvantage [6], indirect discrimination can often be justified as being a proportionate means of achieving a legitimate goal (e.g., in hiring decisions) [1]. Direct discrimination, on the other hand, focuses not so much on the impacts but on the *reasons* behind a given decision. In other words, a person not being hired because of their belonging to a particular social group would constitute a case of direct discrimination. While direct discrimination is illegal both under EU and US law[1], cases of direct discrimination often go unchallenged due to the difficulty of establishing a causal link between protected characteristics and decision outcomes. Within the context of algorithmic decision making, the direct discrimination doctrine is often translated into the requirement to abstain from using protected characteristics as input variables. In practice, however, such attempts of "fairness–through–unawareness" rarely work since protected features are often encoded through other features, giving rise to potential proxy discrimination [18].

Such proxy discrimination further exacerbates the challenge of establishing potential causal links between protected characteristics and less favorable decision outcomes. The identification of proxies and their relationship to protected characteristics is therefore crucial to identify cases of directly discriminating algorithms [1].

While proxy discrimination plays an important role for direct discrimination, it is more often considered in the context of indirect discrimination by algorithms [6,50]. Indirect discrimination has a strong focus on the *outcome* of a given decision (as opposed to the *reason* behind it) and so it more readily connects to the fairness literature's large focus on algorithmic outputs. The tra-

---

[1] Anti-discrimination law in the US speaks of "disparate treatment" which, while similar to direct discrimination, additionally requires there to be discriminatory intent [45].

ditional approach involves translating philosophical or political notions of group fairness into a statistical parity metric on the model's output [34].[2] However, output–based fairness evaluations of this kind have several shortcomings. First, many notions of group fairness are incompatible, except for highly constrained special cases [26]. Second, the problem of many fairness notions only worsens as there is often substantial philosophical disagreement on which ones are genuinely fair in each specific context [8]. Third, by reducing the evaluation to a single number, output–based metrics make it hard to verify the validity of the results and to understand exactly why the model is unfair [37]. Fourth, most output–based fairness evaluations make it difficult to detect intersectional discrimination as they are limited to a specific selection of protected features. This selection entails the risk of missing discrimination against people at the intersection of different protected features [11,27] or against groups that do not share a protected feature [9]. Finally, the computation of these parity metrics often depends on a benchmark data set that may be biased or unbalanced to some extent [33,42]. These shortcomings motivate the research on complementary fairness evaluation methods, which offer additional transparency into the sources of discrimination and are agnostic towards an a priori decision on the choice of protected features, as this is often case-dependent and policy–related [20].

In this paper, we build on the LUCID (Locating Unfairness through Canonical Inverse Design) method proposed by Mazijn et al. [36]. LUCID generates canonical inputs by performing gradient descent on the input space, revealing a trained model's desired input given a preferred output. The resulting canonical set contains valuable information about the model's mechanisms, i.e., which feature values are essential to obtain specific outputs. This allows us to expose potential unethical biases in its internal logic by inspecting the distribution of the protected features. Despite LUCID's appealing properties as a fairness evaluation method, the canonical sets generated by gradient–based inverse design have some critical shortcomings. First, while the canonical sets in their current form are specifically suitable for tabular data, they require differentiable models. LUCID thereby omits the class of tree–based models, which are very effective for tabular data [47]. Additionally, the current gradient–based approach may lead to non–realistic canonical inputs, and it is not straightforward to assess proxy or intersectional discrimination [14].

We present **LUCID–GAN**, which generates canonical inputs via a conditional generative model instead of gradient–based inverse design. LUCID–GAN generates canonical inputs conditional on the predictions of the model under fairness evaluation (see Fig. 1a). Using a conditional generative model has two clear benefits. First, we only require a set of (test) samples and corresponding predictions from the model under fairness evaluation, making it a model–agnostic approach. Second, LUCID–GAN generates realistic samples as defined by its objective function. Furthermore, the flexibility of LUCID–GAN is twofold. First,

---

[2] Note that we focus on notions of group fairness which are most commonly used in practice, while many other definitions of fairness exist, including individual and counterfactual fairness [16,28].

we can extend the canonical inputs with protected features that are not part of the input space of the model under fairness evaluation. Second, the categorical (one–hot encoded) features are part of the conditional vector in the generator, and we can thus condition the canonical inputs on specific feature values (e.g., setting "Male" for "sex"). The first flexibility allows us to assess proxy discrimination, and the second to explicitly check for sources of intersectional discrimination.

LUCID–GAN is an input–based fairness evaluation method which takes a somewhat reverse approach to the statistical output–based metrics. Instead of comparing the predictions, we compare the (protected) feature distributions corresponding to large positive and negative predictions. LUCID–GAN is agnostic towards an a priori decision on the definition of fairness and choice of protected features and instead provides results that suggest potential sources of discrimination [36]. One can then examine the resulting canonical sets from multiple points of view, which are often case–dependent and policy–related [20]. By learning the joint conditional distribution of the features on the model's predictions, LUCID–GAN generates a diverse set of realistic synthetic samples that get positive and negative outputs. Instead of a single number and focusing on a select number of protected features, we get an overview of the overall preferences of the model. We can detect combinations of feature values that often appear together (e.g., "White", "Male", "Married", and "Husband" in the UCI Adult data set), which gives us insights into the different channels of potential proxy discrimination [1].

While LUCID–GAN and output–based metrics may sometimes convey the same results, LUCID–GAN can shed light on the potential sources for the statistical disparities. This is crucial as enforcing statistical parity for the wrong reasons can actually harm the protected groups [13]. LUCID–GAN reveals a model's preferences for a specific output. In contrast, output–based metrics show the statistical disparities on a benchmark data set that may result from many unknown causes. Overall, we argue that both techniques can be part of the same toolbox as they yield different insights.

We provide a brief overview of the literature on algorithmic fairness, activation maximization, and generative models for tabular data in Sect. 2. In Sect. 3, we present LUCID–GAN and discuss how it solves LUCID's shortcomings. In Sect. 4, we show how to generate canonical sets via LUCID–GAN for various fairness evaluations, including direct, proxy, and intersectional discrimination, on the UCI Adult [15] and COMPAS [2] data sets. We find that LUCID–GAN is a valuable addition to the toolbox of algorithmic fairness evaluation, as it offers additional transparency into the sources of discrimination and is agnostic towards an a priori decision on the definition of fairness and choice of protected features.

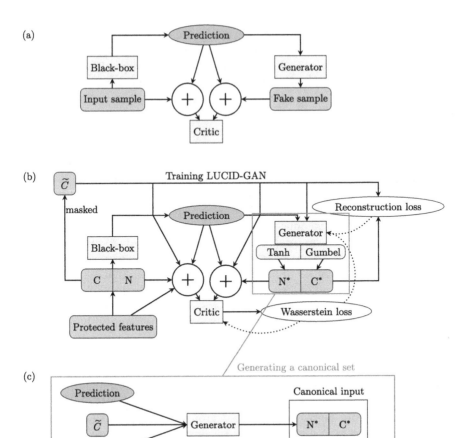

Fig. 1. The LUCID–GAN architecture. (a) High–level overview, (b) LUCID–GAN training mechanism, and (c) the details of the Generator. The input sample may consist of both numerical (N) and one–hot encoded (C) features, which may contain protected features that are not necessarily in the input space of the black–box model. The generator receives random noise, the black–box's predictions, and a masked version of C ($\widetilde{C}$) where only one category of a single one–hot encoded feature is still equal to one. The critic gets real samples from the data and synthetic samples from the generator, where N^* is generated via Tanh functions and C^* via Gumbel–Softmax functions. In addition, it also receives the black–box's predictions and $\widetilde{C}$ to check the validity of the sample. The critic is trained via the Wasserstein loss, while the generator also adds a reconstruction loss on C^* and $\widetilde{C}$. Note that if the protected features are not part of the black–box model's input space, we can still assess proxy discrimination by generating these features (as part of N^* or C^*) and concatenating them to the real samples (as part of N or C) given to the critic. We can use $\widetilde{C}$ to assess cases of intersectional discrimination by generating canonical inputs conditional on fixed values for protected features, such as setting "Male" for "Sex".

2   Background and Related Work

The development of LUCID–GAN to expose unethical biases in a model's internal logic connects ideas from the literature on algorithmic fairness, activation maximization using generative models, and recent advancements in GANs (Generative Adversarial Networks) for tabular data. We discuss these different fields below.

2.1   Algorithmic Fairness

The inherent ambiguity of viewing the concept of fairness spurred the development of many fairness notions, with over 19 widely accepted definitions [34]. Most group fairness notions focus on the equality of outcome by computing statistical parity metrics on a model's output. The two most prominent examples of these statistical output–based metrics are Demographic Parity (DP) and Equality Of Opportunity (EOP) [6]. In DP, we compare the Positivity Rate (PR) of the subpopulations under fairness evaluation, and in EOP, we compare the True Positive Rate (TPR). The choice between DP and EOP entirely depends on the underlying assumptions and worldview of the evaluator [19]. Indeed, even among those two most widely used metrics, substantial philosophical disagreement exists on which one is genuinely fair in each specific context [8]. Moreover, they are incompatible, except for highly constrained special cases [26], and it has been empirically shown that inherent trade–offs exist in many practical situations [35].

In addition, these statistical output–based metrics may suffer from sampling bias and variance as they depend on a benchmark data set [33]. By reducing the fairness evaluation to a single number, it is hard to verify the validity of the results and to understand exactly why the model is unfair. To enhance the transparency of the statistical parity metrics, there is a strong interaction between output–based fairness evaluations and interpretability methods [37]. However, there are many trade–offs and the interpretability methods themselves may suffer from unethical biases [5, 25, 49]. Finally, there is also the selection of protected attributes, which may lead to missing cases of intersectional discrimination, also known as fairness gerrymandering [24]. We argue that LUCID–GAN counters many of these shortcomings by offering additional transparency into the sources of discrimination and being agnostic towards an a priori decision on the definition of fairness and choice of protected features.

2.2   Activation Maximization

Performing gradient descent on the input space generates canonical inputs that maximize a specific output activation [48]. However, this gradient–based inverse design approach often leads to unrealistic inputs that obtain a high–confidence score on a specific class. These so–called fool inputs result from discriminative models allocating large areas of high confidence, often much larger than the area occupied by training samples for that class [41]. To avoid the generation of fool inputs, Nguyen et al. [39,40] perform gradient descent in the latent space of a generator network to maximize the output activation in a separate discriminative model. Finally, Odena et al. [44] and Zhou et al. [53] train an Auxiliary Classifier GAN (AC–GAN) and Activation Maximization GAN (AM–GAN) to maximize the activation of its label in an auxiliary classifier.

Two important distinctions exist with our application of LUCID–GAN on fairness and tabular data. First, our goal is to generate realistic canonical inputs for any black–box model's predictions, not to stabilize the training of the GAN. Moreover, note that the AC– and AM–GAN require access to a differentiable model, which we avoid using a Conditional GAN (CGAN) [38]. Second, most previous methods focus on images, where the resulting canonical inputs are individually interpretable and difficult to aggregate [29]. In contrast, we infer the overall fairness of a model from the feature distributions by generating a set of canonical inputs.

2.3   Tabular GAN

The use of GANs (Generative Adversarial Networks) [21] for tabular data concerns specific challenges, such as mixed data types, non–Gaussian and multi-modal distributions, and sparse and highly imbalanced categorical features [10]. To deal with mixed data types, i.e., numerical and one–hot encoded features, different types of output activation functions are used in the generator. For the numerical features, the hyperbolic tangent function (Tanh) is combined with a min–max normalization as a pre–processing step. However, this does not address the non–Gaussian and multimodal distributions. Therefore, Xu et al. [51] propose a Conditional Tabular GAN (CTGAN) with mode–specific (min–max) normalization by using a variational Gaussian mixture model. For the categorical features, the Gumbel–Softmax function is used to make the softmax operation in the generator differentiable [23]. To handle the sparse and highly imbalanced categorical features, Xu et al. [51] provide a conditional vector to the generator in the form of a masked version of the one–hot encoded features where only one category of a single one–hot encoded feature is still equal to one, and apply a reconstruction loss to the synthetic sample and the masked vector of the selected one–hot encoded feature. They further propose a training-by-sampling technique where the masked one–hot encoded feature is randomly sampled, and its category is sampled from the empirical log–frequency distribution.

The masked vector can be used to control the generation process similarly to the CGAN framework [38]. For example, [17] use the masked vector to oversample specific categories in an imbalanced learning problem. Zhao et al. [52] also add the components of the variational Gaussian mixture model to the masked vector to accommodate features with strict upper and lower bounds, e.g., an income of exactly zero. We continue the work on CTGAN by extending the conditional vector of the generator in LUCID–GAN with the black–box model's predictions, which are continuous values that are not part of the synthetic sample, and examining its interaction with the masked vector.

3 LUCID–GAN

We present LUCID–GAN to expose unethical biases in a model's internal logic by generating canonical inputs. First, we discuss LUCID and the canonical sets as proposed by Mazijn et al. [36]. Then, we introduce LUCID–GAN and show how to generate canonical sets.

3.1 LUCID

Shortcomings in the existing output–based group fairness metrics have spurred the research on complementary fairness evaluation methods, which offer additional transparency into the sources of discrimination and are agnostic towards an a priori decision on the definition of fairness and choice of protected features, as this is often case–dependent and policy–related [20]. In this spirit, Mazijn et al. [36] propose LUCID, and introduce the notion of a canonical set that allows to evaluate the fairness of a model's decision-making processes. Through gradient-based inverse design, LUCID generates canonical inputs, which can be considered the desired input given a preferred output for a trained model. By repeatedly generating canonical inputs, the resulting canonical set reveals which feature values are essential to obtain specific outputs. This allows for exposing potential unethical biases in the model's internal logic by inspecting the distribution of the protected features. In contrast to output metrics, there is no need for a specific fairness metric, a ground truth, or a benchmark data set.

Following Mazijn et al. [36], we use LUCID to generate a canonical set for a trained binary classifier.[3] First, we draw an extensive set of randomly initialized input samples from a uniform distribution. Then, we transform these random input samples into canonical inputs through gradient–based inverse design. Each subsequent transformation results from minimizing the (cross–entropy) loss between the model prediction and the preferred output (e.g., a loan is granted) until the model's prediction is close to its maximum (a predicted probability of 1 in this case). Note that we keep the model parameters fixed throughout the entire procedure. Finally, we inspect the distribution of each protected feature within the canonical set and compare it to the initial random distribution. Several design considerations impact the resulting canonical set, such as the initialization, choice of hyperparameters, and pre- and post–processing of categorical features. Besides these practical considerations, LUCID has some critical shortcomings, such as the requirement of differentiable models, unrealistic canonical inputs, and difficulties in assessing proxy and intersectional discrimination, which we solve by introducing LUCID–GAN.

---

[3] We use the same implementation and default values for the hyperparameters as LUCID. For more details see Mazijn et al. [36]. The code for LUCID is available at: https://github.com/Integrated-Intelligence-Lab/canonical_sets.

3.2 Specifications of LUCID–GAN

LUCID–GAN builds upon the CTGAN [51] framework. In the class of GANs, a generative model is trained through an adversarial process with a critic model (see Fig. 1a). The former aims to create synthetic samples from random noise that fool the latter into judging them as real. Besides the random noise, we provide a conditional vector to the generator, which allows us to control the generation process to some extent [38]. The CTGAN uses a Wasserstein GAN with gradient penalty (WGAN–GP) to prevent common problems in training GAN models, such as mode–dropping, vanishing gradients, and non–convergence [3,4,22]. Xu et al. [51] further propose stabilizing training by following PacGAN [31] and packaging multiple samples together in the critic. Both the generator and the critic consist of fully–connected hidden layers. In the generator, we use batch normalization, ReLU functions, and residual connections on each hidden layer. In the critic, we use leaky ReLU functions and dropout.[4]

3.3 Training LUCID–GAN

The generator in LUCID–GAN generates canonical inputs conditional on the predictions of the black–box under fairness evaluation (see Fig. 1b). The black–box's input samples may consist of both numerical (N) and one–hot encoded (C) features. Both N and C may contain protected features that are not necessarily in the black–box's input space for models which do not directly discriminate against specific features. The numerical features N are pre–processed via mode–specific min–max normalization using a variational Gaussian mixture model, and the categorical features C are one–hot encoded. Note that the processing of the samples for the training of the black–box model and LUCID–GAN does not need to be similar. For example, many tree–based models do not require the one–hot encoding of categorical features.

The generator receives noise which is drawn from a standard normal distribution, and a conditional vector containing the black–box's predictions and a masked version of C ($\widetilde{C}$) where only one category of a single one–hot encoded feature is equal to one. The critic gets real samples from the data and synthetic samples from the generator, where N^* is generated via Tanh functions and C^* via Gumbel–Softmax functions.[5] In addition, it also receives the black–box's predictions and $\widetilde{C}$ to check the validity of the sample.

We use $\widetilde{C}$ to handle the sparse and highly imbalanced categorical features via a training–by–sampling technique. It is constructed by randomly sampling a one–hot encoded feature, and subsequently sampling a category from the empirical

---

[4] We use the same implementation and default values for the hyperparameters as CTGAN. For more details see Xu et al. [51]. The code for CTGAN is available at: https://github.com/sdv-dev/CTGAN.

[5] The generator also outputs the components of the variational Gaussian mixture model for each numerical feature as a one–hot encoded vector. The components are part of the input for the critic to address the non–Gaussian and multimodal distributions. They are further used to reverse the mode–specific min–max normalization.

log–frequency distribution.[6] All the others values are set to zero. To enforce the generator to generate the sampled category in $\widetilde{C}$, we apply a reconstruction loss to C^* and $\widetilde{C}$. To ensure the validity of the conditional vector, we pick the prediction corresponding to the sample from the empirical distribution. After training, we can use $\widetilde{C}$ to generate canonical inputs conditional on fixed values for a single category, such as setting "Male" for "Sex".

The critic is trained via the Wasserstein loss, while the generator also adds the reconstruction loss. The reconstruction loss is the cross–entropy between the sampled one–hot encoded feature and its synthetic counterpart in C^*. The cross–entropy is only computed on a single one–hot encoded feature, which forces the generator to replicate this condition in the synthetic sample.

3.4   Generating Canonical Sets with LUCID–GAN

After training, we use the generator of LUCID–GAN to generate canonical inputs (see Fig. 1c). Similar to the CGAN framework [38], we can use the conditional vector to control the generation process. Indeed, setting the prediction in the conditional vector to a specific value corresponds to maximizing the output activation via gradient descent. For example, in the case of a binary classifier, we can generate a canonical set that reveals the preferred output for receiving a "positive" and "negative" decision by setting the prediction in the conditional vector equal to a predicted probability of 1 and 0, respectively. Instead of comparing the predictions, we compare the (protected) feature distributions corresponding to large positive and negative predictions.

Using a generative model has the benefits of working for any black–box model and generating realistic synthetic samples. Note that if the protected features are not part of the black–box model's input space, we can still assess proxy discrimination by generating these features (as part of N^* or C^*) and concatenating them to the real samples (as part of N or C) given to the critic. We use $\widetilde{C}$ to assess intersectional discrimination by generating canonical inputs conditional on fixed values for protected features, such as setting "Male" for "Sex". This allows us to compare feature distributions for many possible scenarios where otherwise, data would be scarce, and the estimates of output–based metrics would be unreliable [33].

---

[6] For example, let $C_1 = [a, b]$ and $C_2 = [c, d, e]$ be two one–hot encoded features with a possible empirical sample $C = [C_1, C_2] = [0, 1, 0, 0, 1]$, wherein the first one–hot encoded feature we observe the second category b, and in the second one–hot encoded feature the third category e. We construct a masked version of C by first randomly selecting either C_1 or C_2, and then by sampling a category from their respective empirical log–frequency distribution. A potentially masked version of C could be $\widetilde{C} = [1, 0, 0, 0, 0]$ where the first category a of the first one–hot encoded feature C_1 is sampled.

4 Experiments and Discussion

We show how to generate canonical sets via LUCID–GAN for various fairness evaluations, including direct, proxy, and intersectional discrimination, on the UCI Adult [15] and COMPAS [2] data sets. In the UCI Adult data set, we predict if a person earns more or less than $50,000 per year, with more being the preferred output. For COMPAS, the task is to predict if a person will commit recidivism in the next two years, with no recidivism being the preferred output as the person can be released on bail. For both data sets, we consider "Race" and "Sex" to be the (legally) protected features, and for UCI Adult we also consider "Marital Status" and "Relationship". The UCI Adult data set has a fixed test set, while for the COMPAS data set, we sample 20% from the training data as the test set. The samples and predictions of the test set are also used to train LUCID–GAN and to compute the statistical output–based metrics DP and EOP.

We compare LUCID–GAN with LUCID and the statistical output–based metrics DP and EOP (by comparing the TP and TPR, respectively) for the case of direct discrimination (see Fig. 2 and Table 1). We further demonstrate how to apply LUCID–GAN to the cases of proxy (See Fig. 3) and intersectional (see Fig. 4) discrimination. As LUCID only works for differentiable models and DP and EOP are often used for binary classification tasks, we use binary fully-connected neural network classifiers. For LUCID–GAN, the extension to other black–box classifiers is trivial, as it only requires samples and their corresponding predictions, making it a model–agnostic approach.

The classifiers consist of hidden layers with ReLU activation functions and a softmax output layer with two output nodes. The number of hidden layers and nodes is decided by the accuracy on a validation set (20% from the training set) which is 83.9% for UCI Adult and 64.0% for COMPAS. This performance is in line with the standard benchmarks. We choose this standard architecture as the point of this experiment is not to achieve state–of–the–art performance but to demonstrate the capabilities of LUCID–GAN, which does not depend on the quality of the underlying model. Note that the computational complexity of LUCID–GAN lies in the training of the generator and the critic, which for our experiments was only a matter of minutes on a consumer CPU. After training, the generation of canonical inputs for various fairness evaluations is done via single forward passes through the generator.

4.1 Direct Discrimination

We compare LUCID–GAN with LUCID and the statistical output–based metrics DP and EOP (by comparing the disparities between TP and TPR, respectively) for the case of direct discrimination (see Fig. 2 and Table 1). After the classifiers are trained, we train LUCID–GAN on the test set and then generate 1000 synthetic samples for a positive and negative output (i.e., a predicted probability of 1 and 0, respectively). We refer to them as the positive and negative canonical sets. Note that we require no access to the training data and treat the underlying classifier as a black–box. For LUCID, we also generate 1000 synthetic samples for a positive output starting from an initial random uniform distribution (see also Appendix A). Finally, we compute the TP and TPR of all the subpopulations for the protected features. A disparity between these metrics indicates potential discrimination towards the group with lower values.

We locate unfairness in the model's decision–making process with LUCID–GAN by comparing the feature distributions of the positive and negative canonical sets. Only inspecting the feature distributions of either the positive or negative canonical set can lead to misleading results, as the generator is trained to mimic the underlying distribution of its training samples. For example, in both the UCI Adult and COMPAS data sets, more samples correspond to the "Male" category than the "Female" category for the feature "Sex" which results in more males in both the positive and negative canonical sets.

While the results in our experiments are quite clear on visual inspection and the data sets are not high–dimensional, this may not always be the case, and presenting the results as such can be unfeasible and ambiguous. In that case, we suggest using distance metrics, such as the Wasserstein or Jensen–Shannon distance. However, computing these metrics yields no additional insights into our experiments.

In Fig. 2, we see that LUCID–GAN generates more realistic canonical inputs than LUCID. The most prominent examples are the continuous features, where LUCID often generates unrealistic values while LUCID–GAN generates feature distributions that closely match the expected empirical distributions. For example, in the feature "Education Level" of the UCI Adult data set, we see a spike in high–school graduates (9 years), bachelors (13 years), and masters (14 years). The realism is a result of the adversarial process where the critic ensures that the generator outputs a diverse set of synthetic samples which look similar to the training samples. The realism also seems to lead to more outspokenness in LUCID–GAN's canonical inputs for at least two reasons. First, the synthetic samples must respect all the dependencies between the features. For example, the combination of "Male", "Husband", and "Married" is a strongly preferred sample in LUCID–GAN's positive canonical set. The strong co–occurrence of these feature values may indicate a potential for proxy discrimination. Second, it may be easier for LUCID to change the continuous features than the categories, as a small change in categorical features does not make any difference after post–processing. Any change in the continuous features remains, while the categories need to shift from one category to another due to the one–hot encoding.

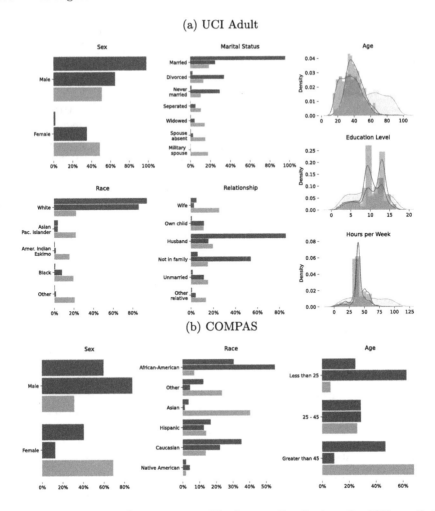

Fig. 2. Locating direct discrimination. The feature distributions for 1000 synthetic samples are shown for the positive and negative outputs in LUCID–GAN (dark blue and dark red, respectively) and positive outputs in LUCID (light green). For the UCI Adult data set, we show the protected features "Sex", "Race", "Marital Status" and "Relationship". We further show the features "Age", "Education Level", and "Hours per Week". For the COMPAS data set, we show the protected features "Sex" and "Race". We further show "Age", which is a categorical feature. Note that to interpret the results of LUCID–GAN, we need to compare the positive and negative canonical sets, while for LUCID we can compare the positive canonical set with an initial random uniform distribution (see also Appendix A). Only inspecting the feature distributions of either the positive or negative canonical set of LUCID–GAN can lead to misleading results as the generator is trained to mimic the underlying distribution of its training samples. (Color figure online)

In Table 1, we see that the DP and EOP disparities do not always point to the same conclusions. For example, the disparity between the PR of "Male" and "Female" indicates a violation of DP, while their TPRs indicate that there is

Table 1. Positivity Rate (PR) and True Positive Rate (TPR) of the subpopulations for the protected features in UCI Adult and COMPAS.

UCI ADULT						
Sex	MALE	FEMALE				
PR	31.0	11.3				
TPR	73.0	72.3				
		ASIAN PAC.	AMER. INDIAN			
Race	WHITE	ISLANDER	ESKIMO	BLACK	OTHER	
PR	26.0	29.7	12.8	11.9	19.7	
TPR	73.2	72.8	66.7	64.9	77.8	
Relationship	WIFE	OWN CHILD	HUSBAND	NOT IN FAMILY	OTHER RELATIVES	UNMARRIED
PR	47.0	1.9	45.6	10.2	3.3	5.6
TPR	71.0	100.0	72.8	78.7	100.0	81.8
			NEVER			SPOUSE / MILITARY
Marital Status	MARRIED	DIVORCED	MARRIED	SEPARATED	WIDOWED	ABSENT / SPOUSE
PR	45.3	9.7	4.7	7.0	9.1	12.6 / 36.4
TPR	72.6	75.0	86.2	55.6	85.7	100.0 / 80.0

COMPAS						
Sex	MALE	FEMALE				
PR	53.6	62.7				
TPR	39.4	38.9				
	AFRICAN				NATIVE	
Race	AMERICAN	ASIAN	CAUCASIAN	HISPANIC	AMERICAN	OTHER
PR	49.2	71.4	61.9	62.5	60.0	54.0
TPR	37.6	0.00	41.9	52.0	60.0	25.0

EOP for both the UCI Adult and COMPAS data sets. Additionally, many categories, including "Military Spouse" in the UCI Adult data set and "Asian" in the COMPAS data set, do not contain sufficient data points to make any conclusions [33]. Finally, the output–based metrics do not give any insights into the actual drivers of the unfairness. There are some notable differences between the output–based metrics and LUCID–GAN. For example, in the UCI Adult data set, the DP metric indicates that "Wife" is the preferred group in the "Relationship" feature. In contrast, the canonical sets indicate a strong preference for "Husband".

4.2   Proxy Discrimination

We retrain the models without the protected features "Race" and "Sex" and obtain a similar accuracy on the test set. We then generate a positive and negative canonical set including the left–out protected features, by generating these features (as part of C^*) and concatenating them to the real samples (as part of C) given to the critic. LUCID–GAN now receives predictions from the black–box model, which does not have "Race" and "Sex" in its input space. For the UCI Adult data set, we keep the protected features "Marital Status" and "Relationship" and assume that there are no protected features left in the COMPAS data set. For the PR and TPR, we obtain similar scores as for direct discrimination and therefore refer to Table 1 for a comparison. This confirms many previous

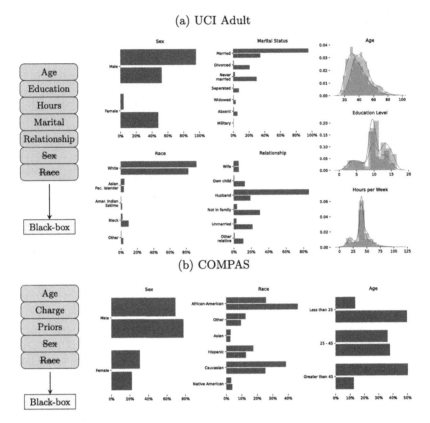

Fig. 3. Locating proxy discrimination. The feature distributions for 1000 synthetic samples are shown for the positive and negative outputs in LUCID–GAN (dark blue and dark red, respectively). For the UCI Adult data set, we show the protected features "Sex", "Race", "Marital Status" and "Relationship". We further show the features "Age", "Education Level", and "Hours per Week". For the COMPAS data set, we show the protected features "Sex" and "Race". We further show the feature "Age". Note that to interpret the results of LUCID–GAN, we need to compare the positive and negative canonical sets. Only inspecting the feature distributions of either the positive or negative canonical set of LUCID–GAN can lead to misleading results as the generator is trained to mimic the underlying distribution of its training samples. (Color figure online)

findings that removing the protected attributes does not generally improve the disparity in the statistical output–based metrics [16].

By comparing the canonical sets from the case of proxy discrimination (see Fig. 3) with those of direct discrimination (see Fig. 2), we see that there are some notable differences (see also Appendix B). For example, in the COMPAS data set, the disparity between "Male" and "Female" in the positive and negative canonical sets has almost entirely disappeared. At the same time, the relative values in the "Race" feature remain mostly unchanged. This may indicate that the previous black–box model was directly discriminating based on "Sex", while the discrimination against "Race" is a combination of both direct and proxy discrimination. For the UCI Adult data set, we find that the discrimination against "Sex" and "Race" remains. This may result from the strong dependencies between many features, such as "White", "Male", "Married", and "Husband".

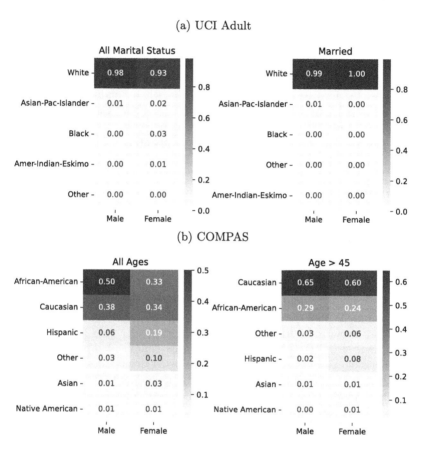

(a) UCI Adult

(b) COMPAS

Fig. 4. Locating intersectional discrimination. The percentage–wise amount of men and women per "Race" category which receive a positive output is shown for 1000 synthetic samples where "Sex" is fixed as "Male" and "Female", respectively. Additionally, for the UCI Adult data set, we show the percentage–wise amount of men and women per "Race" category which receive a positive output when the "Marital Status" is fixed as "Married", and for the COMPAS data set, when "Age" is fixed as ">45".

4.3   Intersectional Discrimination

We use the original models from the direct discrimination evaluation with the protected features "Race" and "Sex" included. In this intersectional discrimination evaluation, we generate 1000 positive canonical inputs where we keep "Sex" fixed as "Male" and 1000 positive inputs where we keep "Sex" fixed as

"Female" by using $\widetilde{C}$ in the conditional vector. Additionally, for the UCI Adult data set, we generate 1000 positive canonical inputs where we also keep "Marital Status" fixed as "Married", and for the COMPAS data set, we keep "Age" fixed as ">45". We show in each case percentage–wise the amount of men and women per "Race" category which receive a positive output (see Fig. 4). On the heat maps, we show a two– and three–dimensional representation of the frequency of protected features at various intersections. For the UCI Adult data set, we find potential discrimination against women conditional on being "White", which entirely disappears if we add the condition of "Married". For the COMPAS data set, we see indications of bias toward women conditional on being "Caucasian" and "African-American". Additionally, when conditioning on "> 45" the number of positive outputs is considerably larger for "Caucasian" compared to "Hispanic" and "African-American". We believe that these heat maps are an ideal method for tracing potential sources of intersectional discrimination, especially when data samples are scarce.

5   Conclusion

The increasing use of Artificial Intelligence (AI) algorithms in (semi–)automated decision–making processes has raised concerns about discriminatory decision patterns. The literature on algorithmic fairness has primarily focused on defining unfairness and eliminating unethical biases, while recent efforts focus on rigorously detecting it. A recent proposal in this direction is LUCID (Locating Unfairness through Canonical Inverse Design), which generates canonical sets by performing gradient descent on the input space, revealing a model's desired input given a preferred output.

We present LUCID–GAN, which generates canonical inputs via a conditional generative model instead of gradient–based inverse design. Using a conditional generative model has several benefits, including that it applies to non–differentiable models, ensures that a canonical set consists of realistic inputs, and allows us to assess proxy and intersectional discrimination. LUCID–GAN is an input–based fairness evaluation method which takes a somewhat reverse approach to the statistical output–based metrics. Instead of comparing the predictions, we compare the (protected) feature distributions corresponding to large positive and negative predictions. The resulting canonical sets contain valuable information about the model's mechanisms, i.e., which feature values are essential to obtain specific outputs. This allows us to expose potential unethical biases in its internal logic by inspecting the distribution of the protected features.

We show how to generate canonical sets via LUCID–GAN for various fairness evaluations, including direct, proxy, and intersectional discrimination, on the UCI Adult and COMPAS data sets. It allows for rigorously detecting unethical biases in black–box models without requiring access to the training data. Overall, we argue that LUCID–GAN is a valuable addition to the toolbox of algorithmic fairness evaluation, as it offers additional transparency into the sources of discrimination and is agnostic towards an a priori decision on the definition of fairness and choice of protected features.

A   LUCID

(See Fig. 5).

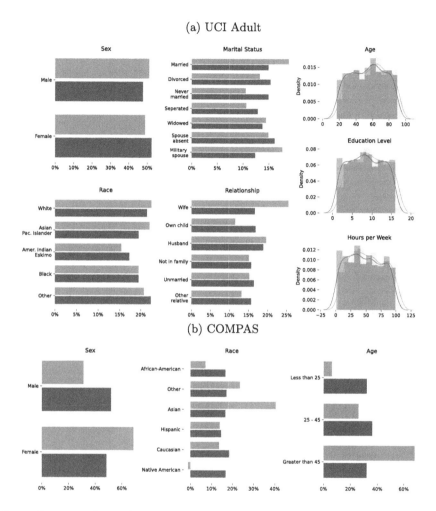

Fig. 5. Locating direct discrimination. The feature distributions for 1000 synthetic samples are shown for the positive outputs in LUCID (light green) starting from an initial random uniform distribution (dark blue). For the UCI Adult data set, we show the protected features "Sex", "Race", "Marital Status", and "Relationship". We further show the features "Age", "Education Level", and "Hours per Week". For the COMPAS data set, we show the protected features "Sex" and "Race". We further show the feature "Age". (Color figure online)

B   Comparing Direct and Proxy Discrimination

(See Fig. 6).

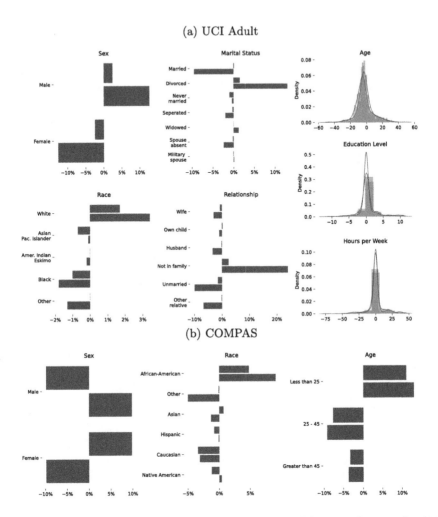

Fig. 6. The difference between the feature distributions of direct and proxy discrimination for the positive and negative outputs in LUCID–GAN (dark blue and dark red, respectively) are shown. For the UCI Adult data set, we show the protected features "Sex", "Race", "Marital Status", and "Relationship". We further show the features "Age", "Education Level", and "Hours per Week". For the COMPAS data set, we show the protected features "Sex" and "Race". We further show the feature "Age". A positive value indicates that the feature appears more frequently in the distribution of direct discrimination. (Color figure online)

References

1. Adams-Prassl, J., Binns, R., Kelly-Lyth, A.: Directly discriminatory algorithms. Mod. Law Rev. **86**(1), 144–175 (2023)
2. Angwin, J., Kirchner, L., Surya, M., Larson, J.: Machine Bias. There's software used across the country to predict future criminals. And it's biased against blacks. In: ProPublica (2016)
3. Arjovsky, M., Bottou, L.: Towards principled methods for training generative adversarial networks. In: International Conference on Learning Representations (2017)
4. Arjovsky, M., Chintala, S., Bottou, L.: Wasserstein generative adversarial networks. In: Proceedings of the 34th International Conference on Machine Learning (2017)
5. Balagopalan, A., Zhang, H., Hamidieh, K., Hartvigsen, T., Rudzicz, F., Ghassemi, M.: The road to explainability is paved with bias: measuring the fairness of explanations. In: Proceedings of the Conference on Fairness, Accountability, and Transparency (2022)
6. Barocas, S., Hardt, M., Narayanan, A.: Fairness and machine learning. fairmlbook.org (2019)
7. Barocas, S., Selbst, A.D.: Big data's disparate impact. Calif. Law Rev. **104**(3), 671–732 (2016)
8. Binns, R.: Fairness in machine learning: lessons from political philosophy. In: Proceedings of the Conference on Fairness, Accountability, and Transparency (2018)
9. Binns, R.: On the apparent conflict between individual and group fairness. In: Proceedings of the Conference on Fairness, Accountability, and Transparency (2020)
10. Borisov, V., Leemann, T., Seßler, K., Haug, J., Pawelczyk, M., Kasneci, G.: Deep neural networks and tabular data: a survey. arXiv preprint arXiv:2110.01889 (2021)
11. Buolamwini, J., Gebru, T.: Gender shades: intersectional accuracy disparities in commercial gender classification. In: Proceedings of the Conference on Fairness, Accountability, and Transparency (2018)
12. Chen, L., Ma, R., Hannák, A., Wilson, C.: Investigating the impact of gender on rank in resume search engines. In: Proceedings of the CHI Conference on Human Factors in Computing Systems (2018)
13. Corbett-Davies, S., Goel, S.: The measure and mismeasure of fairness: a critical review of fair machine learning. arXiv preprint arXiv:1808.00023 (2018)
14. Crenshaw, K.: Mapping the margins: intersectionality, identity politics, and violence against women of color. Stanford Law Rev. **43**(6), 1241–1299 (1991)
15. Dua, D., Graff, C.: UCI machine learning repository (2017)
16. Dwork, C., Hardt, M., Pitassi, T., Reingold, O., Zemel, R.: Fairness through awareness. In: Proceedings of the 3rd Innovations in Theoretical Computer Science Conference (2012)
17. Engelmann, J., Lessmann, S.: Conditional Wasserstein GAN-based oversampling of tabular data for imbalanced learning. Expert Syst. Appl. **174**, 114582 (2021)
18. Fazelpour, S., Danks, D.: Algorithmic bias: senses, sources, solutions. Philos Compass **16**(8), e12760 (2021)
19. Friedler, S.A., Scheidegger, C., Venkatasubramanian, S.: On the (im) possibility of fairness. arXiv preprint arXiv:1609.07236 (2016)
20. Goethals, S., Martens, D., Calders, T.: PreCoF: Counterfactual explanations for fairness. Working paper (2022)
21. Goodfellow, I., et al.: Generative adversarial nets. In: Advances in Neural Information Processing Systems (2014)

22. Gulrajani, I., Ahmed, F., Arjovsky, M., Dumoulin, V., Courville, A.C.: Improved training of Wasserstein GANs. In: Advances in Neural Information Processing Systems (2017)
23. Jang, E., Gu, S., Poole, B.: Categorical reparameterization with gumbel-softmax. In: International Conference on Learning Representations (2017)
24. Kearns, M., Neel, S., Roth, A., Wu, Z.S.: Preventing fairness gerrymandering: auditing and learning for subgroup fairness. In: Proceedings of the 35th International Conference on Machine Learning (2018)
25. Kleinberg, J., Mullainathan, S.: Simplicity creates inequity: implications for fairness, stereotypes, and interpretability. In: Proceedings of the ACM Conference on Economics and Computation (2019)
26. Kleinberg, J., Mullainathan, S., Raghavan, M.: Inherent trade-offs in the fair determination of risk scores. arXiv preprint arXiv:1609.05807 (2016)
27. Kong, Y.: Are "intersectionally fair" AI algorithms really fair to women of color? A philosophical analysis. In: Proceedings of the Conference on Fairness, Accountability, and Transparency (2022)
28. Kusner, M.J., Loftus, J., Russell, C., Silva, R.: Counterfactual fairness. In: Advances in Neural Information Processing Systems (2017)
29. Lang, O., et al.: Explaining in style: training a GAN to explain a classifier in StyleSpace. In: Proceedings of the IEEE/CVF International Conference on Computer Vision (2021)
30. Ledford, H.: Millions of black people affected by racial bias in health-care algorithms. Nature 574(7780), 608–610 (2019)
31. Lin, Z., Khetan, A., Fanti, G., Oh, S.: PacGAN: the power of two samples in generative adversarial networks. In: Advances in Neural Information Processing Systems (2018)
32. Lindholm, M., Richman, R., Tsanakas, A., Wüthrich, M.: Discrimination-free insurance pricing. ASTIN Bull. 52(1), 55–89 (2022)
33. Lum, K., Zhang, Y., Bower, A.: De-biasing "bias" measurement. In: Proceedings of the Conference on Fairness, Accountability, and Transparency (2022)
34. Makhlouf, K., Zhioua, S., Palamidessi, C.: On the applicability of machine learning fairness notions. ACM SIGKDD Explor. Newsl. 23(1), 14–23 (2021)
35. Mazijn, C., Danckaert, J., Ginis, V.: How do the score distributions of subpopulations influence fairness notions? In: Proceedings of the 2021 AAAI/ACM Conference on AI, Ethics, and Society (2021)
36. Mazijn, C., Prunkl, C., Algaba, A., Danckaert, J., Ginis, V.: LUCID: exposing algorithmic bias through inverse design. In: Proceedings of the 37th AAAI Conference on Artificial Intelligence (2023)
37. Meng, C., Trinh, L., Xu, N., Enouen, J., Liu, Y.: Interpretability and fairness evaluation of deep learning models on MIMIC-IV dataset. Sci. Rep. 12, 7166 (2022)
38. Mirza, M., Osindero, S.: Conditional generative adversarial nets. arXiv preprint arXiv:1411.1784 (2014)
39. Nguyen, A., Clune, J., Bengio, Y., Dosovitskiy, A., Yosinski, J.: Plug & play generative networks: conditional iterative generation of images in latent space. In: Proceedings of the IEEE Conference on Computer Vision and Pattern Recognition (2017)
40. Nguyen, A., Dosovitskiy, A., Yosinski, J., Brox, T., Clune, J.: Synthesizing the preferred inputs for neurons in neural networks via deep generator networks. In: Advances in Neural Information Processing Systems (2016)

41. Nguyen, A., Yosinski, J., Clune, J.: Deep neural networks are easily fooled: high confidence predictions for unrecognizable images. In: Proceedings of the IEEE Conference on Computer Vision and Pattern Recognition (2015)
42. Northcutt, C.G., Athalye, A., Mueller, J.: Pervasive label errors in test sets destabilize machine learning benchmarks. In: Advances in Neural Information Processing Systems Track on Datasets and Benchmark (2021)
43. Obermeyer, Z., Powers, B., Vogeli, C., Mullainathan, S.: Dissecting racial bias in an algorithm used to manage the health of populations. Science **366**(6464), 447–453 (2019)
44. Odena, A., Olah, C., Shlens, J.: Conditional image synthesis with auxiliary classifier GANs. In: Proceedings of the 34th International Conference on Machine Learning (2017)
45. Prince, A.E., Schwarcz, D.: Proxy discrimination in the age of artificial intelligence and big data. Iowa Law Rev. **105**, 1257–1318 (2019)
46. Raghavan, M., Barocas, S., Kleinberg, J., Levy, K.: Mitigating bias in algorithmic hiring: evaluating claims and practices. In: Proceedings of the Conference on Fairness, Accountability, and Transparency (2020)
47. Shwartz-Ziv, R., Armon, A.: Tabular data: deep learning is not all you need. Inf. Fusion **81**, 84–90 (2022)
48. Simonyan, K., Vedaldi, A., Zisserman, A.: Deep inside convolutional networks: visualising image classification models and saliency maps. In: Workshop at International Conference on Learning Representations (2014)
49. Slack, D., Hilgard, S., Jia, E., Singh, S., Lakkaraju, H.: Fooling LIME and SHAP: adversarial attacks on post hoc explanation methods. In: Proceedings of the AAAI/ACM Conference on AI, Ethics, and Society (2020)
50. Wachter, S., Mittelstadt, B., Russell, C.: Why fairness cannot be automated: Bridging the gap between EU non-discrimination law and AI. Comput. Law Secur. Rev. **41**, 105567 (2021)
51. Xu, L., Skoularidou, M., Cuesta-Infante, A., Veeramachaneni, K.: Modeling tabular data using conditional GAN. In: Advances in Neural Information Processing Systems (2019)
52. Zhao, Z., Kunar, A., Birke, R., Chen, L.Y.: CTAB-GAN: effective table data synthesizing. In: Proceedings of The 13th Asian Conference on Machine Learning (2021)
53. Zhou, Z., et al.: Activation maximization generative adversarial nets. In: Proceedings of the 35th International Conference on Learning Representations (2018)

Explainable and Interpretable AI with Argumentation, Representational Learning and Concept Extraction for xAI

Explainable Machine Learning
via Argumentation

Nicoletta Prentzas[1]([⊠]), Constantinos Pattichis[1,2], and Antonis Kakas[1]

[1] University of Cyprus, 1 Panepistimiou Avenue, 2109 Nicosia, Cyprus
`nicolep@ucy.ac.cy`
[2] CYENS Centre of Excellence, 23 Dimarchou Lellou Demetriadi, 1016 Nicosia, Cyprus

Abstract. This paper presents a general Explainable Machine Learning framework and methodology based on Argumentation (ArgEML). The flexible reasoning form of argumentation in the face of unknown and incomplete information together with the direct link of argumentation to justification and explanation enables the development of a natural form of explainable machine learning. In this form of learning the explanations are useful not only for supporting the final predictions but also play a significant role in the learning process itself. The paper defines the basic theoretical notions of ArgEML together with its main machine learning operators and method of application. It describes how such an argumentation-based approach can give a flexible way for learning that recognizes difficult cases (with respect to the current available training data) and separates these cases out not as definite predictive cases but as cases where it is more appropriate to explainably analyze the alternative predictions. Using the argumentation-based explanations we can partition the problem space into groups characterized by the basic argumentative tension between arguments for and against the alternatives. The paper presents a first evaluation of the approach by applying the ArgEML learning methodology both on artificial and on real-life datasets.

Keywords: Argumentation in Machine Learning · Explainable Machine Learning · Explainable Conflict Resolution

1 Introduction

As Artificial Intelligence (AI) systems become more autonomous the need for explainability of their decisions and/or actions becomes more important. Solutions without an explanation are for most problems difficult to accept and their usability would easily be questioned. The provision of an explanation for the behavior of the system becomes so important that it is prudent to consider AI systems as generators of explanations just as much as solution providers to a certain task. Given this central role of explanations it is then natural to consider how this would affect our general perspective on learning, where we would require that a learned structure encompasses and facilitates the generation of explanations and indeed, how the need for explanations would affect the learning process itself. How does the need for explanations lead us to re-consider some of the central notions that conventionally drive the machine learning process such as the notions of prediction, accuracy and utility of a learned structure?

L. Longo (Ed.): xAI 2023, CCIS 1903, pp. 371–398, 2023.
https://doi.org/10.1007/978-3-031-44070-0_19

One way to address these questions, is to consider the adoption of a process of reasoning that is closely connected to explanation and justification which could replace the procedural and rigid process of "firing rules" found within conventional machine learning frameworks. Such a case of a more flexible underlying reasoning process that is naturally connected to the notion of explanation but also to the process of constructing explanations is the case of Argumentation.

In this paper, we study how Argumentation can form the basis for a new framework for Explainable Machine Learning, called ArgEML. In the framework of ArgEML, argumentation will be used both as a naturally suitable target language for ML and explanations of the ML predictions as well as the foundation for new notions and metrics that drive the machine learning process. Argumentation offers flexible coverage and prediction notions that are appropriate in the context of learning, where the data from which we are learning may be incomplete and inadequate to reveal the full process or theory generating the data. The emphasis is shifted away from achieving optimal predictive accuracy to that of satisfactory or confident accuracy together with the recognition of difficult cases or subdomains of the problem where a definite prediction cannot be safely taken. Forcing a predictor to take a definite position in all cases including cases where the training data is not sufficiently informative for this can skew the result of the learning even for cases where the training data is sufficiently complete. Within the ArgEML learning process we aim to identify such difficult cases where instead of predicting a definite result the learned theory provides explanations that support several possible alternative predictions. These explanations can then guide us in actively seeking further data examples that would help resolve the dilemma and improve the quality of the learned theory.

The paper will present the basic theoretical notions of the proposed ArgEML framework together with its main machine learning operators and process of application. It will introduce new learning performance metrics that generalize and extend many of the standard metrics used in conventional machine learning and show how an iterative process of learning can be built using these new metrics. The main ArgEML learning methodology is a case of symbolic supervised learning. Importantly though, it can also be applied in a hybrid mode on top of other symbolic or non-symbolic learners that would generate an initial learning theory. Furthermore, using the argumentation-based explanations we can partition the problem space into subgroups characterized by the basic argumentative tension between arguments for and against the alternatives. The paper includes a first evaluation of the ArgEML framework and its learning methodology on artificially generated, as well as real-life, datasets.

1.1 Related Work

The close two-way link between Machine Learning for acquiring knowledge and Argumentation for reasoning with the acquired knowledge has been studied by several works. At the conceptual level, recently the works in [1, 2] argue for the suitability of Argumentation as a defeasible reasoning framework to be applied on the structures or theories resulting from Machine Learning. This connection is based on the simple observation that typically in the context of learning there is a high level of uncertainty in the available data and information and hence a flexible defeasible form of reasoning is warranted.

Both directions of connecting argumentation and ML have been explored. The survey paper of [3] gives a first glimpse of (most of) the landscape of work up to 2016. This survey concentrates more on an analysis of classifying the different works from a technical viewpoint of which particular argumentation framework and semantics each work is based on.

In the early work of [4], we can see how argumentation, with its natural connection to explain the classification of a training data point, can impact on the machine learning process. In this work, an Argumentation-Based Machine Learning (ABML) framework is proposed where standard machine learning methods have been extended to consider further given information about the arguments supporting or explaining the training data points. The approach has been shown [5, 6] to give encouraging results in the performance of ML in a variety of domains. Taking this idea further Concept Learning as Argumentation (CLA) [7] interprets some of the data points themselves as arguments, with premise the situation of the data point and claim the expected prediction. Such observational arguments are taken to be strong compared with arguments that result during the learning process and hence the acceptance of a final learned theory is decided through a dialectic argumentative reasoning process between these different types of arguments. On a similar line, the framework of Argumentation for Multi-Agent Inductive Concept Learning (MAICL) [8] considers subsets of data points and associates to each subset an argument, as the opinion of an agent, for the classification in this subset. Then by taking the corresponding arguments as the models learned by the agents and using argumentation the method aims to reconcile the different models that were learned by the agents, so that they can collectively decide on a prediction in a new situation.

Argumentation is a natural choice as the target language of learning since the task of learning can be viewed as that of uncovering the reasons for why we observe the classification of the training data as that given in the data. Under this perspective several works have studied how to learn argumentation frameworks, whether these are abstract frameworks, as in the case of [9–12], or structured frameworks as in [13–17]. Arguments produced through learning can be evaluated against existing expert arguments to guide the learning process. In the framework of Classification enhanced with Argumentation (CleAr) [18] a possible learned classification with the argument supporting it competes with expert opinion arguments using a scoring system on arguments that would then lead to a final decision. Similarly, in Machine Coaching [19] predictions and arguments supporting these from a learned model are judged by a coach who provides feedback, e.g. counter-arguments or relative strength between arguments, to help steer the learner.

Going beyond using argumentation as the target language of ML argumentation can also be used as a framework for learning explanations for the predictions of the ML system, particularly for opaque learned models. One line of work on this is to study how a neural-network learner at the internal level of its operation can be interpreted as an argumentation framework [20, 21]. Another and important line of work which lies directly along the line of Explainable AI (XAI) in Machine Learning, addresses the potential of using argumentation to provide post-hoc explainability for black-box (neural) learners. [22] show how we can compositionally feed a neural-network output into an external model both for enhancing the training of the network and for producing explainable network prediction. [23] extract rules from neural networks in an ensemble and then use argumentation methods to explain the output of the neural network. The framework of Deep Argumentative eXplanation (DAX) [24] studies how we can explain a neural-network learner by splitting this into smaller parts, using layers of arguments to understand each part and then to integrate these sub-explanations into an explanation for the whole system.

Our approach is motivated by several of the above works and aims to synthesize together different elements from the link between argumentation and learning. It aims to provide an integrated approach where several of the links of argumentation and learning are exploited, such as how argumentation as a defeasible form of reasoning motivates new evaluation metrics for the learning process and how argumentation can provide a framework for ante-hoc or post-hoc explainability for machine learners.

The rest of the paper is organized as follows. In Sect. 2, we review the basic notions of argumentation theory needed to formulate the ArgEML framework. In Sect. 3 we present the ArgEML framework together with the technical details of its learning algorithm and learning operators. Section 4 briefly describes the first version of an ArgEML system. Section 5 presents comparative results of the application of the ArgEML framework and system on three different datasets, one artificial, the IRIS standard dataset and a real-life dataset for diagnosing the possibility of stroke from medical images. Finally, Sect. 6 concludes and discusses future work.

2 Background

In this section we review the basic notions of argumentation that would help us develop a framework of *Explainable Prediction* suitable for machine learning. Specifically, the proposed framework of ArgEML relies on notions from the area of Computational Argumentation (CA) in AI (see e.g. [25, 26] and references therein) and methodologies [1, 27, 28] that link the theory of CA with its practical application. In CA there are several different variations of the basic notions and semantics of argumentation. We will choose a specific framework and semantics to work with. Other choices are equally possible as the framework of ArgEM at the conceptual and theoretical level is independent of the technical details of argumentation, but for the realization and implementation of the theoretical framework a specific choice is needed. Also due to lack of space, we will present here only the basic high-level definitions and notions of argumentation, referring the interested reader to [29, 30] for more technical details.

Our specific choice of argumentation framework for ArgEML is that of the structured argumentation framework of Gorgias [31, 32]. This is a logic-based preference argumentation framework. The Gorgias framework assumes that we have a *language*, L, in which positive or negative literal statements of the problem domain are made. In the language L we also have a notion of *conflict* between statements which contains at least the conflict between a positive statement and its negation. Then an *argumentation theory*, T, consists of a set of *argument rules*. *Argument rules* are parametrized rule associations between a set of statements, called the *Premises* and another statement called the *Position* or *Claim* of the argument. There are two types of argument rules: object-level and priority. *Object-level* argument rules are those whose claim is any statement in the given language L of our problem domain. *Priority* argument rules are those whose claim is of the special form "a1 > a2" where a1 and a2 are any two other argument rules, possibly themselves priority argument rules. Object-level (respectively priority) *individual arguments* are then constructed by instantiating object-level (respectively priority) argument rules. Then given an argumentation theory T an *argument* is a composite subset $D = (D_O, D_P)$ of individual arguments constructed from T, where D_O is a subset of object-level individual arguments and D_P is a subset of priority individual arguments.

To complete the definition of the argumentation framework we need to specify an attack relation between arguments. For this the priority arguments play an important role by providing information on the relative strength between arguments and in this way regulate when an argument can attack or not another argument. Informally, a composite argument, D1, *attacks* another composite argument, D2, whenever they are in conflict, i.e. one argument from D1 and one from D2 have conflicting claims, and the arguments in D1 are rendered by the priority arguments that it contains at least as strong as the arguments contained in D2. More precisely, if the priority arguments in D2 render an argument in it stronger than an argument in D1 then so do the priority arguments in D1: i.e. a relative weak argument in D1 is balanced by a weak argument in D2. Note that the conflict between D1 and D2 can be on their priority arguments, i.e. with D2 containing a priority argument for the claim "a1 > a2" and D1 containing a priority argument for the claim "a2 > a1". The precise formal definition of the attack relation is beyond the scope of this paper and can be found in [31, 32].

Reasoning to conclusions within argumentation is based on the central notion of an *acceptable* set of arguments that supports a certain conclusion of interest, e.g. the prediction of a case in the data of a ML problem. Typically, such an acceptable set of arguments consists of one top-level argument which, based on a set of premises, supports the conclusion of interest, together with other arguments that are needed to *defend* this initial argument against other arguments that attack this, i.e. against its *counter-arguments*. There are several different definitions of the notion of acceptable set of arguments. One of the standard definitions is that of *admissibility* [33]. A set D of arguments in Gorgias is *admissible* iff (i) it is conflict free, i.e. no two of the arguments in D are in conflict and (ii) D attacks back (defends against) all other arguments that attack it. Typically, to construct an admissible set of arguments supporting some desired claim we will first consider attacks against this by object level argument and then include priority arguments to strengthen its object level arguments against the attacking ones. Recursively, we then may need to consider attacks against the adopted priority arguments by other priority arguments claiming the reverse priority and defend against these by adopting yet other higher-level priority arguments between these conflicting priority arguments. The precise formal definition of the attack relation given above and the algorithmic construction of admissible arguments is beyond the scope of this paper and can be found in [31, 32].

Using this central notion of admissible arguments, we can then define plausible and definite *argumentation-based conclusions* or *predictions* according to whether there exists or not an admissible argument that supports the conclusion of interest. If such an admissible argument exists then we say the *conclusion is plausible or possible*. If in addition there exists no admissible argument that supports any other conclusion that is in conflict with the conclusion of interest then we say that this is a *definite conclusion*.

Note that it is possible for a conclusion and some other conflicting conclusion to both be plausible conclusions from the same argumentation theory, in which case we say the theory is *(locally) ambiguous* and the conclusion forms a *dilemma* within the theory.

Argumentation naturally lends itself to being explainable (see e.g. [3, 34–36]). Moreover, explanations built out of argumentation can easily be constructed to be cognitively compatible with the users and to be "socially useful" [37] in exposing the reasons underlying a conclusion. The argument(s), within an admissible set, supporting directly a conclusion, can provide an *attributive* part of an explanation, giving the basic and important reasons justifying why a conclusion would hold and could be chosen. On the other hand, the defending arguments, within an admissible coalition of arguments, can provide a *contrastive* element of the explanation, justifying why the particular conclusion is a good choice in relation to other possible and contradictory conclusions. Within the Gorgias argumentation framework, the process of extracting natural explanations from argumentation is facilitated by the structure of admissible subsets of arguments that support a conclusion. The object-level arguments within the set of a composite argument would give us the basic reasons supporting the claim, i.e. an attributive part of the explanation, while the priority arguments would give the reasons why to prefer this claim over the reasons that support alternative conclusions, thus providing a contrastive element in the explanation.

We close this section by commenting on the relation of the structure of an argumentation theory with the form of (some of) the standard Machine Learning theories. The object-level arguments (rules) are clearly closely related to association rules that ML methods generate. Furthermore, several ML approaches present an ordering, e.g. decision lists [38, 39], on the association rules that they generate. This ordering is typically a global and total ordering. In argumentation the priority argument rules general and extend the possible orderings on the basic object-level associations. They allow *partial* orderings and more importantly *contextual* orderings given by the argumentative reasoning that is carried out on the priority arguments.

3   ArgEML: Concepts and Framework

The argumentation-based framework for Explainable Machine Learning (ArgEML) is based on a novel approach to ML that integrates sub-symbolic methods with logical methods of argumentation to provide explainable solutions to learning problems. ArgEML is based on acknowledging the predictive accuracy difficulties in real-life learning problems and the importance of explanations, as a means of understanding the reasoning behind a prediction and helping the domain expert to take more informed decisions. The approach views the notion of prediction from a different perspective than that of a traditional ML model, by means of relaxing the requirement of accuracy by distinguishing two notions of definite prediction and ambiguity recognition. In this perspective, if we cannot uniquely or definitely predict, but can focus the prediction on a set of alternatives and can give justifications for the alternatives, then we consider that we still have a valuable output of learning.

Utilizing argumentation as a framework for explainable decision making we aim at learning contextual hierarchies starting from general and simple statements to more specific ones and structuring these using priorities between them. The learning process is not driven only by maximizing strict accuracy but also from solutions that would be sufficiently good in terms of accuracy and in those cases, where a definite prediction cannot be given, compensating this with the high-level of explainability of the learned theory. This concept of "sufficiently good but explainable solution" motivates a set of metrics that will govern the learning process of the ArgEML framework, defined and explained in Sect. 3.1.

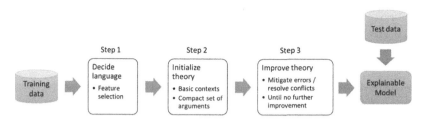

Fig. 1. ArgEML: Overall conceptual description.

The ArgEML methodology is outlined in Fig. 1. The first step decides the language of the learning problem in a similar way to the data processing step in a standard machine learning pipeline. The goal is to select the most relevant features for a given learning problem. The second step aims to identify the basic contexts of the problem domain. To achieve this goal a compact set of arguments with high coverage is selected to initialize the theory. Both steps (1) and (2) can be executed automatically or in a hybrid mode by calling onto a sub-symbolic or symbolic existing learner. The next and final step involves a repeated learning process to produce an argumentation theory as the final output of the learner. At each iteration step two main operators are considered: a mitigation of errors in the definite prediction of (some part of) the current theory and an operator for resolving conflicts in the ambiguity of the current theory. This final step is guided by a learning assessment (metric) that evaluates the quality of different possible new theories in terms of their argumentation-based reasoning performance of the training data. In each iteration of the process the decision whether to mitigate errors or resolve conflicts depends on the learning assessment of the resulting theory in each case.

3.1 Learning Metrics

Learning metrics are defined for an individual argument and its premise conditions or for a collection of arguments, with respect to a dataset D. To define the metrics, we will use the following concepts:

- *Argument*: *Head:- Body*[1] that is read as "Head is supported when Body holds".
  Example: *bird(X):- feat1 = 0* is read as "X is bird is supported when feat1 $= 0$ holds".
- *Theory*: a collection of arguments.
- *Condition*: a set of pairs (feature, value) that reads as feature $=$ value.
- *Frequency (condition, D)*: the number of instances in dataset D where *condition* is true.
- *Definite prediction (theory, D)*: the concept is related to the predictive accuracy that we normally have in a ML model, but here it only applies to the instances in D for which a theory can derive a single definite conclusion.
- *Dilemma (theory, D)*: the concept complements the one of "definite prediction" and refers to the instances in D for which a theory derives multiple conflicting conclusions.

The ArgEML learning metrics are defined in Table 1. We can see that the *Learning Assessment (LA)* of a theory is a generalization of the standard Classification Accuracy metric that includes a weighted element (*dilemmas * w_a*) that reflects the dilemmas of the theory. In general, this weight factor is application depended and chosen accordingly, e.g. for a binary classification learning problem this factor can be chosen to be one-half.

Before giving the overall learning algorithm of ArgEML let us first present informally the role of these different metrics in the ArgEML learning process. *Coverage* metrics are particularly important during the process of theory initialization to define the basic contexts that fully cover the data. Coverage is also important in the process of selecting the premise conditions for a new argument, in combination with accuracy, as defined in the *argument assessment* metric. Then, metrics related to confidence (*definite correct / errors, ambiguity*) are the factors that drive the learning of a theory that represents sufficiently well the knowledge from the data. ArgEML puts the emphasis on coverage first by relaxing the requirement for accuracy allowing conflicts to occur. These conflicts refer to examples in the dataset that a theory cannot provide a definite prediction, it supports multiple conflicting conclusions instead. While ArgEML provides a process for conflicts resolution it is acceptable for some conflicts to remain and this is measured by the *ambiguity* metric. Ambiguity is a new concept that aims to capture cases where a model has difficulty to provide a correct definite prediction. For these cases an argumentation theory will generate a dilemma. Dilemmas include multiple conflicting conclusions with explanations for each particular conclusion. A dilemma can be considered neither a correct nor a wrong prediction. However, its informative part, the explanation, adds value to the prediction. For that reason, dilemmas are included in the *learning assessment* metric to evaluate the performance of a theory.

For any given theory T learned from a dataset D, we have the following vector of metrics v:

$$v = (C, DE, AM, LA) \tag{1}$$

---

[1] We will use a Logic Programming rule notation for the arguments to facilitate the exposition of the realization of the ArgEML framework in the next sections of the paper.

Table 1. Learning metrics

Metric	Definition
Coverage (condition, D) *Coverage* (argument, D)	Percentage of data in a dataset D for which the condition is true, e.g. *Coverage*(feat1 $= 0$, D) $= frequency$(feat1 $= 0$, D)/size(D) Coverage of the premise condition of the argument, e.g. *Coverage*(allow(X):-feat1 $= 0$, D) $= frequency$(feat1 $= 0$, D)/size(D)
Coverage (theory, D)	Percentage of data supported by the set of arguments in a theory *Coverage*(theory, D) $= \bigcup_{i=1}^{m} Coverage(\text{arg}_i, D)$
Accuracy (argument, D)	Percentage of data in a dataset D for which the argument conditions are true and the target value is the same as the head of the argument e.g. *Accuracy*(allow(X):-feat1 $= 0$, D) $=$ $frequency$(allow(X) AND feat1 $= 0$, D)/$frequency$ (feat1 $= 0$, D)
Definite correct (DC) (theory, D)	Percentage of data in D for which a theory provides a definite correct prediction (with respect to the total number of predictions) *(definite correct predictions)/(total number of predictions)*
Definite errors (DE) (theory, D)	Percentage of data in D for which a theory provides a definite wrong prediction (with respect to the total number of predictions) *(definite wrong predictions)/(total number of predictions)*
Definite accuracy (DA) (theory, D)	Percentage of data in D for which a theory provides a definite correct prediction (with respect to the number of definite predictions) *(definite correct predictions)/(total number of definite predictions)*
Ambiguity (theory, D)	Percentage of data on D for which a theory is in a dilemma (with respect to the total number of predictions)
Argument assessment (argument, D)	The weighted sum of coverage and accuracy of argument on D: *Coverage*(argument, D)* w_c + *Accuracy*(argument, D)* w_a
Learning assessment (theory, D)	The sum of the DC with the weighted number of Ambiguity of a theory on D: *Definite correct* (theory,D) + *Ambiguity*(theory,D)* w_d

All weight factors w_c, w_a, w_d correspond to decimal numbers $<= 1$. w_c: weight for coverage, w_a: weight for accuracy, where $w_c + w_a = 1$. We can use different weights to indicate which between coverage and accuracy is more important at a particular stage of the algorithm. w_d: weight factor for ambiguity defined as 1/(number of labels in target class).

where C represents Coverage(T,D), $DE \rightarrow$ Definite-errors(T, D), $AM \rightarrow$ Ambiguity(T, D) and LA $\rightarrow$ Learning-assessment(T,D).

The vector is initialized at the end of 2nd step (initialize theory) where the goal is to develop the initial version of the theory with a compact set of arguments to cover if possible all instances in the dataset D. To illustrate how the vector of metrics is used in the learning process let us consider a binary classification problem on a dataset D with a balanced/equal distribution. A theory can be initialized with the following signature metric vector reflecting that at the start we have complete 100% ambiguity:

$$Theory\_0, v = (100\%, 0\%, 100\%, 0.5) \qquad (2)$$

The next step aims to improve the initial theory to meet the "sufficiently good" requirement which can be defined in terms of the definite-errors and ambiguity metrics, e.g. *Definite-errors(T,D) < 10%* and *Ambiguity(T,D) < 15%*). To achieve this improvement the repeated learning process explores extending the theory using one of the main operators (mitigation of errors/ conflicts resolution) based on the learning assessment of the extended theory that each operator generates. For example, a learning operator that generates a new theory, with signature metric vector Theory_1, will constitute an improvement:

$$Theory\_1, \ v = (100\%\ , 20\%\ , 20\%\ , 0.7) \tag{3}$$

The further application of different learning operators activated by the fact that the predefined thresholds on the levels of both definite-errors and ambiguity are not met can produce different theories with different metric vectors, such as:

$$Theory\_2.1, \ v = (100\%\ , 10\%\ , 20\%\ , 0.8) \tag{4}$$

$$Theory\_2.2, \ v = (100\%\ , 20\%\ , 10\%\ , 0.75) \tag{5}$$

At this stage, the learning process will choose to continue learning with Theory_2.1 because it has the highest LA value of 0.8 (indicating that an improvement on the reduction of errors is preferred over an improvement on the ambiguity).

- **Learning Assessment (LA)**

As we already explained the LA of a theory is a generalization of the standard Classification Accuracy metric,

$$LA(\sim Classification\ Accuracy) = \frac{(\textbf{\textit{definite}}\ correct\ predictions) + \textbf{\textit{dilemmas}} * \textbf{\textit{wa}}}{total\ number\ of\ predictions}$$

(where the new elements are shown in bold). LA gives a holistic evaluation of a theory that balances definite errors (or accuracy) and ambiguity. Similarly, to how classification accuracy increases with the number of correct predictions, ArgEML aims at improving LA by either reducing errors or resolving dilemmas. The most challenging part though is the tradeoff between the two, as the reduction in errors can increase ambiguity, and vice versa. The ArgEML methodology deals with this challenge by gradually reducing errors or dilemmas, based on the LA metric. For example, applying conflicts resolution on *Theory_1, v = (100%, 20%, 20%, 0.7)* can lead to *Theory_2, v = (100%, 25%, 15%, 0.68)*, and then applying errors reduction on Theory_2 can lead to *Theory3, v = (100%, 10%, 15%, 0.75)*.

In Subsect. 5.4 we present a summary of experimental findings and compare the ArgEML learned theories with ML models. The comparison is in terms of accuracy, using the metric of *Definite accuracy* for the ArgEML theories and *Classification Accuracy* for the ML models. We consider the two metrics analogous under the assumption that in a standard machine learning process all predictions are definite.

Table 2. ArgEML Algorithm

input:	D, a dataset with labeled samples $\{(x_1, y_1), (x_2, y_2), .. , (x_n, y_n)\}$ where x_i is a feature vector, and F $\{f_1, f_2, .. , f_z\}$ a feature set P, a list of parameters.
output:	T, argumentation theory learned from D

1:    T_i ← Initialize-Theory (D); $L.add$ (T_i)
2:    $\{definite\text{-}errors, dilemmas, E\}$ ← Evaluate-Theory (T_i, D)
3:    **while** $(definite\text{-}errors > P.errors\text{-}thold$ **or** $dilemmas > P.dilemmas\text{-}thold)$ **do**
4:       **if** $definite\text{-}errors > P.errors\text{-}thold$ **then**
5:           $\{errors\text{-}reduced, T_e\}$ ← Reduce-Errors (T_i, D, E)
6:       **end if**
7:       **if** $dilemmas > P.dilemmas\text{-}thold$ **then**
8:           $\{dilemmas\text{-}resolved, T_d\}$ ← Resolve-Dilemmas (T_i, D, E)
9:       **end if**
10:      **if** $errors\text{-}reduced$ or $dilemmas\text{-}resolved$ **then**
11:          T_{next} ← Best-Learning-Assessment (T_e, T_d); $L.add$ (T_{next})
12:          $\{definite\text{-}errors, dilemmas\}$ ← Evaluate-Theory (T_{next}, D)
13:      **Else**
14:          **exit loop**   ➢   no further learning
15:      **end if**
16:   **end loop**
17:   T ← Best-Learning-Assessment (L)

E: all evaluation results. P: please refer to paragraph 4.2, Table 3.

3.2 ArgEML Top-Level Algorithm

Given a set of n training examples $D: \{(x1, y1), (x2, y2),.., (xn, yn)\}$ where x_i is the input example, a vector of values for features F, and y_i is the class label, the objective is to learn an argumentation theory T, to support the conclusions in y, that covers possibly all instances in D $(coverage(T,D) \approx 100\%)$ and qualifies as a "sufficiently good" theory assuming thresholds $errors\_Thold$ and $ambiguity\_Thold$ for the metrics of definite-errors and ambiguity respectively. The top-level ArgEML algorithm is shown in Table 2. We describe here briefly the main steps of the algorithm: (step 1) Feature set F defines the language of the learning problem and is part of the input. (step 2) The basic contexts of the problem are defined by the process Initialize-Theory. (step 3) Lines 3 – 16 correspond to the repeated learning process of the methodology. At the end, the process Best-Learning-Assessment decides the output of the algorithm, theory T.

The repeated learning process involves two argumentation-based learning operators, the Reduce-Errors and Resolve-Dilemmas operators. The first operator identifies the arguments that erroneously support the target conclusion for a number of instances in D and aims to mitigate these errors with *defeat arguments*. The second operator identifies pairs or arguments in conflict and aims to resolve the conflict by identifying conditional strengths between these arguments. Both operators are applied on a relevant subset of the whole dataset D, the instances supported by the arguments with errors, or the instances supported by the arguments in conflict. These operators are described in more detail in paragraph 3.3 where we will exploit the flexibility of the structured argumentation framework of Gorgias to represent conditional strengths between arguments in terms of *priority arguments*. The repeated learning process terminates when a "sufficiently good" theory is learned or further learning is not possible (errors cannot be reduced or dilemmas cannot be resolved).

- **Initialize-Theory(D)**

The process defines the first set of arguments of the theory to cover possibly all instances in D. Arguments can be defined generic, e.g., *Claim_i.*, which means that the conclusion/prediction *Claim_i* is supported by the theory in general, or specific, e.g. *Claim_j:-Feat1 = 0*, which means that *Claim_j* is supported under the conditions of the premise (Feat1 = 0). The option for generic or specific arguments is defined parametrically. Specific arguments are defined using the "argument construction" algorithm for their premise conditions. The algorithm is described below.

- **Evaluate-Theory(T, D)**

The process evaluates theory T on dataset D and calculates the metrics vector v.

Evaluate-Theory (T, D):
For each instance d_i in D
   For each class label y *(in target feature)*
      solution ← query($T, d\_i, claim\_y$)
      update v with the solution findings (correct/wrong prediction or dilemma)
Return query results + metrics vector.

Evaluate-Theory is called at the end to help determine the quality of the new theory constructed by the learning loop. Its results are used by the *Best-Learning-Assessment(L)* which selects the theory in list L (of candidate theories) with the highest learning assessment. The Evaluate-Theory process can also be used inside the two learning operators of mitigate errors and resolve dilemmas to evaluate (as a look ahead) the quality of the possible resulting local extensions by these operators.

- **Argument construction algorithm**

Given a set of training examples $D: \{(x1, y1), (x2, y2),..., (xn, yn)\}$, where x_i is the input example, a vector of values for features F, and y_i is the class label, the objective is to learn one condition per unique feature value and to select the one that carries the most information about the outcome of interest (a class label, e.g. feat1 = 0 for class label "deny"). The argument construction algorithm is an extension of the OneR [40] (short for "One Rule") classification algorithm that generates one rule for each feature/predictor in a dataset, then selects the rule with the smallest total error as its "one rule". Argument construction generates one rule for each pair of (feature, value) and assigns a "score" value using the *argument assessment* metric.

<u>Argument-construction (D):</u>
For each feature in F
   For each feature value, make a rule as follows:
      Count how often each value of target (class label) appears
      Find the most frequent class
      Make the rule assign that class to this value of the feature
   Calculate the "score" value using the argument assessment metric
Return a list of pairs (rule, score).

Therefore, this algorithm returns a set of arguments for various class labels whose premise have been selected via the extended version of the OneR statistical analysis algorithm that we have chosen to employ in this method. Other algorithms can be used and indeed here we can use an external learning module to generate rules which we import into the ArgEML as arguments, thus running the ArgEML learning methodology in *hybrid* mode.

3.3 Argumentation-Based Learning Operators

The learning process utilizes at various points the *argument construction* algorithm to decide on an appropriate premise condition for building a new argument, either an initial context setting argument or a defeat or priority argument for the specialized argumentation-based operators of Reduce-Errors and Resolve-Dilemmas.

- **Operator: Reduce-Errors**

Given an argumentation theory T, a set of training examples D: $\{(x1, y1), (x2, y2), ..., (xn, yn)\}$, where x_i is the input example and y_i is the class label (target feature value), and the results E of evaluating theory T on dataset D, the objective is to extend theory T with theory T' where for each argument arg_i with errors in T, and for each class label c_j of examples in D supported erroneously by $argi$, a defeater argument arg_{id} exists in T'.

<u>Reduce-Errors (T, D, E):</u>
For each arg_i with errors in T
   D_i is the subset of D that arg_i covers
   $R_i \leftarrow$ Argument-Construction (D_i)
   $Lc \leftarrow$ class labels of examples in D_i that arg_i supports with error
   For each class label c_j in Lc
      Select rule r_{ij} from R_i with the highest score that supports the examples in D_i that
         belong to class cj
      $T' \leftarrow$ extent T with a defeater argument for arg_i using the conditions in r_{ij} and
         the conditions in arg_i
Return T'

An example of a defeater argument for arg_a: $claim\_a:\text{-}feat1 = 0$ that erroneously supports examples that belong to class b is arg_{ab}: $claim\_b:\text{-}feat1 = 0, feat2 = 1$.

We note two important comments that are relevant for the Reduce-Errors operator. Typically, a defeater argument is considered to be of stronger strength that the argument it is defeating, but here this relative strength is not imposed as part of the Reduce-Errors operator. The original and defeater arguments form only a dilemma between them. Thus, at the next iteration of the learning algorithm with the application of the Resolve-Dilemmas algorithm the process will consider the issue of the relative strength of the defeater argument. Furthermore, typically a defeater argument would have a local effect only on the argument that it has been constructed to defeat and not to have a side effect of introducing errors or dilemmas on the rest of the dataset which was not considered when constructing the defeater argument. This localization of the effect of the defeater can be realized by imposing a flat relative strength of anyone of the arguments, apart from the one that the defeater is constructed for, over any defeater argument conflicting with it. It is also possible to localize a defeater argument using specific constructs of the particular argumentation framework in which the learning process is realized.

- **Operator: Resolve-Dilemmas**

Given an argumentation theory T, a set of training examples $D: \{(x1, y1), (x2, y2),.., (xn, yn)\}$, where x_i is the input example and y_i is the class label, and the results E of evaluating theory T on dataset D, the objective is to extend theory T with theory T' where for each pair of arguments in conflict (arg_i, arg_j) in T a pair of priority arguments exists in T'.

> Resolve-Dilemmas (T, D, E):
> **For each** pair (arg_i, arg_j) in conflict in T
> D_{ij} is the subset of D that $arg_i + arg_j$ both cover
> If all instances in D_{ij} belong to the same class c **then**
> $arg_c \leftarrow$ one of the (arg_i, arg_j) that supports claim c
> $arg_{not\text{-}c} \leftarrow$ one of the (arg_i, arg_j) that does not support claim c
> $T' \leftarrow$ extend T with a general priority argument $(arg_c > arg_{not\text{-}c})$
> **Else**
> $R_{ij} \leftarrow$ Argument-Construction (D_{ij})
>   class $c_i \leftarrow$ claim that arg_i supports
>   select rule r_{ic} from R_{ij} with the highest score that supports class c_i
> $T' \leftarrow$ extend T with a priority argument $(arg_i > arg_j)$ under the conditions in r_{ic}
>   class $c_j \leftarrow$ claim that arg_j supports
>   select rule r_{jc} from R_{ij} with the highest score that supports class c_j
> $T' \leftarrow$ extend T with a priority argument $(arg_j > arg_i)$ under the conditions in r_{jc}
> **End if**
> **Return** T'

We note that this algorithm can be applied in the same way between conflicting priority arguments that would have been constructed at an earlier iteration of the learning algorithm. It is applied in the same way where now the claims c_i and c_j are replaced by a claim of priority $p_{ij} = arg_i > arg_j$ and the opposite claim of priority of $p_{ji} = arg_i j > arg_i$. This then allows us to learn hierarchical theories of increasing strength in their predictions.

4 ArgEML: Implemented System

We have implemented the ArgEML methodology in a Java application as shown in Fig. 2. The basic components of the system are briefly described in the next paragraphs. Currently, the system provides two modes of operation, *automatic* and *hybrid* which are also described below.

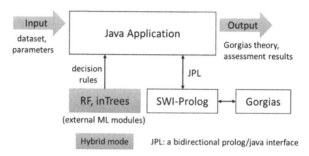

Fig. 2. ArgEML Java Application – Basic Architecture.

4.1 System Components

The Java application includes an API for executing a learning process for a particular set of input. The application provides two modes of operation, (a) automatic, and (b) hybrid. In the *automatic* mode of operation, the application accepts as input a dataset (examples + feature set), while in the *hybrid* mode, the application also accepts as input the results of an external ML model's execution on the input dataset. The current implementation can process the results of the inTrees library. The application interacts with the SWI-Prolog component for the evaluation of the Gorgias argumentation theories learned. This interaction is achieved via the JPL API. A brief description of the basic system components follows:

- *SWI-Prolog*[2] is a versatile implementation of the Prolog language.
- JPL[3] is an API between SWI-Prolog and the Java Virtual Machine. JPL is a set of Java classes and C functions providing a bidirectional interface between Java and Prolog.
- *Gorgias system*[4] is a Prolog meta-interpreter for argumentation.
- *inTrees*[5] is a framework proposed in [38] and implemented as a package in R for extracting interpretable information from tree ensembles such as random forests and boosted trees.

---

[2] https://www.swi-prolog.org/.
[3] https://jpl7.org/.
[4] http://gorgiasb.tuc.gr/.
[5] https://cran.r-project.org/web/packages/inTrees/index.html.

4.2 Modes and Parameters of Operation

In the *automatic* mode of operation learning starts from processing the input dataset. No additional information is provided with regards to the features and their relation to the target variable. On the other hand, in the *hybrid* mode of operation a list of decision rules, extracted by inTrees, is also given as input to the learning process. The system will first process these decision rules to select a compact set that achieves high coverage, possibly 100%. Then the learned theory is initialized by transforming the selected decision rules into arguments.

The execution of the system is highly parametric allowing the end user to fine tune the execution of the process accordingly. The basic parameters are shown in Table 3.

Table 3. System parameters.

Parameter	Values	Parameter	Values
Initialize-theory	args-no-premise/ args-with-premises	Defeaters-with-priority	yes/no
Definite-errors-threshold	percentage	Iterative learning-steps	integer
Ambiguity-threshold	percentage	Data-split (train / test)	percentages
Majority-class-threshold	percentage	Rules-complexity	integer
Balanced-distribution	percentage	Learning-assessment-loss	decimal < 1

These parameters are mainly used to control the search for the learned theory. The details of their function are beyond the scope of this paper.

The ArgEML framework and associated system is currently under continuous development undergoing a thorough evaluation on different learning problems through which we get feedback that can help us tune and improve the approach. Here we present the results of our experimentation on three datasets, (1) an artificial dataset to demonstrate how well the methodology works, (2) a standard dataset for machine learning research to validate the results of ArgEML, and (3) a real-life dataset to show how the methodology works in hybrid mode. We have also trained random forest (RF) models and extracted a Simplified tree ensemble learner (STEL, inTrees) so that we can compare the results, accuracy of prediction and naturality of explanations of ArgEML approach with a standard ML method[6].

4.3 Artificial Dataset Example

To demonstrate how the methodology works we created a synthetic dataset from an argumentation theory that supports scenarios for "staying at home" or "going to the office". The objective was then to use ArgEML to learn the initial theory or an equivalent one back from the dataset without any knowledge of the theory that has generated the data. The purpose of the experiment was to investigate the appropriateness of the ArgEML

---

[6] All datasets presented here are available via request from the authors.

new learning notions on a baseline dataset which we know, by construction, that it has a *contextual hierarchical* structure for which the ArgEML approach should be well-suited.

The dataset generated has 10 binary features, {c1, c2, c3, .., c10}, plus the target variable that defines the scenario supported by the particular instance (*work* or *home*). The dataset contains 120 instances in balanced distribution (60 for work, 60 for home). Learning was done using 100% of the data since the purpose of this experiment was not to estimate the performance of the model rather to demonstrate how the learning evolves. A RF model was also trained on the same dataset, and a compact rule set was extracted as a STEL, a decision list. These were used to compare with the ArgEML learned theory: accuracy of prediction and naturality of explanations that can be extracted from both models.

- **ArgEML execution on the artificial dataset**

Below we show an example trace of the execution of the ArgEML system on this dataset. The parameters of execution where: *{(initialize-theory, args-with-premises), (definite-errors-threshold,0%), (ambiguity-threshold,0%), (majority-class-threshold,60%), (balanced-distribution,20%), (defeaters-with-priority, no), (iterative-learning-steps,10), (data-split-train,100%), (learning-assessment-loss, 0.2)}.*

Step 1: Feature set F = {c1, c2, c3, c4, c5, c6, c7, c8, c9, c10} and *target* variable was given as input.

Step 2: Initialize theory:

Theory_0   rule(r1(Obj), home(Obj), []):-c8(Obj,P8),P8=0.
rule(r2(Obj), work(Obj), []):-c7(Obj,P7),P7=0.
rule(r3(Obj), home(Obj), []):-c7(Obj,P7),P7=1.
rule(r4(Obj), work(Obj), []):-c8(Obj,P8),P8=1.

$$Theory\_0, v = (100\%, 0\%, 46\%, 0.77) \tag{6}$$

Step 3: Improve theory:

Theory_1   rule(p1(Obj), prefer(r1(Obj), r2(Obj)), []):-c1(Obj,P1),P1=0.
rule(p2(Obj), prefer(r2(Obj), r1(Obj)), []):-c3(Obj,P3),P3=0.
rule(p3(Obj), prefer(r3(Obj), r4(Obj)), []):-c9(Obj,P9),P9=1.
rule(p4(Obj), prefer(r4(Obj), r3(Obj)), []):-c10(Obj,P10),P10=1.

$$Theory\_1, v = (100\%, 0\%, 20\%, 0.9) \tag{7}$$

Theory_2   rule(p5(Obj), prefer(p1(Obj), p2(Obj)), []):-c4(Obj,P4),P4=1.
rule(p6(Obj), prefer(p2(Obj), p1(Obj)), []):-c4(Obj,P4),P4=0.
rule(p7(Obj), prefer(p3(Obj), p4(Obj)), []):-c5(Obj,P5),P5=1.
rule(p8(Obj), prefer(p4(Obj), p3(Obj)), []):-c5(Obj,P5),P5=0.

$$Theory\_2, v = (100\%, 0\%, 0\%, 1) \tag{8}$$

At the end of the 2nd iteration of step3 ArgEML exits the learning process because both definite-errors and ambiguity reached the thresholds set (0%). The resulting theory has a learning assessment value 1, which means it supports accurately all instances in the dataset. This trace shows a typical run of the ArgEML method where it gradually reduces the ambiguity level of the theory without introducing any definite errors or more generally keeping an upper bound on the percentage of the definite errors.

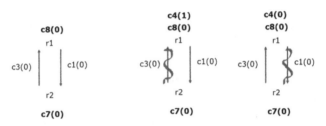

Fig. 3. The hierarchical structure of the learned theory.

The learned theory reveals a hierarchical structure in the data. We can choose to interpret the theory from the perspective of either one of the class values: *home* or *work*. Suppose we choose the value *home*. There are two basic contexts for the class *home* given by c8(0) and c7(1) supporting home via arguments r1 and r3 respectively. In Fig. 3 on the left side, we show the structure of the theory for the first context of c8(0). We see that when the general context of c8(0) is refined with the information c7(0) there is a counter-argument r2 to r1. This is stronger than r1 when c3(0) holds but weaker than r1 when c1(0) holds, as shown by the red arrow attacks between the arguments. When the context is further refined with information about the feature c4 then depending on the value of c4 one of these attacks becomes weaker and effectively it is disabled, as shown in the middle and righthand sides of the figure.

- **Random Forest & inTrees results on the artificial dataset**

A RF model with 500 trees was trained that achieved accuracy 1 on the training set. inTrees was then used to extract the "best" rules from the trees as a decision list (an ordered list of decision rules) known as STEL.

Simplified tree ensemble learner (STEL, extracted by inTrees):

If c7=0 & c8=1 **then** *work*
else if c7=1 & c8=0 **then** *home*
else if c3=0 & c4=0 & c7=0 **then** *work*
else if c8=0 **then** *home*
else if c7=1 & c10=0 **then** *home*
else if c5=0 **then** *work*
else if c8=1 & c9=0 **then** *work*
else *home*

In a decision list a prediction is made by examining the decision rules in their order, the first rule that matches the input data is used to make the prediction.

- **ArgEML theory, STEL - predictions & Explanations on unseen (dilemma) cases**

We have tested both the ArgEM theory and the STEL model on a set of 8 unseen cases which we knew from the generating theory would be difficult dilemma cases. ArgEML predicted "dilemma" for all cases, while STEL gave the same definite prediction of *home* for all cases. This indicates a subtle but important difference of the ArgEML approach particularly for learning problems that would have a contextual hierarchical structure. Another important difference is the nature of the explanations that we can extract from the two different approaches. To illustrate this let us consider two examples, one case from the training set, and one unseen input case.

Input 1: $\{c1 = 0, c2 = 1, c3 = 0, c4 = 0, c5 = 0, c6 = 1, c7 = 0, c8 = 0, c9 = 0, c10 = 0,$ target $=$ work$\}$.

Prediction by STEL: *Work*, **Explanation:** The model predicts *work* because the condition $[c3 = 0 \ \& \ c4 = 0 \ \& \ c7 = 0]$ is true and all of the stronger conditions $\{[c7 = 0 \ \& \ c8 = 1], [c7 = 1 \ \& \ c8 = 0]\}$ are false.

Prediction by ArgEML Theory: *Work*, **Explanation:** The prediction *work* is supported by the fact $c7 = 0$. While the contrary prediction of *home* is also supported by the fact $c8 = 0$, the reason of $c7 = 0$ supporting *work* is stronger when $c3 = 0$. Moreover, although the fact $c1 = 0$ could render the argument for *home* based on $c8 = 0$ stronger this is not so, because $c4 = 0$ holds.

Input 2: $\{c1 = 1, c2 = 0, c3 = 0, c4 = 0, c5 = 1, c6 = 0, c7 = 1, c8 = 1, c9 = 0, c10 = 0\}$.

Prediction by STEL: *Home*, **Explanation:** The model predicts *home* because the condition $[c7 = 1 \ \& \ c10 = 0]$ is true and all of the stronger conditions $\{[c8 = 0], [c3 = 0 \ \& \ c4 = 0 \ \& \ c7 = 0], [c7 = 1 \ \& \ c8 = 0], [c7 = 0 \ \& \ c8 = 1]\}$ are false.

Prediction by ArgEML Theory: *Dilemma*, **Explanation:** A defined prediction cannot be provided because both *home* and *work* conclusions can be supported equally strongly. The conclusion *home* can be supported by argument r3(obj) (*home* $\leftarrow c7 = 1$). The conclusion *work* can be supported by argument r4(obj) (*work* $\leftarrow c8 = 1$).

4.4 Standard Dataset Example

We have experimented with Iris dataset[7], a standard dataset for machine learning research that contains 3 classes of 50 instances each, where each class refers to a type of iris plant (Setosa, Versicolour, Virginica). The original dataset has four numerical features that we discretized with the frequency method: sepal length: {short, medium, long}, sepal width: {narrow, wide}, petal length: {short, medium, long}, petal length: {narrow, wide}.

---

[7] https://archive.ics.uci.edu/ml/datasets/iris.

- **ArgEML execution on the Iris dataset**

Below we show an example trace of the execution of the ArgEML system on this dataset. The parameters of execution where: *{(initialize-theory, args-no-premises), (definite-errors-threshold,0%), (ambiguity-threshold,0%), (majority-class-threshold,60%), (balanced-distribution,20%), (defeaters-with-priority, no), (iterative-learning-steps,10), (data-split-train,80%), (data-split-test,20%), (learning-assessment-loss, 0.2)}.*

Step 1: Feature set F = {sepallength, sepalwidth, petallength, petalwidth, species} was given as input.

Step 2: Initialize theory:

Theory_0   rule(r1(Obj), virginica(Obj), []).
              rule(r2(Obj), setosa(Obj), []).
              rule(r3(Obj), versicolor(Obj), []).

$$Theory\_0, v = (100\% , 0\% , 100\% , 0.33) \tag{9}$$

Step 3: Improve theory:

Theory_1   rule(p1(Obj), prefer(r1(Obj), r2(Obj)), []):-petalLength(Obj,P3),P3=long.
              rule(p2(Obj), prefer(r2(Obj), r1(Obj)), []):-petalLength(Obj,P3),P3=short.
              rule(p3(Obj), prefer(r1(Obj), r3(Obj)), []):-petalLength(Obj,P3),P3=long.
              rule(p4(Obj), prefer(r3(Obj), r1(Obj)), []):-petalLength(Obj,P3),P3=medium.
              rule(p5(Obj), prefer(r2(Obj), r3(Obj)), []):-petalLength(Obj,P3),P3=short.
              rule(p6(Obj), prefer(r3(Obj), r2(Obj)), []):-petalLength(Obj,P3),P3=medium.

$$Theory\_1, v = (100\% , 4\% , 0\% , 0.96) \tag{10}$$

Theory_2   rule(r3d1(Obj), virginica(Obj), []):-sepallength(Obj,P1),P1=short.
              rule(r1d1(Obj), versicolor(Obj), []):-sepalwidth(Obj,P2),P2=narrow.

$$Theory\_2, v = (100\% , 2\% , 44\% , 0.69) \tag{11}$$

At the end of the 2nd iteration of step3 ArgEML exits the learning process because of the significant loss in the learning assessment (from 0.96 to 0.69). The resulting theory has a learning assessment value 0.96 on the training set, and 0.93 on the test set. This trace shows again as in the previous example a typical run of the ArgEML method where it gradually reduces the ambiguity level of the theory. In this case, this introduces a small number of errors. The attempt to mitigate this small number of errors introduced new dilemmas and a major reduction in the learning assessment of the theory. Because of this loss, in the learning assessment, the learning process ended and Theory_1 was selected as the Best-performing-theory.

$$Theory\_1 \text{ assessment on test set}, v = (100\% , 7\% , 0\% , 0.93) \tag{12}$$

A RF model was also trained on the same dataset. The model achieved accuracy 0.96 on the training set and 0.9 on the test set.

4.5   Real-Life Dataset Example

We have experimented with a real-life dataset, the Asymptomatic Carotid Stenosis and Risk of Stroke Study (ACSRS) [41], with 1054 observations of *asymptomatic* (A) and *stroke* (S) patients. Because of the imbalanced class distribution (938 A cases, 112 S cases) in the dataset, 10 subsets of 100 asymptomatic and 100 stroke cases were drawn at random. Here we present the results of running ArgEML application on one of these subsets. The ArgEML system was used in *hybrid* mode where an external learning module was used to give the initial theory. A RF model was trained on the same subset and decision rules where extracted from the model using inTrees. Each decision rule was returned with a set of properties: {length, frequency, error, conditions, prediction, impRRF[8]}. The random forest model was evaluated with accuracy 0.9 on the training set and 0.78 on the test set.

- **ArgEML execution on the ACSRS dataset**

Below we show an example trace of the hybrid execution of the ArgEML system on ACSRS dataset. The parameters of execution where: *{(definite-errors-threshold,5%), (ambiguity-threshold,10%), (defeaters-with-priority, no), (iterative-learning-steps,10), (data-split-train,80%), (data-split-test,20%), (learning-assessment-loss, 0.2),(rules-complexity,2)}.*

Step 1.1: Feature set F = {st, lngsm40, cubrar, dwa1, ctiastr1, target},[9]
Step 1.2 (hybrid): Decision-rules rom RF and inTrees were given as input.

Step 2: Initialize theory by creating a compact set of arguments from the Decision rules list in Step1 to achieve the highest coverage. Only decision rules with length $<= 2$ were considered.

Theory_0   rule(r1(Obj), asympt(Obj), []):-cubrar(Obj,P3),member(P3, [cub1,cub2,cub3]),ctiastr1(Obj,P5),P5=0.
rule(r2(Obj), stroke(Obj), []):-lngsm40(Obj,P2),member(P2, [lng1,lng2,lng3]), cubrar(Obj,P3), member(P3, [cub4]).
...
rule(r11(Obj), asympt(Obj), []):-st(Obj,P1),member(P1, [st3]).
rule(r12(Obj), asympt(Obj), []):-lngsm40(Obj,P2),member(P2, [lng2,lng3]),dwa1(Obj,P4),P4=0.

The full initial theory consists of 12 object-level arguments that were selected from the decision rules from RF and inTrees application.

$$Theory\_0, \ v = (100\%, 4\%, 50\%, 0.71) \tag{13}$$

---

[8] A measure of each rule's relative importance in predicting the correct class.
[9] *st*:Stenosis (%ECST). ECST: European Carotid Surgery Trial. *Lngsm40*: Log(GSM + 40). GSM: Grey Scale Median. *Cubrar*: (Plaque Area)$^{1/3}$ in mm^2. *Dwa1*: DWAs (#of Yes cases).DWA: Discrete White Areas. *Ctiastr1*: History of contr. TIAs and/or Stroke (#of Yes cases). *Target*: {asympt, stroke}.

Step 3: Improve theory:

Theory_1   rule(p1(Obj), prefer(r10(Obj), r2(Obj)), []):-ctiastr1(Obj,P5),P5=0.
             rule(p2(Obj), prefer(r2(Obj), r10(Obj)), []):-lngsm40(Obj,P2),P2=lng3.

             ...

             rule(p19(Obj), prefer(r2(Obj), r11(Obj)), []):-lngsm40(Obj,P2),P2=lng1.
             rule(p20(Obj), prefer(r3(Obj), r11(Obj)), []):-ctiastr1(Obj,P5),P5=1.

$$Theory\_1, v = (100\%, 5\%, 40\%, 0.75) \tag{14}$$

Theory_2   *Theory_2, v=(100%, 8%, 21%, 0.82)*
Theory_3   *Theory_3.1, v=(100%, 3%, 48%, 0.73)*
                     Theory_3.2, v=(100%, 7%, 21%, 0.82)
Theory_4   *Theory_4.1, v=(100%, 3%, 44%, 0.75)*
                     Theory_4.2, v=(100%, 8%, 18%, 0.83)
Theory_5   *Theory_5.1, v=(100%, 4%, 38%, 0.77)*
                     Theory_5.2, v=(100%, 8%, 18%, 0.83)
Theory_6   *Theory_6, v=(100%, 4%, 38%, 0.77)*
Theory_7   *Theory_7, v=(100%, 4%, 28%, 0.82)*
Theroy_8   *Theory_8, v=(100%, 5%, 21%, 0.84)*
9th iteration   No further learning.
                     Best-Performing-Theory: Theory_8

$$Theory\_8 \ assessment \ on \ test \ set \ v = (100\%, 18\%, 23\%, 0.71) \tag{15}$$

At the end of the 9th iteration of step3 ArgEML exits the learning process because it was not able to extend the theory from the previous step. In other words, the operators were not able to learn any new arguments for reducing the errors or resolving the dilemmas. The algorithm selected Theory_8 as the best performing theory with a learning assessment value 0.84 on the training set, and 0.71 on the test set. The random forest model was evaluated with accuracy 0.9 on the training set and 0.78 on the test set.

The above trace shows how ArgEML proceeds to gradually reduces errors and ambiguity levels of the theory. Because of the nature of the data, from the beginning of the process errors and dilemmas coexisted. The execution trace showed in many iterations of step 3 the trade-off between reducing errors/resolving dilemmas. In many cases reducing errors increased dilemmas, or, resolving dilemmas increased errors. However, gradually the learning assessment of the theory improved.

- **ArgEML theory Explanations**

Here we provide two examples of explanations that can be derived from the argumentation theory to illustrative the attributive and contrastive part of the explanations and how these can help the domain expert take a more informed decision.

Input 1: {st = st3, lngsm40 = lng1, cubrar = cub3, dwa1 = 1, ctiastr1 = 1, target = stroke}.

Prediction by ArgEML Theory: *Stroke*, *Explanation*: The conclusion *stroke* is supported by an argument based on the facts lngsm40 = lng1 & cubrar is (cub2 or cub3 or cub4)). This is stronger than an opposing argument based on the fact st = st3, because ctiastr1 = 1 and cubrar = cub3 hold.

Input 2: {st = st4, lngsm40 = lng3, cubrar = cub4, dwa1 = 1, ctiastr1 = 0, target = asympt}.

Prediction by ArgEML Theory: *Dilemma, Explanation:* A definite prediction cannot be provided because both *stroke* and *asympt* conclusions can be acceptably supported by the theory.

The conclusion *stroke* is supported by an argument based on the facts lngsm40 is (lng1 or lng2 or lng3) & cubrar = cub4 and strengthened by the fact lngsm40 = lng3. This argument is stronger than the reason of "lngsm40 is (lng3 or lng4) and ctiastr1 = 0" supporting the conclusion *asympt* when dwa1 = 1.

The conclusion *asympt* is supported by an argument based on the facts lngsm40 is (lng3 or lng4) & ctiastr1 = 0. This argument is stronger than the reason of "lngsm40 is (lng1 or lng2 or lng3) and cubrar = cub4 and lngsm40 = lng3" supporting the conclusion *stroke* when st = st4.

4.6   Summary of Experimental Findings

In Table 4 we summarize the comparison, in terms of accuracy, of ArgEML with the Random Forest approach, on the three datasets.

Table 4. Learning assessment / Accuracy Comparison

Example dataset	Train set			Test set		
	RF	ArgEML		RF	ArgEML	
	CA	DA	LA	CA	DA	LA
Artificial	1	1	1	n/a	n/a	n/a
Iris	0.96	0.96	0.96	0.90	0.93	0.93
ACSRS	0.90	0.94	0.84	0.78	0.77	0.71

RF: Random Forest. CA: Classification Accuracy. DA: Definite Accuracy.
LA: Learning Assessment. CA ~ DA under the assumption that RF predictions are definite.

The comparison is between the metric of *Definite accuracy* for the ArgEML theories and *Classification Accuracy* for the ML models. We consider the two metrics analogous under the assumption that in a standard machine learning process all predictions are definite. Based on this assumption the overall performance of the models is comparable. This is encouraging, given the fact that the ArgEML system is still in its infancy and particularly because the main purpose of this approach is not so much to optimize accuracy but to harness the benefits of informative explanations from the learned theory.

5   Discussion: ArgEML and XAI

The main goal of XAI is to render AI systems transparent at a high cognitive level that links with that of their human users. To achieve this the output of AI systems needs to be placed in a framework that is compatible with that of Human Cognitive Reasoning. One such framework is that of argumentation, given its strong support from Cognitive Science (and other fields) [42] for its suitability to model human reasoning.

In our work, following several earlier works on argumentation for XAI (see [3, 43] for a survey) we have concentrate on the role of argumentation in Explainable Machine Learning. We have studied how adopting argumentation as the target language for ML offers a new perspective on learning with new "explainable evaluation metrics" for the learned output both during the learning process and for its final output. The essence of these new metrics is that they are intrinsically linked with the possible predictions and their explanations by the learned system. For example, we can identify undecided dilemma predictions of the learned output but which still offer valuable information through the explanations for the different prediction possibilities. It is important to stress that the proposed ArgEML methodology with these evaluation metrics does not depend crucially on the specific argumentation framework that we have chosen to realize and implement the framework. The same approach would be possible using other argumentation frameworks from the area of Computational Argumentation in AI. This is because, conceptually, ArgEML uses notions that are intrinsic to argumentation and hence would exist in any argumentation framework.

The ArgEML framework puts an emphasis on the form of the explanations that accompany predictions and other elements in the framework. It exploits the natural link between argumentation and explanation to provide highly informative "peer explanations" of the form that human experts in the domain would. This synthesis of informative explanations comes from the dialectic nature of argumentation allowing us to build explanations containing both an attributive part, giving the basic reasons on which, a prediction is supported (i.e. answering "why this prediction") as well as a contrastive part, which gives additional reasons that strengthen the basic reason against reasons supporting the opposite prediction (i.e. answering "why not a different prediction").

Such explanations go beyond the relatively simple explanations, that we find in standard XAI explainability systems such as LIME [44], SHAP [45] or GLocalX [46], where explanations consist of isolated features that are relevant or significant for the prediction of the learner. Within an argumentation-based framework for ML, like ArgEML, we can form explanations that can synthesize such information for and against the prediction and indeed information for alternative possible predictions. We are currently (not reported in this paper) investigating how ArgEML can provide such a high-level explainability language for black-box (neural-network) machine learning by applying the framework in a hybrid mode on top of the aforementioned standard explainability systems.

The rich and informative nature of explanations from an argumentation-based learner, such as ArgEML, also helps us to analyze the learning problem space and understand how this can be structured into different subparts. We can use the argument-based explanations that we get from the framework to identify subcases of the problem space, where each such subgroup is characterized by a unique type or pattern of explanation. Essentially, this gives us an explanation-based partitioning of the learning space. As an example

Table 5. ACSRS Example Subgroups (on one split of 160 training examples)

Explanation based subgroups	Number of Cases	Accuracy/Dilemma
E1	44	96%
E2	18	95%
E3	9	100%
E4.1, E4.2	5	dilemma
E5.1, E5.2	6	dilemma

of this, we show in Table 5 such "explanation equivalent" largely populated (in terms of number of cases belonging to the group) subgroups of the training set from the ArgEML execution on the ACSRS dataset, presented above in Sect. 5.3. In Groups 1–3 the prediction of the learned theory is definite whereas in groups 4 and 5 the learned theory is in a dilemma and they are specified by two explanations, one for each possible outcome of the prediction. This helps us understand what characterizes difficult cases or cases where we might need more data information to improve the learner, such as in cases that are characterized by the possibly common features of the members of Group 4 or of Group 5.

In general, we can use such a partitioning to grade locally our confidence in the learner for different parts of the problem by, for example, validating the explanation of a sub group of the problem with the help of an expert on the problem domain.

6 Conclusions

Argumentation can play a foundational role in Explainable AI and more generally in Human-centric AI [47] supporting explanations and behavior of systems at a high cognitive level. In this paper we have studied the role of argumentation in explainable machine learning. We have presented a framework for explainable machine learning that uses argumentation as the target language and notion of prediction for learning. We have exposed the main features of this framework and how its results can differ from conventional machine learning approaches. A first set of evaluation experiments have been presented, comparing the accuracy and the nature of explanations for the results with a Random Forest approach on the same problems. We have also illustrated how the explainability element of the argumentation-based approach to machine learning can help us structure and partition the learning problem space into meaningful sub-spaces.

Like any machine learning framework, the application of our approach to real-life problems requires further methods to control and guide the search. The clear conceptual foundation of our approach and its parametric nature with high-level cognitive elements can help in developing better learning algorithms and tuning these to the nature of the problem domain of application. In particular, we aim to study more closely how the quality of the explanations required by a problem domain can affect and perhaps drive the search for argumentation-based solutions to learning. We plan to release soon the first version of our ArgEML system and to encourage its extensive experimentation whose feedback will hopefully help us improve and develop further the approach. We also plan to conduct more experiments by systematically applying the approach to different real-life medical datasets, and engage medical experts to evaluate the quality of explanations. We have already started a preliminary investigation on some of these datasets [48, 49]. Finally, a long-term objective of our work is to examine how an argumentation-based approach to machine learning can be used to provide a post-hoc explainability layer for opaque black-box learned models. Although some work on this exists (see e.g. [50]), this is a major and important challenge that deserves further attention.

Acknowledgements. Part of this work was undertaken under the University of Cyprus internal project, Integrated Explainable AI (IXAI) for Medical Decision Support, ARGEML 8037P-22046. This study is also partly funded by the project 'Atherorisk' "Identification of unstable carotid plaques associated with symptoms using ultrasonic image analysis and plaque motion analysis", code: Excellence/0421/0292, funded by the Research and In-novation Foundation, the Republic of Cyprus.

References

1. Longo, L.: Argumentation for knowledge representation, conflict resolution, defeasible inference and its integration with machine learning. In: Holzinger, A. (ed.) Machine Learning for Health Informatics. LNCS, vol. 9605, pp. 183–208. Springer, Cham (2016). https://doi.org/10.1007/978-3-319-50478-0_9
2. Kakas, A., Michael, L.: Abduction and argumentation for explainable machine learning: a position survey. arXiv (2020). http://arxiv.org/abs/2010.12896
3. Vassiliades, A., Bassiliades, N., Patkos, T.: Argumentation and explainable artificial intelligence: a survey. Knowl. Eng. Rev. **36**, e5 (2021). https://doi.org/10.1017/S026988892100011
4. Možina, M., Žabkar, J., Bratko, I.: Argument based machine learning. Artif. Intell. **171**(10–15), 922–937 (2007). https://doi.org/10.1016/j.artint.2007.04.007
5. Žabkar, J., Možina, M., Videčnik, J., Bratko, I.: Argument based machine learning in a medical domain. Front. Artif. Intell. Appl. **144**, 59–70 (2006)
6. Možina, M., Giuliano, C., Bratko, I.: Argument based machine learning from examples and text (2009). https://doi.org/10.1109/ACIIDS.2009.60
7. Groza, A., Toderean, L., Muntean, G.A., Nicoara, S.D.: Agents that argue and explain classifications of retinal conditions. J. Med. Biol. Eng. **41**(5), 730–741 (2021). https://doi.org/10.1007/s40846-021-00647-7
8. Ontañón, S., Plaza, E.: Coordinated inductive learning using argumentation-based communication. Auton. Agent. Multi. Agent. Syst. **29**(2), 266–304 (2015). https://doi.org/10.1007/s10458-014-9256-2
9. Niskanen, A., Wallner, J.P., Järvisalo, M.: Synthesizing argumentation frameworks from examples. J. Artif. Intell. Res. **66**(503), 554 (2019). https://doi.org/10.1613/jair.1.11758
10. Yras, K.Č., Satoh, K., Toni, F.: Abstract argumentation for case-based reasoning. In: Proceedings of the International Conference on Knowledge Represention and Reasoning, no. Kr, pp. 549–552 (2016)
11. Ayoobi, H., Cao, M., Verbrugge, R., Verheij, B.: Argumentation-based online incremental learning. IEEE Trans. Autom. Sci. Eng. **19**(4), 3419–3433 (2022). https://doi.org/10.1109/TASE.2021.3120837

12. Potyka, N., Bazo, M., Spieler, J., Staab, S.: Learning gradual argumentation frameworks using meta-heuristics. In: CEUR Workshop Proceedings, vol. 3208 (2022)
13. Dimopoulos, Y., Kakas, A.: Learning non-monotonic logic programs: learning exceptions. In: Lavrac, N., Wrobel, S. (eds.) ECML 1995. LNCS, vol. 912, pp. 122–137. Springer, Heidelberg (1995). https://doi.org/10.1007/3-540-59286-5_53
14. Wardeh, M., Coenen, F., Capon, T.B.: PISA: a framework for multiagent classification using argumentation. Data Knowl. Eng. **75**, 34–57 (2012). https://doi.org/10.1016/j.datak.2012.03.001
15. Michael, L.: Cognitive reasoning and learning mechanisms. In: CEUR Workshop Proceedings, vol. 1895 (2017)
16. Prentzas, N., Nicolaides, A., Kyriacou, E., Kakas, A., Pattichis, C.: Integrating machine learning with symbolic reasoning to build an explainable AI model for stroke prediction. In: Proceedings - 2019 IEEE 19th International Conference on Bioinformatics and Bioengineering, BIBE 2019, pp. 817–821 (2019). https://doi.org/10.1109/BIBE.2019.00152
17. Maurizio, P., Toni, F.: Learning assumption-based argumentation frameworks (2022). http://hdl.handle.net/10044/1/98940
18. Carstens, L., Toni, F.: Improving out-of-domain sentiment polarity classification using argumentation (2016). https://doi.org/10.1109/ICDMW.2015.185
19. Loizos, M.: Machine coaching (2019). https://api.semanticscholar.org/CorpusID:236161635
20. Potyka, N.: Interpreting neural networks as quantitative argumentation frameworks. In: 35th AAAI Conference on Artificial Intelligence, AAAI 2021, vol. 7 (2021). https://doi.org/10.1609/aaai.v35i7.16801
21. Riveret, R., Tran, S., Garcez, A.D.A.: Neural-symbolic probabilistic argumentation machines. In: 17th International Conference on Principles of Knowledge Representation and Reasoning, KR 2020, vol. 2 (2020). https://doi.org/10.24963/kr.2020/90
22. Tsamoura, E., Hospedales, T., Michael, L.: Neural-symbolic integration: a compositional perspective. In: 35th AAAI Conference on Artificial Intelligence, AAAI 2021, vol. 6A (2021). https://doi.org/10.1609/aaai.v35i6.16639
23. Sendi, N., Abchiche-Mimouni, N., Zehraoui, F.: A new transparent ensemble method based on deep learning. Procedia Comput. Sci. **159**, 271–280 (2019). https://doi.org/10.1016/j.procs.2019.09.182
24. Dejl, A., et al.: Argflow: a toolkit for deep argumentative explanations for neural networks. In: Proceedings of the International Joint Conference on Autonomous Agents and Multiagent Systems, AAMAS, vol. 3 (2021)
25. Bench-Capon, T.J.M., Dunne, P.E.: Argumentation in artificial intelligence. Artif. Intell. **171**(10–15), 619–641 (2007). https://doi.org/10.1016/j.artint.2007.05.001
26. Rahwan, I., Simari, G.R.: Argumentation in artificial intelligence (2009)
27. Spanoudakis, N.I., Kakas, A.C., Moraitis, P.: Applications of argumentation: the SoDA methodology. In: Frontiers in artificial intelligence and applications, vol. 285 (2016). https://doi.org/10.3233/978-1-61499-672-9-1722
28. Longo, L., Rizzo, L., Dondio, P.: Examining the modelling capabilities of defeasible argumentation and non-monotonic fuzzy reasoning. Knowl.-Based Syst. **211**, 106514 (2021). https://doi.org/10.1016/j.knosys.2020.106514
29. Kakas, A., Moraïtis, P.: Argumentation based decision making for autonomous agents. In: Proceedings of the International Conference on Autonomous Agents, vol. 2 (2003). https://doi.org/10.1145/860575.860717
30. Dietz, E., Kakas, A., Loizos, M.: Computational argumentation & cognitive AI. In: Chetouani, M., Dignum, V., Lukowicz, P., Sierra, C. (eds.) ACAI 2021. LNCS, vol. 13500, pp. 363–388. Springer, Cham (2023). https://doi.org/10.1007/978-3-031-24349-3_19
31. Kakas, A.C., Moraitis, P., Spanoudakis, N.I.: GORGIAS: applying argumentation. Argument Comput. **10**(1), 55–81 (2019). https://doi.org/10.3233/AAC-181006

32. Spanoudakis, N.I., Kakas, A.C., Koumi, A.: Application level explanations for argumentation-based decision making. In: CEUR Workshop Proceedings, vol. 3209 (2022)

33. Dung, P.M.: On the acceptability of arguments and its fundamental role in nonmonotonic reasoning, logic programming and n-person games. Artif. Intell. **77**(2), 321–357 (1995). https://doi.org/10.1016/0004-3702(94)00041-X

34. Cyras, K., Rago, A., Albini, E., Baroni, P., Toni, F.: Argumentative XAI: a survey (2021). https://doi.org/10.24963/ijcai.2021/600

35. Sklar, E.I., Azhar, M.Q.: Explanation through argumentation (2018). https://doi.org/10.1145/3284432.3284470

36. Rago, A., Cocarascu, O., Toni, F.: Argumentation-based recommendations: fantastic explanations and how to find them. In: IJCAI International Joint Conference on Artificial Intelligence, vol. 2018-July (2018). https://doi.org/10.24963/ijcai.2018/269

37. Miller, T.: Explanation in artificial intelligence: Insights from the social sciences. Artif. Intell. **267**, 1–38 (2019). https://doi.org/10.1016/j.artint.2018.07.007

38. Deng, H.: Interpreting tree ensembles with inTrees. Int. J. Data Sci. Anal. **7**(4), 277–287 (2018). https://doi.org/10.1007/s41060-018-0144-8

39. Letham, B., Rudin, C., McCormick, T.H., Madigan, D.: Interpretable classifiers using rules and bayesian analysis: Building a better stroke prediction model. Ann. Appl. Stat. **9**(3), 1350–1371 (2015). https://doi.org/10.1214/15-AOAS848

40. Holte, R.C.: Very simple classification rules perform well on most commonly used datasets. Mach. Learn. **11**(1), 63–90 (1993). https://doi.org/10.1023/A:1022631118932

41. Nicolaides, A.N., et al.: Asymptomatic internal carotid artery stenosis and cerebrovascular risk stratification. J. Vasc. Surg. **52**(6), 1486–1496 (2010). https://doi.org/10.1016/j.jvs.2010.07.021

42. Yáñez, C.S.: Mercier and Sperber's argumentative theory of reasoning: from the psychology of reasoning to argumentation studies. Inform. Log. **32**(1), 132–159 (2012). https://doi.org/10.22329/il.v32i1.3536

43. Čyras, K., et al.: Machine reasoning explainability. arXiv (2020)

44. Ribeiro, M.T., Singh, S., Guestrin, C.: 'Why should i trust you?' Explaining the predictions of any classifier. In: Proceedings of the ACM SIGKDD International Conference on Knowledge Discovery and Data Mining, vol. 13–17-Augu, pp. 1135–1144 (2016). https://doi.org/10.1145/2939672.2939778

45. Lundberg, S.M., Lee, S.I.: A unified approach to interpreting model predictions. In: Advances in Neural Information Processing Systems, vol. 2017-Decem, pp. 4766–4775 (2017)

46. Setzu, M., Guidotti, R., Monreale, A., Turini, F., Pedreschi, D., Giannotti, F.: GLocalX - from local to global explanations of black box AI models. Artif. Intell. **294**, 103457 (2021). https://doi.org/10.1016/j.artint.2021.103457

47. Dietz, E., Kakas, A., Michael, L.: Argumentation: a calculus for human-centric AI. Front. Artif. Intell. **5**, 955579 (2022). https://doi.org/10.3389/frai.2022.955579

48. Prentzas, N., Gavrielidou, A., Neophytou, M., Kakas, A.: Argumentation-based explainable machine learning (ArgEML): a real-life use case on gynecological cancer. In: CEUR Workshop Proceedings, vol. 3208 (2022)

49. Nicolaou, A., Loizou, C.P., Pantzaris, M., Kakas, A., Pattichis, C.S.: Rule extraction in the assessment of brain mri lesions in multiple sclerosis: preliminary findings. In: Tsapatsoulis, N., Panayides, A., Theocharides, T., Lanitis, A., Pattichis, C., Vento, M. (eds.) CAIP 2021. LNCS (LNAI and LNB), vol. 13052, pp. 277–286. Springer, Cham (2021). https://doi.org/10.1007/978-3-030-89128-2_27

50. Albini, E., Lertvittayakumjorn, P., Rago, A., Toni, F.: DAX: deep argumentative explanation for neural networks (2020)

A Novel Structured Argumentation Framework for Improved Explainability of Classification Tasks

Lucas Rizzo(✉) (iD)

Technological University Dublin, Dublin, Ireland
lucas.rizzo@tudublin.ie

Abstract. This paper presents a novel framework for structured argumentation, named extended argumentative decision graph ($xADG$). It is an extension of argumentative decision graphs [10] built upon Dung's abstract argumentation graphs. The $xADG$ framework allows for arguments to use boolean logic operators and multiple premises (supports) within their internal structure, resulting in more concise argumentation graphs that may be easier for users to understand. The study presents a methodology for construction of $xADGs$ from an input decision tree and evaluates their size and predictive capacity for classification tasks of varying magnitudes. Resulting $xADGs$ achieved strong (balanced) accuracy, kept from the input decision tree, while also reducing the average number of supports needed to reach a conclusion. The results further indicated that it is possible to construct plausibly understandable $xADGs$ that outperform other techniques for building $ADGs$ in terms of predictive capacity and overall size. In summary, the study suggests that $xADG$ represents a promising framework to developing more concise argumentative models that can be used for classification tasks and knowledge discovery, acquisition, and refinement.

Keywords: Argumentation · Non-monotonic reasoning · Explainability · Machine Learning

1 Introduction

Several works have employed argumentation and machine learning (ML) in different fashions [8]. Their choice of argumentation framework and purpose of employing argumentation differ, for example, by attempting to improve the performance or the explanatory power of ML models. This paper focus on the problem of explainability. In other words, it proposes an argumentation framework that could be used to improve the understandability of data-driven models. In particular, the emphasis is on decision trees (DT) and on defining argumentative models of equivalent inferential capability but that could be perceived as more understandable. The concept of understandability, as well as the associated notions related to explainability, have a plethora of definitions and can

L. Longo (Ed.): xAI 2023, CCIS 1903, pp. 399–414, 2023.
https://doi.org/10.1007/978-3-031-44070-0_20

be measured in different way [21]. Succinctly, understandability could be linked to the capacity of a model to be understandable from its user point of view. The qualitative analysis of understandability is not performed in this paper. Instead, it provides a quantitative analysis that could indicate a better perceived understandability. It is often inferred that argumentative models are inherently transparent and comprehensible, as they may employ natural language terms and attempt to follow the way humans reason. However, even apparently transparent systems can become convoluted when dealing with large problems. For instance, it is reasonable to assume that an argumentative model with a few arguments is easier to understand than a DT with a plethora of nodes and edges. Hence, it seems worthy to pursue frameworks and automated alternatives for constructing accurate and understandable argumentative models in different contexts.

In summary, this paper presents a novel framework for structured argumentation named extended argumentative decision graph ($xADG$), which enables arguments to use boolean logic operators and multiple supports within their internal structure. The proposed framework is an extension of the argumentative decision graph (ADG) developed by [10], which was itself an extension of Dung's abstract argumentation graphs [11]. The construction of inferential models using $xADG$ is proposed to be made from a given DT. This way, while both the DT and derived argumentative model are guaranteed to maintain the same inferential capability, they may differ in terms of size and comprehensibility. The expectation is that a smaller model will be easier for human reasoners to understand and extend. A preliminary analysis is proposed to investigate whether reasonably smaller structures, in terms of number of arguments/attacks and amount of argument supports, can be achieved for classification tasks of different sizes in the UCI machine learning repository [20].

The remainder of this paper is organised as follows. In Sect. 2, the basics of abstract argumentation semantics and argumentative decision graphs are reviewed. Similar works that have attempted to solve similar problems are also described. Section 3 introduces the formal definition of $xADG$ and describes the experiment proposed to build inferential models using it. Results and discussion are presented in Sect. 4. Finally, Sect. 5 concludes the study and gives a number of indications for future work.

2   Literature Review

When engaging in computational argumentation, the first step is typically to generate a collection of arguments, which can be abstract or structured in various ways. From there, one can establish relationships of attack or support between them, resulting in a network of interrelated arguments known as an argumentation graph. The literature on creating argumentation structures and determining their acceptance in a given context is vast [3]. However, there appears to be a lack of research focused on automatically generating arguments and interactions from data, a critical component for advancing the use and deployment of argumentation systems. The alternative - manual knowledge acquisition from domain experts - is usually prohibitively time-consuming [18]. A few works have performed experiments in this line. For example, the authors in [19] propose the extraction of contradicting rules based on frequent patterns found in the data, followed by their use in structured argumentation, such as ASPIC+ [13]. Preliminary results show that this two-step approach performed well for instances that could be classified, but returned a large amount of undecided records. In [7], the authors put forward a method for extraction of argumentation frameworks for individual unlabelled instances in a dataset, based on other labelled instances. The approach demonstrates competitive predictive capacity for different types of data, but does not analyse the explainability of results in full. In [14], argument attacks are extracted from data-driven proxy indicators through which the probability that a set of arguments is accepted or rejected can be inferred. Experiments are conducted using synthetic data and showing the feasibility of the approach. In [16], the authors propose a process for building a scheme of argument rules initially from ML modules. Additional steps are defined to include attacks that can decrease overall accuracy of arguments but enhance the learning process of a domain expert exploiting the rules. Results demonstrate the potential of the approach but are not evaluated in terms of accuracy loss or by user studies.

Some other works propose the creation of complete or approximate mappings from black-box models to argumentation frameworks. For example, in [4], argumentation is employed as a means of explanation for machine learning outcomes, providing an argumentative interpretation of both the training process and outcomes. In [17] the authors provide a recommender system by extracting argumentation explanations in the form of bipolar argumentation frameworks. In [9] an approach for extracting an argumentation framework from a planning model is given. It is designed in such way to allow its users to query it for explanations about its outputs. Hence, such mappings are usually employed to generate comprehensible explanations or are only assumed, and not investigated, to be more understandable given the inherently transparency of argumentative systems. In contrast, in this work a novel structured argumentation framework is proposed, which is concerned with both predictive capacity and model understandability. A transparent and more concise model could enhance its user capacity of knowledge discovery and refinement. The next subsections introduce the necessary concepts for the definition of the proposed framework.

2.1   Abstract Argumentation Semantics

In this paper, it is important to define the notions of reinstatement and conflictfreeness, as well as the most common Dung semantics [11], such as grounded and preferred. The definitions follow from the works in [5,6].

Definition 1. *Let* $\langle Ar, \mathscr{R} \rangle$ *be an Argumentation Framework (AF),* $a, b \in Ar$ *and* $args \subseteq Ar$. *The following shorthand notations are employed:*

- a^+ as $\{b \,|\, (a, b) \in \mathscr{R}\}$.
- $args^+$ as $\{a \,|\, (a, b) \in \mathscr{R}$ for some $a \in args\}$.
- a^- as $\{b \,|\, (b, a) \in \mathscr{R}\}$.
- $args^-$ as $\{b \,|\, (b, a) \in \mathscr{R}$ for some $a \in args\}$.

a^+ indicates the arguments attacked by a, while a^- indicates the arguments attacking a. $args^+$ indicates the set of arguments attacked by $args^+$, while $args^-$ indicates the set of arguments attacking $args^-$.

Definition 2. *Let $\langle Ar, \mathscr{R} \rangle$ be an AF and $args \subseteq Ar$. args is **conflict-free** iff $args \cap args^+ = \emptyset$.*

Definition 3. *Let $\langle Ar, \mathscr{R} \rangle$ be an AF, $a \in Ar$ and $args \subseteq Ar$. args **defends** an argument a iff $a^- \subseteq args^+$.*

Definition 4. *Let $\langle Arg, \mathscr{R} \rangle$ be an AF and $Lab : Arg \rightarrow \{in, out, undec\}$ be a labelling function. Lab is a **reinstatement labelling** iff it satisfies:*

- $\forall a \in Ar : (Lab(a) = out \equiv \exists b \in Ar : (b$ *defends* $a \wedge Lab(b) = in))$ *and*
- $\forall a \in Ar : (Lab(a) = in \equiv \forall b \in Ar : (b$ *defends* $a \supset Lab(b) = out))$

Definition 5. *Let $args$ be a conflict-free set of arguments, $F : 2^{args} \rightarrow 2^{args}$ a function such that $F(args) = \{a \,|\, a$ is defended by $args\}$ and $Lab : args \rightarrow \{in, out, undec\}$ a reinstatement labelling function. Also consider $in(Lab)$ short for $\{a \in args \,|\, Lab(a) = in\}$, $out(Lab)$ short for $\{a \in args \,|\, Lab(a) = out\}$ and $undec(Lab)$ short for $\{a \in args \,|\, Lab(a) = undec\}$.*

- *$args$ is **admissible** if $args \subseteq F(args)$.*
- *$args$ is a **complete** extension if $args = F(args)$.*
- *$in(Lab)$ is a **grounded** extension if $undec(Lab)$ is maximal, or $in(Lab)$ is minimal, or $out(Lab)$ is minimal.*
- *$in(Lab)$ is a **preferred** extension if $in(Lab)$ is maximal or $out(Lab)$ is maximal.*

The use of argumentation semantics, such as grounded and preferred, can help us examine the justification status of arguments. Essentially, an argument is justified if it can somehow withstand its attackers. Thus, argumentation semantics provide a perspective that one can take, when deciding on the set of accepted, rejected, and undecided arguments. The extension (set of acceptable arguments) can defend itself and remain internally coherent, even if someone disagrees with its viewpoint [22]. The grounded semantics is considered more sceptical, as it takes fewer committed choices and always offers a single extension. For the purposes of this paper, using the grounded semantics is adequate for deriving the inferences from the proposed classification tasks.

2.2   Argumentative Decision Graphs

Formally, the following shorthand notations are employed:

- A dataset $\mathscr{D}$ is represented by a $N \times M$ matrix-like data structure. Each row is called an *instance* of the dataset and each column is called a *feature*.
- The predicates of the form $f_i(v)$ mean *"the feature i has the value v"*.
- The set of all values available for f_i is $\mathscr{V}_{f_i}$.
- One of the features f_i is called the target variable and it is denoted with y.
- The predicates involving the target variable have the form $y(v)$.
- $\mathscr{P}_f$ is the set of predicates regarding the other features $\{f_1, \ldots, f_m\}$.
- $\mathscr{P}_y$ is the set of predicates regarding the target variable y.
- The set of all the predicates is called $\mathscr{P}_f \cup \mathscr{P}_y$.

An *ADG* is proposed in [10] and is defined as following:

Definition 6. *An argumentative decision graph **ADG**, is an argumentation framework $AF = \langle Ar, \mathscr{R} \rangle$, where each $a \in Ar$ is defined as $a = \langle \phi, \theta \rangle$, $\phi \in \mathscr{P}_f, \theta \in \mathscr{P}_y \cup \varnothing$, and $\mathscr{R} \subseteq Ar \times Ar$.*

An *ADG* is a type of abstract argumentation graph that enhances Dung's original model. *ADGs* have a rule-based structure where each argument has a single premise (support) and a conclusion. The support consists of a feature and a corresponding value, while the conclusion represents a value for the target variable. Some arguments may not have a conclusion, and instead, they interact with other predictive arguments. The notion of well-formed *ADGs* is also introduced by [10]:

Definition 7. *Given an ADG $= \langle Ar, \mathscr{R} \rangle$, the ADG is **well-formed** iff $\forall a_1, a_2 \in Ar$ with $a_1 = \langle \phi_1, \theta_1 \rangle$, $a_2 = \langle \phi_2, \theta_2 \rangle$ it holds that:*

1. *if $\phi_1 = f_i(v_1)$ and $\phi_2 = f_i(v_2)$ then $(a_1, a_2) \notin \mathscr{R} \wedge (a_2, a_1) \notin \mathscr{R}$.*
2. *if $\theta_1 = \theta_2 \neq \varnothing$ then $(a_1, a_2) \notin \mathscr{R} \wedge (a_2, a_1) \notin \mathscr{R}$*
3. *if $a_1 = \langle f_1(v_x), y(v_1) \rangle$, $a_2 = \langle f_2(v_y), y(v_2) \rangle$ and $v_1 \neq v_2 \wedge f_1 \neq f_2$ then $(a_1, a_2) \in \mathscr{R} \vee (a_2, a_1) \in \mathscr{R}$*

Informally, these constraints guarantee that: 1) there is no attack between two arguments whose supports contain the same feature; 2) there is no attack between two arguments whose conclusions are the same and not empty; and 3) if two arguments have mutually exclusive conclusions and they use different features in their supports, there must be an attack between them. A well-formed *ADG* can be extracted from a DT following the steps in Algorithm 1. Intuitively, each terminal node in the DT will generate a predictive argument in the *ADG*, while non terminal nodes will generate non predictive arguments. Lastly, arguments with different features and conclusions that are in disjoint paths to distinct terminal nodes will generate attacks. When exploited by an extension-based semantics, such as grounded, the resulting *ADG* will produce the same set of inferences as the DT.

Algorithm 1. Algorithm for building a well-formed ADG from a DT [10]

Input: A DT
Output: A well-formed $ADG = \langle Ar, \mathscr{R} \rangle$
1: $Ar \leftarrow \emptyset$, $\mathscr{R} \leftarrow \emptyset$
2: **for each** directed link l from a node N to a terminal node M **do**
3:     $Ar \leftarrow Ar \cup \langle f_i(v_n), y_m \rangle$ ▷ f_i is the variable tested at node N.
                                 ▷ v_n is the value of f_i identifying the link l connecting N to the terminal node M.
                                 ▷ y_m is the value of the target variable predicted at node M.
4: **end for**
5: **for each** directed link l from a node N to a non terminal node M **do**
6:     $Ar \leftarrow Ar \cup \langle f_i(v_n), \emptyset \rangle$ ▷ f_i is the variable tested at node N.
                                 ▷ v_n is the value of f_i identifying the link l connecting N to the terminal node M.
7: **end for**
8: **for each** $a \in Ar$ associated to a link l_a from node N to M **do**
9:     **for each** $b \in Ar$ associated to a link l_b **do**
10:         **if** l_b is in path p connecting N to a terminal node so that $l_a \in p$ **then**
11:             **continue**   ▷ if l_a and l_b are in a same path from N to a terminal node, then there is no attack
12:         **end if**
13:         **if** a and b features are different or conclusions are different **then**
14:             $\mathscr{R} \leftarrow \mathscr{R} \cup (a, b)$
15:         **end if**
16:     **end for**
17: **end for**
18: **return** $ADG = \langle Ar, \mathscr{R} \rangle$

---

3   Design and Methodology

ADGs are first presented [10] as graph-like models that have the ability to perform classification tasks. In turn, this paper proposes a new model, called *xADG*, which extends *ADGs* by allowing arguments to employ boolean logic operators and multiple supports. Later in this section, the precise definition of a *xADG* is provided. Subsequently, the construction of *xADGs* is proposed to be made from well-formed *ADGs* built from DTs. A simplification procedure is proposed to eliminate any superfluous arguments that may arise from redundant branches within the tree. Afterwards, a set of modifications is introduced to build a *xADG* from the resulting simplified *ADG*. These modifications will allow the removal of arguments and attacks while maintaining the same inferential capability, but incorporating the higher complexity permitted into the argument supports. Other methods have been proposed for the construction of well-formed *ADGs* that do not rely on DTs or any other data-driven approaches [10]. However, these methods have yet to demonstrate superior predictive capacity or model size compared to data-driven classifiers such as DTs. Figure 1 depicts the process proposed for achieving *xADGs* from DTs. The DT can be built by any standard algorithm, such as C4.5 or CART. In turn, a well-formed *ADG* can be derived as detailed in Algorithm 1. The remaining of this section details the subsequent steps: the simplification of *ADGs* and possible modifications to derive *xADGs*.

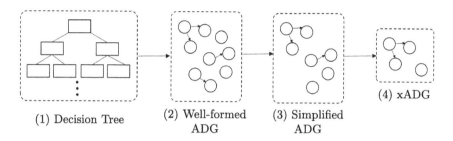

(1) Decision Tree   (2) Well-formed ADG   (3) Simplified ADG   (4) xADG

Fig. 1. Design of the proposed process to build a xADG from a DT while maintaining the same inferential capability. The goal is to achieve a smaller structure, that can be easier to understand and expand by human reasoners.

3.1 ADG Simplification

When considering *ADGs* built from DTs, it is important to note that a DT may contain two different branches that originate from the same starting point and ultimately lead to the same outcome. Hence, all the nodes in these two paths can be removed, while the node in the starting point can be updated in order to draw the same conclusion. Algorithm 1 does not take into account such cases. Therefore, Algorithm 2 can be used to reduce the size of a well-formed *ADG*.

The algorithm is designed to remove predictive arguments with the same conclusion that originate from a same node N in the DT. Since the arguments will be removed, any attacks that make use of them also need to be removed. Finally, the non predictive argument originated from a link of another node M to N needs to have its conclusion updated. This process is repeated while there are arguments to be removed. Figure 2 depicts an example.

3.2 Extended Argumentation Graphs from Data (xADG)

In order to allow for the use of more features by each argument's support, a $xADG$ in introduced here. Basically, a $xADG$ is an ADG where each argument has an internal structure composed of boolean logical operators and one or more supports. It is defined as following:

Definition 8. *An extended argumentative decision graph $\mathbf{xADG}$, is an argumentation framework $AF = \langle Ar, \mathscr{R} \rangle$ where each $a \in Ar$ is defined as $a = \langle (\phi_1$ AND $\phi_2)$ OR $(\phi_3$ AND $\phi_4), \theta \rangle$, $\phi_i \in \mathscr{P}_f, \theta \in \mathscr{P}_y \cup \varnothing$, and $\mathscr{R} \subseteq Ar \times Ar$.*

Algorithm 2. Algorithm for reducing the size of a well-formed ADG built from a DT without considering redundant paths

---

Input: A DT and a well-formed $ADG = \langle Ar, \mathscr{R} \rangle$ built from it
Output: An updated $ADG' = \langle Ar', \mathscr{R}' \rangle$
1: $Ar' \leftarrow Ar, \mathscr{R}' \leftarrow \mathscr{R}$
2: **do**
3:     $Ar'_{old} \leftarrow Ar'$
4:     **for each** pair of arguments $a = \langle f_i(v_1), y_m \rangle$ and $b = \langle f_i(v_2), y_m \rangle$ **do**
        ▷ *Each pair of predictive arguments with same conclusion and support feature*
5:         **if** $f_i(v_1) \cup f_i(v_2) \neq \mathscr{V}_{f_i}$ **then**   ▷ *if v_1 and v_2 do not cover all possible values of f_i, they do not need to be removed*
6:             **continue**
7:         **end if**
8:         **if** links l_a and l_b of a and b do not start from a same node N **then**
9:             **continue**   ▷ *they do not need to be removed*
10:        **end if**
        ▷ *Any pair of arguments at this point needs to be removed*
11:        $Ar' \leftarrow Ar' \setminus \{a, b\}$ ▷ *remove a and b*
12:        $\mathscr{R}' \leftarrow \mathscr{R}' \setminus (x, y)$ where $x \in a, b$ or $y \in a, b$ ▷ *remove attacks with a or b*
13:        **for each** $c = \langle f(v), \emptyset \rangle \in Ar'$ **do**   ▷ *for each non predictive argument*
14:            **if** link l_c starts at M and ends at N **then**
15:                $c \leftarrow \langle f(v), y_m \rangle$ ▷ *Add same conclusion as a and b*
16:                **break**
17:            **end if**
18:        **end for**
19:    **end for**
20: **while** $Ar'_{old} \neq Ar'$ ▷ *Repeat while there are arguments to remove*
21: **return** $ADG' = \langle Ar', \mathscr{R}' \rangle$

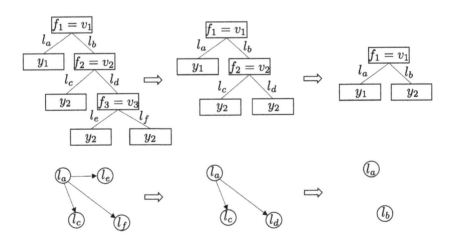

Fig. 2. Example of two steps of Algorithm 2 being employed to simplify an *ADG*. Each DT is depicted on top, with the corresponding *ADG* below. Links between nodes are labelled to identify the arguments in the *ADG*.

Definition 8 characterises an argument in a $xADG$ without compromising its generality. This means that an argument can have a support with any number of predicates $\phi \in \mathscr{P}_f$ in any combination of boolean logical operators AND and OR. Furthermore, an ADG is a specific case of a $xADG$ where all arguments' supports contain only one predicate $\phi \in \mathscr{P}_f$. The notion of well-built arguments in a $xADG$ is also introduced:

Definition 9. *Given an* $xADG$ *represented as an argumentation framework* $AF = (Ar, \mathscr{R})$, *an argument* $a \in Ar$ *with* $a = \langle (\phi_1 \text{ AND } \phi_2) \text{ OR } (\phi_3 \text{ AND } \phi_4), \theta \rangle$ *and* $\phi_i = f_i(v_i)$ *is said to be **well-built** iff it holds that:*

1. *$f_1 \neq f_2$ and $f_3 \neq f_4$.*
2. *One of the two options hold:*
   (a) $f_i \neq f_j$, where $i \in \{1,2\}$ and $j \in \{3,4\}$, or
   (b) $f_i = f_j$ and $v_i \neq v_j$, where $i \in \{1,2\}$ and $j \in \{3,4\}$

Informally, the first constraint guarantees that no same features are concatenated by the AND operator, while the second constraint guarantees that there is no redundancy by different clauses concatenated by the OR operators.

3.3   Building xADGs from ADGs

Given a well-formed ADG, a $xADG$ of equivalent inferential capability can be built by performing a set of modifications. In other words, attacks and arguments can be reduced in a ADG by modifying the internal structure of arguments, as defined by an $xADG$. This can be done while keeping the same set of inferences produced by the original well-formed ADG. Figures 3, 4 and 5 introduce three of such modifications, named m_1, m_2 and m_3.

Concerning the equivalence of inferences, when applying m_1 or m_3, the attacked arguments that were initially rejected (accepted) from some extension-based semantics, will now have their supports in the resulting $xADG$ evaluate to false (true). Hence, the inferences of predictive arguments are preserved. As for m_2, instead of having one or two arguments initially activated, only one in the resulting $xADG$ will be activated (with the same conclusion). Since the attacks of the merged argument remain unchanged, it will be accepted or rejected in the same way as any of the other two in the original structure[1].

Regarding the amount of supports resulting from m_{1-3}, it is worth noting that the examples used to introduce them had initially arguments with only one support, leading to a $xADG$ with arguments having two supports. These simplified examples are easier to comprehend, but it is possible that the changes performed by m_{1-3} may result in a larger number of supports (number of predicates appearing in the argument support). For instance, applying m_2 repeatedly, can lead to an argument having several OR clauses. Hence, the potential advantages and disadvantages of these modifications in terms of number of attacks/arguments and amount of supports is detailed below:

---

[1] This characteristic does not hold for ranking-based semantics [1], in which the number of attackers and attacked arguments may affect the arguments' acceptance.

Modification m_1

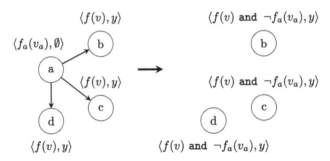

Fig. 3. Example of modification (m_1) for removing non predictive arguments. The support of a non predictive attacking argument (a) is appended in the negative form to the support of the attacked arguments (b, c, and d) using the AND operator. $f(v)$ and y are used to represent any feature with certain value and any conclusion. $f_a(v_a)$ is used to represent a specific feature and value used by argument a.

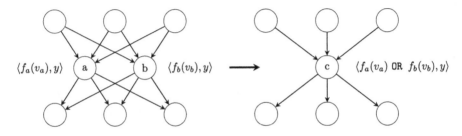

Fig. 4. Example of modification (m_2) for merging two predictive arguments. Two predictive arguments, a and b, with the same conclusion and same set of targets and attackers (including empty sets) can be merged in a single argument. Supports are concatenated by the OR operator and the conclusion is kept the same.

Modification m_3

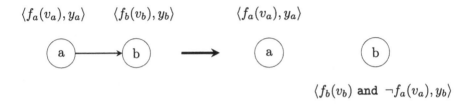

Fig. 5. Example of modification (m_3) for removing an attack. The attack from a to b can be removed by appending the negative support of the attacker to the target argument using the AND operator.

- Modification m_1: this has the potential to remove a single argument and multiple attacks originated from it, by concatenating its negated support to the attacked arguments using the AND operator. When arguments are well-built, it is possible that the number of supports in the resulting argument will not increase.
- Modification m_2: this has the potential to remove a single argument and all the attacks originated and targeted at it. The cost is the addition of its support/s using the OR operator to a second argument with the same conclusion and set of attackers and targets. If arguments are well-built, it is possible that the number of supports in the resulting argument is less than the sum of the supports in the two original arguments. The trade-off between number of arguments/attacks and number of supports will depend on how many attacks can be remove, the amount of supports in the resulting argument, and whether the arguments are enforced to be well-built.
- Modification m_3: this has the potential to reduce a single attack by adding its negative support/s to the attacker using the AND operator.

In terms of enhancing explainability, m_1 and m_2 seem to be more promising, since they have the potential to remove multiple attacks and arguments. m_3 seems to be less promising in terms of size of the resulting $xADG$ and the amount of arguments' supports. The exchange when using m_3 is for one less attack and at least one more support in the attacked argument. Moreover, it can be argued that the visual representation of an attack is a better way of depicting contradictions between arguments instead of negative supports.

3.4 Experimental Setup

To investigate if small $xADGs$ can be achieved, an initial evaluation is proposed. First, a dataset and a respective DT need to be provided. Next, Algorithms 1 and 2 can be applied followed by a series of modifications m_2 and m_1. m_2 is applied before m_1, since merging arguments after removing attacks, could lead to more merged arguments with a high amount of supports. In turn, m_3 is not employed, since it does not offer a good trade-off in terms of explainability. A max number of supports can be set when using m_1 and m_2, so as to avoid the number of supports to be too high. However, this is not limited in this analysis in order to give a better notion of what can be achieved with m_1 and m_2. Algorithm 3 details the steps of this evaluation.

Algorithm 3. Proposed algorithm for the creation of $xADGs$ built from DTs

---
Input: Dataset $\mathscr{D}$
Output: a $xADG$
  1: **Function** WellBuiltArguments($xADG = \langle Ar, \mathscr{R} \rangle$):
  2:     **for each** $a \in Ar$ **do**
  3:         $a \leftarrow$ wellBuilt(a)   ▷ *Updates a by removing any redundancy and making sure it is well-built*
  4:     **end for**
  5: **return** $xADG$
  6: $DT \leftarrow$ A DT classifier($\mathscr{D}$)   ▷ *Some DT algorithm, such as C4.5 or CART*
  7: $ADG \leftarrow$ Algorithm 1 (DT)
  8: $ADG \leftarrow$ Algorithm 2 (DT, ADG)
  9: $xADG \leftarrow ADG$ ▷ *First version of $xADG$ before applying m_1 and m_2*
 10: **do**
 11:     $xADG_{old} \leftarrow xADG$
         ▷ *Merge any single pair of arguments and update it to be well-built*
 12:     $xADG \leftarrow$ WellBuiltArguments($m_2(xADG)$)
 13: **while** $xADG_{old} \neq xADG$ ▷ *Repeat while there are arguments to merge*
 14: **do**
 15:     $xADG_{old} \leftarrow xADG$
         ▷ *Remove any single attacking argument, add its negative support to attacked arguments, and update attacked arguments to be well-built*
 16:     $xADG \leftarrow$ WellBuiltArguments($m_1(xADG)$)
 17: **while** $xADG_{old} \neq xADG$ ▷ *Repeat while there are arguments arguments and attacks to remove*
 18: **return** $xADG$

---

4   Results

In order to assess if small $xADGs$ can be achieved for problems of different magnitudes, four datasets from the UCI machine learning repository [20] were chosen[2]. These datasets were selected based on their number of features and records, so as to provide a more robust indication of the usefulness of $xADGs$. A DT was built for each one with the optimised version of the CART algorithm provided by the `scikit-learn` package [15]. Training and testing sets used a 80%-20% split ratio. The maximum depths of the DTs were chosen based on a preliminary analysis of balanced accuracy. An increasing number of maximum depths were evaluated, and the last one to offer a reasonable improvement in balanced accuracy was chosen. This was done to achieve the highest balanced accuracy without growing the tree for irrelevant gains. Table 1 lists the results for the 4 datasets. The accuracy, balanced accuracy, tree size (nodes and edges), average path length, $xADG$ size (arguments and attacks), and number of supports (min, average and max) are reported. The confidence interval (CI) 95%

---

[2] `archive.ics.uci.edu/ml/datasets/Car+Evaluation`
`archive.ics.uci.edu/ml/datasets/Adult`
`archive.ics.uci.edu/ml/datasets/Bank+Marketing`
`archive.ics.uci.edu/ml/datasets/Myocardial+infarction+complications.`

is presented for all results after running a number of 100 executions for each dataset. The work in [10] performs a similar experiment for building well-formed *ADGs* using the cars and census dataset. A greedy algorithm is employed to build the *ADG* from scratch. Table 2 lists a comparison with this approach.

4.1   Analysis and Discussion

In all experiments, as reported in Table 1, the resulting *xADGs* achieved satisfactory size. That means they are considered small enough to be reasonably understandable by human reasoners. This assumption might not hold if a higher number of supports is employed. However, this should be evaluated with user studies, and it is suggested as future work.

Table 1. Summary statistics of DTs and *xADGs* found for 4 different datasets. Ranges represent the CI 95% of 100 executions. For the cars dataset, class values *acc, good, vgood* were grouped into *acc*. For the myocardial dataset, ZSN was chosen as target feature since it is better balanced, and features with more than 5% missing data were dropped. The DTs were used as input for the creation of the *xADGs*, hence, the (balanced) accuracy is the same for both models.

	Datasets			
	Cars	Census	Bank	Myocardial
Features	6	14	16	59
Records	1728	30152	45211	1436
Tree depth	6	4	3	3
Avg. path length	[5.1, 5.2]	[3.8, 3.9]	[3.0, 3.0]	[3.0, 3.0]
Tree nodes	[26.6, 27.3]	[26.7, 27.4]	[15, 15]	[15,15]
Tree edges	[25.6, 26.3]	[25.7, 26.4]	[14, 14]	[14,14]
xADG args.	[8.3, 9.0]	[8.4, 8.9]	[6.8, 7.0]	[3.2, 3.7]
xADG atts.	[7.7, 9.6]	[6.4, 8.3]	[2.0, 2.0]	[1.0, 1.3]
Supports min	[1.8, 2.0]	[2.0, 2.1]	[2.0, 2.0]	[1.1, 1.3]
Supports max	[3.3, 3.6]	[3.9, 4.0]	[2.9, 3.0]	[1.2, 1.4]
Supports average	[2.6, 2.7]	[2.5, 2.6]	[2.3, 2.3]	[1.1, 1.3]
Accuracy	[0.940, 0.946]	[0.839, 0.841]	[0.898, 0.900]	[0.796, 0.809]
Balanced Acc.	[0.939, 0.946]	[0.728, 0.732]	[0.651, 0.658]	[0.600, 0.611]

When comparing the *xADG* with their counterpart DTs, it is essential to consider both the number of supports and the average path length in the DT. Although the average number of supports may be lower, it is important to note that attacks in the *xADG* might require multiple arguments (if all activated) to produce an inference. Contrarily, the nodes in a DT path can always produce an inference without interacting with the nodes in another path. Therefore, the number of attacks produced should also be considered. This was typically smaller or substantially smaller than the number of arguments reported, suggesting that the evaluation of attacks between arguments might not be necessary to produce an inference in many cases. Hence, when using model size as a metric for assessing users' understandability of both the model and the inferences it generates, there seem to be pros and cons for the DT and for the equivalent $xADG$. The results provided by this quantitative analysis do not seem to offer a decisive outcome. Depending on the available data and prior knowledge of the human reasoner, either the conflict-based representation of $xADG$ or the mutually exclusive rules generated by the paths in the DT could result in a model that is more concise and understandable. However, it is crucial to observe that the $xADG$ allows knowledge to be more easily incorporated, through the addition of arguments and attacks, without any restriction in its topology. Thus, it can be argued that it is more adequate for knowledge discovery, acquisition and refinement.

As for the comparison in Table 2, note that the accuracy and balanced accuracy are better for the $xADGs$ in the cars dataset, and similar in the census dataset. However, the number of arguments and attacks is smaller for the cars dataset and substantially smaller for the census dataset. The number of supports is kept small enough for the arguments to be assumed understandable as previously discussed. This suggests that leveraging the structure and inferential capability of DTs with $xADGs$ might be a good alternative for automating the creation of structured argumentation frameworks with stronger (balanced) accuracy and reasonable size to be used by human reasoners.

Table 2. Comparison of well-formed $ADGs$ built in [10] via a greedy algorithm and $xADGs$ built here via input decision trees and structural modifications. Ranges represent the CI 95% of 100 executions.

	Datasets			
	Cars [10]	Cars	Census [10]	Census
Accuracy	0.88	[0.940, 0.946]	0.83	[0.839, 0.841]
Balanced Acc.	0.88	[0.939, 0.946]	0.75	[0.728, 0.732]
Arguments	8	[8.3, 9.0]	21	[8.4, 8.8]
Attacks	11	[7.7, 9.0]	78	[6.4, 8.3]
Supports min	1	[1.8, 2.0]	1	[2.0, 2.1]
Supports max	1	[3.3, 3.6]	1	[3.9, 4.0]
Supports average	1	[2.6, 2.7]	1	[2.5, 2.6]

5   Conclusions

In this paper, a novel framework for structured argumentation, named extended argumentative decision graph ($xADG$), was proposed. It is an extension of the argumentative decision graph (ADG) proposed by [10] and itself an extension of Dung's abstract argumentation graphs. It enabled arguments to use boolean logic operators and multiple supports within their internal structure. Therefore, it is able to produce more concise argumentation graphs and potentially enhance its understandability from its users' point of view. Results for classification problems of different sizes indicate that xADGs can be built via an input decision tree, while keeping the same (balanced) accuracy and potentially lowering the average number of premises to reach a conclusion. Comparisons with other techniques for construction of $ADGs$ (not derived from an input decision tree) also indicate a better predictive capacity coupled with smaller model size. It is expected that $xADGs$ will provide an initial step for the creation of more concise structured argumentation frameworks that can be learned from data and used for knowledge discovery, acquisition and refinement.

Future work can consider the use of more optimised DTs [12] that could lead to smaller $xADGs$, as well as $xADGs$ modifications that can impact on the models' inferential capability. It is possible that modifications that slightly reduce predictive capacity might allow significant gains in understandability. For instance, it might be possible to reduce the amount of similar (as defined in [2]) arguments. It is also important that user studies are performed to evaluate the understandability of $xADGs$ with a larger number of supports originated from massive decision trees. The addition of human knowledge by domain experts to $xADGs$ could also be tested in various contexts. Finally, $xADGs$ can be employed to reduce the size of large $ADGs$ not linked to monotonic, data-driven models (as in [10]), allowing a more diverse range of understandable solutions to be found.

References

1. Amgoud, L., Ben-Naim, J.: Ranking-based semantics for argumentation frameworks. In: Liu, W., Subrahmanian, V.S., Wijsen, J. (eds.) SUM 2013. LNCS (LNAI), vol. 8078, pp. 134–147. Springer, Heidelberg (2013). https://doi.org/10.1007/978-3-642-40381-1_11
2. Amgoud, L., David, V.: Measuring similarity between logical arguments. In: Sixteenth International Conference on Principles of Knowledge Representation and Reasoning (2018)
3. Baroni, P., Caminada, M., Giacomin, M.: An introduction to argumentation semantics. knowl. Eng. Rev. **26**(4), 365–410 (2011)
4. Bistarelli, S., Mancinelli, A., Santini, F., Taticchi, C.: An argumentative explanation of machine learning outcomes 1. In: Computational Models of Argument, pp. 347–348. IOS Press (2022)
5. Caminada, M.: On the issue of reinstatement in argumentation. In: Fisher, M., van der Hoek, W., Konev, B., Lisitsa, A. (eds.) JELIA 2006. LNCS (LNAI), vol. 4160, pp. 111–123. Springer, Heidelberg (2006). https://doi.org/10.1007/11853886_11

6. Caminada, M.W., Gabbay, D.M.: A logical account of formal argumentation. Stud. Log. **93**(2–3), 109 (2009)
7. Cocarascu, O., Stylianou, A., Čyras, K., Toni, F.: Data-empowered argumentation for dialectically explainable predictions. In: ECAI 2020, pp. 2449–2456. IOS Press (2020)
8. Cocarascu, O., Toni, F.: Argumentation for machine learning: a survey. In: COMMA, pp. 219–230 (2016)
9. Collins, A., Magazzeni, D., Parsons, S.: Towards an argumentation-based approach to explainable planning. In: ICAPS 2019 Workshop XAIP Program Chairs (2019)
10. Dondio, P.: Towards argumentative decision graphs: Learning argumentation graphs from data. In: D'Agostino, M., D'Asaro, F.A., Larese, C. (eds.) AI^3@ AI* IA. CEUR-WS.org (2021)
11. Dung, P.M.: On the acceptability of arguments and its fundamental role in nonmonotonic reasoning, logic programming and n-person games. Artif. Intell. **77**(2), 321–357 (1995). https://doi.org/10.1016/0004-3702(94)00041-X
12. Kotsiantis, S.B.: Decision trees: a recent overview. Artif. Intell. Rev. **39**, 261–283 (2013)
13. Modgil, S., Prakken, H.: The ASPIC+ framework for structured argumentation: a tutorial. Argument Comput. **5**(1), 31–62 (2014)
14. Noor, K., Hunter, A.: A Bayesian probabilistic argumentation framework for learning from online reviews. In: 2020 IEEE 32nd International Conference on Tools with Artificial Intelligence (ICTAI), pp. 742–747. IEEE (2020)
15. Pedregosa, F., et al.: Scikit-learn: machine learning in Python. J. Mach. Learn. Res. **12**, 2825–2830 (2011)
16. Prentzas, N., Gavrielidou, A., Neophytou, M., Kakas, A.: Argumentation-based explainable machine learning (ArgeML): a real-life use case on gynecological cancer. In: Kuhlmann, I., Mumford, J., Sarkadi, S. (eds.) ArgML 2022. CEUR-WS.org (2022)
17. Rago, A., Cocarascu, O., Bechlivanidis, C., Toni, F.: Argumentation as a framework for interactive explanations for recommendations. In: Proceedings of the International Conference on Principles of Knowledge Representation and Reasoning, vol. 17, pp. 805–815 (2020)
18. Rizzo, L., Longo, L.: Comparing and extending the use of defeasible argumentation with quantitative data in real-world contexts. Inf. Fusion **89**, 537–566 (2023). https://doi.org/10.1016/j.inffus.2022.08.025
19. Thimm, M., Kersting, K.: Towards argumentation-based classification. In: Logical Foundations of Uncertainty and Machine Learning, Workshop at IJCAI, vol. 17 (2017)
20. University of California, Irvine: UCI machine learning repository. http://archive.ics.uci.edu/ml. Accessed 18 Apr 2023
21. Vilone, G., Longo, L.: Notions of explainability and evaluation approaches for explainable artificial intelligence. Inf. Fusion **76**, 89–106 (2021). https://doi.org/10.1016/j.inffus.2021.05.009
22. Wu, Y., Caminada, M., Podlaszewski, M.: A labelling-based justification status of arguments. Stud. Log. **3**(4), 12–29 (2010)

Hardness of Deceptive Certificate Selection

Stephan Wäldchen$^{(\boxtimes)}$ [iD]

Zuse Institute Berlin, Berlin, Germany
waeldchen@zib.de

Abstract. Recent progress towards theoretical interpretability guarantees for AI has been made with classifiers that are based on interactive proof systems. A prover selects a certificate from the datapoint and sends it to a verifier who decides the class. In the context of machine learning, such a certificate can be a feature that is informative of the class. For a setup with high soundness and completeness, the exchanged certificates must have a high mutual information with the true class of the datapoint. However, this guarantee relies on a bound on the Asymmetric Feature Correlation of the dataset, a property that so far is difficult to estimate for high-dimensional data. It was conjectured in [26] that it is computationally hard to exploit the AFC, which is what we prove here.

We consider a malicious prover-verifier duo that aims to exploit the AFC to achieve high completeness and soundness while using uninformative certificates. We show that this task is NP-hard and cannot be approximated better than $\mathcal{O}(m^{1/8-\epsilon})$, where m is the number of possible certificates, for $\epsilon > 0$ under the Dense-vs-Random conjecture. This is some evidence that AFC should not prevent the use of interactive classification for real-world tasks, as it is computationally hard to be exploited.

Keywords: Interactive Proof Systems · Formal Interpretability · XAI · Merlin-Arthur classifiers

1 Introduction

Safe deployment of Neural Network (NN) based AI systems in high-stakes applications, e.g., medical diagnostics [12] or autonomous vehicles [21], requires that their reasoning be subject to human scrutiny. One of the most prominent approaches in explainable AI (XAI) is feature-based interpretability, where a subset of the input values are highlighted as being important for the classifier decision in the form of saliency or relevance maps [19]. Feature-based interpretability had some successes, such as detecting biases in established datasets [15]. However, most approaches are motivated primarily by heuristics and come without any theoretical guarantees, which means their success cannot be verified. While they work well on many generic tasks, they fail when some effort is put into hiding

L. Longo (Ed.): xAI 2023, CCIS 1903, pp. 415–427, 2023.
https://doi.org/10.1007/978-3-031-44070-0_21

the true reasoning process. It has also been demonstrated for numerous XAI-methods that they can be manipulated by a clever design of the NNs [1,11,22,23]. This motives formal approaches for interpretability with clearly stated assumptions and guarantees that can be used by auditors to check the reasoning of commercial AI systems.

1.1   Information Bounds on Features

The most prominent approaches to define the importance of an input feature are Shapley Values [16], Mutual Information [8,24] and Precision [20]. All these concepts are closely related to each other, and the precision can be used to lower-bound the mutual information [26]. In principle, they all rely on the idea of partial input to the classifier $f : [0,1]^d \rightarrow \{-1.1\}$ [25]. For input $\mathbf{x} \in [0,1]^d$ and a set $S \subset [d]$, a partial input $\mathbf{x}_S$ consists of the values of $\mathbf{x}$ on the indices in S. Since most classifiers cannot evaluate partial input, it was proposed in [16] to consider the expectations over the input distribution $\mathcal{D}$ conditioned on $\mathbf{x}_S$. In the context of precision, this leads us to the definition

$$\mathrm{Pr}_{f,\mathbf{x}}(S) := P_{\mathbf{y}\sim\mathcal{D}}[f(\mathbf{y}) = f(\mathbf{x}) \mid \mathbf{y}_S = \mathbf{x}_S] = P_{\mathbf{y}\sim\mathcal{D}|_{\mathbf{x}_S}}[f(\mathbf{y}) = f(\mathbf{x})].$$

The challenge for these formal approaches is that $\mathcal{D}|_{\mathbf{x}_S}$ is generally unknown. In fact, inexact modelling of this distribution is exactly what allowed for the manipulation of the methods in [1,11,22,23], as well as for the artefactual explanations produced by the RDE [17] approach in some images [25]. While modelling this distribution for complicated data, e.g. images, can be practically achieved with deep generative networks [7], there is no known way to bound how accurately this models the true distribution. To compare the modelled distribution to some ground truth would require a large amount of samples conditioned on many possible features $\mathbf{x}_S$, which is beyond the scope of even the largest datasets.

As a remedy, interactive classification, inspired by Interactive Proof Systems, has been developed and demonstrated to yield lower bounds on the precision of features without having to calculate $\mathcal{D}|_{\mathbf{x}_S}$ explicitly [26].

1.2   Interactive Classification

Interactive classification is a concept inspired by interactive proof systems applied to the task of deciding whether datapoints belong to a certain class. We refer to Fig. 1 for an illustration. The framework has been put first put forward in [5], after it was noted that without an adversarial aspect, prover and verifier can cooperate to exchange uninformative features [27]. Specifically, the Merlin-Arthur protocol [3] has inspired the formulation of an equivalent Merlin-Arthur classifier in [26]. The prover Merlin receives a datapoint and selects a certificate (usually a relevant feature of the datapoint) to send to the verifier Arthur, who either accepts this as evidence for the class or rejects. The prover can be cooperative, thus trying to convince Arthur of the correct class, or adversarial, trying to get Arthur to accept a datapoint outside the class. The probability

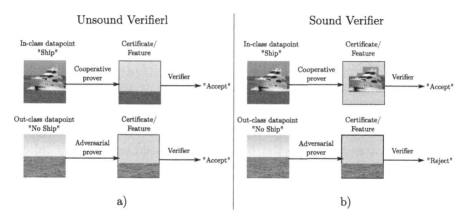

Fig. 1. Illustration of interactive classification with an unsound and a sound verifier. a) The verifier Arthur accepts "water" features as certificates for the "ship" class. While these allow for high completeness, as most ships are on water, the soundness is low since Arthur can be convinced that images without ships belong to the class. Note that this behaviour can actually be observed when classifiers are trained on datasets where boat and water highly correlate [14]. b) Arthur uses the strategy to only accept "boat" features as certificates. This strategy is both complete and sound since an adversarial prover cannot produce these certificates.

that the cooperative prover to convince Arthur for a random in-class datapoint is called the *completeness* of the protocol. The probability that Arthur cannot be convinced for a random out-class datapoint is the *soundness*.

The idea is that a commercial classifier could be mandated to be in interactive classifier with high completeness and soundness. An auditor would establish the soundness themselves by trying to fool Arthur to accept out-class datapoints. Contrary to the precision, completeness and soundness of the Merlin-Arthur pair can be readily estimated on the test dataset. The question is then whether completeness and soundness assure that highly-informative certificates/features are exchanged that can then be further examined for sensitive properties (e.g. sex or race in hiring decisions). In [26], the authors connect the soundness and completeness of the setup to a lower-bound on the average precision of the certificates exchanged between Merlin and Arthur. A crucial quantity that appears in this bound is the Asymmetric Feature Correlation.

1.3   Asymmetric Feature Correlation

Asymmetric Feature Correlation (AFC) was introduced in [26] as a possible quirk of the dataset where features that are individually not informative of the class can indicate the class via their correlation. That means, every feature appears equally likely inside and outside of the class, but the set of features can be highly correlated outside and highly anti-correlated inside. We give an illustration in Fig. 2 b) and define it formally in Definition 4. Merlin and Arthur can use these features to communicate the class. Despite using features with low precision, they retain high completeness since the features are spread out over the in-class datapoints and high soundness since Arthur only fails on the very few out-class datapoints where the features are concentrated. This means that AFC is a crucial quantity that connects high completeness and soundness to high informativeness of the features. We thus require an estimate or at least an upper bound of the AFC of the dataset.

The authors in [26] show that the AFC can be bounded by the maximum number of features in a datapoint. However, if one considers arbitrary subsets of the input as possible features, then this bound becomes exponentially large and thus unusable. One possible remedy is to further exploit the structure of the dataset to get a tighter bound on the AFC. In this work we provide a different argument: Finding such a feature set that realises a large AFC, even if it exists in principle, is closely related to finding highly-dense subgraphs in graphs, which is what we use to argue that this is a computationally hard task and cannot easily be exploited. This was also conjectured in [26].

2   Graph Theoretic Formulation

What reasonably constitutes a useful certificate is subject to ongoing debate. Most common are features in the form of subsets of the input vector, such as cutouts from an image, but others have proposed queries [8], anchors [20] or more abstract functions [2]. For our purposes, we do not need to specify the exact kind of certificate we consider. Rather, we can describe the relationship between datapoints and certificates as that of vertices in a graph. When a certificate can be produced for a datapoint, they share an edge in the graph. An illustration is given in Fig. 2 a).

Definition 1 (Certificate-Selection Instance (CSI)). *A certificate-selection instance is a tripartite graph $G = (V, E)$, where $V = D_1 \cup C \cup D_{-1}$ and $E \subset (D_1 \times C) \cup (D_{-1} \times C)$. We call the vertices in D_1 the in-class datapoints, the ones in D_{-1} the out-class datapoints and the ones in C the certificates.*

We can now give the definition for the cooperative prover (Merlin) in our setup as an certificate assignment for each in-class datapoint. We do not explicitly consider the strategy of the adversarial prover which is assumed to play optimally and for every out-class datapoint selects a certificate that convinces Arthur if he is able to do so.

Definition 2 (Cooperative Prover). *Given an CSI $G = (D_1 \cup C \cup D_{-1}, E)$, a cooperative prover is an assignment $M : D_1 \to C$, such that $\forall x \in D_1 : (x, M(x)) \in E$. The space of all provers of G is $\mathcal{M}(G)$.*

The verifier (Arthur) has the task of deciding to accept a certificate for the class.

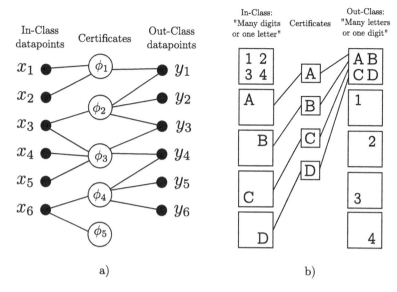

Fig. 2. a) An example instance of the Certificate-Selection problem as a tripartite graph $G = (V, E)$, where $V = D_1 \cup C \cup D_{-1}$ and $E \subset (D_1 \times C) \cup (D_{-1} \times C)$. A datapoint is connected to a certificate when it is possible to produce that certificate from this datapoint. An example would be text data, where the certificates are certain words that are indicative of the class. **b)** An example image dataset with an AFC of 4. The features signifying a letter have low precision (conditioned on "A", in-class and out-class are equally likely). Yet, using letters as certificates for the class, Arthur can classify almost perfectly. He only fails for the top two images, where he cannot be convinced that the image with many digits is in the class, but accepts the image with many letters. Thus, the strategy achieves completeness and soundness of $\frac{4}{5}$, while using features with a low precision of 0.5. It is easy to see that this example can be expanded by including more letters and digits to a case of arbitrarily high soundness and completeness with uninformative features. This also illustrates why the AFC can be upper-bounded by the maximum number of features per datapoint.

Definition 3 (Verifier). *Given an CSI $G = (D_1 \cup C \cup D_{-1}, E)$, a verifier is an assignment $A : C \to \{-1, 1\}$, corresponding to reject/accept of the certificate as evidence for the class. The space of all possible verifiers for G is $\mathcal{A}(G)$.*

We can then define soundness, completeness and the average precision for this setup. The completeness is the probability that Merlin can convince Arthur of the class for the in-class datapoints:

$$\text{completeness}(A, M) := \frac{|\{x \in D_1 \mid A(M(x)) = 1\}|}{|D_1|}.$$

The soundness is the probability that an out-class datapoint does not allow for a certificate that convinces Arthur of the class:

$$\text{soundness}(A) := \frac{|\{x \in D_{-1} \mid \forall \phi \in N(x) : A(\phi) = -1\}|}{|D_{-1}|},$$

where $N(x)$ is the neighbourhood of x, so all certificates connected to this datapoint. We can then define the notion of an (ϵ_c, ϵ_s)-CERTIFICATE-SELECTION INSTANCE, as a CSI for which there exist prover M and verifier A that achieve completeness$(A, M) \geq 1 - \epsilon_c$ and soundness$(A) \geq 1 - \epsilon_s$.

The *precision* of a certificate is defined as:

$$\Pr(\phi) := \frac{|D_1 \cap N(\phi)|}{N(\phi)}.$$

The precision of a feature set F is then $\Pr(F) := \frac{|D_1 \cap N(F)|}{N(F)}$, where $N(F) = \bigcup_{\phi \in F} N(\phi)$. We can then deduce for the precision of the set of certificates accepted by Arthur that

$$\Pr(A) := \Pr(A^{-1}(1)) = 1 - \frac{\hat{\epsilon}_s}{1 - \hat{\epsilon}_c + \hat{\epsilon}_s},$$

where $\hat{\epsilon}_c = 1 - \max_M$ completeness(A, M) and $\hat{\epsilon}_s = 1 - \max_M$ soundness(A, M). The average precision of Merlin is defined as

$$\Pr(M) := \frac{1}{|D_1|} \sum_{x \in D_1} \Pr(M(x)).$$

Note that we only define these quantities wrt. to one class, whereas in [26], these definitions always consider two-classes by maximising or minimising over the two classes.

The general idea is that we would like to draw a conclusion from the precision of Arthur $\Pr(A)$, which can be observed in the interactive classification setup by measuring completeness and soundness, to the unobservable average precision of Merlin $\Pr(M)$. The case of $\Pr(A) \approx 1$ corresponds to a complete and sound protocol, whereas $\Pr(M) \approx 1$ corresponds to the use of informative features. The question is thus: How small can $\Pr(M)$ be made if Arthur and Merlin cooperate to exploit the AFC to still ensure high completeness and soundness?

We now define the graph theoretic version of the asymmetric feature correlation derived in [26].

Definition 4 (Asymmetric Feature Correlation (AFC)). *For a CSI $G = (D_1 \cup C \cup D_{-1}, E)$, the asymmetric feature correlation is defined as*

$$\kappa := \max_{F \subset C} \frac{1}{|F_1^*|} \sum_{y \in F_1^*} \max_{\phi \in N(y) \cap F} \kappa(\phi, F)$$

where

$$\kappa(\phi, F) = \frac{|N(\phi) \cap D_{-1}||N(F) \cap D_1|}{|N(F) \cap D_{-1}||N(\phi) \cap D_1|} \quad and \quad F_1^* = N(F) \cap D_1.$$

To make the intuition clearer: Given a set of certificates F, the quantity $\frac{|N(\phi) \cap D_l|}{|N(F) \cap D_l|}$ is a measure of how correlated the certificates are in class l. If they are all connected to the same datapoint this quantity is close to 1. If they share no datapoints, this quantity becomes minimally $\frac{1}{|F|}$ on average. Thus $\kappa(\phi, F)$ determines the ratio of this correlation between out-class and in-class. The rest of the expression corresponds to an expectation value over a distribution of certificates. This distribution results from taking an in-class datapoint y uniformly at random from the set of all in-class datapoints that are connected to certificates in F, so $N(F) \cap D_1$ and then selecting the worst-case certificate connected to this feature. It is straight-forward to check that the example given in Fig. 2 b) has an AFC of 4.

2.1 Deceptive Feature Selection

Let us assume that Merlin and Arthur collude to use uninformative features (low precision) while achieving acceptable values for completeness and soundness. According to [26], the only way to achieve this is through exploiting the AFC of the dataset. We now want to investigate the computational difficulty of this task.

Definition 5 (Deceptive-Certificate-Selection (DCS)).
We define the DECEPTIVE-CERTIFICATE-SELECTION *problem as follows:*

Given: *Two constants* $\epsilon_c, \epsilon_s \geq 0$ *and an instance G of* (ϵ_c, ϵ_s)*-CSI.*
Task: *Maximise* $1 - Pr(M)$ *over* $M \in \mathcal{M}(G)$ *s.t. there exist $A \in \mathcal{A}(G)$ with* completeness$(A, M) \geq 1 - \epsilon_c$ *and* soundness$(A) \geq 1 - \epsilon_s$.

When we can show that this problem is computationally hard to solve, we can argue that the exploitation of AFC will not be a problem big enough to prevent the use of interactive classification to find certificates with high precision.

3 Inapproximability Bounds

For our inapproximability bound, we make use of inapproximability of DENSEST-k-SUBGRAPH problem (DkS), which is conditional on the DENSE-VS-RANDOM CONJECTURE. This conjecture has been established in [4] and has proven instrumental in deriving a series of inapproximability results, e.g. for MINIMUM-k-UNION [9] and RED-BLUE-SET COVER [10].

Theorem 1. *Assuming* P $\neq$ NP, *there is no polynomial-time algorithm that solves the decision version of* DECEPTIVE-CERTIFICATE-SELECTION. *Assuming furthermore the* DENSE-VS-RANDOM *Conjecture, then for every $\epsilon > 0$ there is no polynomial-time algorithm that achieves a better factor than* $\mathcal{O}(m^{1/8-\epsilon})$ *for the DCS, where m is the number of certificates.*

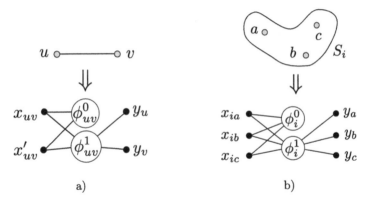

Fig. 3. a) Illustration of the reduction of DENSEST-k-SUBGRAPH to DECEPTIVE-FEATURE-SELECTION. For each vertex in the former, we add an out-class datapoint, and for each edge, we add two certificates and two in-class datapoints. b) Illustration of the reduction of MIN-k-UNION (of degree r) to DECEPTIVE-FEATURE-SELECTION-2. For each element in the former, we add an out-class datapoint, and for each subset S_i we add two certificates and r in-class datapoints.

Proof. We prove Theorem 1 by showing that an α-approximation of DCS implies an α^2-approximation Densest-k-Subgraph, which cannot be approximated better than $\mathcal{O}(|V|^{1/4-\epsilon})$ assuming the Dense-vs-Random Conjecture [4].

Assume we are given a densest-k-subgraph instance $(G = (V, E), k)$. Let $\epsilon_c = \frac{1}{2|E|+1}$ and $\epsilon_s = \frac{k}{|V|}$. Then, we construct an instance of $(\epsilon_c, \epsilon_s) - CSP$ in the following way: For every vertex in V, we add a corresponding vertex in D_{-1}, so

$$D_{-1} = \bigcup_{v \in V} \{y_v\}.$$

For every edge in E, we add two datapoints in D_1, so

$$D_1 = \bigcup_{(u,v) \in E} \{x_{uv}, x'_{uv}\},$$

and two certificates, one connected solely to the two datapoints in x_{uv} and x'_{uv} and one connected to x_{uv}, x'_{uv}, y_u and y_v, thus

$$C = \bigcup_{(u,v) \in E} \{\phi^0_{uv}, \phi^1_{uv}\} \quad \text{where} \quad \begin{aligned} \phi^0_{uv} &= (x_{uv}, x'_{uv}), \\ \phi^1_{uv} &= (x_{uv}, x'_{uv}, y_u, y_v). \end{aligned}$$

Fig. 3 a) provides an illustration. It is easy to see that this instance can be classified with perfect soundness and completeness by just always exchanging the ϕ^0_{uv}.

But to minimise the precision, Merlin wants to choose the uninformative features ϕ^1_{uv}. Since we have chosen ϵ_c smaller than the number of edges, Arthur needs to accept all the certificates assigned by Merlin. Thus, Merlin's certificates can at most cover k datapoints in D_{-1}, for Arthur to fulfil his soundness criterion. The number of edges in the densest-k-subgraph thus determines how often Merlin can assign ϕ^1_{uv} instead of ϕ^0_{uv}.

For Merlin, it makes only sense to assign the same certificate to x_{uv} and x'_{uv}. If he chooses a ϕ^1_{uv} for x_{uv}, which Arthur needs to accept, this already adds y_u and y_v to the datapoints on which Arthur can be fooled. Thus, choosing ϕ^1_{uv} for x'_{uv} reduces the precision with no cost on the soundness. The precision of ϕ^0_{uv} and ϕ^1_{uv} is 1 and $\frac{1}{2}$ respectively. If Merlin chooses ϕ^1 l times, we can calculate

$$1 - \Pr(M) = \frac{l}{2}.$$

Thus the NP-hardness of the decision version of CSP follows directly from the hardness of the decision version of DkS.

Now, let us assume that we had an approximation algorithm that achieves $1 - \Pr(M) \geq \frac{OPT}{f(m)}$, where OPT is the maximum achievable and $f(m)$ is some function in the number of certificates. Then through our construction we would approximate the densest-k-subgraph with factor $f(m)$. Since the number of certificates in our construction is equal to twice the number of edges in the subgraph problem, and the number of edges is at most $|V|$, our algorithm guarantees a factor of $f(2|V|^2)$. But since we know that DkS cannot be approximated better than $\mathcal{O}(n^{1/4-\epsilon})$, we know that we cannot approximate DCSP better than $\mathcal{O}(n^{1/8-\epsilon})$. □

We can define a variant of the DCSP where instead of having low precision as target, we give it as a constraint and target high soundness as to not be detected by an auditor.

Definition 6 (Deceptive-Certificate-Selection-2 Problem (DCS2)). *We define the* DECEPTIVE-CERTIFICATE-SELECTION-2 *problem as follows.*

Given: *An instance G of $(\epsilon_c, \epsilon_s) - CSP$ and constants $\epsilon_c, \epsilon_s, q \geq 0$.*
Task: *Minimise $1 -$ soundness(A) over $A \in \mathcal{A}(G)$ s.t. there exist $M \in \mathcal{M}(G)$ with* completeness$(A, M) \geq 1 - \epsilon_c$ *and* $\Pr(M) \leq 1 - q$.

For this problem, we can derive a conditional inapproximability factor of $\mathcal{O}(m^{1/4-\epsilon})$ via reduction of the MIN-k-UNION problem. The MIN-k-UNION considers a universe of elements U and a selection of subsets $S \subset 2^U$, and searches for a collection of k sets $S_i \in S$ that minimise $|\bigcup_{i=1}^k S_i|$. The inapproximability of the latter problem with a factor of $\mathcal{O}(m^{1/4-\epsilon})$, where $m = |S|$, is conditioned on the stronger assumption that extends the DENSE-VS-RANDOM conjecture to hypergraphs [9].

The reduction is analogous to our reduction for DENSEST-k-SUBGRAPH. It is important to note that the reduction in [9] considers r-uniform hypergraphs, and establishes the hardness of MIN-k-UNION also for the case where all sets S_i have the same size $r = |S_i|$. Again, for every element in U we add an out-class datapoint, and for every subset in S with two certificates and r in-class datapoints, as illustrated in Fig. 3 b). Then we set $\epsilon_c = \frac{1}{r|S|+1}$ and $q = \frac{k}{|S|}$.

Again, Arthur must accept all of Merlin's feature to ensure the completeness criterion. To ensure low average precision, Merlin has to select at least k ϕ^1-certificates while trying to minimise the amount of out-class datapoints they cover. A solution to DCS2 thus solves MIN-k-UNION (of degree r). We do not get the $\frac{1}{2}$-exponent this time, because the inapproximability of MIN-k-UNION is directly stated in the number of sets. Thus, we arrive at an inapproximability factor of $\mathcal{O}(m^{1/4-\epsilon})$ for DCS2, albeit conditional on the stronger HYPERGRAPH-DENSE-VS-RANDOM conjecture.

4   Discussion and Outlook

These results must be interpreted carefully, as they do not yet imply that deceptive certificate selection cannot happen. For a given CSI and given completeness and soundness, let $1 - \text{Pr}^*$ be the solution of the DCS, in other words Pr^* is the lowest possible average precision of the exchanged features. We should expect the average precision of Merlin to lie between the precision of Arthur and the worst case, i.e.

$$1 - \text{Pr}(A) \leq 1 - \text{Pr}(M) \leq 1 - \text{Pr}^*.$$

So far, our analysis shows that it is computationally hard for $1 - \text{Pr}(M)$ to approximate $1 - \text{Pr}^*$. However, in the worst case $\frac{1-\text{Pr}^*}{1-\text{Pr}(A)}$ is of the order of m, the total numbers of certificates, as illustrated in Fig. 2 b). An inapproximability result of $m^{1/8}$ does thus not yet guarantee that $1 - \text{Pr}(M)$ will be close to $1 - \text{Pr}(A)$, the quantity we can practically observe. To ensure that $\text{Pr}(M) \approx \text{Pr}(A)$ we need either a stronger inapproximability with respect to Pr^*, or ideally directly show that certificate selection such that $1 - \text{Pr}(M) \gg 1 - \text{Pr}(A)$ is a computationally hard problem.

On the other hand, for practical purposes it is not necessarily required that $1-\text{Pr}(M)$ will be close to $1-\text{Pr}(A)$, only that $1-\text{Pr}(M) \ll 0.5$ as 0.5 corresponds to uninformative features. Thus, a strong hardness-based separation from $1 - \text{Pr}^*$ will be useful, since $1 - \text{Pr}^*$ is upper-bounded by 1. At this point, we cannot say how informative Merlin's features are, but we can say that they will be far from uninformative.

Furthermore, we want to stress that we are considering worst-case hardness, which does not necessarily imply that deceptive certificate selection will be hard on average. It can be easily shown that the classification problem itself is worst-case NP-hard, yet existing machine-learning approaches successfully solve real-world instances. To make the argument stronger, future work might derive an average-case hardness bound. Of course, much depends on the distribution of the CSI-instances over which the average is taken, and thus it is important to investigate the graph structure of data and features for real-world datasets.

Reductions of the DENSE-VS-RANDOM conjecture hold promise in this direction. The conjecture is based on the hardness of finding dense subgraphs in random graphs, which makes the problem very suitable for average-case hardness reductions [9]. Additionally, the log-density framework [4] on which this conjecture is based, has been successfully used to design worst-case algorithms for a wide range of problems by studying algorithms for average-case instances [13]. For MINIMUM-k-UNION the approximation algorithm matches the lower provided by the conjecture [9]. Ideally, one might analogously design an algorithm to approximate the solution of the DCS-problem and show that any result beyond that approximation factor is NP-hard. This would give a solid understanding of how uninformative the certificates can be made with poly-time effort.

When extended in such a way, our results together with the work in [26] contribute to the establishment of a practically useful theoretical framework for explainable artificial intelligence (XAI). Notably, the interpretability guarantees do not make assumptions on the exact implementation of Arthur and Merlin and are thus applicable to neural network-based classifiers. This compares favourably to frameworks based on properties such as Lipschitz-constants or VC-dimensions, which do not yield useful results for parameter-rich neural networks [28]. We thus expect the design of classifier setups for which interpretability guarantees can be proven, such as interactive classification, to be a fruitful approach for the field of formal interpretability and XAI in general.

Theoretical bounds derived with legible and reasonable assumptions are of great importance to make artificial intelligence-based systems trustworthy. Heuristic interpretability methods have been shown to fail as soon as an effort is made to obscure the reasoning of the classifier. With formal methods, on the other hand, we know under which conditions we can trust their results. Agents with high completeness and soundness could be mandated as commercial classifiers that allow for reliable auditing, e.g., in the context of hiring decisions. We can use past hiring decisions by the Merlin-Arthur classifier as ground truth, which implies perfect completeness. An auditor would use their own adversarial prover to check if Arthur has sufficient soundness. If so, the features by Merlin must be the basis of the hiring decisions. The auditor can then inspect them for protected attributes, e.g., race, sex or attributes that strongly correlate with them [18].

Of course, certificates do not yet explain the whole reasoning process of the model. Crucially, they do not consider whether the certificate is causally related to the class or just correlated with it, which is an important consideration for features that are correlated with sensitive properties. However, there has been progress to adapt interactive classification to find causal features [6]. Extending interpretability to higher-level reasoning, for example via multiple rounds of interaction between prover and verifier, is left for future research.

5   Conclusion

In this work, we abstract interactive classification into an optimisation problem on a tripartite graph. We furthermore consider a deceptive prover-verifier duo that aims to use uninformative certificates and to exploit high asymmetric feature correlation to nevertheless achieve high completeness and soundness. It turns out that this task is computationally hard (assuming NP $\neq$ P), and hard to approximate (assuming the Dense-vs-Random conjecture).

When considering a machine learning task where the verifier will be trained on a training-dataset, then this deceptive strategy is additionally complicated by the learning problem. Soundness and completeness can be evaluated on a test dataset, and the strategy of choosing uninformative certificates developed during training needs to generalise.

These two barriers make it likely that even if the dataset has a high AFC, it will be difficult to exploit. That means, we can draw conclusions from the soundness and completeness of an interactive classification setup about the informativeness of the exchanged features.

References

1. Anders, C., Pasliev, P., Dombrowski, A.K., Müller, K.R., Kessel, P.: Fairwashing explanations with off-manifold detergent. In: International Conference on Machine Learning, pp. 314–323. PMLR (2020)
2. Anil, C., Zhang, G., Wu, Y., Grosse, R.: Learning to give checkable answers with prover-verifier games. arXiv preprint arXiv:2108.12099 (2021)
3. Babai, L.: Trading group theory for randomness. In: Proceedings of the Seventeenth Annual ACM Symposium on Theory of Computing, pp. 421–429 (1985)
4. Bhaskara, A., Charikar, M., Chlamtac, E., Feige, U., Vijayaraghavan, A.: Detecting high log-densities: an o (n 1/4) approximation for densest k-subgraph. In: Proceedings of the Forty-Second ACM Symposium on Theory of Computing, pp. 201–210 (2010)
5. Chang, S., Zhang, Y., Yu, M., Jaakkola, T.: A game theoretic approach to class-wise selective rationalization. In: Advances in Neural Information Processing Systems, vol. 32 (2019)
6. Chang, S., Zhang, Y., Yu, M., Jaakkola, T.: Invariant rationalization. In: International Conference on Machine Learning, pp. 1448–1458. PMLR (2020)
7. Chattopadhyay, A., Slocum, S., Haeffele, B.D., Vidal, R., Geman, D.: Interpretable by design: learning predictors by composing interpretable queries. arXiv preprint arXiv:2207.00938 (2022)
8. Chen, J., Song, L., Wainwright, M., Jordan, M.: Learning to explain: an information-theoretic perspective on model interpretation. In: International Conference on Machine Learning, pp. 883–892. PMLR (2018)
9. Chlamtáč, E., Dinitz, M., Makarychev, Y.: Minimizing the union: tight approximations for small set bipartite vertex expansion. In: Proceedings of the Twenty-Eighth Annual ACM-SIAM Symposium on Discrete Algorithms, pp. 881–899. SIAM (2017)
10. Chlamtáč, E., Makarychev, Y., Vakilian, A.: Approximating red-blue set cover. arXiv preprint arXiv:2302.00213 (2023)
11. Dimanov, B., Bhatt, U., Jamnik, M., Weller, A.: You shouldn't trust me: learning models which conceal unfairness from multiple explanation methods. In: SafeAI@ AAAI (2020)
12. Holzinger, A., Biemann, C., Pattichis, C.S., Kell, D.B.: What do we need to build explainable AI systems for the medical domain? arXiv preprint arXiv:1712.09923 (2017)
13. Jones, C., Potechin, A., Rajendran, G., Xu, J.: Sum-of-squares lower bounds for densest k-subgraph. arXiv preprint arXiv:2303.17506 (2023)

14. Lapuschkin, S., Binder, A., Montavon, G., Muller, K.R., Samek, W.: Analyzing classifiers: fisher vectors and deep neural networks. In: Proceedings of the IEEE Conference on Computer Vision and Pattern Recognition, pp. 2912–2920 (2016)
15. Lapuschkin, S., Wäldchen, S., Binder, A., Montavon, G., Samek, W., Müller, K.R.: Unmasking clever Hans predictors and assessing what machines really learn. Nat. Commun. **10**(1), 1–8 (2019)
16. Lundberg, S.M., Lee, S.I.: A unified approach to interpreting model predictions. In: Guyon, I., Luxburg, U.V., Bengio, S., Wallach, H., Fergus, R., Vishwanathan, S., Garnett, R. (eds.) Advances in Neural Information Processing Systems, vol. 30, pp. 4765–4774. Curran Associates, Inc. (2017)
17. Macdonald, J., Wäldchen, S., Hauch, S., Kutyniok, G.: A rate-distortion framework for explaining neural network decisions. arXiv preprint arXiv:1905.11092 (2019)
18. Mehrabi, N., Morstatter, F., Saxena, N., Lerman, K., Galstyan, A.: A survey on bias and fairness in machine learning. ACM Comput. Surv. (CSUR) **54**(6), 1–35 (2021)
19. Mohseni, S., Zarei, N., Ragan, E.D.: A multidisciplinary survey and framework for design and evaluation of explainable AI systems. ACM Trans. Interact. Intell. Syst. (TiiS) **11**(3–4), 1–45 (2021)
20. Ribeiro, M.T., Singh, S., Guestrin, C.: Anchors: high-precision model-agnostic explanations. In: Proceedings of the AAAI Conference on Artificial Intelligence, vol. 32 (2018)
21. Schraagen, J.M., Elsasser, P., Fricke, H., Hof, M., Ragalmuto, F.: Trusting the X in XAI: effects of different types of explanations by a self-driving car on trust, explanation satisfaction and mental models. In: Proceedings of the Human Factors and Ergonomics Society Annual Meeting, vol. 64, pp. 339–343. SAGE Publications Sage CA: Los Angeles, CA (2020)
22. Slack, D., Hilgard, A., Lakkaraju, H., Singh, S.: Counterfactual explanations can be manipulated. Adv. Neural. Inf. Process. Syst. **34**, 62–75 (2021)
23. Slack, D., Hilgard, S., Jia, E., Singh, S., Lakkaraju, H.: Fooling lime and SHAP: adversarial attacks on post hoc explanation methods. In: Proceedings of the AAAI/ACM Conference on AI, Ethics, and Society, pp. 180–186 (2020)
24. Vergara, J.R., Estévez, P.A.: A review of feature selection methods based on mutual information. Neural Comput. Appl. **24**, 175–186 (2014)
25. Wäldchen, S., Pokutta, S., Huber, F.: Training characteristic functions with reinforcement learning: XAI-methods play connect four. In: International Conference on Machine Learning, pp. 22457–22474. PMLR (2022)
26. Wäldchen, S., Sharma, K., Zimmer, M., Pokutta, S.: Formal interpretability with Merlin-Arthur classifiers. arXiv preprint arXiv:2206.00759 (2022)
27. Yu, M., Chang, S., Zhang, Y., Jaakkola, T.: Rethinking cooperative rationalization: introspective extraction and complement control. In: Proceedings of the 2019 Conference on Empirical Methods in Natural Language Processing and the 9th International Joint Conference on Natural Language Processing (EMNLP-IJCNLP), pp. 4094–4103. Association for Computational Linguistics (2019)
28. Zhang, C., Bengio, S., Hardt, M., Recht, B., Vinyals, O.: Understanding deep learning (still) requires rethinking generalization. Commun. ACM **64**(3), 107–115 (2021)

Integrating GPT-Technologies with Decision Models for Explainability

Alexandre Goossens$^{(\boxtimes)}$ and Jan Vanthienen

Leuven Institute for Research on Information Systems (LIRIS), KU Leuven,
Leuven, Belgium
{Alexandre.Goossens,Jan.Vanthienen}@kuleuven.be

Abstract. The ability to provide clear and transparent explanations for the outcome of a decision is critical for gaining user trust and acceptance, particularly in areas such as healthcare, finance, and law. While GPT-3 and ChatGPT are promising technologies for conversations, they cannot always be used to provide the correct outcome of operational decisions and to give explanations on questions about these decisions. The decision model logic can be employed to explain the decision-making process through various reasoning mechanisms. It is possible to provide automated reasoning and explanations for decisions with the use of chatbots powered by these decision models. However, these chatbots are not always user-friendly as users may struggle to determine the appropriate reasoning and explanation scenario for their questions. This paper explores the potential of GPT-3 technology to identify the appropriate reasoning and explanation scenario for decision-making in chatbots and compares its performance with directly asking the user questions. With GPT-3 technology's ability to identify the appropriate scenario, it will facilitate the development of integrated GPT-3 and decision model powered chatbots that can provide correct and human-understandable explanations for operational decisions.

Keywords: XAI · Chatbots · DMN · Explainable Decision Support Systems

1 Introduction

Operational decisions are an essential aspect of knowledge-intensive organizations and range from loan eligibility decisions, over product pricing decisions to vaccination policies. However, these decisions often require a considerable amount of time and resources to execute properly due to their high volume [1]. In addition, once a final decision has been made, stakeholders often have many questions that cannot always be answered effectively, despite the organization

This work was supported by the Fund for Scientific Research Flanders (project G079519N) and KU Leuven Internal Funds (project C14/19/082).

investing in FAQ pages, help desks, or call centers [2]. Therefore, there is a growing need to automate the execution and explainability of operational decisions to increase efficiency and productivity.

Decision models such as the Decision Model and Notation (DMN) standard [3] can be used to model both the structure and logic of decisions. By making use of various reasoning mechanisms, decision models can be used to answer a plethora of questions explaining operational decisions [4]. One solution to address these automated execution and explainability challenges is the use of decision models to power chatbots [4–6]. DMN chatbots not only execute decisions but can also provide explanations to help employees understand the reasoning behind those decisions. However, a recent survey found that these DMN chatbots are not always user-friendly, and users may not know how to use them correctly [7]. Next, with the rise of new technologies like GPT-3 and ChatGPT, there is a need to investigate whether these can be used to address this issue by either directly answering users' questions or by identifying reasoning scenarios to guide the conversation flow of the chatbot.

The first objective of this paper is to examine the potential of GPT-3 technology in answering user questions with a textual description and without the use of a DMN chatbot. The second objective is to investigate the potential of GPT-3 to identify with which reasoning scenario a user question can be answered. With the use of two problem descriptions, the performance of GPT-3 on answering user questions is evaluated against the actual correct answer. Next, the capabilities of GPT-3 to correctly match a user question with a reasoning scenario are assessed as well. The research aims to add to the existing literature on chatbots and decision models with the goal of improving efficiency and productivity of automated explainability.

The remainder of this paper is structured as follows: Sect. 2 provides a complete overview of the problem at hand by introducing reasoning scenarios, DMN models and DMN chatbots followed by Sect. 3 explaining the specific problem together with the research questions. Section 4 deals with related work and Sect. 5 introduces the methodology and the results. Section 6 illustrates how GPT-3 and DMN chatbots could work together with an example followed by a discussion in Sect. 7. Finally, Sects. 8 and 9 respectively deal with the limitations and future work and conclusion.

2   From Decision Description to Automated Explanations

Organizations execute operational decisions on a daily basis involving various stakeholders. However, the decision-making process is not finished once the final decision is communicated to all the relevant stakeholders. People can have questions and ask for advice on a daily basis about a plethora of issues such vaccination policies or loan approvals. People want to have explanations on how or why a certain decision was reached or how the decision outcome can be changed to something more desirable for them. To meet this demand, organizations set up FAQ pages, helpdesks or call centers, but unfortunately due to for example long waiting times and impersonal answers, this demand is not always satisfied [2]. However, answering these questions is a repetitive task with a streamlined reasoning. Hence, organization would benefit from some kind of automatic explanation tool to serve their stakeholders [8].

The following subsections elaborate on why GPT-3 might not be fitting to directly provide explanations. Next, decision models are introduced as a means to execute as well as explain decisions. Lastly, these decision models are activated with the use of chatbots allowing stakeholders to directly receive answers on their questions.

Running Example. Throughout this section, a running example will be used to illustrate the type of questions users might have and how decision models work. The problem deals with a priority vaccination allocation policy. The following textual description, inspired from [9], explains the problem:

The period in which a person will get vaccinated depends on the number of available doses and the person's assigned group. The person's assigned group is divided into three groups depending on their vulnerability, exposure, medical risks and age. If you are a resident or employee in a residential care centre or if you work in a first line care occupation then you belong to the most vulnerable and exposed people and you will be vaccinated first. Moving on to the second group, if you are older than 65, or if you are between 45 and 65 with an increased medical risk due to healthcare issues, you will get vaccinated next. Lastly, the third group consists of the broader population of people above the age of 18. If you are assigned to group 1, you get the highest vaccination priority at any time. If the available doses is low, then groups two and three are considered to be low priority. But if the available doses is medium then group 2 and group 3 are considered medium and low priority respectively. Lastly, if the available doses is high then group 2 is considered high priority and group 3 is considered medium priority.

Given the above vaccination problem, a first question stakeholders will have is to which group they have been assigned to and when they will be vaccinated. This is the basic decision. It is modeled in the decision model and executed in an intelligent decision execution environment, e.g. a rule-based engine that can import and execute standard DMN decision models. But there is more than this basic decision. After the (complex) operational decision is made, the user still might have some questions which would help them understand the decision better such as:

1. What age should I be to be assigned to group 1?
2. Under what conditions will I be vaccinated first?
3. I don't understand why I am considered high priority, can you explain that to me?

The above questions have different answers depending on a person's situation, but can all be answered using an intelligent reasoning mechanism.

2.1   GPT-3 and Logical Thinking

With GPT-3 [10] and more recently ChatGPT, organizations might be tempted to provide a problem description and use it as an automatic helpdesk to answer questions of stakeholders. However, when given the problem description and the following question: *What age should I be to be assigned to group 1?*, GPT-3 answers the following: *To be assigned to group 1, you must be a resident or employee in a residential care centre or if you work in a first line care occupation.*

It seems that GPT-3 is good at repeating information and providing relevant pieces of information, but not very good at providing very specific answers that might have to be derived from the provided information. The answer of GPT-3 omits or fails to derive based on the textual description that age does not influence whether a person is assigned to group 1 or not, but this should still be communicated clearly to the user. This observation that GPT-3 might not be suitable for directly providing explanations is in line with the conclusion of the study conducted in [10] stating that GPT-3 is not consistently performing excellently nor on par as humans in regards to question answering. But if the complexity of the problem increases, humans also struggle with finding the correct answer.

2.2   Reasoning and Explainability with Decision Models

Despite textual descriptions being a common communication tool between people, they are not ideal for communicating and execution decision logic [8]. Thus, other means of representing decision logic can be used such as decision tables within decision models. Decision tables are commonly used as they easily ensure consistency and completeness and allow for straightforward automation [11,12]. Decision tables are an integral part of the DMN standard which is introduced in Subsect. 2.3.

Figure 1 shows the two tables of the decision model for the vaccination problem described previously. As can be seen, two decision tables have been modeled. This is because the vaccination problem can be split up in two decisions. A first decision called *Person's Assigned Group* determines to which group a person is assigned to based on their *Vulnerability, Exposure, Medical Risk and Age*. A second decision called *Vaccination Priority* needs information related to the *Available Doses* as well as *Person's Assigned Group*, which was determined in the *Person's Assigned Group* decision table, to determine the vaccination priority. The second decision table *Vaccination Priority* requires the output of the first decision table *Person's Assigned Group* and is indicated with an arrow. Each row of a decision table is read as an IF-THEN rule, e.g., the third rule of the *Vaccination Priority* Table is read as follows: IF *Vulnerability= Low* and *Exposure= Low* and *Medical Risk= High* and *Age $\geq$ 45* THEN *Person's Assigned Group = Group 2*.

In the following paragraphs, various execution and explanation reasoning scenarios are introduced that allow to execute and explain decisions with decision models.

U	Vulnerability	Exposure	Medical Risk	Age	Person's Assigned Group
1	High	-	-	-	Group 1
2	Low	High	-	-	Group 1
3	Low	Low	High	>= 45	Group 2
4	Low	Low	Low	> 65	Group 2
5	Low	Low	Low	[18..65]	Group 3
6	Low	Low	High	[18..45[	Group 3

Person's Assigned Group

U	Available Doses	Person's Assigned Group	Vaccination Priority
1	-	Group 1	High
2	Low	Group 2, Group 3	Low
3	Medium	Group 2	Medium
4	Medium	Group 3	Low
5	High	Group 2	High
6	High	Group 3	Medium

Vaccination Priority

Fig. 1. Decision Tables for the vaccination problem

Class 0.1: Complete Reasoning. Decision tables are most commonly known in a context where all the required inputs are provided to determine the final output. Given that rule 3 was triggered in the *Person's Assigned Group* Table and that *Available Doses = Low*, the second rule of the *Vaccination Priority* Table is triggered, determining that *Vaccination Priority = Low*.

Class 0.2: Partial Decision-Making. In some cases, a stakeholder is only interested in the sub-decision of a decision. In this case, a person might only be interested in knowing to which group they have been assigned to. As such, only providing the information related to their *Vulnerability, Exposure, Medical Risk* and *Age* is sufficient to determine the *Person's Assigned Group*.

Class 0.3: Reasoning with Incomplete Information. In a realistic setting, a stakeholder does not always know all the required information beforehand. In such a case, decision tables still allow to reason with incomplete information. It is possible to return all the possibly triggered rules if some information is missing. For example, IF *Person's Assigned Group = Group 2*, but the person does not know the *Available Doses*, it is still possible to determine that *Vaccination Priority* will either trigger rules 2,3 or 5 depending on the value of *Available Doses*. Knowing upfront which outcomes are possible given the current information is very valuable to all stakeholders involved in the decisions.

Explanation Reasonings. Next to the various decision making reasonings most commonly associated with decision models, it is also possible to reason from output to input with decision tables which can be used to provide explanations about a decision. In the following paragraphs, an overview of the explanation questions used in this paper and on how to answer them are illustrated using the decision model of Fig. 1. A more complete overview can be found in [4].

Class 1: How to get? A common question stakeholders can have with the vaccination problem is for example *How do I get vaccinated first?* This can easily be looked up in the *Vaccination Priority* Table in the output column. It can be seen that only rules 1 and 5 result in High priority. Through backwards reasoning it is not complicated to derive for rule 1 that *Person's Assigned Group* should be Group 1 to be vaccinated first, regardless of the value of *Available Doses*. The same reasoning can be applied to understand under which conditions one can be assigned to Group 1. Once all these conditions are found, these can be returned as explanations on how to get a certain outcome.

Class 2: Why? Once a person has been given the final outcome of a decision, they might be interested in why exactly that outcome was achieved. With the vaccination problem a person might ask *Why was I assigned to Group 3* which can then easily be answered with the provided inputs and backwards reasoning. As can be seen in the *Person's Assigned Group* Table, only rules 5 and 6 have group 3 as an outcome, so depending on the provided inputs an explanation on that question can simply be answered with either rule 5 or rule 6.

Class 3: Sensitivity For certain stakeholders, their life or situation might change in a few months. However, these persons might still want to know if the same outcome can be achieved even if certain situational aspects change in the upcoming future. A person might ask: *How old can I be to still be assigned to Group 2?* or *What values can available doses be to still have a medium vaccination priority if I am assigned to group 2?* By knowing the desired outcome of the user and the input that is subject to change, it is possible to check the relevant rules and input value ranges that still provide the same output. The answer on the second question returns that a *Vaccination Priority* = Medium only occurs if *Available Doses* = Medium and *Person's Assigned Group* = Group 2.

Class 4: What if? Once stakeholders receive an answer, fast feedback mechanisms are often not included or often require the re-submission of all their information despite maybe only one thing changing for example *What if I turn 66 next year?*. Given that all the other information is stable but that only the value of *Age* is changing, this can quickly be answered using the same input-output reasoning methods as described in the 'complete' reasoning method.

Class 5: What should? For some stakeholders, certain variables are more flexible than others which in turn means that different outcomes can be achieved depending on that value. A question could be *What should exposure be to be assigned to group 1?* By checking the *Person's Assigned Group*, it can be found that *Exposure* should be high to be assigned to Group 1.

The previous paragraphs illustrated how decision models can be used in various ways to provide users with explanations on how and why certain decision are executed. It can not be expected of people to learn these reasoning methods themselves to find answers in decision tables. This reasoning would therefore benefit from a certain degree of automation.

2.3   More on DMN

In 2015, the Object Management Group (OMG) introduced the DMN standard as a standard to model, communicate and execute operational decisions [3].

Operational decisions are decisions that are executed in high volume by companies with a repeatable logic such as grant eligibilities or loan approvals. These daily decisions are repetitive and therefore offer interesting automating opportunities. A DMN model consists of two parts. A first part contains the decision logic with decision tables (see Fig. 1).

The second part of a DMN model visualizes the decision structure of a decision with a so-called Decision Requirements Diagram (DRD). Figure 2 shows the DRD of the vaccination problem. A DRD shows which inputs are needed for a decision to be made. In a DRD, decisions are represented with rectangles, in this vaccination problem, *Vaccination Priority* and *Person's assigned group* are the two decisions. The required inputs for a decision are represented with rounded rectangles, for example, *Available Doses* is a required input for *Vaccination Priority*. However, *Vaccination Priority* also requires the output of decision *Person's assigned group* as an input to execute its own decision, making *Person's assigned group* an intermediary decision. Inputs are connected to decisions with the use of solid arrows, also called information requirements.

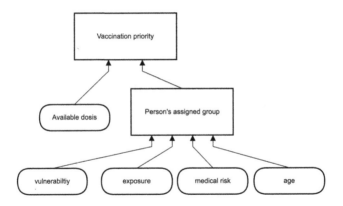

Fig. 2. Decision Requirements Diagram for the vaccination problem

2.4   DMN Chatbot

Various tools support the decision execution mechanism that DMN offers. But as explained previously, by using intelligent reasonings, it is possible to build a DMN chatbot allowing users to directly ask questions about certain decisions and receive explanations. The first main advantage of such a chatbot is its capability to reason with any DMN model without changing anything to the code. Once implemented, the DMN chatbot provides the users with the outcome of a decision based on their own data. The main novelty of DMN chatbots lies in the fact that the explanation classes are incorporated within its reasoning engine allowing users to receive fast and correct explanations on various explanation classes

Automated DMN Chatbot

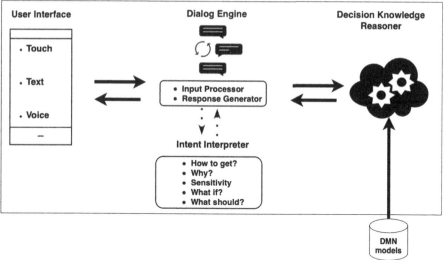

Fig. 3. Automated DMN Digital Assistant Framework [7]

such as the ones explained in Subsect. 2.2. Figure 3 shows the main components of a DMN chatbot [13].

The main components are:

– **User Interface:** A user can interact with the chatbot through either a menu-like fashion with buttons. The chatbot also supports full sentences and allows the user to directly interact with their voice.
– **Dialog Engine:** The dialog engine is responsible for conducting the conversation and adequately asking the right questions. It also provides a user-friendly answer back to the user using the output from the decision knowledge reasoner.
– **Intent Interpreter:** If a person uses full sentences or voice command, the dialog engine sends the text forward to an intent interpreter that needs to identify the required reasoning scenario to answer that question. This in turn is then communicated to the dialog engine which will communicate this to the Decision Knowledge Reasoner.
– **Decision Knowledge Reasoner:** The decision knowledge reasoner is the reasoning engine that analyzes the decision tables. This can be custom-built or accessed through an API [5].

Despite the stable reasoning mechanisms and a functional implementation of the DMN chatbot [13], users have found it not to be user-friendly enough according to a survey [7]. According to the survey [7], the main issue lies with the intent interpreter not consistently triggering the correct reasoning scenario in turn leading to wrong answers. Users on their side do not know which scenario needs to be triggered to get an answer to their question. As such, the intent interpreter needs to be improved so that it consistently and correctly identifies the reasoning scenarios.

3   Specific Problem Statement

The previous section explained how decision models are used to automatically provide decision explanations with the use of DMN chatbots [4]. However, based on a survey, users deemed these chatbots not user-friendly with the main issue being knowing when to use which reasoning method [7]. Therefore, a solution would be to automatically detect which reasoning scenario a user should trigger based on their question and let the reasoning itself be done by the DMN chatbot. Even though deep learning techniques can be used for this problem, they do require a sizeable and labeled dataset of each of these reasoning scenarios which is very difficult to construct. First of all, it would have to cover all possible formulations of a question on the same reasoning scenario and would need to cover a large variety of real-world problems. GPT-3, however, is a few-shot learner [10] which means that with a few examples and solutions of a problem very good performances can be achieved, meaning that the construction of large dataset might not be necessary. Next to that, it is important that the latter solution is indeed a better alternative than directly asking GPT-3 the questions. This leads to the following research questions:

- **Question 1:** To what extent is GPT-3 capable of identifying the appropriate reasoning scenario required to answer a given question?
- **Question 2:** When provided with a problem description, context, and question, can GPT-3 provide the correct answer to the question without the decision model?

4   Related Work

The idea to interact with computers using natural conversations was already proposed in 1966 with the introduction of Eliza [14]. Since then, these computer-human dialogues systems or chatbots have seen a surge in interest [15–17] and were enhanced with more interaction possibilities such as voice recognition[1]. This technology has found its way in a wide array of domains such as the medical domain [18], education [19] or sales [20,21]. These chatbots can be powered by a variety of techniques such as pattern-based Natural Language Processing (NLP), Markov chains, artificial neural networks and more [22]. Because DRDs are acyclic graphs and decision tables are basically rules, DMN chatbots can be considered to be somewhere in between knowledge graph-based and pattern-based chatbots [23].

    When reasoning is involved, the situation becomes more complex. To deal with this complexity, DMN chatbots require a reasoning mechanism to reason

---

[1] https://www.ibm.com/cloud/watson-speech-to-text.

with decision models. These reasoning mechanisms can either be custom-built or accessed through an Application Programming Interface (API). The authors of [5] developed a reasoning mechanism based on Imperative/Declarative Programming (IDP) which was illustrated with a naive chatbots lacking a user-interface or other AI capabilities. The DMN chatbot proposed in [4] makes use of a custom-built reasoning mechanism and is enhanced with AI-capabilities such as voice-recognition[2] and an intent interpreter. Next, a Camunda-based[3] DMN chatbot is introduced in [6], but due to the Camunda reasoning engine it lacks reasoning capabilities compared to the first two approaches. Lastly, a survey was conducted investigating the information retrieval correctness and speed of a DMN chatbot combining the AI capabilities of [4] with the IDP reasoning mechanism of [5] compared to textual descriptions [7]. The survey concludes that the enhanced DMN chatbot is better at providing explanations as well as preferred over textual descriptions. However, the participants reported that the chatbot was not user-friendly because it was difficult to know when to use which reasoning scenario.

5   Experiment

In this section, the methodology and the results of the experiments are laid out. The general idea of the experiment is two-fold.

1. Investigating whether GPT-3 can correctly provide explanations based on a textual description of a problem given a specific situation.
2. Investigating GPT-3's capabilities to correctly identify which questions deal with which reasoning and explanation scenario.

The remainder of this section first introduces a second problem that is used for the evaluation. Next, the set-up of both experiments are explained followed by the hyperparameters of GPT-3. Lastly, the results are compared to a golden standard and reported for both experiments.

5.1   Methodology

With the recent introduction of ChatGPT[4], GPT-3 models and by extension large language models have gained a lot of traction. These models perform very well on a wide variety of NLP tasks [10] and have been trained on a large text dataset gathered from the internet. What makes these models so widely adopted and promising is their generalization capability, given only a few examples of the task they need to perform, impressive results are achieved [10]. Hence why deep learning models such as BERT [24] are not considered in this study as even simply finetuning these models already requires a decently-sized labeled dataset for each problem which in this study-context is not available.

---

[2] see footnote 1.

[3] https://camunda.com.

[4] https://openai.com/blog/ChatGPT.

Discount Problem. For the evaluation, a second problem is introduced. The discount problem deals with a discount eligibility calculation determined by the volume of the order, the time of the year and the client tier that a customer is assigned to such as *Gold* or *Bronze*. The client tier in turn is determined by the years of loyalty of a customer as well as the total value of goods a customer bought over the years. The DMN model of the discount example is shown in Fig. 4 with the according DRD and decision tables.

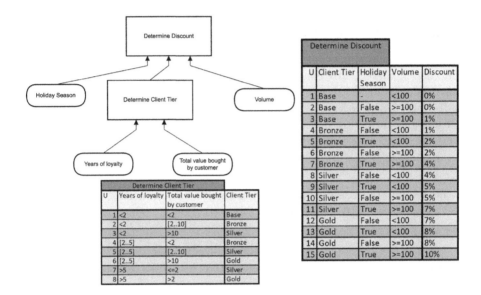

Fig. 4. Discount Example

GPT-3 for Question Answering. In the first experiment, GPT-3 has to answer some questions based on the textual description of the vaccination or discount problem given a certain situation. A situation describes the relevant information to determine the outcome of a decision. This is used as a basis to answer the follow-up questions such as *Why?* or *What if?*. All this information is provided within one prompt to GPT-3. As an evaluation, the answer of GPT-3 is compared to a correct answer determined by a human which is considered a golden standard. An answer is considered correct as long as it provides the same and correct amount of information or more as the human answer. The complete prompt that is given to GPT-3 is as follows:

Complete Prompt: *I provide you with the following text description:* **insert textual description**. *Assume the following information to answer the following questions:* **insert situation**. *Provide for each answer the concerning question:* **insert all questions**.

Table 1 reports the provided situation for both the discount and the vaccination example. The textual description for the vaccination example is the one described in Sect. 2 and the textual description of the discount problem is similar albeit longer. The questions are shown in the second column of Table 2 entitled **Question**.

Table 1. Context of Vaccination and Discount Problem

Problem	Situation
Vaccination	I am 65 years old, my exposure is high, I am not at risk nor vulnerable and the available doses is low
Discount	I have been loyal for three years, have bought goods over time with a total value of 8 and currently placed an order of volume 80 not during the holidays

GPT-3 for Scenario Identification. In the second experiment, GPT-3 has to classify a set of questions into a specific class of reasoning scenarios. It has been decided to focus on explanation scenarios since execution scenarios are not difficult to execute or identify by the user as these follow a rather straightforward approach [7]. The classes were created based on the described reasoning scenarios introduced in [4] and selected on whether they were supported by the most extensive DMN chatbot introduced in [7]. To evaluate the performance of GPT-3, the predicted class is compared to the actual class determined by a human. An answer is considered correct if GPT-3 predicted the same class as the class determined by a human. The classes that GPT-3 is expected to identify are:

- Class 1: How to get Y?
- Class 2: Why?
- Class 3: Sensitivity
- Class 4: What if?
- Class 5: What should?

To ensure better results with GPT-3, each class is accompanied with 3 sample questions and expected output. However, for brevity reasons only one example is mentioned in the prompt below to classify the questions:

Complete Prompt: *There are 5 classes in total. For each class I give you a few examples: Class 1: How to get Y? Examples: Input:"How can I make sure to drink "Guinness"?" Expected output: "Class 1: How to get variable=value?" Class 2: Why?: Examples: Input: "Why did not I not get my loan approved?" Expected output: "Class 2: Explain" Class 3: Sensitivity: Examples: Input: "How much can my daughter still grow to be allowed in the ride?" Expect output: "Class 3: Show all paths" Class 4: What if? Happens when something needs to be changed: Examples: Input: "What would happen if I wear a green t-shirt instead of red? Expected output: "Class 4: What if variable=value?" Class 5: What should?: Examples: Input: What colors should I decorate my room with to get a warmer tone? Expected output:"Class 5: What should?" I will provide you with sentences and return to me for each sentence: the sentence and the expected output; Class Y: Expected output.* **Insert Questions**

Lastly, Table 2 reports the questions that GPT-3 is expected to classify as well as the actual class each question belongs to. Note that the classes of the questions that need to be classified are not given to GPT-3 with the prompt.

Table 2. Prompt questions and respective classes

Example	Question	Class
DISCOUNT	How much value can I still buy without changing client tier?	Class 3: Sensitivity
	How long will I still be the same client tier if I don't buy any more goods?	Class 3: Sensitivity
	What if I order during a holiday season?	Class 4: What if?
	What if the total value bought now exceeded 10?	Class 4: What if?
	Why am I considered a silver customer?	Class 2: Why?
	How come I only got a 4% discount?	Class 2: Why?
	How can I get the discount of 10%?	Class 1: How to get Y?
	How can I become a gold tier customer?	Class 1: How to get Y?
	How many orders should I place to get a golden client tier?	Class 5: What should?
	What holiday season should it be to get a discount of 7%?	Class 5: What should?
Vaccination	How can I get assigned to group 2?	Class 1: How to get Y?
	Under what conditions will I be vaccinated first?	Class 1: How to get Y?
	What if next week it is my birthday and I turn 66 years old?	Class 4: What if?
	What would happen if next week there is a high amount of doses available instead of low?	Class 4: What if?
	Why was I assigned to group 1?	Class 2: Why?
	I don't understand why I am considered high priority, can you explain that to me?	Class 2: Why?
	How much can the available doses change without changing the priority level?	Class 3: Sensitivity
	What is the maximum age I can be without changing group?	Class 3: Sensitivity
	How many doses should there be to get a medium vaccination priority being assigned to group 3?	Class 5: What should?
	What age should I be to be assigned to group 1?	Class 5: What should?

GPT-3 Hyperparameters. The performance of GPT-3 is still dependent on hyperparameters that are set prior to the execution. Table 3 summarizes the hyperparameters used within this study. GPT-3 models can be finetuned for a specific task such as user conversations or code completion and understanding[5]. The most powerful and complete GPT-3 model according to OpenAI is *text-davinci-003* and is therefore picked for the experiments. Secondly, there is also a temperature parameter which determines the randomness of a generated output by the model. A high temperature allows for more randomness and thus more variability in answers for the same question. This however is not desirable in this context as a user should always get the same reply on their questions regardless of when or how many times they ask it. As such this temperature hyperparameter is set to the lowest possible value of 0 which ensures stable answers. The final hyperparameter Max_tokens determines the length a prompt question and the GPT-3 answer can be together. This length is determined by the maximum amount of tokens with a token basically being a word or a punctuation symbol. This parameter has been set to 2400 which completely covers the provided examples, prompt questions and GPT-3 generated answer.

5.2 Results for Question Answering

In the first experiment, GPT-3 had to answer various questions users might have about their own situation within a specific problem namely the vaccination or the discount problem. Table 4 shows the results for GPT-3 answering the explanation questions. To indicate whether an answer has been evaluated as correct or incorrect, the use of a green (correct) and red (incorrect) color scheme has been used. As can be seen only three answers were answered correctly. It is important to note that an incomplete answer can not be considered as correct as an explanation should be complete and not partially complete. For example on question 7 for the discount example: *How can I get the discount of 10%?* the correct answer is: *Holiday Season = True, customer tier = gold and volume ≥ 100* whilst GPT-3 forgets to mention that one needs to be a *Golden tier customer* to benefit from a discount which is crucial information as well. Next, GPT-3 also sometimes replies with a chunk of the text that it deems relevant as an explanation instead of providing a short and clear answer on the question, leaving the interpretation to the user which is also not a desirable situation.

5.3 Results for Scenario Identification

The second experiment researched whether GPT-3 can be used as an intent interpreter. To evaluate this, GPT-3 had to identify to which reasoning class a question belongs to. This was then compared to the actual reasoning class the question belongs to. Table 5 shows the results for GPT-3 identifying the reasoning scenarios on the questions. The same green (correct) and red (incorrect) color scheme as in Table 4 has been used. As can be seen GPT-3 correctly classifies all the questions into the right class.

---

[5] https://platform.openai.com/docs/models/gpt-3.

Table 3. Hyperparameters of GPT-3

Parameter	Value
Model	text-davinci-003
Temperature	0
Max_tokens	2400

Table 4. Results Question Answering

EXAMPLE	Question	Golden answer	Answer GPT-3 logic
DISCOUNT	1	Value can still increase with 2.	2
	2	2 years	5 years.
	3	5% discount	4% discount.
	4	You would be gold tier and receive a discount of 7%.	You would become a silver customer.
	5	Loyalty >5 and value <2 OR loyalty = [2..5] and value is [2..10] OR loyalty <2 and value >10	Because you have been loyal for three years and have bought goods over time with a total value of 8.
	6	Because holiday season = False , Customer tier= silver and volume <100.	Because you ordered 80 units not during the holidays.
	7	Holiday season= True, customer tier= gold and volume >100	Order 100 or more units during a holiday season.
	8	Loyalty is [2..5] and value >10 OR loyalty >5 and value >2	Buy goods over time with a total value of 10 or more and be loyal for 2 to 5 years, or be loyal for more than 5 years and buy more than 2.
	9	You should place orders with value >3	You need to buy goods over time with a total value of 10 or more and be loyal for 2 to 5 years, or be loyal for more than 5 years and buy more than 2.
	10	Holiday season = True + volume >= 100	Silver customers can get a 7% discount when they order 100 or more units during a holiday season.
Vaccination	1	If vulnerability= Low, Exposure= Low, medical risk = High, age>= 45 OR if age >65 and everything else Low	You can get assigned to group 2 if you are older than 65, or if you are between 45 and 65 with an increased medical risk due to healthcare issues.
	2	If assigned group= group 1: vaccination priority = High OR if available doses= high and assigned group = group 2: vaccination priority = High	You will be vaccinated first if You are a resident or employee in a residential care centre or if You work in a first line care occupation.
	3	Nothing changes	If you turn 66 years old, you will be assigned to group 2 and will be vaccinated next.
	4	Still high priority	If there is a high amount of doses available, group 2 will be considered high priority and group 3 will be considered medium priority.
	5	Exposure = High, Risk= Low, vulnerability = Low and age = any	You were assigned to group 1 because you are a resident or employee in a residential care centre or if you work in a first line care occupation, making you the most vulnerable and exposed.
	6	Return rule: Available doses = low + group 1	You are considered high priority because you are a resident or employee in a residential care centre or if you work in a first line care occupation, making you the most vulnerable and exposed.
	7	No change will affect your sensitivity level	The available doses can change depending on the number of available doses and the persons assigned group. If the available doses is low, then groups two and three are considered to be low priority. But if the available doses is medium then group 2 and group 3 are considered medium and low priority respectively. Lastly, if the available doses is high than group 2 is considered high priority and group 3 is considered medium priority.
	8	Any age	The maximum age you can be without changing group is 65 years old.
	9	High	If the available doses is medium then group 2 and group 3 are considered medium and low priority respectively.
	10	Any age is fine, it is dependent on vulnerability, exposure and risk	To be assigned to group 1, you must be a resident or employee in a residential care centre or if you work in a first line care occupation.

Table 5. Results Scenario Identification

EXAMPLE	Question	Golden Class	Answer GPT-3 to classify
DISCOUNT	1	Class 3: Sensitivity	Class 3: Show all paths
	2	Class 3: Sensitivity	Class 3: Show all paths
	3	Class 4: What if?	Class 4: What if variable=value?
	4	Class 4: What if?	Class 4: What if variable=value?
	5	Class 2: Why?	Class 2: Explain
	6	Class 2: Why?	Class 2: Explain
	7	Class 1: How to get Y?	Class 1: How to get variable=value?
	8	Class 1: How to get Y?	Class 1: How to get variable=value?
	9	Class 5: What should?	Class 5: What should?
	10	Class 5: What should?	Class 5: What should?
Vaccination	1	Class 1: How to get Y?	"Class 1: How to get variable=value?"
	2	Class 1: How to get Y?	Class 1: How to get variable=value?
	3	Class 4: What if?	Class 4: What if variable=value?
	4	Class 4: What if?	Class 4: What if variable=value?
	5	Class 2: Why?	Class 2: Explain
	6	Class 2: Why?	Class 2: Explain
	7	Class 3: Sensitivity	Class 3: Show all paths
	8	Class 3: Sensitivity	Class 3: Show all paths
	9	Class 5: What should?	Class 5: What should?
	10	Class 5: What should?	Class 5: What should?

6   Explainable DMN + GPT-3 Chatbot Illustration

This section illustrates an interaction between a user and the DMN chatbot with an integrated GPT-3 intent interpreter. Figure 5 shows how a conversation would work with an integrated GPT-3 intent interpreter on the discount problem for explanation purposes.

The DMN chatbot initiates the conversation by offering to either determine the discount of a user or to explain how a certain discount value can be obtained. By ticking the first button, the user initiates the discount determination decision. The user continues with providing all the relevant information the DMN chatbot asks for. Next, the DMN chatbot returns that the user would be entitled for a 4% discount.

Once the answer has been provided, the DMN chatbot proposes a set of buttons each linked to a reasoning scenario such as *Why?* or *What if?*. This is where the intent interpreter comes in. Because the user does not always know which button can answer their question, the intent interpreter tells the user which button to tick. When the user asks *How much should I order to become a gold customer?*, the GPT-3 intent interpreter detects which reasoning scenario should be triggered and communicates this to the user. The DMN chatbot tells the user to tick the *What should?* button. Afterwards, the DMN chatbot asks the

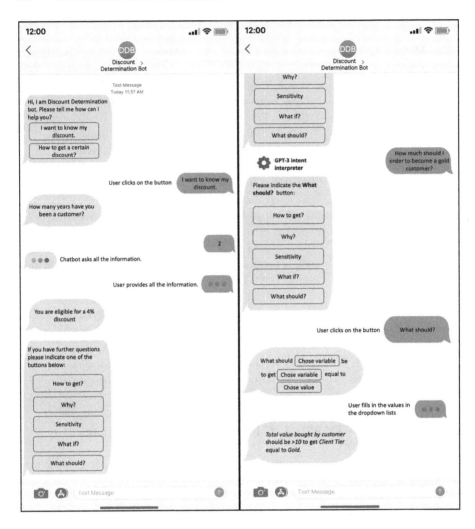

Fig. 5. Sample conversation with GPT-3 as intent interpreter

user to provide the relevant values with the user with drop-down lists. Finally, the user gets the answer and can either continue with asking other questions or stop the conversation there.

7   Discussion

Based on the results, it is clear that GPT-3 performs better at reasoning scenario identification then directly answering the question. This is probably due to the fact that the provided examples of each reasoning scenario were representative enough to correctly classify the questions. It is also important to know that once the correct reasoning scenario has been identified, the correct answer will always be given by the DMN chatbot. This means that if the correct decision tables are given, the correct answer will consistently be returned.

The main issue GPT-3 seemed to have when answering questions was that it did not personalize the answers for the context and question but instead provided a chunk of text in which a user could maybe find their answer. But this still leaves the analysis part for the user which is also not a desirable explanation. One could propose increasing the temperature value of GPT-3 allowing for more creativity but this comes with increased randomness in answers, which is not desirable from an organizational perspective as an organization would want their stakeholders to consistently get a correct answer on their questions. Lastly, GPT-3 is inherently a black box, therefore it is complicated to know whether all the provided information to GPT-3 is processed correctly to answer questions. Because GPT-3 is trained on a large dataset, it already knows certain concepts, but these are not always aligned with the problem that needs to be solved. It is very difficult to know whether GPT-3 is holding on to its own definition for further reasoning or whether it makes use of the newly provided definition.

Based on these results, a good recommendation for organizations would be to use a DMN chatbot if they already have a DMN model available as it ensures consistent answers. The DMN model can then be enhanced with a chatbot and GPT intent detection features for explanation. If the decision logic changes, the chatbot or explanation mechanisms are updated automatically.

8   Limitations and Future Work

Even though GPT-3 performed excellently on the scenario classification, this has been done on a limited dataset and without fine-tuning a GPT-3 model for that problem. A next step would include collecting and labeling a sizeable dataset for those 5 reasoning classes to train a fine-tuned GPT-3 model and evaluate it more extensively. This paper introduces a proof of concept of integrating GPT-3 with a DMN chatbot for scenario identification, however in the future it is planned to refine such an integrated chatbot. Currently, the idea is that a user confirms the predicted scenario as it allows for a better control of the conversation, however this step could also be automated. The benefits of such an automation would have to be evaluated with a survey. It would also be interesting to investigate whether GPT-3 could provide more understandable answers compared to the ones currently returned by the DMN chatbot. Despite the prompts being tested and optimized manually, it is unfortunately not possible to know whether the used prompts are the optimal formulations to classify questions [25,26]. Once the prototype is developed, an evaluation with users in a realistic organizational setting is planned. At the time of this study, GPT-4 did not have a public-access API yet, but investigating the reasoning capabilities of GPT-4 compared to an integrated GPT-3 and DMN chatbot will certainly be done in the future. Given that GPT-4 supports multi-modal inputs, has been trained on more data and performs better than GPT-3, it is likely that it probably performs better at directly answering user questions but the exact performance increase compared to GPT-3 still needs to be researched.

9   Conclusion

This paper starts with the observation that GPT-3 might not always be the most suited solution for question answering regarding operational decisions especially regarding explanations. Next, the capabilities of decision models for flexible reasoning and explanation in an automated fashion with DMN chatbots are shown. Previous research has identified DMN chatbots as challenging to use due to their reliance on users selecting the appropriate explainable reasoning scenario. To address this issue, this study investigates whether GPT-3 can accurately identify the adequate reasoning scenario to answer user questions. Two problem descriptions are used to compare the performance of GPT-3 in identifying the appropriate reasoning scenario versus directly answering user questions. The study concludes that while GPT-3 can correctly identify the reasoning scenario, its performance to directly provide explanations to users is poor. Thus, it is more effective to use GPT-3 to identify the appropriate reasoning mechanism, which can then be forwarded to the DMN chatbot to generate an explanation.

References

1. Vanthienen, J.: On smart data, decisions and processes. In: 2015 7th International Joint Conference on Knowledge Discovery, Knowledge Engineering and Knowledge Management (IC3K), vol. 1. IEEE (2015)
2. Figl, K., Mendling, J., Tokdemir, G., Vanthienen, J.: What we know and what we do not know about DMN. Enterp. Modell. Inf. Syst. Architectures (EMISAJ) **13**, 1–2 (2018)
3. OMG: Omg: Decision model and notation 1.0 (2015) (2008). Accessed 08 Jan 2022
4. Etikala, V., Goossens, A., Van Veldhoven, Z., Vanthienen, J.: Automatic generation of intelligent chatbots from DMN decision models. In: Moschoyiannis, S., Peñaloza, R., Vanthienen, J., Soylu, A., Roman, D. (eds.) RuleML+RR 2021. LNCS, vol. 12851, pp. 142–157. Springer, Cham (2021). https://doi.org/10.1007/978-3-030-91167-6_10
5. Vandevelde, S., Etikala, V., Vanthienen, J., Vennekens, J.: Leveraging the power of IDP with the flexibility of DMN: a multifunctional API. In: Moschoyiannis, S., Peñaloza, R., Vanthienen, J., Soylu, A., Roman, D. (eds.) RuleML+RR 2021. LNCS, vol. 12851, pp. 250–263. Springer, Cham (2021). https://doi.org/10.1007/978-3-030-91167-6_17
6. Estrada-Torres, B., del Río-Ortega, A., Resinas, M.: DemaBot: a tool to automatically generate decision-support chatbots. In: 2021 Best Dissertation Award, Doctoral Consortium, and Demonstration and Resources Track at BPM, BPM-D 2021, pp. 141–145 (2021)
7. Goossens, A., Maes, U., Timmermans, Y., Vanthienen, J.: Automated intelligent assistance with explainable decision models in knowledge-intensive processes. In: Cabanillas, C., Garmann-Johnsen, N.F., Koschmider, A. (eds.) BPM 2022. Lecture Notes in Business Information Processing, vol. 460, pp. 25–36. Springer, Cham (2023). https://doi.org/10.1007/978-3-031-25383-6_3

8. Vanthienen, J.: Decisions, advice and explanation: an overview and research agenda. In: A Research Agenda for Knowledge Management and Analytics, pp. 149–169. Edward Elgar Publishing (2021)
9. Goossens, A., Claessens, M., Parthoens, C., Vanthienen, J.: Deep learning for the identification of decision modelling components from text. In: Moschoyiannis, S., Peñaloza, R., Vanthienen, J., Soylu, A., Roman, D. (eds.) RuleML+RR 2021. LNCS, vol. 12851, pp. 158–171. Springer, Cham (2021). https://doi.org/10.1007/978-3-030-91167-6_11
10. Brown, T., et al.: Language models are few-shot learners. Adv. Neural. Inf. Process. Syst. **33**, 1877–1901 (2020)
11. Vanthienen, J., Mues, C., Aerts, A.: An illustration of verification and validation in the modelling phase of KBS development. Data Knowl. Eng. **27**(3), 337–352 (1998)
12. Huysmans, J., Dejaeger, K., Mues, C., Vanthienen, J., Baesens, B.: An empirical evaluation of the comprehensibility of decision table, tree and rule based predictive models. Decis. Support Syst. **51**(1), 141–154 (2011)
13. Etikala, V., Van Veldhoven, Z., Vanthienen, J.: Text2Dec: extracting decision dependencies from natural language text for automated DMN decision modelling. In: Del Río Ortega, A., Leopold, H., Santoro, F.M. (eds.) BPM 2020. LNBIP, vol. 397, pp. 367–379. Springer, Cham (2020). https://doi.org/10.1007/978-3-030-66498-5_27
14. Weizenbaum, J.: Eliza-a computer program for the study of natural language communication between man and machine. Commun. ACM **9**(1), 36–45 (1966)
15. Zierau, N., Elshan, E., Visini, C., Janson, A.: A review of the empirical literature on conversational agents and future research directions. In: International Conference on Information Systems (ICIS) (2020)
16. Adamopoulou, E., Moussiades, L.: An overview of chatbot technology. In: Maglogiannis, I., Iliadis, L., Pimenidis, E. (eds.) AIAI 2020. IAICT, vol. 584, pp. 373–383. Springer, Cham (2020). https://doi.org/10.1007/978-3-030-49186-4_31
17. Abdul-Kader, S.A., Woods, J.C.: Survey on chatbot design techniques in speech conversation systems. Int. J. Adv. Comput. Sci. Appl. **6**(7) (2015)
18. Divya, S., Indumathi, V., Ishwarya, S., Priyasankari, M., Devi, S.K.: A self-diagnosis medical chatbot using artificial intelligence. J. Web Dev. Web Design. **3**(1), 1–7 (2018)
19. Clarizia, F., Colace, F., Lombardi, M., Pascale, F., Santaniello, D.: Chatbot: an education support system for student. In: Castiglione, A., Pop, F., Ficco, M., Palmieri, F. (eds.) CSS 2018. LNCS, vol. 11161, pp. 291–302. Springer, Cham (2018). https://doi.org/10.1007/978-3-030-01689-0_23
20. Khan, M.M.: Development of an e-commerce sales chatbot. In: 2020 IEEE 17th International Conference on Smart Communities: Improving Quality of Life Using ICT, IoT and AI (HONET), pp. 173–176. IEEE (2020)
21. Janssen, A., Rodríguez Cardona, D., Breitner, M.H.: More than FAQ! chatbot taxonomy for business-to-business customer services. In: Følstad, A., et al. (eds.) CONVERSATIONS 2020. LNCS, vol. 12604, pp. 175–189. Springer, Cham (2021). https://doi.org/10.1007/978-3-030-68288-0_12
22. Hussain, S., Ameri Sianaki, O., Ababneh, N.: A survey on conversational agents/chatbots classification and design techniques. In: Barolli, L., Takizawa, M., Xhafa, F., Enokido, T. (eds.) WAINA 2019. AISC, vol. 927, pp. 946–956. Springer, Cham (2019). https://doi.org/10.1007/978-3-030-15035-8_93

23. Al-Zubaide, H., Issa, A.A.: OntBot: ontology based ChatBot. In: 2011 4th International Symposium on Innovation in Information and Communication Technology, ISIICT 2011, pp. 7–12 (2011)
24. Devlin, J., Chang, M.W., Lee, K., Toutanova, K.: BERT: pre-training of deep bidirectional transformers for language understanding. arXiv preprint arXiv:1810.04805 (2018)
25. Jojic, A., Wang, Z., Jojic, N.: GPT is becoming a Turing machine: here are some ways to program it. arXiv preprint arXiv:2303.14310 (2023)
26. Wei, J., et al.: Chain of thought prompting elicits reasoning in large language models. arXiv preprint arXiv:2201.11903 (2022)

Outcome-Guided Counterfactuals from a Jointly Trained Generative Latent Space

Eric Yeh(✉), Pedro Sequeira, Jesse Hostetler, and Melinda Gervasio

SRI International, Menlo Park, USA

{eric.yeh,pedro.sequeira,jesse.hostetler,melinda.gervasio}@sri.com

Abstract. We present a novel generative method for producing higher-quality counterfactual examples for decision processes using a latent space that jointly encodes observations and associated behavioral outcome variables, such as classification decisions, actions taken, and estimated values. Our approach trains a variational autoencoder over behavior traces to both reconstruct observations and predict the outcome variables from the latent encoding. The resulting joint observation and outcome latent allows for unconditioned sampling of both observations and outcome variables from this space. This grants us the ability to generate counterfactuals using multiple methods, such as gradient-driven updates to move towards desired outcomes, interpolations against relevant cases drawn from a memory of examples, and combinations of these two. This also permits us to sample counterfactuals where constraints can be placed over some outcome variables, while others are allowed to vary. This flexibility also permits us to directly address the plausibility of generated counterfactuals by using gradient-driven updates to raise the data-likelihood of generated examples. We use this method to analyze the behavior of reinforcement learning (RL) agents against several outcome variables that characterize agent behavior. From experiments in three different RL environments, we show that these methods produce counterfactuals that score higher on standard counterfactual quality measures of proximity to the query and plausibility in contrast to observation-only gradient updates and case-based baselines. We also empirically demonstrate that counterfactuals sampled from a jointly trained space are of higher quality than those from the common practice of using latents from reconstruction-only autoencoders. We conclude with an analysis of counterfactuals produced over the joint latent using combinations of latent and case-based approaches for an agent trained to play a complex real-time strategy game, and discuss future directions of investigation for this approach.

1 Introduction

Consider a scenario where a human user needs to decide whether a self-driving vehicle is assessing on-scene risks correctly. Feature importance methods can

Supplementary Information The online version contains supplementary material available at https://doi.org/10.1007/978-3-031-44070-0_23.

highlight portions of the input deemed to govern system decisions, such as the road span in front of the vehicle. While invaluable for development, they are often inadequate for conveying an actionable understanding of agent behavior to users [37]. On the other hand, *counterfactuals*—i.e., contrastive, example-based explanations that *change* specific aspects of the environment to arrive at a different outcome—are well-aligned with how humans develop an actionable understanding of autonomous systems [21]. Several explainable AI studies have also shown them to be effective for conveying explanations about AI systems [4]. A counterfactual adding jaywalkers to the scene increases the agent's perceived risk, assuring the user that the agent recognizes the danger to the pedestrians and is aligned with human expectations.

We present a novel generative model for generating counterfactuals that focuses on "black-box" analyses of observational and behavioral data of machine learning systems. For this work, our focus is on reinforcement learning (RL) agents, although the method itself is broadly applicable beyond RL. Using a corpus of performed trajectories and corresponding outcome variables, we train a variational autoencoder [17], modified to jointly reconstruct the agent's observations and predict outcome variables that characterize its behavior. This joint observation and outcome latent permits unconditioned sampling that reflects correlations between observations and outcomes. This flexibility allows integration of different counterfactual generation methods, such as using interpolations in latent space towards a case-based example while applying gradient-driven updates to increase data-likelihood.

Ensuring plausible counterfactuals is a key challenge: Outside of case-based approaches that draw counterfactuals from a database of existing instances, interpolated or synthesized counterfactuals run the risk of being implausible, which may reduce their credibility. We show that gradient adjustments in the joint latent to increase the data-likelihood of counterfactuals improves plausibility and reduces the number of concrete anomalies generated. We summarize our contributions as follows:

- A novel approach leveraging the use of a latent space jointly trained over observations and outcomes in the generation of counterfactuals, and a demonstration of its importance for improving counterfactual quality.
- A flexible framework for traversal over the latent space with different types of constraints.
- A novel gradient-driven approach using an approximation of the data-likelihood gradient that improves plausibility and decreases the number of anomalous counterfactuals.

2 Related Work

Automated counterfactual generation has been explored by numerous communities. One line of work has focused on case-based approaches: selecting the Nearest Unlike Neighbor (NUN), the instance that is closest to the query based on a proximity measure such as edit distance, whose outcome variable of interest has changed, e.g., has a different label associated with it [15]. In cases where a sufficiently close NUN cannot be identified, transformation templates from good counterfactual pairs in the data are used as a template for interpolation. Another approach uses feature-relevance methods like SHAP [20] to tailor a feature edit schedule for converting the query into a counterfactual [39]. As is common in counterfactual works, a proxy function is trained to predict the outcome variable given the instance and used to ensure that the synthesized counterfactual changes the outcome. Most of this work focuses on tabular data, where data is organized into discrete features (e.g., columns) and copying values has less risk of creating an implausible instance than with less structured data, such as images.

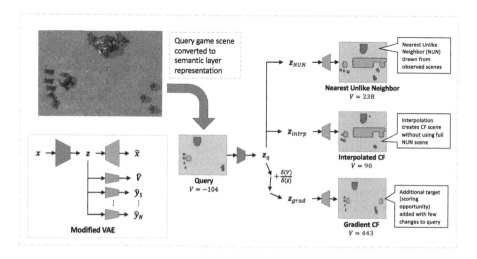

Fig. 1. A variational autoencoder is trained to both reconstruct the input and predict several outcome variables such as the agent's value function (left). As an example, given a *low-value* query instance in the StarCraft II domain encoded as spatial feature layers using PySC2 (agent units are shown in are blue; enemies, red, and assets that can be captured, green), the goal is to obtain a *higher-valued* counterfactual. The query is encoded to its latent (z_q) and counterfactuals (CF) are obtained by three methods (right): identifying the Nearest Unlike Neighbor from data (NUN, top) and then doing a partial latent interpolation to the NUN (middle), or using the gradient information to generate the example (bottom). In these actual examples produced by the methods, adding an additional target (green circle) for the agent raises the value estimate. The interpolation and gradient methods produce alternatives with fewer defending forces and placement of obstacles than the NUN. (Color figure online)

Another body of work stems from the adversarial AI community, where input perturbation and sampling-based methods are used to generate counterfactuals [35]. In particular, a Generative Adversarial Network (GAN) was used to generate counterfactual scenes for Atari game scenes [26]. However, sampling for suitable solutions can be time-consuming, whereas gradient- or example-directed traversals can be more efficient.

Cyclic consistency approaches have also been employed to generate counterfactuals by latent manipulation [16]. However, this approach focuses on a single class transforms, and is currently not amenable to counterfactuals over different combinations of outcome variables.

Gradient descent in the feature space towards the desired outcome has been used for tabular data [23] and, in particular, in the adversarial machine learning community for generating counterfactuals over image data [22,40]. However, these approaches run the risk of generating adversarial counterfactuals, such as shifting a minimal set of pixels, that may be imperceptible to human users and have low utility for understanding the model. Diffusion-based processes have also been explored for counterfactual generation, albeit this line of investigation has focused on pixel-level reconstructions [12], compared with our joint approach which learns a latent that encodes observations and outcomes.

Our approach is motivated by the Plug-and-Play approach, which uses gradient-derived signals from discriminators to iteratively shift the latent of generative models to produce outputs with the desired characteristics; and Plug-and-Play language models (PPLM), which add gradient adjustments to increase the likelihood of generated instances [5,25]. Iterative gradient-based adjustment of a latent space was also explored in xGEMs [13], albeit in that case, the latent was not trained to include outcome information, and reconstructions were not adjusted for plausibility. A similar approach was taken for attribute-based perturbation in the latent space of a conditional variational autoencoder (C-VAE) for counterfactual generation [40]. This approach trained embeddings for observations and outcomes separately, concatenating them as inputs to the decoder. This requires that the full set of outcomes be known for a query and outcome, whereas the joint latent requires only the query observation and allows for adjustments that affect a subset of outcomes, leaving others to vary freely. In addition, previous approaches have neither explicitly measured nor attempted to ensure plausibility. As multiple studies have shown, generative models are not guaranteed to produce samples that are plausible from the in-distribution set, and taking measures to avoid anomalous examples is required [24]. The closest these have approached is through use of computer-vision measures of image quality, such as Fréchet Inception Divergence [8] which uses statistics over feature activations in a network to act as a form of perceptual distance. However, it is used primarily to identify unrealistic artifacts such as blurry images. In addition, these approaches also mostly ignore the issue of proximity, and focus only on whether valid counterfactuals can be produced.

3   Preliminaries

We now describe preliminaries for this work, starting with background on the generative model, followed by how counterfactual queries are formulated. We then describe our metrics for counterfactual effectiveness and how they are implemented in our experiments.

3.1   Variational Autoencoders

Variational autoencoders (VAEs) are probabilistic generative models that encode a high-dimensional input $\mathbf{x}$ into a lower-dimensional latent representation $\mathbf{z}$ from which the original input can be approximately reconstructed [17]. The encoder module of a VAE maps the input to its latent representation, $\mathbf{z} = enc(\mathbf{x})$, and the decoder reconstructs the input, $\mathbf{x} \approx dec(\mathbf{z})$. The latent encoding is regularized by penalizing the KL divergence from a prior distribution $q(\mathbf{z})$ (typically a standard Gaussian) to the conditional distribution $q(\mathbf{z}|\mathbf{x})$ induced by the encoder. The VAE loss is given by

$$\mathcal{L}(\mathbf{x}) = \mathbb{E}_{q(\mathbf{z}|\mathbf{x})} \log p(\mathbf{x}|\mathbf{z}) - D_{KL}(q(\mathbf{z})||p(\mathbf{z}|\mathbf{x})),$$

where the decoder likelihood $p(\mathbf{x}|\mathbf{z})$ is typically implicit from a reconstruction loss, such as the MSE $||\mathbf{x} - dec(\mathbf{z})||^2$. It can be shown [17] that the VAE loss is a lower bound on the data likelihood, $\mathcal{L}(x) \le \log p(\mathbf{x})$. Because the encoder distribution $q(\mathbf{z}|\mathbf{x})$ approximates the known prior distribution $q(\mathbf{x})$, samples from the input space can be generated by drawing $\mathbf{z} \sim q(\mathbf{z})$ and passing the result through the decoder.

3.2   Counterfactual Generation with VAEs

Let M denote the model whose behavior we wish to explore using counterfactual analysis. Given a query input $\mathbf{x}_q$, we want to generate a counterfactual input $\mathbf{x}_c$ that is "related" to $\mathbf{x}$ but for which M would behave differently. We quantify the behavior of M with a vector of outcome variables $\mathbf{y} = (y^{(i)})$, $i \in \{1, \dots, N\}$. When M is a reinforcement learning agent, for example, $\mathbf{y}$ might include the value achieved by the agent, secondary performance measures such as time to reach the goal, and/or categorical measures like whether the agent violated certain constraints.

Our approach to counterfactual generation is based on perturbing the latent representation $\mathbf{z}_q$ of the query input to create a counterfactual latent representation $\mathbf{z}_c$, then decoding $\mathbf{z}_c$ to obtain a counterfactual input $\mathbf{x}_c$, exploiting the ability of VAEs to learn a latent representation space with meaningful axes of variation [9,18]. We extend the basic VAE model to reconstruct both the input $\mathbf{x}$ and the outcome variables $\mathbf{y}$ from the latent representation $\mathbf{z}$, using a separate predictor for each outcome variable, $y^{(i)} = \sigma_i(\mathbf{z})$ (Fig. 1, bottom left). Our intent is to cause the latent representation to encode information about the relationship between the input and the outcome variables, so that traversing the latent space will produce inputs that result in different outcomes. This also provides a trained predictor that can indicate when an example meets the counterfactual outcome criteria. This use of a trained proxy to determine if the outcome is met is a common practice in counterfactual generation from observational data [15].

We say that a counterfactual is *valid* if it achieves a desired change in the outcome variables, and define a validity predicate $\kappa_{i,s,\epsilon}$ that indicates whether the ith outcome variable was changed appropriately, given by

$$\kappa_{i,s,\epsilon} = \begin{cases} \mathbb{I}(y_c^{(i)} \neq y_q^{(i)}) & \text{if } y^{(i)} \text{ is categorical} \\ \mathbb{I}(y_c^{(i)} - y_q^{(i)} \geq s\epsilon) & \text{if } y^{(i)} \text{ is numeric} \end{cases},$$

where $s \in \{-1, 1\}$ is the desired sign of the difference between numeric variables, and ϵ is the desired size of the difference. For brevity, we shorten the validity predicate to κ_i for the rest of this paper. While our experiments consider only a single criterion (a single i), our approach can be extended easily to multiple criteria.

3.3 Counterfactual Quality Measures

For this work, we evaluate counterfactual generation methods along the following measures:

- **Proximity:** How different a generated counterfactual is from its query.
- **Plausibility:** Whether the counterfactual is something one would expect to observe in the domain of interest.
- **Validity:** Whether the counterfactual satisfies the counterfactual criterion κ_i.

Keeping the counterfactual similar to the original instance is important for understanding the relation between the features and the outcome variables and *proximity* is commonly measured through a variety of feature-level edit distance metrics, with counterfactuals having a *sparser* set of differences from the query being better. *Plausibility* is particularly important for systems that synthesize counterfactuals, as anomalous or implausible examples may be discounted by users [15,21]. Is is often measured by how likely the counterfactual is to be drawn from the actual data, Finally, *validity* is necessary since automatically generated counterfactuals may not actually meet the counterfactual criterion κ_i.

We measure the inverse of proximity of a counterfactual to its query via an *observational difference* score. For categorical features, this is computed as a feature edit distance, summed over the number of label changes to convert between observations. For numeric features, we use the absolute score difference, normalized to 0–1. Formally, for an index of all features, the score $i \in I$, odiff(x^1, x^2) is computed as follows:

$$\text{odiff}(\mathbf{y}_1, \mathbf{y}_2) = \sum_i \begin{cases} \mathbb{I}(y_1^{(i)} \neq y_2^{(i)}) & \text{if } i \text{ is categorical} \\ \frac{|y_1^{(i)} - y_2^{(i)}|}{W^{(i)}} & \text{if } i \text{ is numeric} \end{cases},$$

where $W^{(i)}$ is the interval width that normalizes the value.

Finally, there is no guarantee that a given method can produce a *valid* counterfactual, one that satisfies the criterion κ_i. We thus grade each counterfactual generation method by the fraction of queries for which it was able to produce a valid counterfactual, that is $\frac{1}{N} \sum_{i=1}^{N} \kappa_i$ for N queries.

3.4   Plausibility

We assess the plausibility of a latent $\mathbf{z}$ via an anomaly score formed from the observational difference between its decoding and that instance's reconstruction, following the observation that autoencoders act to denoise anomalous inputs [28]:

$$\mathrm{anom}(\mathbf{z}) = \mathrm{odiff}(dec(\mathbf{z}), dec(enc(dec(\mathbf{z}))))$$

This measures the inverse of plausibility in our experiments.[1] Using the hypothesis that autoencoders denoise their inputs, we approximate the data likelihood gradient with the reconstruction loss between the current latent's reconstruction and that scene's reconstruction using the same model:

$$\nabla_{\mathbf{z}} p(dec(\mathbf{z})) \approx -\nabla_{\mathbf{z}} || dec(\mathbf{z}) - dec(enc(dec(\mathbf{z}))) ||$$

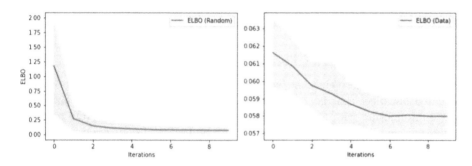

Fig. 2. Evidence lower bound (ELBO) loss against number of round trips for the input, starting from random points (left) and from data-drawn instances (right). The ELBO lower bounds the log-likelihood of the input (as the loss decreases, the input likelihood increases).

We verified the appropriateness of using this approach to increase the plausibility of generated counterfactuals by having our VAE repeatedly encode and decode its own reconstructions. Figure 2 shows the mean and standard deviation of the ELBO loss[2] of the input at each step of the recurrence. The figure shows the curve for 1000 scenes sampled from our StarCraft II minigame data (described in the following sections) and against random latents, using the encoder and decoder for that minigame. The ELBO, in non-loss form, lower bounds the model's log-likelihood of the data and, in both cases, decreases in ELBO loss gives an increase in instance likelihood, with the greatest impact at the first step. Repeating this procedure with 1000 randomly sampled latents also gives the same result. We note that while likelihoods from deep generative

---

[1] We did experiment with One-Class SVMs, but performance on a SC2 Assault scene labeled for anomalous scenes was poor in comparison with the autoencoder approach.

[2] ELBO loss drawn from our training setup, with a KL scaling term of $\beta = 10^{-5}$.

models may not be sufficiently calibrated for outlier detection [38], we are not attempting to estimate a distribution, but instead are looking to increase the likelihood—hence the plausibility—of the reconstructions during counterfactual generation. Indeed, recent work has found that deep network confidence assessments measure how familiar a model is with the features of a scene [6], matching our need to reconstruct using elements the model is more familiar with.

4   Counterfactual Methods

Figure 1 (right) illustrates our counterfactual generation architecture featuring the three methods we investigate in this work. The first draws a suitable example, the Nearest Unlike Neighbor (NUN), from previously observed examples. The second uses a traversal in the jointly trained latent space between the query and the NUN example. By stopping the traversal when the counterfactual criterion is met, this interpolated counterfactual is more proximal to the query (requires fewer feature edits). The third approach uses gradient information provided by the outcome predictors to perform a directed search in the latent space.

4.1   Nearest Unlike Neighbors

The Nearest Unlike Neighbor (NUN) is an example drawn from a library of observed instances that is similar to the query, but has an outcome that meets the counterfactual criterion [15]. It is a reliable way to obtain valid and plausible counterfactuals and serves as a baseline for comparison in our experiments. We draw the NUN $\langle \mathbf{x}_q, \mathbf{y}_{NUN} \rangle$ from the VAE's training instances, minimizing the observational distance while meeting the counterfactual criterion:

$$\mathbf{x}_{NUN} = \arg\min_{\mathbf{x}_c} \text{odiff}(x_q, x_c) \quad \text{s.t. } \kappa_i = 1.$$

4.2   Latent Interpolation

NUNs can ensure plausibility, but may not be sufficiently proximal to the query. Several studies have generated counterfactuals for tabular data by interpolating between the query and the NUN [15,39]. As we are using a generative model, we can perform a similar interpolation in the latent space by interpolating linearly between the latent encodings of the query $\mathbf{z}_q$ and the NUN $\mathbf{z}_{NUN}$ to obtain the interpolated latent representation $\mathbf{z}_\iota$. The scaling factor α is sampled from 0 to 1, set to the first point where the counterfactual criterion is first satisfied, i.e., $\kappa_i(\sigma_i(\mathbf{z}_\iota)) = 1$. If $\alpha = 1$, we consider the interpolation to have failed to produce a valid counterfactual, as the result is the NUN. If a point is found, we then update $\mathbf{z}_\iota$ with a plausibility adjustment, with the magnitude λ selected by a grid search along the unit direction of the gradient for the point with the lowest anomaly score.

$$\mathbf{z}_\iota = \alpha(\mathbf{z}_{NUN} - \mathbf{z}_q) + (1 - \alpha)\mathbf{z}_q, \quad \alpha \in [0, 1]$$
$$\mathbf{z}_\iota = \mathbf{z}_\iota + \lambda \nabla_{\mathbf{z}} p(dec(\mathbf{z}_\iota))$$

4.3   Iterative Gradient Updates

Instead of relying on interpolating toward a concrete example, we can simply follow the gradient signal from the desired outcome predictor to shift it in the desired direction. We then apply a plausibility adjustment to shift the latent to a higher likelihood state:

$$\mathbf{z} = \mathbf{z} + s\lambda_1 \nabla_{\mathbf{z}} y^{(i)}$$
$$\mathbf{z} = \mathbf{z} + \lambda_2 \nabla_{\mathbf{z}} p(dec(\mathbf{z})).$$

where $s \in \{-1, 1\}$ is the desired sign of the change, with scaling terms λ_1, λ_2.[3] We iterate this update until the counterfactual criterion $\kappa_i(\sigma_i(z))$ is satisfied or a maximum number of steps is reached[4]. We note that the gradient update over a latent space trained only for reconstruction, without the plausibility adjustment, is equivalent xGEMs [13] and similar methods in the literature.

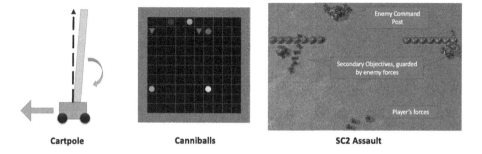

Cartpole   **Canniballs**   **SC2 Assault**

Fig. 3. Environments used in counterfactual generation experiments.

5   Experiment

We now describe the RL environments used, along with the model, training, and counterfactual query setup. We follow with results detailing counterfactual quality across three environments, and show the effect of the plausibility adjustment. We then show how the joint training helps improve counterfactual quality in comparison with a reconstruction only latent. Specific details of the model, training, errors, parameters, and code and data release are given in the Technical Appendix.

---

[3] Set to $\lambda_1 = 5, \lambda_2 = 1$, tuned over the training set.
[4] This was arbitrarily set to 1000 in our experiments.

5.1   Environments

In order to assess generalizability of our counterfactual methods, we conducted experiments in three different reinforcement learning environments: Cartpole [3], Canniballs [33], and a custom minigame in the StarCraft II Learning Environment [36]. Figure 3 illustrates the environments.

Cartpole (left) is a two-dimensional physics simulation, where the agent has to balance a pole on a cart by moving left and right. Reward is given for each timestep the pole remains upright and balanced, with episodes ending when the pole falls over or the cart veers too far from its origin. Observed state consist of four continuous parameters: cart velocity and position, pole angle and angular velocity.

Canniballs (center) [33] is a gridworld game designed to exercise multiple subgoals in a highly stochastic environment. The player controls the red ball, and reward is earned for consuming weaker entities in the game, with a penalty applied for stalling or being consumed. Episodes end when the player is consumed or after a fixed number of steps. All game entities have a strength level, including the player, who can only consume entities weaker than itself. Strength is built up by consuming different entity types (colored balls and triangles), where balls have their own behavior, such as random movement, bouncing across the field, or chasing the player. Observations are in the form of a set of categorical spatial feature layers.

StarCraft II[5] (right) is a multiplayer real-time strategy game that features a variety of unit and building types. Each unit type has strengths and weaknesses, and part of the strategy is to employ the best units to win the game. Buildings provide unique capabilities and can be destroyed or seized. For our experiments, we developed a custom scenario designed to exercise complex decision-making. The agent takes the part of one of the players, and is rewarded for destroying enemy forces, seizing secondary objectives, and destroying the enemy's command post. Capturing a secondary objective provides the player with reinforcements, which can be used to avoid obstacles. The observation space is spatial, but contains multiple layers containing both numerical and categorical data, and is significantly more complex than the two other environments. For the remainder of this paper, we will refer to this scenario as *SC2 Assault*.

5.2   Reinforcement Learning

Both Cartpole and Canniballs were trained using the RLLib framework [19]. For the SC2 Assault agent, we used a V-trace [7] agent trained using the Reaver toolkit [29]. This was implemented in the StarCraft II Learning Environment via the PySC2 interface [36], using a subset of the full action set that is focused on movement and attacks for each type of unit. Having trained the RL agents,

---

[5] https://StarCraft2.com.

we produced 1000 episodes for each environment using the trained policy. This resulted in 189,674 frames for Cartpole, 136,671 for Canniballs, and 213,407 for SC2 Assault.

For the outcome variables used to form counterfactual queries, we based our approach on the concept of interestingness elements [31,32], corresponding to numeric measures that allow highlighting meaningful and potentially explanatory situations as an RL agent interacts with its environment. Each measure is derived from data representing the agent's internal state, such as the value function estimate, V, the action value function Q (depending on the architecture), the action distribution, and others. For these experiments, we used the following interestingness variables as outcomes for exploring counterfactuals:

- **Value:** The value function estimate, measuring the expected discounted cumulative reward at any given state.
- **Confidence:** The action execution certainty of the agent, where we use a measure of statistical dispersion that relies on the entropy of the policy's action distribution.
- **Riskiness:** The margin between highest- and lowest-valued outcomes from taking an action, representing the perceived tolerance for mistakes in the environment.

5.3   Model

We now describe the VAE used to construct the surrogate model from agent trajectories. For the Cartpole agent, we used MLP encoders and decoders over the vector. Canniballs and SC2 Assault use spatial features, so we used a convolutional architecture encoder and decoder. The VAE itself differs from the standard hierarchical model by having all convolutional layers feed into the latent, and using a linear transform after the latent prior to the decoding.

For each environment, we used 95% of the recorded trajectories for training and the remainder for testing. Test mean-squared error for normalized predictions was under 0.1 across the full range of $[-1, 1]$.

We now detail the three major experiments that form the core of our contributions. The first compares gradient-driven counterfactuals across several RL environments. The second examines how plausibility adjustments can improve the likelihood of a generated example and reduce the number of anomalous counterfactuals. Finally, we demonstrate the effectiveness of the jointly training latent space on the quality of counterfactuals. Equivalence to baselines from literature are marked when appropriate.

5.4 Counterfactual Query Setup

For each interestingness variable i and sign of change s, we sampled 100 individual instances from the set of recorded trajectories. Each instance $\langle \mathbf{x}_q, \mathbf{y}_q \rangle$ was filtered so there is sufficient margin in variable i for a valid counterfactual, e.g., $-1 \le \mathbf{y}_q^{(i)} + s\epsilon \le 1$. For the value function, ϵ was two times the standard deviation. The other variables are in the range $[-1, 1]$, and we set $\epsilon = 0.5$. From our inventory of three interestingness variables and two signs of change (increasing or decreasing their value), we experimented with a total of six combinations (600 queries) for each counterfactual generation method and environment.

Table 1. Counterfactual methods for each environment, with microaveraged statistics across counterfactual quality measures. † indicates significant improvement in observational difference against the NUN baseline. * indicates significant improvement in observational difference and anomaly scores against the xGEMs baseline. Best values, including ties, in each domain are bolded.

Method	Obs Diff	Anom Score	Valid CFs
Cartpole			
NUN	1.28 ± 0.71	0.11 ± 0.03	**1.00**
InterpPt	$\mathbf{0.86 \pm 0.82}^{\dagger}$	$\mathbf{0.07 \pm 0.02}$	0.50
Grad	$0.99 \pm 0.89^{\dagger}$	0.31 ± 0.54	0.98
Canniballs			
NUN	1754.91 ± 89.31	$\mathbf{0.00 \pm 0.00}$	0.67
InterpPt	$\mathbf{5.46 \pm 4.10}^{\dagger}$	0.20 ± 0.57	0.67
Grad	$18.94 \pm 20.88^{\dagger}$	12.56 ± 17.13	**0.99**
SC2 Assault			
NUN	1746.12 ± 573.25	$\mathbf{7.52 \pm 3.88}$	**1.00**
InterpPt	$1234.94 \pm 880.92^{\dagger}$	30.38 ± 24.87	0.67
*Grad**	$\mathbf{83.36 \pm 141.25}^{\dagger}$	33.73 ± 45.29	0.97
InterpPt -Pls	1224.06 ± 879.17	48.26 ± 75.52	0.69
*Grad -Pls**	$\mathbf{82.44 \pm 136.11}$	34.41 ± 46.62	0.97
SC2 Assault, Reconstruction-only Latent			
InterpPt	881.94 ± 770.84	72.00 ± 70.78	0.44
Grad	124.17 ± 100.85	83.07 ± 44.34	0.81
xGEMs	123.34 ± 97.66	83.12 ± 44.95	0.81

Table 2. Counterfactual methods for the SC2 Assault task, with microaveraged statistics for each Interestingness Variable across counterfactual quality measures. We find there is significant variance between variables, but the general findings that the joint space improves both the number of valid counterfactuals and their plausibilities still hold.

Method	Obs Diff	Anom Score	Valid CFs
Riskiness			
NUN	1785.89 ± 554.02	5.47 ± 2.77	1.00
InterpPt	1613.77 ± 541.31	24.07 ± 14.12	0.58
Gradient	42.26 ± 45.50	24.42 ± 23.93	0.99
xGEMs	100.13 ± 58.97	83.90 ± 38.55	0.50
Confidence			
NUN	1670.38 ± 566.85	10.90 ± 3.24	1.00
InterpPt	1358.88 ± 771.46	30.82 ± 15.06	0.60
Gradient	52.09 ± 70.31	28.79 ± 33.29	1.00
xGEMs	139.37 ± 85.15	74.84 ± 32.69	1.00
Value			
NUN	1782.08 ± 593.49	6.19 ± 3.11	1.00
InterpPt	889.71 ± 1005.72	34.34 ± 33.84	0.82
Gradient	163.09 ± 217.00	49.44 ± 66.12	0.91
xGEMs	120.76 ± 128.05	91.44 ± 55.31	0.94

5.5 Results

We compared the following methods across the three RL environments:

- Drawing the Nearest Unlike Neighbor from the training set (NUN), which is used as a baseline.
- Latent Interpolation to the NUN, stopping at the first point where κ_i is met (InterpPt).
- Using Iterative Gradient Update to perturb the latent until κ_i is met (Grad).

Table 1 reports the micro-averaged mean and standard deviation of the observational differences, anomaly scores[6], and fraction of valid counterfactual queries for each method against the given query combinations for the three environments. Only values from valid counterfactuals were used to compute these measures. Significance tests are conducted using a two sample t-test with $\alpha = 0.01$. As expected, drawing from a memory of actual instances (NUN) produces the least anomalous and most plausible counterfactuals. However, both latent-based approaches produce counterfactuals with significantly lower observational differences (more proximal) across all three domains. An in-depth analysis of proximity across all three domains is given in the Technical Appendix.

---

[6] Observational difference and anomaly score are the inverses of proximity and plausibility, so lower scores indicate better performance.

The Gradient method produced valid counterfactuals for most queries, missing at most 3% overall. The InterpPt method generated counterfactuals about 67% of the time across all three environments, with the remainder requiring full traversal to the NUN. We examined the impact of a plausible scene gradient adjustment on counterfactuals for the SC2 Assault minigame environment, showing the Latent Interpolation and Gradient methods without the plausibility adjustment (InterpPt -Pls, Grad -Pls). We find the plausibility adjustment significantly reduces the anomaly score without impacting the observational difference for InterpPt. However, we find no significant difference in anomaly scores with Gradient.

To relate anomaly scores to a concrete number of anomalous scenes, we tuned a threshold on the VAE reconstruction scores to detect labeled anomalous SC2 Assault scenes, achieving a test accuracy of 95% over a baseline guess of 66% (plausible)[7]. Out of 600 queries, InterpPt produced 4 anomalous counterfactuals, compared to 20 without the plausibility adjustment. The Gradient method produced 46 with the adjustment, and 48 without.

5.6   Impact of Joint Training

We tested our hypothesis that joint training of input reconstruction and outcome prediction leads to better counterfactuals, as approaches in the literature trained these two tasks sequentially (see Sect. 2). Using the SC2 Assault task, we trained the VAE model with just the reconstruction objective using an otherwise similar setup. We then trained the outcome predictors given the latents produced by the reconstruction-only model, achieving prediction errors comparable to those of the full model. We then re-ran the same set of experiments using the reconstruction-only latent and predictors. Results are presented at the bottom half of Table 1. Here we see that counterfactuals generated from the reconstruction-only latent space produced considerably more anomalous counterfactuals, with fewer valid counterfactuals. We note that the Gradient approach without the plausibility adjustment over the Reconstruction-Only latent is equivalent to xGEMs [13]. In comparison, Gradient derived counterfactuals over the joint space have significantly lower observational differences and anomaly scores, with and without the plausibility adjustment.

In the joint latent, the Interpt and Gradient methods produced a combined total of 50 concrete anomalies, whereas their equivalents from the reconstruction-only latent gave a total of 176 anomalies. xGEMs itself gave 107 anomalies, in contrast to its equivalent in the joint latent, which had 48.

5.7   Analysis by Interestingness Variable

We examine the results by Interestingness Variable for the complex SC2 Assault task (Table 2). We find that there are significant differences between Riskiness, Confidence, and Value across the different methods and quality metrics. However, the general results still hold: Gradient-based approaches are more proximal

---

[7] Model and training are detailed in the Technical Appendix.

to the query, and gradient updates over the joint latent produces significantly better anomaly scores and the number of more valid counterfactuals in contrast with ones produced over a non-joint latent space.

5.8   Counterfactual Analysis

We now present an analysis of counterfactuals drawn from the SC2 Assault minigame task. We first present an overview of how the minigame scenes are structured for the agent.

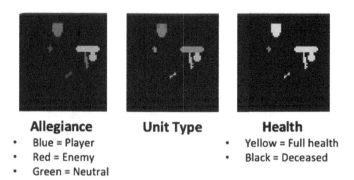

Allegiance

- Blue = Player
- Red = Enemy
- Green = Neutral

Unit Type

Health

- Yellow = Full health
- Black = Deceased

Fig. 4. The SC2 Assault task uses multiple spatial frames to represent different attributes of the units and structures in the game. The leftmost grid represents the allegiance of the unit. The middle encodes the type of unit or structure, while the rightmost describes the health status of that unit. (Color figure online)

Figure 4 describes the observation format. Each scene is described by three spatial *semantic frames* representing different semantic information. The *Allegiance* of the unit determines which faction the unit belongs to. *Unit Type* details the specific type of unit or building at that location. For simplicity, the following analyses will highlight significant unit types directly. Finally, *Health* shows the relative health of the unit using a scale of bright yellow representing full health to black representing no health.

For these analyses, we examine counterfactuals where the value function estimate is either increased by two standard deviations from a sampled low-value scene, or decreased by the same amount from a high-value one. Because the observation space is composed of semantic frames, with each corresponding to a concept such as unit type or allegiance, the differences between a query scene and its counterfactual directly map to understandable and meaningful changes. This can be used to identify the types of changes associated with counterfactuals along an outcome variable: for example, converting enemy defenders into weaker units results in increased value-function estimates. While this example is specific to the SC2 Assault task, similar analyses may be extended to other domains via pre-trained detectors.

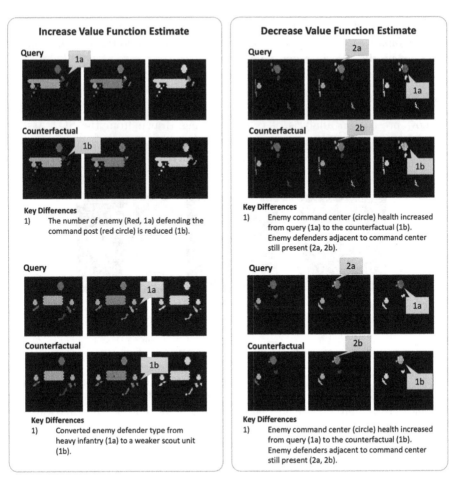

Fig. 5. Four example counterfactuals generated using gradient-based walks in the latent space. The left column shows low-value function estimate query scenes with corresponding higher-valued counterfactuals, while the right shows high-value function estimates and lower-valued counterfactuals. For each example, the top row shows the semantic frames (allegiance, unit type, health) for the query scene, the middle row shows its higher valued counterfactual, and the bottom row shows the highlighted key differences. Key differences are derived by analyzing the differences in each spatially significant semantic frame.

Figure 5 shows four sampled query scenes and the counterfactuals generated by gradient perturbation with the plausibility adjustment. The left column for low-value queries to high-value counterfactuals, with the opposite on the right. We find the generated counterfactuals are both proximal to the query and with minimal artifacts. Deltas in the semantic frames between the queries and counterfactuals show multiple explanations for factors that can increase the value estimate. For example, reducing the number of enemy defenders (top left) or attacking when the enemy defenders are of a weaker type (bottom left) increase the odds of success. On the other hand, situations where the enemy command center is at full health but still has a full complement of defenders reduces the value function estimate, or decreases the agent's perceived ability to destroy the enemy command post.

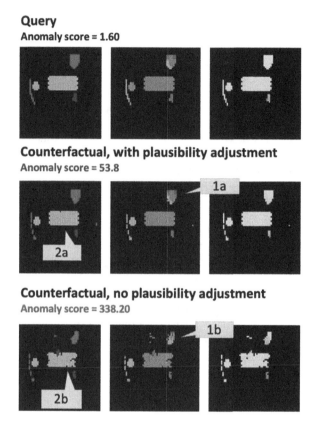

Fig. 6. The impact of plausibility adjustments: The top row shows the query scene, along with its computed anomaly score. The middle row shows a gradient-based counterfactual for increasing the value, with plausibility adjustments, the bottom row shows the equivalent-valued counterfactual without the adjustments. These adjustments preserve the spatial structure of the command structure and defending units (1a vs. 1b) as well as the center set of obstacles and friendly Blue unit placement (2a vs. 2b). (Color figure online)

Figure 6 illustrates the impact of the plausibility adjustment. For a low-valued starting query, the gradient-based counterfactual with the plausibility adjustment results in less noise, and a lower anomaly score, than one run to the same value.

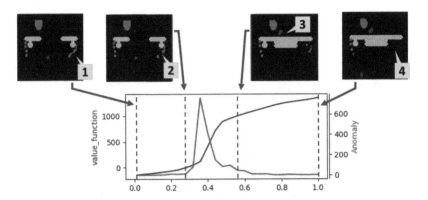

Fig. 7. Traversal in the latent space between the a low-value query (1) and high-value nearest unlike neighbor counterfactual (4). The top row shows the reconstructed scene from the latent, restricted to unit Allegiance for clarity, while the bottom shows the value estimate and the anomaly score for that point in the traversal. The traversal provides a sensitivity analysis showing both the value of the feature and its importance in the original query (Color figure online)

The sequence of feature changes in the scene between the query and a counterfactual also provides information about which features bolster an outcome in the query. Figure 7 gives an example a low-value query and a high-value NUN drawn from the library. Four samples are drawn from the latent trajectory from the query (left) to the NUN (right). The top row shows the scene reconstruction, restricted to the unit allegiance frame for clarity. The bottom shows the value function estimate (blue) and the anomaly score for a reconstruction at that point in the latent traversal (red). The differences between scene features between each of the sampled points illustrates the change in the value function resulting from those feature changes. In addition, the schedule of feature edits can identify correlated features and their impact on the value function.

6   Discussion and Future Work

We presented a latent space that jointly contains information about observations and outcome variables that permits unconditioned sampling. From this, we presented two methods for obtaining counterfactuals: the first employing interpolations between the query and case-based instances drawn from a memory, the second using gradient updates to iteratively update the query to reflect the desired outcomes. We show that the joint latent approach can produce more valid counterfactuals that are also more plausible. We also show that reconstruction error as a proxy for the likelihood gradient can help improve the plausibility of counterfactuals in certain cases. We followed with an assessment of a sampling of generated counterfactuals, demonstrating the ability of the method create meaningful and plausible examples.

Future areas of investigation include a closer examination of these methods in contrast to feature-level adversarial methods. A major concern about that class of methods is that the counterfactuals they generate may be imperceptible to humans, as their perturbations are fuzzing attacks that minimize feature-level changes. While latent space traversal methods can take steps to ensure a minimal amount of feature-level differences, future work should include stronger assurances for preventing the generation of counterfactuals that are imperceptibly different from the query. Our approach allows gradient-based adjustments to have a latent meet different criteria, such as improving data-likelihood. This can be tailored to include adjustments reflecting feature edits corresponding to actionable elements the agent or human operator has control over, such as the disposition of friendly forces in the SC2 Assault environment.

Another area of possible improvement would be the use of classifier-free guidance to improve the quality of the counterfactuals, as gradient-based signals from discriminative classifiers may not be sufficient to capture the shape of certain outcome variable distributions [10]. Use of this method in conditional latent diffusion was also found to improve generated imagery [30].

Finally, we note that this work, like many others, looks at intrinsic measures of counterfactual quality. Proper extrinsic evaluations of how counterfactuals can improve a meaningful task remains to be addressed. One possible avenue would be to use counterfactuals to improve the examples used for machine-teaching and tutoring applications [34]. We are also investigating the use of directed counterfactuals to warn decision-makers of likely or dangerous possible scenarios. In addition, they may also act as a source of additional weak evidence for observational assessments of the causal link between features and outcomes.

Acknowledgements. This material is based upon work supported by the Defense Advanced Research Projects Agency (DARPA) under Contract No. HR001119C0112. Any opinions, findings and conclusions or recommendations expressed in this material are those of the author(s) and do not necessarily reflect the views of the DARPA.

References

1. Agarap, A.F.: Deep learning using rectified linear units (ReLU). arXiv preprint arXiv:1803.08375 (2018)
2. Bowman, S.R., Vilnis, L., Vinyals, O., Dai, A.M., Józefowicz, R., Bengio, S.: Generating sentences from a continuous space. CoRR abs/1511.06349 (2015). http://arxiv.org/abs/1511.06349
3. Brockman, G., et al.: OpenAI gym. arXiv preprint arXiv:1606.01540 (2016)
4. Byrne, R.M.J.: Counterfactuals in explainable artificial intelligence (XAI): evidence from human reasoning. In: Proceedings of the Twenty-Eighth International Joint Conference on Artificial Intelligence, IJCAI-19, pp. 6276–6282. International Joint Conferences on Artificial Intelligence Organization (2019). https://doi.org/10.24963/ijcai.2019/876
5. Dathathri, S., et al.: Plug and play language models: a simple approach to controlled text generation. CoRR abs/1912.02164 (2019). http://arxiv.org/abs/1912.02164

6. Dietterich, T.G., Guyer, A.: The familiarity hypothesis: explaining the behavior of deep open set methods (2022). https://doi.org/10.48550/ARXIV.2203.02486, https://arxiv.org/abs/2203.02486

7. Espeholt, L., et al.: IMPALA: scalable distributed deep-RL with importance weighted actor-learner architectures. CoRR abs/1802.01561 (2018). http://arxiv.org/abs/1802.01561

8. Heusel, M., Ramsauer, H., Unterthiner, T., Nessler, B., Klambauer, G., Hochreiter, S.: GANs trained by a two time-scale update rule converge to a nash equilibrium. CoRR abs/1706.08500 (2017). http://arxiv.org/abs/1706.08500

9. Higgins, I., et al.: Beta-VAE: learning basic visual concepts with a constrained variational framework (2016)

10. Ho, J., Salimans, T.: Classifier-free diffusion guidance (2022)

11. Ioffe, S., Szegedy, C.: Batch normalization: accelerating deep network training by reducing internal covariate shift. In: Bach, F., Blei, D. (eds.) Proceedings of the 32nd International Conference on Machine Learning. Proceedings of Machine Learning Research, vol. 37, pp. 448–456. PMLR, Lille (2015). https://proceedings.mlr.press/v37/ioffe15.html

12. Jeanneret, G., Simon, L., Jurie, F.: Diffusion models for counterfactual explanations. In: Asian Conference on Computer Vision (2022)

13. Joshi, S., Koyejo, O., Kim, B., Ghosh, J.: xGEMs: generating examplars to explain black-box models. CoRR abs/1806.08867 (2018). http://arxiv.org/abs/1806.08867

14. Karras, T., Laine, S., Aittala, M., Hellsten, J., Lehtinen, J., Aila, T.: Analyzing and improving the image quality of StyleGAN. CoRR abs/1912.04958 (2019). http://arxiv.org/abs/1912.04958

15. Keane, M.T., Smyth, B.: Good counterfactuals and where to find them: a case-based technique for generating counterfactuals for explainable AI (XAI). CoRR abs/2005.13997 (2020). https://arxiv.org/abs/2005.13997

16. Khorram, S., Fuxin, L.: Cycle-consistent counterfactuals by latent transformations. In: 2022 IEEE/CVF Conference on Computer Vision and Pattern Recognition (CVPR), pp. 10193–10202 (2022)

17. Kingma, D.P., Welling, M.: Auto-encoding variational bayes (2013). https://doi.org/10.48550/ARXIV.1312.6114, https://arxiv.org/abs/1312.6114

18. Klys, J., Snell, J., Zemel, R.: Learning latent subspaces in variational autoencoders. In: Advances in Neural Information Processing Systems, vol. 31 (2018)

19. Liang, E., et al.: Ray RLlib: a composable and scalable reinforcement learning library. CoRR abs/1712.09381 (2017). http://arxiv.org/abs/1712.09381

20. Lundberg, S.M., Lee, S.: A unified approach to interpreting model predictions. CoRR abs/1705.07874 (2017). http://arxiv.org/abs/1705.07874

21. Miller, T.: Explanation in artificial intelligence: insights from the social sciences. CoRR abs/1706.07269 (2017). http://arxiv.org/abs/1706.07269

22. Moore, J., Hammerla, N., Watkins, C.: Explaining deep learning models with constrained adversarial examples. CoRR abs/1906.10671 (2019). http://arxiv.org/abs/1906.10671

23. Mothilal, R.K., Sharma, A., Tan, C.: Explaining machine learning classifiers through diverse counterfactual explanations. CoRR abs/1905.07697 (2019). http://arxiv.org/abs/1905.07697

24. Nalisnick, E., Matsukawa, A., Teh, Y.W., Gorur, D., Lakshminarayanan, B.: Do deep generative models know what they don't know? (2018). https://doi.org/10.48550/ARXIV.1810.09136, https://arxiv.org/abs/1810.09136

25. Nguyen, A., Yosinski, J., Bengio, Y., Dosovitskiy, A., Clune, J.: Plug & play generative networks: conditional iterative generation of images in latent space. CoRR abs/1612.00005 (2016). http://arxiv.org/abs/1612.00005

26. Olson, M.L., Khanna, R., Neal, L., Li, F., Wong, W.: Counterfactual state explanations for reinforcement learning agents via generative deep learning. CoRR abs/2101.12446 (2021). https://arxiv.org/abs/2101.12446

27. Paszke, A., et al.: PyTorch: an imperative style, high-performance deep learning library. In: Wallach, H., Larochelle, H., Beygelzimer, A., d'Alché-Buc, F., Fox, E., Garnett, R. (eds.) Advances in Neural Information Processing Systems, vol. 32, pp. 8024–8035. Curran Associates, Inc. (2019). http://papers.neurips.cc/paper/9015-pytorch-an-imperative-style-high-performance-deep-learning-library.pdf

28. Pomerleau, D.A.: Input reconstruction reliability estimation. In: Hanson, S., Cowan, J., Giles, C. (eds.) Advances in Neural Information Processing Systems, vol. 5. Morgan-Kaufmann (1992). https://proceedings.neurips.cc/paper/1992/file/b7bb35b9c6ca2aee2df08cf09d7016c2-Paper.pdf

29. Ring, R.: Reaver: modular deep reinforcement learning framework (2018). https://github.com/inoryy/reaver

30. Rombach, R., Blattmann, A., Lorenz, D., Esser, P., Ommer, B.: High-resolution image synthesis with latent diffusion models. In: Proceedings of the IEEE Conference on Computer Vision and Pattern Recognition (CVPR) (2022). https://github.com/CompVis/latent-diffusion, https://arxiv.org/abs/2112.10752

31. Sequeira, P., Gervasio, M.: Interestingness elements for explainable reinforcement learning: understanding agents' capabilities and limitations. Artif. Intell. **288**, 103367 (2020). https://doi.org/10.1016/j.artint.2020.103367

32. Sequeira, P., Yeh, E., Gervasio, M.: Interestingness elements for explainable reinforcement learning through introspection. In: Joint Proceedings of the ACM IUI 2019 Workshops, p. 7. ACM (2019)

33. Showalter, S.: Cameleon canniballs environment (2021). https://github.com/SRI-AIC/cameleon#environments

34. Simard, P.Y., et al.: Machine teaching: a new paradigm for building machine learning systems. CoRR abs/1707.06742 (2017). http://arxiv.org/abs/1707.06742

35. Szegedy, C., et al.: Intriguing properties of neural networks. In: ICLR (2014)

36. Vinyals, O., et al.: Starcraft II: a new challenge for reinforcement learning. CoRR abs/1708.04782 (2017). http://arxiv.org/abs/1708.04782

37. Wachter, S., Mittelstadt, B.D., Russell, C.: Counterfactual explanations without opening the black box: automated decisions and the GDPR. CoRR abs/1711.00399 (2017). http://arxiv.org/abs/1711.00399

38. Wang, Z., Dai, B., Wipf, D., Zhu, J.: Further analysis of outlier detection with deep generative models (2020). https://doi.org/10.48550/ARXIV.2010.13064, https://arxiv.org/abs/2010.13064

39. Wiratunga, N., Wijekoon, A., Nkisi-Orji, I., Martin, K., Palihawadana, C., Corsar, D.: DisCERN: discovering counterfactual explanations using relevance features from neighbourhoods. CoRR abs/2109.05800 (2021). https://arxiv.org/abs/2109.05800

40. Yang, F., Liu, N., Du, M., Hu, X.: Generative counterfactuals for neural networks via attribute-informed perturbation. CoRR abs/2101.06930 (2021). https://arxiv.org/abs/2101.06930

An Exploration of the Latent Space of a Convolutional Variational Autoencoder for the Generation of Musical Instrument Tones

Anastasia Natsiou[✉], Seán O'Leary, and Luca Longo

School of Computer Science, Artificial Intelligence and Cognitive Load Research Lab, Technological University Dublin, Dublin, Republic of Ireland
{anastasia.natsiou,sean.oleary,luca.longo}@tudublin.ie

Abstract. Variational Autoencoders (VAEs) constitute one of the most significant deep generative models for the creation of synthetic samples. In the field of audio synthesis, VAEs have been widely used for the generation of natural and expressive sounds, such as music or speech. However, VAEs are often considered black boxes and the attributes that contribute to the synthesis of a sound are yet unsolved. Existing research focused on the way input data can influence the generation of latent space, and how this latent space can create synthetic data, is still insufficient. In this manuscript, we investigate the interpretability of the latent space of VAEs and the impact of each attribute of this space on the generation of synthetic instrumental notes. The contribution to the body of knowledge of this research is to offer, for both the XAI and sound community, an approach for interpreting how the latent space generates new samples. This is based on sensitivity and feature ablation analyses, and descriptive statistics.

Keywords: Explainable Artificial Intelligence (XAI) · Variational Autoencoders (VAE) · Audio Representations · Audio Synthesis · Latent Feature Importance

1 Introduction

Generative models in the field of sound synthesis have enabled musicians, and sound designers to create and manipulate sounds in new and innovative ways [20,32]. Variational Autoencoder (VAE) is a type of deep generative model that has been widely used in the field of audio generation [12,15,26]. VAEs can be trained on a dataset of sound recordings to learn a compressed representation of the sounds in the latent space. The latent space can then be manipulated to generate new, similar sounds. The design of VAEs is considered successful when samples with similar principles map closer to each other in the latent space, and new sounds can be generated by interpolating between previous sounds with specific properties. However, this is not always the case. The model extracts information from the audio samples forming a latent space that does not always match human perception. Explainable artificial intelligence (XAI) is an emerging area of research that aims to develop techniques to make deep learning models transparent and interpretable to humans [4,37,38]. Explainability can be used in generative models for sound synthesis for the creation of audio samples in a more understandable and controllable way. However, according to [29], XAI for arts, and more specifically generative music, is still in its early stages. Most of the existing publications focus on controlling the synthesis of the generative model by regularizing its latent space to specific characteristics [23,36,40].

In this manuscript, we attempt to explain how latent dimensions are linked to the generation of discreet instrumental musical tones for monophonic, and harmonic audio samples. First, we provide explanation techniques for understanding the impact of different parameters on the resulting sound using VAEs, and then we explore the contribution of each attribute of the latent space to the synthesis of a specific instrument. Section 2 overviews the existing methodology used in this manuscript while briefly providing a literature review on the most prominent techniques. The chapter provides a concise overview of the prevalent audio representations commonly used and our proposed representation, along with an explanation of the architecture of VAE. Additionally, it delves into the examination of statistical methods and visualization techniques employed to uncover the significance of latent attributes. Through careful analysis, these approaches enable the identification and assessment of the importance of latent variables in the context of audio synthesis. Section 3 describes the dataset and hyper-parameterization of the VAE, along with evaluation methods for sound reconstruction. Finally, the results are reported in Sect. 4 and the conclusion and future directions in Sect. 5.

2   Methodology and Related Work

Our goal is to permit the manipulation of latent representations of discreet instrumental notes created by deep generative models and provide an explanation for the synthesis of musical tones. In Sect. 2.1, we demonstrate the importance of input representations for sound synthesis followed by the development of a new representation for monophonic and harmonic sounds. Section 2.2 outlines the benefits of Variational Autoencoders compared to the classic autoencoders and introduces ways to create the latent space. The proposed methodology for the generation of the latent space is illustrated in Fig. 2. Finally, Sect. 2.3 provides techniques for the interpretation of VAEs based on methods for latent feature importance.

2.1   Audio Representations

Audio representations are mathematical representations of acoustic signals that are used to analyze, process, and manipulate sound. The fundamental form of an acoustic signal is the discretized version of the waveform which is created by sampling the continuous wave in time and amplitude. In deep learning applications, this waveform is called raw audio and it represents the acoustic wave as a sequence of numbers, each number representing an amplitude sample at a chosen sampling frequency. Although raw audio is the most accurate representation of sound, it is often considered unsuitable for deep learning models due to its high dimensionality and lack of interpretability.

To overcome these obstacles, recent studies propose high-level forms that offer more meaningful descriptions [27]. Time-frequency representations such as spectrograms, mel-spectrograms, or Constant-Q Transformations (CQT) have been proven beneficial for deep generative models [2,3,35]. Their success is mainly achieved because of their ease to be stored and processed. In deep learning models, where memory and computational limitations can slow down the training process, time-frequency representations provide an efficient solution. Finally, spectrograms provide a visual representation that captures important characteristics such as frequency content, harmonics, timbre, and temporal dynamics. They provide a physically and perceptually meaningful representation making them more useful for deep generative models [13]. An overview of spectrograms is depicted in Fig. 1. In an attempt to reduce even more the wealth of acoustic information, various studies extract perceptual features from the original signal. Compact representations such as acoustic features [11] or spectral coefficients [14] capture the essential spectral information of the audio signal while reducing the amount of data required for analysis and processing. Spectral coefficients can be used to represent the spectral envelope of an audio signal, which contains information about the shape of the frequency spectrum and the relative amplitudes of the various frequency components.

In this work, we design a new audio representation based on acoustic features that is able to represent monophonic, and harmonic instrumental notes. The proposed representation is created by the fundamental frequency and the logarithm of the amplitudes of the first 7 harmonics in overlapping frames of sound. The first 7 harmonics are able to capture the most perceptually significant part of a note providing information about the spectral shape of the acoustic signal. Since the dataset is monophonic and harmonic, the waveform can be synthesized with the given amplitudes and the integer multiples of the fundamental frequency:

$$f_n = n f_0 \qquad (1)$$

where $n \in [1, 7]$ represents the number of the harmonic for every frame i of the sound. The suggested representation offers a lower-dimensional alternative to spectrograms, enabling further compression by autoencoders. Moreover, its meaningful structure is expected to result in a latent space that is more interpretable, allowing for a better understanding and analysis of the learned representations.

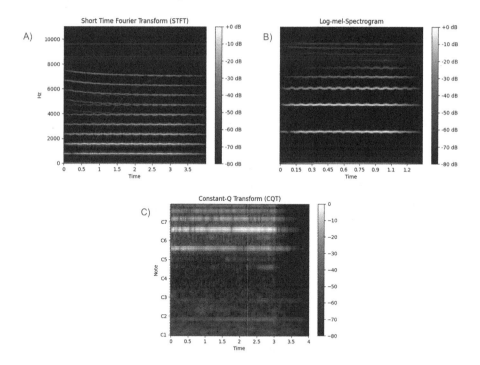

Fig. 1. Demonstration of time-frequency representations of sound: A) Magnitude spectrogram (using STFT) B) Log-mel-spectrogram and C) Constant-Q Transform (CQT)

2.2   From Autoencoders to Variational Autoencoders

An autoencoder [5] is a type of neural architecture used for unsupervised learning. The fundamental idea behind an autoencoder is to learn a compressed representation of the input data that captures its most important features, in order to reconstruct the original input data as accurately as possible. Autoencoders consist of two main parts: an encoder that attempts to reduce the dimensionality of the original samples producing a compressed or *latent representation*, and a decoder that aims to reconstruct the original input data given the latent representation. For a feedforward single layer model, the encoder maps an input vector $x \in \mathbb{R}^d$ to an encoding $z \in \mathbb{R}^e$ where $d > e$ using a non-linear activation function $f(.)$

$$y = f(Wx + b) \tag{2}$$

where $W \in \mathbb{R}^{(e \times d)}$ represents the weights of the connections between the neurons and $b \in \mathbb{R}^e$ accounts for the bias term. The decoder maps z back to the reconstructed $\widehat{x} \in \mathbb{R}^d$ using a similar approach

$$\widehat{x} = f(W_{out}y + b_{out}) \tag{3}$$

where $W_{out} \in \mathbb{R}^{(d \times e)}$ and $b_{out} \in \mathbb{R}^d$. The reconstruction is achieved by a training procedure where the autoencoder attempts to minimize the difference between the input data and the reconstructed output data, using a loss function such as mean squared error or binary cross-entropy.

Although autoencoders can achieve a low reconstruction error, these types of architectures do not promise a meaningful learned representation. The latent space created by an autoencoder often lacks interpretability and similar samples can be mapped at different regions in the space. To solve this problem, Variational autoencoders (VAEs) [18] convert the input data to a latent space through a stochastic distribution, making it more "smooth" and interpretable. In the vanilla VAE, the encoder maps a latent variable $z \in \mathbb{R}^e$ with an input variable $x \in \mathbb{R}^d$ where $d > e$ by using a distribution $q(z|x)$ to approximate $p(z|x)$. This approximation is named *Variational Inference*. The prior distribution of z is $p(z)$ and therefore the decoder is parametrized to approximate the distribution $p(x|z)$. More specifically, the encoder outputs the mean μ_M and the covariance σ_M as the inputs of the Gaussian distribution function $N(z; \mu_M, \sigma_M^2 I)$ over a latent space with M number of dimensions. The objective of the network is to minimize the KL divergence between $q(z|x)$ and $p(z)$ by maximizing the evidence lower bound:

$$\mathbb{E}[\log p(x|z)] - KL(q(z|x) \parallel p(z)) \leq \log p(x) \tag{4}$$

In the above equation, the first term measures how well the reconstructed data matches the original, while the second term measures the difference between the approximate posterior distribution $q(z|x)$ and the prior distribution $p(z)$. The KL divergence term encourages the learned posterior distribution to be close to the prior distribution, which in turn regularizes the learned latent space representation. By sampling from a distribution, VAEs have the ability to generate new data samples that are similar to the input data. Furthermore, the generated latent space is regularized by a specific distribution making it more structured and continuous. This means that similar input data will be closer in the latent space and small changes in the latent space correspond to small changes in the generated data. Finally, interpolation between two points in the latent space is feasible. This way, a new sample can be created by combining the properties of the multiple original data. VAEs have demonstrated their potential in multiple audio applications including real-time synthesis [7], polyphonic synthesis [21], or instrumental tones generation controlled over their pitch [33].

2.3   Latent Feature Importance

In deep generative models, such as VAEs, latent variables can play a critical role in capturing complex relationships in the data and generating high-quality outputs. However, these variables are not directly observable and the task to interpret their role in the model can be challenging [1]. Latent feature importance refers to the relative importance of hidden or latent variables, as opposed to the input or output data [8]. For the investigation of latent feature importance, a variety of techniques have been proposed. *Sensitivity analysis* involves the process of perturbing the values of the latent features and observing the resulting changes in the output variables. By measuring the reconstruction error of the generated data when a slight variation of the latent feature is applied, we gain insights into which latent features are more important for producing the correct output. Gradient-based investigation of each feature of the latent space [28] constitutes a prominent technique for sensitivity analysis of the VAEs.

Feature ablation involves the procedure of removing individual latent features from the model and measuring the resulting changes in the output variables. In VAEs, feature ablation studies can be conducted to calculate and visualize the encoded samples for the most significant parts of the latent space that lead to the generation of synthetic data [19]. In a similar approach, *feature attribution techniques* involves the process of assigning a score to each latent feature based on its contribution to the final output. Several methods have been proposed for computing feature attribution scores, including Local Interpretable Model-Agnostic Explanations (LIME) [30], SHapley Additive exPlanations (SHAP) [22], and Integrated Gradients [34]. A more contemporary method for quantifying the reliance of a model on each feature is the Shapley Additive Global importancE (SAGE) [9]. This approach assigns a score to each feature based on five desirable properties, namely efficiency, symmetry, dummy, monotonicity, and linearity.

Other methods for experimenting with latent feature importance include a variety of clustering techniques. *Clustering* involves grouping similar points in the latent space together based on their output variables. Clustering has been used as an integrated method of the architecture of VAEs to regularize the latent space based on existing distributions [16,31,41] or as a regularization method based on specific characteristics of the training data [6,29]. Finally, valuable insights into the importance of the latent features can be gained through visualization of the latent variables. However, since the latent space usually indicates a high dimensionality, visualization can be achieved by projecting the high-dimensional latent space onto a lower-dimensional space that can be easily plotted and interpreted. Two of the most popular visualization techniques are the Principle Component Analysis (PCA) [25] and the two- or three-dimensional Stochastic Neighbor Embedding (t-SNE) [24]. In this manuscript, we investigate many of the above methods to analyze and understand the way latent features contribute to the generation of synthetic instrumental notes. Our experimentation includes a sensitivity analysis along with a feature ablation analysis for the understanding of the influence of each feature of the latent space on the properties of the generated sound. Furthermore, we provide statistical analysis and visualization of the latent space for identifying the latent attributes related to each instrument.

3   Experimental Setup

In this section, we describe the experimental setup, including details of the dataset and its pre-processing, model configuration, and evaluation methods

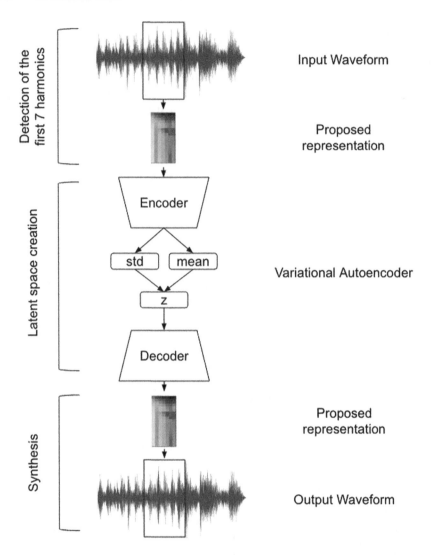

Fig. 2. Proposed architecture for the generation of the latent space using Variational Autoencoders and an audio representation based on the first 7 harmonics.

for the reconstruction. Figure 2 illustrates the overall reconstruction schema for the extraction of the latent features of audio samples and the reconstruction of instrumental notes.

3.1 Dataset

The experiments were conducted using the NSynth dataset[1], a collection of four-second monophonic notes from a variety of instruments in acoustic, electronic, or synthetic form in different categories as per their velocity or acoustic quality. The training and testing data had a pitch in the range of 80 Hz–2100 Hz. Furthermore, an analysis of the samples revealed that many of the data were not harmonic and they were excluded from the experiments along with some samples that had variations in the fundamental frequency or amplitude. The remaining dataset is composed of 101911 training samples and 1324 testing samples of guitar, bass, brass, keyboard, flute, organ, mallet, reed, and string.

The waveform of these samples was pre-processed to generate a representation that includes the fundamental frequency and the logarithm of the amplitude of the first 7 harmonics for overlapping segments of sound. The fundamental frequency was computed using the YIN algorithm [10] with a post-processing step to ensure that the pitch will not vary more than 3% between consecutive frames. The amplitudes of the first 7 harmonics were calculated by a peak detection technique in the time-frequency domain. For the conversion of the waveform to the time-frequency domain, we used the Short Time Fourier Transform (STFT) with a normalized Blackman window of 690 samples, an FFT window of 1024, and a hop size of 172. The final representation was later normalized using the min-max scaling to be transformed into the range $[0, 1]$.

3.2 Model Configuration

For the audio reconstruction, we used convolutional VAEs with a mirrored encoder and decoder as it is presented in Fig. 3. The two components are composed of two 2D convolutional layers with 32 filters each, a kernel size of 3, a stride of 2, and the same padding. Two dense layers are used to calculate the mean and variation and the latent space is the vector created after sampling from the distribution. Our experiments found an optimum of 8, for the dimensionality of the latent space, after which the performance of the reconstruction decreased. The ReLU is used as an activation function for the convolutional layers while the softmax function is applied to the output layer to form the generated normalized representation. The network is trained using the ADAM optimizer [17] with an initial learning rate of 0.001 in batches of size 128. For the reconstruction loss, we use binary cross-entropy, and an early stopping patience limit is set equal to 20 to avoid wasting resources during training. Additional regularization techniques such as dropout, or L1 and L2 regularization did not improve the quality of the generated samples. All models were implemented using the TensorFlow library[2] on a Tesla P100 GPU.

---

[1] https://magenta.tensorflow.org/datasets/nsynth.
[2] https://www.tensorflow.org/.

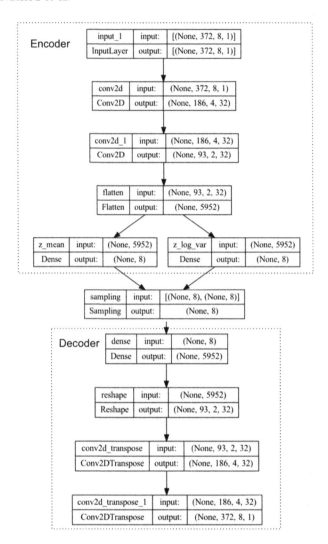

Fig. 3. The architecture of the Convolutional Variational Autoencoder VAE. Parameters and dimensions of the audio representation for every step of dimensionality reduction.

3.3   Reconstruction Quality

We evaluated the reconstruction capacity of the VAE using the Mean Squared Error (MSE) between the original and generated audio representation of the fundamental frequency plus the first 7 harmonics. However, MSE is not always sufficient as a metric for the reconstructed samples since it measures the pixel-wise difference between the original and reconstructed images, without taking into account the high-level structure and semantics of the data. Therefore, we additionally computed the Structural SIMilarity (SSIM) [39] between the two representations. SSIM is a method for computing the structural similarity between two images, which takes into account the luminance, contrast, and structural information. The SSIM index ranges between -1 and 1, with values closer to 1 indicating higher similarity between the two images.

4 Results and Discussion

To interpret the way VAEs generate new samples, we conducted two types of experiments. In the first set of experiments, we performed a global analysis measuring the reconstructive capabilities of each attribute of the latent space. The second type of experiment is an attempt of interpreting the contribution of each latent feature to the synthesis of musical notes from a specific instrument.

4.1 Global Analysis

The goal of this section is to provide experimental results on the generation of instrumental notes using VAEs. It is also an attempt to analyze and interpret the latent space of the generative network. As it is illustrated in Fig. 3, the encoder projects the audio samples into a high-level representation by sampling from the distribution using the mean and the standard deviation predicted for each attribute. Then, the decoder uses as input the generated latent features trying to reconstruct the original samples. The ability of the network to generalize and create new samples that are similar to the original is affected by many parameters. One of the most important parameters is the size of the latent space. A relatively small latent space can increase computational efficiency while improving the ability to interpret its results. In our architecture, by decreasing the number of latent parameters, we concluded to a latent space with a dimensionality of 8 since it provided the right balance between the size of the latent space and the reconstruction error. The trained network achieved an average MSE of 0.039 and an average SSIM of 0.948 across all the samples of the testing dataset. To gain some knowledge of the latent features, we initially depicted the distribution of a testing dataset of notes for a variety of instruments along with some statistical information. Figure 4 illustrates the boxplot of all possible values for the 8 attributes of the latent space. According to this figure, the second and third attributes have more clustered data around the median obtaining fewer possible values for the instrumental notes. Continuing with the interpretation of the latent space, we conducted a feature ablation analysis. In this set of experiments, we investigated the importance of each attribute of the latent space by enabling each time a single feature and measuring the SSIM with the original samples. The results from this analysis are demonstrated in Fig. 5 while the reconstructed images by permitting only one feature at a time are illustrated in Fig. 6. Based on these experiments, the first three attributes of the latent space demonstrate higher similarity with the original samples implying higher importance for the reconstruction of new samples.

A final examination of the latent space of the VAE covers a sensitivity analysis by applying the method of perturbation and observing the resulting changes

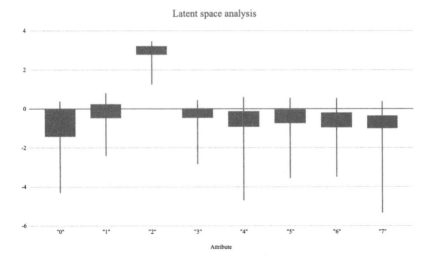

Fig. 4. Boxplot of the attribute analysis of the latent space. It illustrates all possible values of the 8 latent attributes.

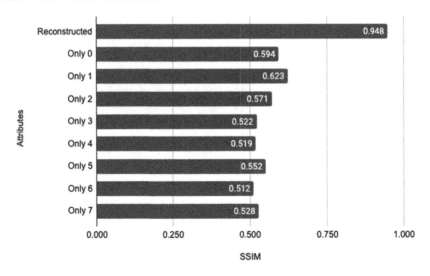

Fig. 5. SSIM between the original samples and the samples generated by only one enabled attribute.

in the synthesized samples. More specifically, we modified each attribute by 10%, 20%, 30%, 40%, 50%, and 60% respectively, and measured the percentage of SSIM decrease. The results of these experiments are depicted in Fig. 7. This analysis provides information about the sensitivity of each attribute, pointing out that features one, two, and five are less resilient to change. The conducted global analysis provided information about the overall behavior of the model and the importance of the features of the latent space. It showed that the attributes

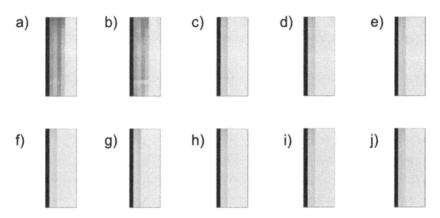

Fig. 6. Visualization of the reconstructed representation using one feature at a time. a) Original representation. b) Reconstructed representation. c) Only the "0" attribute. d) Only the "1" attribute. e) Only the "2" attribute. f) Only the "3" attribute. g) Only the "4" attribute. h) Only the "5" attribute. i) Only the "6" attribute. j) Only the "7" attribute.

do not have the same importance and do not contribute equally to the generation of new samples. Finally, it proved that the latent features do not have the same resilience to change. Most of the analyses conducted resulted in similar results proving that the attributes "0", "1", "2", and "5" play the most significant role in the reconstruction of the sound.

4.2   Instrument-Based Analysis

In this section, we provide an instrument-based analysis for analyzing sound signals to identify the underlying musical instrument or instruments that produced the sound from the latent representation. Notably, we investigate the association of latent features with musical instruments. In order to do that, we statistically analyzed the latent space separately for every instrument class to address the significance of each latent feature for each instrument. Table 1 provides the mean and the standard deviation of every attribute for each instrument. It presents the variable range demonstrating that a specific range of some attribute can imply a particular instrument. For example, if the value of the feature "2" of the latent space is 4, the instrument will be more probably a flute or have some properties of flutes.

Another way to investigate instruments from their latent features is by visualizing the latent space. Figure 8 depicts the projection of the 8-dimensional latent space in the 2-dimensional space indicating every instrument with a specific annotation. For the dimensionality reduction, we used the t-SNE algorithm with PCA initialization and perplexity of 49. The visualization indicates that the model is able to learn high-level representations with respect to instruments since sounds from a specific instrument present a smaller distance in the latent

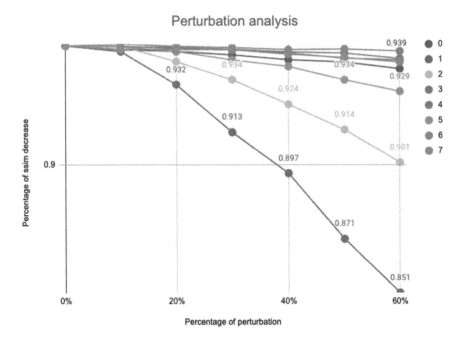

Fig. 7. Perturbation analysis of the latent attributes. Each line shows the percentage of the SSIM decrease by modifying each attribute from 0% to 60%.

Table 1. Mean and standard deviation of each latent feature for every instrument class.

Class	"0"	"1"	"2"	"3"	"4"	"5"	"6"	"7"
Guitar	0.23 ± 0.56	-0.39 ± 0.74	3.32 ± 0.24	0.04 ± 0.58	0.3 ± 0.74	0.41 ± 0.72	-0.84 ± 1.05	0.14 ± 0.69
Keyboard	-0.26 ± 0.84	-0.34 ± 0.76	3.26 ± 0.24	-0.17 ± 0.86	0.29 ± 0.96	0.75 ± 0.73	-0.31 ± 0.91	-0.12 ± 0.91
Vocal	-2.49 ± 1.59	0.54 ± 0.89	2.71 ± 0.61	-0.12 ± 0.68	-0.3 ± 0.67	-0.73 ± 1.03	0.16 ± 1.05	-1.16 ± 1.39
Organ	-0.56 ± 1.37	0.32 ± 0.96	3.09 ± 0.65	0.05 ± 0.56	0.06 ± 1.06	-0.18 ± 0.77	0.15 ± 1.44	-0.03 ± 1.12
Bass	-1.11 ± 0.97	0.31 ± 1.48	2.77 ± 0.72	-0.38 ± 1.09	-0.3 ± 1.19	-0.25 ± 1.43	-0.31 ± 0.82	-0.53 ± 1.01
Brass	-0.55 ± 0.78	0.29 ± 0.85	2.98 ± 0.41	0.11 ± 0.62	-0.88 ± 1.01	0.21 ± 0.96	0.11 ± 0.9	-0.81 ± 0.89
Flute	-0.34 ± 0.73	1.01 ± 1.09	3.81 ± 0.86	0 ± 0.38	0.4 ± 1.07	0.06 ± 0.45	-0.69 ± 0.67	-0.13 ± 0.94
Reed	-0.1 ± 0.83	0.35 ± 0.78	3.14 ± 0.36	0.12 ± 0.73	-0.76 ± 1.02	-0.39 ± 1.2	-0.07 ± 0.83	-0.42 ± 0.87
String	-0.92 ± 0.8	0.14 ± 1.39	3.02 ± 0.22	0.36 ± 0.7	-0.65 ± 0.83	-0.45 ± 0.73	-0.17 ± 0.77	0.04 ± 1.06

space. However, some clusters, such as string and brass, are not completely disentangled. This could be due to either reducing the dimensionality of the data or the model lacking sufficient information to identify instrument-based features. Enhancing the precision of the generative model for synthesizing sound from a lower-dimensional space, or incorporating additional regularization methods that offer timbre information, may result in a latent space with clusters that are more spread out.

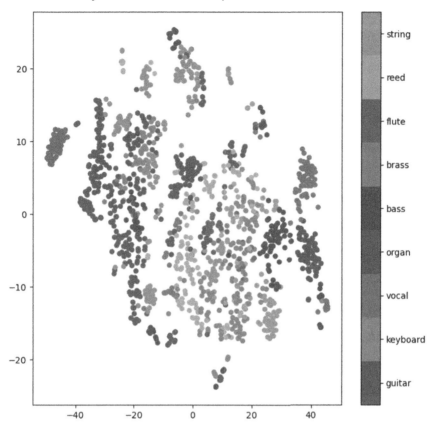

Fig. 8. Visualization of the projection of the latent representation in a 2-dimensional space using t-SNE.

4.3 Contribution to the Body of Knowledge

The research presented in this manuscript has yielded a notable dual contribution to the fields of explainable AI and audio synthesis. Through a comprehensive series of experiments, the study introduces an analysis protocol that offers the XAI community a systematic approach to assess the significance of individual latent attributes in the generation of new samples using Convolutional Variational Autoencoders. Furthermore, it extends its impact to the realm of sound synthesis by investigating the underlying mechanisms employed by deep generative networks to create novel audio outputs. Explainability techniques such as sensitivity analysis and feature ablation methods are useful for comprehending how latent features contribute to generating synthetic samples. Moreover, statistical measures and visualization techniques can aid in distinguishing the way different classes of samples are represented in the latent space. Overall, this research provides valuable insights and practical knowledge, enriching the existing body of literature in both domains and advancing our understanding of explainable AI and audio synthesis.

5   Conclusion

Explainable artificial intelligence (XAI) methods offer promising tools for analyzing and interpreting the complex processes underlying sound synthesis. By providing greater transparency into the inner workings of deep learning models, XAI techniques can help researchers and musicians better understand the factors that contribute to the creation of sound, and how to optimize models to produce high-quality, diverse, and musically meaningful sounds. In this manuscript, we used XAI methods such as feature importance analysis, latent feature visualization, and sensitivity analysis to interpret the latent space of Variational Autoencoders (VAEs) for the synthesis of new musical notes produced by a specific instrument, which gives rise to its unique timbre and tonal quality. The conducted study pointed out that the attributes of the latent space do not contribute equally to the process of generating new samples, and demonstrated that the features of the latent space retain information about the instrument. Furthermore, visualizing the latent space indicated that sounds generated from a specific instrument exhibit a shorter distance between them. However, some instruments presented partial entanglement of clusters that could be attributed to the dimensionality reduction or inadequate information in the model to discern features based on instruments. Therefore, potential future work would include augmenting the precision of the generative model to synthesize sound in a lower-dimensional space or introducing further regularization techniques that provide timbre information. Finally, additional explainability methods can be adopted to interpret the synthesis of new samples.

Acknowledgement. This work was funded by Science Foundation Ireland and its Centre for Research Training in Machine Learning (18/CRT/6183).

References

1. Ahmed, T., Longo, L.: Examining the size of the latent space of convolutional variational autoencoders trained with spectral topographic maps of EEG frequency bands. IEEE Access **10**, 107575–107586 (2022). https://doi.org/10.1109/ACCESS.2022.3212777
2. Aouameur, C., Esling, P., Hadjeres, G.: Neural drum machine: an interactive system for real-time synthesis of drum sounds. In: International Conference on Computational Creativity (2019)
3. Arık, S.Ö., Jun, H., Diamos, G.: Fast spectrogram inversion using multi-head convolutional neural networks. IEEE Sig. Process. Lett. **26**(1), 94–98 (2018)
4. Arrieta, A.B., et al.: Explainable Artificial Intelligence (XAI): concepts, taxonomies, opportunities and challenges toward responsible AI. Inf. Fusion **58**, 82–115 (2020)

5. Baldi, P., Hornik, K.: Neural networks and principal component analysis: learning from examples without local minima. Neural Netw. **2**(1), 53–58 (1989)
6. Caillon, A., Bitton, A., Gatinet, B., Esling, P.: Timbre latent space: exploration and creative aspects. In: Timbre International Conference (2020)
7. Caillon, A., Esling, P.: RAVE: a variational autoencoder for fast and high-quality neural audio synthesis. In: International Conference on Learning Representations (2022)
8. Chikkankod, A.V., Longo, L.: On the dimensionality and utility of convolutional autoencoder's latent space trained with topology-preserving spectral EEG head-maps. Mach. Learn. Knowl. Extr. **4**(4), 1042–1064 (2022). https://doi.org/10.3390/make4040053. https://www.mdpi.com/2504-4990/4/4/53
9. Covert, I., Lundberg, S.M., Lee, S.I.: Understanding global feature contributions with additive importance measures. In: Advances in Neural Information Processing Systems, vol. 33, pp. 17212–17223 (2020)
10. De Cheveigné, A., Kawahara, H.: YIN, a fundamental frequency estimator for speech and music. J. Acoust. Soc. Am. **111**(4), 1917–1930 (2002)
11. Défossez, A., Zeghidour, N., Usunier, N., Bottou, L., Bach, F.: SING: symbol-to-instrument neural generator. In: Advances in Neural Information Processing Systems, vol. 31 (2018)
12. Dhariwal, P., Jun, H., Payne, C., Kim, J.W., Radford, A., Sutskever, I.: Jukebox: a generative model for music. arXiv e-prints (2020)
13. Engel, J., Agrawal, K.K., Chen, S., Gulrajani, I., Donahue, C., Roberts, A.: GAN-Synth: adversarial neural audio synthesis. In: International Conference on Learning Representations (2019)
14. Engel, J., Gu, C., Roberts, A., et al.: DDSP: differentiable digital signal processing. In: International Conference on Learning Representations (2019)
15. Franzson, D.B., Shepardsson, V., Magnusson, T.: Autocoder: a variational autoencoder for spectral synthesis (2022)
16. Graving, J., Couzin, I.: VAE-SNE: a deep generative model for simultaneous dimensionality reduction and clustering. BioRxiv (2020)
17. Kingma, D.P., Ba, J.: Adam: a method for stochastic optimization (2017). http://arxiv.org/abs/1412.6980. arXiv:1412.6980
18. Kingma, D.P., Welling, M.: Auto-encoding variational bayes. arXiv preprint arXiv:1312.6114 (2013)
19. Kobayashi, K., Miyake, M., Takahashi, M., Hamamoto, R.: Observing deep radiomics for the classification of glioma grades. Sci. Rep. **11**(1), 10942 (2021)
20. Kumar, K., et al.: MelGAN: generative adversarial networks for conditional waveform synthesis. arXiv:1910.06711 (2019). http://arxiv.org/abs/1910.06711
21. Lee, S., Kim, M., Shin, S., Lee, D., Jang, I., Lim, W.: Conditional variational autoencoder to improve neural audio synthesis for polyphonic music sound. arXiv preprint arXiv:2211.08715 (2022)
22. Lundberg, S.M., Lee, S.I.: A unified approach to interpreting model predictions. In: Advances in Neural Information Processing Systems, vol. 30 (2017)
23. Luo, Y.J., Agres, K., Herremans, D.: Learning disentangled representations of timbre and pitch for musical instrument sounds using Gaussian mixture variational autoencoders. arXiv preprint arXiv:1906.08152 (2019)
24. Van der Maaten, L., Hinton, G.: Visualizing data using t-SNE. J. Mach. Learn. Res. **9**(11), 2579–2605 (2008)
25. Maćkiewicz, A., Ratajczak, W.: Principal components analysis (PCA). Comput. Geosci. **19**(3), 303–342 (1993)

26. Natsiou, A., Longo, L., O'Leary, S.: An investigation of the reconstruction capacity of stacked convolutional autoencoders for log-mel-spectrograms. In: 2022 16th International Conference on Signal-Image Technology & Internet-Based Systems (SITIS), pp. 155–162 (2022). https://doi.org/10.1109/SITIS57111.2022.00038

27. Natsiou, A., O'Leary, S.: Audio representations for deep learning in sound synthesis: a review. In: 2021 IEEE/ACS 18th International Conference on Computer Systems and Applications (AICCSA), pp. 1–8. IEEE (2021)

28. Nguyen, Q.P., Lim, K.W., Divakaran, D.M., Low, K.H., Chan, M.C.: GEE: a gradient-based explainable variational autoencoder for network anomaly detection. In: 2019 IEEE Conference on Communications and Network Security (CNS), pp. 91–99. IEEE (2019)

29. Reed, C., et al.: Exploring XAI for the arts: explaining latent space in generative music (2022)

30. Ribeiro, M.T., Singh, S., Guestrin, C.: "Why should i trust you?" Explaining the predictions of any classifier. In: Proceedings of the 22nd ACM SIGKDD International Conference on Knowledge Discovery and Data Mining, pp. 1135–1144 (2016)

31. Saseendran, A., Skubch, K., Falkner, S., Keuper, M.: Shape your space: a Gaussian mixture regularization approach to deterministic autoencoders. In: Advances in Neural Information Processing Systems, vol. 34, pp. 7319–7332 (2021)

32. Shan, S., Hantrakul, L., Chen, J., Avent, M., Trevelyan, D.: Differentiable wavetable synthesis. In: ICASSP 2022–2022 IEEE International Conference on Acoustics, Speech and Signal Processing (ICASSP), pp. 4598–4602. IEEE (2022)

33. Subramani, K., Rao, P., D'Hooge, A.: VaPar Synth-a variational parametric model for audio synthesis. In: ICASSP 2020–2020 IEEE International Conference on Acoustics, Speech and Signal Processing (ICASSP), pp. 796–800. IEEE (2020)

34. Sundararajan, M., Taly, A., Yan, Q.: Axiomatic attribution for deep networks. In: International Conference on Machine Learning, pp. 3319–3328. PMLR (2017)

35. Tatar, K., Bisig, D., Pasquier, P.: Latent timbre synthesis: audio-based variational auto-encoders for music composition and sound design applications. Neural Comput. Appl. **33**, 67–84 (2021). https://doi.org/10.1007/s00521-020-05424-2

36. Vigliensoni, G., McCallum, L., Fiebrink, R.: Creating latent spaces for modern music genre rhythms using minimal training data. In: Conference on Computational Creativity (2020)

37. Vilone, G., Longo, L.: A quantitative evaluation of global, rule-based explanations of post-hoc, model agnostic methods. Front. Artif. Intell. **4**, 160 (2021). https://doi.org/10.3389/frai.2021.717899

38. Vilone, G., Rizzo, L., Longo, L.: A comparative analysis of rule-based, model-agnostic methods for explainable artificial intelligence. In: Longo, L., Rizzo, L., Hunter, E., Pakrashi, A. (eds.) Proceedings of the 28th Irish Conference on Artificial Intelligence and Cognitive Science, Dublin, Republic of Ireland, 7–8 December 2020. CEUR Workshop Proceedings, vol. 2771, pp. 85–96. CEUR-WS.org (2020)

39. Wang, Z., Bovik, A.C., Sheikh, H.R., Simoncelli, E.P.: Image quality assessment: from error visibility to structural similarity. IEEE Trans. Image Process. **13**(4), 600–612 (2004)

40. Watcharasupat, K.N., Lerch, A.: Evaluation of latent space disentanglement in the presence of interdependent attributes. In: International Society for Music and Information Retrieval Conference (ISMIR) (2021)

41. Xu, J., et al.: Multi-VAE: learning disentangled view-common and view-peculiar visual representations for multi-view clustering. In: Proceedings of the IEEE/CVF International Conference on Computer Vision, pp. 9234–9243 (2021)

Improving Local Fidelity of LIME by CVAE

Daisuke Yasui[(✉)], Hirosh Sato, and Masao Kubo

National Defense Academy, 1-10-20 Hashirimizu, Yokosukashi, Kanagawa, Japan
zyukuryodannko@gmail.com

Abstract. Knowing the basis of decisions is essential for using Machine Learning (ML) in various regions, such as medical diagnosis, automated driving, and organizational decision-making. The LIME algorithm is an XAI method that can be applied to many black-box models. However, there is a problem in that the local fidelity of the interpretable model decreases. The problem is due to the sampling and weighting step of LIME; using an autoencoder is an effective way to improve this. In this study, we aim to simultaneously improve the sampling and weighting of LIME in a classification task by using a conditional variational autoencoder and filtering samples by classes. Experiments were conducted to compare the local fidelity of the proposed and existing methods for neural network classifiers trained on three medical diagnostic data sets. The results show that the proposed method improves the local fidelity compared to the existing methods. In addition, we visualized the distribution of samples in the autoencoder latent space and conducted comparative experiments by attaching and detaching components of the existing and proposed methods to analyze the factors that improve fidelity.

Keywords: LIME · Local fidelity · Conditional variational autoencoder

1 Introduction

Although the performance of Machine Learning (ML) has been improving, the inability to explain the reasons for decisions has become a bottleneck in its practical application, and there is a social need to improve the explanation of ML [9]. In particular, it is important for users to be able to understand and accept the decision basis of ML models in high-risk fields such as medicine [2,9], automated driving [8,9], and organizational decision-making [9]. In addition, when an ML model makes a wrong decision, knowing the basis of the decision facilitates the maintenance of the ML model. Furthermore, the explanation promotes the awareness of experts and the discovery of new knowledge [8,9]. Against this background, research on Explainable AI (XAI) has been active.

XAI can be classified according to three criteria [8]. The first criterion is local or global. A local explanation is a method that explains the basis of the output

© The Author(s), under exclusive license to Springer Nature Switzerland AG 2023
L. Longo (Ed.): xAI 2023, CCIS 1903, pp. 487–511, 2023.
https://doi.org/10.1007/978-3-031-44070-0_25

y for a particular instance x by presenting a model that can be interpreted by humans, such as a linear model [13,14,16], as shown in Fig. 1(a). In contrast, a global explanation describes the overall decision tendency by approximating an entire complex model. As shown in Fig. 1(b), multiple instances and outputs of the target model can be used to transform complex models into highly readable models such as linear models and decision trees [18].

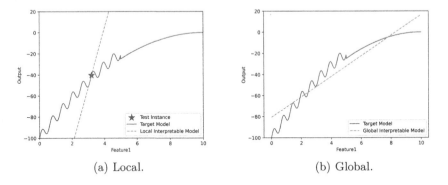

(a) Local.   (b) Global.

Fig. 1. Example to present local and global explanation.

The second criterion is whether it is intrinsic or post hoc [8]. Intrinsic methods refer to approaches in which the model itself expresses the basis for the decision, such as linear models and decision tree models. In the case of a linear model, the coefficients explain the importance of each feature to the output. Conversely, post hoc methods involve using a more explanatory model as a substitute or examining sensitivity based on the inputs and outputs of the target model [4,13–16]. The third criterion is model-specific or model-agnostic [8]. For example, in computer vision, Grad-CAM [15], which can show a heatmap of the influence of a particular instance on a decision, can be applied to CNN, but not to other models.

We focused on local explanations because highly accurate ML models, including deep learning models, are often nonlinear models, and the basis for decisions differs from instance to instance. In addition, considering that various ML models will be developed in the future, the model-agnostic method can contribute more to the development of ML models. Therefore, in this study, we focused on XAI, which is a local and model-agnostic explanation.

LIME [13] is an XAI method that can be applied to various models and provides local and post hoc explanations of the target model. But LIME has the problem of deteriorating the local fidelity of interpretable models [8]. This is due to the sampling and weighting step of the LIME, and the use of an autoencoder is an effective way to improve it [14,16]. Although it can be said that the autoencoder locally approximates the distances between the test instance and samples in the feature space of the target model, we considered that there is room for improvement. In this study, we show that the fidelity of the local interpretable model can be improved by using a conditional variational autoencoder (CVAE) [17] and filtering samples by classes.

The structure of this paper is described as follows. In Sect. 2, we describe the LIME algorithm, the causes of local fidelity degradation in LIME, and a method called ALIME and VAE-LIME, which improve local fidelity. Section 3 proposes CVAE-LIME, an improved method of ALIME and VAE-LIME. In Sect. 4, we conduct a comparison experiment between the existing method and the proposed method. In addition, comparative experiments are conducted to analyze each component's effect by removing the components of the proposed method. Section 5, discusses the mechanisms by which each component of the proposed method affected local fidelity, and Sect. 6 provides a summary and future perspectives.

2   Related Work

This chapter describes the LIME algorithm and the causes of the local fidelity deterioration, which is a problem of LIME. In addition, we describe ALIME and VAE-LIME, in which the deterioration of local fidelity is improved by using an autoencoder.

2.1   LIME

LIME [13] is an algorithm that provides a local explanation g (e.g., a linear regression model) of a target model f (e.g., a deep neural network model) at a particular instance x. Expressed as a minimization problem, it can be shown in Eq. 1 and 2. $\mathcal{L}$ is a measure of how close the explanation g is to the prediction of the target model f. The complexity of g is denoted by $\Omega(g)$. G is the family of interpretable models. z and z' is one of the samples Z sampled from the distribution of the entire data set. W_x defines how large the neighborhood z around instance x is that we consider for the explanation g.

$$\xi(x) = \arg\min_{g \in G} \mathcal{L}(f, g, W_x) + \Omega(g) \tag{1}$$

$$\mathcal{L}(f, g, W_x) = \sum_{z, z' \in Z} W_x(z)(f(z) - g(z'))^2 \tag{2}$$

x : Instance
f : Target model
g : Interpretable model
z : Perturbed sample (z' is discretized)
W_x : Weights by similarity to instance$x$

Now, we visually consider how LIME searches for an interpretable model g of a target model f. For example, suppose we have a binary classification dataset with two features as shown in Fig. 2(a). As a result of training with a neural network, etc., a function like Fig. 2(b) is obtained.

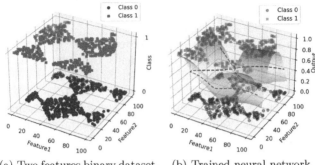

(a) Two features binary dataset.   (b) Trained neural network.

Fig. 2. Example to present ML model learning from training data. (Color figure online)

The blue and pink surface in Fig. 2(b) represents a function of the target model f. The dashed line represents the decision boundary. If the number of features is only two, it can be visualized. But if the number of features is three or more dimensions, it is difficult to visualize. And as a result, the ML model becomes a black box whose decision basis is unknown to humans. In Fig. 2(b), the entire surface of f cannot be well approximated by a linear model. However, assuming that even the most complex surface can be locally linearly approximated, the target model f can be represented by an interpretable model g in a very close neighborhood of the test instance x.

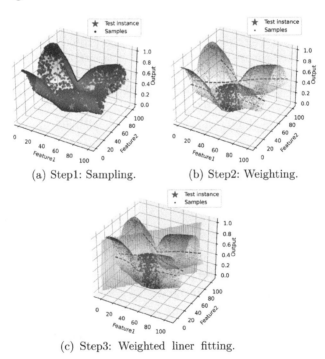

(a) Step1: Sampling.   (b) Step2: Weighting.

(c) Step3: Weighted liner fitting.

Fig. 3. How to make a local interpretable model by LIME.

Therefore, LIME acquires an explanatory model g around instance x by following the three steps shown in Fig. 3.

- **Step 1:** Generate a large number of perturbed samples z (purple) over the distribution of the dataset. Then, get outputs of the target model f for z.
- **Step 2:** Calculate the samples weighting W_x according to the distances between the samples and the test instance x. (Also expressed as marker size of samples here).
- **Step 3:** A weighted linear fitting of the samples yields a local linear approximation model g.

In this example, the linear model g is as in Eq. 3. Since the linear model g locally approximates the target model f, the coefficients allow the user to know which features are important at instance x. Figure 4 is a summary of the explanation at instance x. Feature 1 and 2 are feature values of the test instance x which was normalized. The output of the target model f is 0.38. However, since g is an approximate formula, substituting the Feature Value into Eq. 3 does not result in values for f and g that are perfectly consistent.

$$g = 0.19 \times \text{Feature1} + 0.15 \times \text{Feature2} + 0.45 \tag{3}$$

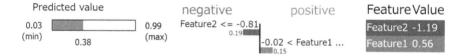

Fig. 4. LIME explanation at a test instance x.

For a user to trust a local approximation model g, it is important that the output of the model g approximates well the output of the model f around the instance x. This is called local fidelity [1,8,13,14,16]. In LIME, there are two ways to measure local fidelity [14,16]. The first measure is whether the output of the approximation model g is similar to the output of the target model f for the entire N samples of z, after taking the weights W into account. This can be evaluated by R_w^2, which expresses the goodness of fit of the estimated regression equation to the data, as in Eq. 4. The higher this value, the higher the local fidelity.

$$R_{\mathrm{w}}^2 = 1 - \frac{\sum_{i=1}^{N} w_i \left(\hat{f}_i - \hat{g}_i \right)^2}{\sum_{i=1}^{N} w_i \left(\hat{f}_i - \bar{f} \right)^2} \tag{4}$$

The second measure of local fidelity is the difference between the output f and the output g for the instance x. This can be evaluated by MSE (Eq. 5). As you can see in Fig. 3(c), a small MSE only means that the model g is passing through test instance x: the coefficients of the local approximation model g (the slope of model g) are not evaluated. Therefore, this is a supplementary indicator.

$$MSE = \frac{1}{2}\left(\widehat{g}_{(x)} - \widehat{f}_{(x)}\right)^2 \tag{5}$$

In LIME, there is a problem with local fidelity worsening. This is caused by the sampling and weighting step in the LIME algorithm [8]. In Fig. 5(a), the area in the red circle is insufficiently sampled. If one wanted to explain the inputs in the red-circle area, the linear regression model would generate model g with low fidelity because there would not be enough data points to use in the regression itself. In addition, Fig. 5(b) shows that the blue-box area is weighted even though it is not near the test instance x. This may cause samples that are not similar at all to be judged as similar. In other words, it does not define locality correctly, which also leads to reduced local fidelity. We will then analyze the factors that cause these two problems from the LIME source code.

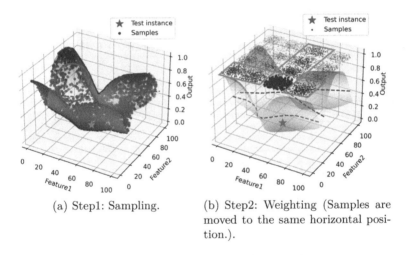

(a) Step1: Sampling.   (b) Step2: Weighting (Samples are moved to the same horizontal position.).

Fig. 5. Causes of reducing local fidelity. (Color figure online)

The sampling and weighting steps of the LIME are shown in Eq. 6 to 10. First, all continuous variables of a dataset are discredited by Eq. 6 and 7. Equation 6 is defined to find the maximum value of each value range when the maximum and minimum values of feature m in the data set are divided into four equal parts.

$$q(m, i) = MIN(m) + (MAX(m) - MIN(m)) * \frac{i}{4}, (i = 0, 1, 2, 3) \tag{6}$$

Equation 7 is a function that determines to which value range the feature m of instance x corresponds. Equation 6 and 7 discretize each feature of the continuous variable for all instances of dataset D to integers between 0 and 3. If the feature m is originally a discrete value, it is still the same.

$$\text{Quartile } (x_m) = \begin{cases} 0 \, (MIN(m) \le x_m < q(m,1)) \\ 1 \, (q(m,1) \le x_m < q(m,2)) \\ 2 \, (q(m,2) \le x_m < q(m,3)) \\ 3 \, (q(m,3) \le x_m < \text{MAX}(m)) \end{cases} \quad (x_m = \text{ Value of feature } m)$$

(7)

The probability of feature m in the generated sample z being equal to i is given by Eq. 8. It is expressed as the number of instances where the feature m is i in dataset D divided by the number of instances in the dataset D. When re-converting to a continuous variable, each value is sampled from a uniform distribution over the corresponding value range. The sample z is sampled from the entire dataset without considering the instance x. Therefore, if the dataset contains few samples similar to the instance x, an insufficient number of samples are generated.

$$P(z_m = i) = \frac{Num(D_m, i)}{Num(D)}$$

(8)

Weights W of each sample z is computed using Eq. 9 and 10. M is the number of features the dataset has. The more features are sampled from the same value range or discrete value as the feature of the test instance x, the more weight is given.

$$W(z) \sim \sum_{m=1}^{M} \text{Match}(x_m, z_m)$$

(9)

$$\text{Match}(a, b) = \begin{cases} 1(a = b) \\ 0(a \ne b) \end{cases}$$

(10)

As shown in Eq. 9, it is considered difficult to perform the similarity calculation directly in a high-dimensional space [10]. Therefore, if the similarity calculation can be performed in a low-dimensional space with dimensionality reduction, more appropriate weighting can be achieved [5,6,17,19].

2.2   ALIME, VAE-LIME

ALIME. A study that has improved the local fidelity of the LIME is a method called ALIME [16], which uses an autoencoder. Autoencoder (AE) learns to transform the input into low-dimensional latent variables by the encoder and to recover the input from the latent variables by the decoder. As a result, the encoder acts as a feature extractor of the input data. ALIME improves the problem of calculating the similarity between the test instance x and sample z by reducing the dimension with the encoder portion of the denoising autoencoder [19]. A flowchart of the ALIME algorithm is shown in Fig. 6.

ALIME

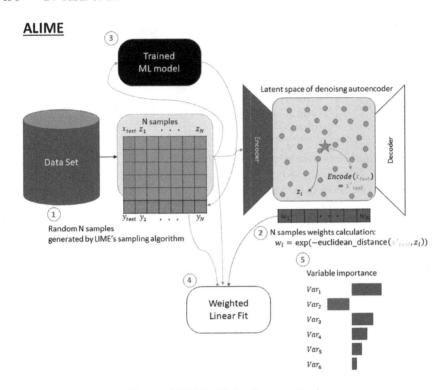

Fig. 6. ALIME. (Color figure online)

In advance, the denoising autoencoder (DAE) is trained on the dataset used to train the target model. Samples are generated using the LIME sample generation algorithm as mentioned in Eq. 8. Samples are converted into latent variables by the encoder, and the distance in latent space determines the weights (purple) of each sample. The outputs (orange) of the target model for the generated samples are then computed. Weighted linear regression is performed based on the weights, samples, and outputs. The coefficients of the generated linear model are used to estimate the importance of the features. Thus, ALIME improves the similarity calculation between test instance x and sample z, but ALIME does not solve the problem of inadequate sampling around test instance, which is one of the two reasons that deteriorate the local fidelity of LIME.

VAE-LIME. There is another method called VAE-LIME [14], which uses a variational autoencoder (VAE) [5]. VAE-LIME has also improved the local fidelity of the explainable model of LIME. DAE which is used in ALIME works as a feature extractor but is not suitable for generating samples. Because the distribution of the latent variables is not controlled. VAE improves this problem. VAE trains to maximize the lower bound $\mathcal{L}_{\mathrm{VAE}}$. The objective function of VAE is shown in Eq. 11.

$$\mathcal{L}_{\mathrm{VAE}}(X, p, q) \equiv E_q[\log p(X|Z)] - D_{KL}[q(Z|X)\|p(Z)] \tag{11}$$

p and q represent the probability distribution of the data, respectively. VAE penalizes the encoding of inputs X into latent variables Z with a distribution that does not follow a normal distribution with D_{KL}. This penalty enables the latent variable to vary continuously in latent space. Therefore, VAE can obtain an excellent latent space that enables generative processing.

Taking advantage of VAE's superiority in data generation, VAE-LIME aims to improve local fidelity by generating more realistic samples to train locally interpretable linear approximation models. A flowchart of the VAE-LIME algorithm is shown in Fig. 7. In advance, the variational autoencoder (VAE) is trained on the dataset used to train the target model. Using this learned VAE, instance x (green) is mapped into latent space and decoded with noise to generate samples (gray). The weights (purple) of each sample are determined by its distance in latent space. The outputs (orange) of the target model for the generated samples are then computed. Based on these weights, samples, and outputs, weighted ridge fitting is performed. VAE-LIME enables focused sampling around test instances but does not use class information.

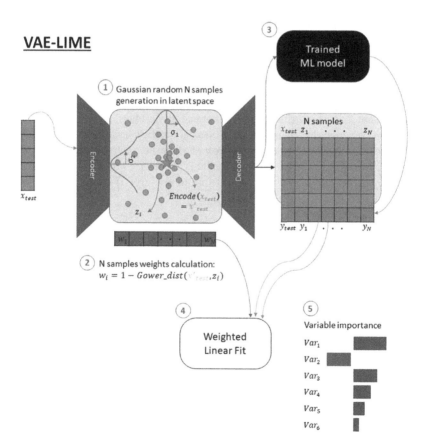

Fig. 7. VAE-LIME. (Color figure online)

3   Proposed Method (CVAE-LIME)

In this chapter, we first describe the conditional variational autoencoder (CVAE), which is a semi-supervised learning method. Then, we explain the advantages of CVAE over the autoencoders used in ALIME and VAE-LIME. Finally, we propose CVAE-LIME.

3.1   Conditional Variational Autoencoder (CVAE)

Conditional Variational Autoencoder (CVAE) [17] is an extension of VAE to semi-supervised learning. CVAE can be expressed by Eq. 12 with $\mathcal{L}_{\mathrm{CVAE}}$ as the objective variable.

$$\mathcal{L}_{\mathrm{CVAE}}(X, y, p, q) \equiv E_q[\log p(X|Z, y)] - D_{KL}[q(Z|X, y)\|p(Z, y)] \qquad (12)$$

CVAE also learns by maximizing the lower bound $\mathcal{L}_{\mathrm{CVAE}}$. One major difference from VAE is that the function q can transform the input X and class y into the latent variable Z, and the function p can transform the latent variable Z and class y into X. This makes it possible to separate class and latent variables, which was not possible with VAE. For example, if X is a handwritten numeral picture and y is the class of the numeral, the latent variable Z is learned to represent the slant of the numeral, writing habits, and so on. In this way, CVAE is a model that can learn distributions for the same class.

In Fig. 8, we visually compare the data generation capabilities of VAE and CVAE. The blue and red markers represent dataset with two-dimensional features. VAE and CVAE were trained on this dataset. The purple markers are samples generated by projecting several instances (green) into the latent space, adding Gaussian noise, and then decoding.

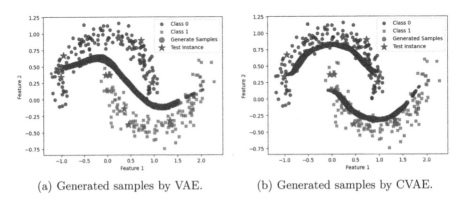

(a) Generated samples by VAE.   (b) Generated samples by CVAE.

Fig. 8. Comparison of generated samples by VAE and CVAE. (Color figure online)

Generated samples by CVAE are similar to the distribution of the dataset, while VAE generates samples that do not exist. This suggests that the CVAE decoder, which learns class information, is superior to the VAE in generating LIME samples.

Next, consider the encoder's dimensionality reduction capability. ALIME and VAE-LIME use the latent space of autoencoders to compute the similarity between the test instance and the samples in the feature space of the target model. Figure 9(a) shows the results of the dimensionality reduction of the breast cancer dataset [7] to two dimensions using t-SNE [6]. The same dataset was split 7 to 3 for training and test data, and VAE and CVAE were trained on the training data. The distribution of the test data in the two-dimensional latent space of VAE and CVAE is shown in Fig. 9(b) and 9(c). Figure 9(a) shows that the data of the same class are clustered together. However, in the case of VAE and CVAE, the samples of different classes are mixed.

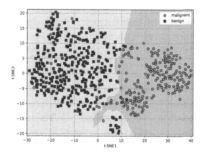

(a) Dimensionality reduction by t-SNE.

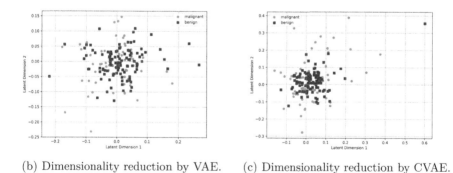

(b) Dimensionality reduction by VAE.   (c) Dimensionality reduction by CVAE.

Fig. 9. Differences in dimensionality reduction in breast cancer dataset.

Suppose that the data of the same class are close in the feature space of the target model, as shown in Fig. 9(a). In such a case, if the similarity is calculated based on the latent space of VAE and CVAE as shown in Fig. 9(b) and 9(c), it is expected that the discrepancy from the similarity in the feature space of the target model will be large.

Here, we restrict ourselves to samples of the same class. For CVAE, in contrast to VAE, the latent variables corresponding to the inputs can be obtained for each class. This indicates that the similarity between test instances and samples computed by CVAE is superior to VAE when restricted to the same class.

3.2   CVAE-LIME

As mentioned before, CVAE is believed to be able to generate samples more likely to be present in the dataset than VAE. Therefore, we thought that the decoder of CVAE could improve sampling from the vicinity of the test instances over existing studies. We assume that the neighborhoods of the test instance are the same class in the feature space of the target model. In this case, by restricting the samples to the same class as the test instance, it is possible to restrict them to the neighborhood of the test instance. In addition, as mentioned in the previous section, the encoder of CVAE could improve the similarity calculation between the test instance and samples of the same class as the test instances over VAE. Furthermore, the locality is ensured by restricting the sample to the top-weighted samples. Therefore, we propose CVAE-LIME as shown in Fig. 10 and the following steps. At each step, the image diagram in the feature space of the target model looks like Fig. 11.

- **Preprocess:** Training a CVAE using the dataset employed for the target model's training.
- **Step 1:** The test instance x with its class is encoded. N latent variables are generated by adding Gaussian noise to the encoded test instance x. Then, we obtain N samples of z by decoding latent variables with the test instance's class. We call this step **Sampling by decoder**.
- **Step 2:** Obtain the outputs y of the N samples of z by the target model f.
- **Step 3:** The samples z are re-encoded. The Euclidean distances between the test instance x and the N samples of z are calculated in the latent space. The distances are converted to weights from 0 to 1 by an exponential kernel. We call this step **Weighting by encoder**.
- **Step 4:** Only the same class as the test instance is selected. In this paper, this is called **Filtering by class**.

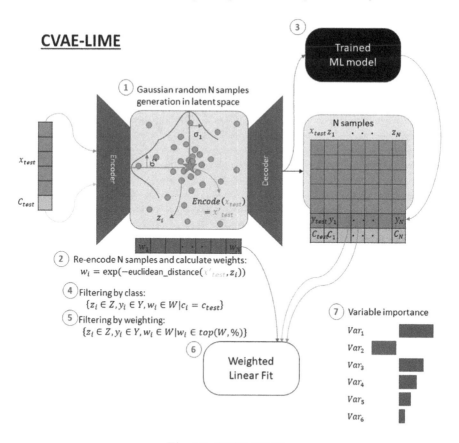

Fig. 10. CVAE-LIME.

- **Step 5:** The weighted ones are also filtered in arbitrary proportions. In this paper, this is called **Filtering by weighting**.
- **Step 6, 7:** Finally, ridge regression is performed on the samples z, outputs y and their weights w to generate an approximate linear model g that is locally explainable.

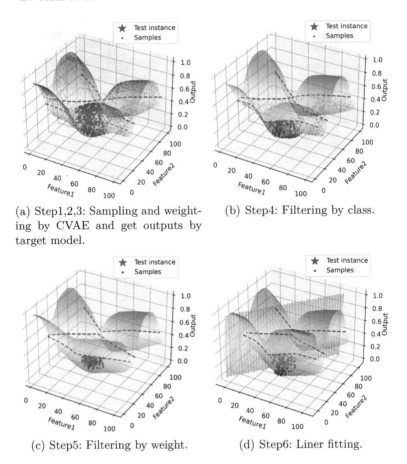

(a) Step1,2,3: Sampling and weighting by CVAE and get outputs by target model.

(b) Step4: Filtering by class.

(c) Step5: Filtering by weight.

(d) Step6: Liner fitting.

Fig. 11. An image diagram of CVAE-LIME in the feature space of the target model. These figures show how a linear model is generated for the target model at each step of the proposed method shown in Fig. 10.

4   Experiment

Three experiments were conducted. In the first experiment, we compared the proposed method (CVAE-LIME) with existing methods (LIME, ALIME, and VAE-LIME) to confirm the improvement of local fidelity (R_w^2, MSE). In the second experiment, we detached the components of the proposed method in order to clarify the effect of improving the local fidelity. In the third experiment, we checked the distribution of generated samples in the latent space of the autoencoder to assist in analyzing the second experiment.

4.1 Comparative Experiments with Existing Methods

Experimental Setup. A probable situation where accountability is required is a medical diagnosis by ML. For this purpose, three medical diagnosis datasets were used: breast cancer dataset [7], hepatitis patients dataset [12], and liver patients dataset [3]. They were divided 7 to 3 into training and test data. Table 1 presents dataset parameters. The neural network trained as a binary classification problem was used as the target model. The hidden layer has 30 neurons, the output layer has 2 neurons, and the activation function is a sigmoid function. Forty instances of the test data in each dataset were used as test instances to generate local linear approximation models for the proposed method, VAE-LIME, ALIME, and LIME, respectively.

Table 1. Datasets.

Dataset	Observations	Feature	Class
Breast cancer	699	30	2
Hepatitis patients	155	20	2
Liver patients	583	11	2

The number of samples generated by the existing method and the proposed method was set to 5000, which is the default setting of LIME. As described in Sect. 2.1, we use R_{w}^2 for measuring the local fidelity of LIME and MSE as an auxiliary measure. Table 2 summarizes the experimental setup.

Table 2. Experimental Setting 1.

	Condition
Dataset	· Breast cancer dataset · Hepatitis patients dataset · Liver patients dataset
Target model	· Neural network
Test instances	· Forty of the test data

Experimental Results. The results of the comparison experiment are shown in Table 3 and 4. The values represent the average of the R_{w}^2 and MSE of the local linear approximation models on the 40 instances for each dataset. The value of the best method is **bold**. The p-value of the Mann-Whitney U-test between each method for the 40 evaluated values was also calculated. There was no predominant difference when VAE-LIME and LIME were evaluated with MSE in the three datasets (p > 0.05), but there was a predominant difference for the other combinations (p < 0.05).

Table 3. R_w^2 of interpretable model (Higher is better).

Dataset	CVAE-LIME	VAE-LIME	ALIME	LIME
Breast cancer	**0.83**	1.1×10^{-3}	0.38	0.14
Hepatitis patients	**0.95**	1.1×10^{-3}	0.55	9.3×10^{-2}
Liver patients	**0.96**	5.5×10^{-4}	0.72	0.23

Table 4. MSE of interpretable model (Lower is better.).

Dataset	CVAE-LIME	VAE-LIME	ALIME	LIME
Breast cancer	$\mathbf{6.0 \times 10^{-4}}$	5.9×10^{-2}	2.6×10^{-2}	5.6×10^{-2}
Hepatitis patients	$\mathbf{1.0 \times 10^{-3}}$	4.8×10^{-3}	4.6×10^{-3}	6.3×10^{-3}
Liver patients	3.3×10^{-3}	6.1×10^{-3}	$\mathbf{3.0 \times 10^{-3}}$	1.5×10^{-2}

4.2 Samples Generated by LIME's Algorithm and the Decoder in the Latent Space

We visualized the sample's distribution of the breast cancer dataset generated by LIME's sampling algorithm and each decoder in the latent space of each autoencoder (Fig. 12,13 and 14). The left sides were generated by LIME's sampling algorithm, and the right sides were generated by each decoder. The red crosses indicate test instances in the latent space, and the rest indicate the 5,000 generated samples. Blues indicate that the generated samples are labeled 0 (malignant), and oranges are labeled 1 (benign). Because of space limitations, the results are shown for one instance out of forty test data.

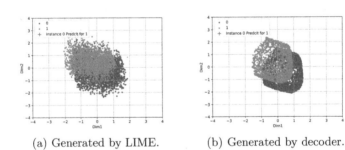

(a) Generated by LIME.   (b) Generated by decoder.

Fig. 12. Generated samples in CVAE latent space. (Color figure online)

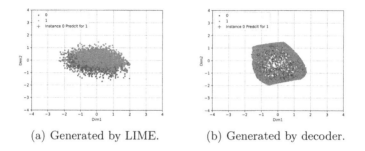

(a) Generated by LIME.   (b) Generated by decoder.

Fig. 13. Generated samples in VAE latent space. (Color figure online)

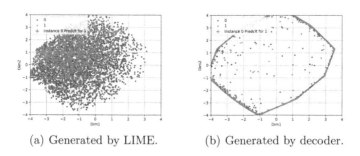

(a) Generated by LIME.   (b) Generated by decoder.

Fig. 14. Generated samples in DAE latent space. (Color figure online)

4.3 Effects of Proposed Method Components

Experimental Setup. We analyze the effects of each element of the proposed method (weighting by the encoder, sampling by the decoder, filtering by class, filtering by weighting) and the types of the autoencoder. Since sampling by encoder must be used in combination with weighting by the encoder, four ways (weighting by the encoder, sampling by the decoder + weighting by the encoder, weighting by the encoder + filtering by class, and all of them) were tested. And three ways were tested when the autoencoder was changed from CVAE to DAE or VAE, for a total of 12 patterns. For each pattern, the values of R_{w}^2 and MSE for each test data are displayed in a box-and-whisker diagram when filtering by weighting is varied from 10% to 100%. For LIME, experiments were conducted on the same instances and the same results are posted for comparison. Table 5 summarizes the experimental setup.

Table 5. Experimental setting 2.

	Condition
Dataset	· Breast cancer dataset · Hepatitis dataset · Liver patient dataset
Target model	· Neural network
Instances	· 40 of the test data
Combination of each element	· Weighting by encoder · Weighting and sampling by auto encoder · Weighting by encoder and filtering by class · All of the above elements
Autoencoder	· CVAE · VAE · DAE
Filtering by weighting	· Sample of top 10–100% of weightings

Weighting by Autoencoder

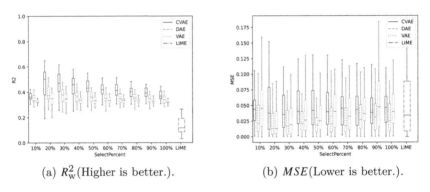

(a) R^2_{w}(Higher is better.). (b) MSE(Lower is better.).

Fig. 15. Breast cancer dataset.

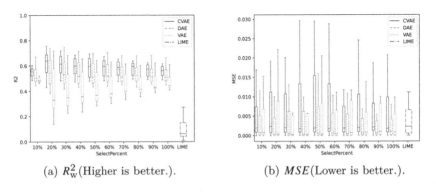

(a) R^2_{w}(Higher is better.). (b) MSE(Lower is better.).

Fig. 16. Hepatitis patients dataset.

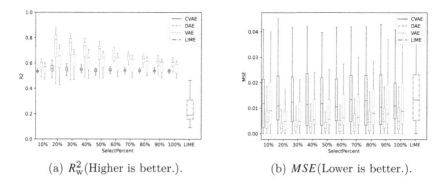

(a) R^2_{w}(Higher is better.).

(b) MSE(Lower is better.).

Fig. 17. Liver patients dataset.

Weighting and Sampling by Autoencoder

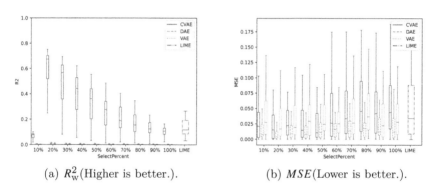

(a) R^2_{w}(Higher is better.).

(b) MSE(Lower is better.).

Fig. 18. Breast cancer dataset.

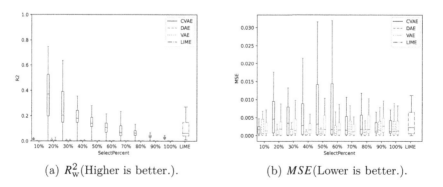

(a) R^2_{w}(Higher is better.).

(b) MSE(Lower is better.).

Fig. 19. Hepatitis patients dataset.

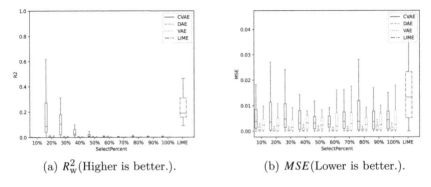

(a) R^2_{w}(Higher is better.).   (b) MSE(Lower is better.).

Fig. 20. Liver patients dataset.

Weighting by Autoencoder and Filtering by Class

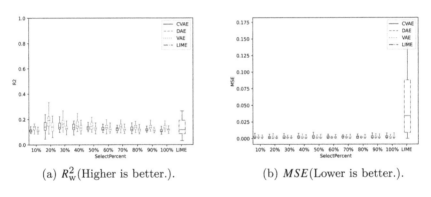

(a) R^2_{w}(Higher is better.).   (b) MSE(Lower is better.).

Fig. 21. Breast cancer dataset.

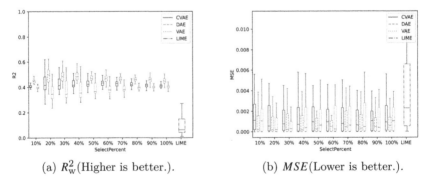

(a) R^2_{w}(Higher is better.).   (b) MSE(Lower is better.).

Fig. 22. Hepatitis patients dataset.

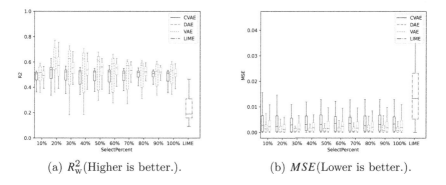

(a) R^2_{w}(Higher is better.).

(b) MSE(Lower is better.).

Fig. 23. Liver patients dataset.

Weighting and Sampling by Autoencoder and Filtering by Class

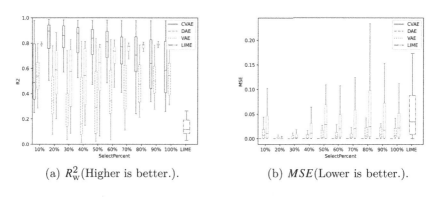

(a) R^2_{w}(Higher is better.).

(b) MSE(Lower is better.).

Fig. 24. Breast cancer dataset.

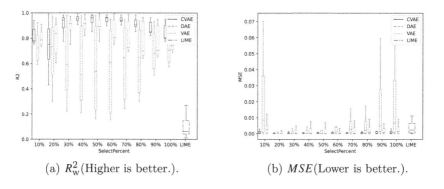

(a) R^2_{w}(Higher is better.).

(b) MSE(Lower is better.).

Fig. 25. Hepatitis patients dataset.

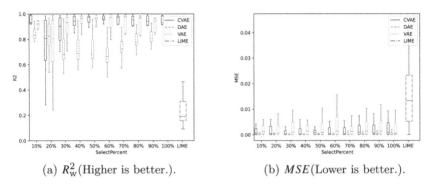

(a) R_{w}^2 (Higher is better.).   (b) MSE (Lower is better.).

Fig. 26. Liver patients dataset.

5   Discussion

Table 3 shows that the proposed method has the highest fidelity compared to the existing methods. In order to examine this factor, we first check the tendency of the distribution of samples in the latent space and consider how it affects R_{w}^2 and MSE as shown in Sect. 4.2. Based on this, we discuss the results of each experimental condition.

5.1   Tendencies in the Distribution of the Generated Samples and Their Impact on R_{w}^2 and MSE

In Fig. 13(b), both class samples are almost equally present around the test instance. Assuming that instances of different classes are far apart in the feature space of the target model, this situation makes R_{w}^2 degrade. On the other hand, in Fig. 12(b), since the different class is farther apart, the deterioration of R_{w}^2 is expected to be less than the others. We call this **IMPACT 1**.

Looking at the number of samples surrounding the test instances (red crosses) in Fig. 12(a), 13(a), and 14(a), it becomes evident that there are only a few generated by LIME. However, in Fig. 12(b), 13(b), it can be observed that a significant number of samples are generated by the autoencoder. This is thought to be because the decoder of CVAE and VAE generates samples by considering test instances. Since a large number of samples are generated around the test instance in this way, R_{w}^2 and MSE are expected to improve. We call this **IMPACT 2**. On the other hand, in the case of DAE, not enough samples are generated around the test instance, as shown in Fig. 14(b). This is because latent variables in DAE are not controlled as in VAE and CVAE.

Furthermore, in Fig. 12(b), 13(b), the region where the samples exist is clearly defined. VAE and CVAE learned to move the latent variables closer to the origin. Thus, the decoders decode latent variables outside the existence region as samples at the edges of the existence region. Therefore, a large number of samples that must be far from the test instance are too close. Accordingly, it results in a deterioration of R_w^2. We call this **IMPACT 3**. Therefore, removing samples at the edges of the existing area is expected to improve R_w^2.

5.2 Discussion of Proposed Method

Effect of Weighting by Encoder. Figure 15, 16 and 17 show that R_w^2 and MSE are improved by changing the LIME weighting method to the encoder. This tendency is similar to the result of ALIME [16]. Comparing among autoencoders, CVAE has a better R_w^2, but MSE is sometimes inferior to other methods. A large R_w^2 and small MSE is most desirable. Conversely, a small R_w^2 and small MSE can be taken to mean that the gradient of the model being explained is not captured.

Effect of Sampling by Decoder. Comparing Fig. 15, 16, 17 and Fig. 18, 19, 20, R_w^2 decreases for VAE and DAE, but improves for CVAE. The reason is that when using VAE and DAE, numerous different class samples are generated close to the test instance as mentioned in **IMPACT 1**. In CVAE, however, this negative effect is mitigated because the distribution is shifted from class to class.

Effect of Filtering by Class. Comparing Fig. 15, 16, 17 and Fig. 21, 22, 23, the results show that the addition of filtering by class keeps it almost unchanged. This can be attributed to the fact that LIME's sample generation algorithm does not originally have many samples around the test instances.

Synergy of All Elements. Figure 24(a), 25(a), and 26(a) show that local fidelity is greatly improved by combining all elements. Sampling by decoder generates a large number of samples around the test instance, and filtering by class eliminates samples that are far from the test instance in the feature space of the target model. As a result, it is suppressing the negative effects of **IMPACT 1** while receiving the positive effects of **IMPACT 2**.

Figures 24, 25, and 26 show that local fidelity is improved as samples are filtered by weight, while it decreases when the samples are filtered too much. This is thought to be because the selection of samples by weighting can reduce **IMPACT 3** by eliminating samples gathered at the edges of the region where the latent variable exists. On the other hand, too much selection will result in the loss of samples around the test instances, thus lowering local fidelity. When comparing CVAE, VAE, and DAE, CVAE has a higher local fidelity. This may be because CVAE is more suitable than VAE or DAE in terms of sampling and weighting, in situations where only samples of the same class.

6 Summary and Future Issues

XAI is necessary for the wide use of machine learning models in society. Among XAI methods, we focused on a method called LIME. LIME has a problem with poor local fidelity when approximating the target model with an interpretable model around the test instance, which requires improved sampling and weighting.

Our contributions are the following two. The first contribution of this paper is to propose a new method to improve the fidelity of local linear approximation models by assuming that the neighborhood of the test instance is of the same class in the feature space of the target model. We accomplished this by sampling and weighting samples with a conditional variational autoencoder and filtering the samples by weights and classes. The second contribution is the comparison between the existing studies and the proposed method, and the clarification of the mechanism by which the proposed method improves local fidelity.

Future work is to improve this method into a global explanation. A global explanation can be achieved by collecting multiple local explanations. If we consider a situation in which multiple local explanations are stitched together to generate a global explanation, we believe that the fidelity of the individual local explanations becomes a necessary technique to improve the fidelity of the global explanation [11].

References

1. Parimbelli, E., Buonocore, T.M., Nicora, G., Michalowski, W., Wilk, S., Bellazzi, R.: Why did AI get this one wrong? Tree-based explanations of machine learning model predictions. Artif. Intell. Med. **135**, 102471 (2023)
2. Ahmad, M.A., et al.: Interpretable machine learning in healthcare. In: 2018 IEEE International Conference on Healthcare Informatics (ICHI), pp. 447–447 (2018). https://doi.org/10.1109/ICHI.2018.00095
3. Diaconis, P., et al.: Computer-intensive methods in statistics. Sci. Am. **248**(5), 116–131 (1983). http://www.jstor.org/stable/24968902
4. Greenwell, B.M., et al.: A simple and effective model-based variable importance measure. ArXiv arXiv:1805.04755 (2018)
5. Kingma, D.P., et al.: Auto-encoding variational bayes. arXiv preprint arXiv:1312.6114 (2013)
6. van der Maaten, L., et al.: Visualizing data using t-SNE. J. Mach. Learn. Res. **9**(86), 2579–2605 (2008)
7. Mangasarian, O.L., et al.: Breast cancer diagnosis and prognosis via linear programming. Oper. Res. **43**(4), 570–577 (1995)
8. Molnar, C.: Interpretable Machine Learning: A Guide for Making Black Box Models Explainable (2019)
9. Information Technology Promotion Agency Japan: AI white paper (2019). (in Japanese)
10. Rajaraman, A., et al.: Mining of Massive Datasets. Cambridge University Press, Cambridge (2011)
11. Ramamurthy, K.N., et al.: Model agnostic multilevel explanations. In: Proceedings of the 34th International Conference on Neural Information Processing Systems, NIPS 2020, Red Hook, NY, USA. Curran Associates Inc. (2020)
12. Ramana, B.V., et al.: A critical study of selected classification algorithms for liver disease diagnosis. Int. J. Database Manag. Syst. **3**(2), 101–114 (2011)
13. Ribeiro, M.T., et al.: "Why should i trust you?": explaining the predictions of any classifier. Association for Computing Machinery, New York (2016)

14. Schockaert, C., Macher, V., et al.: VAE-LIME: deep generative model based approach for local data-driven model interpretability applied to the ironmaking industry. CoRR arXiv:2007.10256 (2020)
15. Selvaraju, R.R., et al.: Grad-CAM: visual explanations from deep networks via gradient-based localization. In: Proceedings of the IEEE International Conference on Computer Vision (ICCV) (2017)
16. Shankaranarayana, S.M., Runje, D.: ALIME: autoencoder based approach for local interpretability. In: Yin, H., Camacho, D., Tino, P., Tallón-Ballesteros, A.J., Menezes, R., Allmendinger, R. (eds.) IDEAL 2019. LNCS, vol. 11871, pp. 454–463. Springer, Cham (2019). https://doi.org/10.1007/978-3-030-33607-3_49
17. Sohn, K., et al.: Learning structured output representation using deep conditional generative models. In: Cortes, C., Lawrence, N., Lee, D., Sugiyama, M., Garnett, R. (eds.) Advances in Neural Information Processing Systems. Curran Associates Inc. (2015)
18. Vidal, T., et al.: Born-again tree ensembles (2020)
19. Vincent, P., et al.: Extracting and composing robust features with denoising autoencoders. In: Proceedings of the 25th International Conference on Machine Learning, pp. 1096–1103 (2008)

Scalable Concept Extraction
in Industry 4.0

Andrés Felipe Posada-Moreno[1]([envelope]) [ID], Kai Müller[2], Florian Brillowski[2] [ID],
Friedrich Solowjow[1] [ID], Thomas Gries[2] [ID], and Sebastian Trimpe[1] [ID]

[1] Institute for Data Science in Mechanical Engineering, RWTH Aachen University,
Dennewartstr. 27, 52068 Aachen, Germany
{andres.posada,solowjow,trimpe}@dsme.rwth-aachen.de
[2] Institut für Textiltechnik of RWTH Aachen University, Otto-Blumenthal-Straße 1,
52074 Aachen, Germany
{kai.mueller,florian.brillowski,thomas.gries}@ita.rwth-aachen.de

Abstract. The industry 4.0 is leveraging digital technologies and machine learning techniques to connect and optimize manufacturing processes. Central to this idea is the ability to transform raw data into human understandable knowledge for reliable data-driven decision-making. Convolutional Neural Networks (CNNs) have been instrumental in processing image data, yet, their "black box" nature complicates the understanding of their prediction process. In this context, recent advances in the field of eXplainable Artificial Intelligence (XAI) have proposed the extraction and localization of concepts, or which visual cues intervene on the prediction process of CNNs. This paper tackles the application of concept extraction (CE) methods to industry 4.0 scenarios. To this end, we modify a recently developed technique, "Extracting Concepts with Local Aggregated Descriptors" (ECLAD), improving its scalability. Specifically, we propose a novel procedure for calculating concept importance, utilizing a wrapper function designed for CNNs. This process is aimed at decreasing the number of times each image needs to be evaluated. Subsequently, we demonstrate the potential of CE methods, by applying them in three industrial use cases. We selected three representative use cases in the context of quality control for material design (tailored textiles), manufacturing (carbon fiber reinforcement), and maintenance (photovoltaic module inspection). In these examples, CE was able to successfully extract and locate concepts directly related to each task. This is, the visual cues related to each concept, coincided with what human experts would use to perform the task themselves, even when the visual cues were entangled between multiple classes. Through empirical results, we show that CE can be applied for understanding CNNs in an industrial context, giving useful insights that can relate to domain knowledge.

Keywords: industry 4.0 · digital shadow · concept extraction · global explanations · explainable artificial intelligence

L. Longo (Ed.): xAI 2023, CCIS 1903, pp. 512–535, 2023.
https://doi.org/10.1007/978-3-031-44070-0_26

1   Introduction

Industry 4.0 represents a change in how industries operate through the integration of digital technologies, interconnectivity, and artificial intelligence. This paradigm shift is made possible through three key factors. First, the maturity of sensor and communication technology has facilitated seamless monitoring of machines and communication through integrated systems, evolving into the concept of the *Internet of Things* (IoT) [44]. Second, the increase in available computational resources has enabled pervasive and complex data processing in real-time decision-making. Third, the advancements of big data and artificial intelligence technologies allows industries to extract valuable insights from large amounts of complex data [15]. Together, these factors are the foundations of the Industry 4.0, where data, interconnected processes, and information processing algorithms are the cornerstone of decision-making in a more efficient, productive, and sustainable future.

In this context, convolutional neural networks (CNNs) have been instrumental for making sense out of image data. CNNs have found numerous applications due to their ability to automatically learn relevant features and patterns from data, enabling applications in visual inspection, quality control, predictive maintenance, and robot vision. However, one of the challenges of implementing CNNs in industrial applications is their "black box" nature, referring to the lack of understanding how their prediction process works. This issue is highlighted when CNNs behave unexpectedly, due to issues such biases, shortcut learning, and data leakages [18]. This situation underscores the challenge of automatically generating valuable insights from complex data while ensuring the reasons behind them align with expert knowledge and comply with industry standards.

As a practical example, let us consider a textile quality control process, where a CNN is trained to classify images into normal textiles, folded textiles, or textiles with gaps [7]. This quality control step can be part of the product lifecycle of a carbon-fiber process, where the folds or gaps in the used textiles can indicate a detriment in the mechanical properties of a final product. During operations, the model will classify whether new textile parts contain gaps, folds, or they are normal textiles. Nonetheless, biases can exist in the dataset, such as different lighting conditions for the classes, specific markers, or even spurious correlations. Thus, the model can learn to classify the samples based on the unintended bias, as it's an effective mechanism learned during training. Eventually, it will cause unexpected behaviors, generating issues in the production process, and lead to a general loss of trust in the CNN models.

To address this issue, the field of eXplainable Artificial Intelligence (XAI) focuses on developing techniques to increase the interpretability and understandability of model's prediction processes [3,9,11]. Depending on the context, these techniques can be classified as local or global. On one hand, local explanations focus on understanding the reasoning behind a single image prediction, e.g., by computing the contribution of each feature for the current prediction. This type of explanations can be used for detecting critical or non-important factors, providing insights on a single prediction [3,9,11]. In the context of CNNs, these types of explanations are known as saliency maps, but have been found to be noisy and unreliable [1,47]. On the other hand, global explanations aim to provide a general understanding of how a model functions across multiple datapoints, e.g., by automatically extracting the patterns learned by a model, providing a set of visual cues that a model has learned to differentiate, and how important they are in the prediction process of the model. In the case of CNNs, *concept extraction* (CE) techniques provide sets of patterns learned by CNNs named *concepts*, which refer to visual cues that the models have learned to differentiate in their prediction process [20,27,33]. These types of explanations have been used for the early detection of biases, and for ensuring the alignment of expert knowledge. Yet, their computational requirements can be an obstacle for scaling their usage to larger industrial datasets. Overall, the usage of local and global explanations can fulfill a critical role in making CNNs more transparent, understandable, and useful in industrial applications.

The core process of CE aims at identifying a set of high-level features or representations learned by a CNN during training. It is based on the assumption that through the layers of a CNN, the network learns to represent increasingly complex and abstract features which are functional to the task being learned. In this process, each high-level feature or concept is represented by three components. First, a vector in the latent space of the CNN, used to determine if a concept is present in an image (and sometimes where). Second, an importance score, describing how relevant is the concept for the prediction process of the network. Third, a set of example images containing the concept, which serves as a human understandable medium for making sense of which visual cues are associated with the concept. These methods aim to understand and visualize these learned representations, to gain insights in the functioning of the CNN, and to assess how aligned they are compared to experts knowledge.

Current research on applications of XAI methods for industrial applications has focused on using local explanation techniques, such as SHAP [30] to explain timeseries or tabular data based models. In contrast, global explanation techniques have been primarily used in the medical domain to search for global biases and artifacts [17,22]. However, global explanation techniques have rarely been applied in the context of the industry 4.0. This represents a relevant gap because global explanations can provide a general overview of what a model learns, allowing a clear comparison with domain knowledge, this makes them relevant for the industry 4.0. Furthermore, how such explanations relate in the context of a digital shadow or digital twin has not been discussed.

In this work, we extend a recent CE method for better scalability and apply it on three representative datasets. We select datasets in the context of material design, product manufacturing and maintenance. First, we select a dataset related to material production, this is, a dataset on quality control during textile/weave production of 2D semifinished composites. Second, we select a dataset one step further in a product manufacturing process, this is, a dataset on carbon fiber three-dimensional form reinforcement. Finally, we choose a dataset on visual inspection during maintenance, this is, a dataset on photovoltaic modules defect detection. In addition to demonstrating how CE helps for the validation of the trained models/CNNs, we also discuss how the concepts can be an integral part of model development and quality control. There are three key contributions in this work. First, we modify the concept extraction technique *Extracting Concepts with Local Aggregated Descriptors* (ECLAD) to reduce its computational requirements by reformulating its concept extraction step. Second, we provide three use cases of industrial applications where concept-based explanations can be used, providing empirical results significant in the context of the industry 4.0. Third, we discuss the relation between global explanations with the notion of digital shadows. We highlight how the usage of global explanations can relate to expert knowledge, and how this allows a more informative usage in operations.

2 Background

Our work explores the intersection of two topics within the realm of artificial intelligence. The first topic focuses on the field of explainable artificial intelligence, where we further develop a type of concept-based explanation technique based on local aggregated descriptors. The second topic relates to the applications of XAI techniques in an industrial context, specifically, exploring the connection between explanations, industry 4.0, and knowledge generation from data.

In this section we briefly explore the current literature of both topics, providing an overview of the state-of-the-art research related to both concept-based explanations, and XAI techniques in the industry 4.0.

2.1 Concept-Based Explanations

In the field of XAI, **post-hoc explanations** refer to methods used to provide insights into the inner workings of a model after it has been trained, and without modifying its architecture or training process. Post-hoc explanations are generally divided in two categories, local explanations (concerning a single data point), or in global explanations (concerning the general behavior of the model) [3,9,11]. Concerning of CNNs, local explanations are known as saliency maps. These explanations are able to increase the transparency of a single prediction, but are unable of providing any direct insight regarding the future behavior of a model, nor it's generalization capabilities to other datapoints. In contrast, global explanations, and specifically concept extraction techniques, provide a series of references of how a model encodes information, which types of visual cues it learned to detect, and how important are these patterns in the prediction process. In this context, we have based our work in concept-based explanations, as these provide high-level abstractions, serving as bits of generated knowledge which human experts can assess and confirm.

As a generality, **concept extraction** refers to techniques aiming to identify and represent in human understandable visualizations, high level abstraction within the latent space of a CNN. This family of post-hoc techniques, have been developed following the work on "Testing with Concept Activation Vectors" (TCAV) [27], where Kim et al. propose a method for testing whether a human defined concept was learned by a CNN by statistically testing latent representations (flattened activation maps) of the concept's examples.

A representative technique is "**Automatic Concept-based Explanations**" (ACE) [20], complimenting TCAV by automatically extracting concepts. The base mechanism of ACE consisted on extracting and clustering representations of multiple patches of each image, obtained using a superpixel segmentation technique. In contrast, **Concept-Shap** [46] proposes the learning of a concept representation, by inserting a bottleneck layer of lower dimensions between two layers of a CNN. This method also suggested the usage of Shapley values [30] instead of TCAV for scoring the importance of each concept. Other similar techniques such as PACE [26], MACE [28] and CACE [21] have proposed similar approaches of training an encoder towards a lower dimensional space. In comparison, these techniques are more computationally expensive, as the learning of this representation space requires training through multiple epochs of the complete analyzed dataset. In comparison, "**Extracting Concepts with Local Aggregated Descriptors**" (ECLAD) [33], proposed the identification of concepts through pixel-wise descriptors obtained from the latent space of models named "Local Aggregated Descriptors". This technique introduced the possibility of not only extracting concepts, but also localize them in new sample images.

Nonetheless, the current techniques are computationally expensive, requiring a significant number of evaluations of the CNN for each image in a dataset, as indicated in the complexity analysis by Posada-Moreno et al. [33]. In the case of ACE, this number scales proportional to the number of concepts and superpixels (20–50). For Concept-Shap, MACE, and PACE, this number scales with the number of epochs required for learning the concept representation. As well as the number of samples used to estimate the concepts importance, e.g., Concept-Shap uses Shapley values (Monte Carlo approximation [41]), depending also on the number of concepts. Similarly, for ECLAD, these evaluations scale with the number of classes of the dataset and the number of concepts (to compute their relative importance measure). In our work, we aim to conserve the benefit of concept extraction and localization of ECLAD, while diminishing its required computational cost. We achieve this replacing the importance measurements of the concepts, requiring only one evaluation per image during concept identification, and one evaluation for concept scoring.

2.2   Industrial Applications of XAI Techniques

On a practical side, most industrial applications of XAI techniques center around local explanations, which provide insights into individual predictions made by AI models. These focus has been observed in previous works [2,25,35,48], where a significant ration of the cited examples on each survey relate to local explanation techniques such as SHAP [30], LIME [34], and Grad-CAM [38]. To our knowledge, there is a gap in the literature on the usage of global explanations in the context of industrial applications.

The primary applications of XAI techniques relate to the understanding and validation of AI models though their development process. More specifically, current works have focused on the interpretability and transparency of these models as a mean to debug models and detect biases. Previous works have explored the usage of XAI techniques in the context of quality control [7,39], anomaly detection [8,10,31], or maintenance [23,36,40]. These works have focused mainly in analyzing models based on tabular data or timeseries. In our work, we focus not only on using XAI methods as a tool for testing and detecting biases, but also on the capability of generating knowledge, validating it with human experts and reusing said knowledge to provide valuable insights during operations.

A subset of previous publications has tackled the usage of XAI methods for analyzing models based on image data in industrial applications. These studies employ XAI methods to understand the main features used by models for making predictions, with the goal of enhancing interpretability and detecting possible biases. Notably, Brillowski et al. [7] explored the usage of Grad-CAM [38] to study a CNNs decision logic, focusing on enhancing interpretability, and detecting possible misalignment with human experts. Similarly, Ho Sun et al. [42] tackle the usage of CAM [49] methods, for enhancing vibration video based fault diagnostics. Nonetheless, these applications focus on local explanations, which limits significantly the scope of the insights, exposing any hypothesis to possible confirmation biases. These approaches seek to enhance predictions, but leave aside any knowledge that can be abstracted on a global scale, such as the identification of the visual cues learned by the model. In our work, we seek not only to enhance the predictions of the original model by extending them through explanations, but also to profit from the validation process of the model to generate coherent knowledge about the visual cues related to experts knowledge.

Researchers have designed multiple frameworks on the concept of industry 4.0 [5]. Specially, the term Digital Twin (DT) refers to the models related to physical entities, and the term Digital shadow refers to the data trace generated by the sensors [6]. In our work, we propose including explanation methods not only as part of these entities, but also as tools for the direct generation of knowledge from data. This is, predictive models and explanation methods become part of the digital twins, whereas the predictions and explanations become part of digital shadows. Additionally, the interaction with human experts provides the assurance that concepts generate domain knowledge during operations.

3   Concept Extraction

The term *concept-extraction* refers to a process of analyzing a trained model $y = f(x)$ and a dataset $E = \{(x_i, y_i)\}_{i=1}^{N}$ to identify and score a set of high-level features or concepts that the model learned to differentiate during training. As a result, a set of concepts $C = \{c_j\}_{j=1}^{n_c}$ is extracted, where each concept c_j, is described by a latent representation v_{c_j} within the analyzed CNN, an importance score I_{c_j} denoting its relevance towards the prediction process, and a set of examples ε_{c_j} containing the visual cues related to the concept. The process of concept extraction, highly depends on (i) the choice of latent representation to use, (ii) the process of concept identification, and (iii) the metric used for concept importance scoring. In this section, we will introduce our choices for providing a scalable and effective concept extraction technique.

In this work, we use ECLAD [33] as a method for concept extraction. We then modify its concept importance scoring phase, to diminish its computational cost. Thus, we start by describing the latent representation (Subsect. 3.1) and the concept identification (Subsect. 3.2) as introduced in ECLAD. Finally, we introduce a novel improved importance score (Subsect. 3.3), which we propose to diminish the computational cost of assessing the relevance of concepts.

3.1   Latent Representations

The latent representations in concept extraction are a choice which has direct influence on how the concepts are abstracted, identified, and scored. We use the notion of Local Aggregated Descriptors (LADs) introduced in ECLAD [33]. This descriptor $d_{(a,b)}$ refers to each pixel-wise element of the tensor d, which can be obtained by concatenating the upscaled activation maps of a set of arbitrary layers L. in contrast with other latent representations (e.g. flatten activation maps for TCAV and ACE [20,27]), LADs provide information on how the CNN encodes a region of the images in multiple levels of abstraction, while maintaining the positional information of each spatial region. As LADs are computed for each pixel in an image, they allow for an intrinsic concept localization, informing users not only about what is in an image, but also where. This advantage over other methods enables the posterior usage of concept vectors to generate local explanations (for a single instance), through concept localization masks.

3.2   Concept Identification

The concept identification process, requires the partial or total computation of latent representations for a dataset and the usage of a pattern mining method. In contrast with other types of latent representations, LADs are computed on a per-pixel basis for each image. Thus, the computation of LADs for all images in a dataset would pose a significant memory requirement. To mitigate this requirement, the process of concept identification is performed by computing the LADs of batches of images, and using the clustering algorithm minibatch k-means [37] to obtain a set $\Gamma = \{\gamma_j\}_{j=1}^{n_c}$ of n_c centroids defining each concept.

In a practical sense, the concept identification step proposed in ECLAD [33], consists on performing minibatch k-means over the set D of all descriptors $d_{x_i,(a,b)}$ of all images of the dataset E,

$$\Gamma = \{\gamma_j\}_{j=1}^{n_c} = \text{minibatch k-means}(D, n_c). \tag{1}$$

As a highlight, we can obtain a binary mask $m_{x_i}^{\gamma_j}$ ($m_{x_i}^{c_j}$) by extracting the LADs of the image x_i, and comparing which pixel-wise representations are closer to the centroid γ_j. Similarly, the example set of which visual features in the images correspond to a concept can be computed, by attenuating unrelated regions of the images by a factor λ as introduced in ECLAD,

$$\varepsilon_{c_j} = \{(1 - \lambda)\, m_{x_i}^{c_j} \odot x_i + \lambda x_i \mid x_i \in E\}. \tag{2}$$

where $\odot$ denotes the element-wise product between matrices.

3.3 Improved Importance Score

The importance score of a concept is a numerical value quantifying the relevance of its related visual cues towards the prediction of the analyzed model f. This score helps understand which visual cues have the most significant impact on the model's output. Nonetheless, the relative importance score RI_{c_j} proposed in ECLAD, is computationally expensive to compute, requiring $n_c \times n_k$ evaluations of the model for each analyzed image, where n_c denotes the number of concepts, and n_k the number of output classes of the model f. **We propose a new importance metric**, which can be computed through a single evaluation of the model f for each analyzed image. To this end, we introduce the function $g(y)$,

$$g(y) = \|y \cdot \mathbf{1}^\top - \mathbf{1} \cdot y^\top\|_2. \tag{3}$$

where $y \in \mathbb{R}^{n_k}$ is the output of the model f, and $\mathbf{1}$ is a vector of ones the of the same size as y. $g(y)$ reduces the final output of the model f, to a single value related to the difference between the logits of each output dimension.

The function $g(y)$ or $g(f(x))$ aims to highlight how distinctive an image is with respect to all classes in a single score. In this context the result of $y \cdot \mathbf{1}^\top - \mathbf{1} \cdot y^\top$ yields a matrix where each item represents the difference between the logits of two classes. Thus, the elements will be zero in the diagonal, and will represent the difference between classes in the rest of positions. Thus, $\nabla_x g(f(x))$ gives a quantitative measure, how much each pixel in x contributes to differentiating one class from another.

To estimate the relevance of the concept c_j per image, we aggregate the gradient $g(f(x))$ of the pixels related to said concept, as seen in Eq. 4. We obtain the mean relevance of the concept for all images containing the concept in the dataset, as seen in Eq. 6.

$$r_{x_i}^{c_j} = \|\nabla_x g(f(x_i)) \odot m_{x_i}^{c_j}\|_1. \tag{4}$$

$$\overline{r^{c_j}} = \frac{1}{n_{c_j}} \sum_{x_i \in E} r_{x_i}^{c_j}. \tag{5}$$

where $n_{c_j} = \|\{\|m_{x_i}^{c_j}\| > 0 \mid x_i \in E\}\|$ is the number of images in the dataset E containing pixels related to c_j; And $\odot$ denotes the element-wise product between matrices. As an intuition, $r_{x_i}^{c_j}$ refers to how much the pixels belonging to the concept c_j contribute towards the difference in logits, in other terms, towards the prediction of the model. Similarly, $\overline{r^{c_j}}$ refers to the average contribution of a concept, along a complete dataset. Finally, we introduce the importance score I_{c_j} as the scaled absolute value of the mean relevance of each concept,

$$I_{c_j} = \frac{|\overline{r^{c_j}}|}{\max_{c_j}(|\overline{r^{c_j}}|)}. \tag{6}$$

After the execution of our method, a set $C = \{c_j\}_{j=1}^{n_c}$ of n_c concepts are extracted. Each concept is defined by its latent representation, γ_j defining the pattern learned by the CNN; The importance score I_{c_j}, defining the relevance of the concepts in the prediction process of the model; and the example set ε_{c_j}, containing masked images, showing which visual cues relate to each concept. Our method retains the extraction and localization capabilities from ECLAD, while reducing significantly its computational. Specifically, we reduce the number of evaluations of the model for computing the importance scores of the concept, from $n_c \times n_k$ per image for ECLAD, to once per image for ours.

4 Use Cases

In this section, we present three representative industrial use cases where we apply our concept extraction method. We first present a case where CE is used in the context of fiberglass textiles, where the analyzed model was trained to detect common material errors within samples during a materials design process. Then, we explore an application of carbon fiber reinforcement quality control, where models are used during production, as a mean for detecting placement errors which can directly impact the mechanical properties of a resulting product. Finally, we study a case in the context of maintenance, where we analyze a dataset of photovoltaic modules, depicting an automatic inspection process in large solar plants. As a highlight, the choice of use cases, relates to three key industrial topics, material design and production, product manufacturing, and maintenance processes for asset management.

For each use case, we start with a brief introduction, explaining the relevance of the applications. Then, we introduce the dataset used as a representative problem in each context. Research on image classification has advanced significantly over the past decades, allowing the training of high accuracy models without significant issues. We solve the tasks of images classification through a standard Densenet121 [24] architecture, training each model until convergence.

In the three cases, the classification problem can be solved through the used architecture and training scheme. Yet, for the usage of these models, it is important to understand how the predictions are being made. It is only through the explanation processes that we can ensure whether the models are performing the tasks as intended. Thus, for each use case, we follow the training with the execution of our concept extraction technique, and obtain explanations on how each models' prediction process work. Finally, we discuss each set of results, performing visual inspection and comparing them with human experts knowledge.

4.1   Tailored Textiles

The tailored textiles (TT) use case concerns a quality control problem during the development of custom reinforcement composite materials. The value of TT arises from the increase of the global fiber-reinforced plastics (FRP) market, which was approximately 8% in 2021 [45]. In this market, the high cost of producing fiber reinforced polymers (FRPs) has led to efforts to find ways to reduce manufacturing costs while maintaining structural performance. In these market needs, TT are a promising solution for achieving weight reduction, as they can be locally reinforced with additional material, reducing weight while maintaining strength. Reinforcements are incorporated during production, leading to cost savings during preforming. Due to their properties, TT have the potential to improve the cost and weight efficiency of FRPs [43]. Quality controls are necessary to ensure that TTs meet load-path-compliant reinforcement requirements, such as fiber angle, freedom from defects, and proper setting [13,14]. This issue can be tackled through the usage of automatic visual inspection systems, which enable non-destructive and fast inline testing [16,19,32].

In this context, a TT dataset was generated to represent a practical quality control scenario. In this experiment, continuous material rolls of glass fiber fabric with plain weave were cut into sizes of 300×200 mm. Among these samples, half were reinforced with a single carbon fiber. The samples were classified into six classes of 300 images of 4288×2848 pixels each, based on the presence of common defects or error free textiles, as seen in Fig. 1.[1]

The problem detecting quality issues in the fiber glass images was formalized as an image classification problem. In a practical sense, this allows for the usage of different kinds of CNN architecture, training procedures, and data augmentations, which finally allow the training of a model attaining a high accuracy. In this use case, we used a Densenet121 [24], training it with a train-test split of 0.8 until convergence. We used an initial learning rate of 0.1, a reduce on plateau scheduler, and weight decay. During training, the images were resized to a shape of 512×512, making them small enough for an efficient evaluation, yet big enough not to lose the details of the fiber glass errors. The final model achieved perfect accuracy, yet, the question rises of whether it learned the task as intended, or there was an unintentional bias on the provided data.

Thus, to verify if the model was working as intended, we executed our concept extraction method to generate a global explanation of its prediction process. Our algorithm was executed using mini batches of 8 images to obtain 20 concepts. Afterward, the resulting concepts were inspected, taking into account their importance score, and their example sets. The top five concepts with the highest importance scores are shown in Fig. 2, other concepts represent different subregions of the images with importance scores lower than 0.01, thus deemed as unimportant. Subsequently, we provided a human expert with the obtained concepts, and analyzed whether they coincided with the visual cues he used during an inspection process.

---

[1] The dataset is available under the link: https://doi.org/10.5281/zenodo.7970596.

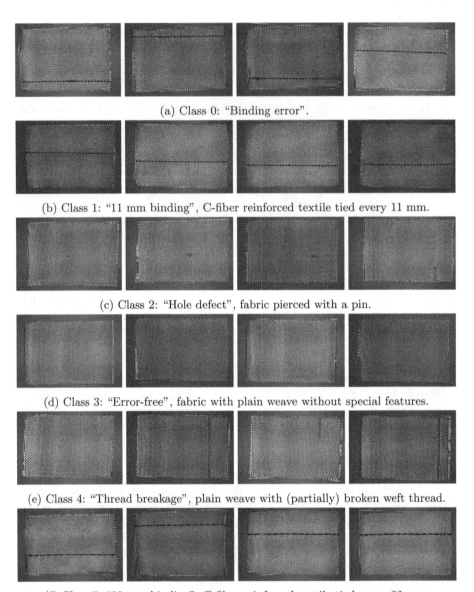

(a) Class 0: "Binding error".

(b) Class 1: "11 mm binding", C-fiber reinforced textile tied every 11 mm.

(c) Class 2: "Hole defect", fabric pierced with a pin.

(d) Class 3: "Error-free", fabric with plain weave without special features.

(e) Class 4: "Thread breakage", plain weave with (partially) broken weft thread.

(f) Class 5: "22 mm binding", C-fiber reinforced textile tied every 22 mm.

Fig. 1. Samples images from the fiber glass errors dataset. Figures above depict the different types of error in fiberglass production. Figure 1d depicts error free fiber glass textiles. Figure 1e contains textiles with a thread partially broken. Figure 1c depicts textiles with a puncture hole. Whereas Figs. 1a, 1b, 1f contain three different types of binding errors.

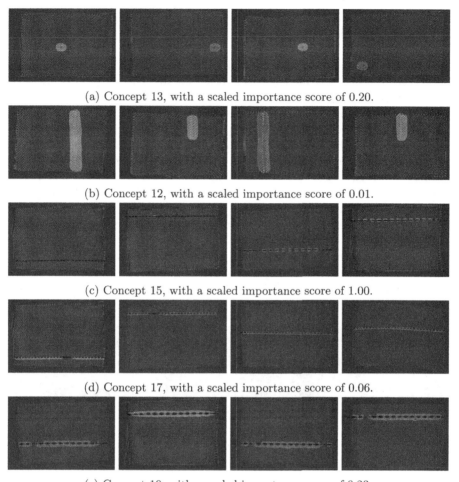

(a) Concept 13, with a scaled importance score of 0.20.

(b) Concept 12, with a scaled importance score of 0.01.

(c) Concept 15, with a scaled importance score of 1.00.

(d) Concept 17, with a scaled importance score of 0.06.

(e) Concept 19, with a scaled importance score of 0.23.

Fig. 2. Sample images of top extracted concepts. All five top concepts related to the visual cues used by human experts. Concepts 13 in Subfigs. 2a related to punctures present in class 2. Concept 12 in Subfig. 2b refer to thread breakages from class 4. Concepts 15, 17, and 19 in Subfigs. 2c, 2d, and 2e relate to the visual cues of missing thread bindings, 11 mm bindings, or 22 mm bindings respectively.

The main observation found from inspecting the concepts was that they corresponded with the visual cues that an expert would use for performing the quality control task. Two concepts (punctures Fig. 2a and thread breakage Fig. 2b) related directly to the key visual cues of classes 2 and 4 respectively. Although the other visual cues are entangled between multiple classes, the model learned their concepts accordingly. Specifically, the visual cues in the different "binding" classes, are shared. This is, the same binding thread appears in all three classes, yet, what changes is the spacing or the lack of binding threads. The extracted concepts, directly relate to missing thread bindings (concept 15), binding threads with a spacing of 11 mm (concept 17), and binding threads with a spacing of 22 mm (concept 19). The resulting concepts, provide evidence to the human experts that the model performs the task using the intended regions. Moreover, it also learned which specific features appeared across classes and disentangled them in distinctive representations.

In addition to generating a better understanding of what the model learned, and where does it react to the different patterns, CE techniques also allow for a better understanding of the original dataset. Within the example sets of multiple concepts, mixed samples were observed. This is, concepts related to the visual feature of a single class, were detected in other images. As shown in Fig. 3, regions that the model encode as punctures were detected at the beginning of thread breakages. Similarly, regions that the model encodes as thread breakages were detected adjacent to puncture. From a practical perspective, this confirms general knowledge that thread breakages can be caused by punctures, and thus, both visual cues can indeed appear together. Nonetheless, as a result of this observation, experts can further discuss edge cases in the dataset, ensuring that they are labelled correctly.

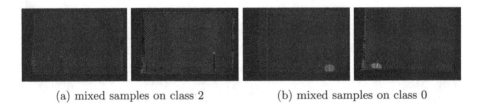

(a) mixed samples on class 2   (b) mixed samples on class 0

Fig. 3. Sample images from concepts found in non-related classes. Subfig. 3a shows detections of concept 13 associated with punctures, but appearing in thread breakage images. Conversely, Subfig. 3b shows detections of concept 12 related to thread breakages appearing adjacent to punctures.

Concept based explanations, provided a medium for experts to understand the prediction process of the model, increasing their trust. Additionally, the visual evaluation of models, also highlighted that they could be used as a source of knowledge for better decision-making during production.

4.2   Carbon Fiber Quality Control

This section presets a use case related to carbon fiber reinforcement quality control. The carbon fiber (CF) use case relates to a quality control process posterior to a reinforcement procedure. In general, carbon fiber textiles are a popular reinforcing material for plastics, due to its high stiffness, which makes it possible to craft a lightweight, yet powerful composite. The main application of fibre-reinforced composites are safety-critical domains like aviation or mobility.

In these domains, it is crucial to protect passengers' lives at all costs, which is why high quality levels are demanded per legislation.

Quality control of textiles and textile reinforced plastics is mainly executed in a manual manner, as existing intelligent quality control systems often fail silently when faced with changing errors appearances or different textile structures. This results in a tedious and tiresome visual inspection for workers in quality control, leading to exhaustion and increasing error proneness over time worked. In this context, it is imperative for any trained CNN, to not only make accurate predictions, but also to make them for the right reasons. Moreover, to increase trust from human experts, it is a necessity to have a better understanding of a model's capabilities and limitations in a more detailed manner.

To represent a practical quality control problem of carbon fiber reinforcement, a dataset was generated. The dataset was obtained using a commonly used carbon plain weave with a grammage of $200\,g/m^2$. First, the weave was cut to $300 \times 300\,mm^2$ samples using a CNC cutter table. Then, two sample sheets were placed on top of each other to form a stack. Next, in between the two textile layers, a binder (EPIKOTE EP 05311 from Hexion Inc.) with a grammage of $5\,g/m^2$ was applied to maintain shape stability after the three-dimensional forming process. The forming process was executed on an asymmetric form set (positive and negative) mounted on a press, shaping 25 stacks three-dimensionally. Due to its asymmetric characteristic (curvatures and edges), the form was prone to different types of errors. Subsequently, using a high resolution camera (Apodius HP-C-V3D) mounted on a robotic arm (Hexagon ROMER Absolute Arm), 500 images with a resolution of 2048×1536 pixels, were taken of the textiles' surfaces in three-dimensional shape. Afterwards, the surface scan images were cropped to 341×384 pixels patches and transformed to grayscale. Each patch was then labeled according to one of three classes, normal textile, gap, or fold, as seen in Fig. 4. Finally, the patches were manually inspected and images that were blurred, out of focus, or had bad contrast were sorted out.[2]

Similar to the previous use case, the quality control process was formulated as an image classification problem. A Densenet121 model [24] was used and trained until convergence with a train-test split of 0.8. The training procedure was maintained, using a learning rate of 0.1 and a reduce on plateau scheduler. Given the original size of the patches, the images were resized to 224×224 pixels, applying random rotations and photometric data augmentations. After training, the model achieved perfect accuracy in the testing set. Which, given the complexity of the task, raises the question of whether such minimal visual cues as gaps were learned by the model, or other biases such as the average intensity of the pixels could be used to perform the classification.

Thus, our concept extraction method was used to provide human experts with the means for better understanding the prediction process of the model. Our method was executed to mine for 10 concepts using mini-batches of 8 images. Afterwards, the example sets of the concepts and their respective importance scores were presented to the human expert. The three concepts with the highest

---

[2] The dataset is available under the link: https://doi.org/10.5281/zenodo.7970490.

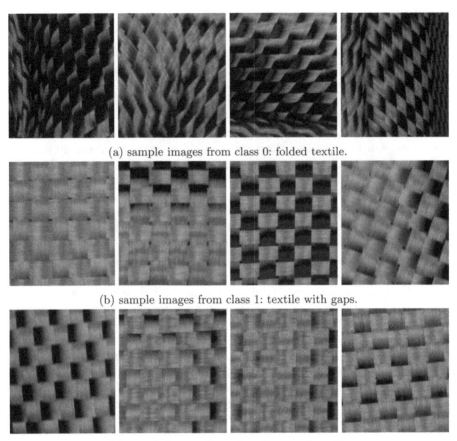

(a) sample images from class 0: folded textile.

(b) sample images from class 1: textile with gaps.

(c) sample images from class 2: normal textile

Fig. 4. Carbon fiber quality control dataset. The images on Fig. 4a, depict patches of a textile with folded regions. Similarly, the images on Fig. 4b, contain patches where gaps exist between the textile threads. Finally, the images on Fig. 4c, represent normal patches of textile. Both folded regions and gaps have adverse impact in the mechanical properties of a final product.

importance scores are shown in Fig. 5, where the two most important concepts (5 and 6) relate to folded regions of the textiles in different directions, and the third one (8) relates to gaps in the textiles. Other concepts had importance scores below 0.3, with a minimal contribution towards the prediction process of the model.

As a key finding, the obtained concepts aligned with the visual cues that human experts would use to perform a similar task. Particularly, it was possible for human experts to verify that the gap regions were indeed used as a key visual cue for differentiating the types of errors. Moreover, although the model has distinctive representations for folded regions on different angles, it was possible

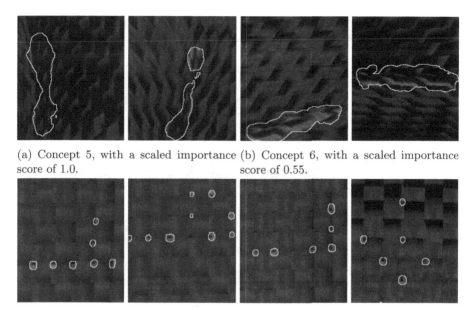

(a) Concept 5, with a scaled importance (b) Concept 6, with a scaled importance
score of 1.0.   score of 0.55.

(c) Concept 8, with a scaled importance score of 0.14.

Fig. 5. Top concepts extracted from Densenet121, trained on the carbon fiber quality control dataset. From the top concepts, the two most important ones (concept 5 and 6), relate to the visual cues present in folded regions of the textiles. In addition, concept 8, refers to gaps, or the darker regions present in the intersection point between fibers. Other unrelated concepts had scaled importance scores lower than 0.03. Indicating that visual cues learned by the CNN coincide with those used by a human expert while performing the visual quality control.

to verify that what mattered to the model was indeed the center of the fold, and not the intensity of the region itself. This provided insights into the generalization capabilities of the model, increasing experts trust.

Furthermore, the capabilities of the CE technique to localize concepts in new samples, provide the experts with knowledge regarding the correctness of the predictions. This is specially important in cases where textiles differ from the original dataset, or when a specific prediction is challenged.

Similar to before, the analysis provides insights not only on the decision process of the model, but also on edge cases found in the dataset. In this case, regions related to concept 8 (associated with gaps) were found in samples of the other classes, seen in Fig. 6. In one case, textiles which were bent on specific ways, forced some gaps while deforming the textile threads. This confirmed that, although the visual cues of folded textiles are given priority by the model, it still detects the regions containing gaps. In other cases, it was detected that some images initially labelled as normal, contained gaps of different sizes. This detections allow a dual refinement of both, models and dataset, while at the

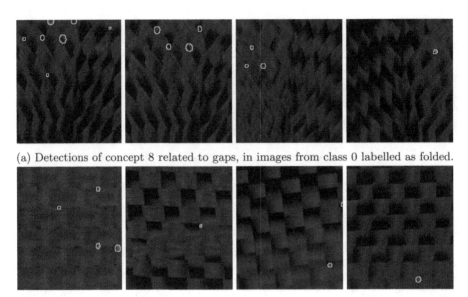

(a) Detections of concept 8 related to gaps, in images from class 0 labelled as folded.

(b) Detections of concept 8 related to gaps, in images from class 2 labelled as normal.

Fig. 6. Samples off cross appearance of visual cues. These images depict edge cases on both folded and normal classes, where visual cues related to gaps (concept 8) are detected. These edge cases provide valuable feedback for experts to decide if any mislabelling has occurred.

same time, allowing human experts to contribute in the training process of the models.

Finally, the obtained concepts, provide experts with a tool for understanding the model and other future predictions. This proves valuable in cases where experts want models to adapt to other textiles (e.g. glass, aramide, basalt, flax), and want to validate whether the original visual cues are still detected for the new types of materials.

4.3   Photovoltaic Panels Maintenance

The final use case relates to the inspection processes in photovoltaic (PV) power plants. Within the context of the industry 4.0, efforts in pursuing low-carbon energy have boosted recent adoption of large scale photovoltaic (PV) systems [12]. Nonetheless, the adoption of PV systems can be complex, as their viability highly depends on a robust and scalable monitoring of the photovoltaic modules [29]. These solar modules have multiple physical safeguards such as a glass lamination and metal frames. Yet, the modules are still vulnerable to mechanical damages, obstructions, as well as installation and manufacturing errors [29]. In an effort to implement large scale inspection of PV systems, recent approaches have used unmanned aerial vehicles (UAV) for the acquisition of high resolution images of the installed solar modules. In this context, deep learning visual inspection systems provide an alternative for the large scale monitoring of PV modules. Nonetheless, Visual identification of defects is still challenging, even for experts [12,29].

In this context, we represent a practical case using the dataset provided by Bao et al. [4], mimicking a real world photovoltaic power plant, where images containing multiple types of defects were provided. As seen in Fig. 7, the used dataset contains PV panels images which are either defect free, contain broken panels, foreign objects, or missing panels. The dataset is composed of 5000 images from different perspectives of 512 × 512 pixels. This dataset, represents the common case of having to inspect the solar panels installed in a large scale PV system though a set of images obtained using UAVs. It is common for these inspections to be performed manually, as the classification of which panels contain defects can be challenging, and the predictions from automated models can be unreliable. In this context, it is critical to understand not only the capabilities of any used model, but also to have more information on why a prediction was made, and where was an issue detect. This becomes a first step towards understanding why a model is performing unreliably, and towards making the necessary changes to retrain a working system.

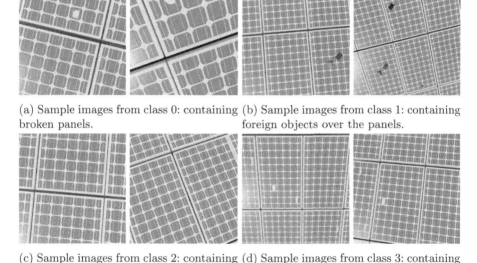

(a) Sample images from class 0: containing broken panels.

(b) Sample images from class 1: containing foreign objects over the panels.

(c) Sample images from class 2: containing normal panels.

(d) Sample images from class 3: containing panels with complete missing sections.

Fig. 7. Photovoltaic module dataset, depicting images of solar panels, emulating an automatic inspection in a large scale panel system [4]. The images in Figs. 7a and 7d contain panels where one of the subsections is partially broken or fully missing. The images from Fig. 7b, depicts images where foreign objects have landed over the panels. Finally, the images on Fig. 7c contain normal solar panels without any defect.

This task of visual inspection was formulated as an image classification problem. A similar architecture as before was used (Densenet121 [24]), following the same training process as the previous use cases. The images were resized to 224×224 pixels, and random rotations as well as color jitter were added as data augmentations. This procedure highlights the flexibility of CNN techniques, and their power to learn patterns from different types of data. Regardless, it also highlights the importance of understanding why predictions are being made, as a high accuracy score does not necessary mean that the model is performing the task as intended.

Thus, after training the model until convergence, we used our concept extraction technique for explaining the inner workings of the model. The main objective for analyzing this model is not only to provide mediums for understanding the models' behavior, but also for highlighting, for specific predictions, where are the defects detected, facilitating human inspectors assets management. In this regard, our concept extraction technique was executed to extract 10 clusters, using mini batches of 8 images. From this process, the three main concepts are shown in Fig. 8, as other concepts were scored with importance lower than 0.04, contributing minimally to the prediction of any class. In highlight, the resulting concepts align directly with the main visual cues relate to each class, giving a basic confirmation that the image classification task was solved using the desired visual cues.

In more detail, the resulting explanation assured the human expert, that the network was able to differentiate foreign objects, broken panels, and missing panels. As seen in Fig. 8, not only was the network capable of classifying each class correctly, but internally, within its latent space, it has the capabilities of a coarse segmentation of defects from raw images. This is specially significant, given the similarities between broken and missing panels, where the difference lays in the "completeness" or not of the missing section. Thus, though the concept extraction process, human experts can have an assurance that, not only is the model performing the detections as they intend, but that for any new images, the prediction can be extended to localize where the defects are. This detection, is the results of the network abstraction, without the need of any extra label or the training of other object detection algorithms.

As a final remark, global explanations allowed the better understanding of the three use cases, providing human experts with the key visual cues used in the models' prediction. Moreover, the explanations allowed the processing of raw data to generate knowledge, by localizing concepts for any new prediction.

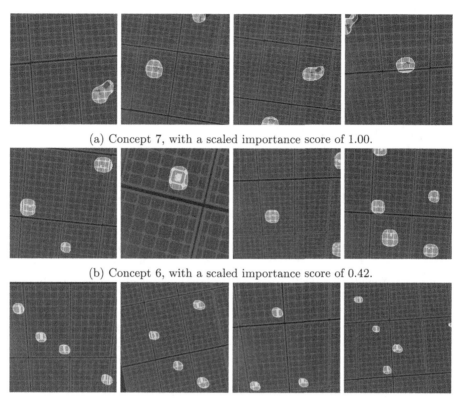

(a) Concept 7, with a scaled importance score of 1.00.

(b) Concept 6, with a scaled importance score of 0.42.

(c) Concept 9, with a scaled importance score of 0.28.

Fig. 8. Top concepts extracted from a Densenet121, trained on the Photovoltaic module dataset. The three most important concepts are directly aligned with the labelled classes, containing either missing panels (concept 7), broken panels (concept 6), or the foreign objects (concept 9). Other concepts had scaled importance scores lower than 0.04. These explanations provide extra information complimenting the initial predictions, with an indication of what was detected and where.

5   Conclusions

This manuscript explores the usage of concept-based explanations in the context of the industry 4.0. To this end, we discuss the relation between the industry 4.0 and explainability techniques, we state the connection of explanations, digital shadows, explainability methods and digital twins. Then, we base our study on the concept extraction method ECLAD, modifying its concept scoring process and making it more scalable. Finally, we apply our CE method on industry related data and demonstrate the viability of its usage in this context.

First, we discuss the connection between concept based explanations and the framework of the Industry 4.0. Specifically, that concept extraction methods can be part of digital twins, and the generated explanations are part of digital shadows. More so, that high level concepts provide domain experts with means to assess alignment. Moreover, further concept localization can provide valuable insights during manufacturing operations.

Second, we modify the concept extraction method ECLAD to improve its scalability. We propose a new concept scoring procedure, based on a novel CNN wrapping function, and the aggregation of the gradients at the input of the model. With our method, we decrease the number of evaluations in the concept scoring phase by a factor of $n_k \times n_c$.

Third, we explore the application of our method in the context of tailored textiles, carbon fiber quality control, and maintenance of photovoltaic modules. In the three use cases, after training and explaining models, the obtained concepts aligned with the visual cues pertinent to each task. We show how models trained to differentiate fiber glass errors, learn the visual cues of punctures, thread breakages, and binding issues. Similarly, models trained on carbon fiber errors, learn the folding regions of textiles, as well as abnormally big gaps. In addition, we show how models trained for detecting photovoltaic panel issues, learned the visual cues related to foreign objects, broken panels, and missing panels. Through empirical results, we show that concept extraction methods provide usable explanations in the context of industrial data. These explanations can be used to better understand the prediction process of models and to ensure the models' alignment with expert knowledge.

The current work shows promising results on the usage of concept-based explanations for industrial applications, opening multiple possible research directions. On a practical perspective, it opens the opportunity for using high-level concepts, as understandable mediums in industrial applications for detecting domain shifts, anomalies, class differences, and in general, for an analysis of possible biases and data leakages present in datasets. On an abstract perspective, it hints towards a structured integration of explanation methods in industry 4.0 frameworks and processes. Finally, it opens a discussion about measuring the value of these explanations, by estimating the increase of trust generated, or the possibility of detecting different kinds of biases present in data.

Acknowledgements. Funded by the Deutsche Forschungsgemeinschaft (DFG, German Research Foundation) under Germany's Excellence Strategy-EXC-2023 Internet of Production-390621612.

References

1. Adebayo, J., Gilmer, J., Muelly, M., Goodfellow, I.J., Hardt, M., Kim, B.: Sanity checks for saliency maps. In: Bengio, S., Wallach, H.M., Larochelle, H., Grauman, K., Cesa-Bianchi, N., Garnett, R. (eds.) NeurIPS, pp. 9525–9536 (2018)
2. Ahmed, I., Jeon, G., Piccialli, F.: From artificial intelligence to explainable artificial intelligence in industry 4.0: a survey on what, how, and where. IEEE Trans. Ind. Inform. **18**(8), 5031–5042 (2022)
3. Arrieta, A.B., et al.: Explainable artificial intelligence (XAI): concepts, taxonomies, opportunities and challenges toward responsible AI. Inf. Fusion **58**, 82–115 (2020)

4. Bao, T., et al.: MIAD: a maintenance inspection dataset for unsupervised anomaly detection. CoRR abs/2211.13968 (2022)
5. Becker, F., et al.: A conceptual model for digital shadows in industry and its application. In: Ghose, A., Horkoff, J., Silva Souza, V.E., Parsons, J., Evermann, J. (eds.) ER 2021. LNCS, vol. 13011, pp. 271–281. Springer, Cham (2021). https://doi.org/10.1007/978-3-030-89022-3_22
6. Bibow, P., et al.: Model-driven development of a digital twin for injection molding. In: Dustdar, S., Yu, E., Salinesi, C., Rieu, D., Pant, V. (eds.) CAiSE 2020. LNCS, vol. 12127, pp. 85–100. Springer, Cham (2020). https://doi.org/10.1007/978-3-030-49435-3_6
7. Brillowski, F.S., et al.: Explainable AI for error detection in composites: knowledge discovery in artificial neural networks. In: SAMPE EUROPE Conference and Exhibition 2021. SAMPE EUROPE Conference and Exhibition, Baden/Zürich (Switzerland), 29–30 October 2021 (2021). https://publications.rwth-aachen.de/record/848836
8. Brito, L.C., Susto, G.A., Brito, J.N., Duarte, M.A.V.: An explainable artificial intelligence approach for unsupervised fault detection and diagnosis in rotating machinery. CoRR abs/2102.11848 (2021)
9. Burkart, N., Huber, M.F.: A survey on the explainability of supervised machine learning. J. Artif. Intell. Res. **70**, 245–317 (2021)
10. Chowdhury, D., Sinha, A., Das, D.: XAI-3DP: diagnosis and understanding faults of 3-D printer with explainable ensemble AI. IEEE Sens. Lett. **7**(1), 1–4 (2022)
11. Das, A., Rad, P.: Opportunities and challenges in explainable artificial intelligence (XAI): a survey. CoRR abs/2006.11371 (2020)
12. Deitsch, S., et al.: Automatic classification of defective photovoltaic module cells in electroluminescence images. Sol. Energy **185**, 455–468 (2019)
13. DIN Deutsches Institut für Normierung e.V.: DIN 65147: Kohlenstoffasern Gewebe aus Kohlenstofffilamentgarn. beuth Verlag, Berlin (1987)
14. DIN Deutsches Institut für Normierung e.V.: DIN 65673: Luft- und Raumfahrt Faserverstärkte Kunststoffe. beuth Verlag, Berlin (1999)
15. Duan, Y., Edwards, J.S., Dwivedi, Y.K.: Artificial intelligence for decision making in the era of big data - evolution, challenges and research agenda. Int. J. Inf. Manag. **48**, 63–71 (2019)
16. Duboust, N., et al.: An optical method for measuring surface roughness of machined carbon fibre-reinforced plastic composites. J. Compos. Mater. **51**(3), 289–302 (2017)
17. Gamble, P., et al.: Determining breast cancer biomarker status and associated morphological features using deep learning. Commun. Med. **1**(1), 14 (2021)
18. Geirhos, R., et al.: Shortcut learning in deep neural networks. Nat. Mach. Intell. **2**(11), 665–673 (2020)
19. Gholizadeh, S.: A review of non-destructive testing methods of composite materials. Procedia Struct. Integrity **1**(2), 50–57 (2016)
20. Ghorbani, A., Wexler, J., Zou, J.Y., Kim, B.: Towards automatic concept-based explanations. In: Wallach, H.M., Larochelle, H., Beygelzimer, A., d'Alché-Buc, F., Fox, E.B., Garnett, R. (eds.) NeurIPS, pp. 9273–9282 (2019)
21. Goyal, Y., Shalit, U., Kim, B.: Explaining classifiers with causal concept effect (CaCE). CoRR abs/1907.07165 (2019)
22. Graziani, M., Andrearczyk, V., Müller, H.: Regression concept vectors for bidirectional explanations in histopathology. CoRR abs/1904.04520 (2019)

23. Hong, C.W., Lee, C., Lee, K., Ko, M., Hur, K.: Explainable artificial intelligence for the remaining useful life prognosis of the turbofan engines. In: ICKII, pp. 144–147. IEEE (2020)

24. Huang, G., Liu, Z., van der Maaten, L., Weinberger, K.Q.: Densely connected convolutional networks. In: CVPR, pp. 2261–2269. IEEE Computer Society (2017)

25. Islam, M.R., Ahmed, M.U., Barua, S., Begum, S.: A systematic review of explainable artificial intelligence in terms of different application domains and tasks. Appl. Sci. **12**(3), 1353 (2022)

26. Kamakshi, V., Gupta, U., Krishnan, N.C.: PACE: posthoc architecture-agnostic concept extractor for explaining CNNs. In: IJCNN, pp. 1–8. IEEE (2021)

27. Kim, B., et al.: Interpretability beyond feature attribution: quantitative testing with concept activation vectors (TCAV). In: Dy, J.G., Krause, A. (eds.) ICML. Proceedings of Machine Learning Research, vol. 80, pp. 2673–2682. PMLR (2018)

28. Kumar, A., Sehgal, K., Garg, P., Kamakshi, V., Krishnan, N.C.: MACE: model agnostic concept extractor for explaining image classification networks. IEEE Trans. Artif. Intell. **2**(6), 574–583 (2021)

29. Li, X., Yang, Q., Chen, Z., Luo, X., Yan, W.: Visible defects detection based on UAV-based inspection in large-scale photovoltaic systems. IET Renew. Power Gener. **11**(10), 1234–1244 (2017)

30. Lundberg, S.M., Lee, S.: A unified approach to interpreting model predictions. In: Guyon, I., et al. (eds.) NeurIPS, pp. 4765–4774 (2017)

31. Meas, M., et al.: Explainability and transparency of classifiers for air-handling unit faults using explainable artificial intelligence (XAI). Sensors **22**(17), 6338 (2022)

32. Mueller, K., Greb, C.: Machine vision: error detection and classification of tailored textiles using neural networks. In: Andersen, A.-L., et al. (eds.) CARV/MCPC 2021. LNME, pp. 595–602. Springer, Cham (2022). https://doi.org/10.1007/978-3-030-90700-6_67

33. Posada-Moreno, A.F., Surya, N., Trimpe, S.: ECLAD: extracting concepts with local aggregated descriptors. CoRR abs/2206.04531 (2022)

34. Ribeiro, M.T., Singh, S., Guestrin, C.: "Why should I trust you?": explaining the predictions of any classifier. In: Krishnapuram, B., Shah, M., Smola, A.J., Aggarwal, C.C., Shen, D., Rastogi, R. (eds.) SIGKDD, pp. 1135–1144. ACM (2016)

35. Saranya, A., Subhashini, R.: A systematic review of explainable artificial intelligence models and applications: recent developments and future trends. Decis. Anal. J. 100230 (2023)

36. Sayed Mouchaweh, M., Rajaoarisoa, L.H.: Explainable decision support tool for IoT predictive maintenance within the context of industry 4.0. In: Wani, M.A., Kantardzic, M.M., Palade, V., Neagu, D., Yang, L., Chan, K.Y. (eds.) ICMLA, pp. 1492–1497. IEEE (2022)

37. Sculley, D.: Web-scale k-means clustering. In: Rappa, M., Jones, P., Freire, J., Chakrabarti, S. (eds.) Proceedings of the 19th International Conference on World Wide Web, WWW 2010, Raleigh, North Carolina, USA, 26–30 April 2010, pp. 1177–1178. ACM (2010)

38. Selvaraju, R.R., Cogswell, M., Das, A., Vedantam, R., Parikh, D., Batra, D.: Grad-CAM: visual explanations from deep networks via gradient-based localization. In: ICCV, pp. 618–626. IEEE Computer Society (2017)

39. Senoner, J., Netland, T.H., Feuerriegel, S.: Using explainable artificial intelligence to improve process quality: evidence from semiconductor manufacturing. Manag. Sci. **68**(8), 5704–5723 (2022)

40. Serradilla, O., Zugasti, E., Cernuda, C., Aranburu, A., de Okariz, J.R., Zurutuza, U.: Interpreting remaining useful life estimations combining explainable artificial intelligence and domain knowledge in industrial machinery. In: FUZZ-IEEE, pp. 1–8. IEEE (2020)
41. Strumbelj, E., Kononenko, I.: Explaining prediction models and individual predictions with feature contributions. Knowl. Inf. Syst. **41**(3), 647–665 (2014)
42. Sun, K.H., Huh, H., Tama, B.A., Lee, S.Y., Jung, J.H., Lee, S.: Vision-based fault diagnostics using explainable deep learning with class activation maps. IEEE Access **8**, 129169–129179 (2020)
43. Uthemann, C., Jacobsen, L., Gries, T.: Cost efficiency through load-optimised and semi-impregnated prepregs. Lightweight Des. Worldwide **10**(6), 18–21 (2017)
44. Wang, J., Lim, M.K., Wang, C., Tseng, M.: The evolution of the internet of things (IoT) over the past 20 years. Comput. Ind. Eng. **155**, 107174 (2021)
45. Witten, E., Mathes, V.: Der europäische markt für faserverstärkte kunststoffe/composites 2021: Marktentwicklungen, trends, herausforderungen und ausblicke (2022). https://www.avk-tv.de/files/20220503_avk_marktbericht_2022_final.pdf
46. Yeh, C., Kim, B., Arik, S.Ö., Li, C., Pfister, T., Ravikumar, P.: On completeness-aware concept-based explanations in deep neural networks. In: Larochelle, H., Ranzato, M., Hadsell, R., Balcan, M., Lin, H. (eds.) NeurIPS (2020)
47. Yona, G., Greenfeld, D.: Revisiting sanity checks for saliency maps. CoRR abs/2110.14297 (2021)
48. Zhang, Z., Hamadi, H.M.N.A., Damiani, E., Yeun, C.Y., Taher, F.: Explainable artificial intelligence applications in cyber security: state-of-the-art in research. IEEE Access **10**, 93104–93139 (2022)
49. Zhou, B., Khosla, A., Lapedriza, À., Oliva, A., Torralba, A.: Learning deep features for discriminative localization. In: CVPR, pp. 2921–2929. IEEE Computer Society (2016)

Author Index

L. Longo (Ed.): xAI 2023, CCIS 1903, pp. 537–540, 2023.
https://doi.org/10.1007/978-3-031-44070-0

.

Printed in the United States
by Baker & Taylor Publisher Services